THE SCIENCE OF
PERSONALITY

THE SCIENCE OF PERSONALITY

Lawrence A. Pervin

Rutgers University

John Wiley & Sons, Inc.
New York • Chichester • Brisbane • Toronto • Singapore

Acquisitions Editor   Karen Dubno
Marketing Manager   Rebecca Herschler
Senior Production Editor   Bonnie Cabot
Designer   Harry Nolan
Cover Illustration   Robert Neubecker
Manufacturing Coordinator   Dorothy Sinclair
Photo Researcher   Hilary Newman
Illustration Coordinator   Sandra Rigby

This book was set in 10/12 pt. Garamond Light by Ruttle, Shaw, & Wetherill and printed and bound by Donnelley & Sons (Crawfordsville). The cover was printed by Lehigh Press.

Library of Congress Cataloging in Publication Data
Pervin, Lawrence A.
     The science of personality / Lawrence A. Pervin.—1st ed.
          p.   cm.
     Includes bibliographical references.
     ISBN 0-471-57850-9 (cloth : alk. paper)
     1. Personality.   I. Title.
     BF698.P377   1996
     155.2—dc20   95-5144
                                                                  CIP

Printed in the United States of America
10 9 8 7 6 5 4 3 2 1

PREFACE

My goal in writing this text is to present to students the field of personality as it exists today, with all of the sense of excitement and challenge that personality psychologists face in their efforts to understand people. One might ask: How could the goal of a current personality text be otherwise? The fact is, however, that since the 1960s personality texts have been based, to a large extent, on grand theories of personality, such as Freud's psychoanalytic theory and learning theory. Some texts consist only of the description of perhaps a dozen or so theories of personality. The text I studied from as a student was of this sort and was considered a landmark for its time. Other texts focus on a few major theoretical approaches and bring in relevant research, but the focus remains on the grand theories.

The field of personality has changed dramatically over the past 30 years, however. It no longer is dominated by grand theories. Rather, it focuses its efforts on the investigation of a number of questions concerning personality that may be influenced greatly or minimally by a grand theory. The following questions are of current concern to personality psychologists: To what extent is personality stable over time and across situations? How can we account for stability and change? How do genes and environment, nature and nurture, interact to produce an individual's personality? How, and to what extent, do unconscious processes influence what we feel and do? What is the nature of the self and to what extent does the concept of the self differ across cultures? Do thoughts and feelings influence physical health? These and other compelling questions are the subject matter of current personality research and form the basis for what is presented in this text.

THE NEED FOR CHANGE IN HOW PERSONALITY IS TAUGHT

To my knowledge, personality is the only area in psychology in which the leading texts do not present the field as it currently exists. Despite being the author of another personality text that is focused on grand theories, I believe that it is time for the teaching of the field to reflect current research more accurately. There is a drama to research as we seek to understand and explain the complex person. Today there are a large number of investigators involved in this drama and dedicated to the scientific study of the person. This text is an effort to engage and inform the student in this process, and thereby to transform the teaching of the field to reflect its current status more accurately.

When I began work on this book a few years ago, I felt as if I might be a lone voice in the field. Clearly this is not the case. I was pleased to learn of a paper given by Gerald Mendelsohn of the University of California (Berkeley) at a symposium on "Teaching Personality Psychology" at the 1993 meetings of the American Psychological Association. Mendelsohn indicated that the typical, time-honored approach to teaching personality to undergraduates—namely a Theories of Personality course—is misleading and uninformative. The material presented in such a course is outdated and of limited scientific relevance and has little to do with research actually done by personality psychologists. He suggested that we do a disservice to students and to the field by continuing to present such an outdated picture and that it is time we did better.

More recently, an article by Mark Leary of Wake Forest University appeared in the professional newsletter *Dialogue* with the title "How Should We Teach Undergraduates About Personality?" He too noted that the current classic theories course does not adequately reflect contemporary personality psychology. In addition, he indicated that many of the theories covered in such a course are unsubstantiated. He suggested that students who take a single course in personality are better served by a text organized around major topics of current concern than one organized around grand theories.

I agree with these analyses but am aware that what is being suggested will meet with some resistance. I have deliberated about just how I would change the content of my personality course when I switch from a traditional theories course to one that reflects current work in the field. The task was well stated by an anonymous reviewer of a draft of this book:

> If we instructors of personality are honest with ourselves, I believe that we must acknowledge that the old schema, our old way of presenting the field, has outlived its utility. The use of this text will require that we "old dogs" learn new tricks. But, after all, we must consider what is best for the "young dogs" we teach. And I believe that for them, the new schema offers a better foundation on which to assemble the mushrooming data in this field.

As one of the "old dogs," I will have to follow this reviewer's advice and approach the teaching of the course somewhat differently. After some resistance, which I believe is typical for such efforts, I eagerly look forward to the adventure.

ORGANIZATION OF THE TEXT AND CHAPTER CONTENT

People are complex. No two are alike. How can we capture such complexity and diversity while still formulating general laws for all? This is the essence of the challenge facing personality psychologists. The research presented in this book represents my own sense of where we currently stand in relation to this challenge and is the focus of the text. At the same time, I have made an effort to familiarize the student with some of the major theories current in the field by discussing them in relation to relevant research. I also have made an effort to be fair in presenting alternative approaches while periodically expressing my own point of view and evaluation of these efforts.

Finally, while focusing on the work of individuals who identify themselves as personality psychologists, I also have included the research of many individuals who might be considered social psychologists, developmental psychologists, or behavioral geneticists. I think that many of these labels are arbitrary and do not make much sense. Beyond this, I think that we must make use of knowledge from any source. Human personality is sufficiently complex that we cannot afford to ignore relevant work in other parts of psychology or, for that matter, in other disciplines such as anthropology and biology.

Chapter 1 is an introduction to the field—how we all are personality psychologists and how personality scientists differ from "the person in the street" in being more systematic about gathering data and testing hypotheses. The first chapter focuses on the major approaches to research (i.e., clinical, correlational, experimental), outlining the history and contributions of each. The emphasis is on the strengths and limitations of these approaches and the need for a multimethod approach to the study of personality.

Part One includes three chapters on the units of personality—traits, cognitions, and motives. Psychologists historically have emphasized what people do, think, and feel. The three chapters in this part illustrate how psychologists have attempted to understand personality through an emphasis on one or another of these units. Relations among the units also are discussed. A concluding section suggests that a full understanding of how people function will necessarily involve an appreciation of relations among behaviors, thoughts, and feelings.

Part Two focuses on personality development. Chapter 5 discusses evidence concerning the contributions of genes and environments to the development of personality. Although genes and environment, nature and nurture, are typically placed in opposition to one another, the chapter emphasizes the interdependence of the two—we never have genes without an environment or an environment without genes. Thus, our task is to understand relations between the two rather than attempt to decide whether one is more important than the other. Chapter 6 discusses the development of personality over time and focuses on the issue of its stability over extended periods. The results of a number of longitudinal studies are presented as illustrative of current work in the field.

Part Three focuses on specific areas of research. Here I was faced with the task of deciding which research was important to present to students and how the research could be presented in terms of coherent categories. I have attempted to be broad and representative in coverage but obviously selectivity is necessary. The first six chapters in this section cover topics that I beleive to be of fundamental importance to the field as well as active areas of current research—the unconscious, the self, motivation, emotion and health, psychopathology and psychotherapy, and assessment. In each of these chapters attention is given to the questions being addressed by researchers and how they are attempting to answer them. Alternative theoretical and research approaches are considered, once more with an emphasis on the strengths and limitations of each.

The concluding chapter of the text addresses fundamental questions that I believe confront personality psychologists and also discusses prospects for the field. This chapter most clearly sets forth my own thoughts as I attempt to return to various issues covered in the text and consider the future course of the field. In this chapter I emphasize the importance of being aware of cultural differences and diversity while attempting to formulate general laws.

As noted, my effort has been to be representative in presenting the field as it exists today. Dealing with such a large amount of material is potentially an overwhelming task for both the writer and the reader. Therefore, I have made an effort to present the research in terms of coherent categories and to structure each chapter in ways that will facilitate learning. Each chapter begins with a chapter overview that provides the context within which the material in the chapter can be considered. Each overview is followed by a list of questions to be addressed in the chapter. I have found such questions to be useful in stimulating interest and in helping to relate research to broader issues. Almost every chapter includes a "Spotlight on the Researcher" box featuring a researcher whose work is covered in the chapter. The researchers offer a personal statement concerning the development and current significance of their work and the future direction of their research. Finally, each chapter concludes with definitions of the major concepts covered and a summary of the major points.

A CONCLUDING PERSONAL NOTE

In science, as in life, I believe that we must mix commitment with humility—commitment to particular goals and views, humility in appreciation that we may be totally wrong and our views will have to change. I am fond of saying that life without commitment is passionless, and life without humility leaves one possessed by ideology and resistant to change. I hope that the student reading this text will develop not only an understanding of the field of personality as it exists today but also a commitment to particular ideas and approaches to research, a commitment tempered, however, by an appreciation for the complexity of the field and the challenges that lie ahead.

I invite students and faculty to join with me in what I see as a new approach to the field for beginning personality students. While most of the grand theories of the field have existed for more than a quarter of a century, most of the research covered in this text has been conducted in the last decade. While most text revisions done every 4 or 5 years require relatively minor changes, a second edition of this text likely will require much more significant change. If not, this will be a disappointing statement about lack of progress. Given how much is yet to be learned about human personality, changes in the field need not reflect progress, but we can be sure that a lack of change reflects a lack of progress. The material covered in this text represents progress beyond what might have been included in such a text written 5 to 10 years ago. I have faith in the progress that will be made in the next 5 to 10 years.

ACKNOWLEDGMENTS

My efforts to complete this text were inadvertently assisted by the squirrels in my backyard. Anyone who has observed squirrels trying to steal bird food cannot but be impressed with their motivated, goal-directed, tenacious behavior. In trying to design a squirrel-proof bird feeder, I fell off a ladder, tore my achilles tendon, and had to spend a summer on crutches. I used the time writing the text I had been planning to write, although at an accelerated pace encouraged by my lack of mobility. So, these fascinating animals deserve a word of acknowledgment, and a period of observation by those who doubt the goal-directed quality of animal behavior.

I have been assisted in developing this text by the students in my personality classes. In particular, I appreciate the efforts of three students, Cheryl DeFeo, William Duffie II, and Valerie Gellene, who read and gave me feedback on portions of the text. I appreciate the contributions of the prominent and busy psychologists who contributed to the Spotlight on the Researcher sections in the text. As with my work on my other text, Karen Dubno, editor at Wiley, has been of tremendous help, prodding me in a gentle way to do what required more work but helped to improve the text. The helpful reviews and suggestions for revision of the following colleagues are gratefully acknowledged:

James Averill
University of Massachusetts—Amherst

Brian Hayden
Brown University

Jeff Burroughs
BYU—Hawaii

Lawrence Lilliston
Oakland University

David Christian
University of Idaho

Joseph Lowman
University of North Carolina—Chapel Hill

Jerrold Downey
University of South Alabama

Steve Spencer
SUNY—Buffalo

Sherryl Goodman
Emory University

And finally I acknowledge the following colleagues, whose response to a survey helped Wiley and I decide that the time was right for a new way to track the personality course:

Susan Andersen
New York University

Robert Bornstein
Gettysburg College

Darryl Bem
Cornell University

Mary Brabeck
Boston College

James Calhoun
University of Georgia

John Campbell
Franklin & Marshall College

Etzel Cardeña
Trinity College

Anne Constantinople
Vassar College

W. G. Dahlstrom
University of North Carolina—Chapel Hill

Robert Dolliver
University of Missouri

Eugene Doughtie
University of Houston

Jerrold Downey
University of South Alabama

William Drennen
University of South Carolina

Harold Einhorn
San Francisco State University

Ron Fisher
Miami—Dade Community College

Iris Fodor
New York University

William Gayton
University of Southern Maine

Uwe Gielen
St. Francis College

Sherryl Goodman
Emory University

David Harder
Tufts University

Brian Hayden
Brown University

M. Hemphill
College of St. Francis

Cooper Holmes
Emporia State University

Jurgis Karuza
SUNY at Buffalo

Gregory Kolden
Colby College

Michael Lambert
Brigham Young University

Kevin Lanning
University of New South Wales, Australia

Peter Lennon
Seton Hall University

Lawrence Lilliston
Oakland University

Anthony LoGiudice
Frostburg State College

Dennis Madrid
University of Southern Colorado

James Mancuso
SUNY at Albany

Karen Mark
Illinois State University

Claudia McDade
Jacksonville State University

Dale Neaman
Wichita State University

Daniel Nelson
Siena College

Jim Nelson
Valparaiso University

L. Orlofsky
University of Missouri

E. L. Paul
Wellesley College

Paul Poppen
George Washington University

Ross Robak
Pace University

J. Rodriguez
Occidental College

Jack Shaffer
Humboldt State University

Barry Silverstein
William Patterson College

Jefferson Singer
Connecticut College

Jaine Strauss
Williams College

Frank Vitro
Texas Women's University

Lloyd Williams
Lehigh University

Stanley Woll
California State University at Fullerton

Lawrence A. Pervin

BRIEF CONTENTS

CONTENTS

PART TWO: PERSONALITY DEVELOPMENT

INTRODUCTION: THE SCIENTIFIC STUDY OF PERSONALITY

CHAPTER OVERVIEW

How are we to study the complexity of human personality? Personality psychologists follow diverse paths in their research efforts. Sometimes these paths overlap, but often they diverge in terms of what is studied as well as in how it is studied. But whichever path researchers choose to pursue, and whichever aspects of personality are of particular interest to them, they must seek to ensure that their observations are reliable and accurate. In this chapter we consider the differing research strategies pursued by personality psychologists as they seek to unravel the mystery of human personality functioning. We also consider why some investigators prefer one strategy over another and the scientific goals held in common by all investigators.

Questions to Be Addressed in This Chapter

1　What are the research methods available to personality psychologists?

2　What is the history of these methods?

3　What are the strengths and limitations of each of the methods?

4　Which goals do these methods share despite the divergent paths taken in the scientific study of personality?

Humans have been personality psychologists since the development of consciousness and a sense of self. All of us, in our everyday lives, observe other people, formulate ideas as to their characteristics and reasons for behaving, make predictions about their behavior, and adjust our own behavior accordingly. Probably all of us, to one degree or another, note individual differences among people and categorize others into types. Probably all of us have ideas about the fundamental nature of humans, for example, whether they are basically good or bad, altruistic or selfish, generous or greedy, as well as ideas about how easily they can be changed to do good or evil.

From the earliest times there is evidence of efforts to systematize such views about people, often in the form of a religion and a social code of behavior. The Old Testament, for example, includes descriptions of the personalities of individuals and the reasons for their behavior. From the time of the Greek civilization, there were efforts to relate individual differences in personality (temperament) to the functioning of the body, a view in principle not that different from current biological views of personality. Historically philosophers have been concerned with the fundamental nature of humans and the reasons for human action, and many psychology departments in universities evolved out of philosophy departments.

It is, however, to the end of the nineteenth century and the beginning of the twentieth that we trace the beginnings of psychology as a science, and it is here too that we can begin to find the roots of the scientific study of personality as we know it today. As we shall see, it was not until the 1930s that personality began to be recognized as a distinct part of psychology, largely due to the publication of such great works as Allport's (1937) *Personality: A Psychological Interpretation* and Murray's (1938) *Explorations in Personality.* In this sense, personality as a discipline is a very young science, close to 60 years old. Yet, its roots as a science date back another fifty years, a century or so ago, to the beginnings of psychology as a science. It is here, at the dawn of the twentieth century, that we find the beginnings of three traditions in personality research—the clinical, the correlational, and the experimental.

THREE RESEARCH TRADITIONS

In this book we are exploring the scientific study of personality. Thus, we are interested in the systematic investigation of individual differences and the organized functioning of the person as a whole. Whereas most personality texts begin with a definition of personality, we will leave this for the end, content at this point to say that we are concerned with both individual differences and the organization of parts into a functioning whole. In emphasizing personality as a science, we are concerned with systematic observation and investigation as opposed to what might be called "arm-chair speculation" or philosophical debate. Personality as a science rests largely on observations concerning human functioning that can be replicated by other observers and on efforts to formulate principles and laws that can be tested through further observation.

Within the field of personality as a science, there are three distinct research traditions, each with its own approach to observation —the *clinical,* the *correlational,* and the *experimental.* In this chapter we trace each tradition from its beginnings to its place in the field of personality today, noting along the way the problems that have arisen and the contributions that have been made. We will then be in a position to consider the relative strengths and limitations of the three approaches and the role they can play in a modern science of personality.

THE CLINICAL APPROACH TO PERSONALITY

Clinical research involves the systematic, in-depth study of individuals.

Jean Charcot and His Students

We begin our story of this approach with the work of the French physician Jean Charcot (1825–1893) at a neurological clinic in Paris. Charcot was interested in understanding the problems of hysterical patients who came to his clinic, individuals who, for example, had paralyses that did not make anatomical sense, problems with seeing despite a healthy visual apparatus, periods of fainting of unknown cause, and inexplicable amnesias or gaps in memory. Charcot began to study these patients, to classify their symptoms, and to treat them, largely through the use of hypnosis. Could one rule out the possibility of physical, organic difficulties? Yes. Could one conclude that they were faking their difficulties? No.

Charcot also trained other physicians, three of whom went on to make their own important observations and are part of the history of personality. One student was Pierre Janet (1859–1947), who succeeded Charcot as director of the neurological clinic and continued Charcot's study of hysterical disorders and his work with hypnosis. Janet attempted to systematize the clinical observations of hysteria and relate them to concepts in psychology. Janet found that patients under hypnosis could recall experiences completely forgotten under normal awake conditions. Suggestions from him to hypnotized patients could often be therapeutic to them in their awake state, even if they had no recall of the suggestions. Thus, Janet was led to the view that there is a splitting of consciousness in hysteria; that is, Janet's clinical observations led him to posit the existence in hysterics of two or more streams of mental functioning that are split off from one another rather than being united as in normal functioning. It was as if the individual could have ideas, "fixed ideas," that were dissociated from one another. Because of this dissociation, conscious awareness and control of the fixed ideas were not possible. It was the existence of these dissociated or split-off parts of consciousness that led to the symptoms of hysteria. Thus, the symptom, such as the paralyzed hand, was under the control of a split-off fixed idea rather than under the voluntary control of the rest of the personality. Although Janet's dissociation theory of hysteria and mental processes was neglected for a long period of time, it has now regained considerable interest from cognitive psychologists interested in unconscious processes (Kihlstrom, 1990).

Another student of Charcot's was the American Morton Prince (1854–1929). Prince is of particular importance to the field of personality for two reasons. First, his book *The Dissociation of Personality* (1906) contained case descriptions of **multiple per-**

sonalities, or individuals within whom two or more distinct and separate personalities exist, often with some personalities being unaware of the existence of other personalities. His detailed case presentation of the treatment of Miss Beauchamp provides many important observations concerning the functioning of multiple personalities. It is the forerunner of such later famous cases as *The Three Faces of Eve* (Thigpen & Cleckley, 1954) and *Sybil* (Schreiber, 1973).

Today, there is tremendous interest in multiple personalities for a number of reasons: Many clinicians think that there has been a significant increase in the number of such cases, and such cases raise questions concerning the self, consciousness, and volitional control. For example, we can ask first how it is that these different personalities get split off from one another rather than being integrated into some organized sense of self. Different selves exist within all of us; why then aren't we all multiple personalities? Second, how is it that parts of one's life, lived by one personality, can be completely split off from other parts of one's life and shielded from knowledge by another personality? And, finally, how is it in such cases that each personality can exert control over the actions of some but not other personalities? How can the wishes and intentions of one personality be blocked from expression by another personality? In *The Three Faces of Eve,* how was Eve Black at times able to block the conservative intentions of Eve White and instead act in flirtatious, seductive ways? Does the explanation for such phenomena offer us any insight into the problem all of us face at times when one part of our personality interferes with the wishes of another part, as when our desire to diet is overridden by the craving for food or our intention to get started on a paper is blocked by procrastination and delay?

A second reason for the importance of Morton Prince was his establishment of the Harvard Psychological Clinic in 1927. Here Prince continued his research and provided the climate for clinical research by other psychologists. One such psychologist was Henry Murray (1883–1988), author of the monumental *Explorations in Personality* (1938) and forefather of a generation of personality psychologists interested in the intensive study of the individual. As Prince's successor as director of the Harvard Psychological Clinic, Murray played an important role in furthering efforts to study individuals intensively through the combination of clinical and other methods of investigation.

Sigmund Freud

The third Charcot pupil of note was Sigmund Freud (1856–1939). Freud was one of the intellectual giants of the twentieth century. His theory of personality and method of therapy, psychoanalysis, have influenced millions of lives and our society as a whole. Virtually all students who have taken an introductory course in psychology are familiar with the basics of his theory—his emphasis on unconscious processes, the importance of the sexual and aggressive instincts, the importance of early experience in the formation of personality, and the role of anxiety and the mechanisms of defense in the formation of neuroses. His terms for the parts of personality, *id, ego,* and *superego,* are virtually a part of the everyday parlance of our culture and the focus for cartoons in popular magazines. Yet, many would argue that it is his clinical observations, rather than his theoretical formulations, that show Freud's true genius (Klein, 1976; Schafer, 1976). As someone who has practiced as a clinician for over 30 years, I share this point of view—the greatness of Freud was in his observations and descriptions of aspects of personality functioning ignored by some but also challenged by many to this day.

What is it that Freud did? Stripped away from the complexities of theory, Freud listened to people. He listened not just for a few minutes but for an hour or so at a time and for weeks, months, and years with the same individual. During this time he encouraged his patients to let their minds wander and to follow but one rule, to say everything that came to mind and withhold nothing. This seems to be an easy task for therapist and patient alike, the therapist required just to listen and the patient to talk or free associate. Yet, as many who have tried it have discovered, neither is necessarily easy. Therapists often find it difficult to be silent and just observe, and patients always experience times when they are reluctant to share thoughts that come to mind and feelings that are experienced. As is true for all of us in our everyday lives, there are times when we have thoughts and feelings that we are afraid to recognize and ashamed to share with others. It was Freud's genius, then, to take seriously and attempt to understand just these thoughts and feelings, and to encourage individuals to join in this endeavor with him.

In its essence, then, psychoanalysis as a clinical method of investigation is about the wishes and fears that people have, about their memories of the past and the sense they make of these memories in relation to their current functioning, about memories of their relationships in childhood and how these memories color their relationships in the present, about their struggles to cope with painful feelings such as anxiety and shame (Lewis, 1992a), and about their reluctance to share many thoughts and feelings with others, at times even themselves. Stripped of abstract and metaphorical terms such as *libido* and *Oedipus complex*, psychoanalysis is about the drama of life played out in each of us, about the inexplicable symptoms we develop and senseless things we find ourselves doing, about why some of us are driven to succeed and others cannot allow themselves success, about how we can both crave intimacy and also be afraid of it.

As is well known, Freud's observations and his theories have been challenged from the time of their initial presentation to today. What is particularly troubling about this is that the challenge comes not only from those who reject psychoanalysis outright but from those who may begin with a commitment to it. Thus, early disciples

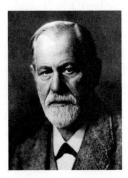

The roots of the clinical approach
to personality can be
traced to Sigmund Freud.

of Freud, such as Adler and Jung, broke with him and established their own schools of analysis based on their own observations and theories. And, more recently, we have analysts who question the "scientific truth" of what patients recall in psychoanalysis (Spence, 1982, 1987) and others, such as Albert Ellis and Aaron Beck, who reject psychoanalysis altogether in favor of more cognitive approaches to the field. What is particularly troubling is that it is not just the theoretical formulations that are being challenged, but the very nature of the observations themselves. In other words, for all of the brilliance of Freud and his efforts at careful observation and description, there are many who would still ask: Where are the data? And it is here that we run into the nub of the problem with some forms of clinical data—unless the observations can be confirmed by others, in systematic and specified ways, they are useless from a scientific standpoint.

Henry Murray

I suspect that Henry Murray, Prince's successor at the Harvard Psychological Clinic, was very much aware of these issues as he attempted to build upon many of the observations reported by psychoanalysts such as Freud and Jung. Murray was sensitive to the value of clinical observation through his training as a physician but also aware of the value of scientific research through his training in biochemistry. He was a person of broad interests and enormous creativity, delving into psychoanalysis through his own analyses with Carl Jung and Franz Alexander and into the fantasy life of others through the development, with Christiana Morgan, of the **Thematic Apperception Test (TAT).** In this test subjects are shown a scene on a card, such as a young man turned away from an older woman, and asked to tell a story about the scene. Since there is so little actual material on which to base a story, much of the subject's response can be treated as fantasy expressing the needs (wishes and fears) of the individual. To provide for more systematic investigation, there is an established method for scoring the stories so that subjects can be compared in terms of the strength of various needs or motives. For Murray, then, the TAT provided a means of accessing the world of the person emphasized by psychoanalysts, a world that could not be accessed through self-report alone: "Children perceive inaccurately, are very little conscious of their inner states and retain fallacious recollections of occurrences. Many adults are hardly better" (Murray, 1938, p. 15).

It is interesting to note that the subtitle of Murray's 1938 book *Explorations in Personality* is "A Clinical and Experimental Study of Fifty Men of College Age." This subtitle brings to our attention Murray's effort to utilize both the clinical and experimental methods in his studies of the person. It also is interesting to note that the book is dedicated to, among others, Morton Prince, Sigmund Freud, and Carl Jung.

In Murray's pioneering research, over the course of three years a group of investigators studied fifty subjects with the common purpose of arriving at a formulation of the personality of each subject and through analysis of the data a guide to the personality functioning of people generally. Data were obtained from interviews, questionnaires, fantasy measures such as the Thematic Apperception Test, and situational tests such as responses to the frustration of not being able to solve a puzzle. Thus, Murray and his co-workers departed from typical clinical investigations in their use of a variety of controlled conditions. However, it also is true that what distinguished this research from more traditional academic research was the variety of data obtained on each subject and the case conference method used to formulate a comprehensive picture of each individual. Murray's effort was to "penetrate below the level of what is evident to the ordinary layman" (1938, p. 33) and to develop a comprehensive picture of the person as a whole. It is this interplay between the effort to capture the comprehensiveness of the clinical and the rigor of the experimental that most represents the genius and creativity of Murray's research. In accordance with the methods of clinical researchers, Murray called for personality psychologists to not lose sight of human nature as it operates in everyday existence. For more traditional academic researchers, he called for orderly methods of investigation and proper statistical treatment of findings. In accord with psychoanalytic investigations, there was in-depth study of individuals and an emphasis on unconscious tendencies. In addition, there was an effort to relate current personality functioning to experiences in childhood. On the other hand, more attention was paid to the conscious, manifest personality than would be typical for psychoanalysts and greater effort to test hypotheses in systematic ways. Capturing the tensions associated with such an effort, Murray described his work as follows:

> In short, then, we might say that our work is the natural child of the deep, significant, metaphorical, provocative and questionable speculations of psychoanalysis and the precise, systematic, statistical, trivial and artificial methods of academic psychology. Our hope is that we have inherited more of the virtues than the vices of our parents.

> 1938, pp. 33–34

Murray was involved in a World War II effort to select individuals to serve in the Office of Strategic Services, the forerunner of the Central Intelligence Agency (CIA). The war proved important for the development of personality psychology because it greatly expanded the role of personality psychologists in the assessment and treatment of individuals. Personality psychologists established their skill in developing tests that could be used to measure individuals on important personality traits and, as clinical psychologists, established their place in the treatment of psychological disorders. An outgrowth of this was the further development of grand theories of personality based primarily on clinical investigation.

Carl Rogers and George Kelly

Two theories of particular note in this regard are Carl Rogers's self-actualizing theory of personality and George Kelly's personal construct theory of personality. These clinically based theories point to important aspects of personality functioning. They also illustrate the ways in which such clinically based theories are derived from important social forces current at the time of investigation.

Carl Rogers (1902–1987) may be the most influential personality theorist representative of what has been called the **Human Potential Movement.** Responding to the psychoanalytic view of the person as driven by dark, unconscious forces, and the behaviorist, Skinnerian view of the person as merely responding to external reinforcers, Rogers emphasized the movement of the organism toward growth and self-actualization. The focus for Rogers was on the *self*, on the ways in which the individual perceives and experiences the self. Rogers maintained that he did not begin his work with the concept of the self. In fact, at first he thought it was a vague, scientifically meaningless term, a view often expressed by others in the field. However, as he listened to clients express their problems, he found that they talked in terms of the self. Thus, the self became his focus of inquiry and the center of his description of personality.

Rogers attempted to be both a sensitive clinician and a rigorous scientist. He believed that clinical material, obtained during psychotherapy, offers valuable insights into the nature of human functioning. In attempting to understand human behavior, he always started with clinical observations. From there, however, he believed that it was necessary to formulate specific hypotheses that could be tested in a rigorous way. Thus, in his practice as a therapist, he would emphasize the subjective, attempting as much as possible to experience and empathize with the experiential world of the client. However, in his functioning as a researcher interested in the process of psychotherapy and how people change, he would emphasize objectivity and what he described as the elegant methods of science. He was as committed to the former as a source for hypotheses as he was to the latter as a tool for their confirmation. In the end, however, it was what he observed as a clinician that he trusted most of all.

There are a number of interesting parallels between Carl Rogers and George Kelly (1905–1966). Born within a few years of one another and obtaining their Ph.D.'s in the same year, 1931, they both began their careers by working with children and developed theories of personality and approaches to psychotherapy based on their experiences with clients. Yet, they were led to emphasize vastly different phenomena in their theories of personality and quite different methods in their approaches to psychotherapy. Kelly published *The Psychology of Personal Constructs* in 1955, a set of books that was reviewed as the greatest single contribution to the theory of personality functioning of the decade between 1945 and 1955 (Bruner, 1956).

In this work Kelly described his view of the person as a scientist, ever seeking to make better predictions concerning the behavior of people and to expand the range of phenomena covered by his or her theory. Kelly emphasized the **constructs** or ways of construing (interpreting) the world that people have and the problems created when they have maladaptive constructs or apply their constructs in maladaptive ways. Examples of the latter include people rigidly applying the same way of viewing events despite changing circumstances or applying their constructs in such random ways that life becomes chaotic. Although Kelly rejected any simplistic characterization of his theory, most people would describe it as a cognitive theory of personality, emphasizing as it does the ways in which people think about and process information concerning the world, including themselves. In this, he anticipated the cognitive, information-processing approach to personality by perhaps two decades.

As noted, despite parallels in their histories, Rogers and Kelly were led to distinctly different points of emphasis and approaches to therapy. Both were interested in people's perception of the world about them and of themselves, but for Rogers the emphasis was on *experience* whereas for Kelly it was on *constructs*. For Rogers the ideal was the self-actualizing person, whereas for Kelly it was the well-functioning scientist. For Rogers the goal of psychotherapy was to help the person become more in touch with his or her own feelings and more empathic with others, whereas for Kelly the goal was to help the person make better predictions and be more open to testing his or her theory of personality (construct system) against the data of events. Whereas Rogers as a therapist tried to provide a climate in which clients would grow as people, Kelly as a therapist played a more active role in encouraging clients to examine their constructs and conduct their lives in the atmosphere of experimentation. Whereas Rogers believed that Kelly's approach was "almost entirely an intellectual function" (1956, p. 358), Kelly viewed the Rogerian therapist as having too much faith in an emerging being and as being too little involved in helping clients to do new things that would result in better data (1955, p. 401).

Considering the contributions of Freud, Rogers, and Kelly, we have a treasure of clinical observations and three enormously creative grand theories of personality. I suspect that followers of each approach would accept many of the observations made by followers of the other approaches. As a practicing clinician, I am no less impressed with the observations made by Rogers and Kelly than I am with those made by Freud. Yet, the observations and theories are vastly different, as are the approaches to psychotherapy. The three approaches lead to different kinds of observations and to the testing of different kinds of hypotheses. Thus, it is hard to make exact comparisons between them or to make direct tests of whether one theory's hypotheses are better than those of another. It even is hard to establish rules for determining whether one or another approach to therapy is better at helping people to change.

Strengths and Limitations of the Clinical Approach

So, it is here that we come to the strengths and liabilities of the clinical method as it typically has been used in the field of personality. To its credit, the clinical method provides the opportunity to observe a great variety of phenomena as well as the functioning of the person as a whole, and it is capable of generating new observations and a wealth of hypotheses. As a practicing clinician, I am continuously impressed with new observations concerning people and what I believe are new insights into personality functioning. Yet, to its detriment the clinical method often makes it difficult for others to confirm the observations or to formulate specific hypotheses that might be tested under more rigorous empirical conditions. In other words, as scientists we always are seeking *reliable observations* and *tests of hypotheses* that follow agreed upon rules of evidence. We need not be rigid about what the observations are or where they take place—they can be cognitions, fantasies, emotions, or behaviors that occur in the therapist's office, in a testing session, or in the laboratory. However, we must be insistent that others can replicate the observations and that we have a way of testing whether the suggested relationships do indeed exist. It is here that the scientist all too often is frustrated with the contributions of the clinician.

Lest the contrast be drawn too dramatically, it should be noted that most clinically based theories of personality were developed by individuals trained in the methods of science and devoted to the goals of reliability of observation and the testing of hypotheses. Freud had been an excellent biological researcher before he became an analyst and was quite sophisticated about scientific procedures. Murray was trained in research in biochemistry before he became a psychologist, and Rogers made significant contributions to the scientific study of the process of psychotherapy. Kelly so valued the functioning of the scientist that he sought to make his clients better scientists in their daily lives. Thus, it is not the case that clinicians such as these were unaware of scientific procedures or rejecting of them. However, for the sake of observation, they were prepared to relax some rules of evidence and, in their efforts to map out the broad terrain of personality, often were prepared to forgo the formulation of hypotheses that could be put to the test.

The clinical method can be used in conjunction with the other methods of investigation that we are about to consider. Examples of such efforts will appear throughout this book. However, generally this has not been the case; that is, individual personality psychologists typically have emphasized one or another method of investigation. Whether the trade-offs clinicians often make are necessary and worthwhile, students can decide for themselves, once they have considered the alternative research strategies and the findings in the field to date.

THE CORRELATIONAL APPROACH TO PERSONALITY

Correlational research typically involves the use of statistical measures to establish the association, or correlation, between sets of measures on which individuals have been found to differ. In other words, the correlational approach emphasizes individual differences and the effort to establish relationships among those differences on various personality characteristics. For example, individual differences in anxiety might be related to test performance. Or, individual differences in temperament might be related to career choice. In contrast to the clinical emphasis on observation, the correlational approach emphasizes measurement. In contrast to the clinical emphasis on the study of the individual or a few subjects, the correlational approach emphasizes the use of data obtained on large numbers of subjects. Instead of the holistic emphasis of the clinical approach to personality, the correlational approach emphasizes relationships among a few elements of personality functioning.

We will have a chance to examine these differences in greater detail later. For now, it is important to keep in mind the emphasis on measurement of individual differences and the effort to establish statistical relationships among these differences—the key terms being *individual differences, measurement,* and *statistical relationships*.

Sir Frances Galton and His Followers

Let us begin the history of this approach to personality with the work of Sir Francis Galton (1822–1911). About the same time that Charcot was conducting clinical studies of hysteria, Sir Francis Galton was involved with studies that would lead him to be called the "founder of individual psychology" (Boring, 1950). A half-cousin of Darwin's, Galton was influenced by Darwin's discoveries and his theory of evolution. Thus, he set out to study differences in humans and whether those differences were due to heredity. In tracing some of the history of Galton's work, it is important to keep in mind his emphasis on three things—individual differences, measurement,

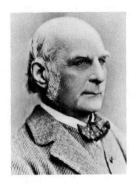

The roots of the correlational approach to personality can be traced to Francis Galton.

and heredity, as well as his emphasis on the use of tests, ratings, questionnaires, and large numbers of subjects. As we shall see, most, if not all, of these factors have remained basic characteristics of the correlational approach to personality.

Galton began with an interest in the inheritance of human attributes, in particular the inheritance of intellectual abilities. He strongly believed that human characteristics were inherited and that these characteristics could be systematically measured. For example, he developed the "Galton whistle" to measure the ability to hear high-pitched tones. He also developed a means for rating genius and eminence (i.e., superior accomplishment in fields such as law, literature, politics, science, and art), as well as a measure of the boringness of speakers. With a background in meteorology, he believed that quantitative measurement was a necessary characteristic of a truly scientific endeavor. His early work was on the question of whether genius and eminence tend to run in families. Through the use of defined criteria for rating such accomplishments, and the careful biographical study of families of men of accomplishment, Galton found a strong relationship between the biological closeness of two men and the probability of their both being eminent.

On the basis of his findings of the tendency for genius and eminence to run in families, Galton concluded that individual differences in intelligence and talent are largely inherited. In this regard he contrasted "nature" (heredity) with "nurture" (environment), a contrast that remains with us to this day. He also emphasized the importance of studying resemblances between twins and siblings separated environmentally as a result of adoption.

Following this research, Galton set up a laboratory to measure individuals on a great variety of characteristics. Over the course of time he measured thousands of individuals on a variety of physical and psychological characteristics. In this research he used tests, ratings, and questionnaires. To establish relationships among the data, he developed the concept of the **correlation coefficient** or the quantitative measure of the association between two sets of data. Thus, for example, one could compute the statistical association or correlation between height and weight or between parental intelligence and offspring intelligence. This work was further developed by his disciple Karl Pearson (1857–1936), resulting in the statistical procedure known today as the *Pearson product moment correlation*.

Galton's work on the measurement of mental abilities was further pursued by another British psychologist, Charles Spearman (1863–1945). Inspired by Galton's work, Spearman set out to determine whether there was something that might be called *general intelligence* or whether individual differences in intelligence were due to differences in multiple, independent, separate abilities. To do this he gave many different tests of mental ability to hundreds of people and conducted correlation tests to determine whether those high on one ability also tended to be high on other abilities. His answer to the question concerning intelligence was that there is a general intelligence or *g factor*. In this work he also created the statistical procedure known as *factor analysis,* through which one finds commonalities, called *factors*, in a large mass of data. The question for personality researchers is whether there are basic groups of characteristics, or factors, on which people differ. If we measure people on lots of personality characteristics, do the many differences really boil down to a few groupings, and, if so, what are they? As we shall see, it is the development of factor analysis that has been fundamental to the correlational approach to personality.

Raymond B. Cattell and Hans J. Eysenck

The importance of World War II for the development of clinical psychology as a profession, and the increased role of psychologists as therapists, has already been mentioned. Earlier, World War I played an important role in the development of psychologists as assessors of human characteristics. During the war a committee of psychologists was established within the medical department of the U.S. Army to devise ability and personality tests for the classification of recruits. This work led to the development of a group intelligence test, the Army Alpha, and a personality inventory, the Personal Data Sheet, designed to select out individuals with serious neurotic difficulties. Although the latter was not based on factor analysis, it represented a milestone in the use of personality questionnaires for important personnel decisions.

At this point we move ahead to the 1940s when we see the blossoming of the correlational approach to personality. This period brings together the use of ratings and questionnaires as sources of personality data, the use of factor analysis as a statistical technique, and the concept of the *trait* as a fundamental unit of personality. Since the 1940s this combination of a statistical technique—factor analysis, particular kinds of data—ratings and questionnaires, and a concept—the trait has exerted a powerful influence on the field. It is here that we can continue to see the emphasis on measurement and individual differences noted as fundamental to the correlational approach to personality. It is here that we can see at least partial fulfillment of Allport's prediction in 1937 that Galton's view "seems destined to dominate the psychology of personality during the twentieth century" (Allport, 1937, p. 97).

Our story can begin with the effort of Raymond B. Cattell (1905–) to develop a useful taxonomy (classification) of personality units or traits. Trained in chemistry, Cattell believed that it was necessary to develop a classification of basic units of personality comparable to the periodic table of elements in chemistry. Born and trained in England, he was influenced by Spearman's work on factor analysis, which was to become the tool for establishing personality psychology's periodic table of elements. The elements of personality were to be traits or behaviors that typically covaried (increased and decreased together). In other words, traits referred to behaviors that were correlated with one another. The method for finding traits was factor analysis.

How was one to go about finding the basic elements of personality—its basic table of the elements? Cattell (1943) built upon an earlier effort by Allport (Allport & Odbert, 1936) to use personality descriptors found in the English language. What better place is there to look for the basic units of personality than in the language people use to describe one another. What Cattell did was develop a list of personality terms, mainly personality traits, found in common usage and in the professional literature. One hundred adults then were rated on 171 such terms, and these ratings were subjected to a factor analysis to determine the basic groupings or units. Cattell concluded that there were 12 basic personality factors (Cattell, 1943, 1945).

Cattell's work with ratings was followed by the factor analysis of responses by large numbers of subjects to thousands of personality questionnaire items. This led to the finding of 16 personality factors and publication of the Sixteen Personality Factor Questionnaire (Cattell, 1956, 1965).

Hans J. Eysenck (1916–), another British psychologist, similarly pursued the correlational approach to personality through the factor analysis of responses to questionnaire items. Based on his research Eysenck emphasized three basic trait dimensions of personality: *introversion-extraversion, neuroticism* (stable-unstable), and *psychoticism* (insensitive-sensitive) and devised questionnaires to measure individual differences on the three dimensions (Eysenck, 1970, 1990).

The Five-Factor Model of Personality

Since the beginning of the 1990s, many factor-analytic studies of personality ratings and questionnaire responses have been conducted. The history is a long one with many detours concerning the number of units or factors basic to personality and the names of these units. A consensus seems to be emerging among proponents of this approach that there are five basic factors or dimensions of personality—this is known as the **five-factor model (FFM)** of personality (Costa & McCrae, 1992; John, 1990; McCrae & John, 1992). Since these units are discussed in depth in Chapter 2, they will only be listed at this time: They are Neuroticism, Extraversion, Conscientiousness, Agreeableness, and Openness to Experience. Also, although this too will be considered in greater detail later in the text, it is suggested that individual differences in these personality traits are to a large extent inherited (Loehlin, 1992). Thus, in terms of the emphasis on individual differences, measurement, statistical procedures to establish correlations, and an interest in heredity, we can trace the roots of this approach to personality back to the efforts of Galton.

As was true of the clinical approach to personality research, it would be a mistake to expect absolute uniformity among researchers within the correlational research tradition. These researchers study different aspects of personality and often utilize different kinds of data (e.g., ratings, questionnaires, objective tests). Further, although factor analysis has been emphasized here, there are followers of the tradition who prefer to use other procedures to establish relations among individual differences variables. What is common to all followers of this approach, and what separates such research from clinical or experimental research, is the effort to establish statistical associations or correlations among measures of individual differences.

Strengths and Limitations of the Correlational Approach

The focus of the correlational approach is on individual differences. As with the clinical approach, interest is in the functioning of the person over a wide range of situations and in all aspects of personality. However, whereas the clinical approach makes use of both self-report data and actual observations of behavior, at least in the clinical setting, the correlational approach is typically limited to self-report data. Also, whereas the clinical approach generally leaves considerable latitude for what the clinician will ask and how the patient or subject will respond, the correlational approach restricts self-report to the items on questionnaires and the alternatives given for responses. For example, a trait questionnaire typically asks the subject to respond to each item in terms of whether or not it is characteristic of them (see Table 2.1). In return for this limitation and potential liability, psychologists using the correlational approach are able to give subjects numerical scores on specific traits and use statistical procedures to establish relationships between trait scores and other variables (e.g., between scores on Neuroticism and performance difficulty in anxiety-arousing situations). In other words, whereas clinicians are forced to use their heads to observe patterns of relationships, those using the correlational approach make use of statistical procedures to establish relationships. Both, however, are vulnerable to the potential distortions that are a part of all self-report data (Wilson, 1994).

At its core, the correlational approach to personality seeks to define the basic structure of personality, what Cattell viewed as personality's basic table of the elements. As noted, the specific method to be used is factor analysis. Ultimately, then, the value of this approach will be defined by the extent to which personality psychologists agree that the factors derived from using the method of factor analysis make sense as basic units of personality. At the present time many personality psychologists are encouraged by the progress being made, but agreement by no means exists among all personality psychologists. The evidence in support of the utility of traits as units of personality is considered in Chapter 2. Other units of personality, such as cognitive and motivational variables, derived from other approaches, are considered in Chapters 3 and 4.

THE EXPERIMENTAL APPROACH TO PERSONALITY

Experimental research involves the systematic manipulation of variables to establish causal relationships. Such manipulation does not occur in the clinical and correlational approaches. The experimenter may manipulate one variable, the independent variable, and measure the effects on the second variable, the dependent variable. For example, degree of threat or anxiety (independent variable) can be experimentally increased and its observed effects on learning or performance (dependent variable) measured. In contrast to the clinical emphasis on the individual, the experimental approach typically involves the study of many subjects. In contrast to the correlational approach, with its emphasis on individual differences, the experimental approach emphasizes general laws of psychological functioning that apply to all people. In contrast to both clinical and correlational research, there is direct experimental control over the variables of interest to the investigator.

The roots of the experimental approach to personality can be traced to Wilhelm Wundt.

Wilhelm Wundt, Hermann Ebbinghaus, and Ivan Pavlov

At about the same time that Charcot was conducting his clinical investigations in France, and Galton was conducting his studies in England, Wilhelm Wundt (1832–1920) was establishing the first laboratory of experimental psychology in Germany. Whereas Galton has been described as the founder of individual psychology, Wundt has been described as the "founder of general psychology" (Boring, 1950, p. 487). Trained in chemistry and physiology, Wundt stressed the place of psychology as a science—an experimental science with procedures similar to those followed in the natural sciences. Wundt defined psychology as the *science of immediate experience* and investigated the effects of changes in stimuli (e.g., lights, sounds) on the intensity and quality of subjects' experiences.

Also near the end of the nineteenth century, two other individuals conducted experimental research that was to be influential in the history of the field. In Germany, Hermann Ebbinghaus (1850–1909) studied memory. He invented the nonsense syllable, which was formed by two consonants surrounding a vowel (e.g., zag, feb, rit). Subjects learned a list of nonsense syllables and then were tested after various time periods for their recall of the original list. This experiment allowed him to study such things as the effects of repetition on memory and forgetting as a function of time. What is of significance here is the emphasis on experimental control and the establishment of principles of memory for all subjects. His result was a *forgetting curve* that typified the forgetting of material over time. Such a curve ignored or "smoothed out" individual differences. Also of significance was the use of nonsense syllables that removed the effects of meaning, and the different meanings the same words can have for different people, on how material is learned and remembered. Although one rarely reads today of research involving the use of nonsense syllables, they were routinely used as late as the 1950s.

In Russia, Ivan Pavlov (1849–1936) was conducting his experimental research on classical conditioning. All psychology students must by now be familiar with Pavlov's classic research on the conditioning of a dog's responses to stimuli that originally were neutral or uninfluential with regard to those responses. Thus, a bell sounded before the presentation of food to a dog could eventually itself produce the salivary response associated with food and a bell sounded before an electric shock that was administered to the dog's paw could produce the withdrawal response associated with the shock. Among the phenomena investigated by Pavlov that are of particular interest to personality psychologists was his study of conflict and **experimental neurosis**. Here Pavlov conditioned one stimulus to a positive reinforcer and a second stimulus to a neutral or aversive stimulus. The question asked was what would happen when the dog could not discriminate between the two stimuli. For example, suppose a circle is conditioned to food and an oval-shaped stimulus to shock, and then stimuli that are between a circle and an oval are presented.

What are the effects? What Pavlov found was that the presentation of such conflictual stimuli, involving the breakdown in ability to discriminate between signals of positive and negative events, led to the development of emotionally disturbed behavior on the part of the dogs.

Although Pavlov was interested in individual differences in dogs as they related to the conditioning of responses, the major thrust of his research was on the development of general laws of classical conditioning. In its emphasis on the experimental manipulation of variables and the establishment of causal relations between pairings of stimuli with responses, Pavlov's work clearly illustrates the experimental approach. It also is of interest here because of the use of animals to establish general principles of psychological functioning, something that is more characteristic of the experimental approach than of the clinical and correlational approaches. Finally, as noted, Pavlov's work illustrates the application of general principles to such important personality phenomena as conflict and the development of a neurosis.

J. B. Watson, Clark Hull, and B. F. Skinner

To the extent that the experimental approach to research is fundamental to all of psychology, its history is that of the history of psychology. Since our emphasis here is on personality research, we will briefly consider some of the highlights of this broader history as they relate to the field of personality. Thus, we can first note the importance of John B. Watson (1878–1958) and the development of behaviorism. Watson, in his book *Psychology from the Standpoint of a Behaviorist* (1919), emphasized the objective study of overt behavior as opposed to the use of introspection and the study of internal events (e.g., dreams). For him psychology was the study of the development of stimulus-response (S-R) connections. In addition, partly because he was uncomfortable with being a subject himself and with the artificial instructions given to subjects, Watson emphasized the use of animals in research. At the same time, he did conduct some research with humans, such as his famous study of the conditioning of emotional reactions in infants (J. B. Watson & Rayner, 1920).

Watson's emphasis on behaviorism and S-R psychology was important in relation to the work of Clark Hull (1884–1952). After an early interest in hypnosis, Hull devoted himself to the development of an S-R theory of learning. It is hard for today's students to appreciate the power that S-R psychology had over the field of psychology generally, and parts of personality psychology in particular, during the 1940s and early 1950s. The prevailing model of human functioning at the time was that of the telephone switchboard—stimuli got plugged in and responses came out. The S-R model was applied not only to animal learning but to child development, social psychology, and, of course, personality. It included both the experimental investigation of phenomena of interest to personality psychologists, such as the study of approach-avoidance conflicts in rats, and the translation of clinical theories such as psychoanalysis into S-R terms (Dollard & Miller, 1950). Of particular interest here is a general review at the time of experimental tests of psychoanalytic theory (Sears, 1944). It may be of interest to note that although some S-R psychologists were eager to submit psychoanalytic observations and hypotheses to experimental investigation, Freud and other analysts believed such experimental tests could prove little—the clinical observations stood on a solid foundation by themselves.

Another important development from Watson's behaviorism was B. F. Skinner's (1904–1990) operant conditioning. Skinner's emphasis on the shaping of observable responses through various schedules of reinforcement had a particularly powerful impact on the field of clinical psychology during the 1950s and 1960s. The interpretation of abnormal behavior as the result of maladaptive learning, and the application of principles of operant conditioning to the modification of behavior, an approach to treatment known as **behavior modification,** was a powerful force during this time. It was seen as a rival in both theory and application to more clinically based approaches such as psychoanalysis and Rogers's client-centered therapy. Its emphasis on the experimental study of variables affecting overt behavior also was seen by its proponents as more scientific than the correlational use of questionnaires to study traits that often were difficult to observe directly.

Cognitive Approaches

As we shall see in Chapter 3, the experimental approach has been used to study a wide variety of personality phenomena, both within and outside the context of S-R theory and operant conditioning theory. Since the cognitive revolution in the 1960s, many problems of importance to personality psychologists have been studied through the application of principles and procedures borrowed from experimental cognitive psychology. In particular, we can note such areas as the study of unconscious processes, the self, and motivation (Pervin, 1990). Although we have not seen the development of comprehensive theories of personality such as those that grew out of clinical approaches, or the development of a "consensual" view such as the five-factor model from the correlational approach, we have seen the development of social cognitive and information-processing approaches to personality (Bandura, 1986; Cantor & Zirkel, 1990; Mischel, 1973, 1990).

The psychologists associated with these cognitive approaches to personality depart radically from the principles and procedures emphasized by the early experimental learning psychologists such as Hull and Skinner. They make use of concepts of internal processes, such as goals, and often are eclectic in their methods of research, including at times the use of questionnaires. Generally they emphasize the study of human subjects rather than animals, sometimes in the natural environment rather than in the laboratory. What binds them together, however, and allows us to include them within the experimental tradition, is their emphasis on links with experimental psychology and the use of systematic research to establish general principles of personality functioning. Although accepting of the use of clinical material for suggesting hypotheses to be investigated, they reject the clinical approach as the fundamental basis for a science of personality. And, although accepting of the use of self-report in some research, they reject a primary emphasis on questionnaires and the use of personality concepts derived from correlational approaches such as factor analysis.

Strengths and Limitations of the Experimental Approach

In many ways the experimental approach represents the scientific ideal. The experimenter manipulates specific variables to establish cause-effect relationships. To the extent that self-report data are not used, there is no need to worry about whether the subject is telling the truth or is able to report accurately on what is being experienced.

So why aren't all personality psychologists committed to the experimental approach? We will have more to say about this in the following section, but here we can note that many personality psychologists see the experimental situation as limited in regard to what can be studied. To what extent can such important personality phenomena as fantasies and romantic relationships be studied in the laboratory? To what extent can findings in the laboratory be extrapolated to the behavior of individuals in their daily lives? And, just as the clinical and correlational approaches have potential limitations because of their reliance on self-report data, so too does the experimental approach have potential limitations because of the nature of the experimental situation. We would like to believe that subjects come to the experimental situation without preconceived notions as to what the experiment is about and are completely conscientious in their efforts to be good subjects. Any student who has served as a subject in an experiment knows, however, that subjects often bring their own hypotheses to the experiment and act in accordance with them or pick up what they perceive to be cues as to what the research is about and, for the good of science, behave in accordance with what they think is the experimenter's hypothesis. Or, for other reasons, some subjects may decide to behave in ways that will disconfirm what they believe to be the experimenter's hypothesis. In a certain sense, for human subjects the experiment is a social situation in which their own personalities may enter in ways unforeseen by the experimenter.

For many personality psychologists, however, the most troubling aspect of the experimental approach is the limitation on studying the richness of relationships among the elements of an individual's personality. In limiting investigation to a few well-controlled variables, the experimental approach misses what is a fundamental aspect of personality functioning, the functioning of the parts in the context of a total system. Thus, even after defining cause-effect relationships among specific variables, the personality psychologist is left with the task of considering how all the pieces fit together, that is, of determining how the personality as a whole functions. After breaking down personality into the pieces, we are left with the task of putting Humpty-Dumpty back together again.

SHARED GOALS, DIVERGENT PATHS

We have had the opportunity to examine briefly the history of three approaches to personality—the clinical, the correlational, and the experimental. Starting at roughly the same time, just before the turn of the century, the three traditions have continued into the present, at times overlapping but more generally being pursued independently of one another. To put the matter in broader and richer perspective, let us consider the following three points: (1) Throughout the history of the field there have been debates concerning which is the better or best approach to research. (2) At the same time, personality research often makes use of combinations of the clinical, correlational, and experimental approaches. (3) All personality research shares certain goals.

Strengths and Limitations of the Three Approaches

Throughout the history of the field of psychology, there has been controversy concerning the relative strengths and weaknesses of the various approaches to research. Early note was taken of these differences in a 1939 presidential address to the American Psychological Association (Dashiell, 1939). Here a distinction was made between the *experimental attitude* and the *clinical attitude.* The experimental attitude involved careful experimentation through which the scientist was able to gain control over variables and understand the conditions under which phenomena occur. In contrast, the clinical attitude involved speculation in which the individual rather than general principles was the primary subject matter. Whereas the one focused on an understanding of a phenomenon, the other focused on an understanding of the individual.

Fifteen years later, a distinction was drawn between the *experimental* and *psychometric* (correlational) approaches in psychology (Bindra & Scheier, 1954). The experimenter is interested in how to produce phenomena; the psychometric researcher is interested in differences that already exist, such as differences among individuals. Advocates of each approach tended to go their own ways, and the suggestion was made that a combination of experimental and psychometric approaches might be useful.

Shortly thereafter, a paper on "The Two Disciplines of Scientific Psychology" was published (Cronbach, 1957). Written by a highly regarded member of the scientific community, the paper again contrasted the experimental and correlational approaches as two streams of method, thought, and affiliation. Whereas the experimenter seeks to manipulate variables and establish uniform results, the correlational psychologist studies phenomena as they occur and is interested in individual differences as a central matter of concern. Thus, what is a matter of annoyance for one (i.e., individual variation) is a matter of particular interest for the other.

Finally, a more contemporary observer of the field of personality again noted the existence of two traditions of research—each typified by a specific subject matter, methodology, and theoretical orientation (Hogan, 1982). In one tradition there is an emphasis on experimental methodology, single aspects of behavior, and what is true for people generally. In the other tradition, there is an emphasis on clinical case study or questionnaire research, individual differences, and relationships among the parts.

Thus, over the course of more than 50 years various psychologists have emphasized the differences between the clinical, correlational, and experimental approaches to research, as well as the divisions that exist among adherents of each approach. Let us consider, for example, the views of Raymond Cattell concerning the three approaches and why he is such a strong supporter of the correlational approach. Cattell (1965) distinguished among three methods in the study of personality: clinical, bivariate (experimental), and multivariate (correlational). He viewed the clinical method as having the virtue of studying important behaviors as they occur and as looking for lawfulness in the total organism. He noted the value of description and pointed to Darwin's theory of evolution as a masterful outgrowth of careful observation. However, for Cattell the clinical method suffered from two major limitations: (1) It uses too few subjects to differentiate between the idiosyncratic and the universal and (2) it lacks quantitative methods to establish relationships and test competing hypotheses.

Cattell viewed the bivariate (experimental) method as expressing a concern for scientific rigor and as having been useful in other sciences as well as in areas of psychology such as perception and learning. However, for him the experimental method was flawed in relation to the study of personality by its focus on but a few variables and its inability to study important phenomena as they occurred in everyday life. Not surprisingly then, Cattell viewed the multivariate (correlational) method as the best of all worlds, combining the virtues of the clinical and experimental approaches without the limitations of either. Thus, for Cattell, the correlational method, via factor analysis, could establish quantitative relationships through the study of many subjects as they experienced many important events. That factor analysis might have its own limitations, that the correlational method has neither the observational power of the clinical method nor the power of the experimental method to establish causal relations, did not seem to bother Cattell. For him the "beautiful and complex" method of factor analysis was sufficient to find the basic elements and build the structure of personality.

Lest one think that Cattell is unusual in this regard, we could, of course, find comparable representatives of the clinical and experimental points of view. Nor should one think that many of these issues are peculiar to the personality field. Recently, for example, there was debate among investigators of memory as to whether the laboratory or the natural environment was the best place to study memory. Remember our earlier mention of Ebbinghaus's research on memory using nonsense syllables in a laboratory setting. How does such research compare with the investigation of autobiographical memory—what people remember from their past, or eyewitness memory—what people remember from observing a crime being committed?

In a relevant series of articles, the issue was framed as follows: "How shall we study memory? Should we look to the real world and concentrate on naturalistic everyday approaches? Or should we concentrate on more controlled laboratory experimentation" (Loftus, 1991, p. 16)? Those who favored the laboratory approach expressed the view that

> the more complex a phenomenon, the greater the need to study it under controlled conditions and the less it ought to be studied in its natural complexity . . . the superficial glitter of everyday methods should not be allowed to replace the quest for truly generalizable principles.
>
> Banaji & Crowder, 1989, p. 1192

Those who favored the naturalistic approach suggested that the biological field studies of Darwin were a better model for psychology than the laboratory studies of experimental physics. A third view was that the naturalistic approach was acceptable to begin with but that the controlled experiment was the only way to uncover the factors at work. A fourth, ecumenical view was that the two approaches were complementary—there was no reason to believe that there was only one correct way to study memory.

In sum, throughout the history of the field there have been differing views as to how research is best conducted. Clearly there are potential advantages and limitations to each approach (Table 1.1), and in principle there is no reason why they cannot be used in conjunction with one another. Yet, the fact is that researchers do tend to become committed to one or another approach. What is of significance beyond this, however, is that the approach chosen tends to lead to certain observations and to exclude others, and the findings of one approach are all-too-often rejected by the adherents of another. What the clinician observes may not readily lend itself to study through correlational or experimental methods. For example, Freud's observations of the importance of unconscious factors in emotion and memory have been difficult to test through the use of these methods. This is discussed further in Chapter 7. What the correlational researcher finds may lack depth to the clinician and sharpness to the experimentalist. We learn, for example, that overweight students, particularly females, have more difficulty paying for college and receive less family financial support than do normal-weight students (Crandall, 1991), but why on earth should this be the case? Finally, the findings of the experimentalist may seem trivial and artificial to clinicians and correlationists.

TABLE 1.1 Summary of Potential Strengths and Limitations of Alternative Research Methods

Potential Strengths	Potential Limitations
CASE STUDIES AND CLINICAL RESEARCH	
1. Avoid the artificiality of laboratory.	1. Lead to unsystematic observation.
2. Study the full complexity of person-environment relationships.	2. Encourage subjective interpretation of data.
3. Lead to in-depth study of individuals.	3. Involve entangled relationships among variables.
CORRELATION RESEARCH AND QUESTIONNAIRES	
1. Study a wide range of variables.	1. Establish relationships that are associational rather than causal.
2. Study relationships among many variables.	2. Lead to problems of reliability and validity of self-report questionnaires.
EXPERIMENTAL RESEARCH	
1. Manipulates specific variables.	1. Excludes phenomena that cannot be studied in the laboratory.
2. Records data objectively.	2. Creates an artificial setting that limits the generality of findings.
3. Establishes cause-effect relationships.	

Source: Personality: Theory and Research (6th ed., p. 52), by L. A. Pervin, 1993, New York: Wiley.

USING MORE THAN ONE APPROACH

Despite the emphasis placed here on the different approaches, personality research-ers often attempt to combine aspects of more than one approach. For example, the trait psychologist Eysenck has used a questionnaire to study individual differences in the introversion-extraversion trait, as the trait relates to performance in many laboratory situations. In one such study it was found that relative to one another, introverts are more sensitive to pain and extraverts are more sensitive to rewards (G. Wilson, 1978). This work combined the use of questionnaire measures of individual differences determined through factor-analytic techniques, part of the Galton corre-lational tradition, with differences in performance in a laboratory situation, part of the Wundt experimental tradition.

Murray's (1938) work was previously noted as an attempt to combine in-depth interviews with situational tests and the quantitative treatment of findings, methods that included some of the virtues of the more observationally minded clinician with those of the more empirically minded experimentalist. Thus, he concluded that "Our hope is that we have inherited more of the virtues than the vices of our parents" (Murray, 1938, p. 34). Following in Murray's tradition, David McClelland (1961) at-tempted to study the role of achievement motivation in performance through the combined use of TAT-like pictures, laboratory tests of risk-taking behavior, and measures of periods of economic growth in various societies. In one of the grandest research efforts in the field of personality, McClelland found a relationship between individual differences in the need for achievement and risk-taking, entrepreneurial behavior as well as a relationship between periods of high achievement motivation and periods of economic growth within a society. In other words, in an extended line of investigations, he combined the use of fantasy measures favored by clinicians (TAT), with measures of behavior in laboratory experiments, with recorded data of periods of economic growth for various societies and drew associations or correla-tions among them.

Let us turn now to two more recent illustrations of the combined use of more than one research approach. The first involves the development of the concept of the **Type A behavior pattern** and the study of its relation to coronary heart disease. The initial observation of a possible link between personality characteristics and risk of heart disease was made on a clinical basis by two medical cardiologists (M. Friedman & Rosenman, 1974). Indeed, some of the initial observations were made by a secretary who noticed that many of the patients were wearing out the front of the seats while waiting to see the doctors. The cardiologists went on to observe that many younger patients suffering from cardiac disorders had a particular constellation of behavioral characteristics including competitive achievement striving, a sense of time urgency, and aggressiveness. Observation of this pattern in clinical interviews was followed by development of a structured interview to measure individual differ-ences in this regard. The interview asked standard questions designed to elicit com-petitiveness, impatience, and hostility. In addition to content, measures of expressive style were developed for characteristics such as vocal speed, volume, and explosive-ness. Later, a questionnaire was developed by other investigators to measure indi-vidual differences in the characteristics associated with the Type A behavior pattern.

Research on the Type A behavior pattern, measures of it, and its relation to coronary heart disease covers a 20-year period. During this time research in the laboratory was conducted to determine whether Type A individuals, defined in terms of the structured interview or questionnaire, performed differently from non–Type A individuals on various tasks. For example, it was found that relative to individuals scoring low on Type A measures, those scoring high tended to solve more problems and work at levels closer to the limits of their endurance while reporting less fatigue (Glass & Carver, 1980). In a more naturalistic study it was found that bus drivers in the United States and India who scored high on questionnaire measures experienced more stress, had more accidents, and showed more impatient driving behavior relative to individuals with low scores (Evans, Palsane, & Carrere, 1987). Additional observational and questionnaire data showed high scorers to respond with greater hostility when provoked or frustrated although they did not necessarily become more aggressive.

In other words, what we have here is a clinical observation that led to the development of a structured interview measure and a questionnaire measure of individual differences in the proposed pattern of personality characteristics. Individual differences on these measures then were studied in relation to differences in performance on laboratory tasks as well as on other questionnaires and in real-life situations. This research still is in progress but at least two findings seem conclusive. First, the structured interview measure and the questionnaire measure are not in full agreement and one cannot be used as a substitute for the other. In other words, scores on the two measures do not correlate as well as would be expected or desired. The structured interview measure correlates with other data in more theoretically meaningful ways than does the questionnaire measure. Second, the hostility component of the Type A pattern appears to be the most central. There does appear to be evidence of a relationship between hostility, in particular suppressed hostility, and increased risk for coronary heart disease (Booth-Kewley & Friedman, 1987; H. S. Friedman & Booth-Kewley, 1988).

A second illustration of the combined use of various approaches to research involves the concept of **learned helplessness.** Here the story begins with experimental research on fear conditioning and learning with dogs. Martin Seligman (1975) found that when dogs experienced uncontrollable shock in one situation, they transferred their sense of helplessness to another situation in which shock was avoidable— that is, they developed the learned helplessness response. This was true for about two-thirds of the dogs, with the remaining third not developing this pattern, at least not as readily.

Further research demonstrated that the same phenomenon found in dogs could be produced in humans (Hiroto, 1974). College students exposed to a situation of uncontrollable noise had greater difficulty learning to escape the noise in a second situation in which escape was possible than did subjects who had not been exposed to the first situation. Further, an effort was made to determine if individual differences on a questionnaire measure of internal-external locus of control would relate to performance in the laboratory situation. Internal locus of control individuals believe in their ability to control life's events whereas external locus of control individuals believe that chance, luck, or fate control life's events—in other words, they are relatively helpless in influencing them. Individuals who scored as externals on the questionnaire were slower to escape or avoid the unpleasant noise than were internal locus of control subjects. An association or correlation thus was found between a measure of a personality difference and performance in a laboratory test situation. This personality difference in locus of control presumably corresponded to the experimental condition producing the learned helplessness in the dogs, suggesting that individuals high on external locus of control had a past history of experiencing helplessness in relation to negative events.

Once more the history of the relevant research covers a period of over 20 years. During this time there was a focus on the relation between the sense of helplessness and depression that led to the hypothesis that depression is caused by the attribution of helplessness to the self ("It is due to me that I am helpless"), to stable factors ("It will always be this way"), and to global factors ("I am a helpless person, not just helpless about this particular thing") (Abramson, Seligman, & Teasdale, 1978). In addition, a questionnaire was developed, the Attributional Style Questionnaire (Peterson, 1991; Table 1.2), to measure individual differences in the tendency to attribute positive and negative events to internal, stable, and global factors. Individual difference scores on these measures were then correlated with scores for depression as well as performance measures in laboratory and nonlaboratory situations. At this point the evidence of a link or association between depression and internal, stable, and global attributions for negative events appears to be fairly strong (Peterson & Seligman, 1984; Segal & Dobson, 1992). However, it remains unclear as to whether there is a causal relationship between these attributions and depression.

The point of the brief presentation of each of these areas of research is that the investigation of a personality characteristic can, and often does, involve the use of more than just one approach to research. The personality researcher can be interested

TABLE 1.2   Illustrative Item—The Attributional Style Questionnaire (ASQ)

You have been looking unsuccessfully for a job for some time.
1. Write down the *one* major cause. _____
2. Is the cause of your unsuccessful job search due to something about you, or to something about other people or circumstances? (circle one number)
   Totally due to other
   people or circumstances   1 2 3 4 5 6 7   Totally due to me
3. In the future, when looking for a job, will this cause again be present? (circle one number)
   Will never again be
   present   1 2 3 4 5 6 7   Will always be present
4. Is the cause something that influences just looking for a job, or does it also influence other areas of your life? (circle one number)
   Influences just this   Influences all
   particular situation   1 2 3 4 5 6 7   situations in my life
5. How important would this situation be if it happened to you? (circle one number)
   Not at all important   1 2 3 4 5 6 7   Extremely important

Source: "The Attributional Style Questionnaire," by C. Peterson et al., 1982; *Cognitive Therapy and Research, 6,* p. 292.

in general laws and individual differences, in questionnaire measures of individual differences and in performance in laboratory situations, in clinical observations and quantitative measurement. At the same time, these research traditions remain and tend to stand apart, with proponents of each tradition equally committed to the view that the data from their approach provide the best answers to the questions of interest to the student of personality.

SHARED SCIENTIFIC GOALS

Despite these divergent paths, personality psychologists share certain scientific goals. Primary among them are the extension of fields of observation and the development of theories that suggest lawful relationships among variables. We can focus here on the concepts of *reliability* and *validity*, which are basic to the science of personality as well as all other scientific efforts. **Reliability** refers to the extent to which observations are stable and dependable and can be replicated. The foundation of any science is the observations that are made by investigators. For observations to be of scientific merit they must be replicable. Periodically one hears of a finding reported in the scientific literature that is then followed by reports from other investigators that they were not able to replicate the finding. Sometimes such reports come from major laboratories and create headlines, as when a biologist from an outstanding laboratory reported a finding related to AIDS research that subsequently could not be replicated by others and was found to be in error. The important point here is not that there was an error in the reported observation but that the error could be detected by the efforts of others to replicate the observation. Thus, reliability, in terms of replicability of findings, is a basic essential of scientific research.

The other fundamental concept, **validity,** refers to the extent to which we can be sure that our scientific concepts and laws are reflected in our observations. Our scientific concepts, such as motives and personality traits, are defined by observations tied to these concepts. Our scientific laws, such as one that expresses a relationship between a motive and performance, are also tied to observations. To establish the validity of a concept, our observations must fit those suggested by the concept. To establish the validity of a concept such as the need for achievement, our observations must fit those suggested by the concept. To establish the validity of a law concerning personality, our observations must confirm the relationships suggested by the law.

Laws of relationships among variables are parts of theories. Theories are ways of unifying observations, suggesting lawful relationships among variables, and pointing the way toward further observations. Thus, theories are ways of defining what is known and pointing us in fruitful directions toward exploration of the unknown. Theories lead to the formulation of *hypotheses* or suggested relationships among variables. Generally, hypotheses are stated in the form of "If . . . then" relationships: *If* there is change in this variable, *then* this change or difference will be observed in this other variable. Or, *if* individuals differ on this characteristic, *then* they should also differ in these other ways. There might be the hypothesis that an increase in achievement motivation will lead to increased preference for risky investment situations, or the hypothesis that individuals high on the trait of extraversion will prefer to study with others relative to individuals low on this trait.

It should be clear that observations, concepts, theories, and hypotheses are tied to one another. Observations lead to the formulation of concepts that are then unified in terms of a theory. The theory leads to the statement of hypotheses of relationships among variables that are then tested through further research. Ideally there is a continuous process of further observation and the development of new concepts and better theories. In this way, science, including the science of personality, is a continuously unfolding and evolving enterprise.

The three traditions discussed in this chapter (clinical, correlational, experimental) emphasize different paths toward making observations and establishing lawful relationships among variables. As we shall see in Part One of this text, it is for this reason that the research based on these three traditions often leads to somewhat different observations and the formation of different concepts. At the same time, any scientific enterprise emphasizes reliability and validity, the replicability of observations, and lawful relationships among variables. Thus, while following different paths, participants in these three traditions share a commitment to the pursuit of personality research as a scientific enterprise.

MAJOR CONCEPTS

Clinical research. An approach to research involving the intensive study of individuals in terms of naturally occurring behavior or verbal reports of what occurred in the natural setting.

Multiple personality. A psychological disorder in which two or more fairly distinct separate personalities are present within the same person.

Thematic Apperception Test (TAT). A projective test, developed by Morgan and Murray, in which subjects tell stories to a standard set of pictures.

Human Potential Movement. A popular movement during the 1960s and 1970s that emphasized the fulfillment or actualization of individual potential, including openness to experience.

Construct. In Kelly's theory, a way of perceiving, construing, or interpreting events.

Correlational research. An approach to research in which individual differences are measured and related to one another.

Correlation coefficient. A statistical measure of the degree of association or correlation between sets of data.

Factor analysis. A statistical method for determining those variables or test responses that increase or decrease together. Used in the development of personality tests and of some trait theories (e.g., Cattell, Eysenck, FFM).

Trait. A disposition to behave in a particular way, as expressed in a person's behavior over a range of situations.

Five-factor model (FFM). An emerging consensus among many trait theorists suggesting five basic factors within the human personality: Neuroticism, Extraversion, Openness to Experience, Agreeableness, and Conscientiousness.

Experimental research. An approach to research in which the experimenter manipulates the variables and is interested in establishing cause-effect relationships and general laws.

Experimental neurosis.   The development in a laboratory setting, generally with animals, of analogues to human neurotic phenomena.

Behavior modification.   A method of therapy, following learning theory principles, particularly Skinnerian, for the changing of problematic behaviors.

Type A behavior pattern.   A behavior pattern consisting of a constellation of behavior characteristics (competitive achievement striving, sense of time urgency, aggressiveness) thought to be related to risk of coronary heart disease.

Learned helplessness.   Seligman's concept expressing an animal's or person's learning that outcomes are not affected by behavior.

Reliability.   The extent to which observations are stable and dependable and can be replicated.

Validity.   The extent to which observations reflect the concepts, phenomena, or variables of interest.

SUMMARY

1. The scientific study of personality involves the systematic investigation of individual differences and the organized functioning of the person as a whole.

2. Three research traditions can be distinguished within the field of personality as a science—the clinical, the correlational, and the experimental.

3. The clinical approach to personality involves the systematic, in-depth study of individuals. The clinical work of Freud, Rogers, and Kelly is illustrative of this approach to research.

4. The correlational approach to personality involves the use of statistical measures to estimate the association, or correlation, between sets of measures on which individuals have been found to differ. The trait research of Cattell, Eysenck, and proponents of the five-factor model of personality is illustrative of this approach to research.

5. The experimental approach to personality involves the systematic manipulation of variables to establish causal relationships. The work of Pavlov on classical conditioning and of S-R learning psychologists as well as current social cognitive, information-processing approaches to personality are illustrative of this approach to research.

6. Often personality researchers use aspects of more than one of these approaches to research. Such efforts are illustrated in achievement motivation research, investigation of the Type A behavior pattern, and research related to the concept of learned helplessness.

7. Each of the three research traditions is associated with specific potential strengths

and limitations (see Table 1.1). Although following divergent paths, personality psychologists from the three research traditions share the common goals of achieving reliability and validity in their work.

8.   Theories are ways of suggesting lawful relationships among variables, of defining what is known, and of pointing us in fruitful directions toward exploration of the unknown. The three traditions represent different paths toward making observations and establishing lawful relations among variables. They share, however, a commitment to the pursuit of personality research as a scientific enterprise.

P A R T

I

UNITS OF PERSONALITY

E very science makes use of conceptual units that provide the basis for theory and investigation in the field—for example, the periodic table of the elements in chemistry, the parts of the body in anatomy, the units of matter in physics.

What are the units of the science of personality? This question, addressed by Gordon Allport in 1958, will be of concern to us in the next three chapters. Allport listed 10 basic units: intellectual capacities, temperament traits, unconscious motives, social attitudes, cognitive styles and schema (ways of viewing the world), interests and values, expressive traits, stylistic traits, pathological trends, and factorial clusters of traits derived from factor analysis (Allport, 1958). Allport suggested that complex units rather than very small or molecular units were needed, as well as units that could account for the regularities in behavior and also the variabilities of behavior from situation to situation. In addition, he noted that we were not always able to observe directly the units of interest, such as unconscious motives or some traits. This inability, of course, is not unique to personality research since many sciences include units that cannot, at least initially, be observed directly.

The personality psychologist David McClelland, already noted in Chapter 1 in regard to his work on achievement motivation, considered the issue of basic units in his 1951 personality text. Three units received particular emphasis— traits, schema, and motives (McClelland, 1951). Although containing fewer items than Allport's list, McClelland's units actually are quite similar since virtually all of Allport's units could be included in the three categories suggested by McClelland. For example, Allport's interests and values unit, as a way of organizing experience, could be included within McClelland's schema category.

How similar are the units of personality studied today and how far have we come in our observations and measurements in regard to these units? How do the units relate to one another and how far do they seem to take us in our efforts to understand personality—the organized, system aspects of the functioning of the person that provide for individual differences? To answer the first question, it can be suggested that the basic units of research in the field of personality today remain very similar to those noted by Allport and McClelland, particularly if we include emotions within the motivation category, as McClelland did. Thus, in the following chapters we consider traits, cognitions-schemas, and motives as basic units of personality. Answers to the other questions, concerning the relationships among the units and how far we have come in our research on them, will await consideration of the units themselves. It is, then, to such consideration that we now turn.

TRAIT UNITS OF PERSONALITY

2

CHAPTER OVERVIEW

In this chapter we consider traits as units of personality. Traits describe broad regularities or consistencies in the functioning of people. We commonly use such traits to portray the personalities of others and of ourselves. Are such concepts also useful to us as personality scientists? Many personality researchers think so and have accumulated an impressive amount of evidence in support of traits as basic units of personality. However, other personality psychologists suggest that personality is too complex and variable to be captured by such basic units. In this chapter we consider the evidence in support of traits as basic units of personality as well as the questions raised by critics of the trait concept.

Questions to Be Addressed in This Chapter

1. How is the trait concept used to describe the basic units of personality?

2. How have different trait psychologists studied the trait concept and how similar have their findings been?

3. Are there a few basic trait units that represent the fundamental building blocks of personality? What is the evidence in support of such a view?

4. If traits represent broad consistencies in behavior over time and across situations, how are we to account for variability of behavior in response to the demands of particular situations?

We begin our study of the units of personality with the concept of a trait. **Traits** are descriptors we use to characterize someone's personality. They include terms such as outgoing, friendly, reserved, hostile, competitive, generous, and so on. We find these terms to be useful summary descriptions whether we have just met someone or know that person well, whether we have seen him or her in a wide range of situations or just in one setting. It is not always clear to us just how we arrive at this assessment of a person—one answer perhaps is that "she just seemed that way." Even though we are surprised to find that someone is very different in situations other than the one we knew him in, generally we find ourselves comfortable using traits to describe people. Apparently this is true for people around the world and starts at a fairly early age (John, 1990; Yik & Bond, 1993).

The use of trait terms to describe individual differences started with the earliest efforts to categorize people. The emphasis on the trait concept as a fundamental unit of personality also dates back to the beginning of personality as a distinct part of psychology. Thus, in his groundbreaking book on personality, Allport (1937) suggested that traits were the fundamental units of personality. Another book on personality written in the same year similarly suggested that "Traits are the units of personality" (Stagner, 1937, p. 12). Since that time the trait concept has gone through periods of popularity and disfavor among personality psychologists, but it always has remained an important part of the field. Even though traits have never been totally accepted as the basic units of personality, there have always been leaders in the field who believe them to be so.

Although, as we shall see, trait psychologists do not always agree as to how to define and measure a trait, they do agree on two points: (1) Traits refer to regularities or broad behavioral consistencies in the conduct of people. As such, traits represent basic categories of individual differences in functioning. Thus, to describe someone as outgoing is to describe a general characteristic and to distinguish that person from others who are characterized as being shy. (2) As descriptors of such broad differences in functioning, traits are useful as the basic units of personality. Following from this, the task for personality psychologists is to discover the basic traits of personality, develop ways to measure them, explore how traits develop, and then determine whether the concept offers a satisfactory explanation for individual differences in functioning in a wide variety of contexts.

Before considering some of the more recent research on the trait concept, let us briefly review the theories and procedures of investigation of three important figures in its history.

THE TRAIT PSYCHOLOGY OF GORDON W. ALLPORT

Gordon Allport (1897–1967) viewed traits as the basic structural elements of personality. He considered a trait to be a *predisposition to respond* in a particular way. A trait led to consistency in response because it rendered many stimuli "functionally equivalent" and brought together many forms of adaptive and expressive behavior. For example, sociable people are friendly and outgoing because many situations are viewed by them as opportunities to relate to people and because relating to others is part of their style of functioning in the world. In other words, traits represent a readiness to respond in a particular way because, on the input side, various situations are treated as similar and, on the output side, the person has an expressive and adaptive style.

Do traits actually exist or are they merely useful descriptors of behavioral generalities? Allport believed that traits actually existed in that they were based in the "neuropsychic systems" of people. Although they could not be observed and measured at the time, Allport believed that traits were based in biological and physical differences among people. At the same time, it was in the "observable stream of behavior" that traits were to be seen.

Allport suggested many different categories of traits. One distinction had to do with whether traits could be used to describe people in general or just a single individual—this known as the *nomothetic-idiographic* issue. Allport believed that it was important to develop trait units that applied to all people—the **nomothetic** emphasis. However, he also insisted upon the importance of the individual and suggested that there were traits that could be unique to the individual—the **idiographic** emphasis. A second distinction had to do with how central and broadly descriptive a trait was. Here Allport distinguished among *cardinal traits, central traits,* and *secondary dispositions.* A **cardinal trait** expresses a disposition that is so pervasive in a person's life that virtually every act is traceable to its influence. For example, we speak of the Machiavellian person named after Niccolò Machiavelli's portrayal of the successful Renaissance ruler, of the sadistic person named after the Marquis de Sade, and of the authoritarian personality who sees virtually everything in black-and-white stereotyped ways. Generally, people have few such cardinal traits. **Central traits** (e.g., honesty, kindness, assertiveness) express dispositions that cover a more limited range of situations than cardinal traits but still represent broad consistencies in behavior. Finally, **secondary dispositions** represent tendencies that are the least conspicuous, generalized, and consistent. In other words, people possess traits with varying degrees of significance and generality. Different traits may be cardinal, central, or secondary dispositions in different people.

Allport did not make use of the method of factor analysis to determine trait units or categories. In fact, from his earliest writings he rejected factor analysis on the ground that it so emphasized the average that the individual got lost in the process. He suggested that factor analysis treats the person as composed of independent elements rather than as a unified system of interdependent substructures. Again, he was concerned with the total, organized, patterned aspects of individual functioning more than with what he viewed as abstract units that might not relate to individuals in a meaningful way.

Although critical of factor analysis, Allport did make a noteworthy effort to develop a taxonomy of trait terms (Allport & Odbert, 1936). What he did was develop a list of such terms found in an English dictionary, add some additional slang terms, and then classify the almost 18,000 terms into categories. The categories consisted of stable and enduring characteristics, temporary mood states and activities, social evaluations, and a mixed category of physical characteristics and talents or abilities. The first category, stable and enduring characteristics, is the one that is most closely related to the trait concept as it is generally used. Although somewhat unsystematic in the way that categories were formed, the research was important in its use of ordinary language as a basis for developing a taxonomy of trait terms.

A few additional points are noteworthy in relation to Allport as a trait theorist. First, he was critical of psychologists who focused on measures of individual differences to the neglect of the organization of the individual as a whole. This fit with his rejection of factor analysis as a method for studying personality. Allport suggested that it might be more important to know about traits unique to the person, and about the organization of traits within the person, than to know where the person stands relative to others on some common traits. More generally, he emphasized the importance of idiographic research that involved the in-depth study of pattern and organization in individual functioning, relative to nomothetic research, or the study of individual differences on a few standard personality measures. For Allport any legitimate theory of personality had to be capable of capturing the uniqueness of the individual.

Second, Allport was very much aware of the variability and complexity of behavior, but he did believe that people behave consistently and thus the trait concept was useful. At the same time, he recognized that people are influenced by situations and that most behaviors express the influence of multiple traits. In addition, he suggested that every person has conflicts that can be expressed in antagonistic dispositions. Thus, consistency was a matter of degree and "perfect and rigid self-consistency is not to be expected" (1937, p. 332).

Finally, Allport struggled with the issue of the relation of the motive concept to the trait concept. We will return to this issue when we consider the concept of motive and the relation of traits to motives. However, it is important to recognize here that Allport was concerned with what activated the organism as well as with what guided its response to stimuli, the distinction he made between motivation and style of response (Allport, 1937, p. 323). At times he viewed the person in motivational terms. At the same time, he rejected then traditional views of needs and motives as too limited depictions of personality. These traditional views were seen as suggesting that all motivation could be reduced to the operation of but a few motives (e.g., sex and aggression) and all behavior was in the service of tension reduction. Could such a view do justice to the varied functioning of the person? He thought not. Thus, Allport rejected the conventional view of motives and attempted to include motives within the domain of traits. At the same time, he suggested that not all motives were traits and not all traits were motives. What, then, was the relation between the two? This was a question that he never resolved to a satisfactory degree (Pervin, 1993c).

Allport was a personality psychologist of considerable wisdom. His writings can still be read with profit today. However, for the most part his work is of historical interest rather than being noteworthy for its impact on current trait theory. This likely is because of Allport's emphasis on the idiographic relative to the nomothetic, on pattern and organization within the individual relative to differences between individuals, and to his criticism of factor analysis. Although Allport considered the units discovered through factor analysis to "resemble sausage meat that has failed to pass the pure food and health inspection" (1958, p. 251), subsequent trait psychologists have relied on factor analysis as a major tool in the discovery of the basic units of personality.

THE TRAIT PSYCHOLOGY OF RAYMOND B. CATTELL

Raymond B. Cattell is one of the great figures in the history of trait psychology. His interests and contributions are incredibly wide ranging and include not only the application of factor analysis to personality traits and personality assessment, but also contributions in the areas of intelligence and the inheritance of personality, as well as other areas.

Cattell's college major was in chemistry and, when he turned to a career in psychology, his goal was to develop a taxonomy of personality traits comparable to chemistry's periodic table of the elements. Trained in England, he was influenced by Spearman's work with factor analysis. Thus, factor analysis was seen as the method of choice for determining the basic units of personality. His early research involved using many of the trait terms already employed by Allport (Allport & Odbert, 1936) but in addition using factor analysis to determine groups of terms that seemed to go together. In this research (Cattell, 1943) he had adults rated by acquaintances or judges and then used factor-analytic techniques to determine which groups of traits were highly correlated. He concluded that 15 factors appeared to account for most of personality.

Not content with analyses of trait terms as used in everyday language, Cattell set out to determine if the same groups of trait terms (factors) could be found in questionnaires. This research was to serve as a check on the earlier research and also as the basis for the development of a questionnaire to measure individual differences in the basic elements of personality. Thousands of questionnaire items were written and administered to large numbers of subjects. Factor analyses were used to determine which questionnaire items went together. In analyzing these data Cattell concluded that there were 16 factors or groups of items and on this basis developed the **Sixteen Personality Factor (16 P.F.) Questionnaire** to measure individual differences on the relevant trait dimensions (Catttell & Eber, 1962). Some of these trait dimensions were Reserved-Outgoing, Stable-Emotional, Expedient-Conscientious, and Conservative-Experimenting.

How well did these factors agree with those obtained from the earlier research involving ratings based on trait terms used in everyday language? Cattell concluded that 12 showed considerable correspondence whereas 4 appeared to be unique to the questionnaires. Continuing with this line of investigation, he set out to determine whether the same factors would be obtained from using objective test data. Once more many subjects were tested, in this case on laboratory-type tests, to determine which performances went together to form trait factors. The factor analysis of the behavioral test data resulted in the finding of 21 trait factors. How well did these correspond with the factors obtained in ratings and questionnaires? Although there was considerable overlap, there was no simple "point-to-point" correspondence (Skinner & Howarth, 1973).

It may be hard to appreciate the magnitude of Cattell's efforts to determine the basic structure of personality. To do so, it is important to recognize that today factor analyses are done completely on a computer—the data are entered along with the factor-analytic program and the output indicates how many factors there are and which trait terms go together on each factor. However, in the 1940s, when Cattell was doing this research, computers were not available and he had to do these analyses by hand (John, 1990)! Beyond this, Cattell was not content with data of one kind alone—ratings, questionnaire responses, or laboratory-type tests. Rather, he dared to determine whether the same basic elements came up in all three realms of data, as he suggested should be the case. To this day such a monumental effort has not been replicated. As we shall see, subsequent investigators have been content to use one type of data or, at best, to check on the relations between ratings and questionnaire data.

Now we just briefly touch upon two additional contributions by Cattell to trait theory and research. First, Cattell was interested in the determinants and the development of traits. To study the former, he developed a method to determine how much heredity and environment influence the development of different traits. Although the relative influences of heredity and environment were found to vary considerably, overall personality was estimated to be two-thirds determined by environment and one-third by heredity (Hundleby, Pawlik, & Cattell, 1965). As we shall see, research in this area, now known as *behavior genetics research,* has advanced considerably since these studies by Cattell. However, his research in this area is noteworthy, particularly in that it occurred at a time when most psychologists in the United States were taking an almost exclusively environmentalist position.

In addition to this interest in the determinants of traits, Cattell explored the progression of trait development over time. Thus, he was interested in questions such as whether the same traits were relevant to personality at all ages and whether trait scores were stable over time. Much of this research suggested that the same basic trait factors could be found in children, adolescents, and adults (Coan, 1966). On the other hand, a study of nursery school children indicated that only about one-third of the traits found in adults could be found in children age four or younger (Damarin & Cattell, 1968). Cattell also found evidence of a fair amount of stability on a trait, particularly as the individual becomes older (Cattell, 1965).

The second contribution is Cattell's concern with the dynamic aspects of personality as well as its structural aspects—with the fluid, changing aspects of personality as well as its stable aspects. Thus, Cattell clearly did not see the person as a static entity who behaved the same way in all situations. He recognized that how a person behaves at any one time depends on many motivational and situational factors. Thus, he also used factor-analytic techniques to derive a taxonomy of motives and attempted to develop a formula to predict behavior based on the relevant trait and situational variables.

We have considered the work of Cattell at some length both because of its historical significance and because it highlights a number of issues that will concern us later in the chapter—the basic trait units, the comparability of traits from different data domains, the determinants of traits, and trait stability and change over time. Although not previously discussed, we can add here his research on whether the same traits show up in different cultures. Taken together, his work represents a remarkable record of accomplishment.

THE TRAIT PSYCHOLOGY OF HANS J. EYSENCK

Many of Hans Eysenck's contributions have paralleled those of Cattell, and he also makes extensive use of factor analysis. In addition, Eysenck, like Cattell, has been incredibly wide ranging in his interests—discovery of basic trait units, development of personality questionnaires, investigation of the genetic determinants and the biological bases of personality (Eysenck, 1990) and the determinants of creativity (Eysenck, 1993). However, he differs from Cattell in two fundamental ways. First, he emphasizes fewer trait dimensions than does Cattell, preferring to operate at the level of **types** that underlie the factors or traits emphasized by Cattell. Second, more recently he has made a greater attempt to relate individual differences in traits to differences in biological functioning.

Let us consider these differences in greater detail. As noted, like Cattell, Eysenck makes use of factor analysis to determine the basic dimensions of personality. Like Cattell, Eysenck emphasizes traits as habitual responses that tend to go together. At a higher level of organization, however, Eysenck describes types (Eysenck, 1970; Figure 2.1). Although the term *type* is used, it is important to recognize that in fact it represents a dimension with a low end and a high end and people may fall along various points between the two extremes.

Figure 2.1   Diagrammatic Representation of Hierarchical Organization of Personality.

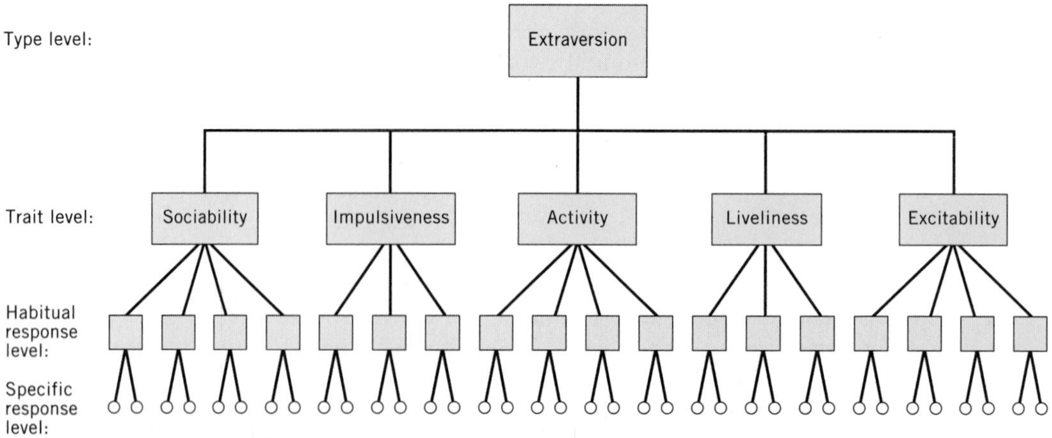

Source: The Structure of Personality (p. 13), by H. J. Eysenck, 1970, London: Metheun. Reprinted by permission of Metheun & Co.

Figure 2.2   The hierarchical structure of Psychoticism (P).

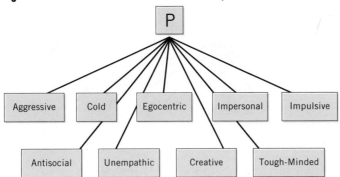

Eysenck emphasizes three basic dimensions of personality—*Introversion-Extraversion, Neuroticism, and Psychoticism* (Figures 2.2, 2.3, 2.4; Eysenck, 1990, p. 246). The initials E (Extraversion), N (Neuroticism), and P (Psychoticism) are used to denote these three type dimensions and the acronym PEN is used to refer to the three-dimensional model of personality. The Eysenck Personality Questionnaire (EPQ) has been developed as a measure of individual differences on these three basic trait dimensions (Eysenck & Eysenck, 1975; Table 2.1).

Before considering each of these dimensions in greater detail, it may be noted that the first two dimensions (E,N) are similar to what is found if the 16 factors suggested by Cattell are subjected to further factor analysis. In other words, a further condensing or grouping of Cattell's traits, derived from questionnaires, leads to second-order factors that are similar to Eysenck's Introversion-Extraversion and Neuroticism dimensions. As we shall see, these two factors or dimensions show up as important in virtually every factor-analytic trait study. The third dimension, Psychoticism, turns out to be much more controversial.

Briefly considered, the Introversion-Extraversion dimension relates to differences in sociability and impulsiveness. The typical extravert is sociable, likes parties, has

Figure 2.3   The hierarchical structure of Extraversion-Introversion (E).

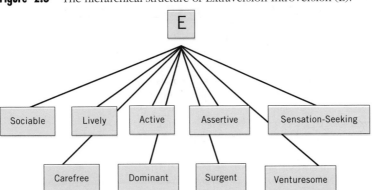

Figure 2.4 The hierarchical structure of Neuroticism (N).

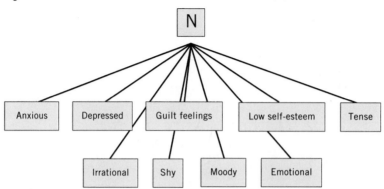

Source: "Biological Dimensions of Personality," by H. J. Eysenck, 1990, in L. A. Pervin (ed.), *Handbook of Personality: Theory and Research,* p. 246, New York: Guilford. Reprinted by permission, Guilford Publications.

many friends, craves excitement, and acts on the spur of the moment. The introvert tends to be quiet, introspective, reserved, reflective, and distrustful of impulsive decisions and prefers a well-ordered life to one filled with chance and risk. A wide variety of studies indicate fundamental differences in the functioning of introverts and extraverts: Introverts are more sensitive to pain, are more easily fatigued, find that excitement decreases performance, do better in school, prefer more solitary vocations, are less suggestible, and are less sexually active both in terms of frequency and variety of partners than are extraverts (Eysenck, 1990; Wilson, 1978; Zuckerman, 1991). As we have noted, Eysenck suggests that individual variations in personality reflect differences in biological functioning. In relation to E, he suggests that introverts are more easily aroused by events and more easily learn social prohibitions than do extraverts. As a result, introverts are more restrained and inhibited. There also is evidence that introverts are more influenced by punishments in learning whereas extraverts are more influenced by rewards (Eysenck, 1990).

TABLE 2.1 **Illustrative Items for Extraversion, Neuroticism, and Psychoticism from the Eysenck Personality Questionnaire-Revised (Eysenck, Eysenck, & Barrett, 1985)**

	Yes	No
1. Do you usually take the initiative in making new friends?	____	____
2. Does your mood often go up and down?	____	____
3. Do you prefer to go your own way rather than act by the rules?	____	____
4. Are you mostly quiet when you are with other people?	____	____
5. Are your feelings easily hurt?	____	____
6. Do you take much notice of what people think?	____	____
7. Can you easily get some life into a rather dull party?	____	____
8. Are you a worrier?	____	____
9. Would you like other people to be afraid of you?	____	____

Note: These items would be scored in the following way: *Extraversion:* 1 Yes, 4 No, 7 Yes; *Neuroticism:* 2 Yes, 5 Yes, 8 Yes; *Psychoticism:* 3 Yes, 6 No, 9 Yes.

Introversion–Extraversion. A basic trait dimension of personality that involves individual differences in the extent to which people are introverts (unsociable, quiet, passive) or extraverts (sociable, outgoing, active).

In relation to Neuroticism, people high on N tend to be emotionally labile and frequently complain of worry and anxiety as well as of bodily aches (e.g., headaches, stomach difficulties, dizzy spells). As noted, the exact nature of the Psychoticism dimension is less clear but for the most part relates to a tendency to be aggressive, cold, egocentric, impersonal, unsocialized, and unconventional. In some ways the term itself is unfortunate, since it makes people think that what is being measured is the psychopathology known as psychosis. Although the trait may predispose people to psychosis, individual differences on it follow a normal distribution that to some degree is independent of the clinical state of psychosis. Also, although many of these trait characteristics have negative social value, Eysenck (1993) suggests a link between high scores on this dimension and creativity. Presumably the essential link here is the ability to think in unconventional ways that is essential to creativity, although obviously it is not the only prerequisite for such accomplishment.

Turning to the biological aspects of these trait dimensions, it can be noted that Eysenck's emphasis on establishing the biological foundations for the existence of each trait preceded by some time the current popularity of this area of research. This also is true of his emphasis on the evolutionary significance of traits:

> I feel that the major, most fundamental dimensions of personality are likely to be those on which variation has had evolutionary significance, and that this evolutionary history is likely to manifest itself in strong genetic determination of individual differences along these dimensions.

1977, pp. 407–408

Whereas deriving trait categories from ratings and questionnaires is useful descriptively, Eysenck notes the need for a causal analysis of why these trait dimensions appear. As evidence that biological factors play an important role in the development of P, E, and N, Eysenck (1990) cites the presence of the factors cross-culturally and the strong genetic (inherited) component to them. In addition, there is evidence that the factor analysis of the behavior of monkeys leads to factors similar to E (play), N (fearful, withdrawal), and P (aggression) (Zuckerman, 1991, p. 42).

Discussion of the biological roots of P, E, and N is complicated by the need for a sophisticated understanding of the biological functioning of the body and measures of such functioning. In addition, many of the studies in this area lead to inconclusive or inconsistent results, depending on the population studied, measures used, and conditions of testing. To date the most consistent results seem to suggest that the E dimension relates to the regulation of sensory input (Eysenck, 1990). On the whole the data suggest that extraverts are normally at a lower level of arousal and are less easily aroused than are introverts. The same level of stimulation thus leads to greater arousal in introverts. Conversely, extraverts need more stimulation to reach the same level of arousal as introverts. This accounts for the strong tendency for extraverts to become bored with low levels of stimulation and to seek higher levels of stimulation than is true for introverts. Less work has been done on the N and P dimensions than on E, and there is less to report concerning their biological roots at this time (Eysenck, 1990). This area, however, is one of growing importance and we will return to it when other, more recent, trait models are considered. One authority in the field suggests that "Eysenck can rightly claim that his system rests on a body of psycho-biological research not even approached by advocates of other dimensional models" (Zuckerman, 1991, p. 11).

THE FIVE-FACTOR MODEL (FFM)

Although the major concepts of Allport, Cattell, and Eysenck had been developed by the 1960s, a common view or trait taxonomy had not been achieved. Since then other three-factor models have been developed, some based on factor analysis and others based on individual differences in the functioning of physiological systems (Cloninger, 1987; Gray, 1987; Tellegen, 1993). Some of these models, particularly those emphasizing individual differences in the functioning of biological systems, are similar to Eysenck's three factors, although they are not identical to them or to one another. In addition, there are other trait models that emphasize seven factors.

Over the course of the years, many factor-analytic studies were performed by a variety of investigators, without unanimity concerning the basic trait units. John (1990) has written an excellent history of this research, in particular emphasizing repeated investigations between 1949 and 1981 that suggested the existence of five trait factors. Yet, agreement concerning a basic trait taxonomy remained elusive. In the light of subsequent events, it remains somewhat of a mystery as to why so little agreement could be achieved after so many studies. These subsequent events relate to a consensus that is emerging around what has been called the **Big Five** (Goldberg, 1981, 1993) or the **five-factor model (FFM)** of personality:

> Today we believe that it is more fruitful to adopt the working hypothesis that the five-factor model of personality is essentially correct in its representation of the structure of traits. . . . If this hypothesis is correct—if we have truly discov-ered the basic dimensions of personality—it marks the turning point for per-sonality psychology.

McCrae & John, 1992, p. 177

What is the five-factor model, this possible turning point for personality psychol-ogy, and what is the evidence in support of it? Although slightly different terms have been used for the Big Five factors, we use the terms *Neuroticism, Extraversion, Openness to Experience, Agreeableness,* and *Conscientiousness* (Table 2.2) because they, and an associated questionnaire, have provided the basis for a good deal of recent research. In addition, a rearrangement of the beginning letters of each term provides an easy way of remembering them—**OCEAN** (John, 1990, p. 96). The ques-tionnaire associated with the five-factor model is the **NEO-PI Five-Factor Inventory** (Costa & McCrae, 1992). The NEO-PI consists of 300 items for which subjects indicate, on a five-point scale (from strongly agree to strongly disagree), the extent to which the statement is characteristic or representative of them. In addition to scores on the five factors, individuals receive scores on six subscales or facets associated with each of the five factors. These facets offer greater differentiation concerning behavior

TABLE 2.2 The Big Five Trait Factors and Illustrative Scales

Characteristics of the High Scorer	Trait Scales	Characteristics of the Low Scorer
NEUROTICISM (N)		
Worrying, nervous, emotional, insecure, inadequate, hypochondriacal	Assesses adjustment vs. emotional instability. Identifies individuals prone to psychological distress, unrealistic ideas, excessive cravings or urges, and maladaptive coping responses.	Calm, relaxed, unemotional, hardy, secure, self-satisfied
EXTRAVERSION (E)		
Sociable, active, talkative, person-oriented, optimistic, fun-loving, affectionate	Assesses quantity and intensity of interpersonal interaction; activity level; need for stimulation; and capacity for joy.	Reserved, sober, unexuberant, aloof, task-oriented, retiring, quiet
OPENNESS TO EXPERIENCE (O)		
Curious, broad interests, creative, original, imaginative, untraditional	Assesses proactive seeking and appreciation of experience for its own sake; toleration for and exploration of the unfamiliar.	Conventional, down-to-earth, narrow interests, unartistic, unanalytical
AGREEABLENESS (A)		
Soft-hearted, good-natured, trusting, helpful, forgiving, gullible, straightforward	Assesses the quality of one's interpersonal orientation along a continuum from compassion to antagonism in thoughts, feelings, and actions.	Cynical, rude, suspicious, uncooperative, vengeful, ruthless, irritable manipulative
CONSCIENTIOUSNESS (C)		
Organized, reliable, hard-working, self-disciplined, punctual, scrupulous, neat, ambitious, persevering	Assesses the individual's degree of organization, persistence, and motivation in goal-directed behavior. Contrasts dependable, fastidious people with those who are lackadaisical and sloppy.	Aimless, unreliable, lazy, careless, lax, negligent, weak-willed, hedonistic

NEO-PI-R Facet Scales Associated with the Big Five Trait Factors

Neuroticism: anxiety, angry hostility, depression, self-consciousness, impulsiveness, vulnerability

Extraversion: warmth, gregariousness, assertiveness, activity, excitement seeking, positive emotions

Openness to Experience: fantasy, aesthetics, feelings, actions, ideas, values

Agreeableness: trust, straightforwardness, altruism, compliance, modesty, tendermindedness

Conscientiousness: competence, order, dutifulness, achievement, striving, self-discipline, deliberation

Source: The NEO Personality Inventory Manual (p. 2), by P. T. Costa Jr. and R. R. McCrae, 1985, Odessa, FL: Psychological Assessment Resources; *NEO-PI-R, Professional Manual,* (p. 3), by P. T. Costa Jr. and R. R. McCrae, 1992, Odessa, FL: Psychological Assessment Resources.

within each of the five broad factors (Table 2.2). The authors argue strongly for the use of questionnaires to assess personality and are critical of the use of projective tests and clinical interviews (McCrae & Costa, 1990).

VALIDATING EVIDENCE

What is the evidence for the validity of this model and the associated questionnaire? Proponents of the five-factor model suggest a number of converging lines of evidence.

Cross-Cultural Agreement on Factors

First, factor analyses of natural-language trait descriptors show good agreement across diverse cultures (Goldberg, 1993; John, 1990). Not only do these five factors show up in English, but in other languages as well. This has led Goldberg to suggest the **fundamental lexical hypothesis:**

> The variety of individual differences is nearly boundless, yet most of these differences are insignificant in people's daily interactions with others and have remained largely unnoticed. Sir Francis Galton may have been among the first scientists to recognize explicitly the fundamental lexical hypothesis—namely that the most important individual differences in human transactions will come to be encoded as single terms in some or all of the world's languages.

Goldberg, 1990, p. 1216

The suggestion here is that over time humans have observed which individual differences are particularly important in their interactions with one another and have developed terms for easy reference to them. The Big Five trait factors capture those aspects of interaction that are particularly central to people. They address questions concerning who can be counted on for what and, more generally, how people can be expected to relate to one another.

Self-Ratings and Ratings by Others

A second line of evidence concerns the relation of self-ratings to how individuals are rated by others. Here there is evidence of substantial agreement of self-ratings with ratings by peers and spouses on all five factors (Table 2.3) (McCrae & Costa, 1990). Apparently agreement between self-ratings and ratings by others can be achieved after only minimal social interaction. Exactly how some judgments can be made on the basis of minimal social contact is not fully understood and remains an area for further investigation. At the same time, however, agreement with self-ratings is greatest with well-acquainted individuals rather than with relative strangers (Funder & Colvin, 1988; D. Watson, 1989). The importance of this finding is that it suggests that self-ratings are related to actual behavior rather than being fictitious self-representations on the part of the person being rated.

Motives, Emotions, and Interpersonal Functioning

A third line of evidence concerns the relation of the five-factor model and the associated NEO-PI questionnaire to other personality characteristics such as motives,

TABLE 2.3 **Correlations Between Peer Ratings, Spouse Ratings, and Self-Reports**
Correlations represent evidence of substantial agreement between self-ratings and ratings by others (i.e., peers and spouse).

NEO-PI factor	AGREEMENT BETWEEN			
	Peer and peer	Peer and spouse	Peers and self	Spouse and self
Neuroticism	.36	.45	.37	.53
Extraversion	.41	.26	.44	.53
Openness	.46	.37	.63	.59
Agreeableness	.45	.49	.57	.60
Conscientiousness	.45	.41	.49	.57

Note: All correlations are significant at $p < .001$. $Ns = 144$ to 719.
Source: Personality in Adulthood (p. 38), by R. R. McCrae and P. T. Costa Jr., 1990, New York: Guilford. Reprinted by permission of Guilford Publishers.

emotions, and interpersonal functioning. Concerning trait-motive relationships, a relation has been found between a high score on certain traits and the pursuit of certain goals-motives (B. R. Little, Lecci, & Watkinson, 1992; Read, Jones, & Miller, 1990). For example, a person described as *gregarious* would be likely to pursue the goal of being with other people and a person high on the *dominance* trait would likely pursue goals such as controlling other people and getting his or her own way. In addition, a relation has been found between scores on the NEO-PI and scores on the Personality Research Form, a measure of Murray's needs (Costa & McCrae, 1988). Although Murray distinguished between the trait and motive concepts, a distinction that is followed in this book, many trait theorists suggest that motives are parts of traits and no such distinction is necessary.

Relations have also been found between scores on the five-factor traits and the tendency to experience specific emotions. For example, an association has been found between high scores on N and the tendency to experience negative affects, and high scores on E and the tendency to experience positive affects (D. Watson & Clark, 1992). In addition, N has been found to be associated with negative psychological well-being whereas E has been found to be associated with positive psychological well-being (McCrae & Costa, 1991). High scores on O (Openness to Experience) were associated with more of both positive and negative affect. High scores on A (Agreeableness) and C (Conscientiousnes) were less clear in their associations but generally were related to positive affect and psychological well-being. Although one cannot argue conclusively for cause-effect relations from correlational data, the authors suggest that "loving and hard-working people have more positive experiences and fewer negative experiences because these traits foster social and achievement-related successes; their traits contribute to a life with more daily uplifts and fewer daily hassles" (McCrae & Costa, 1991, p. 231).

Turning to interpersonal behavior, the suggestion has been made that the representation of interpersonal behavior can be viewed as complementary to the five-

SPOTLIGHT ON THE RESEARCHER

PAUL T. COSTA, JR. AND ROBERT R. McCRAE:

The Five-Factor Model (FFM) of Personality

In the mid-1970s most personality and social psychologists seriously believed that personality traits were cognitive fictions, and that responses to the personality questionnaires so laboriously constructed over the previous 50 years reflected nothing more than stereotypes, response styles, and impression management.

When we began to work together in 1975, we had two things that most psychologists did not: (1) a strong intuition that traits were real and (2) access to the data of the Normative Aging Study, a longitudinal study sponsored by the Veterans Administration in Boston. The data consistently supported two conclusions: (1) Trait measures were related in meaningful ways to define at least three broad dimensions of personality (N, E, O), and (2) individuals' scores on these dimensions were remarkably stable over long periods of time. Combined with our early findings that personality scales predicted such important outcomes as medical complaints and life satisfaction, these results led us in 1980 to announce a renaissance of trait theory.

Our subsequent research at the Baltimore Longitudinal Study of Aging dovetailed with the work of many colleagues, from whom we learned that our three-factor model needed to be expanded to a five-factor model (N, E, O, A, C), that traits were to a substantial degree inherited, and that very similar factors could be found in many different languages and cultures. We developed an instrument to measure the five factors, the NEO Personality Inventory, which appears to be a useful tool in research on a wide range of psychological phenomena, from psychopathology to creativity to occupational interests and job performance.

Trait psychology, one of the oldest paradigms for understanding human nature, has now returned to prominence. Work so far has established the broad outlines of a theory of personality in which individual differences can be understood in terms of five innate and universal factors, stable over time, with important consequences across the life span. Much remains to be done to fill in the details: What specific traits best define the global factors? How should disagreements between two observers' ratings of personality be recognized and reconciled? How do cultural variations shape the expression of traits? What are the conceptual links between traits, needs, and motives? Are additional factors beyond the five needed to explain personality disorders? What psychological processes coordinate the expression of different traits in the same individual?

Not all personality psychologists see the value of a trait perspective, and not all trait psychologists have adopted the five-factor model. But there is a vitality in the field today that stems in large part from the successes of this model and the challenges it poses for alternative models and paradigms. This is an exciting time for personality psychology.

factor model (Trapnell & Wiggins, 1990; Wiggins, 1992; Wiggins & Pincus, 1992). According to Wiggins, interpersonal behavior can be understood in terms of two dimensions—a Dominance-Submission (Agency) dimension and a Nurturance-Hostility (Communion) dimension. In a sense, interpersonal behavior consists of combinations of power and love. Individual differences in interpersonal behavior can be understood, then, as a function of the extent to which each of the two dimensions is involved. For example, an arrogant or calculating interpersonal style would represent a combination of Dominance and Hostility; a gregarious, extraverted style a combination of Dominance and Nurturance; and an aloof, introverted style a combination of Submission and Hostility. Scores on the five trait factors can then be related to styles of interpersonal behavior formed by the two dimensions. In addition, there is evidence of a link between scores on the five factors and the type of attachments individuals form in their adult love relationships (Shaver & Brennan, 1992). In particular, individuals who form secure romantic relationships tend to be less neurotic and more extraverted than are individuals who form anxious attachments or individuals who avoid romantic attachments altogether.

For some time psychologists have attempted to determine whether people prefer others who are similar or opposite to themselves—do "birds of a feather flock together" or do "opposites attract"? For example, does a dominant person prefer people who also are dominant or people who are submissive and easily dominated? According to Wiggins (1991), "correspondence" occurs in relation to the Nurturance-Hostility dimension and "reciprocity" occurs in relation to the Dominance-Submission dimension. In other words, friendliness pulls friendliness and hostility pulls hostility whereas dominance pulls submission and submission pulls dominance. Evidence for this relation remains equivocal, however. Generally it is more supportive for the correspondence rather than the reciprocity aspect of interpersonal relations (Wiggins & Pincus, 1992).

Diagnosis of Personality Disorders

A fourth line of validating evidence concerns a recent effort to relate the five-factor model and the NEO-PI to the diagnosis of personality disorders (Costa & Widiger, 1994; Widiger, 1993). Some clinicians view personality disorders as separate, distinct categories of psychopathology, unrelated to normal personality traits. Proponents of the five-factor model view personality disorders as falling on a continuum with normal personality. For example, the compulsive personality might be seen as someone extremely high on the Conscientiousness factor and the antisocial personality as someone extremely low on the Agreeableness factor. Beyond scores on single-factor dimensions is the pattern of scores on the five factors that may be of considerable significance for diagnosis.

There are two particularly important points in this approach to personality disorder classification and diagnosis. The first, already mentioned, is that the disorders in personality are viewed as extremes on a continuum with normal personality traits. The second is that personality disorders are seen as the result of patterns of traits that result in a particular personality style. These points contrast with the view that personality disorders represent distinct categories, a view that is more similar to a medical model than a psychological model of disorder.

Although still in its early stages of development, what is called the *dimensional approach to personality disorder diagnosis* is important because it is based on a general model of personality functioning, and it may offer a basis for the assignment of patients with different personality disorders to different treatments (Wiggins & Pincus, 1992). Finally, it is important because it represents a potentially important contribution by psychologists in an area that previously has been dominated by medical models and psychiatrists.

Genetics and Evolutionary Theory

A fifth line of evidence involves studies of the genetic contribution to personality traits. Both Eysenck and Cattell emphasized a strong genetic, inherited aspect of traits. Over the past decade, an impressive amount of evidence has been gathered to support the view that many important personality traits have a strong inherited component (Loehlin, 1992; Plomin, Chipuer, & Loehlin, 1990). At this point we need not consider at great length the basis for the determination of the genetic and environmental contributions to a trait. It is sufficient here to emphasize that comparisons are made of the similarity of personality test scores of individuals varying in degree of genetic similarity and degree of environmental similarity. For example, identical twins are identical genetically whereas fraternal twins and ordinary siblings share about 50% of their genes in common. Unrelated individuals, such as adopted siblings, share no genes in common. Individuals reared together are assumed to share a greater environmental similarity than do individuals reared apart. Considering the degree of personality similarity to be related to genetic and environmental similarity allows researchers, called *behavioral geneticists,* to estimate the percentage of variance in test scores that can be accounted for on the basis of genes alone, environment alone, and gene-environment interactions. A critical concept, **heritability,** refers to the proportion of variance (i.e., individual differences) of a particular trait that is due to the contribution of genes.

About 40% of individual differences in personality can be accounted for on the basis of inheritance (Loehlin, 1992). At the same time, the degree of inheritance varies somewhat from trait to trait. Thus, the suggestion of some newspapers that "Personality Traits Are Mostly Inherited" or that "People Are Born, Not Made" has some validity, but it also represents an oversimplification of the issue (Loehlin, 1992). Indeed, even some psychologists who emphasize the genetic contribution to personality are concerned that, as an overcorrection to past extremes of environmentalism, the pendulum may swing too far in the direction of "nature over nurture" (Plomin et al., 1990). If 40% of individual differences in personality traits is due to inheritance, that still leaves the majority of personality as the result of other than strictly genetic variables.

Along with general estimates of the heritability of personality, we can consider heritability estimates for specific traits. There has been more research done on the Extraversion and Neuroticism factors than on the other three factors—Openness to Experience, Agreeableness, and Conscientiousness. A sense of the varying degrees of personality similarity as a function of genetic and environmental similarity can be obtained from Table 2.4. The data represent the summation of multiple investigations by different investigators in different countries (Bloom, 1964; Loehlin, 1992; Rowe, 1993; Zuckerman, 1991). For comparative purposes, data for height and weight are given as well as for E and N.

TABLE 2.4   **Familial Correlations for Height (H), Weight (W), Extraversion (E), and Neuroticism (N)**

Correlations indicate a significant genetic contribution to personality (E, N), although the contribution is not as large as that for height or weight. The data also suggest, with the possible exception of weight, minimal effects of being reared together (Adoptive siblings—together correlations).

Median Correlations	H	W	E	N
MZ twins reared together	.95	.90	.54	.46
DZ twins reared together	.52	.50	.19	.22
Mean Correlations				
MZ twins reared together	.90	.80	.48	.41
DZ twins reared together	.56	.46	.12	.25
MZ twins reared apart	.92	.69	.41	.41
DZ twins reared apart	.67	.46	.03	.23
Biological siblings—together	.52	.50	.20	.28
Adoptive siblings—together	− .07	.24	− .06	.05
Midparent—biological child		.26	.19	.25
Midparent—adopted child		.04	.00	.05

Sources: *Stability and Change in Human Characteristics* by B. S. Bloom, 1964, New York: Wiley; *Genes and Environment in Personality Development,* by J. C. Loehlin, 1992, Newbury Park, CA: Sage; "Genetic Perspectives on Personality," by D. C. Rowe, 1993, in R. Plomin and G. E. McClearn (Eds.), *Nature, Nurture and Psychology,* Washington, DC: American Psychological Association; *Psychobiology of Personality,* by M. Zuckerman, 1991, New York: Cambridge University Press.

Table 2.4 shows the median correlations for identical and fraternal twins on E and N. It is clear that the median correlations are much higher for identical (MZ) twins than for fraternal (DZ) twins. However, in neither case do the correlations approach those for height and weight. The data in this table also make clear that it does not make much of a difference whether the siblings are reared together or apart. Further evidence of the genetic component is the fact that biological sibling scores generally show higher correlations than do adoptive sibling scores. In addition, parent scores are more highly correlated with scores of their biological offspring than with scores of their adoptive children.

There is evidence of a genetic contribution to all the Big Five factors, which appears to be greatest for O (Openness to Experience) and least for C (Conscientiousness) (Loehlin, 1992; Table 2.5). The former may be the result in part of the association of intelligence with O since intelligence has a strong genetic basis to it (Bouchard & McGuer, 1981; McGuer, Bouchard, Iaconor, & Lykken, 1993). This subject is considered in more detail in Chapter 5.

Evidence of a genetic contribution to these traits lends itself to an evolutionary interpretation, that is, that there is survival value to the traits. Thus, many trait theorists now view the five-factor model, and traits generally, within an evolutionary perspective. There are two components to this picture. First, returning to Goldberg's (1990) fundamental lexical hypothesis, there is the view that trait terms have emerged to help people categorize behaviors basic to the human condition. For example, people

TABLE 2.5 Heritability Estimates for the Big Five Traits

Big Five Factor	h^2
Extraversion	.36
Agreeableness	.28
Conscientiousness	.28
Neuroticism	.31
Openness to Experience	.46
Mean for the Big Five	.34

Source: Genes and Environment in Personality Development (p. 67), by J. C. Loehlin, 1992, Newbury Park, CA: Sage.

want to know whether others are agreeable (A), can be counted on (C), and are stable or unstable (N).

Second, there is the view that important individual differences exist because they have played some role in the process of evolution by natural selection (D. M. Buss, 1991, 1994). The fundamental question asked is: How did traits evolve to solve adaptive tasks; if not for this reason, why would they exist at all? Presumably individual differences relate to such basic evolutionary tasks as survival and reproductive success. Traits such as dominance, friendliness, and emotional stability (the other end of the N dimension) might be particularly important, for example, in relation to mate selection (Kenrick, Sadalla, Groth & Trost, 1990). Emotional stability, conscientiousness, and agreeableness might be particularly important in relation to group survival. Thus, individual differences in traits and trait terms reflect the tasks humans have had to face in the long history of their evolutionary development.

The evolutionary perspective within trait theory is relatively recent, and much more theoretical and research work needs to be done. At the same time, it is an important development in that it seeks to anchor personality theory in biological principles common to other species. In the words of one of its proponents: "There is no reason to believe that we are somehow exempt from the organizing forces of evolution by natural selection. Personality theories inconsistent with evolutionary theory stand little chance of being correct" (D. M. Buss, 1991, p. 461). Together with the work on inheritance and that on individual differences in biological functioning associated with traits, the evolutionary perspective holds the potential for valuable links between trait psychology and the field of biology (Table 2.6).

CONSISTENCY OF PERSONALITY AND THE PERSON-SITUATION CONTROVERSY

We now come to an issue concerning the validity of the trait concept that appears to be both simple and complex. It involves the consistency of personality. The trait

TABLE 2.6 Evidence in Support of the Five-Factor Model

1. Cross-cultural agreement on basic factors—the fundamental lexical hypothesis.
2. Agreement between self-ratings and observer ratings.
3. Correlations between trait scores and measures of motives, emotions, and interpersonal behavior.
4. Personality disorder diagnoses as dimensions and clusters of personality traits rather than categories.
5. Genetic evidence and evolutionary theory.

concept suggests that personality is consistent, that is, that there is stability to individual differences in personality functioning. Throughout the history of the field, personality psychologists have been concerned with this issue: Is personality stable and consistent (Pervin, 1984, 1985, 1990)? Or, alternatively, are situational forces so powerful as to override personality variables and be more important for behavior? Do people determine their lives or are they shaped by situational events? Do people express their personalities in all situations in much the same ways, or do they play roles according to the demands of the situation? How would you understand the ways in which you are similar and different in various situations in light of the trait concept? Before turning to the relevant evidence, let us consider some of the history of a debate that shaped much of the field over a period of 20 years and, to a certain extent, continues as an undercurrent to this day.

Much of the trait work of Allport, Eysenck, and Cattell had been done by the 1960s. In addition, a number of investigators already had reported factor analyses congruent with the eventual five-factor model. However, during the 1960s a growing dissatisfaction with trait concepts and trait assessment devices arose. In part this was based on differing findings concerning the number and kinds of traits found by different investigators. Remember we already have observed differences among Allport, Eysenck, Cattell, and five-factor theorists concerning the number of fundamental traits and the nature of some of these basic units. In part the growing dissatisfaction was based on problems in predicting performance through the use of trait questionnaires. After a period of considerable enthusiasm concerning what trait questionnaires might be able to do in the way of prediction of performance, a number of studies concluded that such prediction was far more complicated than would be suggested by a simple trait perspective. The kinds of personality variables that entered into performance, and how these variables related to one another, appeared to be far more complicated than suggested by then traditional personality theory. This was true for such important areas as the prediction of success as a fighter pilot or as a clinical psychologist (Wiggins, 1973).

At the same time, models emphasizing the control of behavior through manipulation of reward contingencies in situations, following from Skinner's work, were gaining in importance. And, at the same time, personality psychologists were beginning to be influenced by the cognitive revolution and the importance of ways in which people discriminate among situations. These forces came together in 1968 in the form of an attack on "traditional personality theory" by Walter Mischel. Both psychoanalytic theory and trait theory were included in traditional personality theory.

What Mischel suggested was that there was much less evidence of consistency in behavior than was suggested by trait theorists and that associated questionnaire scores were poor predictors of performance in real-life situations. Mischel suggested that what was important was the situational specificity of behavior rather than assumed broad dispositions (traits) in the person. The battle lines had thus been drawn for what came to be known as the **person-situation controversy,** a controversy that, as noted, dominated much of the field for the next 20 years and to this day remains largely unresolved.

As indicated, the issue is both simple and complex. It is simple because we all recognize both stability and variability in behavior, our own as well as that of others. We assume that people have personalities and feel reasonably comfortable attributing traits to them; yet we also recognize that sometimes the same person is sociable and at other times unsociable, sometimes dominant and at other times submissive. The matter is complex because we do not have agreement about how stable or variable people are or, even more important, how to account for the stability and variability. Is there sufficient evidence of stability, or consistency, to warrant use of the trait concept? If so, how do we go about accounting for times when a person does not behave in ways consistent with the trait?

Much of the person-situation controversy revolves around what is meant by consistency and what degree of consistency one takes as adequate evidence for the existence of a trait. No trait theorist would argue that a person behaves the same way in all situations. We already have seen that both Allport and Cattell recognized the importance of situational factors in the regulation of behavior, a point emphasized by Eysenck as well. However, they would argue that there is sufficient consistency, that is, that people are reliable "enough" in their individual differences, to warrant use of trait terms to describe them. Is there evidence that this is the case?

There are two types of consistency that may be considered, longitudinal consistency and cross-situational consistency. The former, which can be termed **stability,** refers to whether people are stable over time in their trait characteristics. Measured over weeks and years, do people score the same on traits? The latter, for which we reserve the term **consistency,** refers to whether people express the same traits over a range of situations.

There is good evidence of the longitudinal stability of traits, even over extended periods of time (Block, 1981; Conley, 1985). A study related to the five-factor model reports the conclusion that personality changes little after age 30 in most people:

> In the course of thirty years, most adults will have undergone radical changes in their life structures. They may have married, divorced, remarried. They have probably moved their residence several times. . . . And yet, most will not have changed appreciably in their standing on any of the five dimensions.
>
> McCrae & Costa, 1990, p. 87

Indeed, the authors of this study are so emphatic concerning personality stability after age 30 that they characterize it as, in most cases, unchanging, fixed, and "set like plaster" (Costa & McCrae, 1994).

One must consider such statements with a certain degree of caution. First, the

TABLE 2.7   Stability of NEO-PI Scales for Younger and Older Men and Women

The data indicate significant stability in adult personality as defined by the NEO-PI five factors.

NEO-PI Scale	AGE 25–56		AGE 57–84		Total
	Men	Women	Men	Women	
N	.78	.85	.82	.81	.83
E	.84	.75	.86	.73	.82
O	.87	.84	.81	.73	.83
A	.64	.60	.59	.55	.63
C	.83	.84	.76	.71	.79

Note: All correlations are significant at $p < .001$. $Ns = 63$ to 127 for subsamples. Retest interval is 6 years for N, E, and O scales, 3 years for short forms of A and C scales.
Source: Adapted from *Personality in Adulthood* (p. 88), by R. R. McCrae and P. T. Costa Jr., 1990, New York: Guilford.

authors are considering personality after age 30. Second, they are restricting their observations to personality as defined by five factors or traits. Finally, they are defining stability-fixity in terms of a median correlation of .6 on the five factors (Table 2.7). Note that a correlation of .6 between scores on one factor leaves sufficient room for change such that one might not want to characterize personality on that factor as "fixed" or "set in plaster." Beyond this, however, a correlation of that order on each of the five factors leaves room for change in the pattern, organization, or configuration of personality (Pervin, 1993c). Finally, even if personality typically does not change, this does not mean that it cannot change. There may be factors that typically mitigate against change that, if altered, would provide for greater change.

Accepting these words of caution, the expressed stability nevertheless is impressive. Why should there be considerable longitudinal stability to personality? In part it may result from the genetic contribution to traits. Probably of greater importance, however, is the tendency for people to lock themselves into life situations and to define themselves in certain terms once they have reached a certain age. People select and shape their environments so as to reinforce their traits. An extravert does not just wait for situations to happen but seeks out others and often encourages them to be extraverted as well. In addition, once perceived as an extravert, others are likely to behave in ways that perpetuate that characteristic. In other words, a person with a certain self-image will behave in ways that confirm that self-image and others with that image of the person will behave in ways that confirm it as well. Often this is why it is so hard for people to behave differently and then to have others treat them differently. Thus, although perhaps personality can change, there are powerful forces operating to maintain stability over time.

The matter becomes somewhat more complex when we consider cross-situational consistency. It would not make sense for a person to behave the same way in all situations, nor would trait theorists expect this to be the case. Rather, trait theorists would expect a person to behave consistently over a range of situations; that is, various behaviors would be expressive of the same trait and in most situations a person would behave in a way expressive of that trait. Thus, we have the principle of **aggregation:** A trait does not refer to a specific behavior in a specific situation, but rather to a class of behaviors over a range of situations. People high on Extraversion express a range of extraverted behaviors over a range of situations, even though they may vary in the way they express their extraversion from situation to situation and may not be extraverted in a single, specific situation. To assess someone on a trait, therefore, one has to sample a range of behaviors and situations; that is, one must take an aggregate measure of behavior.

The point is well made in an important study by Epstein (1983). Epstein asked 30 college students to rate their feelings, their behavioral impulses, and actual behavior for each of 28 days. Ratings were made for 14 positive and negative feeling states (e.g., secure, happy, angry). For behavioral impulses and actual behavior, ratings were made of 64 response tendencies (e.g., stimulus seeking, aggression, social withdrawal). The question asked was how much behavior on one set of occasions was predictive of behavior on another set of occasions, and whether this varied with the time interval between the two.

What was found was that there was greater correspondence as larger samples of behavior were included in the two sets of observations. Behavior sampled on one day was minimally predictive of behavior sampled on another day. However, behavior sampled over a two-week interval was quite predictive of behavior sampled over another two-week interval. In other words, a person's behavior over two weeks could be better predicted from behavior over a previous two weeks than could behavior on one day be predicted from behavior on the previous day. This was particularly true for feelings and was not affected by the time interval (i.e., one-week, two-week, or three-week intervals). Epstein concluded that the data provided

> strong evidence for the existence of broad, cross-situational dispositions, or traits. Expressed otherwise, there is enough cross-situational stability in behavior to allow one meangfully to refer to personality attributes without having to specify the situations in which they occur. Such a conclusion does not deny that situational factors exert an important influence on behavior.
>
> 1983, p. 112

Epstein's data are interesting and important. They support the principle of aggregation. Note, however, that they do not address the issue of how variable people are from situation to situation—the situational specificity of behavior. Through aggregation the variability of behavior from situation to situation is washed out. But what happens if one attends to this? How variable are people and can we specify the determinants of such variability? At this point, after considerable research, we can conclude that how variable people are depends on the measures used and the range of situations investigated. For example, greater behavioral consistency will be shown if a range of measures for a trait rather than only one measure is used (Funder & Colvin, 1991). People express the same trait differently in various situations.

Concerning range of situations, people behave more similarly to the extent that situations are similar. For example, people will behave more similarly from laboratory situation to laboratory situation and from daily life situation to daily life situation than from laboratory to daily life situation (Funder & Colvin, 1991) and more consistently with friends than with strangers (Moskowitz, 1988).

Not surprisingly, people will behave more consistently in situations that are low in constraint or weak in pressure to conform than in situations in which behavior is highly constrained by strict behavioral norms (Monson, Hesley, & Chernick, 1982). In other words, for the trait to come out the situation must provide room for a range of alternative behaviors. Similarly, traits will be more expressive where people are free to select situations than when situations are imposed on them. Indeed, one of the clearest expressions of a trait can be found in the situations the person self-selects (Snyder, 1981).

What we find, then, undoubtedly will not come as a surprise to the student who has pondered the question of consistency and variability of behavior. People are both stable and changing, consistent and variable. People are more stable later in life and over shorter time intervals than they are earlier in life and over longer time intervals. People are more consistent over situations that are similar than they are over situations that are different.

IMPLICATIONS FOR THE PREDICTION OF BEHAVIOR

What are the implications of these findings for the prediction of behavior? From the previous discussion we can conclude that the best predictor of behavior in a situation is past behavior in a comparable situation, thus providing for similarity of influence of both personality and situation variables. Prediction of aggregate behavior from past aggregates of behavior also appears to be possible. However, prediction of a person's behavior in a specific situation from samples of behavior in other isolated situations is difficult, particularly if those situations are very different from the one to which predictions are being made. Generally the better we know people, the better we are able to predict their behavior, both because we are able to use aggregate measures and because we can make use of data from past behavior in similar situations. However, even with people we know well, periodically we are surprised to learn that they behave quite differently in contexts in which they were not previously observed by us.

It may be useful here to draw a distinction between the concepts of bandwidth and fidelity. **Bandwidth** refers to the breadth of behaviors to which one can predict while **fidelity** refers to the accuracy with which one can make specific predictions. By analogy one can think of a radio that is evaluated in terms of the range of stations it can pick up (bandwidth) and the clarity with which it can pick up specific stations (fidelity). The ideal radio, of course, has both excellent bandwidth and excellent fidelity, but sometimes one has to play off one strength against the other, deciding which is of greater importance. Similarly, a test can have broad bandwidth but poor fidelity, meaning that it can predict to a wide variety of behaviors but not with a great degree of accuracy to any specific behavior. Alternatively, a test can have excellent fidelity in predicting a specific piece of behavior but be poor in the range of behaviors it can be used to predict. As a general statement we can suggest that the trait concept and associated tests have good bandwidth but poor fidelity; that is, as an aggregate concept, traits relate to behavior over a broad range of situations. To increase fidelity, situational factors need to be taken into consideration and, as noted, the best predictor of behavior in a situation is past behavior in a comparable situation. Such fidelity, however, does not give one much bandwidth.

In fact, the prediction of behavior in daily life is exceedingly difficult, particularly in more complex situations. This is both because of the influence of unknown, unforeseen events and because of the many determinants of complex behavior. One can understand a great deal about a person but have difficulty predicting his or her behavior in novel situations because one is missing a critical ingredient or does not know how to combine the various ingredients. Weather forecasters understand a great deal about weather but, as we all know, often make serious mistakes because of a slight shift in a weather pattern or ingredient. Thus, the ability of trait psychologists to predict the behavior of individuals may be an important indicator of the value of the trait concept, but it is not a final indicator of its validity.

In sum, trait psychology is limited in its ability to predict behavior. However, this should not surprise us or limit our consideration of its potential as a fundamental building block of personality.

A CRITICAL OVERVIEW OF TRAITS AND FACTOR ANALYSIS

The record of recent research accomplishment in relation to the trait concept is indeed impressive. Much has been accomplished from the time of Mischel's challenge to the utility of the trait concept to the present. But all is not well in this regard. Despite the enthusiasm of proponents of the trait concept, who suggest it is a "basic discovery" of personality psychology (McCrae & John, 1992), there are some fundamental questions that can still be asked.

WHAT IS A TRAIT?

Throughout this discussion we have considered the trait concept as if there were agreement among trait theorists concerning its conceptual status. This is not the case, however, particularly in regard to two matters. First, is a trait a *predisposition to respond* or *actual behavior*? In other words, can a latent response propensity that becomes manifest only under very limited conditions still be considered a trait? Or, must predispositions to respond become manifest in actual behavior over a wide range of situations in order to assume trait status? From the way traits are discussed and measured, the latter appears to be the case; that is, the trait concept appears to relate to overt behavior. However, this issue rarely is addressed.

Second, what aspects of personality functioning are included in the trait concept? Do traits relate exclusively to overt behavior or do they relate to feelings, thoughts, and values as well? Although early trait theorists described traits in terms of classes of responses, referring to overt behaviors, proponents of the five-factor model seem to include feelings and motives in the concept as well. If traits include all aspects of personality on which individuals may differ in consistent ways, then is there anything distinctive about the trait concept?

Tests used to measure traits typically include items from diverse areas of personality functioning. For example, on the NEO-PI, items such as the following are included: "I have a low opinion of myself." "I often worry about things that might go wrong." "Others think of me as modest and unassuming." "Frightening thoughts sometimes come into my head." Such items can be contrasted with others that relate more directly to overt behavior: "I waste a lot of time before settling down to work." "I am a very active person." "I follow the same route when I go someplace." Some items appear to relate to behavior but in fact are ambiguous in this regard, for example, the item "I often crave excitement." Does this refer to the craving alone, regardless of whether it leads to exciting behavior, or is there the assumption that the craving leads to behavior? One can probably think of things that are "craved" but do not lead to behavior, so this may not be a trivial distinction.

In sum, the first question we can ask concerns which aspects of personality are included within the trait concept and whether all trait theorists show agreement in this regard.

HOW MANY TRAITS? WHICH ONES?

As noted earlier in this discussion, trait theorists disagree concerning the number of basic units. Allport called for the use of many traits; Cattell emphasized sixteen, Eysenck three; and now there are the Big Five. Proponents of the five-factor model suggest that a consensus is emerging around this model, but clearly the three-factor model has its adherents. Some suggest that the three-factor model can be expanded into the five-factor model, but once more there is not total agreement in this regard. In addition, whereas three-factor proponents have attempted to relate the factors to biological systems, this has not been true for five-factor proponents. The latter have been much more focused on rating and questionnaire data.

Even within three-factor and five-factor models, there is not perfect consensus concerning the nature of the factors. Three-factor theorists seem to show good but not universal agreement concerning the first two factors but do not agree on the third. Five-factor theorists similarly show disagreement concerning some of the five factors, in particular the nature of the Openness to Experience factor. Although at times disagreement appears to be more a question of how the factor is labeled than one of substance, this is not always the case. In the words of one supporter of trait theory, "the resemblance is more fraternal than identical" (Briggs, 1989, p. 248). In addition, although there is some cross-cultural evidence in support of the five-factor model, some data do question whether the model is completely universal or pan-cultural (Yang & Bond, 1990).

In sum, a consensus concerning how many and which traits has not as yet emerged. There are broad areas of reasonable agreement, but differences remain.

THE METHOD—FACTOR ANALYSIS

To a great extent, much of current trait theory is dependent upon the method of factor analysis. Questions can be raised, however, concerning just what factor analysis can and cannot do for us. Is it the method that will lead to the discovery of the underlying structure of personality? Although the method clearly has its adherents, others are much less optimistic. As noted earlier, although Allport was committed to trait theory, he was critical of the use of factor analysis. Others are equally critical, suggesting that the method is comparable to putting people through a centrifuge and expecting the "basic stuff" to come out (Lykken, 1971; Tomkins, 1962). My own view is that although factor analysis is extremely useful in determining clusters (groups) of behaviors or items that go together, it is doubtful that one can rely upon it for the discovery of personality's periodic table of the elements.

One can also consider here the data that are put into the factor analysis. Remember that the data consist almost exclusively of trait ratings and questionnaire data, both highly dependent upon language and the behaviors-traits that people think go together. Would any other science—biology, physics, chemistry, or geology, for example—begin with natural language in the search for its basic units? Is personality fundamentally different from other sciences in this regard? Is it possible that what is being studied is "folk psychology" or beliefs people have about the world rather than the actual structure of personality (Tellegen, 1991, 1993)? This is a question raised even by proponents of the five-factor model, although they suggest that as a minimum, it is a good place to begin the search (John, 1990).

DESCRIPTION OR EXPLANATION?

Finally, there is the question of the explanatory status of the trait concept. Are traits *descriptions* of behavioral regularities or *explanations* of observed regularities (Briggs, 1989; Wiggins, 1973). In its simplest form, we can ask whether traits are "real" or whether they are "convenient fictions by which we communicate" (Briggs, 1989, p. 251). Eysenck (1992) has been concerned with this matter, suggesting that without a theory there is the danger of circularity—the use of a trait concept to explain behavior that serves as the basis for the trait concept in the first place. People behave in an extraverted way "because" they are extraverts but we know that they are extraverts because of their behavior. If this is the case, how much do we add to our understanding of personality?

Proponents of the three-factor model have made an effort to provide a theoretical underpinning for the three factors. As noted, for the most part this involves an emphasis on genetically determined differences in biological functioning (Zuckerman, 1991). Although proponents of the five-factor model have emphasized the inherited component of the factors and have attempted to place the model within an evolutionary perspective, the model still lacks an underlying explanatory structure. At the same time, some suggest that "the global designation of these efforts as 'atheoretical' seems both inaccurate and unfair" (Wiggins, 1992, p. 531).

CONCLUSION

We come now to the end of our discussion of the first suggested unit of personality—the trait. Clearly traits make sense to us since we use them in our daily lives all the time. In my experience, students typically find trait theory attractive, often the most appealing of all personality theories. We have had a chance here to consider the many forms of trait theory and the evidence in support of traits as a basic unit of personality. It is time now to turn to consideration of other units, and ultimately to consider possible relations among the units.

MAJOR CONCEPTS

Trait. A disposition to behave in a particular way, as expressed in a person's behavior over a range of situations.

Nomothetic. An approach to research and personality description in which individual differences on standard measures are emphasized.

Idiographic. An approach to research and personality description, emphasized by Allport, in which the emphasis is on the uniqueness of the individual in terms of specific traits and the organization of traits.

Cardinal traits, central traits, secondary dispositions. Allport's distinction among traits of varying descriptiveness for the person. Cardinal traits refer to dispositions so pervasive that virtually every act of the person is traceable to their influence. Central traits refer to dispositions to behave over a range of situations. Secondary traits refer to dispositions to behave that are relevant to only a few situations.

Sixteen Personality Factor (16 P.F.) Questionnaire. The personality questionnaire developed by Cattell to measure individuals on 16 basic traits.

Type. The classification of people into a few groups, each of which has its own de-fining characteristics (e.g., Eysenck's introverts and extraverts).

PEN model. Eysenck's model of personality emphasizing the three trait dimensions of Psychoticism, Extraversion, and Neuroticism.

Five-factor model (FFM). An emerging consensus among trait theorists suggesting five basic factors to human personality: Neuroticism, Extraversion, Openness to Experience, Agreeableness, and Conscientiousness.

Big Five. The five major traits that are represented in the five-factor model.

OCEAN. The acronym for the five traits in the five-factor model of personality.

NEO-PI Five-Factor Inventory. A questionnaire measure of the five traits associated with the five-factor model.

Fundamental lexical hypothesis. The hypothesis that over time the most important individual differences in human interaction have been encoded as single terms in language.

Heritability. The concept expressing the proportion of variation among individuals on a trait that can be attributed to genetic differences.

Person-situation controversy. A controversy between psychologists who emphasize the importance of personal (trait) variables in determining behavior and those who emphasize the importance of situational influences.

Stability. The maintenance of a trait characteristic over time.

Consistency. The maintenance of a trait characteristic across situations.

Aggregation. The use of a class of behaviors over a range of situations to measure a trait.

Bandwidth. The range of behaviors covered by a personality concept or personality measure.

Fidelity. The specificity with which a personality concept or personality measure can be used to describe or predict behavior.

SUMMARY

1. Traits refer to broad regularities or consistencies in the behavior of people. They are commonly used by people in their personality descriptions and are seen by trait psychologists as constituting the basic units for describing individual differences in personality.

2. Allport viewed a trait as a predisposition to respond in a particular way. He was concerned with the pattern and organization of traits within the individual and rejected the method of factor analysis for the discovery of basic personality units.

3. Cattell used the method of factor analysis to discover and compare traits in ratings, questionnaire responses, and laboratory tests. He also was interested in the contributions of heredity and environment to the development of traits and in the progression of trait development over time.

4. Using factor analysis, Eysenck developed the PEN model, emphasizing the trait dimensions of Psychoticism, Extraversion, and Neuroticism. He also emphasized the biological foundations of these trait dimensions.

5. Many current trait psychologists suggest that a consensus is emerging around the Big Five or five-factor model (OCEAN). Supportive evidence includes cross-cultural agreement on factors found in ratings and questionnaires, agreement between self-ratings and ratings by others, correlations between trait scores and other aspects of personality functioning, relationships between trait scores and personality disorders, and results from research on the inheritance of traits.

6. The trait concept suggests that personality is consistent. Although there is evidence of longitudinal trait stability, the evidence concerning cross-situational consistency is much more controversial. This is reflected in the person-situation controversy.

7. For purposes of prediction, the trait concept and associated tests have good bandwidth but poor fidelity.

8. The record of recent trait research is impressive. At the same time, questions are raised concerning the definition of a trait, agreement concerning the number and content of basic traits, the method of factor analysis, and whether traits constitute explanations as well as descriptions of behavior.

COGNITIVE UNITS OF PERSONALITY

3

CHAPTER OVERVIEW

In this chapter we consider cognitive units of personality—ways in which people think about themselves and the world. This approach was influenced by the development of computers and uses the computer as a metaphor for personality functioning. Personality is defined in terms of the concepts and beliefs people hold, and the ways in which they process information and develop explanations for events. In contrast to the trait approaches, there is a much greater emphasis on how people vary their behavior to meet the demands of specific situations.

Questions To Be Addressed In This Chapter

1 How does an emphasis on cognitive units of personality lead to different views of personality functioning than those suggested by an emphasis on trait units?

2 What are the implications of using the computer as a metaphor for human personality functioning? What cognitive or information-processing units of personality can be derived from the use of such a metaphor?

3 What are the implications of how we perceive the causes of events for emotions and motivation?

In this chapter we consider units of personality that are very different from traits. Here we consider units associated with the cognitive functioning of the person. The term **cognition** refers to the person's thought processes, including perception, memory, and language. It is used to refer to the ways in which the organism processes information concerning the self and the surrounding world. Whereas the model for trait theorists was chemistry's table of elements, the model for cognitive theorists is a computer that takes in, stores, transforms, and produces information.

Cognitive units of personality involve both the kind of information that is received and the ways in which the information is processed; that is, both *content* and *process* aspects of cognition are important for understanding personality. In relation to content, some people focus their attention on the interpersonal world, whereas others focus on the impersonal world; and some people focus on the world of feelings while others do not focus on feelings at all. It often is difficult for people to understand one another when the content of their cognitive functioning is so vastly different. In relation to process, some people process information in a detailed, analytical way while others focus on broad generalities. Once more, it often is difficult for people to understand one another when they process the same information in different ways. When the same information is "packaged" differently, it comes out looking different.

As has already been indicated, the term *cognition* is not new to the field; it has been in use almost from the beginnings of psychology. Yet, what is referred to as the "cognitive revolution" began in roughly the 1960s (Boneau, 1992). Since that time, cognition has formed an increasingly important part of psychology generally, and personality in particular. We consider here some of the historical developments in cognitive approaches to personality, to appreciate both the diversity of approaches and the changes over time.

THE CONCEPT OF COGNITIVE STYLE

Much of the early work on cognition and personality, begun during the 1950s, focused on individual differences in cognitive style. For example, consider the work of Herman Witkin on what was first known as field independent–field dependent cognitive styles and then as analytical–global cognitive styles (Witkin et al., 1962).

Witkin began his research with experimental work in the area of perception. The problem of interest to him was how individuals maintain a proper orientation toward the upright in space; that is, how do we know whether our body or another object in the environment is upright? Do we rely on visual cues from the surrounding environment, on bodily cues that tell us when we are upright, or on some combination of the two? What happens if we only have one set of cues or if the cues conflict with one another—our body is telling us we are straight but the environment is telling us we are tilted, or vice versa?

To investigate the issue, Witkin used a Rod and Frame Test (RFT) in which the subject sat in a completely darkened room and observed a luminous frame that surrounded a luminous rod. The experimenter tilted the frame and rod to a variety of angles and the subject's task was to bring the movable rod to a position that was upright. To do this, the subject had to disregard the tilt of the field (frame) and make use of cues from his body position. A large tilt of the rod in the direction of the tilted frame suggested a reliance on visual cues whereas an accurate positioning of the rod through the use of bodily cues and the disregard of visual cues suggested a reliance on bodily cues. Would people make use of visual cues or bodily cues, tilt the rod in the direction of the frame on in relation to the upright body?

Although Witkin was interested in general laws of perception, he found great variation among individuals. A simple generalization concerning visual or bodily cues was impossible because the relevant question was "which cues were more important for whom?" (Witkin et al., 1954). Thus began a 25-year period of research on individual differences in perception and the relation of these differences to overall personality organization.

First, there was an effort to determine whether the same perceptual mode of orientation was used in a variety of perceptual situations. For example, consider the Embedded Figures Test (EFT; Figure 3.1). This is a paper-and-pencil test that requires the subject to find a simple figure or shape that is hidden within the complex pattern of the larger figure or field. Can the subject locate the simple figure within the more complex one or will the subject be bound by the surrounding context? Is performance on this test related to that on the RFT where there is a similar task of separating an element of the field from the surrounding context? Witkin concluded that performance on a variety of such tests was consistent and defined the **field independence– field dependence** construct in terms of individual differences in the ability to perceive a part of the field independently of its surroundings. Field independent individuals are much more able than field dependent subjects to perceive parts of the field independently of the surroundings. In a sense, they are able to see the forest from the trees. Although it may seem as if it is better to be field independent than

Figure 3.1   Picture of problem from the Embedded Figures Test used to measure field dependence and field independence.

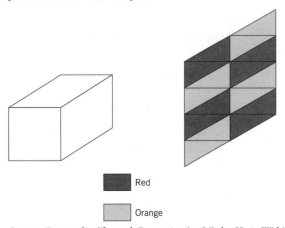

Red

Orange

Source: Personality Through Perception (p. 34), by H. A. Witkin et al., 1954, New York: Harper & Row. Reprinted by permission of HarperCollins Publishers, Inc.

field dependent, as we shall see, each type of cognitive style has its own advantages and disadvantages.

Second, there was an effort to determine whether such differences in perception were related to other differences in personality functioning. Here it was found that individual differences in perception were indeed related to differential functioning in other areas. For example, relative to field dependent people, field independent people were found to be more active in their coping efforts, more able to control their impulses in a flexible manner, and less bothered by feelings of inferiority (Witkin, et al., 1962). In addition, cognitive style was found to be an important variable in students' selection of majors and in performance in courses. Thus, field independent subjects preferred and did better in courses requiring analytical skills (e.g., sciences, mathematics, engineering), while field dependent subjects preferred and did better in areas that required involvement with people (e.g., social sciences, counseling, teaching) (Witkin, 1973). In sum, there was evidence that differences in perceptual orientation were associated with broad differences in personality organization.

Further research led to development of the concept of **analytical versus global style** of cognitive functioning. The person with an analytical style experiences stimuli as discrete from their backgrounds and is able to overcome the embedding context. Beyond this, the world contains well-delineated parts and the field as a whole is well organized. In contrast, the person with a global style of cognitive functioning experiences the environment as more of a vague, undifferentiated field and the qualities of the whole dictate the experience of the parts. Thus, analytical individuals experience the body and the self as structured and distinct from the environment to a greater extent than is true for global individuals. The latter show a greater tendency to experience the body as a vague "mass" and the self as fused with its surroundings. In addition, global individuals tend to be more dependent on the external environment for self-definition and for attitudes and feelings than are analytical individuals. Thus, they are more apt to change their views on social issues to conform to the views of those in positions of authority (Witkin et al., 1962).

In sum, Witkin began with the experimental study of perception and moved on to establish a pattern of correlations that was viewed as reflecting consistent differences in cognitive style. Although he accumulated an impressive array of findings, relatively little progress was made with the concept subsequent to his death in 1979.

Other concepts describing cognitive styles also were developed during this period. For example, there were *levelers* and *sharpeners,* referring to sensitivity to differences between objects; and *repressors* and *sensitizers,* referring to differences in sensitivity to feelings; and people who were *cognitively complex* and others who were *cognitively simple,* referring to differences in the complexity with which individuals structured their world.

Today, one rarely hears of such differences in cognitive style. The closest recent such concept was **self-monitoring:** High self-monitors are individuals who are highly sensitive to cues of situational appropriateness and regulate their behavior accordingly, in contrast to low self-monitoring individuals who are less attentive to social information and behave more in accord with internal feelings and attitudes (Snyder, 1979). What has happened to these earlier concepts of cognitive style? For the most part, they have disappeared from the literature. One rarely sees reference to them in personality journals or personality texts. Most current graduate students probably never heard of them!

Why did they disappear from the literature? This always is a complex matter, no doubt the result of many factors. However, three appear to be of particular import. First, as more research was done, inconsistent findings began to emerge. In addition, it often was hard to define ways in which similar-sounding cognitive styles were different from or related to one another. Second, questions were raised concerning the generality of these cognitive styles (Cantor & Kihlstrom, 1987). Individuals were not found to be as consistent from task to task, and from area of personality functioning to area of functioning, as was suggested by the concept of cognitive style. In other words, whereas cognitive style theorists treated such individual differences as traits, questions were raised concerning the cross-situational generality of the differences. Finally, as we shall see, such concepts were replaced by others less stylistic in nature and more reflective of developments in the cognitive revolution.

TWO PRE-COGNITIVE REVOLUTION THEORISTS: KELLY AND ROTTER

During the 1950s, prior to the start of the cognitive revolution, two important cognitive theories emerged in the personality field. Not only that, but they came from two theorists at the same university, Ohio State, although apparently they were developed independently of one another and in many ways were quite dissimilar. However, it is their common emphasis on cognitive units that warrants their joint consideration at this time.

KELLY'S PERSONAL CONSTRUCT THEORY

The personal construct theory of George Kelly (1955) emphasizes the way in which the person construes or interprets events. For Kelly, there was no objective truth, only ways of interpreting or construing events. As indicated in Chapter 1, the person was viewed as a scientist, that is, an observer of events who formulates concepts to organize phenomena and uses these concepts to predict the future. What distinguishes the scientist from the ordinary person is that the former makes more systematic observations, is more explicit about hypotheses being tested, and is more systematic in the testing of hypotheses. The goal for every person is to become as good a scientist as possible, that is, to become increasingly able to describe, explain, and predict events. The goal is to increase the range of convenience of one's theory as well as sharpen the focus of convenience. Returning to concepts noted in Chapter 2, the goal is to increase both bandwidth and fidelity.

Kelly's personal construct theory is an extremely imaginative enterprise. There are two features that are particularly noteworthy. First, it deals with both structure and process, with both stability and change in the organism. Second, it focuses on both the uniqueness of the individual and the processes common to all people. Thus, to a far greater extent than most personality theories, it is both *idiographic* and *nomothetic*. The construct theory is primarily idiographic in its emphasis on the unique ways in which the person interprets the world. The meaning of events is highly idiosyncratic. It is primarily nomothetic in its emphasis on processes of cognitive functioning common to all people. Our concept systems can be enormously varied in content, but limited to a certain number of processes.

The central unit for Kelly was the **construct**—a way of perceiving, construing, or interpreting events. For example, good-bad is a construct frequently used by people as they consider events. A construct always has two poles. However, one pole need not be the logical opposite of the other. For example, one person may have the construct give-receive and another the construct give-take, one person may have the construct assertive-unassertive and another the construct hostile-unassertive, and one person the construct love-hate and another the construct love-lust. Once a construct becomes part of a person's cognitive structure, it potentially can be applied to anything. Thus, whatever constructs one applies to others are potentially applicable to the self, and vice versa: "One cannot call another person a bastard without making bastardy a dimension of his own life also" (Kelly, 1955, p. 133).

Kelly differentiated among many different types of constructs. There are core constructs that are basic to a person's functioning and peripheral constructs that are less central. For example, good-bad might be a core construct and funny-serious a peripheral construct, although what is a core construct for one person can be a peripheral construct for another person. Also, there are verbal constructs that can be expressed in words and preverbal constructs that are used even though the person has no words to express them. Finally, there are superordinate constructs that include other constructs within their context and subordinate constructs that are included within the context of other (superordinate) constructs.

A person's constructs are organized to form a construct system. A person may have a very complex or a very simple construct system. A complex construct system involves many constructs that are connected to one another, with multiple levels of organization. In contrast, a simple construct system has few constructs that are not connected with one another and have but one or two levels of organization. A complex construct system provides for much greater differentiation in perception of the world and for more fine-grained predictions. A simple construct system means that all people and all things are lumped into categories such as good-bad or successful-unsuccessful, and predictions are the same without regard to circumstances.

Kelly developed the **Role Construct Repertory Test (Rep test)** to assess the content and structure of the person's construct system. In this test the person is given a list of titles to which names of people known to him or her are attached (e.g., mother, father, teacher most liked). Then the person is given three of the figures from the list and asked to indicate how two are alike and different from the third. For example, two of the people might be seen as outgoing, and different from the third person who is seen as shy. Thus, the construct outgoing-shy is elicited. Through further steps the constructs used by the person and the relations among them are determined. Illustrative constructs given by one person are presented in Table 3.1.

Of interest to us is how far Kelly was able to take a cognitive perspective. For example, rather than using a motive concept such as drive or need, he suggested

TABLE 3.1   **Role Construct Repertory Test: Illustrative Constructs**

Similar Figures	Similarity Construct	Dissimilar Figure	Contrasting Construct
Self, Father	Emphasis on happiness	Mother	Emphasis on practicality
Teacher, Happy person	Calm	Sister	Anxious
Male friend, Female friend	Good listener	Past friend	Trouble expressing feelings
Disliked person, Employer	Uses people for own ends	Liked person	Considerate of others
Father, Successful person	Active in the community	Employer	Not active in the community
Disliked person, Employer	Cuts others down	Sister	Respectful of others
Mother, Male friend	Introvert	Past friend	Extravert
Self, Teacher	Self-sufficient	Person helped	Dependent
Self, Female friend	Artistic	Male friend	Uncreative
Employer, Female friend	Sophisticated	Brother	Unsophisticated

that people are intrinsically active and seek to anticipate events, that is, to predict the future. For Kelly *anxiety* is the experience associated with finding that events lie outside the construct system, and *fear* is experienced when a new construct is about to emerge. *Threat* is associated with comprehensive change in the construct system.

There are many other elements to Kelly's personal construct theory that could be considered. He described disordered or pathological aspects of construct system functioning and ways of changing construct systems. For now, however, we can limit ourselves to the elements that have been described. These are sufficient to see just how far Kelly was able to take a cognitive perspective: The unit of personality is the construct. Individuals can be described in terms of their constructs, the organization of their constructs into systems, and the functioning of their construct systems. A person behaves similarly in situations construed as similar. A person's construct system can show considerable flexibility and adaptiveness while retaining its basic structure: A superordinate construct can become subordinate, or less important, for a while and then return to its former superordinate position. Whether people are intelligent or unintelligent may ordinarily be a superordinate construct, but it can assume a subordinate status in a recreational situation. For example, athletic-unathletic may achieve superordinate status in an athletic event, and sociable-unsociable at a party, although ordinarily they may be of lesser importance than the construct intelligent-unintelligent. Finally, over time people are stable in their functioning to the extent that their construct system remains the same.

To return to the points made earlier, Kelly's theory is noteworthy in its emphasis on both structure and process and on both idiographic and nomothetic aspects of people. Structure resides in the constructs and construct system, while process involves the ways in which constructs are used to predict events as well as in the dynamics of construct system functioning. People are unique in the ways in which they interpret events but similar in the extent to which they have similar construct systems. Ultimately, every person is unique in the constructs used and the elements that are included in each construct. Thus, every person has his or her own unique reality. However, certain processes are common to all people. We all seek to antici-pate events and we all seek to reduce anxiety, fear, and threat. To a certain extent, then, for all of us living involves the challenge of constantly seeking to expand our construct system while avoiding threats to the already established structure.

We end this section on Kelly with a discussion of his impact on later theory and research. First, although Kelly influenced later personality theorists, such as his stu-dent Mischel, personal construct theory has developed little since its initial formula-tion. Current cognitive personality psychologists pay tribute to Kelly's work but, as we shall see, have gone in a somewhat different direction. Second, for the most part, personal construct theory is not a major part of current personality research. Kelly himself developed his ideas out of clinical experience rather than systematic corre-lational or experimental research. Much of the subsequent research based on per-sonal construct theory revolved around the Rep test. Although the theory is recog-nized as a major contribution, and there remains an organization devoted to personal construct theory and research, relatively little current research that is reported in the major journals is based on Kelly's work.

ROTTER'S SOCIAL LEARNING THEORY

As noted, Julian Rotter (1954) developed his social learning theory at the same time that Kelly was developing his personal construct theory. Rotter worked as both a clinician and an experimental researcher. In addition, he had been influenced by the work of analysts such as Freud and Adler, as well as the work of experimental learning theorists such as Hull and Tolman. Adler's influence is particularly important in relation to Rotter's emphasis on the *social* component of psychological functioning. For Rotter it is important to recognize that the majority of our learning occurs within a social context and the majority of our motivation involves other persons. The influences of Hull and Tolman are noteworthy in terms of Rotter's emphasis on both reinforcers and cognitions in human functioning.

During the 1940s there was considerable debate among traditional learning the-orists about *what* is learned and *how* it is learned. Hullians, following the theory of Clark Hull, emphasized S-R connections that were formed on the basis of reinforce-ment. Tolmanians, following the theory of Edward Chase Tolman, emphasized the learning of cognitive maps that occurred in the absence of reinforcement. According to Tolman, reinforcement influenced motivation and behavior but learning occurred in the absence of reinforcement. In addition, what was learned were "cognitive maps" rather than S-R connections. Thus, rats running a maze learned a map of the maze rather than more mechanistic right-left turns. Tolman was far ahead of his time in this emphasis on the importance of cognitive variables in learning and performance.

What Rotter attempted to do was combine the importance of reinforcement, associated with Hull, with the importance of cognition, associated with Tolman. Thus, he suggested that in a situation the individual may have a number of behavioral options. Each potential behavior is associated with an outcome. The outcome has a *value* associated with it, a reinforcement value. For example, acting in either an aggressive or a dependent manner may result in a variety of possible outcomes, each of which is associated with a certain reinforcement value. Thus, we have the importance of the reinforcers emphasized by Hull in learning and performance. In addition, however, people have *expectancies* concerning the likelihood of the reinforcers following each behavior. It is as if the person, or rat, says, "The likelihood of my getting this reinforcer for this behavior is *x*."

What we have here is the suggestion that behavior outcomes, reinforcers, have both greater or lesser value and higher or lower probabilities (expectancies). The likelihood of a behavior then is a function of both the value of the reinforcer associated with it and the probability of the reinforcer occurring. We have what is known as an **expectancy-value model** of behavior (Feather, 1982). To return to the earlier example, acting in either an aggressive or a dependent manner may result in a variety of possible outcomes, each of which is associated with a reinforcement value and a probability of occurrence. The specific behavior chosen represents the greatest combination of value and expectancy.

It is important to recognize that in Rotter's model, the value and probability of various reinforcers are unique to the individual. It is not some objective measure of value and probability that is important but rather the individual's value and expectancy calculations. Thus, we often are surprised to learn of the seemingly unusual value a person associates with an outcome or the seemingly strange expectancies a person has about certain outcomes. Surprising or unusual behavior can only be understood in terms of the expectancies and reinforcement values of the individual, as is true of all behavior. A very aggressive person associates high reinforcement value and/or high probability of reinforcement with behaving aggressively, whereas a very timid, inhibited person associates negative outcomes, in terms of value and probability, with acting aggressively.

Rotter suggested that these reinforcement values and expectancies are unique not only to the individual but to the situation as well. The same behavior will not have the same outcome, in terms of reinforcement value and expectancy, in every situation. Behaving aggressively has different outcomes in social and athletic situations, for example. Thus, it is not surprising that people vary their behavior from situation to situation, depending on the reinforcement contingencies associated with behaviors in each situation. This also suggests that situations can be understood and assessed in terms of the outcomes (value and expectancy of reinforcers) associated with specific behaviors (Rotter, 1981). Again, however, it is the psychological situation that is unique to the individual that is important in determining behavior.

Although Rotter emphasized the importance of reinforcement values and expectancies unique to the situation, he also suggested that people develop expectancies that hold across many situations—**generalized expectancies** (Rotter, 1966, 1971, 1990). One generalized expectancy emphasized by Rotter is **interpersonal trust**—the extent to which one can rely on the word of others. Compared to those low on interpersonal trust, those high on interpersonal trust have a generalized expectancy that people can be trusted to keep their word and not betray others. This concept has received minimal research attention. A generalized expectancy that has received enormous research attention is **internal versus external locus of control of reinforcement,** or **locus of control.** People high on internal locus of control have a generalized expectancy that reinforcers or outcomes will depend largely on their own efforts, whereas people high on external locus of control have a generalized expectancy that outcomes will depend largely on luck, fate, chance, or other external forces. Internal locus of control people have a generalized expectancy that personal effort will make a difference, whereas external locus of control people have a generalized expectancy that their efforts will make little difference. External locus of control people feel relatively helpless in relation to events.

The enormous amount of research conducted in relation to the concept of locus of control is due both to its theoretical and applied importance as well as to the fact that there is a questionnaire associated with it. The *Internal-External (I-E) Scale* was developed to measure individual differences in generalized expectancies concerning the extent to which rewards and punishments are under internal or external control (Table 3.2). For a decade or so it probably was the most frequently used questionnaire in personality research! In addition, more specific variants of the scale were developed to measure generalized expectancies in children and in areas such as health (Lau, 1982; Lefcourt, 1984; Strickland, 1989; Wallston & Wallston, 1981).

Rotter's work has had an enormous impact on the field, in terms of its influence both on the thinking of other personality psychologists and on research. However, the latter influence has declined of late. In part this is because the locus of control scale was found to be more complex than originally expected. In addition, as will be seen in the following sections, research has tended to shift to different topics and measuring instruments. In particular, many social learning psychologists have preferred to study more specific expectancies and to tie their research to developments in cognitive psychology. Although Rotter's work has spanned the period of the cognitive revolution, his major theoretical effort preceded it and his thinking has been left largely untouched by it.

TABLE 3.2   Illustrative Items from Rotter's Internal-External Locus of Control Scale

1a. Many of the unhappy things in people's lives are due partly to bad luck.
1b. People's misfortunes result from the mistakes they make.
2a. One of the major reasons we have wars is that people don't take enough interest in politics.
2b. There will always be wars, no matter how hard people try to prevent them.
3a. Sometimes I can't understand how teachers arrive at the grades they give.
3b. There is a direct connection between how hard I study and the grades I get.
4a. The average citizen can have an influence in government decisions.
4b. This world is run by the few people in power and there isn't much the little guy can do about it.

Source: Rotter, 1966.

TWO POST–COGNITIVE REVOLUTION THEORISTS: MISCHEL AND BANDURA

In this section we consider two cognitive theorists whose views clearly have been influenced by the cognitive revolution and developments in cognitive psychology. It is interesting that their personal roots are very different. Mischel was born in Vienna and grew up in New York; Bandura was born and grew up in northern Alberta, Canada. Mischel was a student of Kelly and Rotter at Ohio State University, whereas Bandura was a student of Kenneth Spence, a follower of the S-R learning theorist Clark Hull. For 20 years, however, they were colleagues at Stanford University and from there spearheaded developments in a cognitive approach to personality.

MISCHEL'S COGNITIVE SOCIAL LEARNING THEORY

Walter Mischel, already familiar to us through his 1968 critique of trait theory, has attempted to develop an alternative conceptualization of personality. There are perhaps three key points of emphasis to this view (Mischel, 1990, Mischel & Shoda, 1995). First, there is an emphasis on **situational specificity.** An individual's behavior is seen as highly variable and relatively situation-specific. Second, there is an emphasis on the **discriminativeness** of human perceptual-cognitive functioning. People generally are able to discriminate among the rewards and demands associated with different situations, and to vary their behavior accordingly. This discriminativeness among situations is what leads to the situational specificity of behavior. It is the disregard of such cognitive functioning that leads to problems associated with trait approaches. Third, there is an emphasis on the *adaptive,* **self-regulatory** aspects of personality functioning. Mischel is interested in how people are able to vary their behavior from situation to situation in adaptive ways, that is, in how they are able to vary their functioning to meet the demands of the particular situation. And, Mischel is interested in how people are able to delay gratification and maintain commitments to goals over extended periods of time.

As noted, Mischel did his graduate work at Ohio State University, where he was influenced by Kelly and Rotter. He has described them as being his "dual mentors" who influenced his thinking in enduring ways. In 1973, once the cognitive revolution had gained momentum, Mischel published a "cognitive social learning" reconceptualization of personality. Five units were basic to this reconceptualization, many showing the influences of Kelly and Rotter. Over the course of 20 years, Rotter and some of his students, most particularly Nancy Cantor (1990; Cantor & Zirkel, 1990), have attempted to develop and extend this view of personality.

What might such cognitive-social units be? First, people have *personal constructs* and **encoding strategies.** What is emphasized here is the ways in which people construe and process information relevant to the self, others, and events in the world. The emphasis on personal constructs clearly relates to Kelly's thinking and that on encoding strategies to information-processing models associated with the cognitive revolution.

Second, there are *subjective values, preferences,* **goals.** This unit expresses individual differences in the value given to different outcomes. It also expresses the ability of people to have mental representations of end points, or goals, and thereby to engage in purposive, goal-directed behavior (Cantor & Zirkel, 1990). Cantor (1990) in particular has directed her research efforts toward understanding how people select and direct themselves toward **life tasks.** Life tasks represent cognitive-motivational units that draw attention to the future-oriented aspects of personality. For college students the life task of working toward independence is generally of particular importance, although individuals vary in the importance associated with it. Other life tasks for college students involve doing well academically and socially. Here too individuals differ in the importance given to these tasks. What is important about the life task–goal concept is that it focuses attention on what people are trying to do rather than on what they have, the latter being more characteristic of the trait concept (Cantor, 1990).

Third, individuals have *expectancies* concerning the probable consequences of action. As suggested by Rotter, to predict people's behavior in a particular situation one must consider their specific expectancies concerning possible behavior outcomes in that situation. Again, the emphasis is on specific expectancies in specific situations. People develop "If ____, then ____" outcome expectancies that guide the selection of behavior in a situation. As does Rotter, Mischel suggests that behavior will be quite different when the expectancies associated with two situations differ: "The child who has been rewarded regularly in preschool for 'dependency' with the teacher but not with peers is unlikely to provide evidence for a high correlation between 'dependency' assessed in these two situations" (Mischel, 1990, p. 119).

Fourth, people have **cognitive and behavioral competencies.** People differ in the information they have, in the ways in which they are able to make use of information, and in their specific behavioral skills. Mischel (1990) suggests that cognitive and behavioral competencies relate to *potential* achievements rather than actual achievements, which are governed by many variables. Thus, the emphasis is on what a person *can do* rather than what the person *typically does*. In addition, although cognitive competencies show considerable stability over time and some generality across situations, it is important not to consider them as fixed, traitlike entities.

The concept of cognitive competencies is given particular emphasis in Cantor and Kihlstrom's (1987) concept of **social intelligence.** According to them, social intelligence represents "the concepts, memories, and rules—in short, the knowledge—that individuals bring to bear in solving personal life tasks" (1987, p. ix). Social intelligence involves the ability to use knowledge in relation to specific problem-solving situations. It is adaptive and task-oriented. In addition, it is viewed as task-specific or *domain-specific*. Thus, one person has expertise in academic tasks, another in mechanical tasks, another in social relationships, and another in family matters. In contrast to a view of generalized intelligence or a generalized cognitive style, it is suggested that people often develop knowledge and expertise that is task- or domain-specific. The "smart" person in one domain may be rather "dense" in another. The "scholarly" academic may perform well in some situations but, relative to the "shrewd" investor, perform poorly in others, and both may perform poorly in comparison to the "smart" athlete in still other situations. Cantor and Kihlstrom consider this unit to be so important that it is placed at the center of their view of personality.

Finally, we have the concept of *self-regulatory systems*. Here the emphasis is on how complex, long-term goals are developed and maintained over long periods of time, even when there is little external support for their pursuit. What is emphasized here is individuals' ability to develop and enact long-term plans, to set standards and hold to them, and to resist temptation and stay on course despite frustration. Individuals establish their own goals and select their own plans for achieving these goals. In the course of their pursuit of these goals, individuals monitor their performance and evaluate their accomplishments, rewarding themselves with praise for gains made and punishing themselves with criticism for failures that could have been avoided.

Mischel (1990) has been particularly interested in the strategies developed by young children attempting to delay gratification. For example, what is a child to do when he or she is given the choice between an immediately available object, say a cookie or toy, but can have an even better cookie or toy if he or she is prepared to wait for it? This is a situation with which children, as well as adults, are frequently faced: "I know it pays to wait, but how do I get myself to do it?" Not surprisingly, Mischel has found that children are better able to wait for a preferred outcome relative to an immediately available but less desirable outcome if they can shift their attention away from the immediately available but less valued object. As most of us probably are aware, it is easier to delay if the desired object is not staring us in the face all the time.

These, then, are Mischel's candidates for the units of personality: constructs and encoding strategies, goals, expectancies, competencies, and self-regulatory systems (Table 3.3). Although some, such as goals, have a motivational component to them, they all clearly involve an emphasis on cognition. They are the units emphasized by what Cantor and Kihlstrom (1987) call "cognitive personologists." In addition to the emphasis on cognition, they stress the highly idiosyncratic meaning that individuals can attach to situations. Thus, as well, they emphasize the situational specificity of behavior as people discriminate among situations, adapt to them, and use them as opportunities to achieve desired goals.

Two frequently neglected points are important in relation to this cognitive-social

TABLE 3.3   Suggested Units of Personality—Social Cognitive Theory

1. Constructs and encoding strategies.
2. Goals.
3. Expectancies.
4. Competencies.
5. Self-regulatory systems.

Source: "Toward a Cognitive Social Learning Reconceptualization of Personality," by W. Mischel, 1973, *Psychological Review, 80;* "Personality Dispositions Revisited and Revised: A View After Three Decades," by W. Mischel, 1990, in L. A. Pervin (Ed.), *Handbook of Personality: Theory and Research* New York: Guilford.

SPOTLIGHT ON THE RESEARCHER

WALTER MISCHEL

Perhaps knowing that Sigmund Freud's residence in Vienna was near where I lived as a child predisposed me to become fascinated by his theories. Although my proximity to Freud ended in my eighth year when the Nazis took over Austria and my family fled to New York, a decade later I still wanted to apply his ideas to help people as a clinician. It was my interest in psychodynamic theory that motivated my study of clinical psychology.

Ambivalence emerged, however, as I saw that many of the "facts" that I was learning might reflect the shared faith of true believers rather than the findings of science. My skepticism escalated when I tried to apply what I was taught to help troubled adolescents and lonely, isolated elderly people as a social worker on New York's lower East Side and found what I had learned was not relevant in these real-world contexts.

These concerns were reinforced in both my research and clinical experience after my training was completed. As a consultant for the Peace Corps in the early 1960s, I discovered that under some conditions—such as when people really trust psychologists—they are willing and able to assess themselves and can predict their own behavior as accurately as the best available formal tests or clinical judgments by experts. These surprising results led me to think that while the available assessment methods were useful for describing broad overall differences between types or groups of people, they were not sufficiently accurate and sensitive to make useful predictions and treatment decisions about individuals and the specific life situations they faced.

Characterization of individuals on common trait dimensions (such as Conscientiousness or Sociability) provided useful overall summaries of their average levels of behavior but missed, it seemed to me, the striking discriminativeness often visible within the same person closely observed over time and across situations. Might someone who is more caring, giving, and supportive than most people in relation to his family also be less caring and altruistic than most people in other contexts? Might these variations across situations be meaningful stable patterns that characterize the person enduringly rather than random fluctuations? If so, how could they be understood and what did they reflect? Might they be worth taking into account in personality assessment for the conceptualization of the stability and flexibility of human behavior and qualities? These questions began to gnaw at me and the effort to answer them has become a fundamental goal for the rest of my life.

At the same time I began to see that the effects of the stimuli or situations and rewards or stresses that people encounter depend on how they encode or represent them in their heads cognitively and emotionally. For example, the same child who could not wait for more than a few moments for a desired outcome that required delay of gratification might be able to wait longer than the researcher if she could just mentally represent and think about the reward in slightly different ways. If the way in which people cognitively represent the stimuli or situations they encounter crucially influences their impact, the study of individual differences in personality needs to focus on this and other "mediating person variables." That is, the personality psychologist needs to identify the basic psychological variables that underlie behavior, and not just summarize the overall level or type of behavior the person typically displays.

Cumulative research findings have been converging for many years to suggest a set of basic person variables that underlie individual differences in people's social behavior and affective states. In my view, these are the ways in which individuals encode or represent situations and themselves; the expectancies, beliefs, values, goals, and feelings that become activated in a given context; and the competencies and skills that are available for coping. It is the interaction among these variables within the context of the particular situation that underlies the distinctive patterns of behavior and feeling that come to characterize the individual.

Yuichi Shoda and I have recently formalized this view as a "cognitive-affective system theory" of personality (Mischel & Shoda, 1995). In this theory, each person is conceptualized as a distinctive cognitive-affective system whose interactions with the social environment generate the individual's characteristic patterns of behavior. Although this system is itself stable, it generates highly variable patterns of behavior that depend on the situation and the information being processed as well as on the individual who interprets and reacts to them. Thus the variability of behavior, rather than reflecting the inconsistency of personality, can reflect its distinctive behavioral signature. The challenge for future research is to understand how the interactions between the person system and the situation generate that signature.

conceptualization of personality. First, it does not neglect or underemphasize individual differences. Because Mischel was critical of trait approaches to personality, he sometimes is viewed as attacking the concept of individual differences. Clearly this is not the case. Mischel believes in the existence of individual differences, even in the existence of dispositions (Mischel, 1990). What he is against, however, is the trait view of cross-situational consistency that ignores the discriminativeness of cognitive functioning and the associated situational specificity of behavior. Indeed, he suggests that it often is only when people are excessively anxious or limited in their behavioral repertoire that they behave in the way suggested by trait theorists.

Second, Mischel's conceptualization does not emphasize situational influences over personality variables. Because of his attack on trait theory and his suggestion that behavior is relatively situation-specific, Mischel often is seen as the enemy of personality psychology. However, clearly Mischel believes in the importance of personality variables, including the ability of individuals to select and choose situations, as well as their ability to reconstrue situations that cannot otherwise be changed or avoided. Thus, Mischel is not antipersonality, but rather for a different conceptualization of personality—a cognitive-social one.

Research Illustrating Situational Specificity

To what extent is our behavior fairly uniform across situations, as suggested by trait theory, and to what extent is our behavior specific to the situation, as suggested by Mischel? Consider some recent research on the behavior of boys in a camp setting (Shoda, Mischel, & Wright, 1994). The point of this study was to demonstrate the "If ____, then ____" pattern of individual person–situation relationships, that is, to demonstrate that people have stable patterns of behavior that vary according to how situations are perceived. In contrast to the trait emphasis on overall, aggregate consistency across situations, there is the emphasis on consistency within domains of situations but discrimination among categories or domains of situations. In sum, the purpose of the study was to demonstrate that behavior is both stable or consistent and varying or context dependent.

In this study, observations were made of the behavior of boys during the course of the day at a summer camp for children with behavioral problems. Observations of behavior were recorded for five situations: (1) when a peer initiated positive contact; (2) when a peer teased, provoked, or threatened; (3) when praised by an adult; (4) when warned by an adult; and (5) when punished by an adult. These five situations were selected because they involved both positive and negative situations as well as peer and adult interactions. In each situation a recording was made of whether the boy responded with any of five behaviors: (1) verbal aggression; (2) physical aggression; (3) whining; (4) compliance; and (5) prosocial talk. The observations were recorded daily throughout the summer as each type of psychological interpersonal situation occurred. This was done for 5 hours a day, 6 days a week, for an entire 6-week summer program—an average of 167 hours of observation per child. An incredible effort!

The question the investigators addressed concerned the stability of individual behavior in and across the five psychological situations. In terms of the data, the questions addressed included the following: How likely is the individual boy to respond with each of the five behaviors to each of the five psychological situations? Is there evidence of stability of individual behavior within each of the five categories of interpersonal situations? Is there evidence of stability of individual behavior across the five categories of interpersonal situations? The data indicated the following:

1. Behavior was stable or consistent within psychological situation categories but not across these categories; that is, a boy who responded with verbal aggression to being teased by a peer was likely to express this behavior whether the teasing occurred at a cabin meeting, on the playground, or in the classroom, but not necessarily likely to express this behavior if warned by an adult or in any of the other observed psychological situations.

2. Individuals tended to be more consistent in their behavior across psychological situations that were more similar to one another than across situations that were not similar to one another. Similarity was defined in terms of whether the situations shared features such as positive-negative interaction and peer-adult involvement (Figure 3.2). Corresponding to this, individual differences in behavior tended to be more consistent across psychological situations that were more similar to one another than across situations that were not similar to one another.

3. Over time, individuals were found to have stable profiles of behavior in terms of types of situations in which they expressed each of the five interpersonal behaviors; that is, each individual had an identifiable pattern of variation in expressing the five behaviors in the five situations.

4. Aggregation, or the combination of a class of behaviors over a range of situations, increased stability of individual differences in behavior, but the effect of situational context on behavior remained.

Figure 3.2 Consistency of individual differences in behavior (r) according to similarity of situations (shared features). agg. = aggression.
The data indicate, with the exception of prosocial talk, greater consistency of individual differences in behavior as situational similarity increases.

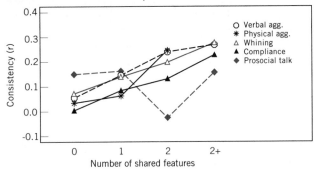

In sum, the authors concluded that, in agreement with the cognitive-social conception of personality, individuals have stable behavioral tendencies that are contextualized in terms of particular types of psychological situations. Support was found for the assumption of stable but discriminative "If ____, then ____" relationships. Finally, it was suggested that although the trait emphasis on aggregation may be useful for demonstrating individual differences in average behavior trends, such an approach ignores the situational discriminativeness and unique behavior signature that characterizes the individual.

What is suggested by this research is that each of us has a characteristic style of behaving similarly within certain groups of situations and differently in other groups of situations. It is the rare person who is extraverted or introverted in *all* social situations. Rather, most of us have characteristic patterns of sociability in some groups of situations and shyness in other groups of situations. Two people may have the same average degree of sociability, but the groups of situations in which they are sociable or shy may be very different. It is this pattern of stability and variability that is seen by Mischel as central to each individual's personality. According to him, people have stable personalities, but they make use of cognitive competencies to adapt to the perceived requirements of specific situations or categories of situations. Indeed, it is the use of such competencies that gives the unique stamp to each personality.

BANDURA'S SOCIAL COGNITIVE THEORY

Albert Bandura's theoretical emphasis parallels that of Mischel in many ways, although his roots in the field are very different. First called a social learning theory (Bandura & Walters, 1963), with minimal attention given to cognitive variables, Bandura's work increasingly has emphasized the importance of cognitive variables and now is called a social cognitive theory of personality (Bandura, 1986).

Although Bandura's views have changed over time, they have evolved more than they have gone through radical transformations. In addition, two other features are noteworthy. First, changes in the theory have been tied to new areas of research. Although trained as a clinician, and interested in processes of therapeutic change, Bandura always has emphasized experimental investigation. He believes that clinical concepts and procedures should be made amenable to experimental tests.

Second, in attempting to develop a comprehensive theory of personality, Bandura has drawn from developments in other areas, most particularly cognitive psychology and social psychology. At a time when grand theories are becoming rare in the field, Bandura's social cognitive theory approaches that status. Until the 1960s, there were many grand theories, covering virtually all aspects of personality. Thus, we had the theories of Freud and other analysts; Rogers; trait theorists such as Allport, Eysenck, and Cattell; and more cognitively oriented theorists such as Kelly and Rotter. Beginning around the 1960s, personality research increasingly emphasized specific variables, or at best minitheories, rather than such grand theories. Yet, in Bandura's work we find an emerging outline of a grand theory of personality, and, as suggested by one reviewer, "what more can we ask from a single colleague and scholar" (Baron, 1987, p. 415).

Rather than going into the theory in detail, we consider here three components of it that relate to the emphasis on cognitive units of personality: (1) cognitive elements in learning or the acquisition of behavior, (2) self-efficacy beliefs, and (3) standards or goals. These three components, in fact, relate sequentially to developments in the theory and points of emphasis in research.

Bandura's early work was devoted to the study of **observational learning,** or the process whereby people learn merely by observing the behaviors of others. Much of this thinking goes back to the work of the learning theorist Tolman, who emphasized cognitive variables in learning. Tolman distinguished between the acquisition of behaviors and the performance of behaviors, reinforcers being essential to the latter but not to the former. This was a position at odds with S-R reinforcement theory as well as Skinner's operant approach, both of which emphasized the essential role of reinforcers in all learning.

What Bandura did was to demonstrate, in experimental research with children, how behaviors could be learned in the absence of rewards but demonstrated only in the presence of rewards (Bandura, Ross, & Ross, 1963). Thus, in one study children observed a model express aggressive behavior, in this case punching a plastic Bobo doll. To study the effects of rewards on the model, one group of children observed the model being rewarded for the aggressive behavior; a second group of children observed the model being punished for the aggressive behavior; and a third group of children observed a model for whom no consequences followed the aggressive behavior. In a subsequent condition, children from all three groups were left alone in a room with the Bobo doll, as well as other toys, and observed to see if they would express aggressive behavior toward the doll. First the children were observed without incentives for any particular behavior and then they were observed while being given incentives for reproducing the model's behavior. In sum, in this experimental study there were three groups of children who observed differing consequences to the model (model rewarded, model punished, no consequences) and then were observed in two different conditions (no incentive, incentive).

Two questions were asked: First, did the children show more aggressive behavior when given incentives for such behavior? The data clearly indicated that for each of

Observational Learning. Aggressive behavior can be learned from the observation of models, including models observed on television.

the three groups of children, many more aggressive behaviors were displayed under the incentive condition than the no incentive condition. In other words, the children had learned (acquired) many aggressive behaviors that were not performed under the no incentive condition but were performed under the incentive condition. Rewards were necessary for performance, but not for the acquisition of behavior.

Second, did the consequences to the model affect the children's display of aggressive behavior? The three groups of children did differ in their display of aggressive behavior in the no incentive condition. Children who observed the model rewarded for aggressive behavior displayed the most aggressive behavior and those who observed the model punished displayed the least aggressive behavior. However, these differences were wiped out once all of the children were put in the incentive condition. Here, children from the three groups (model rewarded, model punished, no consequences) were very similar in their aggressive behavior toward the Bobo doll. The children in the model punished group, who in the no incentive condition produced far fewer aggressive behaviors than children in the other two groups, produced about the same number of aggressive behaviors once they were given the incentive for doing so. Thus, the data clearly indicated that the consequences to the model had an effect on the children's performance of the aggressive behaviors but, once more, not on the learning of them.

Bandura suggested that children learn many things merely by observing parents and others, called models, and referred to this process as **modeling.** He went on to investigate areas to which the concept could be extended. One extremely important line of research demonstrated that children could acquire emotional responses as well as behavioral responses through the observations of models, a process called **vicarious conditioning.** For example, human subjects who observed a model express a fear response were found to develop a vicariously conditioned fear response to a previously neutral stimulus (Bandura & Rosenthal, 1966). Research on monkeys similarly demonstrated that emotional reactions of young monkeys could be vicariously conditioned through observation of the emotional responses of older monkeys. What is particularly striking about this research is that it demonstrated that the period of observation of emotional reactions can be very brief and still produce intense,

SPOTLIGHT ON THE RESEARCHER

ALBERT BANDURA:
Self-Efficacy Theory

My interest in perceived self-efficacy was an unintended out-growth of a different line of research. Psychological treatments have traditionally attempted to change human behavior by talk. In the sociocognitive view, human functioning can be enhanced more dependably and fundamentally by mastery experiences than by conversation. In translating this notion to therapeutic practice for phobic disorders, my students and I evolved a pow-erful guided mastery treatment. It eradicates phobic behavior and biochemical stress reactions, eliminates phobic ruminations and recurrent nightmares, and creates positive attitudes toward formerly dreaded threats. These striking changes are achieved by everyone in a brief period. The changes endure.

Having developed a powerful treatment, we launched a series of studies on how to reduce vulnerability to negative experiences with phobic threats should they occur in the future. We reasoned that if people have no contact with the phobic threats after functioning is fully restored, an aversive experience could well reinstate the phobic disorder. However, if they have had many masterful encounters with the phobic threats immediately after completing treatment, the impact of later negative experiences would be neutralized by the numerous positive ones. To test this notion, we structured opportunities for self-directed mastery experiences with varied phobic threats after the phobic disorder was eradicated. In follow-up assessments we were discovering that the participants not only maintained their therapeutic gains, but also made notable improvements in domains of functioning quite unrelated to the treated dysfunction. For example, after mastering an animal phobia, participants had reduced their social timidity, expanded their competences in different spheres, and boosted their venturesomeness in a variety of ways. Success in overcoming, within a few hours of treatment, a phobic dread that had constricted and tormented their lives for 20 or 30 years produced a profound change in participants' beliefs in their personal efficacy to exercise better control over their lives. They were putting themselves to the test and enjoying their successes much to their surprise.

I redirected my research efforts to gain a deeper understanding of personal efficacy. To guide this new mission, I formulated a theory that addressed the key aspects of human efficacy. These aspects include the origins of efficacy beliefs, their structure and function, their diverse effects, the psychosocial processes through which they operate, and the modes of influence by which human efficacy can be developed and enhanced. Efficacy beliefs have been shown to play a central and pervasive role in personal causation. They affect how people think, feel, motivate themselves, and behave.

Self-efficacy theory has spawned large programs of research in diverse spheres of human functioning far removed from its serendipitous origin. This substantial body of literature is reviewed in a volume I am presently completing on *Self-Efficacy: The Exercise of Control.*

The theorizing and research on perceived self-efficacy are being extended in several directions. Self-efficacy beliefs operate in concert with other determinants within the broader framework of social cognitive theory. Analyses of codetermination of human functioning will add to our understanding of how beliefs of personal efficacy operate in personal causation.

Personal adaptation and change are rooted in social systems. Sociological theories and psychological theories are often regarded as rival conceptions of human behavior or as representing different levels of causation. Human behavior cannot be fully understood solely in terms of social structural factors or psychological factors. A full understanding requires an integrated perspective in which societal influences operate through psychological mechanisms to produce behavioral effects. Recent research conducted within this expanded framework of causation is showing that, indeed, socioeconomic conditions affect human functioning partly through their effects on people's beliefs of their efficacy. This line of research will give us a better sense of how people are producers as well as products of social systems.

Human lives are intimately linked to the sociocultural environments in which people are immersed. Many of the challenges of life center on common problems that require people working together to change their lives for the better. The strength of families, communities, social institutions, and even nations lies partly in people's sense of collective efficacy that they can solve the problems they face and improve their lives through unified effort. People's beliefs in their collective efficacy influence the type of social future they seek to achieve, how much effort they put into it, and their endurance when collective efforts fail to produce quick results. Knowledge on collective efficacy and how to develop it carries considerable socal implications. Life in the societies of today is increasingly affected by transnational interdependencies. What happens economically and politically in one part of the world can affect the welfare of vast populations elsewhere. Perceived collective efficacy is, therefore, becoming increasingly important to a broad understanding of how people can exercise some control over the direction and quality of their lives.

long-lasting consequences in the observer (Berger, 1962; Mineka, Davidson, Cook, & Klein, 1984). In sum, intense and long-lasting emotional reactions can be acquired from observing models and need not be acquired exclusively on the basis of direct experience. Many of our likes and dislikes, attractions and fears, can be based on vicarious conditioning rather than direct experience.

In 1977 Bandura published a paper that in many ways appeared to represent a radical departure for him and his work. In fact it represented part of a gradual transformation toward a greater cognitive emphasis in his thinking and research. The paper emphasized the concept of **self-efficacy** and placed it at the center of all change in psychotherapy (Bandura, 1977b). Bandura's concept of self-efficacy relates to the perceived ability to cope with specific situations. It relates to judgments people make concerning their ability to act in a specific task or situation. According to Bandura, self-efficacy judgments influence which activities we engage in, how much effort we expend in a situation, how long we persist at a task, and our emotional reactions while anticipating a situation or being involved in it. We think, feel, and behave differently in situations in which we feel confident of our ability than in situations in which we are insecure or feel incompetent. Thus, self-efficacy beliefs influence thoughts, motivation, performance, and emotional arousal.

What is important to recognize about Bandura's self-efficacy concept is that it does not refer to a "self" that someone has but rather to cognitive processes in which the

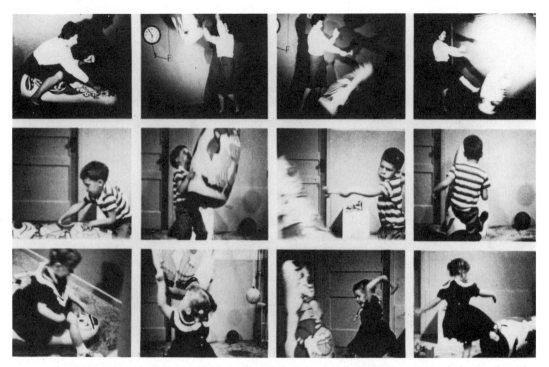

Observational Learning. Children who observe a model express aggressive behavior (punch a plastic Bobo doll—top row), learn (acquire) these behaviors and perform them when given incentives for doing so (middle and bottom rows).

concept of self is involved. In other words, the self is a concept, construct, or mental representation like any other concept, except that it is more important than most in its influence on our thought, feeling, and action. As such, it can be studied in the same way that we study other such mental representations. Thus, we can be interested in the factors influencing the development of self-efficacy beliefs and how self-efficacy beliefs can be changed.

A second important point about Bandura's self-efficacy concept is that it does not refer to a global self-concept. People make self-efficacy judgments in relation to specific tasks and situations. People may believe that they are effective in handling some situations and not others. In other words, once more there is an emphasis on situational specificity. Although some psychologists talk about a person's self-concept and self-esteem, Bandura suggests that such concepts are too global and do poorly at predicting how a person will perform in a specific situation. Such global concepts may have some degree of generality, or bandwidth, but they have little fidelity, or ability to predict to specific situations. This is because they do not adequately recognize the many differentiations people make among situations and their ability to master the differing requirements associated with them.

The third area to be considered is that involving cognitive contributions to motivation (Bandura, 1989b). For some time, social cognitive theory ignored the area of motivation. However, this area has since been addressed in terms of goals and

Modeling. Social cognitive theorists emphasize the importance of observing others in the acquisition of behavior.

standards. A *goal* relates to a desired end point. A **standard** relates to a reference point for desired behavior or performance. Standards may be external, representing evaluations imposed by others, or they may be internal, representing evaluations imposed internally. Praise and criticism, whether external or internal, represent responses to meeting or not meeting standards. Thus, standards represent goals for us to achieve and bases for expecting reinforcement from others or from ourselves.

Cognitive processes are important in relation to motivation in at least three ways. First, in experimental research Bandura has demonstrated that people rely upon performance feedback to maintain commitment to a goal. We are able to remain more motivated when we have information about progress toward a goal than in the absence of such information. Second, self-efficacy judgments play an important role in motivational effort and commitment. We are able to remain more motivated when we have high self-efficacy judgments for goal attainment. Either the absence of information concerning progress or low perceived self-efficacy can lead to poor effort. On the other hand, people will sustain effort toward reaching a goal when they are provided with adequate feedback and have high perceived self-efficacy in relation to the task (Bandura & Cervone, 1983).

The third way in which cognitive processes are important in motivated behavior is through expectancies. According to Bandura, behavior is maintained by expectancies or anticipated consequences, rather than just by immediate consequences. Through the cognitive development of expectancies concerning the results of various actions, people are able to anticipate the consequences of behavior before undertaking action. Through such cognitive development they also are able to anticipate rewards and punishments far into the future. These and other cognitive developments are important to the process of *self-regulation*. How is it that we are able to maintain commitment to a goal over extended periods of time, particularly in the absence of external rewards? We are able to do so through our cognitive capacity to keep a goal in mind and to anticipate future rewards, partly based on positive self-efficacy judgments, and through our ability to reward ourselves for progress toward the goal. Alternatively, commitment to long-term goals is problematic when we have limited cognitive abilities to keep the goal in mind, when we have limited capacity for anticipating the future, when we do not believe we have much chance of attaining the goal, and when we do not receive external or internal rewards for progress made.

In this section, we clearly are touching on the unit to be considered in the next chapter—motives. However, at times it is difficult to maintain an absolute distinction among the units of personality. What is important to recognize at this point is the emphasis on cognitive variables—expectancies, performance feedback, cognitive representations of goals and standards, and self-efficacy beliefs.

Bandura's work has become increasingly cognitively oriented and influential. His concept of self-efficacy has been particularly important in the areas of psychotherapy and health. There has been investigation of therapeutic procedures that enhance patient self-efficacy (Bandura, 1986), as well as extensive investigation of the relation of perceived self-efficacy to undertaking health-promoting behaviors and to responses to stress. Research clearly suggests that perceived self-efficacy relates to people's preparedness to undertake behaviors that promote health (Bandura, 1992). Other research suggests that low self-efficacy beliefs are associated with the stress response and with poorer functioning of the body's disease-fighting system (A. O'Leary, 1990, 1992). For Bandura and other cognitive personality psychologists, such research accomplishments give adequate testimony to the importance of cognitive variables in personality functioning.

Before completing our discussion of Bandura's work, it may be useful to consider the relation of his work to the study of individual differences. Note that for the most part Bandura does not make individual differences the focal point of his research. He does not start with groups differing on a personality characteristic and certainly does not make use of groups differing on a trait. Like Mischel, he is not interested in such broad characterizations or taxonomies of individuals. Instead, his work focuses on cognitive structures and processes that are important for all people and in relation to which individuals may differ. For the most part, his work is experimental rather than correlational in nature. Personality is believed to be important and individual differences are recognized. However, it is in the adaptiveness of people to specific situations and tasks, particularly as cognitive processes are involved, that the emphasis lies.

ADDITIONAL COGNITIVE UNITS: SCHEMA, ATTRIBUTIONS, AND BELIEFS

In the preceding section we considered personality theories that heavily emphasize cognitive concepts. In this section we consider three additional concepts that are important in relation to cognitive approaches to personality. Considerable attention is devoted to these concepts in later chapters; therefore, only a brief discussion is given to them here as examples of additional concepts useful in the cognitive approach to personality.

SCHEMA

The world is filled with information. Our minds are filled with information. Given the enormous scope of this information, we must find ways of forming categories to treat it in a reasonably economical way. For example, rather than treating every vehicle as different we can group them into categories such as *car* and *truck*. Even though there are differences among the vehicles we see, we can group some as cars and others as trucks. We know that cars are useful for some purposes, trucks for other purposes. This simplifies the world in terms of what we perceive, what we remember, and how we go about making decisions. Think what it would be like if we had to consider each stimulus as a completely novel one, with no way of treating it as something similar to what we already know. Think what it would be like if each time we had to act we had no way of organizing the information available to us. Without ways of organizing the world, we would be overwhelmed with information and unable to act in an adaptive way. Thus, categories are useful ways of organizing information.

Schema refers to such categories or ways of perceiving the world, including the self. A schema is a cognitive structure that organizes information. As such it affects how new information is perceived, organized, and remembered. In information-processing terms, it affects how information is encoded, stored, and retrieved. It is similar to a concept or a construct in Kelly's terms. The trait factors discussed in Chapter 2 represent schema (the same term is used for the plural and the singular). From a personality standpoint, individuals differ in the schema they form, in the relations among these schema, and in the ways in which they process information relevant to their schema. As noted in the discussion of Kelly's theory, two people may have difficulty understanding one another if they do not share the same schema. They may also have problems if they have the same name for a schema but include different things in it. This often is the case when two people go along thinking they understand one another only to learn eventually that they are talking about different things. For example, two people may both have a schema for loyalty, but one might include lying to protect a friend as part of the schema whereas the other may not. Or, two people might have a hostility schema and one would include sarcasm in it whereas the other would not.

For cognitive personality psychologists, schema define the ways in which people are able to view others and themselves. There are culturally shared schema and at times schema unique to the individual. For cognitive personality psychologists, the schema concept is useful for studying, often through experimental procedures, the ways in which people process information. For example, do men and women have different schema and process information in different ways? Does having a certain schema for the self influence the way in which we perceive events relative to ourselves? Can we become something if we do not have a schema for it? For example, can we lose weight if we do not have a schema of ourselves as thinner than we are? Do depressed individuals have different schema and thereby process information differently than do nondepressed individuals? These are the kinds of questions that are of concern to cognitive personality psychologists. As noted, we will have the chance to consider many of these questions in later chapters.

ATTRIBUTIONS

Most cognitive personality psychologists emphasize the importance of expectancies. But what are expectancies based on? In part our expectancies are based on our memory of past events and our *attributions* or explanations for these events. According to attribution theorists, when an event occurs, particularly a meaningful or surprising event, we ask ourselves why it occurred (Weiner, 1990). Why did Jane not accept my invitation? Why did Jack act in such a critical way? Why was Fred so nice today? Our explanations for these events, called **causal attributions,** play an important role in our emotional reactions to events and our expectancies for the future.

Attribution theorists have been concerned with how people go about making causal attributions. Are there particular explanations people rely upon and, if so, what determines which explanation is used? Personality psychologists interested in attributional processes similarly are interested in such questions, but they also are interested in individual differences in attributions. Do some people tend to rely more upon some explanations and other people more upon other explanations? And, if so, what are the consequences of such differences for personality functioning?

In Chapter 1 we considered the work of Seligman and others on the relation of learned helplessness and attributions to depression. The Attributional Style Questionnaire (ASQ) was described as a method for determining the extent to which people attribute positive and negative events to internal, stable, and global causes. It was suggested that such attributions have implications for understanding depression. Additional research suggests that a pessimistic explanatory style (i.e., internal, stable, global attributions for negative events) is associated with poor academic and athletic performance relative to an optimistic explanatory style (Peterson, 1991). Thus, this work illustrates individual differences in attributions and the importance of such differences for emotion and motivation. In the next chapter we have the opportunity to consider the work of other attribution theorists and to consider further the implications of differing attributions for motivation and personality functioning more generally.

BELIEFS

The final cognitive unit to be considered in this section is the *belief.* Once more it is a concept that has been considered previously, for example, in the discussion of Bandura's emphasis on self-efficacy beliefs. **Beliefs** express the conviction that something is or is not true—that the world is or is not a just place, that one is or is not competent in certain areas, that one is or is not a good person. Individuals differ in the content of their beliefs, in the conviction with which they hold to their various beliefs, and in the emotions associated with them. Once more we have a cognitive unit of significance for personality.

The concept of beliefs is quite broad and thereby can be used to cover many areas. We briefly touch upon two illustrative areas relevant to personality functioning, both of which will be covered in greater detail later in the text. The first illustration concerns stress. Stress researchers suggest that the amount of stress experienced is influenced by our beliefs concerning the dangers before us and our ability to cope with them. Lazarus (1991), a leading figure in the stress area (see Chapter 10), uses the term **appraisal** to define the process whereby people evaluate what is at stake in a potentially stressful encounter and whether their resources are adequate to meet the demands of the situation. Individuals differ in the appraisals they make of the potential for harm or benefit in various situations as well as in their appraisals of resources for influencing whether benefit or harm occurs. Beyond the area of stress, such appraisals are seen as being important in determining specific emotions experienced in situations and thereby the emotional life of the person more generally.

Discussion of the cognitive units of schema and attributions suggested important implications for the emotional well-being of individuals. Clearly this is true as well for beliefs. Cognitive personality psychologists interested in abnormal personality functioning and therapeutic change have emphasized concepts such as *maladaptive beliefs* and *irrational beliefs* (see Chapter 12). **Maladaptive beliefs** interfere with adaptive functioning. For example, a total belief that life's events cannot be influenced by one's actions interferes with taking adaptive action. Maladaptive beliefs often may have the quality of a *self-fulfilling prophecy,* whereby the belief leads to actions that confirm it. For example, the depressed person who believes that he or she will be rejected may behave in ways that lead to rejection. The belief is confirmed but the person is unaware that the problem lies in the belief itself.

Irrational beliefs are beliefs that are not logical. Illustrative irrational beliefs are "If good things happen, bad things must be on the way" and "If I express my needs, others will reject me" (Ellis & Harper, 1975). Here too the belief may have a self-fulfilling quality to it. Often it is difficult to evaluate the rationality of a belief. If a person believes he or she is being persecuted, it may be a delusion (false belief) but it also may be true. In most cases, however, irrational beliefs are less open to evidence than are rational beliefs. At least this would appear to be true for the irrational beliefs that trouble individuals with psychological difficulties. Often such individuals are themselves aware of the irrationality of their belief but are unable to do anything about it, saying "I know this doesn't make sense, but . . ."

In sum, many cognitive personality psychologists are interested in the appraisals people make and in the extent to which their beliefs are adaptive or maladaptive, rational or irrational. Some beliefs form major parts of individual theories, as is true for self-efficacy beliefs in Bandura's theory and locus of control beliefs in Rotter's theory. Other beliefs are more specific to a particular area of research, as in Seligman's work on depression and causal explanations for events.

ANALYSIS OF COGNITIVE UNITS

We thus conclude our discussion of cognitive units of personality, although we certainly will continue our consideration of them in relation to various aspects of personality functioning. What can be said about them at this time? First, although cognitive concepts are not new, cognitive conceptions of personality are new, dating back to just before the cognitive revolution and increasing in importance ever since. Second, there is no one cognitive conception of personality, just as there is no one trait theory. If there is a consensus emerging around the five-factor model in trait theory, one might suggest that a social cognitive perspective is generally accepted among cognitive personality psychologists. The main points of emphasis in such a common perspective would appear to be the importance of cognitive processes in personality functioning, the social nature of personality functioning, and the domain specificity of personality functioning. At the same time, clearly the specific cognitive units emphasized by different theorists vary considerably.

What are these cognitive units of personality? They include what appear to be fairly pure cognitive units such as expectancies, self-efficacy beliefs, and causal attributions. However, they also include units, such as values and goals, that could equally well be considered motivational units. In fact, as we shall see, goals have become an important motivational unit of personality. And, cognitive units include abilities, such as cognitive competencies in assessing situations and planning strategies to meet task demands. Finally, they involve processes of self-regulation that place emphasis on the ability to anticipate the future and tolerate delay of gratification. In the broadest terms, they include all adaptive efforts of the organism that involve taking in information, processing information, and then using information to meet tasks and demands.

What should be clear to the student at this point is the difference in focus between trait and cognitive units. Whereas trait units start from an individual differences perspective, cognitive units start from the perspective of common processes in relation to which individuals will differ, particularly in relation to specific situational demands. Whereas trait theorists emphasize individual differences in their use of factor-analytic techniques, cognitive theorists emphasize common processes in their experimental research. Whereas trait theorists are prepared to aggregate and make general predictions, cognitive theorists focus on the situation-specific aspects of individual functioning and are comfortable only with situation-specific predictions. Interestingly enough, however, for the most part neither trait nor cognitive personality psychologists have emphasized the patterned, organized functioning of the individual. Thus, intensive studies of individuals have been rare for both contemporary trait and contemporary cognitive personality psychologists. In both cases, the units are emphasized more than the organization among the units.

MAJOR CONCEPTS

Cognition.   The person's thought processes, including perception, memory, and language—the ways in which the organism processes information.

Field independence–field dependence. Witkin's concept of a cognitive style involving individual differences in an emphasis on bodily as opposed to surrounding contextual cues.

Analytical versus global cognitive style. Witkin's concept of a cognitive style involving differences in the extent to which individuals experience contexts as well defined in their parts as opposed to amorphous wholes.

Self-monitoring.   A cognitive individual difference variable involving the extent to which the person regulates his or her behavior according to situational cues.

Construct. In Kelly's theory, a way of perceiving, construing, or interpreting events.

Role Construct Repertory Test (Rep test). Kelly's test to determine the constructs used by a person, the relationships among constructs, and how the constructs are applied to specific people.

Expectancy-value model. A model that emphasizes the probability of behavior as a function of the expected outcome and the value of the outcome.

Generalized expectancies. Rotter's concept for expectancies that hold across many or most situations.

Interpersonal trust. Rotter's concept of a generalized expectancy for the extent to which one can rely on the word of others.

Internal-external locus of control. Rotter's concept of a generalized expectancy concerning the determinants of rewards and punishments.

Situational specificity, domain specificity. The emphasis on behavior as varying according to the situation or domain, as opposed to the emphasis by trait theorists on consistency in behavior across situations.

Discriminativeness. Mischel's emphasis on the ability of people to discriminate among situations and vary their behavior accordingly.

Self-regulation. The utilization of cognitive processes to regulate one's own behavior.

Encoding strategies. The ways in which people organize incoming information.

Goals. In social cognitive theory, desired future events that motivate the person over extended periods of time and enable the person to go beyond momentary influences.

Life tasks. Cantor's concept for cognitive-motivational units that draw attention to major future goals.

Cognitive and behavioral competencies. Mischel's emphasis on the skills people have in processing information and behaving adaptively in situations.

Social intelligence. Cantor and Kihlstrom's concept for the knowledge individuals bring to bear in solving personal life tasks.

Observational learning. Bandura's concept for the process through which people learn merely by observing the behavior of others, called models.

Modeling. Bandura's concept for the process of reproducing behaviors learned through the observation of others.

Vicarious conditioning. Bandura's concept for the process through which emotional responses are learned by observing them in others.

Self-efficacy. Bandura's concept for the perceived ability to cope with specific situations.

Standard. In social cognitive theory, a reference point for desired behavior or performance.

Schema. A cognitive structure that organizes information and affects how information is encoded, stored, and retrieved.

Causal attribution. The perceived cause of events.

Belief. The conviction that something is or is not true.

Appraisal. Lazarus's concept for the evaluation of what is at stake in a situation and the person's resources to determine whether harm or benefit occurs.

Maladaptive beliefs. Beliefs that interfere with adaptive functioning and are suggested to play an important role in disturbed psychological functioning.

Irrational beliefs. Beliefs that are not logical and not open to proof or disproof. Viewed by cognitive personality psychologists as playing an important role in disturbed psychological functioning.

SUMMARY

1. Cognitive approaches to personality focus on the ways in which people process information concerning the self and the surrounding world—that is, how people take in, store, transform, and produce information. The computer is used as a metaphor for such functioning.

2. Early work on cognition and personality focused on the concept of cognitive style, illustrated by Witkin's work on field independence–field dependence and analytical-global styles of cognitive functioning. Such work was replaced by other concepts that placed less emphasis on the generality of individual differences in cognitive functioning and more emphasis on situational specificity.

3. Kelly's personal construct theory and Rotter's social learning theory illustrate personality theories with a strong cognitive emphasis that preceded the cognitive revolution in psychology. Kelly viewed the person as a scientist and his theory emphasized personal constructs or ways of perceiving, construing, or interpreting events. Rotter emphasized the importance of both reinforcement and cognition in the social functioning of people, as expressed in an expectancy-value model of behavior. He also emphasized the importance of generalized expectancies such as trust and locus of control.

4. Mischel and Bandura illustrate two personality theorists whose work was influenced by the cognitive revolution. Mischel's cognitive social learning theory emphasizes situational specificity, discriminativeness among situations, and self-regulatory aspects of personality functioning. Units of personality emphasized are encoding strategies, goals, expectancies, competencies, and self-regulatory systems. They are seen as relatively situation- or domain-specific. Bandura's social cognitive theory emphasizes the importance of cognition in the acquisition of behavior, in the development of self-efficacy beliefs, and in the development and pursuit of standards or goals. These concepts have been important in extending the theory into the areas of motivation and health.

5. Other units emphasized by cognitive personality psychologists are schema, attributions, and beliefs. Schema represent organizations of information that influence how we perceive, remember, and use information. Individuals differ in the content of their schema as well as in the ways in which they process information. Attributions, involving causal explanations for events, have important implications for the emotional and motivational lives of people. Similarly, beliefs people hold, as in their appraisals of situations and themselves, may be adaptive or maladaptive, rational or irrational, with important implications for psychological well-being.

6. There is no one cognitive theory of personality. However, cognitive personality psychologists share an emphasis on the importance of cognitive processes in personality functioning as well as an emphasis on situational or domain specificity. Relative to trait psychologists, they tend to emphasize processes common to people and experimental research. Although relatively recent in development, cognitive approaches to personality have gained considerable influence in the field.

MOTIVATIONAL UNITS OF PERSONALITY

CHAPTER OVERVIEW

In this chapter we consider motives as basic units of personality. Motives address the question of *why* we behave as we do. The need for such a concept might seem obvious. Yet, at times, motives have been emphasized by personality psychologists and at other times abandoned. In this chapter we consider alternative theories of motivation and whether the trait, cognitive, and motive concepts are competing personality concepts or whether all are necessary for a comprehensive analysis of personality.

Questions to Be Addressed in This Chapter

1 Is the concept of motivation necessary for personality theory?

2 Are people totally motivated by the pursuit of pleasure and the avoidance of pain, a hedonic orientation, or are other motives possible?

3 Which motives or categories of motives appear to be basic to human functioning?

4 What is the relation of the motive concept to the trait and cognitive concepts previously discussed?

In this chapter we consider a third unit of personality, **motives.** Traditionally the concept of *motivation* has been used to address three questions: (1) What *activates* the organism? (2) Why does the organism *select* or choose one response over another, one direction of activity over another? For example, given a choice between food and water, why does a dog choose one or the other? Or, given a choice between becoming a business executive or a college professor, why does a person choose one or the other? (3) Given the same stimulus, why does the organism sometimes *respond* one way and sometimes another? Why does a dog sometimes seem very interested in food and sometimes not at all? Or, why is a person sometimes interested in being with people and at other times interested in being alone?

These are the *activation, selection-direction,* and *preparedness of response* aspects of motivation: what activates the organism, why one or another direction is chosen, and why differential responses are given at various times to the same stimulus. The concept of motivation suggests that there are internal qualities that play an important role in the activation and regulation of behavior. From the standpoint of personality psychology, the concept of motivation suggests that these internal qualities act upon other aspects of the person's functioning. Thus, motives are seen as influencing cognition and action, thinking and behavior. Clearly, for example, altruistic and aggressive motives have different implications for what we think, how we feel, and how we act. Given individual differences in motives, our motives and ways of expressing them play an important role in giving a particular stamp to us as persons. In other words, our motives are an important part of our personality, both in and of themselves as well as in relation to their influence on other parts of the personality.

In its most basic terms, the concept of motivation addresses the question of *why*—why we behave as we do. Put this way, it might seem obvious that we need such a concept. Yet, this is not necessarily the case. Although motivation has generally been an area of keen interest on the part of psychologists, there have been times when its utility as a scientific concept has been questioned (Cofer, 1981; Mook, 1987; Pervin, 1983). During the 1950s and 1960s there was a noticeable decline in interest in the concept. This had to do with both the demise of interest in the concept of *drive* and the cognitive revolution. The decline in interest in motivation, and shift toward a cognitive model, was so great that in the 1970s the editors of the distinguished *Nebraska Symposium on Motivation* series considered dropping the term *motivation* from the title. A concerned motivation theorist was led to ask: "Where, in cognitive theory, are the strong urges and the 'hot' emotions or passions that have been central to our thinking in respect to motivation and emotion for so long?" (Cofer, 1981, p. 52).

The name of the series was not changed, more for practical than conceptual reasons—libraries had standing orders for the series and a change in name threatened these standing orders. Thus, it is interesting that the 1990 edition of the *Nebraska Symposium* indicates that it has returned to its roots and will again confront the concept of motivation directly (Dienstbier, 1990). After a drought of around 20 years, interest in motivation has returned. The issues it addresses could not be dealt with by other approaches. Just as the learning theorist Tolman was criticized for leaving his rats "left in thought" (Guthrie, 1952), without an explanation for what activated, energized, and directed them, so the cognitive models of the early cognitive revolution threatened to leave humans left in thought. Motivation is back, both as a concept of interest in its own right as well as an important influence on how we process information concerning the world.

Most, although not all, theories of personality include a theory of motivation. Some theories postulate one motive, others a few basic motives, and some a hierarchy of motives. Maslow (1954, 1971), for example, suggests a hierarchy of motives ranging from biological needs such as hunger, sleep, and thirst to psychological needs such as self-esteem and self-actualization. Given the diversity of approaches, are there categories or groups of theories that have important elements in common? Let us consider the view of the cognitive personality theorist George Kelly, who, while rejecting the need for a concept of motivation, offered the following system for categorizing the various theoretical models:

> Motivational theories can be divided into two types, push theories and pull theories. Under push theories we find such terms as drive, motive, or even stimulus. Pull theories use such constructs as purpose, value, or need. In terms of a well-known metaphor, these are the pitchfork theories on the one hand and the carrot theories on the other. But our theory is neither of these. Since we prefer to look at the nature of the animal himself, ours is probably best called a jackass theory.
>
> Kelly, 1958, p. 50

To a certain extent, all categorizations of theories of motivation are somewhat arbitrary since there generally is some overlap among the theories and differences within a category. However, Kelly's categories do make some sense even if, as we shall see, his own theory was hardly that of a jackass. So, let us consider push and pull, pitchfork and carrot, theories of motivation, as well as others that have been important in the field.

PITCHFORK-DRIVE THEORIES OF MOTIVATION

Perhaps the best example of pitchfork theories of motivation are those associated with **drive** states and tension reduction. Traditional drive theories suggest that an internal stimulus drives the organism. The drive typically is associated with a biological state, such as hunger or thirst, that creates a state of tension in the organism. In its simplest form, being without food produces a physiological deficit and tension state associated with the hunger drive, whereas being without water produces a physiological deficit and tension state associated with the thirst drive. These states of tension are associated with displeasure or pain, whereas the process of tension reduction is associated with positive reinforcement or pleasure. Thus, drive theories typically are tension-reduction models of motivation. They also can be considered *hedonic* or pleasure-oriented theories of motivation in that they emphasize the organism's efforts to seek pleasure and avoid pain.

FREUD'S DRIVE THEORY

Freud's theory of motivation is an example of a drive, tension-reduction, hedonic theory. According to Freud, the source of all energy lies in states of excitation within the body that seek expression or tension reduction. These states of excitation are called *instincts* or *drives* and represent constant, inescapable forces. The instincts (drives) are characterized by a source, an aim, and an object. As noted, the source of the instincts is in bodily states of excitation or tension. The aim of all instincts is tension reduction, which is associated with pleasure. The object of the instinct is the way in which it is satisfied or the way in which the tension is released and reduced. As we shall see, for psychoanalysts the ways in which instincts are satisfied play a key role in personality development.

Freud's earlier theory included ego instincts, relating to tendencies toward self-preservation, and sexual instincts, relating to tendencies toward preservation of the species. His later theory included the *life instinct*, made up of both the ego and sexual instincts, and the *death instinct*, which is the aim of the organism to die or return to an inorganic state. The energy of the life instinct was called **libido.** No such term has come to be commonly associated with the energy of the death instinct. In fact, the death instinct remains one of the most controversial and least accepted parts of the theory, with most analysts referring instead to *aggressive instincts*. Analysts also have used the terms *instinct* and *drive* interchangeably, some preferring one term and some the other. For the balance of this discussion of Freud's theory of motivation, we will use the term *drive*, although it should be remembered that the term *instinct* could be used as well.

Most students of personality are familiar with Freud's structural model of personality, defined by the concepts of id, ego, and superego. The *id* represents the source of all drive energy. It "seeks" the release of excitation or tension and thereby functions according to the *pleasure principle*. In marked contrast to the id is the *superego*, which represents the moral branch of our functioning, containing the ideals we strive for and the punishments (guilt) we expect when we have gone against our ethical code. Finally, the third structure is the *ego*. The ego responds to reality. Its function is to express and satisfy the desires of the id in accordance with reality and the demands of the superego. In this sense the ego is seen as serving an "executive" function in terms of coordinating the demands of the id for pleasure with the demands of the superego for socialized behavior and the demands of reality.

Psychoanalysis is known as a dynamic theory of personality. The dynamics of personality involve the motivational forces in the individual and the interplay among those forces. Thus, in psychoanalysis the dynamics of personality involve the efforts of the person to satisfy the drives of the id in accordance with the demands of the superego and reality. This is not always possible if there is *conflict* between two or more drives or between drives and moral prohibitions (superego) or reality (ego). Of particular importance are conflicts between the wish to express the drives and the fears of harm from within (e.g., guilt, shame) or from the external world. A person may wish to express sexual desires but may feel guilty or fear criticism and rejection from others. Or, the person may wish to express anger but feel ashamed of feeling angry or fear retribution from others.

"Double Scotches for me and my super-ego, and a glass
of water for my id, which is driving."

Psychoanalytic Theory. Freud's theory of motivation emphasized the drives of the id as regulated by forces from the ego and super-ego.

Such states of conflict are associated with anxiety and sometimes with the development of neuroses. Anxiety represents a signal that danger exists and that harm or injury may result. Such a signal follows earlier experiences in which expression of the drive was associated with punishment and pain. Thus, the person experiences, at some level, the sense of "If I do this I will be hurt and experience pain." To deal with the painful state of anxiety, the person may employ what are known as **mechanisms of defense,** which are ways of attempting to cope with the drives without injury or pain. Thus, the person may use the mechanism of *denial* and say that he or she does not have the wish (e.g., sexual or aggressive desire), or the mechanism of *projection* and project the wish onto others (e.g., it is others who have sexual desires or are hostile), or use the mechanism of *repression* and remove the wish from consciousness.

These mechanisms of defense are employed rapidly and unconsciously so that the person is aware of neither the wish nor the use of the mechanism of defense. Neuroses are formed when there is too much conflict, that is, when there is excessive energy diverted from the gratification of the instincts to protection against anxiety. Because of excessive anxiety and excessive use of mechanisms of defense, neurotics live constricted lives and are limited in their freedom to express their drives and gain pleasure from doing so.

To summarize, Freud's theory of motivation involved instincts or drives that had a source (i.e., states of bodily excitation), an aim (i.e., release of energy or tension reduction), and an object (i.e., the means by which energy is released and tension reduced). When things are going well, the person experiences pleasure from the expression of the drives, often engaging in activities that involve multiple sources of gratification. When things are not going well, the person experiences conflict, anxiety, and distress.

Within such a framework, what gives the individual a distinctive character? That is, where do individual differences enter in? For the most part, within the psycho-analytic theory of motivation, individual differences appear in the intensity of the individual's drives, how the drives are expressed, the extent of conflict and anxiety, and the ways in which the person defends against anxiety. Let us consider each in turn. First, because of reasons of constitution and experience, individuals differ in the strength of their sexual and aggressive drives. Second, individuals differ in the objects or ways of expressing their sexual and aggressive desires. According to Freud, the ways in which sexual and aggressive energy can be transformed and expressed are virtually limitless. People can be sexually aroused by an enormous diversity of visual, auditory, and tactile stimuli; and they can gain pleasure from expressing their aggressive drives in an enormous number of ways, including such diverse activities as watching horror movies, playing competitive sports, and engaging in sarcastic sparring. Further, people can simultaneously gain both sexual and aggressive grati-fication in a variety of ways, including teasing one's lover and feeling stimulated by battle. It should be clear that although these illustrations relate to a fairly conventional understanding of sexual arousal, Freud used the term much more broadly to include activities such as eating, smoking, and many forms of work. In any case, the point here is that with two basic forms of drive, sexual and aggressive, Freud was able to suggest enormous individual differences in the form or means of gratification. What "drives" a person is, in that sense, truly idiosyncratic to the individual.

The third source of individual differences lies in both the extent and ways of coping with conflict and anxiety. At one extreme, for some individuals the various ways in which the drives are to be gratified operate in a harmonious, integrated fashion. At the other extreme, virtually every effort at drive gratification leads to conflict with another drive or with a barrier in the form of anxiety. In the former case, the person can gain sexual and aggressive gratification through various pursuits relatively free of anxiety and the need to utilize mechanisms of defense. In its simplest terms, the person can love and work. In the latter case, the person experiences conflicts between drives and the threat of anxiety associated with many approaches to drive gratification. These represent extreme cases. We all, however, experience some degree of anxiety. Thus, an important aspect of individual differences lies in how we defend against anxiety—our preferences for particular mechanisms of de-fense.

Freud's theory, then, is a pitchfork theory of motivation in its emphasis on drives or states of bodily excitation and tension. The focus is on our efforts to gratify our drives in the form of tension reduction. The theory is hedonic in its emphasis on the role of pleasure and the avoidance of pain. It is a dynamic theory in the attention given to motives and the interplay among the various forces within the individual, in particular those seeking pleasure and those seeking the avoidance of pain (e.g., anxiety). It is a very simple theory in that few drives are posited. However, it is a highly complex theory in terms of the ways in which the drives can be gratified or blocked from expression, as well as in the ways in which drives can be combined. Finally, it suggests that each individual has a *character structure* or a particular structure of drives, ways of gratifying drives, and means of avoiding anxiety. This character structure is what gives the individual his or her stamp of personality. And, it is this character structure that remains relatively stable both across situations as well as over the life span.

A final note concerning Freud's drive theory of motivation concerns the energy model expressed in it. According to the theory, motivation consists of energy derived from the drives. This energy can be discharged, sidetracked, or dammed up. If the drive energy is blocked from one channel of expression, it finds another. If the person works too hard at defending against the drives, energy is used for the purposes of defense and the person ends up exhausted without gaining pleasure. Using knowledge derived from the study of physics, Freud conceptualized human motivation as being like a hydraulic system in which energy flows along multiple paths, released here and blocked there, generally following the path of least resistance. It is a powerful metaphor, one that continues to be used by many analysts to this day, despite changes in our knowledge of physics and our understanding of biological processes in the organism.

Freud's drive theory forms an essential ingredient of classical psychoanalytic theory. In order to be considered a true "Freudian," one must accept the theory of the instincts, only parts of which have been presented here. In the history of psychoanalysis, many individuals began as followers of Freud and his theory of the instincts but then developed their own theories of motivation, often theories that placed less emphasis on biological forces and greater emphasis on social and cultural ones. Beyond this, Freud's theory of motivation had relatively little direct impact on academic research. In contrast to the impact it had on clinical work, with enormous effort devoted to understanding how drives are formed, organized, expressed, and inhibited in patients, personality psychologists in academic settings have conducted relatively little experimental and correlational research on these issues.

STIMULUS-RESPONSE THEORY

Following the work of Watson, many behaviorists rejected mental concepts such as motivation, including the concept of drive. For example, the learning theorist B.F. Skinner rejected all such concepts and focused exclusively on reinforcing conditions in the environment. However, other behaviorists suggested that the drive concept could be useful as long as it was tied to specific external circumstances associated with objective measurement. These external circumstances could then be associated with internal drive states. For example, the hours an organism would go without food could be tied to the strength of the hunger drive. Many stimulus-response (S-R) theorists, such as the learning theorist Clark Hull, made use of such a model.

Clark Hull probably was the preeminent learning theorist of his time. Although hard to appreciate today, during the 1940s and early 1950s his S-R theory was the major force in many areas of psychology. Not only animal learning but many social psychological and personality phenomena were interpreted within the S-R framework. According to Hull (1943), organisms are activated by drives. A distinction was drawn between innate primary drives and learned secondary drives. The **primary drives,** such as pain and hunger, generally are associated with physiological conditions within the organism. **Secondary drives** represent drives that have been acquired on the basis of their association with the satisfaction of the primary drives. For example, the acquisition of money can become a secondary drive associated with the satisfaction of a primary drive. Another example of a secondary drive would be anxiety or fear, based on its association with the primary drive of pain. Anxiety is an important secondary drive because it can be learned quickly and strongly, thus becoming a powerful motivational force.

According to Hull's model of *instrumental learning*, responses are associated with stimuli as a result of reinforcement through the reduction of drive stimuli (e.g., reward, escape from pain, avoidance of pain). The pairing of a response with a stimulus is called a **habit;** personality is composed of the habits, or S-R bonds, that are learned through drive reduction.

A better feeling for Hull's model can be gained from consideration of a typical instrumental learning experiment conducted with rats to maximize experimental control over the variables. In such an experiment, the intensity of a drive and the amount of reinforcement would be manipulated to see the effects on learning. For example, an experimenter might seek to study maze learning in a rat. The experimenter could manipulate the number of hours of food deprivation (hunger drive) in a rat, as well as the amount of food reward for making a correct response in the maze, and determine the effects on maze learning. The instrumental responses (correct turns in the maze) are reinforced through reduction of the hunger drive stimuli.

Another illustration would be that of instrumental escape learning. In this type of experiment (N. E. Miller, 1951), a rat is put into a box with two compartments: a white compartment with a grid as a floor and a black compartment with a solid floor. The compartments are separated by a door. At the beginning of the experiment, the rats are given electric shocks while in the white compartment and are allowed to escape into the black compartment. Thus, a fear response is learned in association with the white compartment. A test is then made as to whether the fear of the white compartment can lead to the learning of a new response; that is, can the secondary drive of fear act as the basis for learning? Now, in order for the rat to escape to the black compartment, it must turn a wheel placed in the white compartment. The turning of the wheel opens the door to the black compartment and allows the rat to escape. After a number of trials, the rat begins to rotate the wheel with considerable speed, demonstrating the learning of a response in association with reduction of the secondary fear drive. Just as food operated as a reinforcer in the first illustration, reduction of the fear drive operated as a reinforcer in this experiment.

At this point the reader may be impressed with the experiments but left wondering about how such work with rats relates to human personality. The contrast to Freud, of course, is dramatic. Both Hull and Freud used the concept of drive and emphasized the importance of drive reduction in learning. Both tied the drive concept to physiological functioning. However, Freud's concept was a metaphor tied to many clinical observations, whereas Hull's concept was based on objective measurements and experimental research. Thus, despite the similarity of concepts, the gap between the two would appear to be enormous. Yet, it was just this gap that John Dollard and Neal Miller (1950) tried to bridge. Both followers of Hull and trained as psychoanalysts, Dollard and Miller were among the first to relate principles of instrumental learning theory to personality phenomena, in particular phenomena described by psychoanalysts.

To illustrate the approach of Dollard and Miller, let us consider the concept of *conflict*, so central to the thinking of both Hull and Freud. N. E. Miller (1944), working with rats, explored what would happen if the same response was associated with both pleasure and pain. Suppose a hungry rat runs a maze and is rewarded with food at the end of the maze. The maze-running responses are learned on the basis of positive reinforcement. One can also see that the closer the rat gets to the end of the maze the stronger its response (the rat runs more quickly). Thus, one can draw a line representing an approach gradient that reflects the greater strength of response as the rat approaches the reward (Figure 4.1).

Now, however, suppose the rat sometimes is shocked at the end of the maze. Here the maze-running responses are associated with punishment and, instead of an approach response, an avoidance response is learned. Once more one can see that the closer the rat gets to the end of the maze, the stronger the response, in this case the fear response. Thus, one can draw a line representing the avoidance gradient that reflects the greater strength of this response as the rat approaches the shock (see Figure 4.1). A rat put into such a maze now faces a conflict situation—the same end point is associated with positive reinforcement and with punishment, with pleasure and with pain. Running toward the end point is associated with reduction of the hunger drive but avoidance is associated with reduction of the fear drive. What is the rat to do? Since the approach and avoidance gradients have different slopes, they

Figure 4.1   Graphic representation of an approach-avoidance conflict.
The tendency to approach is stronger far from the goal, while the tendency to avoid is stronger near to the goal. Conflict is greatest where the lines intersect.

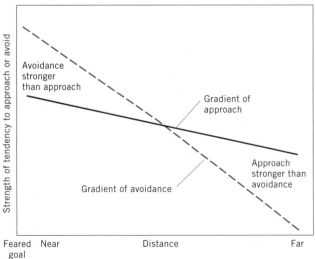

(From *Personality and Psychotherapy* [p. 356], by J. Dollard and N. E. Miller, 1950, New York: McGraw-Hill. Reprinted by permission of HarperCollins Publishers, Inc.)

intersect at a particular point and it was here that N. E. Miller (1944) predicted that the rat would stop, with the opposing approach and avoidance forces being equal. Indeed, this was exactly what was found. Rats would run toward the end point but then stop as the fear response became stronger (see Figure 4.1). Further, by strengthening the hunger drive or weakening the fear drive through reduced punishment, the animals could be made to move further along toward the end point of the maze.

Dollard and Miller used this experiment as a model of how people can acquire conflicts, namely through the acquisition of both approach and avoidance responses in relation to the same object. It has always struck me as a powerful model for the conflicts people face and descriptive of how people function in relation to these approach-avoidance conflicts. I recall a patient who had conflicted sexual feelings toward women. In part he associated pleasure and gratification of his sexual urges with contact with women. On the other hand, he had a problem having erections and experienced shame in this regard. Thus, he associated both pleasure and shame with sexual contact with women. It should be noted that his shame response was partly based on the response of one woman with whom he attempted to have intercourse, and whether other women would respond similarly was not clear to him. In any case, what he would typically do is meet a woman, date her a few times, and lose interest as the relationship deepened and a sexual relationship might develop. He reached what he called his "comfort zone," where he enjoyed the contact but did not have to experience the anticipated shame of an erectile dysfunction.

Through the concepts of drive, drive conflict, anxiety, and reinforcement, Dollard and Miller translated many psychoanalytic concepts into Hullian instrumental learning principles. What appeared to be vague, metaphorical concepts could perhaps be put into systematic terms and hypotheses tested in experimental ways. Although a brilliant contribution, this effort never went very far, mostly because psychologists were losing interest in the drive concept, clinical psychologists were becoming more interested in Skinnerian principles, and the cognitive revolution was approaching.

MURRAY'S NEED-PRESS MODEL

We already have come across the work of Henry Murray (1938, 1951) in relation to his important book on personality and the development of the Thematic Apperception Test (TAT). Here we consider Murray's theory of motivation, which formed an essential part of his personality theory. In fact, it has been suggested that Murray was primarily a motivational psychologist (Hall & Lindzey, 1957, p. 171).

In his discussion of the variables of personality, Murray gave major attention to the concept of **need,** which he used in the same sense that others used the term *drive.* Murray assumed that a need was derived from a force in the brain that organized perception and action and could be aroused by internal or external stimuli. Murray distinguished between *primary* and *secondary needs*, similar to the previously mentioned distinction between primary and secondary drives. He also distinguished between *overt needs* that are permitted direct expression and *covert needs* that are inhibited or blocked from expression. Further, he tied needs to states of tension within the organism and need satisfaction to the reduction of tension. However, Murray suggested that the focus on the end state of tension reduction gave an incomplete picture of the motivational processes of humans. According to him, it is not a tensionless state that is desired, but rather the *process* of reducing tension that is satisfying. Thus, the individual may increase tension as a way of gaining the pleasure that accompanies tension reduction.

Murray, with his background in biology and chemistry, was interested in the classification of needs. Aware that others believed that such classification was unnecessary or impossible, Murray suggested that describing, defining, and classifying are necessary steps in the development of a science. Thus, following the intensive study of a small number of subjects, he derived a list of 20 manifest needs and 8 latent needs. Each need had associated with it a desire or intended effect, feelings, actions, and trait names. For example, the need for dominance is associated with the desire to control, influence, or direct the behavior of others; with the feeling of confidence; with actions that influence, lead, persuade, and prevail upon; and with trait names such as forceful, assertive, and decisive. Other suggested manifest needs were achievement, affiliation, aggression, nurturance, play, and sex.

An important contribution by Murray was his focus on the environment as well as the individual. Murray suggested that characteristics of the environment could be associated with the satisfaction or frustration of a need. These environmental characteristics were called **press,** defined as aspects of the environment that affected the well-being of the person. The press of the environment formed the external counterpart to the internal need. Individuals with particular needs, then, would find environments with particular press more or less gratifying. Since individuals differ in their needs, they also will differ in the environments they find most satisfying. People and environments can then be considered in terms of the degree of need-press congruence, that is, the degree of fit between the needs of the individual and the characteristics of the environment. An environment with lots of social interaction would be congruent with the needs of an extravert but incongruent with the needs of an introvert.

As noted, Murray believed that an important aspect of personality is the organization of the individual's needs. Together with Christiana Morgan, he developed a system for scoring needs in relation to TAT stories given by subjects. The TAT was used as a fantasy measure of needs because Murray believed that people often are not able to report their own needs. Although clinicians have focused on the pattern or organization of needs within the individual, personality researchers have tended to focus on the action of one or a few specific needs.

We already have noted briefly the work of McClelland in this regard (McClelland, 1961; McClelland, Atkinson, Clark, & Lowell, 1953). What McClelland and his colleagues did was to develop a fantasy measure of the need for achievement (*n* Ach), using cards with pictures on them specifically designed to relate to this need and scoring categories based on differences between stories told under achievement-arousing conditions and neutral conditions. Achievement motivation (*n* Ach) was defined as a need to do things better or to surpass standards of excellence. For example, a story describing a person striving to achieve a difficult goal or competing with others for success would be scored high on *n* Ach relative to a story describing a person thinking about getting together with family for a fun weekend. It was viewed as functioning like a biological drive in the sense of energizing, directing, and se-

Illustrative Card Used to Measure the Need for Achievement (n Ach). Subjects are asked to write a story indicating what is going on, what led up to it, and what will happen in the future. Stories are scored according to a formal scoring system.

lecting behavior. Individual differences in achievement motivation are viewed as enduring dispositions that are activated under specific conditions. Individuals high on *n* Ach have been found to differ from those low on *n* Ach in a variety of ways. Those high on *n* Ach prefer moderately difficult tasks (as opposed to very easy or very difficult tasks), prefer tasks on which they are responsible for the outcome, and prefer entrepreneurial activities that provide challenge and responsibility for outcome (Koestner & McClelland, 1990). Scores on *n* Ach have not been predictive of academic success because such performance often depends on different motivational forces.

In addition to work on the achievement motive, work has been done on the power motive and the intimacy motive (McAdams, 1988; Winter, 1973, 1988). Once more, individual differences in motive strength are assessed by scoring TAT stories for themes relevant to the particular motive. Individuals high on power motivation have been found to seek leadership roles and offices, to be assertive and controlling in interactions with others, including friends, and to have problems in love relationships (Winter, 1988). Relative to low scorers, individuals high on intimacy motivation have been found to spend more time involved with and thinking about people and relationships, to issue fewer commands to peers, to position themselves in closer physical proximity to others in a group, and to make more references to "we" and "us" in group meetings (McAdams, 1988). These two motives are of particular interest since

Illustrative Card Used to Measure the Need for Intimacy. Subjects are asked to write a story indicating what is going on, what led up to it, and what will happen in the future. Stories are scored according to a formal scoring system.

they parallel the two trait dimensions noted in Chapter 2 in relation to interpersonal behavior.

Before ending our review of Murray's motivational model, two points are worthy of consideration. The first involves a comparison of self-report measures of motivation with fantasy measures. Recall that Murray was mistrustful of subjective reports: "Children perceive inaccurately, are very little conscious of the inner states and retain fallacious recollections of occurrences. Many adults are hardly better" (1938, p. 15). McClelland has gone on to suggest that self-report measures of motivation represent different measures than do fantasy measures of motivation (Koestner & McClelland, 1990; McClelland, Koestner, & Weinberger, 1989). Self-report measures and fantasy measures of the same motive seldom correlate significantly and instead correlate with different behaviors. The suggestion is made that fantasy measures of motivation are more expressive of the motivational concept whereas self-report measures are more reflective of values and social norms. Thus, fantasy measures are more accurate in predicting behavior in unconstrained situations, whereas self-report measures are more accurate in predicting attitudes. Also, fantasy measures are more accurate than self-report measures in predicting action over an extended period of time. It is suggested that this is because motives assessed in this way reflect a more basic level of motivational functioning.

The second point relates to Murray's position regarding the relation of the motive

SPOTLIGHT ON THE RESEARCHER

DAN P. McADAMS:
The Study of Narratives

Perhaps because I have always been moved most by the power of a good story, the central focus of my work in personality psychology is *narrative*. As a graduate student working with David McClelland in the late 1970s, I developed a narrative measure of individual differences in "intimacy motivation," the recurrent desire for warm, close, and communicative interactions with others. By coding for certain themes in narrative fantasies told in response to pictures (the Thematic Apperception Test), a researcher may obtain an estimate of the strength of intimacy motivation in a given individual's life. Throughout the 1980s, my students and I conducted a number of studies showing that people who score high in intimacy motivation are indeed different in theoretically predictable and important ways from people who score lower on the motive. For example, high-intimacy persons tend to be seen by others as especially loving and natural; to spend more of their normal day thinking about relationships with others; to engage in more smiling and eye contact in the presence of others; to report higher levels of subjective well-being; and to reconstruct their own lives as narratives exemplifying the value of warm, close, and communicative interactions with others. Women tend to score higher than men in intimacy motivation, going back at least as far as sex differences observed among fourth-grade girls and boys.

My early work on intimacy motivation, therefore, illustrated the usefulness of employing a narrative methodology (content analysis of TAT stories) for studying individual differences in personality. The narrative methodology, furthermore, connected me to the tradition of "personology" and the "study of lives," as represented in the writings of Henry A. Murray and Robert White. Urging personologists to embark on biographical studies, Murray once wrote that "the history of the organism is the organism." Following Murray's promptings, I proceeded to invent and validate coding systems for analyzing autobiographical narratives of earliest memories, peak experiences, and life turning points. The data from these studies suggest that, as Murray and White maintained, narrative reconstructions of human lives show considerable, though by no means perfect, thematic coherence. When people tell stories about their lives, they tend to organize those narrative accounts along the great thematic lines of "agency" (power/achievement/autonomy) and "communion" (love/intimacy/union).

Therefore, narrative accounts can provide clues to personality dispositions, such as motives. But narratives can also be construed as units of personality themselves—as psychological phenomena that merit careful consideration on their own terms. In the last 10 years, I have become increasingly fascinated with the ways in which people naturally construct life stories, or personal myths, to provide their lives with what Erik Erikson called an *identity*. Today, I primarily study people's internalized and evolving life stories—the inner narratives of self they create to selectively reconstruct the past, understand the present, and anticipate the future so that their lives may be endowed with a sense of unity and purpose. I study life stories *not* because life stories tell me about motives and traits but instead because these narratives *are* our identities. Beginning in late adolescence and young adulthood, we live, we tell about it (to ourselves and others) in story, and then we live according to the stories we tell. Life and story evolve together, dialectically, each informing the other. My own life-story theory of identity is part of a growing intellectual movement today in the human sciences focusing on the narrative patternings of human lives, represented in the writings of such scholars as Jerome Bruner, Silvan Tomkins, and Hubert Hermans.

People create different kinds of stories to make sense of their lives. No two stories are exactly the same. But there are certain standard characters, themes, settings, and plots that people appropriate into their own life stories, to make their lives sensible. I have been working for the past few years to develop a taxonomy of story forms—a classification system of the different kinds of stories people create as their identities. I have also been struggling to understand the extent to which some stories may be deemed to be psychologically, socially, or even morally "better" than other stories. In this regard, I have focused attention most recently on the life stories constructed by mature men and women who have distinguished themselves for their valuable contributions to helping others, especially those others of the younger generation. These especially *generative* adults tend to fashion life stories in which they were "chosen" or "called" to help others at an early age, leading them to become committed to a clear ideology or belief system that has enabled them to "redeem" or make better the many bad experiences they encounter in life. It is a story of believing that I was blessed at an early age, singled out to do something special, so that I can pursue life's goals and confront life's challenges with a clear sense of mission or destiny. Generative adults have chosen to narrate their lives in this way. Their stories do not necessarily tell what "really happened" in their past but what instead they have *chosen* to make as their identity today.

More than traits, motives, schema, or any other dispositional construct in personality psychology, it is the *stories* people create about their lives that are the key to understanding personality coherence. The main challenge for my work in the future is to document in a scientifically legitimate manner the similarities and the differences among the many kinds of stories people construct to provide their lives with unity and purpose. As something of a biographer of everyday men and women, I see my own work as potentially enhancing people's lives and contributing to society's well-being to the extent that I am able to understand how people may create the noblest, the most heroic, and the most exemplary stories to live by.

concept to the trait concept. Murray clearly distinguished between the two and favored the motive concept. He described a trait as relating to consistencies in behavior whereas a need referred to an internal process that might or might not be reflected in behavior:

> According to my prejudice, trait psychology is over-concerned with recurrences, with consistency, with what is clearly manifested (the surface of personality), with what is conscious, ordered, and rational. It minimizes the importance of physiological occurrences, irrational impulses and beliefs, infantile experiences, unconscious and inhibited drives . . . . It stops short precisely at the point where a psychology is needed, the point at which it begins to be difficult to understand what is going on.

1938, p. 715

In sum, Murray's theory of motivation had many features in common with other drive, tension-reduction models. However, he was more interested than Freud or Dollard and Miller in the classification of drives and in the assessment of individual differences. Although the cognitive revolution brought a decline in interest in drive models and in unconscious motivation, through the work of McClelland and others some interest remained in the study of a few motives and the use of fantasy measures. In addition, a self-report measure based on Murray's list of needs, the Personality Research Form (PRF), is used in many research efforts (Jackson, 1974). In contrast to Murray's motive-trait distinction, an effort has been made to relate scores on this instrument to measures of the Big Five traits and, more generally, to include motive concepts within trait theory (Borkenau & Ostendorf, 1989; Costa & McCrae, 1988; Ostendorf & Angleitner, 1990).

FESTINGER'S THEORY OF COGNITIVE DISSONANCE

We now consider briefly a cognitive theory with a tension-reduction basis. In 1957 Leon Festinger published a book called *A Theory of Cognitive Dissonance* that greatly influenced thinking in the field of social psychology for the next two decades. According to Festinger, cognitive dissonance refers to a state of tension that is created when two or more cognitions are inconsistent or in conflict with one another (e.g., "I smoke." "I want to be healthy." "Smoking is bad for your health"). When such a state of tension exists, people are motivated to reduce the state of tension created by the dissonance. As noted recently by a follower of Festinger's, by the 1970s the theory of **cognitive dissonance** was recognized as perhaps the most important development in social psychology to that time (Aronson, 1992). It is presented here, in a personality text, because it also influenced personality researchers and illustrates how cognitive processes can be considered within a tension-reduction framework.

As noted earlier, the S-R reinforcement framework was the dominant view within the field during the 1940s and 1950s. Then along came Festinger's theory of cognitive dissonance. Let us follow the history as described by Elliot Aronson, Festinger's student and himself an important contributor to the research literature:

> Because the field was so thoroughly dominated by this simplistic brand of reward/reinforcement theory, whenever an individual performed a behavior it had to be because there was a concrete reward lurking somewhere in the background—so the name of the game, in those days, was let's find the reinforcer . . . .
>
> Then along came Leon Festinger, and social psychology has not been the same since . . . . Leon started with a very simple proposition: *If a person held two cognitions that were psychologically inconsistent, he or she would experience dissonance and would attempt to reduce dissonance much as one would attempt to reduce hunger, thirst, or any drive.* What Leon realized, in 1956, was the importance of forging a marriage between the cognitive and the motivational.

Aronson, 1992, pp. 303–304

To illustrate cognitive dissonance theory, and how radically it departed from traditional reinforcement theory, let us consider an early piece of research. Suppose you are rewarded for making statements contrary to your political beliefs, will that result in a change in these beliefs? Reinforcement theory would suggest so, and the bigger the reward for the response (statement of the belief), the bigger the change in belief. Presumably through reinforcement you would associate positive value with the stated belief. However, research demonstrated that people are more likely to change their beliefs to conform to their public statements if they are underrewarded than if they are given large rewards (Festinger, 1965). Additional research demonstrated that people who go through a severe initiation to join a group come to like the group better than those who go through a mild initiation. Whereas reinforcement theory would suggest that we dislike things associated with pain, dissonance theory showed that we can come to like those things for which we suffer.

How are such results to be understood? What Festinger suggested was that public statements that were contrary to private beliefs represented dissonant cognitions and produced a state of tension within the person. Receiving a large reward for the public statements allows the person to reduce the dissonance by saying: "Well, I'm just doing this for the money. I don't really believe it." The greater the sum of money, the easier to reduce the dissonance in this way. On the other hand, a very small reward leaves the person uncomfortable about the private-public discrepancy and creates pressure to adjust the private view to conform to the public view. Similarly, withstanding the ordeal of a grueling initiation period is dissonant with the picture most of us have of ourselves, unless we see ourselves as basically masochistic. Why then go through the procedure? It must be because the group is so wonderful that it makes this all worthwhile. The more grueling the initiation, the more wonderful we must believe the group to be, something the U.S. Marine Corps has known for years.

Let us consider one more illustrative piece of research. How do cigarette smokers reconcile the cognition that smoking causes cancer with the cognition that they wish to live? Of course, one dissonance-reducing mechanism would be to reject the information, and many smokers do this. However, research demonstrated that people can be much more subtle in their dissonance-reducing efforts. Groups of smokers and nonsmokers were asked a variety of questions, including the following: How serious is the threat of cancer due to smoking? How much smoking is truly dangerous? When will a cure for cancer be found? How many years does one have to smoke for it to be truly dangerous? The results are illustrated in Table 4.1. Not surprisingly, smokers rated the smoking-cancer risk lower than nonsmokers. In addition, smokers suggested a higher number of cigarettes as truly dangerous, with the more they smoked the greater the number they gave as truly dangerous. Finally, smokers thought a cure for cancer would come sooner than did nonsmokers and thought one had to smoke a greater number of years for it to be dangerous. What was particularly impressive here was that if one considers how many years smokers had been smoking, how many years of smoking were necessary before it was truly dangerous, and when a cure for cancer would be found, smokers thought that a cure would be found before it was truly dangerous for them! As indicated, nonsmokers thought that fewer years of smoking were dangerous and a cancer cure was further away, with the cure coming

TABLE 4.1   Smoker and Nonsmoker Estimates of the Danger from Smoking

Relative to nonsmokers, smokers estimate a greater number of cigarettes and a greater number of years of smoking for cigarette smoking to be dangerous, as well as an earlier discovery of a cure for cancer. Smokers appear to reduce cognitive dissonance by underestimating the dangers associated with smoking cigarettes and by assuming a cure for cancer will come before they are at risk.

Item	SMOKERS		NONSMOKERS	
	Mean	Median	Mean	Median
1. Estimate of number of cigarettes smoked per day that is truly dangerous.	26.5	30	20.1	20
2. Estimate of minimum number of years an individual predisposed toward cancer must smoke to get cancer at some time.	24.5	15	22.8	10
3. Estimate of number of years within which a cure for all cancer should come.	22.6	20	33.1	20

Source: "Cigarette Smoking and Alternative Methods of Reducing Dissonance," by L. A. Pervin and R. J. Yatkor, 1965, *Journal of Personality and Social Psychology, 2,* p. 33. Copyright 1965 by the American Psychological Association. Reprinted by permission.

after the dangerous number of years. Thus, cigarette smokers reduced dissonance by minimizing the threat, not only by rejecting the smoking-cancer link but by believing that they were not vulnerable or that a cure would be available (Pervin & Yatko, 1965).

Although influential mainly within social psychology, cognitive dissonance theory was seen as having important implications for personality theory as well (Elliot & Devine, 1994). If people were motivated to reduce the tension created by dissonant beliefs, then what about beliefs about the self? Would a person with a positive self-image be motivated to reject information dissonant with that self-image? Would a person with a negative self-image be more prone to accept negative feedback than positive feedback, and perhaps even be motivated to behave in ways that would confirm the negative self-image? Indeed, research suggests that this can be the case. For example, people with low opinions of themselves have been found to behave in ways that will confirm their negative self-image (Aronson & Mettee, 1968). Could we have here a cognitive explanation for what Freudians would see as masochistic behavior?

What happened to cognitive dissonance theory? Once more the reasons for the decline in interest in a theory are complex. But part of the explanation may have to do with its focus on tension reduction. Remember, in the quote presented earlier it was suggested that the person experiencing cognitive dissonance "would attempt to reduce dissonance much as one would attempt to reduce hunger, thirst, or any drive." In other words, dissonance theory was a drive, tension-reduction model of motivation. As Aronson tells the story, by the mid-1970s the allure of the theory began to wane as interest in the entire topic of motivation faded and the journals were all but overwhelmed by the incredible popularity of purely cognitive approaches . . . . Those of us who have survived the more recent era dominated by pure cognition in social psychology are well aware of the fact that, for a great many years, it has become fashionable to pretend that motivation does not exist, but, of course, that was merely a convenient fiction.

1992, pp. 303–304

We will have a chance to consider more purely cognitive approaches shortly, but first let us consider the "carrot," pull theories noted by Kelly.

CARROT-INCENTIVE THEORIES OF MOTIVATION

Now, persistent, goal-directed behavior is a fact of observation and not an inference . . . . It is something to be explained. We must ask: How does the goal situation arise? What regulates and directs persistent goal-oriented activities? These are straightforward questions and they deserve straightforward answers.

P.T. Young, 1961, p. 58

The theories of motivation considered earlier emphasized the disquieting state of affairs caused by internal tension and the efforts of the organism to discharge tension, express an instinct, or reduce the level of a drive. In contrast, the theoretical view to be considered here emphasizes the motivational pull of incentives, that is, the motivational pull of end points anticipated by the organism. It is not so much that the organism is being pushed as it is that it is being pulled toward something. An end point associated with pleasure has the quality of a "carrot" or incentive that pulls the organism toward it. An end point associated with pain pulls the organism in another direction, away from the pain. Although different in this sense from drive, tension-reduction models, it should be clear that incentive theories of motivation still emphasize the importance of striving for pleasure and avoiding pain. In this sense they too are hedonic theories of motivation.

HISTORICAL NOTE

Incentive theories of motivation go back some time in the field of psychology. McDougall (1930) was so struck with the directed, goal-seeking quality of behavior that he announced himself to be a purposive psychologist. He rejected a mechanistic, reflex, stimulus-determined view of behavior in favor of an emphasis on active strivings toward anticipated goals: "We foresee a particular event as a possibility; we desire to see this possibility realized, we take action in accordance with our desire, and we seem to guide the course of events in such a way that the foreseen and desired event results" (1930, p. 5). It was the persistent, variable, but goal-directed quality of behavior that led McDougall to characterize it as **purposive.**

About the same time, Tolman (1932) was emphasizing purpose and cognition in animal learning. He too was impressed with the goal-seeking, purposive character of behavior—including rat behavior. He emphasized the general, integrated nature of the organism's action rather than the accumulation of specific S-R habits and thereby was in sharp disagreement with the Hullian view. Like McDougall, Tolman was struck with the patterned, organized, purposive quality of behavior. Organisms strive to achieve goals, which are made up of a hierarchy of superordinate and subordinate goals. These goals are associated with reward or value and also with a probability of achievement. Behavior is determined by the expectancy of attaining a goal and the value of the goal—the expectancy-value model noted in Chapter 3.

Other theorists also emphasized the purposive, goal-directed quality of behavior. Yet, these views fell into decline for three reasons. First, they seemed very mentalistic (i.e., emphasizing what was going on in the mind rather than observable behavior) and teleological. **Teleology** refers to the direction of functioning toward some end point. For example, we may seek to have a specific career or a particular family life or to live a moral life. For some psychologists, this was taken to mean that future events determine present events. Such a view, of course, was rejected by psychologists. Behavior can be governed only by the present, which can include, however, one's images of the future. Despite this argument, purposive views were rejected. Second, the S-R view was so powerful as to dominate the field and relegate other positions, such as the purposive view, to a minor status. Third, as noted, with the demise of drive theory and the beginning of the cognitive revolution, there was a general decline in interest in motivation. Purposive theories of motivation experienced the same fate as other theories of motivation even though they included a strong cognitive element—the anticipation or mental representation of the future.

Interestingly enough, developments in the area of cognition eventually led the field back to a strong interest in goal-directed behavior. During the 1940s, there were major advances in cybernetics—the study of how complex machines can be directed in their functioning toward some target or end point (Wiener, 1948). Consider, for example, a home thermostat that turns the heat or air-conditioning on and off to maintain a steady temperature or end point. Or, consider an anti-aircraft gun automatically guided by radar toward a moving plane. Today, these machines have become so complex that at times their functioning is indistinguishable from that guided by humans, so that as passengers on a plane we are not aware that the plane is being landed mechanically.

In addition, and related to cybernetics, was the development of computers in the 1950s. Computer models of human functioning were suggesting that people use broad principles to guide behavior toward goals (Newell, Shaw, & Simon, 1958). Then, in 1960, a very influential book, entitled *Plans and the Structure of Behavior,* suggested a model of functioning whereby people kept a standard or end point in mind and then kept adjusting their behavior to meet that standard (Miller, Galanter, & Pribram, 1960). What the authors suggested was that we consider how an ordinary day is put together. The structure of an ordinary day includes plans for what needs to be done and what is expected to happen; that is, the day has an organized, patterned, goal-directed quality. They suggested that the person's goals are represented by images of end points or targets that direct the person's behavior, just as is true of a thermostat or radar-directed anti-aircraft gun. Plans are developed to achieve the goal and actions are tested against the mental representation of the end point to see whether we are remaining on course and getting closer to the goal. For example, someone might organize their day around an important business meeting, taking care to make sure that the staff is ready, the necessary documents have been put together, and the presentation rehearsed. Or, someone might organize their day around an important athletic event, taking care to eat specific foods, have adequate rest, take adequate time to warm up, and make plans for a party following the anticipated success.

What was striking about this development was that it became legitimate to think in terms of purposive, future-oriented, goal-directed behavior. Behavior was not being directed by the future but by some mental representation of the future. If machines could function in terms of some standard or end point, why not humans? However, what was left out of this model was how goals get established and how we select among goals or desired outcomes. Although providing for purposive behavior, the model remained cognitive in nature and lacked the power of a motivational force. To a certain extent, the person was left in thought just as Guthrie (1935, 1952) suggested was true of Tolman's rats. However, in this case it was not necessary to turn to an S-R, drive-reduction model.

CURRENT WORK IN GOAL THEORY

Over time, developments in the cognitive revolution moved from a focus on "cold cognition," or purely cognitive processes, to a focus on "hot cognition," or the relation of emotion and motivation to cognition. Associated with this has been an interest in goal theories of motivation. Today, the concept of **goal,** in one or another form, has become a major part of motivation and personality theory (Carver & Scheier, 1982; Emmons, in press; Pervin, 1989). It is expressed in various concepts such as *life tasks* (Cantor, 1990a), *personal strivings* (Emmons, 1989b), *personal projects* (Little, 1989), *current concerns* (Klinger, 1977), *possible selves* (Markus & Ruvolo, 1989), *standards* (Bandura, 1989b; Higgins, 1990), and *goals* (Ford, 1992; Locke & Latham, 1990; Pervin, 1983, 1989). What is common to these concepts is an emphasis on purposive, goal-directed behavior, that is, the view that the person's behavior is organized around the pursuit of desired end points or goals.

How does goal theory relate to personality? First, goal theory returns the concept of motivation to center stage as an area of concern for personality psychologists. It suggests that in order to understand human behavior, in particular its patterned, organized, and directed quality, we must consider its motivation. The concept of a goal and the view of humans as organized goal systems are suggested as useful motivational perspectives. Second, there are individual differences in the kinds of goals that people pursue. Third, there are individual differences in the ways that people pursue their goals, that is, in the strategies and plans they use in goal-system functioning. Fourth, goals are seen as playing an important role in other aspects of personality functioning. Let us consider some of the relevant research.

What kinds of goals do people have? At least five goal categories appear in a variety of goal studies (Emmons & Diener, 1986; Ford, 1992; Novacek & Lazarus, 1989; Pervin, 1983):

1. *Relaxation/Fun* (desire for enjoyment: "Many of my daily activities involve doing things just to have fun or relax.")
2. *Aggression/Power* (self-assertiveness and dominance: "I generally try to take a leadership role in situations that are important to me.")
3. *Self-Esteem* (development and protection of self: "Many of my activities are directed toward maintaining or improving my self-esteem.")
4. *Affection/Support* (desire for relatedness, affiliation: "I seek friendships and intimate relationships.")
5. *Anxiety/Threat Reduction* (avoidance of stress: "A lot of my time is spent avoiding situations that are fearful or threatening to me.")

Note that both positive, approach goals and avoidance goals are included; that is, a goal can be something we seek to obtain as well as something we seek to avoid. Note also that although some of these goals are related to some of Murray's needs as well as to some interpersonal traits, they are not identical to them. In addition, in contrast to drive or need theories, the emphasis is on the motivated, purposive, goal-directed nature of action rather than on tension reduction. In contrast to trait theories, the emphasis is on a motivational explanation for behavior rather than on a description of behaviors that appear to go together.

Beyond these categories, individuals have highly idiosyncratic goals and goal structures. It is possible for almost anything to become a goal, something to be attained or avoided. What is a goal of major priority for one person may be of minor priority for another; and where two or more goals are integrated for one person, they may be in conflict for another. At the same time, a number of principles appear to be well established in research:

1. People are more likely to engage in behavior associated with goals high in value and probability of attainment than in behavior associated with goals low in value and probability of attainment (Locke & Latham, 1990; Pervin, 1983).
2. Progress toward standards (goals) is associated with positive affect and movement away from them is associated with negative affect (Bandura, 1986; Higgins, 1987; Locke & Latham, 1990; Pervin, 1983).
3. Goal-system functioning is related to subjective well-being and health; that is, individuals with specific, obtainable goals that are integrated experience better health and subjective well-being than individuals without goals or individuals whose goals are vague or experienced as unattainable or in conflict with one another (Emmons, 1986; Emmons & King, 1988; Palys & Little, 1983).
4. Individuals discriminate among areas (domains) in their lives and select goals for specific domains (e.g., achievement goals in school or work and affiliative goals in social situations) as well as specific strategies in association with different goals and situations (Cantor, 1990a; Cantor & Langston, 1989). In other words, as suggested by social cognitive theorists, goal-system functioning is

characterized by discriminativeness and flexibility. At the same time, people are able to retain overall goal structures. In this sense, goal-system functioning relates to both stable and varying aspects of individual behavior (Pervin, 1983).

These results are illustrative of the kinds of research being conducted by personality psychologists interested in using a goal model of motivation. Again, what joins them together is an emphasis on the importance of motivation in understanding personality and an emphasis on behavior as organized in the direction of end points or goals. At the same time, this is a very diverse group. Some clearly come from a social cognitive perspective while others do not. Some seek to establish links with trait theorists while others suggest that traits and motives are fundamentally different concepts. Some emphasize that goals are conscious while others suggest that some goals, including some important ones, may be unconscious or unavailable to awareness. Some emphasize the cognitive component of goals while others emphasize the affective, emotional component. And, some suggest that pleasure is associated with progress toward a goal while others emphasize the pleasure associated with the goal itself.

In sum, current work in the area of goals is robust. There are areas of common conceptualization but also areas of disagreement. Two areas of particular concern can be noted at this time. First, what is it that gives goals their motivating power? How are goals acquired? Most goal theories are silent in this regard, although a few emphasize that goals are based on the association of positive and negative affect with people and things (Pervin, 1983, 1989). Second, how are goals related to action and problems in action (Cantor, 1990a; Kuhl & Beckman, 1985; Pervin, 1991)? Most activities involve the action of multiple goals. Thus, the question of how goals are organized becomes an important issue. Also, at times people are unable to act upon their goals—they cannot get themselves to do what they "want" to do (e.g., they procrastinate in writing a paper) or they cannot stop themselves from doing what they "don't want" to do (e.g., eating compulsively). Such breakdowns in goal-directed behavior, or what have been called problems in volition, remain puzzling phenomena for researchers in this area. We will return to these issues and related research in Chapter 9.

COGNITIVE THEORIES OF MOTIVATION: KELLY'S JACKASS

In the beginning of this chapter we considered Kelly's views concerning motivation. We used his categories of pitchfork and carrot theories to describe push and pull theories of motivation, noting that both were hedonic theories based on the principles of gaining pleasure and avoiding pain. Recall that Kelly favored looking at the animal itself and named his theory a "jackass" theory. However, as we shall see, his was hardly a jackass theory, nor are other cognitively based theories of motivation.

In this section we consider theories of motivation based on cognitive factors. Two attributes distinguish these theories from those already considered: They do not emphasize hedonic, pleasure-pain principles, and, second, they emphasize the importance of cognitive considerations.

At times cognitive theorists speak of a "need for consistency" or a "need to know." For example, the self psychologist Prescott Lecky (1945) emphasized the person's motivation to maintain the unity, organization, or consistency of the self. Although this may seem similar to Festinger's emphasis on the need for cognitive consistency, Lecky did not associate any tension or noxious state with the lack of consistency. We are motivated to maintain consistency because that is the way we function. Pleasure may be a by-product of such achievement of consistency, but it is not the motivating force. Thus, although the term *need* may be used by some cognitive theorists, there is not an emphasis on tension reduction or drive principles. In Kelly's terms, the organism seeks cognitive clarity and cognitive consistency because that is the nature of the beast.

What, then, do cognitive theorists have to offer concerning our understanding of motivational issues? Let us consider here two points of view, Kelly's and that based on attributional principles.

KELLY'S EMPHASIS ON ANTICIPATING EVENTS

We already have noted how the personal construct theorist George Kelly repudiated the concept of motivation. Kelly did this because he wanted to break from traditional drive theories and other traditional ways of viewing human behavior. However, he did recognize the need to address issues such as activation, selection, and differential response. How, then, did he explain what activated the person, why one or another path is selected, and why there are differential responses to the same stimulus?

Kelly (1955, 1958) suggested that rather than needing some explanatory concept such as drive or incentive to get the person going, we accept the person as active because it is in the nature of the organism to be active. One needs a starter to get a machine such as a car going, but that is not the case for living creatures—they are active by virtue of being alive. A rather startling suggestion, but then how do we account for the direction and preparedness of response aspects of motivation? Kelly suggested that people act like scientists in that they seek to anticipate or predict events. Recall Kelly's emphasis on the person's construct system as a way of representing the world that leads them to make predictions or bets about what is likely to occur. In making predictions, people seek to be increasingly accurate in their predictions. Like all good scientists, people seek elaboration of their theories or personal construct systems. Like all good scientists, people seek to make better and better predictions over a wider range of phenomena. In other words, they seek both increased fidelity and bandwidth in their theory. Or, in Kelly's terms, they seek increased elaboration of their construct system. In sum, according to Kelly the person chooses the course of action that promises the greatest further development of his or her construct system. In our daily functioning we seek to make better predictions concerning our own behavior and that of others.

And what of preparedness of response? Kelly did not directly address this issue in as much detail. However, he did consider the implications of having one's predictions confirmed or disconfirmed. According to Kelly, we seek to have our predictions confirmed but do not seek the boredom of always making the same predictions and always having the same things happen. At the other extreme, Kelly suggested that encountering a situation without a relevant construct, without a way of anticipating events, produces anxiety. Beyond this, people experience threat if they encounter events that present the potential for total, comprehensive change in their construct system. According to Kelly, terror is the threat that everything one believes to be true is all wrong. Thus, Kelly suggested that our response to a stimulus or situation differs according to its relation to the predictions we have made. We seek the elaboration of our construct system and seek to avoid the boredom of the routine and the terror of complete uncertainty.

Note that although the term *seek* is used in relation to the functioning of the construct system, it is not being used in the sense of seeking some end point (goal) associated with positive value. Once more, it is just in the nature of the cognitive functioning of the organism that this occurs. According to Kelly, we seek better predictions because that is what we are about—jackasses, scientists, or whatever. We do not seek better predictions to satisfy our drives or to better obtain some incentive. Nor do we seek consistency to reduce cognitive dissonance and the tension created by it. Rather we seek consistency and dissonance-free cognitions so as to make better predictions. No further assumptions are necessary.

The observing student may have wondered whether Kelly does not still utilize a hedonic principle by suggesting that we seek to avoid monotony on the one hand and anxiety and threat on the other hand. As indicated elsewhere (Pervin, 1993a), this is the case. In his emphasis on the painful emotions associated with not having relevant constructs or finding important constructs invalidated, Kelly does utilize a hedonic principle, even if not a drive or tension-reduction principle. Kelly presented the view that people act as scientists and seek to predict events as a fundamental postulate, and there is no research to support or refute this view. There is research indicating that uncertainty under conditions of threat creates anxiety and motivates the person to reduce uncertainty (Mineka, 1985; Pervin, 1963). What remains unclear is whether uncertainty and inconsistency per se are motivating or whether they are motivating because of the tension or threat that can be associated with them—whether a strictly cognitive need for consistency is involved or a need to predict and control in the service of other needs (Swann, 1991).

In sum, what we have here in Kelly's theory is a bold attempt to account for motivational issues in cognitive terms. Regardless of conclusions concerning the issue of uncertainty addressed just before, it is clear that his account represents a radical departure from traditional hedonic push and pull theories.

ATTRIBUTIONAL MODELS

In Chapter 3 we considered attributions as cognitive units, emphasizing research relating internal, stable, and global attributions for negative events to depression. Although the focus there was on cognitive units, it was noted that attributions can have implications for motivation. Thus, it is appropriate that we consider attributional models within the context of cognitive theories of motivation.

Weiner's Attributional Model

Recall that attribution theory concerns the causal explanations people make for events. Like Seligman, Bernard Weiner (1985, 1990, 1993) is interested in such causal explanations and their implications for motivation and emotion. His attributional dimensions are similar, but not identical, to those emphasized by Seligman. Weiner asks the following questions: What kinds of causal explanations do we give for events? What are the implications of different causal explanations for how we feel and what we do? Does it make a difference if we believe that success was due to luck or hard work? Does it make a difference in how we treat others if we attribute their difficulties to something they could have avoided as opposed to accident? To what extent does the attribution of responsibility for events influence how we feel about and respond to ourselves and others?

What kinds of causal explanations do we give for events? Weiner suggests that there are three dimensions relevant to causal explanations. The first dimension, related to Rotter's work on locus of control, concerns whether causes are perceived as coming from within (internal) or from outside (external) the person. This dimension has been named *locus of causality.* A second dimension, *stability,* concerns whether the cause is perceived to be stable and relatively fixed, as opposed to being unstable and variable. The implications for causal attributions from combining these two dimensions can be seen in Table 4.2. Accordingly, we can attribute success or failure to *ability* ("I am bright"), *effort* ("I tried hard"), *task difficulty* ("The test was easy"), or *chance* or *luck* ("I was lucky in guessing right").

The third dimension, **controllability,** has to do with whether events are subject to control or influence through additional effort. For example, social rejection because of physical unattractiveness might be attributed to internal, stable, and uncontrollable causes, whereas social rejection because of obnoxious behavior might be attributed to internal, stable, and controllable causes. In each case it is the person's causal attributions that are important. Thus, some people might see their physical appearance as uncontrollable, whereas others might see it as controllable; some people might see their intellectual performance as the result of fixed intelligence, whereas others might see it as the result of effort and acquired knowledge (Dweck, 1986). As is probably clear, and as we will see demonstrated in research, such differing atttributions have important implications for how people function in social and learning situations.

Are there emotional and motivational implications of differing attributions? As noted, Weiner suggests that this is very much the case. It makes a great deal of

TABLE 4.2   Possible Causal Attributions for Success and Failure

Cause	Internal	External
Stable	Ability	Task difficulty
Variable	Effort	Chance or luck

Source: "A Theory of Motivation for Some Classroom Experiences," by B. Weiner, 1979, *Journal of Educational Psychology, 71.*

difference for how we feel and what we do whether we attribute success to effort or chance. Successful outcomes attributed to ourselves lead to greater self-esteem than do such outcomes attributed to external causes such as an easy task or good luck. On the other hand, such attributions for unsuccessful, negative outcomes also lead to greater self-blame and lessening of self-worth. Of particular importance, according to Weiner, are attributions made along the dimension of controllability, for it is here that the issue of personal responsibility appears. Attributions of controllability for personal failure are associated with emotions such as guilt, shame, and humiliation, whereas attributions associated with uncontrollability for personal failure do not lead to such self-criticism. Similarly, attributions concerning controllability for the failures of others are important in relation to social motivation and action. We hold others responsible for failures attributed to controllable causes and feel angry toward them. On the other hand, we feel sympathy toward those whose failures are seen as the result of circumstances beyond their control. If failure or illness is seen as the result of needlessly risky behavior, we may feel angry toward the person and stigmatize him or her; whereas if it is seen as the result of heredity or other circumstances beyond the person's control, we may feel sympathy and seek to be of assistance. In sum, the attributions we make determine whether we see the problem as one of sin (controllable) or sickness (uncontrollable). More generally, the feelings we have toward ourselves and others, and the consequent motives and actions, are significantly influenced by the causal attributions we make for events.

Dweck's Model of Implicit Beliefs About the Self and the World

Another model that is heavily influenced by cognitive, attributional considerations is Carol Dweck's social cognitive approach to motivation (Dweck, 1990, 1991; Dweck, Chiu, & Hong, 1995; Dweck & Leggett, 1988). Dweck's work began with the observation that schoolchildren differed in their response to failure on an academic task (Diener & Dweck, 1978, 1980). Two response styles seemed particularly noteworthy—a *helpless* style and a *mastery-oriented* style. In response to failure, the helpless style children quickly experienced negative self-cognitions (e.g., "I'm no good," "It's my fault"), boredom, anxiety, and task aversion. Because of these negative cognitions and negative affect, there was a marked decrement in further performance. On the other hand, mastery-oriented children confronted with difficult problems experienced these problems as challenges to be mastered through effort. They would say to themselves such things as "I did it before, I can do it again." Whereas the helpless style children viewed their difficulties as failures, indicative of low ability and poor prognosis for the future, the mastery-oriented style children viewed their difficulties as temporary setbacks and as opportunities for further development of competence. The attributions given for the difficulties were very different, with important implications for emotions and motivation.

Why such differences in response style? Dweck found that the two groups of children were pursuing different goals (Elliot & Dweck, 1988). Whereas helpless style children pursued *performance* goals, mastery-oriented style children pursued *learning* goals. Whereas the former were seeking to establish their *ability* and to avoid feeling inadequate, the latter were seeking to improve their *competence.* Underlying these differences were differing views or theories of the nature of intelligence. Whereas the former group of children viewed intelligence as an **entity,** that is, fixed, the latter group of children viewed intelligence as **incremental,** that is, as malleable. Viewing intelligence as fixed left those children feeling anxious and vulnerable, whereas viewing intelligence as something malleable left the other children prepared to face challenges with effort and enthusiasm. The implications of entity and incremental beliefs concerning intelligence are compared in Table 4.3.

In sum, Dweck's research suggested that attributions for events are important, but that underlying attributional styles are beliefs about oneself and the world. Such beliefs, or implicit theories about the self and the world, are viewed as more basic than attributions, in fact as underlying the causal, attributional processes described by Weiner. Do such theories apply to nonacademic domains as well? Dweck suggests that responses to social rejection show similar differential responses (Goetz & Dweck, 1980). To take the illustration she used in her research, consider the following question: "Suppose you move to a new neighborhood. A girl/boy you meet does not like you very much. Why would this happen to you?" Although the setting may differ, this is a situation virtually everyone faces periodically. Whereas some blame rejection on personal social incompetence, others blame it on less personal factors. In observations of actual behavior, Dweck found that children who blame rejection on personal social incompetence (entity belief) show withdrawal and poor social flexibility, whereas children who blame rejection on less personal factors (incremental belief) are less disrupted by rejection and more able to adapt their behavior to changed circumstances. In sum, a similar helpless versus mastery-oriented pattern of response to social rejection as that found in response to failure on an intellectual task occurs.

TABLE 4.3   **Comparison of Entity and Incremental Beliefs Concerning Intelligence**

Entity Beliefs	Incremental Beliefs
1. Intelligence is fixed or uncontrollable.	1. Intelligence is malleable.
2. Person is not sure he or she can solve problems on which there was previous success.	2. Person anticipates little difficulty in solving problems on which there was previous success.
3. Performance reflects ability: "If you have to work at something, you must not be very good at it." "Great discoveries come easily to people who are true geniuses."	3. Performance reflects effort and utility of strategy for the task: "Even geniuses have to work hard for their discoveries."
4. If you are smart, you will succeed regardless of task difficulty or effort.	4. You are smart if you master something difficult or figure out something new.
5. Obstacles indicate a lack of ability.	5. Obstacles represent challenges and opportunities for mastery.
6. Criticism is a reflection on the self.	6. Criticism is information that is useful for improved performance.

Source: Adapted from "Self-Theories and Goals: Their Role in Motivation, Personality, and Development," by C. S. Dweck, 1990, *Nebraska Symposium on Motivation, 38.*

SPOTLIGHT ON THE RESEARCHER

CAROL S. DWECK:
Implicit Theories About the Self and the World

When I was a graduate student at Yale in the late 1960s, doing research in animal learning, my imagination was captured by the animal work on learned helplessness. I realized that the concept had relevance for how people cope with negative events, and I turned my research to that issue. I wanted to explain why some children show a "learned helpless" reaction when they fail, while others, of equal ability, show a more "mastery-oriented" pattern. My research took me first to how the children interpreted their failure: Some saw it as an indictment of their intelligence, but others saw it as sign that they should step up their effort or try a new strategy.

Over time, as my students and I probed more and more deeply, we began to find that children held even more basic beliefs about themselves ("implicit theories") that seemed to set up these interpretations in the first place. What we found was that those who believe their intelligence is a fixed trait are the ones who are most likely to question that trait when they fail (and to show a helpless response). Those who believe their intelligence is a malleable quality, one they can cultivate, are led to question their strategies and not their underlying intelligence when they meet obstacles.

This work shows how people's implicit theories can create a framework for understanding themselves and what happens to them, so that two people with equal ability confronting identical circumstances can have dramatically different interpretations and reactions.

The implicit theory model has taken us in many new directions. It has helped us understand the development of helpless reactions in very young children (who were thought to be invulnerable to helplessness). It has helped us understand reactions to social setbacks. Maybe the most interesting new dirction is the study of people's social judgments—how people who believe in fixed versus malleable traits understand and judge others. Which implicit theories foster flexible judgments and which foster more rigid stereotypes? All in all, we are trying to shed light on the basic beliefs we all carry around with us that guide our thoughts and actions as we move through the world.

Taking these research results as our starting point, let us round out Dweck's model of motivation. What Dweck suggests is that people develop implicit theories about themselves and the world. These theories then orient them toward different *goals*. Illustrative of such differences are those noted in relation to the domain of intellectual achievement—performance goals versus learning goals. The theories and goals then lead individuals to make different attributions for outcomes as well as to have differential affective and behavioral responses to events:

theory———➤goal orientation———➤cognitive, affective, behavioral pattern

Again, attributions are emphasized as important, but as based on underlying goals that are based on underlying implicit theories concerning the self and the world. Individuals differ in their implicit theories and therefore in their goals and response patterns. However, it is important to note that, in keeping with social cognitive theory, individuals are assumed to develop different theories and goals in relation to different domains. Thus, there is no reason to assume that a person demonstrating a helpless style in relation to academic situations will not demonstrate a mastery-oriented style in relation to social situations.

In its emphasis on the importance of implicit theories, goals, and cognitive responses to goal achievement or nonachievement, Dweck's model represents a social cognitive model of motivation. The personality units emphasized are those previously noted in Chapter 3—beliefs, goals, attributions. Although Dweck emphasizes goals as an important motivational unit, the primary emphasis is on cognitive variables rather than the pleasure-pain (hedonic) principles associated with incentive theories of motivation. It is for this reason that it is presented here in the discussion of cognitive theories of motivation.

GROWTH, SELF-ACTUALIZATION THEORIES OF MOTIVATION

It is time to consider a fourth, and final, general model of motivation: growth, self-actualizing theories of motivation. Theories proposing this model were particularly popular in the 1960s, forming what was described in Chapter 1 as the Human Potential Movement. This movement was seen as a third force in American psychology, countering what were seen as the negative, pessimistic, and limited conceptions of human nature found in the other two forces, psychoanalysis and behaviorism. What joined the various theoretical positions in this movement together was an emphasis on a basic tendency of the organism toward growth and **self-actualization.**

Like most such developments, the Human Potential Movement was an outgrowth of both scientific and societal developments. The decade of the 1960s was one of idealism, and the emphasis on growth and the realization of one's full human potential were part of that idealism. In terms of scientific developments relating to psychology, evidence was making clear the limits of a drive, tension-reduction model of personality. Working with monkeys, Harlow (1953) was struck with evidence that monkeys learned most efficiently if they were given food before testing rather than after, in contradiction to the supposed facilitative effects of drive (hunger) and reinforcing effects of drive reduction. In addition, Harlow and his students found that animals would explore for the sake of exploration, even working for the opportunity to explore. Was one to posit an exploratory drive and a separate drive for each such type of activity? This hardly seemed to make sense.

Shortly thereafter, R. W. White (1959) published a paper challenging traditional views of motivation. In this paper, which became a classic, White suggested that the fundamental human motive is that of **competence motivation**—the motivation to deal competently or effectively with the environment. Motivation to explore, to smanipulate objects, to meet challenges, and to develop skills all are part of the organism's efforts to grow and flourish rather than expressions of tissue deficits or drive tensions. Coming from a vastly different theoretical framework, White anticipated by almost 20 years Bandura's emphasis on self-efficacy motivation.

The two main leaders of the Human Potential Movement were Carl Rogers and Abraham Maslow. As noted in Chapter 1, Rogers postulated self-actualization as the single motivation to life. Maslow (1968) suggested a hierarchical view of human motivation. He accepted the importance of biological needs (e.g., hunger, sleep, thirst) involving tension and movement toward tension reduction. However, Maslow also suggested that higher in the hierarchy of human motives are those that often involve an increase in tension—motives that are expressed when people are being creative and fulfilling their potential.

The views of Maslow and Rogers had relatively little direct impact upon research. The spirit of their views probably is best expressed today in the work of Deci and Ryan (1985, 1991) on *intrinsic motivation* and *self-determination theory*. According to Deci and Ryan, humans have an innate, natural tendency to engage their interests, to exercise their capacities, and to conquer optimal challenges. This movement toward self-determination is expressed in **intrinsic motivation,** or the motive to engage in a task because of an interest in the task itself. The contrast to intrinsic motivation is *extrinsic motivation*, in which the person is engaged in a task because of the rewards that will follow from its successful completion. Learning for the sake of learning is illustrative of intrinsic motivation, whereas learning for the sake of extrinsic rewards such as praise and financial gain is illustrative of extrinsic motivation.

In their early research, Deci and Ryan demonstrated that subjects engaged in a task without an offer of reward showed greater subsequent interest in such tasks than did subjects receiving a reward for their efforts. In contrast to reinforcement theory, rewards were not necessary for learning. Beyond this, the presence of rewards could actually interfere with task performance (Lepper & Greene, 1978). In other words, there may be a "hidden cost of reward," something about reward that decreases motivation and turns play into work.

Deci and Ryan then extended their view of the effects of reward more generally to the issue of social control and feelings of self-determination. They suggest that when tasks are performed because of external forms of social control (e.g., threats, deadlines, explicit competition, evaluation), there is diminished intrinsic motivation. On the other hand, when individuals are given a chance to increase their competence and experience the task as self-determined, intrinsic motivation is likely to increase. In a research study testing this view, fourth-grade children were exposed either to teachers who pressured them to maximize their performance or to teachers who simply told them to learn. In addition, teacher behavior was assessed in terms of the extent to which controlling strategies were used. Following this, student performance was assessed on the tasks initially taught as well as on other, related tasks. What was found was that students exposed to teachers using pressured, controlling strategies performed poorly relative to students exposed to teachers emphasizing learning and

Self-Actualization and Intrinsic Motivation. Some models of motivation are neither "push" nor "pull" theories, emphasizing instead the person's movement toward fulfillment of their potential and interest in activities independent of external rewards.

using noncontrolling approaches (Flink, Boggiano, & Barrett, 1990). Similar to the work of Dweck, an emphasis on learning goals (intrinsic motivation) had a beneficial effect relative to an emphasis on performance goals (extrinsic motivation). More generally, research suggests that controlling strategies negatively impact intrinsic motivation, creativity, and achievement.

Also related to this view is the work of Mihaly Csikszentmihalyi (1975) on **optimal experiences** and the experience of **flow.** In such experiences the person is involved in activities for which there are few, if any, rewards in the conventional sense. The person is engaged in the activity because of the pleasure derived from such engagement, as is the musician who plays for the joy of playing or the scientist fascinated with the process of discovery. People engaged in such activities often describe a "flow" experience in which attention is completely focused on the task and there is a loss of self-consciousness. In the flow experience everything seems "in synch" and hours may pass without awareness of the time. In such efforts there is pleasure in the involvement and a wish to continue, in contrast to the boredom and anxiety associated with tasks performed under conditions of pressure and threat.

The views discussed in this section not only differ from hedonic views, but often are in direct conflict with them. According to these views, there may be tissue needs and drives, but they are not the essence of human motivation. Some activities may start off based on the satisfaction of biological needs or the wish to obtain external incentives, but, in the words of Allport (1961), they attain **functional autonomy:** "What was once extrinsic and instrumental becomes intrinsic and compelling. The activity once served a drive or some simple need; it now serves itself, or in a larger sense, serves the self-image (self-ideal) of the person" (p. 229). In sum, not only are external rewards and incentives not necessary for motivation, but they may actually interfere with it. People may not be pushed by pitchforks or pulled by carrots, but that doesn't make them jackasses either.

COMMENTS ON MOTIVATIONAL UNITS

In this chapter we have considered the concept of motivation and alternative theoretical views—drive, tension-reduction theories; incentive-goal theories; cognitive theories; and self-actualization theories. These theories address the question of *why* people behave as they do, in particular the questions of what activates the person, what directs and maintains activity, what accounts for differential responses to the same stimuli, and what terminates activity. They represent both broad theoretical answers to these questions that apply to all people as well as bases for individual differences. Within each model is an emphasis on individual differences in the organization and expression of motives.

Although these views have been presented separately, it is clear that there often is overlap among them. Thus, the concept of need at times has been associated with tension reduction and at other times with an incentive or goal, and the concept of a goal at times associated with an incentive, hedonic view and at other times with a more purely cognitive view. Whereas Weiner's attributional model emphasizes cognitive factors but includes an emotional component that is important in motivation, Dweck's model emphasizes cognitive factors and goals but without a clear emotional component. Whereas some, such as Murray and McClelland, emphasize the necessity of using fantasy measures of motives and the limitations of self-report, others suggest that self-report devices are satisfactory for the investigation of most motives.

These theories are a diverse group, with overlap among the categories, and no one theory representing a comprehensive analysis. In addition, motivation theorists differ in how they view the relation between motivation and the other suggested units of personality—traits and cognitions. Although Allport presented himself as a trait theorist, he also emphasized the importance of motives. Social cognitive theorists such as Bandura, Mischel, and Cantor emphasize motivational units such as goals, but in their emphasis on domain specificity reject the idea of traits. Other illustrations of these complex relationships could be given, but perhaps it is time now to direct ourselves to the question of the relationship among the units of personality—traits, cognitions, and motives.

RELATIONSHIPS AMONG THE UNITS OF PERSONALITY: TRAITS, COGNITIONS, AND MOTIVES

What is the relationship among the suggested units of personality—traits, cognitions, and motives? Are they really all the same and just different ways of cutting the same pie? Alternatively, are they separate and distinct units, completely independent of one another? Or, are they conceptually separate units that are understood to always be interrelated? Here I try to present some of the differing views that exist in the field, while at the same time indicating my own point of view.

Let us begin with one opinion, that all personality consists of traits. According to trait theorists, personality consists of regularities in functioning and traits represent the concept defining these regularities. Thus, according to this view, traits are the fundamental structural units of personality. Some trait theorists suggest that there are different kinds of traits, such as temperament traits, ability traits, and motivational traits (Guilford, 1975). Others suggest that most, perhaps all, traits have cognitive, emotional-motivational, and behavioral components to them. Although it is useful to recognize these components as distinct aspects of personality, these trait theorists suggest that they still are components of traits and there is little need for other structural units (McCrae, 1994).

Murray came to a quite different conclusion. He clearly distinguished between the concept of a trait and that of a motive and suggested that although a motive (need) might operate but once in a person's life, a trait referred to a recurrent action pattern. And, although a motive might rarely express itself in behavior, particularly in a direct form, it might still be an important part of the dynamic organization of the person's personality.

Although they would not agree with all of Murray's points, social cognitive theorists certainly would be in agreement with his critique of the trait concept's emphasis on consistency. For social cognitive theorists, it is the variability of behavior, the discriminative abilities and domain-specific functioning of humans that is the starting point for an understanding of personality. For such theorists, the concept of trait, as traditionally defined by trait theorists and as studied within the context of factor analysis, does an injustice to basic aspects of personality functioning and can never be the basic unit of personality.

Yet, can one disregard evidence in support of traits, evidence gathered through analyses of language, ratings, and questionnaires, and as supported by findings in the area of behavioral genetics? I think not and, therefore, am led to the conclusion that the fundamental traits emphasized by trait theorists, the Big Five, for the most part represent temperament aspects of personality that have a strong genetic component to them. In other words, I believe that traits exist, that we are born with temperament dispositions that play an important role in the unfolding of our personalities, and that many aspects of our functioning may also be related to temperament and show traitlike qualities. At the same time, like Murray, I believe that traits and motives are fundamentally distinct concepts, and the latter are particularly necessary for an understanding of the dynamic aspects of personality and for an answer to many *why* questions. And, with social cognitive theorists, I believe that an exclusively trait view does an injustice to the variability of behavior. As a patient of mine said to me recently: "I am perfectly able to be aggressive and ask direct questions in work situations, where I feel empowered, but become numb and am unable to behave that way in close personal relationships where I feel much more vulnerable." To understand and explain such phenomena, we must employ both cognitive and motivational concepts.

So, I am led to reject the view of hegemony of one concept over the others, of the dominance of trait concepts over all others, and equally well to reject the view of complete independence of the units from one another. Cognition plays a role in motivation in the form of representations of goals and plans or strategies to achieve goals. Motivation plays a role in cognition in terms of directing our thoughts to particular areas and in influencing the ways we organize and utilize information (Kunda, 1987). And, if we can accept traits as based on temperament, traits influence the development of our cognitive and motivational functioning. Certainly the temperamentally active infant is set on a different cognitive and motivational path than the temperamentally inhibited infant, even if these temperamental differences are not all-determinant of later developments.

I am led, then, to the view that traits, cognitions, and motives are separate but interrelated units of personality. They can be considered separately and studied as if they were independent of one another. However, at times there are fuzzy boundaries between the concepts, and any complex piece of a person's behavior likely involves trait, cognitive, and motivational components. Thus, they are convenient conceptual units for us to use at this time, while understanding that one or more of them may be dropped and others added as we continue our search for the fundamental units of personality.

Finally, we must understand that whatever the units we employ, we are left with the task of understanding the organization of personality. The nature of the units is just one part of the problem, the organization of the units and the functioning of the person as a system is another part of the problem. People, no less than machines or other species, are not just units but are organizations of components. As indicated in the introduction, we must always attend to the organization of units as well as the delineation of the units themselves.

MAJOR CONCEPTS

Motive.   A concept used to explain the activation, direction, and preparedness of response aspects of behavior or the *why* of behavior.

Drive.   An internal stimulus associated with a state of tension that leads to efforts toward tension reduction.

Libido.   The psychoanalytic term for the energy associated first with the life instincts and then with the sexual instincts.

Mechanisms of defense.   The psychoanalytic concept for those devices used by the person to reduce anxiety, resulting in the exclusion from awareness of some thought, feeling, or wish.

Primary and secondary drives.   In S-R theory, primary drives are biologically based internal stimuli that activate and direct behavior (e.g., hunger drive) and secondary drives are learned internal stimuli that are acquired on the basis of association with the satisfaction of primary drives (e.g., anxiety).

Instrumental learning.   In S-R theory, the learning of responses that are instrumental in bringing about pleasure in the form of tension reduction.

Habit.   In S-R theory, an association between a stimulus and a response formed on the basis of reinforcement (tension reduction).

Need.   A concept, similar to motive, that is used to explain the *why* of behavior.

Press.   Murray's concept for describing environmental characteristics that were associated with need satisfaction.

Cognitive dissonance.   Festinger's concept for the state of tension created when two or more cognitions are inconsistent with one another.

Purposive.   Describes behavior that is directed toward obtaining some end point or goal.

Teleology.   The view that action is directed toward future end points, at times also seen as suggesting that future events determine events in the present.

Goal.   A desired future event that motivates the person.

Locus of causality, stability, and controllability.   Weiner's three attributional dimensions that are important for emotion and motivation. The locus of causality dimension concerns whether causes are perceived as coming from within (internal) or from outside (external) the person, the stability dimension (stable-unstable) to how fixed the cause is perceived to be, and the controllability dimension (controllable-uncontrollable) to whether the events are subject to influence through additional effort.

Entity and incremental beliefs.   Dweck's concepts for differing beliefs concerning aspects of the self such as intelligence, the former expressing the view that something is fixed and the latter that it is malleable.

Self-actualization.   The concept emphasized by Rogers and others suggesting that the fundamental tendency of the organism is to actualize and enhance the self.

Competence motivation.   White's concept expressing the motivation to deal competently or effectively with the environment.

Intrinsic motivation.   The view that people can be motivated by an interest in a task itself, independent of rewards that may be associated with successful completion of it.

Optimal experience, flow.   Csikszentmihalyi's concept for the experience of pleasure associated with the intense focusing of attention and lessened self-consciousness while engaged in activities of great interest (e.g., music, art).

Functional autonomy.   Allport's concept that a motive may become independent of its origins; in particular, motives in adults may become independent of their earlier basis in tension reduction.

SUMMARY

1. The concept of motive has been used to address the questions of activation, selection-direction, and preparedness of response aspects of behavior, that is, the question of *why* we behave as we do. Four major categories of motivational theories have been considered: drive, tension-reduction theories; incentive theories; cognitive theories; and self-actualization theories.

2. Drive theories of motivation are based on the model of biological states of tension that lead the organism to seek tension reduction. Such tension reduction is associated with positive reinforcement or pleasure and thus such theories are considered hedonic or pleasure oriented.

3. Freud's theory of sexual and aggressive drives is an illustrative drive theory. The theory emphasizes the dynamic interplay among drives and mechanisms of defense used to reduce anxiety that may be associated with drives.

4. Drive theory also is illustrated in S-R learning theory, Murray's need-press theory, and Festinger's theory of cognitive dissonance. The emphasis on drive, tension-reduction theories declined beginning in the 1960s with increasing evidence of motives that did not fit the model and with developments in the cognitive revolution.

5. Incentive theories of motivation emphasize the motivational pull of end points anticipated by the organism. Although different from drive theories in their emphasis on goals rather than biologically based internal stimuli, incentive theories of motivation are similar in their hedonic basis. Currently there is considerable interest in a number of goal-related concepts.

6. Cognitive theories of motivation emphasize the importance of cognition either in terms of a cognitive need, such as the need for consistency or the need to be able to anticipate events, or in terms of the implications of cognitions for emotion and motivation. Kelly's theory illustrates the former, while Weiner's emphasis on attribution and Dweck's emphasis on entity and incremental beliefs illustrate the latter. In contrast to hedonic theories such as drive and incentive theories, the emphasis in such theories is on cognitions and their implications for motivation rather than on pleasure or reinforcement.

7. The fourth category of motivation theories consists of those that emphasize a motive toward growth or self-actualization. The motivation theories of two leaders of the Human Potential Movement, Rogers and Maslow, are illustrative of such theories. Also illustrative are theories that emphasize the importance of intrinsic motivation (Deci and Ryan) and the experience of flow associated with intense engagement in some activities (Csikszentmihalyi).

8. Having considered trait, cognitive, and motive units of personality, the question can be raised of the relationship among the units; that is, are they competing concepts or are they distinct concepts related in complex ways to one another? The view suggested in the text is that the three concepts relate to different but interrelated aspects of personality functioning and that most important human activities involve interactions among them.

PART

II

PERSONALITY
DEVELOPMENT

I n this part we consider two basic issues concerning personality development—the determinants of personality and the degree to which personality
development follows a clearly defined path from childhood to adulthood
and beyond. The first issue often is framed in a somewhat simplistic fashion as
the nature-nurture controversy; that is, is personality primarily determined by
genes (nature) or environment (nurture)? The second issue is framed, in an
equally simplistic fashion, as the stability-change controversy; that is, is change
always possible in personality or is one's basic personality defined, and "set in
stone," by some point in time? Both are issues of controversy in the field, and
the nature-nurture controversy has become a broader social and political issue
as well.

In the following two chapters we seek to define the issues, review the most
up-to-date research findings that bear upon them, and attempt to arrive at the
conclusions that currently make the most sense in light of these findings. In
doing so, we must be prepared to do two things. First, we must think about the
problems in more complex ways. For example, we must view genes and environments, nature and nurture, as always operating in conjunction with, rather
than in opposition to, one another. That is, it is never nature *versus* nurture, and
always nature *and* nurture. And, we must be prepared to consider the possibility
that personality change may be more or less possible for different characteristics
and more or less possible given different environmental circumstances. Thus,
ultimately we want to understand the processes governing personality stability
and change rather than just knowing whether personality generally remains
stable or changes.

Second, in considering these two issues we must be prepared to give up old
ways of thinking about them and possibly currently held beliefs as well. For
example, most of us come to the issues with general biases concerning how
important genes are for personality development and how much change is
possible. I know that when I was a college student my general disposition was
to believe that environment was far more important than heredity for personality
development and that although personality change in adulthood was possible,

the basic personality structure had been determined by one's early environment. Not only did I have a bias, but I tended to view the issues in relatively undifferentiated, absolute terms. In all likelihood, most college students have some biased beliefs in one or another direction as well. The truth be told, I suspect that I still have some general biases in my beliefs on these two issues, tempered, I hope, by a more disciplined form of raising questions and evaluating the evidence. It is this more disciplined form of asking questions and evaluating evidence that is encouraged as we consider these two important and controversial issues.

THE NATURE AND NURTURE OF PERSONALITY

5

CHAPTER OVERVIEW

In this chapter we consider genetic (nature) and environmental (nurture) determinants of personality. Historically this has been an area filled with controversy despite the major gains in understanding genetic contributions to personality. Research suggests that environment is important in shaping personality, but one important part of the environment, the family, does not affect all children in the family in the same way. The overall theme of this chapter is that genes and environments are always interacting; that is, there is never gene without environment or environment without gene.

Questions to Be Addressed in This Chapter

1 What is the relation between heredity and environment, nature and nurture?

2 What can evolutionary theory contribute to our understanding of human personality?

3 What methods are available to determine the contributions of genes to personality and what does research suggest concerning these genetic contributions?

4 To what extent do individuals growing up in the same family share the same environment, leading to similar personalities?

5 Do individuals with different genetic characteristics experience different environments? Why?

To a great extent, people throughout the world share many features in common. This certainly is true in relation to structural characteristics (e.g., organs of the body), and many would suggest that it is true as well for many aspects of psychological functioning that are tied to our common evolutionary heritage (D. M. Buss, 1991, 1995). At the same time, clearly there are major differences among people, both in structural characteristics such as height and weight and in personality characteristics such as sociability and tendency to experience anxiety. How to account for such similarities and differences has been the task of both biologists and psychologists, the former tending to focus on the causes of similarities and the latter on the causes of differences. Today, in particular through the work of behavioral geneticists, there has been a joining of the two types of endeavors. Thus, **behavioral geneticists** are individuals who attempt to determine the genetic contributions to behaviors of interest to psychologists. Just how this is done, and what we have come to understand about the genetic and environmental determinants of personality, is the subject of this chapter.

In approaching this issue of the genetic and environmental determinants of personality, it should be clear to the student that this is an issue that historically has been extremely controversial. In Chapter 1 it was noted that Galton, a cousin to Darwin, framed the issue in terms of "nature versus nurture." On the basis of his family pedigree studies, Galton concluded that "nature prevails enormously over nurture." In pitting nature versus nurture, or heredity versus environment, he set the tone for the controversy that raged over the next century. This controversy has involved not just scientific questions, but political and social questions as well, and the issues continue to be debated to this day (Baumrind, 1993; Herrnstein & Murray, 1994; J. F. Jackson, 1993; Pervin, 1984; Scarr, 1992, 1993).

The initial question was: Is it due to nature or nurture, heredity or environment? Then, the question became: Is it due *more* to nature or to nurture? Then: *How* do heredity and environment interact to form psychological characteristics (Anastasi, 1958)? Despite Anastasi's call, over 30 years ago, for a more reasoned and differentiated approach to the issue, and despite the suggestion of many biologists and psychologists that heredity never operates in the absence of environment and environment never operates in the absence of heredity, people to this day tend to pit one against the other—nature against nurture, heredity against environment. And, historically we see periods in which one emphasis holds sway against the other. For example, during the 1920s there was considerable interest in, and emphasis on, the importance of genetic factors. During the 1930s and 1940s, these views became extremely unpopular, in part because of their association with events in Nazi Germany (Degler, 1991). More recently, there has been a return to an interest in evolutionary and genetic contributions to human psychological functioning. Indeed, the emphasis on genetic factors has become so great that at least one major behavioral geneticist, Robert Plomin, has warned that the pendulum may be swinging too far in the direction of an emphasis on nature:

Despite the reluctance of the behavioral sciences to acknowledge genetic influences even through the 1970s, genetic influence has become increasingly accepted during the 1980s. It is good for the field of personality that it has moved away from simple-minded environmentalism. The danger, now, however, is that the rush from environmentalism will carom too far—to a view that personality is almost completely biologically determined.

Plomin, Chipuer, & Loehlin, 1990, p. 225

Given the tendencies for the issue to be framed in either-or terms, for the pendulum to swing in one or the other direction, and for views to become polarized, it is necessary for us to try and chart a balanced and differentiated course. In charting this course, it is important to understand exactly what concepts do and do not mean and which implications and conclusions can and cannot be drawn from the data. In charting this course, it is useful to think in terms of an image suggested by the biologist Waddington (1957). Intent upon emphasizing the ongoing interaction between genes and environment during the course of development, Waddington used the analogy of the movement of a ball down a landscape. The landscape, representing what is genetically determined, may have many or few hills and valleys, each varying in height or depth and steepness. The ball rolling down the landscape represents development and the influence of environmental forces. The ball can move only within the contours of the landscape. It will be difficult for it to move up a hill or out of a valley with steep walls. Thus, such a path of movement or development can occur only through considerable environmental impact. There is a "natural" progression, or path of least resistance, for the ball, but it can be deflected in various directions. The number of possible paths depends on the number of different slopes or valleys available to the ball at a particular point. Thus, at some stages of development many options or courses of development are left open. Generally, each path taken represents some foreclosure or narrowing of potential for some other courses of development. As the ball moves down the landscape, then, one can expect its final position to be increasingly defined, just as one would expect that with age various personality characteristics become increasingly defined and less open to change. The key point, however, is that the movement of the ball, at any one point in time or over time, can be understood only in terms of the contours of the landscape and the forces operating on the ball, that is, in terms of the joint action of heredity (the landscape) and environment (forces operating on the ball).

In sum, in considering the nature *and* nurture of personality, we must keep in mind that the development of personality is always a function of the interaction of genes with environments, that there is no nature without nurture and no nurture without nature (Plomin, 1990a). We can separate the two, as will be done in this chapter, for purposes of discussion and analysis, but the two are never operating independently of one another.

THE "NATURE" OF PERSONALITY: GENETIC CONTRIBUTIONS

Whatever we inherit that is common to us as humans, as well as what we inherit that makes us unique, is inherited through the action of **genes.** We inherit 23 pairs of chromosomes, one of each pair from each of our biological parents. The chromosomes contain thousands of genes. Genes are made up of a molecule called DNA and direct the synthesis of protein molecules. Genes may be thought of as sources of information, directing the synthesis of protein molecules along particular lines. It is the information contained in the genes that directs the biological development of the organism. It is this information that directs the biological development of the fertilized egg into a fetus, a fully formed neonate, an adolescent with secondary sex characteristics, and an elderly person with characteristics associated with the aged.

The amount of information contained in the genes is truly remarkable. In appreciating the relation of genes to behavior, it is important to understand that genes do not govern behavior directly. Thus, there is no "extraversion gene" or "introversion gene" and there is no "neuroticism gene." To the extent that genes influence the development of personality characteristics such as the Big Five described in Chapter 2, they do so through the direction of the biological functioning of the body.

Within this context, the amount of behavior-relevant information stored in genes is tremendous. For example, genes determine the anatomical differences between different species and lay the groundwork for many species-specific behaviors. One of the most complex and fascinating pieces of animal behavior is the dance of the honeybee. When honeybees discover food, they return to the beehive and signal to the other bees, through what has been called a dance, the location of the newly discovered food supply. Both the distance and direction of the food supply relative to the hive is signaled through the kind of dance that is performed and the angle of the signaling bee in relation to the sun—quite a remarkable communicative act! Although the development of such behaviors likely depends on some experience, the basis for such species-specific behaviors lies in the biological processes directed by the genes (Goldsmith, 1991). The point being made here is that the behavior of the organism that is directed by biological processes governed by information contained in the genes can be quite complex.

In the past, a distinction often was made between instinctive and learned behavior. Instinctive behavior was tied to gene functioning and learned behavior to nongene functioning. Such distinctions today are seen as quite artificial and misleading. What formerly were seen as instinctive behaviors today are seen as involving some degree of experience, particularly at a critical or sensitive period in the development of the animal. For example, the development of songs in birds is directed by both information contained in the genes and experiences during periods critical for bird-song development. Particular birds are "wired" for the development of particular bird songs, but such development requires particular sensory experiences during particular periods of development. If these experiences do not occur, the "wired" development also does not occur. Thus, genes may determine the development of species-specific biological processes that require environmental experiences to develop into species-specific behaviors (Goldsmith, 1991).

On the other hand, behaviors that show great diversity among members of a species, and that often are referred to as learned, can be built upon biological processes that are genetically governed. For example, one cannot help but be struck by the enormous diversity of languages spoken around the world and the enormous range of sounds made within these languages. As adults listening to individuals speaking a foreign language, it often is impossible for us to hear differences in sounds considered to be quite fundamental by speakers of that language. In addition, it often is difficult, at times impossible, for us to perform sounds fundamental to that language. Yet, all humans are born "wired" to learn a language and able to perform all of the sounds found in any language (Werker, 1989). The biological basis for the learning of language and performing the sounds found in languages throughout the world is provided by the genes, but the specific language learned and whether certain sounds can be made depend on experience—in the case of language learning, experience that occurs during the first few years of life. In sum, once more we have complex behaviors whose development is contingent both upon biological processes governed by genes and upon experience.

Before completing this section on the relation of genes to behavior, it is important to note that most behaviors of interest to personality psychologists are influenced by many genes rather than by the functioning of any single gene. Periodically we hear of the discovery of a gene that determines a particular characteristic, often a gene that determines a particular disease in humans. Such discoveries may lead to the mistaken assumption that most important human characteristics, including those on which we differ as individuals, are determined by single genes. In fact, most such characteristics are likely determined by the interaction of multiple genes. The idea that many personality characteristics of interest to us may be influenced by a configuration of genes rather than by single genes is important to our understanding of why some characteristics that are genetically influenced may not run in families. The members of the family, including those of different generations, may have various combinations of genes, but only the occasional member with the particular configuration will show the specific characteristic (Lykken, McGue, Tellegen, & Bouchard, 1992). Thus, the characteristic may show up only rarely in a family and yet be genetically determined. For many important characteristics, therefore, there may be no simple link between genetic determination and appearance within a family.

This section on genes and their relation to behavior has focused on genes as sources of information that govern the direction of development and the functioning of biological structures and processes. It is the functioning of these biological structures and processes, in conjunction with environmental events, that governs the development of observed behavior. It is the functioning of the genes, in conjunction with experience, that makes us similar to one another as members of the same species and different from one another as unique individuals. This is true for both simple and complex pieces of behavior, for that which seems to be true of all of us and for that which seems unique to the individual. Finally, it has been suggested that most behaviors of interest to psychologists are likely caused by a configuration of genes rather than by any single gene.

Biologists and psychologists distinguish between two kinds of explanations for behavior—*ultimate causes* and *proximate causes*. **Ultimate causes** refer to explanations associated with evolution, that is, why the behavior of interest evolved and the adaptive function it served. Darwin's theory of evolution serves as the foundation for such ultimate cause explanations of behavior. **Proximate cause** explanations refer to biological processes operating in the organism at the time the behavior is observed. In other words, one kind of explanation takes a historical view of the development of the species, in this case an evolutionary view, whereas the other kind of explanation focuses on processes operating in the present. The common denominator of both views, however, is the importance of genes in the context of an organism's attempts to solve an adaptive problem. In terms of evolution, organisms that solve adaptive tasks pass their genes on to successive generations. In a certain sense, genes contain "designs for living" that have enabled organisms to reproduce successfully. In terms of proximate causes, it is genes that provide the biological foundations for an organism's attempts to solve adaptive tasks in the present. Presumably it is the genes that provided the basis for adaptive functioning in the past that continue to provide that basis in the present. Thus, we consider how the information contained in genes can offer ultimate and proximate explanations for many of the phenomena of interest to personality psychologists.

EVOLUTIONARY, ULTIMATE EXPLANATIONS

Evolutionary psychologists seek to understand aspects of human functioning in terms of their relation to evolved solutions to adaptive problems faced by the species over millions of years (D. M. Buss, 1991, 1995). According to this view, basic psychological mechanisms are the result of evolution by selection; that is, they exist and have endured because they have been adaptive to survival and reproductive success. The key questions then are: Which psychological mechanisms have evolved through selection and which adaptive problems did they evolve to solve (D. M. Buss, 1995)? In other words, evolutionary psychologists suggest that we look at fundamental psychological mechanisms and the functions they serve. To illustrate such efforts, we consider here the evolutionary interpretation offered by D. M. Buss (1989, 1991, 1995) of two important aspects of male-female relationships—male-female differences in mate preferences and male-female differences in causes of jealousy.

Male-Female Mate Preferences
According to evolutionary theory, dating back to Darwin, males and females have evolved different mate preferences as a result of prior selection pressures. Basically the theory revolves around two fundamental differences between men and women. First, there is the **parental investment theory**—the view that women have a greater parental investment in offspring than do men because women pass their genes on to fewer offspring. This is because of both the limited time periods during which they are fertile and, relative to men, the more limited age range during which they can produce offspring. Thus follows the suggestion that females will have stronger preferences about mating partners than will males (Trivers, 1972). Also, there is the suggestion that males and females will have different criteria for the selection of mates, the former focusing more on the reproductive potential of a partner (i.e., youth) and the latter on the mate's potential for providing resources and protection.

Second, there is the matter of **parenthood probability.** Since women carry their fertilized eggs, they can always be sure that they are the mothers of the offspring. On the other hand, males cannot be so sure that the offspring is their own and therefore must takes steps to ensure that their investment is directed toward their own offspring and not those of another male (D. M. Buss, 1989, p. 3). Thus follows the suggestion that males have greater concerns about sexual rivals and place greater value on chastity in a potential mate than do females.

Following are some of the specific hypotheses that have been derived from parental investment and parenthood probability theories (D. M. Buss, 1989; D. M. Buss, Larsen, Westen, & Semmelroth, 1992):

1. A woman's "mate value" for a man should be determined by her reproductive capacity as suggested by youth and physical attractiveness. Chastity should also be valued in terms of increased probability of paternity.
2. A man's "mate value" for a woman should be determined less by reproductive value and more by evidence of the resources he can supply, as evidenced by characteristics such as earning capacity, ambition, and industriousness.
3. Males and females should differ in the events that activate jealousy, males being more jealous about sexual infidelity and the threat to paternal probability, and females more concerned about emotional attachments and the threat of loss of resources.

D. M. Buss (1989) obtained questionnaire responses from 37 samples, representing over 10,000 individuals, from 33 countries located on 6 continents and 5 islands. There was tremendous diversity in geographic locale, culture, ethnicity, and religion. What was found? First, in each of the 37 samples males valued physical attractiveness and relative youth in potential mates more than did females, consistent with the hypothesis that males value mates with high reproductive capacity. The prediction that males would value chastity in potential mates more than females was supported in 23 out of the 37 samples, providing moderate support for the hypothesis. Second, females were found to value the financial capacity of potential mates more than did males (36 of 37 samples) and valued the characteristics of ambition and industriousness in a potential mate to a greater extent than did males (29 of 37 samples), consistent with the hypothesis that females value mates with high resource-providing capacity.

Male-Female Differences in Causes of Jealousy

In subsequent research, three studies were done to test the hypothesis of sex differences in jealousy (D. M. Buss et al., 1992). In the first study, undergraduate students were asked whether they would experience greater distress in response to sexual infidelity or emotional infidelity. Whereas 60% of the male sample reported greater distress over a partner's sexual infidelity, 83% of the female sample reported greater distress over a partner's emotional attachment to a rival.

In the second study, physiological measures of distress were taken on undergraduates who imagined two scenarios, one in which their partner became sexually involved with someone else and one in which their partner became emotionally involved with someone else. Once more males and females were found to have contrasting results, with males showing greater physiological distress in relation to imagery of their partner's sexual involvement and females showing greater physiological distress in relation to imagery of their partner's emotional involvement.

In the third study, the hypothesis that males and females who had experienced committed sexual relationships would show the same results as in the previous study but to a greater extent than would males and females who had not been involved in such a relationship was explored. In other words, actual experience in a committed relationship was important in bringing out the differential effect. This was found to

SPOTLIGHT ON THE RESEARCHER

DAVID M. BUSS:
An Evolutionary Psychology of Personality

My interest in the evolutionary psychology of personality started during my undergraduate days with my fascination with "big questions." Although not clearly formed at the time, it struck me that taking an evolutionary perspective offered the possibility of shedding light on some of the big questions in psychology, such as: What is the nature of human nature? In what ways do men and women differ, and *why* do they differ? What are the most important ways in which individuals within each sex differ? Furthermore, my specific interest in human mating stemmed in part from my observation that mating, dating, and sex seemed to be major preoccupations of people—dominating discussions with friends, inspiring fantasies and longings for love, and bringing psychological pain when things go awry. However, psychology seemed to ignore the very things that most concerned women and men in everyday life. And perhaps not by coincidence, mating happens to lie at the nexus of evolutionary approaches.

The significance of my work, I believe, lies first in demonstrating that some of the dominant assumptions of our field are radically wrong. In particular, despite the mainstream presumption that cultures are infinitely and arbitrarily variable, and that they are all-determining of our desires, my research on the mating desires of people in 37 cultures was the first to show empirically that there is remarkable universality to men's and women's desires. In other words, contrary to the view that "humans have no nature, except for the capacity to learn and the capacity for culture," it turns out that humans universally have clearly defined desires that are part of our human nature. This work was also critical in establishing the fact that some sex differences are universal—a finding that is disconcerting to those whose ideologies or theoretical perspectives somehow require men and women to be psychologically identical. At a more conceptual level, my work has been important in showing that evolutionary psychology is an important, viable, and empirically testable paradigm for psychological science.

Where is this research headed? My research is moving in two related directions. One is the study of prestige, status, and reputation—a cluster of critical, but also ignored, topics within psychology. So far I have collected data on "human prestige criteria" from Germany, Poland, China, and Guam and have data collections underway in Ethiopia, Kenya, Albania, and Turkey. Psychology, in my view, needs to become cross-cultural. The second direction, in some ways a return to my roots, involves greater attention to the evolutionary psychology of individual differences—something that has not received enough attention from evolutionary psychologists. The biggest and most exciting challenge lies ahead—creating the "ultimate theory of personality" by integrating human nature, sex differences, and individual differences.

be the case for males for whom sexual jealousy was found to be increasingly activated by experience with a committed sexual relationship. However, there was no significant difference in response to emotional infidelity between females who had and had not experienced a committed sexual relationship.

In sum, the authors interpreted the results as supportive of the hypothesis of sex differences in activators of jealousy. Although alternative explanations for the results were recognized, the authors suggested that only the evolutionary psychological framework led to the specific predictions.

Evolutionary Explanations

As previously noted, for some time evolutionary, Darwinian explanations for human behavior fell into disfavor. Today, they again are being suggested as the basis for understanding basic aspects of human psychological functioning. For some, such as Buss, they offer virtually the only hope for bringing the field of psychology into some kind of theoretical order. According to him, human behavior depends on psychological mechanisms and the only known origin of such mechanisms is evolution by natural and sexual selection. According to some, anyone interested in the social behavior of humans must take into account the evolutionary history of the behavior. According to this view, the biological roots of human nature, as expressed in the genes, are the link between evolution and behavior (Goldsmith, 1991; Kenrick, 1994).

At the same time, there are others who question just how much evolutionary theory has to say about human functioning and who also caution about the implications that may be drawn from such a view. While not denying that we have an evolutionary history, these psychologists suggest humans have progressed to the point where they are much freer of genetically programmed responses. Such psychologists also caution us concerning the interpretation of social patterns as biologically and evolutionarily based when they may be based on other grounds. For example, Cantor (1990) suggests that in focusing on the problems of survival and reproduction, evolutionary psychologists have ignored much of the diversity of social interaction and efforts to solve contemporary problems. Thus, many feminists are particularly concerned about D. M. Buss's interpretation of his data, concerned that such an interpretation ignores cultural factors and *may* suggest that such male-female differences are inevitable. What we have, then, is a powerful biological theory that is being extended to include many phenomena of interest to psychologists, the future of which remains unclear.

BEHAVIORAL GENETICS

As noted earlier, behavioral geneticists conduct research to determine genetic linkages to behavior. As we shall see, of late there also has been an effort to use the methods of behavioral genetics to study environmental effects. However, for the most part the efforts remain focused on demonstrating genetic-behavior relationships.

Three major methods are used by behavioral geneticists to establish genetic-behavior relationships: *selective breeding, twin studies,* and *adoption studies.* **Selective breeding** studies are conducted with animals. In this research animals with the trait to be studied are selected and mated. This same selection process is used with successive generations of offspring until a strain of animals is produced that is consistent within itself for the desired characteristic. It is basically this process that is used in breeding race horses and accounts for the high price bid for winning horses that will be used for stud purposes. It also is the process that has been used to establish different breeds of dogs, each of which has specific characteristics that appeal to various dog owners (Figure 5.1).

Within psychology, an early and important illustration of selective breeding was Tryon's (1940) development of strains of "bright" and "dull" rats. Tryon was able to develop two different strains such that the dullest of the bright group was brighter than almost every member of the dull group. Although subsequent research suggested that factors other than "bright-dull" were being selected for, the research demonstrated that selective breeding procedures could be used to produce groups differing on particular characteristics. With advances in the understanding and measurement of genetic effects, such procedures have become much more sophisticated. Thus, today there are efforts underway to create a map of the dog genome, that is, to determine the exact gene and combinations of genes responsible for each characteristic of dogs—anatomical structure, coat color and quality, temperament, herding or retrieving instinct, and so on.

Figure 5.1   *"We Come in Many Shapes and Sizes."* Selective breeding procedures have been used to develop animals with specific desirable characteristics.

In selective breeding research it also is possible to subject genetically different strains of animals to different developmental experiences and then to sort out the effects of genetic differences and environmental differences on the observed later behavior. For example, the roles of genetic and environmental factors in later barking behavior or fearfulness can be studied by subjecting genetically different breeds of dogs to different environmental rearing conditions (Scott & Fuller, 1965). Thus, the method of selective breeding and manipulation of developmental environments can be used to determine the genetic basis for behavioral differences, the extent to which the behavior can be modified by the environment, and the process through which such modification occurs.

Although such methods are possible with animals, ethical principles of research obviously preclude their utilization with humans. With humans we must look for "natural experiments" in which there are known variations in degree of genetic similarity and/or environmental similarity. If two organisms are identical genetically, then any later observed differences can be attributed to differences in their environments. On the other hand, if two organisms are different genetically but experience the same environment, then any observed differences can be attributed to genetic factors. While with humans we never have the ideal combination of known variations in genetic and environmental similarity, identical (monozygotic, MZ) twins and fraternal (dizygotic, DZ) twins offer an approximation to this research ideal. Monozygotic twins develop from the same fertilized egg and are identical genetically. Dizygotic twins develop from two separately fertilized eggs and are as genetically similar as any pair of siblings, sharing about 50% of their genes on the average.

The rationale for the use of **twin studies** to demonstrate the importance of genetic factors in personality can be stated as follows:

1. Since MZ twins have identical genes, any difference between them must be due to environmental differences.
2. While DZ twins differ genetically, they have many environmental conditions in common and thereby provide some measure of environmental control.
3. When both MZ and DZ twins are studied, it is possible to evaluate the effect of differing environments on the same genotype and the consequence of differing genotypes being acted upon by the same or similar environments.

In a simplified form, differences between MZ twins are environmentally determined and differences between DZ twins are genetically determined. Therefore, comparison of the extent and nature of both of these effects in relation to the same personality characteristic enables one to estimate the extent to which the characteristic is genetically determined and the extent to which it can be modified by different environmental contingencies.

The necessary conditions for making these arguments are rarely, if ever, met and the results of twin studies are not always as conclusive as one might hope. In particular, special efforts often are made to treat identical twins differently, and fraternal twins, despite their identical ages, cannot be assumed to experience the same environments. As we shall see, assessing the similarity of environments turns out to be a quite complicated matter, both because individuals with different genetic makeups experience the same environment differently and because they act in ways to create different environments. However, the results of twin studies can, at a minimum, be considered suggestive.

The study of twins has been further extended by consideration of similarities and differences between MZ twins who have been raised together and MZ twins who have been raised in different environments. Measured similarities despite rearing in different environments suggest the action of genetic factors whereas measured differences despite identical genes suggest the action of environmental factors. The rearing of MZ twins in different environments generally occurs because they have been given up for adoption and, more broadly, **adoption studies** offer another method for studying genetic and environmental effects. When adequate records are kept, it is possible to consider the similarity of adopted children to their natural (biological) parents, who have not influenced them environmentally, and the similarity to their adoptive parents, who share no genes in common with them. The extent of similarity to their biological parents is indicative of genetic factors while the extent of similarity to their adoptive parents is indicative of environmental factors.

Finally, such comparisons can be extended to families that include both biological and adoptive children. Take, for example, a family with four children; two of the children are the biological offspring of the parents and two of the children have been adopted. The two biological offspring share a genetic similarity with one another and with the biological parents that is not true for the two adopted children. Assuming the two adopted children are unrelated, they share no genes in common but share a genetic similarity with their own biological parents and any siblings who might exist in other environments. It thus is possible to compare different parent-offspring and biological sibling–adoptive sibling combinations in terms of similarity on personality characteristics. For example, one can ask whether the biological siblings are more similar to one another than are the adoptive siblings, whether they are more similar to the parents than the adoptive siblings, and whether the adoptive siblings are more similar to their biological parents or to their adoptive parents. A "yes" answer to such questions would be suggestive of the importance of genetic factors in the development of the particular personality characteristic.

It should now be clear that in twin and adoption studies we have individuals of varying degrees of genetic similarity being exposed to varying degrees of environmental similarity. By measuring these individuals on the characteristics of interest, we can determine the extent to which their genetic similarity accounts for the similarity of scores on each characteristic. For example, we can compare the IQ scores of MZ and DZ twins reared together and apart, biological (nontwin) siblings reared together and apart, adoptive siblings and biological siblings with parents, and adoptive siblings with their biological and adoptive parents. Some representative correlations are presented in Table 5.1. The data clearly suggest a relationship between greater genetic similarity and greater similarity of IQ.

It is here that we come to a statistic of great importance, that of h^2 or **heritability,** previously discussed in Chapter 2. Behavioral geneticists take correlations such as those illustrated for IQ and use them to come up with an estimate of the extent to which the variation in scores is due to genetic factors. This estimate is known as a *heritability estimate* and is represented by the figure h^2. Strictly defined, the herita-

TABLE 5.1   Average Familial IQ Correlations (R)

As genetic similarity increases, so does the magnitude of the correlations for IQ, suggesting a strong genetic contribution to intelligence.

Relationship	Average R	Number of pairs
REARED-TOGETHER BIOLOGICAL RELATIVES		
MZ twins	.86	4,672
DZ twins	.60	5,533
Siblings	.47	26,473
Parent-offspring	.42	8,433
Half-siblings	.35	200
Cousins	.15	1,176
REARED-APART BIOLOGICAL RELATIVES		
MZ twins	.72	65
Siblings	.24	203
Parent-offspring	.24	720
REARED-TOGETHER NONBIOLOGICAL RELATIVES		
Siblings	.32	714
Parent-offsping	.24	720

Note: MZ-monozygotic   DZ-dizygotic

Source: Adapted from "Familial Studies of Intelligence: A Review," by T. J. Bouchard and M. McGue, 1981, *Science, 250,* p. 1056. © American Association for the Advancement of Science. Reprinted from McGue et al., 1993, p. 60.

bility estimate is the proportion of observed variance in scores that can be attributed to genetic factors. Before turning to some of the evidence concerning the heritability of personality, it is important to keep this definition in mind and to understand the origin of the concept. The concept of heritability has its origins in biology where, for example, different seeds of the same plant could be put in the same soil and grown under the same environmental conditions. Differences in plant growth and characteristics could then be attributed to genetic differences in the seeds, with the heritability estimate reflecting the extent to which differences in plant characteristics could be attributed to genetic factors. The rationale for this procedure has been taken over by behavioral geneticists to apply to investigations of heritability of characteristics in humans.

An important point to keep in mind in relation to heritability estimates is that they refer to specific populations; that is, they relate to the variance accounted for by genetic factors *in the particular population studied.* If a different pattern of relationships were observed in two different studies, the result would be two different heritability estimates! The difference between the two different estimates might be great or small, depending on various aspects of the two populations investigated and the measures used. In addition, there are alternative ways of calculating heritability estimates that can result in somewhat differing estimates. For example, Plomin (1990a, p. 70) describes six different bases for calculating the heritability of IQ. The resulting heritability estimates vary from .30 to .72, or from 30% to 72% of the variance being attributed to genetic variance. Although we will have more to say about the heritability estimate later on, it is important to recognize what it is and what it is not—it *is* an *estimate of the variance* in a characteristic *in a particular population* that can be attributed to genetic factors and it *is not* the discovery of how much of a characteristic is due to heredity! The important point is that it is an estimate associated with a population and not a definitive measure of the action of genes.

Let us turn now to the conclusions of behavioral geneticists concerning the inheritance of personality. The following two quotes represent the overall position of current behavioral geneticists: "It is difficult to find psychological traits that reliably show no genetic influence" (Plomin & Neiderhiser, 1992) and "For almost every behavioral trait so far investigated, from reaction time to religiosity, an important fraction of the variation among people turns out to be associated with genetic variation. This fact need no longer be subject to debate" (Bouchard, Lykken, McGue, Segal, & Tellegen, 1990). By now a number of twin and adoption studies have been conducted on a wide variety of personality variables, in some cases extended over a period of time for the sample of subjects studied. At times almost startling observations are made, as when identical twins reared apart and brought together as adults are found not only to look and sound alike but to have the same attitudes and share the same hobbies and preferences for pets (Lykken, Bouchard, McGue, & Tellegen, 1993). But beyond such almost eerie observations is a pattern of results strongly suggesting, as indicated in the two quotes, an important role for heredity in almost all aspects of personality functioning.

In Chapter 2 we had the chance to consider some of the suggested genetic contributions to the Big Five personality traits, as well as the suggestion that the overall heritability of personality is 40%. Table 5.2 presents heritability estimates for a wide variety of characteristics. For comparative purposes, heritability estimates for height and weight are included, as well as a few other characteristics that may be of interest. Although single heritability estimates are given, for each characteristic a range of heritability estimates could be given indicating the varying estimates derived by different investigators studying different populations or using different estimate methods. For example, heritability estimates for IQ have ranged from .3 to .8 (30% to 80% of the variance), and for Extraversion from .32 to .65 (32% to 65% of the variance). Variation in attitude heritability has been found depending on the attitude studied. Attitudes concerning punishment of criminals and premarital sex have been found to have much higher heritability estimates than attitudes concerning economic policies and educational issues such as co-education (Eaves, Eysenck, & Martin, 1989; Tesser, 1993). Once more, however, the data suggest the overall conclusion that heredity plays an important role in virtually every aspect of personality functioning, including most attitudes.

Most psychologists familiar with the behavioral genetic data probably would agree with this conclusion and with the essence of the two previously presented quotes—

TABLE 5.2   **Heritability Estimates**

The data indicate a strong genetic contribution to personality (overall estimate of 40% of the variance), a contribution not as large as that for height,
weight, or IQ but larger than that for attitudes and behaviors such as TV
viewing.

Trait	h^2 estimate
Height	.80
Weight	.60
IQ	.50
Specific cognitive ability	.40
School achievement	.40
Big Five	
Extraversion	.36
Neuroticism	.31
Conscientiousness	.28
Agreeableness	.28
Openness to Experience	.46
EASI Temperament*	
Emotionality	.40
Activity	.25
Sociability	.25
Impulsivity	.45
Personality overall	.40
Attitudes	
Conservatism	.30
Religiosity	.16
Racial integration	.00
TV viewing	.20

* EASI = Four dimensions of temperament identified by Buss & Plomin
(1984). E = emotionality; A = Activity; S = Sociability; I = Impulsivity.
Sources: Bouchard et al., 1990; Dunn & Plomin, 1990; Loehlin, 1992;
McGue et al., 1993; Pedersen et al., 1988; Pedersen et al., 1992; Plomin,
1990; Plomin et al., 1990; Plomin & Rende, 1991; Tellegen et al., 1988; Tesser, 1993; Zuckerman, 1991.

genetic, inherited factors are important for personality. The rub comes when estimates
of the importance are given, particularly estimates of genetic importance relative to
environmental importance. Thus, some behavioral geneticists have characterized the
evidence as indicating a "strong heritability of most psychological traits" (Bouchard
et al., 1990, p. 223) and also have concluded that the family environment does
relatively little to shape personality. We will consider the issue of environmental
influences in the next section, but for now we must note the contrast between an
"important" role for genes and a "strong" heritability. There is a subtle but important

difference between the two, the latter suggesting a great deal more weight or emphasis.

Beyond these differences in interpretation, it is important to be aware of two inappropriate conclusions that can be drawn from the behavioral genetic data, *conclusions that no behavioral geneticist would consider*. First, it is possible to draw the inappropriate conclusion that the heritability estimate indicates the extent to which a characteristic is determined by heredity. Our earlier discussion was meant to safeguard against this, but further discussion is warranted. Even were one to accept the overall heritability estimate of 40% for personality, this would not mean that 40% of one's personality is inherited, or that 40% of some aspect of one's personality is inherited, or that 40% of the difference in personality between two individuals or groups of people is inherited. Similarly, a heritability estimate of 80% for IQ does not mean that 80% of intelligence is inherited, or that 80% of one's own intelligence is inherited, or that 80% of group differences in intelligence is due to heredity. Remember that the heritability estimate is a population statistic that varies with the characteristic measured, how the characteristic is measured, the age and other characteristics of the population investigated, and whether twin or adoption study data are used. Again, the heritability index is an estimate of the proportion of the variance in a characteristic, measured in a particular way, in a specific population, that can be attributed to genetic variance. It is a concept far more popular with psychologists than with biologists. Thus, the biologist Goldsmith cautions:

> Heritability does not mean the degree to which a trait is genetically determined. Consequently, a measure of heritability says exactly nothing about why any individual does or does not possess the trait. It does not speak to the role genes play in controlling the expression of the trait. Failure to understand these distinctions has a way of perpetuating the nature-nurture morass.
>
> 1991, p. 32

While appreciating such distinctions, and understanding the limits of heritability estimates, behavioral geneticists still see them as a useful first step in understanding the genetic contribution to behavior (Plomin, 1990a, p. 23).

A second inappropriate conclusion concerning heritability estimates would be the suggestion that because a characteristic has an inherited component, it cannot be changed. There is a very common assumption that if something is biological and inherited, it is fixed. Even sophisticated individuals, well aware of the flaw in this view, slip into making such a connection. Even if something is altogether determined by heredity, this does not mean that it cannot be altered by the environment. Dogs can be bred for specific characteristics but this does not mean that a particular environment cannot alter the characteristic. Similarly, individuals may be born with certain temperaments but this does not mean that their temperaments are set for life (Kagan, 1994; Kagan & Snidman, 1991a,b). Height is significantly determined by genes but can be influenced by the nutrition available in the environment. It is useful here to keep in mind Waddington's analogy of a ball rolling down a landscape. Heredity provides a contour within which the unfolding of the organism can proceed along many different paths.

THE NURTURE OF PERSONALITY

In this section we consider evidence of the effects of environment on personality. In a sense, evidence in support of the importance of the environment has already been presented in the previous section. To the extent that behavioral genetic data indicate that roughly 40% of the variance for single personality characteristics and personality overall are determined by genetic factors, then the rest of the population variance is made up of some combination of environmental effects and measurement error. Indeed, one of the interesting aspects of recent developments in behavioral genetics has been the effort to use twin and adoption study data to determine environmental effects on personality variables. Thus, although Plomin (1990a) suggests that "genetic influence is so ubiquitous and pervasive in behavior that a shift in emphasis is warranted: ask not what is heritable; ask instead what is not heritable" (p. 112), at the same time he suggests that "the other message is that the same behavioral genetic data yield the strongest available evidence for the importance of environmental influence" (p. 115).

In his book *Nature and Nurture*, Plomin (1990a) suggests that behavioral genetics has two messages: nature *and* nurture. Behavioral genetics research leads to evidence concerning the importance of genes and of the environment. It is from these two messages that the title of this chapter is derived.

The question can then be asked: What in the environment makes a difference? For example, in relation to personality, does growing up in the same family environment make a difference for personality development; that is, beyond shared genes, are siblings similar in personality as a result of being reared in the same family? What behavioral geneticists are doing is not only estimating the proportion of the population variance of a characteristic that is due to heredity, but estimating the proportion that is due to different kinds of environments. A distinction is made between *shared environments* and *nonshared environments*. **Shared environments** consist of those environments shared by siblings as a result of growing up in the same family. For example, family values and child-rearing practices may be common across siblings. **Nonshared environments** consist of those environments that are not shared by siblings growing up in the same family. For example, siblings may be treated differently by parents because of sex differences, birth order differences, or life events unique to a particular child (e.g., illness in the child or financial difficulties during the youth of one of the children).

Which environmental characteristics might be important in influencing personality development in siblings? In behavioral genetics research this is studied by comparing biological siblings who grow up in the same family environment to biological siblings who grow up in different family environments, and by comparing adopted siblings raised in the same family environment to biological siblings raised in different environments. In other words, differing degrees of resemblance in personality are studied as a function of both degree of genetic similarity and degree of shared family environment. If shared environments are important, then biological siblings raised together will be much more similar than biological siblings raised apart. They also should be much more similar to their biological parents than are the siblings raised apart. In essence, biological siblings raised together should resemble one another,

ROBERT PLOMIN:
Nature and Nurture

I attended graduate school in the personality development program of the Department of Psychology at the University of Texas at Austin in the early 1970s. Graduate students were required to enroll in a series of "core" courses. One of these core courses was behavioral genetics, and I have been hooked ever since on questions of nature (genetics) and nurture (environment).

I wanted to apply behavioral genetic research strategies to the study of development, especially personality development (Plomin, 1986). (For an introduction to behavioral genetics methods and results, see Plomin, 1990a.) I began by studying mouse behavior rather than human behavior because more powerful genetic designs are possible. However, as happens to many mouse researchers, I developed a severe allergy to mice that brought a quick end to that plan. I then began using the twin method to study inherited personality characteristics in infancy and early childhood. Arnold Buss and I wrote two books on our temperament theory of personality development that focus on parental ratings of emotionality, activity, and sociability/shyness as the most heritable personality traits early in life (A. H. Buss & Plomin, 1975, 1984). However, we now know that parental ratings of temperament are problematic. For example, an adoption study using parental ratings shows no genetic influence (Plomin, Coon, Carey, DeFries, & Fulker, 1991). Observational measures are needed (e.g., Braungart, Plomin, DeFries, & Fulker, 1992; Plomin et al., 1993).

My current research focuses on the interface between nature and nurture, that is, using behavioral genetic strategies to understand more about the environment. One topic of research is nonshared environment (Plomin & Daniels, 1987). Genetic influence on personality is important, but so too is the environment. However, the way the environment works is to make children growing up in the same family different from, not similar to, one another. Why are children growing up in the same family so different in personality? The search for such nonshared environmental influences has stimulated much recent research (e.g., Dunn & Plomin, 1990; Hetherington, Reiss, & Plomin, 1994).

A second topic at the interface between nature and nurture has been called the nature of nurture (Plomin & Bergeman, 1991). Twin and adoption studies have shown that diverse measures widely used in psychology as measures of the environment show genetic influence. Personality is likely to be part of the reason why measures of the environment show genetic influence (Plomin, 1994). For example, parenting measures might reflect genetically influenced personality characteristics of their children.

Finally, an area of increasing interest to me is the application of molecular genetic research strategies to begin to identify some of the many genes responsible for widespread genetic influence in psychology (Plomin, 1990b). Although finding genes for simple single-gene disorders is now straightforward, it is by no means easy to find genes in complex systems such as personality. Nonetheless, some personality research of this type has begun (Plomin & Saudino, 1994) and much more molecular genetic research can be expected in the near future as the human genome project continues its breathtaking progress (Plomin, 1993).

and their parents, beyond the degree that could be accounted for by common genes alone. In addition, if shared environments are important, then two adopted siblings raised together should be more similar than two such siblings raised apart. If non-shared environments are important, then these relationships should not hold. In essence, if nonshared environments are important, then siblings raised together will be no more similar than are such siblings raised apart.

On strictly intuitive, subjective grounds, we may think about the following questions: How similar are brothers and sisters in the same family beyond what would be expected by common inheritance? To what extent can we speak of a family environment in the sense of an influence common to all members of the family? Although we all recognize differences between siblings, at times striking differences, intuition tells us that when all is said and done, children in the same family do share things in common as a result of sharing the same family environment. Although we recognize sibling differences, and sometimes ask how two siblings raised in the same family can be so different, our overall impression is that generally we can say: "You know that they came from the same household." Yet, in one of the most striking findings from behavioral genetics, there is considerable evidence that shared environmental effects, experiences shared as members of the same family, are not nearly as important as nonshared environmental effects. Put differently, the unique experiences siblings have inside and outside the family appear to be far more important for personality development than the shared experiences resulting from being in the same family. Although we will go on to explore this matter in greater detail, fundamentally this is the answer suggested to the question: Why are children from the same family so different (Plomin & Daniels, 1987)? The answer: Nonshared environments!

Does the suggestion that children from the same family are different because of the effects of nonshared environments mean that family experiences are unimportant? Does this mean that early experiences are unimportant for personality development, in contrast with what psychoanalysts would have us believe? Although such conclusions have been drawn by some, this is not in fact what is suggested. Rather, the interpretation is that family influences are important, as are experiences outside the family, but it is the experiences unique to each child that are important rather than the experiences shared by children in the same family (Dunn, 1992; Dunn & Plomin, 1990). Rather than the family unit being important for investigation, it is the unique experiences of each child in the family that are important:

> Experiences in the family do not make siblings similar. The only factors important to children's development are those that are experienced differently by children in the same family. . . . In other words, environmental influences that affect development operate on an individual-by-individual basis, not on a family-by-family basis. . . . What runs in families is DNA, not shared experiences in the family.
>
> Dunn & Plomin, 1990, pp. 42–43

The evidence in support of the conclusion of little importance of shared environmental experiences comes from correlation data comparing biological and adoptive siblings growing up in the same family. These data (Table 5.3) indicate that biological

TABLE 5.3 Correlations for Siblings Growing Up in the Same Family

A comparison of similarity of biological siblings and adoptive siblings suggests an important genetic contribution to personality and a very small effect due to shared environmental experience (see Figure 5.2).

Characteristic	Correlation
Height	.50
Weight	.50
Width of mouth	.30
IQ	.47
School achievement	.50
Hypertension	.07
Asthma	.07
Diabetes	.06
Extraversion	.25
Neuroticism	.07
Personality overall	.15
MZ twins personality overall	.50
DZ twins personality overall	.30
Adoptive siblings personality overall	.05
Adoptive siblings height	.02
Adoptive siblings weight	.05

Source: Adapted from *Separate Lives: Why Siblings Are So Different,* by J. Dunn and R. Plomin, 1990, New York: Basic Books.

siblings are not all that similar in height or even in weight. However, primarily because of common genes, their correlations for both are about .50. On the other hand, the correlations for adopted siblings growing up in the same family are almost zero! This is particularly surprising for weight. One would assume that because of common eating patterns and attitudes toward weight and body shape that growing up in the same family would lead to some similarity in weight. The average sibling correlation for personality is about .15, whereas that for adoptive siblings is .05 (Dunn & Plomin, 1990, pp. 15, 48). Data such as these lead Dunn and Plomin (1990) to the conclusion that about 40% of the variance in personality is due to genetic factors, about 35% to nonshared environmental experiences, about 5% to shared environmental experiences, and the remaining 20% to error of measurement (Figure 5.2).

If family experiences are so different, and there have been challenges to this conclusion, then it becomes important to understand the environmental experiences that make children from the same family so different. One approach has been the effort to study the different experiences of children in the same family. As part of this effort, a self-report questionnaire known as **SIDE–Sibling Inventory of Differential Experiences** (Daniels & Plomin, 1985) has been developed. Individuals are asked to compare their experiences to those of their siblings in areas such as parental

Figure 5.2 Components of variance in personality.
The variance of personality is due primarily to genetic factors; environmental influence is almost entirely nonshared.

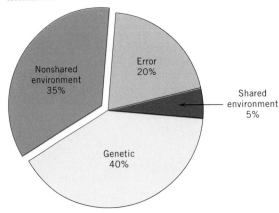

(From *Separate Lives: Why Siblings Are So Different,* by J. Dunn and R. Plomin, 1990, New York: Basic Books. ©1990, Basic Books, Inc. Reprinted by permission of Basic Books, a division of HarperCollins Publishers, Inc.)

treatment and peer relationships. Table 5.4 contains some of the questionnaire items. Not suprisingly, there is evidence of clear differences in siblings' perceptions of their parents' relationships with them (Dunn & Plomin, 1990, p.64).

Beyond any differences in *actual* parental treatment is the importance of *perceived* differences. One component is that a child experiences parental treatment at one age but observes parental treatment of a sibling when the sibling is either older or younger. It is this difference between self-observation at one age and observation of treatment of a sibling at another age that may be key to the differential sibling experiences. A study that might be of interest in this regard would involve a com-

TABLE 5.4   Illustrative Items from the Sibling Inventory of Differential Experience (SIDE)

	Toward Sibling Much More		Same		Toward Me Much More
Mother:					
Has been strict with us	1	2	3	4	5
Has enjoyed doing things with us	1	2	3	4	5
Has been sensitive to what we think and feel	1	2	3	4	5
Has disciplined us	1	2	3	4	5
Father					
Has been strict with us	1	2	3	4	5
Has enjoyed doing things with us	1	2	3	4	5
Has been sensitive to what we think and feel	1	2	3	4	5
Has disciplined us	1	2	2	4	5

Note: Scores are obtained for Affection (e.g., second and third items) and Control (e.g., first and fourth items).
Source: Separate Lives: Why Siblings Are So Different, by J. Dunn and R. Plomin, 1990, New York: Basic Books. ©1990, Basic Books, Inc. Reprinted by permission of Basic Books, a division of HarperCollins Publishers, Inc.

parison of agreement concerning parental treatment by siblings differing in age discrepancies. In other words, the question would be whether siblings closer in age show greater agreement concerning parental treatment than do siblings with a greater age disparity.

What other experiences of developmental importance do siblings from the same family not share in common? Here, of course, there is a wide range of possibilities. Depending on the age disparity, two siblings can be growing up during different cultural times—the conservative 1950s as opposed to the more radical 1960s, the "me generation" of the 1980s as opposed to the more socially involved generation of the 1990s. School experiences and experiences with peers often are quite important in personality development and here too there is enormous opportunity for differential experiences by siblings. Some of these experiences may result in good part from genetic differences between siblings. For example, the likely differential peer experiences between one child who is very attractive or very athletic as compared to the experiences of the sibling who is much less attractive or athletic. Other differential experiences may result from familial experiences that play a role in the two siblings behaving differently with peers. Finally, some of these experiences may result from chance alone—the one sibling who has an excellent teacher but the other sibling does not, the one sibling who experiences the death of a friend but the other sibling does not, the one sibling who goes on an influential trip but the other sibling does not. For better or for worse, chance encounters may play a much greater role in personality development than most of us suspect (Bandura, 1982; Lewis, 1995).

Before concluding our discussion of the nurture of personality, it is important to consider another view of the influence of family environment on personality. Hoffman (1991) is critical of the previously discussed behavioral genetics emphasis on two major grounds. First, Hoffman suggests that there are problems with such research that may result in an underestimation of the effects of shared family environments. Second, Hoffman suggests that the complexity of shared family environment effects in interaction with other effects can mask the common effects of general family styles.

Let us consider each of these points in turn. First, Hoffman challenges a number of assumptions of behavioral genetics research. For example, she questions the assumption that monozygotic and dizygotic twins have equally similar environments. She suggests that MZ twins are treated more similarly by parents than are DZ twins and, because of their greater physical similarity, are also treated more alike by peers. In addition, Hoffman notes that adoption studies often come up with different results than do twin studies and that the measures of environmental influence used in such studies are open to question. Finally, she notes that there are unique aspects to adoptive families and that some studies do show a significant role for common experiences (Rose, 1988; Tellegen et al., 1988).

Turning to the second point, Hoffman suggests that developmental psychologists have a different conception of the family environment than do behavioral geneticists. According to Hoffman, differences in perception of the same environment are recognized as are differential effects that result from the children's different ages and different genetic characteristics. Beyond this, however, is the suggestion that the same environment can have a different effect on two siblings because of differences that exist in them, differences caused by both genetic and environmental variables.

In other words, a common environmental experience might not result in a shared personality trait if such an experience is acting upon already existent differences. In addition, the effects of common environmental experiences may be masked by subsequent environmental experiences that are unique to each child. The end result is that "it is possible that there is an aspect of the family environment that has affected all of the children, but that it is expressed in different ways" (Hoffman, 1991, p. 192).

In sum, Hoffman does not question that siblings from the same family are different. Rather, she asks, why would siblings be alike? Given that the family dynamics are altered by each additional child, that the family environment is acting upon, and being acted upon, by children with already existent different characteristics, and given the multiple influences from within and outside the family that contribute to personality development, can we really expect siblings from the same family to look alike on personality traits?

To this, we can add a caveat. Measures of personality may result in siblings looking more different than they actually are. Surface differences may mask underlying similarities, that is, phenotypic differences may mask genotypic similarities. Phenotypic refers to those characteristics that are observable; genotypic to the underlying structure. For example, two siblings may share a dominance-submissive conflict or issue surrounding control. One may handle the conflict by being overly compliant and the other by being overly domineering. Or, two siblings may struggle with issues concerning the expression of anger. One may handle the conflict through the expression of explosive anger while the other may handle it through excessive inhibition. In both cases the measurement of personality in terms of observable traits may mask underlying similarities that result from common family dynamics.

Despite the differences in the Plomin-Dunn and Hoffman views, it should be noted that major common points remain. Thus, they, as well as other psychologists, agree that nurture is important—that experiences within and outside the family have important effects on personality development. They also agree that personality characteristics are multidetermined, that is, determined by multiple factors operating at one time and over time. Finally, they agree that genetic factors and environmental factors always are interacting. It is to this interactive aspect of nature and nurture that we now turn.

THE INTERACTION OF GENES WITH ENVIRONMENTS

Until now we have considered the nature and nurture of personality, treating the effects of each separately. However, as noted early in this chapter, nature and nurture always are interacting. Along with the continuous unfolding of the effects of genes and experience, three particular forms of gene-environment interactions have been distinguished (Plomin, 1990a,b; Plomin & Neiderhiser, 1992). First, there is the case of the same environmental experiences having different effects on individuals with different genetic constitutions. For example, the same behavior on the part of an anxious parent may have different effects on an irritable, unresponsive child than on a calm, responsive child. Rather than a straightforward effect of parental anxiety that is the same for both kinds of children, there is an interaction between parental behavior and child characteristic. In this case the individual is a passive recipient of environmental events. Genetic factors are interacting with environmental factors but only in a passive, reactive sense.

In a second kind of nature-nurture interaction, individuals with different genetic constitutions may evoke different responses from the environment. For example, the irritable, withdrawn child may evoke a different response from the parent than will a calm, responsive child. It often is interesting to see a group of relatives looking at just-born infants in the hospital nursery. Aside from their interest in their own new relatives, as a group they tend to show more or less interest in the other infants. They immediately identify some as cute and others as having a face "only a mother could love," some as being very active and others as being very quiet, some as looking intelligent and others as looking unintelligent. Such initial differences can have important implications for the developing parent-child bond. For example, take the newly born infant who is irritable and an anxious parent interacting with a neonate for the first time. Contrast this to same parent interacting with a calm neonate. In the former case, the irritable neonate is likely to increase the anxiety of the parent while in the latter case the anxiety of the parent is likely to be diminished. In the former case, the parent may feel that he or she is "a terrible parent," while in the latter case the parent may be reassured that he or she is "a good parent," even though the neonate's behavior had nothing to do with the parent's behavior! However, the different parental behaviors evoked by the two infants can now set in motion two completely different patterns of parent-child interaction.

The importance of evoked environmental effects continues throughout development. Probably the first such difference has to do with gender—"It's a boy" as opposed to "It's a girl." But beyond this, at an early age children start to associate personality characteristics with body builds and thereby treat peers differently depending on these associations. Children of medium build are expected to be more assertive and athletic than children of slender build or of heavy, round build. Attractive children or athletic children call forth different peer responses than do less attractive or athletic children (Brehm, 1992). In each case, a genetically determined characteristic evokes a differential response from the environment. In these cases, physical features have been used for illustrative purposes. However, personality characteristics with genetic components operate along similar lines. The constitutionally shy, inhibited child elicits different peer responses than does the constitutionally extraverted child.

In a third form of gene-environment interaction, individuals with different constitutions seek out, modify, and create different environments. Once the individual is able to interact actively with the environment, which occurs at a fairly early age, genetic factors influence the selection and creation of environments. The extravert seeks out different environments than does the introvert, the athletic individual different environments than the nonathletic individual, and the musically gifted individual different environments than the individual gifted in visual imagery. These effects increase over the course of time as individuals become increasingly able to select their own environments. By a certain point in time, it is impossible to determine the extent to which the individual has been the "recipient" of an environmental effect as opposed to the "creator" of the environmental effect.

In sum, individuals can be relatively passive recipients of environments; they can play a role in environmental events through the responses they evoke; and they can play an active role in selecting and creating environments. In each case, there is a nature-nurture, gene-environment interaction. Because of such interactions, behavioral geneticists now emphasize the genetic influences on environmental measures, or *environmental genetics* (Plomin & Bergeman, 1991; Plomin & Neiderhiser, 1992; Plomin & Rende, 1991). In other words, in studying the effects of nature on nurture, we can no longer assume that our measure of the environment is free of genetic influences. This is true for both the perception of environments as well as the objective assessment of environments. In terms of the subjective experiencing of environments, individuals with different genetic endowments will give different descriptions of what are objectively the same environments. In terms of the objective assessment of environments, observations of parents interacting with their children make clear just how much the children influence the unfolding of the parental environment (Kagan, 1994). Early on nature and nurture begin to interact, starting a process that continues throughout the life of the individual.

THE NATURE AND NURTURE OF PERSONALITY: CONCLUSION

This chapter has considered the nature and nurture of personality. We began by considering the importance of genes for personality, in terms of ways that the operation of genes makes us similar as humans and the ways in which it makes us unique as individuals. Our evolutionary history suggests that there is something common to us all as members of the human species, while our genetic inheritance tells us that each of us is unique in many ways. We then went on to consider the importance of the environment, suggesting that there is considerable evidence of environmental influences on personality, although it has been hard to define the relation of specific environmental effects to specific personality characteristics. Part of the reason for this is the multiple determinants of personality—the multiple genes influencing most important personality characteristics, the multiple environmental forces operating at any given time, and the multiple ways in which heredity and environment interact.

In thinking about complex issues, it is easy to fall into either-or forms of thinking, as seen in the nature versus nurture controversy. The emphasis here, instead, has been on the continuous interplay between genes and experience, between heredity and environment, between nature and nurture in the formation of behavior. Thus, the biologist Timothy Goldsmith (1991) suggests that to attribute behavior to one or the other is about as fruitful as arguing whether it is the sugar or the flour that makes the cake. He further goes on to suggest that "understanding is not furthered by trying to allocate a percentage of human behavior that can be accounted for by the genes, with the balance to be attributed to culture" (p. 87). According to him, as well as other biologists, we probably will never be able to determine to what extent any human action is genetically or culturally determined. In fact, many would suggest that such a question has no meaning in the first place. Whether or not we continue to use heritability estimates, we must always keep in mind that they are but estimates of genetic contributions to variance in a particular population, not facts concerning how much of personality is genetically determined. It is hoped that by now the complexity of the interaction between nature and nurture is so apparent that such simple answers are understood to be impossible.

MAJOR CONCEPTS

Behavioral genetics.   The study of genetic contributions to behaviors of interest to psychologists, mainly through the comparison of degrees of similarity among individuals of varying degrees of biological-genetic similarity.

Genes.   Elements in chromosomes by which hereditary characteristics are transmitted.

Ultimate causes.   Explanations for behavior associated with evolution.

Proximate causes.   Explanations for behavior associated with current biological processes in the organism.

Parental investment theory.   The evolutionary theory that males and females differ in degree of investment in offspring.

Parenthood probability.   The evolutionary view that male-female differences in behavior are associated with differences in certainty concerning parenthood.

Selective breeding.   An approach to establishing genetic-behavior relationships through the breeding of successive generations with a particular characteristic.

Twin studies.   An approach to establishing genetic-behavior relationships through the comparison of degree of similarity among identical twins, fraternal twins, and nontwin siblings. Generally combined with adoption studies.

Adoption studies.   An approach to establishing genetic-behavior relationships through the comparison of biological siblings reared together with biological siblings reared apart through adoption. Generally combined with twin studies.

Heritability (h^2).   The proportion of observed variance in scores in a specific population that can be attributed to genetic factors.

Shared and nonshared environments. The comparison in behavior genetics research of the effects of siblings growing up in the same or different environments. Particular attention is given to whether siblings reared in the same family share the same family environment.

SIDE—Sibling Inventory of Differential Experiences.   A questionnaire used to study perceptions of siblings of their family environment.

Environmental genetics.   The study of genetic influences on environmental measures.

SUMMARY

1.   This chapter considers the genetic and environmental determinants of personality, an area that historically has been filled with controversy involving scientific,

political, and social issues. Although we can consider the importance of genes and environments separately, personality characteristics are always developing as a function of their joint operation.

2.   Inherited characteristics are influenced by the operation of genes that direct the biological functioning of the body. Most personality characteristics are likely influenced by the interaction among multiple genes.

3.   Evolutionary theory concerns ultimate causes of behavior, that is, why the behavior of interest evolved and the adaptive function it served. Work in the area of male-female mate preferences, emphasizing sex differences in parental investment and parenthood probability, and in male-female differences in causes of jealousy, illustrate research associated with evolutionary interpretations of human behavioral characteristics.

4.   Three methods used to establish genetic-behavior relationships are selective breeding, twin studies, and adoption studies. Twin and adoption studies lead to significant heritability estimates for intelligence and most personality characteristics. The overall heritability for personality has been estimated to be approximately .4, that is, approximately 40% of the variance in personality characteristics is due to genetic factors. However, there is evidence of variability of heritability estimates depending on the population studied, personality characteristic studied, and measures used.

5.   While recognizing the important contribution of genes to personality, it also is important to keep in mind that heritability estimates refer to population estimates rather than estimates of the contributions of genes to individual characteristics or estimates of genetic contributions to individual or group differences. In addition, it is important to keep in mind that "genetically influenced" should not be equated with fixed or nonmalleable.

6.   Behavioral genetic research also suggests an important environmental influence on personality. Such research has led behavioral geneticists to conclude that biological siblings are different not only because of genetic differences but also because of the importance of nonshared environments relative to shared environments. In part, as evidenced in research with the SIDE questionnaire, children from the same family report different parental treatment and peer relationships. Such research need not, however, lead to the conclusion that family experiences and early experience are unimportant in personality development.

7.   In terms of gene-environment interactions, the same environment has different implications for individuals with different genetic constitutions. In addition, individuals with different genetic constitutions evoke different responses from the environment and select different environments in which to function.

8.   The interaction between nature and nurture is such that simple answers to complex questions are impossible. There is never gene without environment or environment without gene; that is, we must always be aware of the nature and nurture of personality.

CHARTING PEOPLE'S LIVES OVER TIME

6

CHAPTER OVERVIEW

In this chapter we consider the ways in which people are stable over time, the ways in which they change, and the factors contributing to stability and change. The questions here are complex, involving the issues of defining and measuring stability and change. In addition, research suggests significant individual differences in degree of stability or change. Studies of people over time are useful in considering such questions and a number of studies are considered. Ultimately, the issue facing us is understanding the processes involved in personality stability and change over time.

Questions to Be Addressed in This Chapter

1 How stable is personality over time? Can we predict from one point in time what a person will be like at a later point in time?

2 How do we recognize underlying continuities in personality despite seeming (phenotypic) changes?

3 How can we make sure that our measures of the same characteristic at different ages are comparable?

4 Why is longitudinal research so difficult and what is distinctive about what we can learn from it?

It is interesting to think about people's lives over time and to consider whether we could have predicted what would unfold. Given a particular starting point, whether birth, childhood, or adolescence, can we anticipate the unfolding of an individual's life? How many of the presidents of the United States would have been recognized in their youth as potential leaders of their country? Consider three of the most influential scientists of the century—Darwin, Einstein, and Freud. At what point could one have recognized the magnitude of their future contributions and influence? Freud's admiring biographer Ernest Jones commented that by the time Freud was age 30, he was "a first class neurologist, a hard worker, a close thinker, but—with the exception perhaps of the book on aphasia—there was little to foretell the existence of genius" (E. Jones, 1953, p. 220).

One hears people express two opposite points of view: On the one hand, "I always knew he would be a . . ." or "From the day she was born, you knew she was headed for . . ." On the other hand, people also say, "Who would have figured that he would end up doing . . ." or "I never would have guessed she would become a . . ." Some believe you can anticipate the path of the life of at least some people. Others believe you cannot. As the great Yankee catcher Yogi Berra once said: "It ain't over 'til it's over." Or, as the great movie producer Samuel Goldwyn is reported to have said: "Only a fool would make predictions, especially about the future."

Consider the unfolding of the lives of some of the most well-known figures of the 1960s. Two of the leaders of the demonstrations at the Democratic National Convention in 1968 were Abbie Hoffman and Jerry Rubin. They were advocates of radical political reform. In subsequent years neither became an influential figure, but what is interesting is that Hoffman remained committed to his radical views while Rubin became a Wall Street investor. Consider another pair. Timothy Leary and Richard Alpert were two of the leaders of the drug-using, mind-expanding, psychedelics movement. They came from very different backgrounds, worked together as psychologists at Harvard University, and gained notoriety by involving Harvard graduate students in their use of psychedelics for "mind-expanding" purposes. In subsequent years, Alpert became interested in Eastern religion and is now known as Ram Dass. Leary became an entertainer. A further note of interest here is that many psychologists were amazed at Alpert's dramatic transformation from a conventional psychologist and son of a wealthy and influential family to a cultfigure. Yet, the well-known personality psychologist David McClelland, who headed the program at Harvard where Leary and Alpert worked, commented that the change was not as remarkable as people might have thought—underlying the vast overt, **phenotypic** differences were underlying, **genotypic** commonalities. For example, underlying the seeming personality changes were motives to be influential, recognized, and esteemed. Although different in manifestation, the underlying motives remained the same.

These vignettes bring two groups of questions to mind. First, *how stable is personality over extended periods of time?* Is it more stable over some periods than others? Are some aspects of personality more stable than others? Are the personalities of some people more stable than those of others? Why? Second, *how do we recognize underlying continuities in personality despite seeming (phenotypic) discontinuity?* As the person develops, how can we measure personality characteristics in age-appropriate ways so that comparisons are possible? For example, if we are interested in sociability or aggression, how should we measure such personality characteristics in adults relative to their measurement in childhood and perhaps even in infancy? Can measures of intelligence in infancy be comparable to measures of intelligence in adulthood? Are we to consider personality change as any difference in behavior between two points in time or can we distinguish between quantitative changes and qualitative changes? And, even within qualitative changes, can we distinguish between a qualitative change that is *continuous* with an earlier pattern, such as the assertive person who expresses this characteristic in a different way, and a qualitative change that is *discontinuous* with an earlier pattern, such as the shy person who becomes very sociable? And, perhaps most difficult of all, can we distinguish between change in a particular characteristic or aspect of a person's functioning and change in the overall organization of the person's personality?

In what follows, we first consider stage theories that suggest a natural progression to the development of personality. Then we consider longitudinal studies of personality and the evidence for stability and change, continuity and discontinuity, in personality development. Finally, we consider factors operating to promote change and development as opposed to those factors that operate to keep the organism as it is.

STAGE THEORIES OF PERSONALITY

Some psychologists view development in terms of stages. **Stage theories** of development have three defining qualities. First, they view development in terms of *stages* or periods of time during which the organism can be described in terms of specific characteristics. Different stages are associated with different qualitative characteristics. In other words, the stages represent qualitative changes in the nature of the organism. Second, each stage is assumed to occur during a specific time period. This time period generally has a range, beginning earlier in some individuals and later in others but it typically has some boundaries defining the time during which the stage is expected to occur. Some boys and girls develop secondary sex characteristics earlier than others, some later than others, but there is a period of time during which these characteristics are expected to develop in all boys and girls. Third, there is a *fixed sequence* or *fixed progression* of stages. Each stage, with its own defining set of characteristics, is assumed to follow upon a specific previous stage and to be followed by a specific later stage.

Most psychological theories of developmental stages are based on observation. Within developmental psychology, the best-known stage theorist is Jean Piaget (1896–1980). Piaget proposed that infant and child cognitive development can be described in terms of a series of stages, each with its own defining characteristics and period of time during which it is expected to occur. Piaget's theory of cognitive development was based on clinical observations, followed by systematic research to explore the development of cognitive abilities in children.

FREUD'S PSYCHOSEXUAL STAGES OF DEVELOPMENT

The best-known stage theory of personality development is Freud's theory of the *psychosexual stages of development.* According to Freud, the source of the instincts or drives is in states of bodily tension. The area of the body that serves as a source of bodily tension, and thereby instinctual (drive) energy is called an **erogenous zone.** Developmentally there is a biologically determined shift in the major erogenous zones of the body. Thus, at any one time the major source of excitation and energy tends to be located in a particular erogenous zone, with the location of that zone changing during the early developmental years. The first erogenous zone is the mouth, the second the anus, and the third the genitals. The mental and emotional growth of the child is dependent on the social interactions, anxieties, and gratifications that occur in relation to these zones.

During the oral stage of development, when the source of bodily excitation is focused on the mouth, there is gratification in feeding, thumb sucking, and other mouth movements characteristic of infants. In adult life, traces of orality are seen in chewing gum, eating, smoking, and kissing. In other words, the form of expression changes, but there is a tie to the earlier stage and mode of gratification. According to this theory of character development, which suggests that personality development is strongly influenced by gratifications and frustrations experienced during the first five years of life, excessive frustration during this period leads to the development of the *oral personality.* Personality characteristics associated with this character type include being demanding, impatient, envious, covetous, jealous, mistrustful, pessimistic, and depressed (feeling empty). This is not to say that an individual characterized as an oral personality has all of these personality characteristics, but rather that many of them occur together to form a pattern.

Perhaps most descriptive of the personality type associated with the oral stage of development is the **narcissistic personality** (Emmons, 1987; Raskin & Hall, 1981). Basic to the functioning of the narcissistic personality is a focus on the self and an interest in others in terms of how they can "feed" the individual's self-esteem. These individuals tend to have an exaggerated feeling of being *entitled* to things from others, of *deserving* the admiration and love of others, and of being *special* or unique. They tend to make frequent references to themselves in their speech (Raskin & Shaw, 1987) and to be demanding of the attention of others. Once more, in terms of the theory, there is a change in the adult manifestation (phenotype) of the characteristics, but the basic, underlying personality structure (genotype) remains the same.

Returning to the other stages in the psychosexual theory of personality development, the second stage is the *anal stage* (ages 2 amd 3), during which excitation is located in the anus. During this stage pleasure is associated with the expulsion of the feces, which stimulates the mucous membranes of that region. However, the pleasure associated with such movement brings the child into conflict with the requirements of others to delay. Associated with the gratifications and frustrations of this period is the development of the *anal personality.* The traits of the anal personality relate to the bodily and interpersonal processes occurring during the anal stage of development—the accumulation and release of feces and the struggle of wills over toilet training. Thus, some of the traits associated with the anal personality are striving for power and control, pleasure in possessions, anxiety over waste and loss of control, and concern with whether to submit or rebel.

Finally, in the *phallic stage* (ages 4 and 5) of development, excitation and tension come to focus in the genitals. The male child develops erections, and the new excitations in this area lead to increased interest in the genitals and the realization that the female lacks a penis. This, together with the development of a rivalry with the father for the affections of the mother (Oedipus complex), leads to *castration anxiety*—the fear that he may lose his penis. For the female child during this period there is similarly an experiencing of excitation in the genitals. For her, however, this is associated with the awareness of the lack of a penis. For the female this stage is associated with the development of a rivalry with the mother for the affections of the father. The biological differentiation between the sexes during this stage is associated with different psychological developments. Thus, for the male child later traits associated with this period include competitiveness and an emphasis on being strong or potent, whereas for the female child later traits associated with this period include exhibitionism and a combination of seductiveness with naivete (Table 6.1).

Freud's theory of the psychosexual stages of development has been criticized in general for its excessive emphasis on biological developments and by feminists in particular for the way in which it portrays women. It also has been criticized on research grounds, although some evidence in support of the theory can be found (Pervin, 1993a). The point of presentation here, however, is not to evaluate its merits as a theory but rather to illustrate a stage theory of personality development. From this standpoint we can see how Freud suggested that early biological and psychological development consists of a fixed sequence of stages, each occurring at an approximate point in time and each with its own set of defining characteristics. In addition, each is associated with a pattern of adult personality characteristics. The form of expression of these adult personality characteristics represents a change from their expression in childhood. However, according to the theory, the basic underlying character structure remains the same regardless of the change in outer manifestation (phenotype) of the same underlying personality structure (genotype).

ERIKSON'S PSYCHOSOCIAL STAGES OF DEVELOPMENT

In contrast to Freud's emphasis on biology and the development of the instincts, Erik Erikson focused on the social developments that occur at various stages. In addition, he extended the list of stages of development and their implications for personality through adulthood and the later years (Table 6.2).

TABLE 6.1 Personality Characteristics Associated With Psychoanalytic Personality Types

Personality Type	Personality Characteristics
Oral	Demanding, impatient, envious, covetous, jealous, rageful, depressed (feels empty), mistrustful, pessimistic
Anal	Rigid, striving for power and control, concerned with shoulds and oughts, pleasure in possessions, anxiety over waste and loss of control, concern with whether to submit or rebel
Phallic	*Male:* exhibitionistic, competitive, striving for success, emphasis on being masculine-macho-potent *Female:* naive, seductive, exhibitionistic, flirtatious

TABLE 6.2   Erikson's Eight Psychosocial Stages of Development and Their Implications for Personality

Psychosocial Stage	Age	Positive Outcomes	Negative Outcomes
Basic Trust vs. Mistrust	1	Feelings of inner goodness, trust in oneself and others, optimism	Sense of badness, mistrust of self and others, pessimism
Autonomy vs. Shame and Doubt	2–3	Exercise of will, self-control, able to make choices	Rigid, excessive conscience, doubtful, self-conscious, shame
Initiative vs. Guilt	4–5	Pleasure in accomplishments, activity, direction, and purpose	Guilt over goals contemplated and achievements initiated
Industry vs. Inferiority	Latency	Able to be absorbed in productive work, pride in completed product	Sense of inadequacy and inferiority, unable to complete work
Identity vs. Role Diffusion	Adolescence	Confidence of inner sameness and continuity, promise of a career	Ill at ease in roles, no set standards, sense of artificiality
Intimacy vs. Isolation	Early Adulthood	Mutuality, sharing of thoughts, work, feelings	Avoidance of intimacy, superficial relations
Generativity vs. Stagnation	Adulthood	Ability to lose oneself in work and relationships	Loss of interest in work, impoverished relations
Integrity vs. Despair	Later Years	Sense of order and meaning, content with self and one's accomplishments	Fear of death, bitter about life and what one got from it or what did not happen

Consider the first stage. According to Erikson this stage is significant not just because of the localization of pleasure in the mouth, but because in the feeding situation a relationship of trust or mistrust develops between the infant and the caregiver. Similarly, the anal stage is significant not only for the change in the nature of the major erogenous zone, but also because toilet training is a significant social situation in which the child may develop a sense of autonomy or succumb to shame and self-doubt. In the phallic stage the child must struggle with the issue of taking pleasure in, as opposed to feeling guilty about being assertive, competitive, and successful.

Whereas Freud viewed the first 5 years of life as determining the basic character structure of the individual, Erikson is less deterministic in this regard. As noted, later stages of development have their own associated issues and offer opportunities for new developments and positive outcomes. For example, the crucial task of adolescence is the establishment of a sense of ego identity, an accrued confidence that the way one views oneself has a continuity with one's past and is matched by the perception of others. In contrast to people who develop a sense of identity, people with role diffusion experience the feeling of not really knowing who they are, of not knowing whether who they think they are matches what others think of them, and of not knowing how they have developed in this way or where they are heading in the future. During late adolescence and the college years, this struggle with a sense of identity may lead to joining a variety of groups and to considerable anguish about the choice of a career. If these issues are not resolved during this time, the individual is, in later life, filled with a sense of despair; life is too short, and it is too late to start all over again.

Erikson is perhaps best known for his emphasis on the **identity versus role diffusion** stage, and it is this stage that has attracted some of the greatest research interest. Erikson's stage theory was based on clinical observation. In an interview study of college students, Marcia (1966, 1980) extended Erikson's work on this stage by defining four possible identity outcomes: Identity Achievement, Moratorium, Identity Diffusion, and Foreclosure. Ideally the person leaves this stage with the achievement of an identity. This includes some exploration of alternative values and career goals, including some that may be in opposition to those of his or her parents, and the readiness to make a commitment. In the case of Moratorium, the exploration and examination continue, often with considerable obsessive preoccupation and anxiety, without the movement toward a commitment. In the case of Identity Diffusion, there is a lack of sense of direction but without the continued struggle characteristic of those in the Moratorium outcome. Finally, in the case of Foreclosure there is a commitment to values and goals but without consideration of alternatives. The commitment here is premature and may be based on an excessive need to adhere to parental values and goals or an excessive fear of dealing with the uncertainty associated with exploration.

As is true of most stage theorists, Erikson does not view the stages as completely independent of one another. The individual develops as a totality. Thus, each stage is influenced by what has occurred in prior stages and has implications for developments in the stages that follow. For example, the individual capable of establishing a stable identity may be helped to do so by earlier being able to take pleasure in accomplishments and direction (initiative) as opposed to feeling guilty about goals and achievements (guilt). And, the individual who established such a stable identity is in a better position than one who leaves that stage without such an identity to go on to form stable and intimate interpersonal relationships (Kahn, Zimmerman, Csikszentmihalyi, & Getzels, 1985).

A young man in his twenties who came to me as a patient illustrates this principle of stage-relatedness. He was experiencing severe depression following the inability to complete some work necessary to finalize his career choice. It was not that he lacked the ability but instead was so overcome with anxiety about his choice, and what it meant to him, that he could not complete the necessary tasks. Following this he felt enormous guilt since his family had always expected him to pursue this career. In addition, he felt that he was a total failure and that life now was over for him—without a career he was nothing. Interestingly enough, in adolescence he never had gone through the exploration and crises so often associated with satisfactory establishment of an ego identity. Rather, he forced himself to adopt his parents' values and to pursue the path chosen for him. At the time he both took pleasure in this commitment but also recognized his relief at not having to deal with the struggle of exploration. And, his premature foreclosure of the identity issue could be tied to earlier childhood experiences in which he always compared himself unfavorably to his father but felt guilty about embarking upon an independent path.

In sum, Erikson's contributions are noteworthy in three ways:

1. He emphasized the psychosocial as well as the biological basis for personality development;
2. He extended the psychoanalytic stages of development to include the entire life cycle and articulated the major issues to be faced in the later stages;
3. He recognized that people look to the future as well as to the past, and that how they construe their future may be as significant a part of their personality as how they construe their past.

At the same time, in keeping with other stage theorists, he emphasized a sequence of stages, occurring during prescribed times, with defining issues and possible positive and negative outcomes. And, while defining the opportunities for development associated with each stage, he also noted the dependence of developments during one stage on those of earlier stages and their influence on developments during later stages. As with other personality stage theorists, his interest was in the broad, system-wide effects of developments during each stage. In other words, how the issue associated with each stage was resolved was seen as having broad implications for personality development rather than only influencing the development of an isolated component.

CRITIQUE OF STAGE THEORIES OF DEVELOPMENT

Stage theories of development emphasize a fixed sequence of stages, each with its own characteristics and beginning and ending at an approximate age point. In addition, many such stage theories suggest that the stages represent **critical periods** in development; that is, if the prescribed development does not occur during that period, then it will not develop in the appropriate form during later periods of development. The theories presented, as well as other stage theories of development, vary in the extent to which they emphasize each of these features. Thus, the psychoanalytic theory of psychosexual stages expresses all of these characteristics while other developmental views place greater emphasis on gradual successions of development and less emphasis on critical periods.

Although graphic in their stage images, and useful in delineating the importance of certain processes occurring at different points in time, stage theories have come in for considerable criticism. First, questions have been raised as to whether development must occur in a fixed sequence and the relation between developments at various points in time. For example, is it possible to skip one stage or pass through it rapidly while making up time? Are developments at one stage transformed as the individual moves on to the next stage or are developments of each stage layered on top of one another? For example, does one always have various levels of self-perception and self-consciousness or does the development of self-consciousness replace earlier levels of development?

Another point of criticism, in particular by social cognitive theorists, is the generality of development implied by stage theories. While stage theories tend to imply a uniform level of development at a particular stage, social cognitive theorists emphasize that developments in various areas or domains can proceed at different rates. Bandura (1986) argues that development occurs in specialized areas rather than in global structures. One develops specific rather than global competencies. Regarding cognitive development, Bandura suggests that

> cognitive stages presumably comprise qualitatively different modes of thinking that are uniform within each stage. Higher stages are achieved by transforming lower ones. The assumption of stratified uniformities of thought, however, is at variance with empirical findings. The level of cognitive functioning commonly varies across different domains of content.

> 1986, p. 484

Finally, we come to the issue of critical periods, which "imply a sharply defined phase of susceptibility preceded by and followed by lack of susceptibility" (Bateson & Hinde, 1987). The term was used by the distinguished ethologist Konrad Lorenz to describe the importance of particular experiences at specific periods of development. For example, there is the phenomenon known as *imprinting*—a young duckling quickly learns to direct its following behavior toward its mother when it observes her movement. The period during which imprinting occurs begins soon after hatching and ends some days later. What is striking is the specific time period during which such imprinting will occur and how, during that time, the young duckling will imprint itself (i.e., learn to follow) other moving objects if not exposed to the mother. Both before and after this period, the imprinting phenomenon does not occur. Or, to take another example, birds will learn their species-characteristic song only if it is heard during a specific early period of development.

Observations such as these led to the view of critical periods as fixed time periods for environmental effects with ominous consequences for development if these environmental inputs did not occur during the prescribed time. The psychoanalytic view of stages of character development is in accord with such a view. Today, however, such a view is being called into question and the concept of critical periods is being replaced by that of *sensitive periods* (Bornstein, 1987, 1989; Wachs, 1992). At this point there appears to be little general support for the view of fixed periods of development with permanent negative effects if the appropriate environmental stimuli are not present during that time. Instead, greater, although not necessarily unlimited, flexibility and plasticity are recognized. Thus, the concept of **sensitive periods** "implies a phase of greater susceptibility preceded and followed by lower sensitivity, with relatively gradual transitions" (Bateson & Hinde, 1987, p. 20).

It should be clear that the concept of sensitive periods does not completely do away with the importance of developmental periods, nor does it suggest unlimited openness and plasticity in the development of the organism. Rather, it softens the relatively fixed influence of particular effects suggested by the critical periods concept. Thus, the concept of sensitive periods suggests that the organism is particularly sensitive to particular environmental effects during limited periods of time. However, it also suggests that this influence need not be permanent or irreversible under any later circumstances. The concept of sensitive periods recognizes that not all forms of stimuli are equally important at all stages of development. It also recognizes that the importance of such stimuli at particular times does not mean the effects of its presence or absence are irreversible. However, change at later points in time may require very special conditions. For example, it is suggested that periods of high stress and considerable environmental impact may be necessary to alter in adulthood the behaviors established in early childhood (Bateson & Hinde, 1987).

In sum, we may wish to make use of the concept of stages of development as descriptive of the importance of certain periods of time and of sequences of typical quantitative and qualitative changes. Certain periods of time are more important than others for the development of particular characteristics, and certain kinds of environmental input are more important than others during these periods. And, there does appear to be a natural sequence to the unfolding of many characteristics. At the same time, the process of development does not appear to be as global, fixed, and rigid as a literal translation of stage theories might suggest. Although not unlimited, there does appear to be considerable flexibility and plasticity to development. We will have a chance to consider these issues in further detail in the next section as we review findings from longitudinal research.

LONGITUDINAL STUDIES OF DEVELOPMENT

Longitudinal research consists of studies of the same individuals over extended periods of time with repeated measurements at various time intervals. Such studies can be contrasted to one-shot pieces of research and to **cross-sectional research,** in which the variables of interest are studied simultaneously in different age groups. For example, in cross-sectional research on aggression, measures of aggression might be obtained at the same time on children, adolescents, and adults to look at changes in level and expression of aggression from childhood through adulthood. In contrast, in longitudinal studies of aggression the same individuals are assessed at these differing points in time.

Cross-sectional research allows one to consider age trends in personality characteristics and is easier to conduct than longitudinal research. In such research one also hopes to be able to infer causal links between the variables of interest, such as patterns of child rearing and the development of patterns of aggression. However, cross-sectional research has two major limitations. First, one has to infer causal links rather than actually following the links as they are established. Second, differences in scores between age groups may be more a function of social changes than of age trends. For example, if one measured interest in rock music in adolescents, young adults, and middle-aged adults, one might conclude that there is a shift toward decreased interest over time. However, in fact, this might have to do with changes in music interest with different social times. Similarly, members of a particular generation may be affected by such dramatic events as depressions and wars, with differential scores on variables reflecting the effects of these specific events rather than changes based on age (Elder, 1974, 1979; Elder & Caspi, 1988).

In contrast to these limitations of cross-sectional research, longitudinal research allows one to study the developmental process as it unfolds. Such research allows not only the study of the progression of single variables, but also the development of patterns of relationships over time. Although the findings of any one longitudinal study need to be replicated by other such studies, in particular other studies at different points in time and in different cultures, clearly the potential advantages of longitudinal research are many. At the same time, such studies are not conducted as often as one might expect because of the many difficulties associated with them. As with any such research, there is the problem of finding equivalent measures for the personality characteristic of interest for different age groups. How are intelligence, sociability, ego strength, and so on to be measured in children, adolescents, young adults, middle-aged adults, and the aged? But, beyond this, longitudinal research requires a long time horizon and considerable financial commitment. The investigators will not know their results for a considerable period of time, and this is difficult to endure in a field that requires constant evidence of productivity. And, one has to be confident that funds will be available on a continuing basis to make possible follow-up studies 10, 20, 30 years down the road. Finally, one has to hope that subjects will still be alive, can be located, and are willing to participate as subjects at later points in time. All of these are reasons why studying people the longitudinal way is also seen as studying people the hard way (J. Block, 1993; Funder, Parke, Tomlinson-Keasey, & Widaman, 1993).

STABILITY AND CHANGE IN PERSONALITY DEVELOPMENT

In reviewing the results of longitudinal research, we are particularly concerned with patterns of stability and change in personality. The issue of stability and change is not a simple one, and many psychologists have biases toward viewing personality as relatively stable or as relatively flexible. Thus, whereas some believe that "the zebra can as easily change his stripes as the adult his personality" (J. B. Watson, 1928, p. 138), others are much more optimistic in this regard. Sometimes the influence of such biases is subtle: The Personality Science Weekend program at the 1992 convention of the American Psychological Association was titled, Can Personality Change? Sometimes, as will be pointed out later, such biases influence which personality variables are studied, how they are studied, and how the results are interpreted. Therefore, before beginning our consideration of some longitudinal studies, it may be useful to consider just what is meant by stability and change in personality.

Let us begin this discussion by examining some illustrations. If we consider changes in height and weight over time, it is clear that children get taller and gain weight; that is, there are changes in height and weight. However, suppose a group of individuals remains average in height and weight. Do we say that their height and weight have changed, because of absolute changes, or do we say that their height and weight have remained stable, because of their relative position? To take another example, throughout childhood, perhaps throughout life, people gain in knowledge, but does their intelligence change? Consider some other examples. If we pour some water into the kettle, turn the gas on, and observe steam come out of the kettle as the water boils, do we say that change has occurred (i.e., the water has changed into steam)? Or, instead of putting the water into the kettle, we put it outside on an extremely cold day. As we observe the water turn into ice, do we say that change has occurred? The water, steam, and ice seem so very different, yet we know that structurally they all are made up of H_2O, in which case perhaps we should not be suggesting that change has occurred at all. Or, what about the larva that becomes a caterpillar and then a moth? There is structural change, but it is the same animal. Or is it? Is the situation different with humans when we observe their transformation from infant into adult? Should we say that they are the same person, emphasizing stability, or are we to emphasize how much they have changed? Note the following question: "What about you would have to change for you to no longer consider yourself to be you?" In other words, how much change and what kind of change is necessary for one to say that "real" change has occurred?

As these examples illustrate, an answer to what is meant by stability and change is not straightforward. There are all different kinds of stability and change, and different means of measuring them. In relation to personality development, we can contrast four kinds of change. First, there is *absolute change* and *relative change*. A person may change in absolute height or weight but remain the same relative to others. Or, a person might become more uninhibited over time but still remain average for their age and peer group. In each case there has been an absolute change for the individual but not a change relative to others in his or her age and peer group.

Another distinction to be considered is that between *quantitative change* and *qualitative change*. To return to another illustration given earlier, people might gain more knowledge over time but not think about things any differently. On the other hand, there might occur a fundamental change in their way of thinking, in terms of being able to think in more complex ways. The development of self-consciousness can be described as a qualitative change rather than merely a change in scores on some variables. Bodily changes associated with adolescence, such as the development of secondary sex characteristics, represent qualitative changes of considerable psychological importance. Such changes go beyond quantitative changes such as gains in height or weight.

Perhaps the distinction of greatest import for personality theory is that between *phenotypic change* and *genotypic change*. Phenotypic change involves change at the observable level whereas genotypic change involves change at the underlying structural level. The change from water to ice or steam represents a phenotypic change. Since the underlying structure, H_2O, remains the same, we do not speak of a genotypic change. In relation to personality, because a person becomes aggressive in different ways, a phenotypic change, does not mean that there has been a change at the basic structural, genotypic level. Similarly, a shift in the areas in which a person is competitive represents a phenotypic but not a genotypic change. This distinction is important for personality development because there are many phenotypic changes that may occur that do not represent structural, genotypic changes. On the other hand, we often may observe a change without being clear whether it is phenotypic or genotypic. Can we be as sure that different behaviors represent different manifestations of the same personality characteristic as we are that structurally water, steam, and ice are the same?

Finally, we can distinguish between *continuous change* and *discontinuous change*. Continuous change is gradual and lawful and follows a consistent pattern that can be identified. Although a person changes in bodily characteristics and appearance over the course of a lifetime, one can describe this change as continuous or consistent. In some cases one can see the boy in the man or the girl in the woman. In other cases, comparing photos from widely separated times, it may seem as if they could hardly be of the same person. Yet, following the process more closely allows us to see a gradual, consistent, continuous process of evolution from child to adult. In contrast, discontinuous change is abrupt and fundamental. A person experiencing a serious accident may undergo a significant change in appearance, leaving his or her appearance discontinuous with what it was previously. Or, if people are placed in a "total environment" that is substantially different from their previous environment, such as going into battle conditions, they may undergo a radical personality change that is discontinuous with their past personality. People describe such monumental experiences and their consequent effects as having changed them forever, often making them into virtually new people.

Following the person at close intervals allows us to distinguish between continuous and discontinuous change, between change in which the coherence of the personality is maintained and change in which there is a fundamental shift in system functioning. Seeing the person at two widely separated points in time may permit us to measure the amount of change but remain unclear about the kind of change that has occurred and the intervening processes involved. What at widely separated points in time appears to be discontinuous change may, upon closer inspection, reveal itself to be continuous change.

Considering distinctions such as these, it is easy to see why it can be overly simplistic to speak only in terms of stability or change. Together with the task of finding equivalent personality measures for different age groups, we have to be clear about the criterion we are using for speaking in terms of stability or change. In studying personality longitudinally, we want to appreciate both stability and change. And, we want to be able to differentiate among the different kinds of change that are possible, since these will have implications for our understanding of personality development. In studying personality longitudinally, we want to appreciate the change from childhood to adulthood, just as we want to appreciate the change from a caterpillar to a butterfly, while recognizing the gradual transformation that has occurred. In sum, we want to be able to consider the continuity, consistency, or coherence that can be present in the midst of apparent change while at the same time leaving room for recognition of radical, discontinuous change.

ILLUSTRATIVE LONGITUDINAL STUDIES

In this section we consider a few longitudinal studies that illustrate longitudinal research and principles of personality development. Then we consider the results of studies that suggest stability and change in personality.

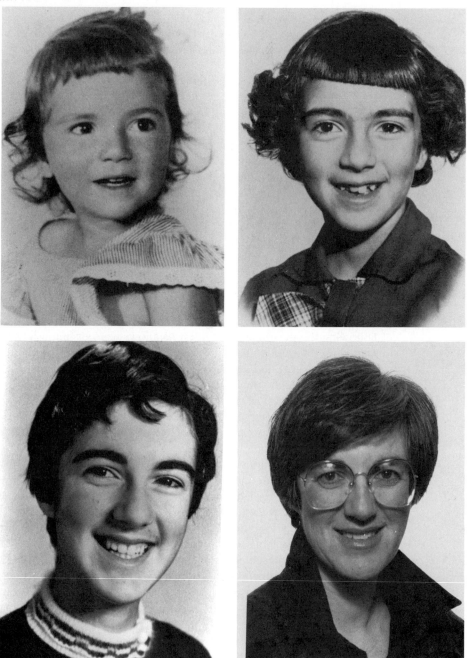

Longitudinal Research. Studies of people over time suggest evidence for both stability and change, depending on which characteristics are studied, how stability and change are measured, and the life history of the individuals involved.

Magnusson's Swedish Study of Individual Development and Adjustment (IDA)

The first longitudinal study to be considered is that by David Magnusson (1988, 1990, 1992; Magnusson, Andersson, & Torestad, 1993; Magnusson & Torestad, 1993). This study is presented because it shows how longitudinal research is conducted, considers both biological and social factors in personality development, and is concerned with individuals and development of the organism as a whole.

Magnusson began the Individual Development and Adjustment (IDA) study in 1965. The objective of the research was to detail how individual and environmental factors interact to govern development from childhood to adulthood. There was particular interest in the developmental processes underlying social maladaptation as expressed in problems such as alcoholism, crime, and psychological difficulties. The research, now in progress for 30 years, began with the study of all boys and girls attending the third, sixth, and eighth grades in school in a community in central Sweden. Thus, the majority of the students were 10, 13, and 15 years of age when the study began in 1965. This group included a total of about 1,400 individuals!

Most of the data consisted of information obtained from the subjects themselves. In addition, information was obtained from parents, teachers, peers, and public records such as those covering crime, alcohol abuse, and psychiatric admission and diagnosis. Most of the data were obtained from tests, inventories, and ratings given in group administrations, but some data were obtained from interviews, observations, and individual tests. Data were obtained on biological factors such as hormonal response to stress and electrophysiological brain activity (EEG) as well as on environmental factors such as characteristics of the home and school.

As one might imagine, a project such as this raises enormous pragmatic and ethical problems. How does one get the cooperation of the subjects and maintain this cooperation over the course of 30 years? How does one get access to files? How does one protect confidentiality in a project involving over a thousand subjects and many investigators, some of whom change as the project continues? What Magnusson did was to begin the project with the formation of a committee consisting of the chair of the Parent-Teacher Association, the school medical officer, the school psychologist, three teacher representatives, one headmaster (principal), and a representative of the National Board of Education. All parts of the study were approved by this committee before they were printed and distributed. Parents were informed of all details of the project at a general meeting and when they were asked to complete the questionnaires. Students were informed of the study and urged to participate but were not required to respond to any questions they preferred not to answer. The editors of local newspapers were given extensive information about the project and received copies of the tests and questionnaires distributed to the students, parents, and schools. In later, follow-up testings, feedback was given to subjects about the progress to date. In sum, this was a monumental effort to ensure the participation and cooperation of all parties to the longitudinal research. Although perhaps they seem irrelevant to the major purposes of the study, longitudinal research can succeed or fail on the basis of such efforts.

In terms of ethics, every possible effort was made to protect the confidentiality of the subjects. All information on individual subjects was coded as soon as it was obtained, making it impossible for anyone without the code key to identify a particular subject. The data were stored in safes in a room with a burglar alarm. Results always were reported in ways that did not allow for the identification of the specific individuals involved.

What are some illustrative findings of this research and how are they conceptualized by Magnusson? We can consider here two sets of findings, one concerning biological maturation and social development in girls, the other concerning the development of social problems in boys. In terms of the former, Magnusson and his associates were interested in the role played by biological maturation in social development. Specifically, what was investigated were the effects of early as opposed to late biological maturation in adolescent girls. Would there be any association between such differences in biological development and problem behavior in the home (e.g., running away), school (e.g., truancy), or leisure life (e.g., use of drugs and alcohol)? At the age of 15 there were clear differences in such problem behavior in the direction of more problems for early as opposed to late maturing girls. For example, at age 15, 35% of the early maturing girls as opposed to 6% of the late maturing girls had been drunk on multiple occasions. Early maturing girls also showed much more conflict with adults and were less interested in school and future careers. To a much greater extent than late maturing girls, the early maturing girls were focused on their social relationships, generally with older males and females.

Although such differences were dramatic at age 15, by the end of adolescence and early adulthood many of them had been reduced considerably. Thus, in adulthood there were few differences between the two groups in terms of problem behavior and social relationships. In other words, the problem behavior of the early maturing girls lasted over a limited period of time. On the other hand, some long-term consequences of early development did appear to hold. For example, such girls tended to marry earlier, have children earlier, enter the labor market earlier, and leave school earlier than did late maturing girls. These differences could not be attributed to differences in intelligence or family background.

To study the development of problem behavior in boys, Magnusson and his associates divided their sample of over 500 boys into groups in terms of their pattern of scores on measures of personality variables such as aggressivenes, motor restlessness, poor concentration, and poor peer relations. Would differences in patterns of scores on such measures taken at age 13 relate to later problematic social behavior such as alcoholism and criminality? Two groups of boys were found to have poor relationships with peers, one group with this problem alone and the other group with the additional problems of excessive aggressiveness and hyperactivity. Whereas the boys in the former group did not show later problematic behavior, the boys in the latter group showed a far greater tendency in this regard. For example, whereas the boys in the first group did not differ from chance in the probability of their later development of alcohol and criminal problems, the probability of such problems was far greater than chance in boys who were also characterized by hyperactivity and aggressiveness. In contrast, boys at 13 years of age who had no problems developed later alcohol and criminal problems at a rate far less than would be expected by chance.

Here too a biological component entered into an understanding of the later developments. Boys with an early pattern of hyperactivity and aggressiveness were also found to have comparatively low levels of adrenaline secretion in their urine. This was important because the secretion of adrenaline is associated with the perception of situations as stressful or threatening. Individuals with low adrenaline output have been viewed by psychologists as low in physiological reactivity and therefore as less likely to perceive situations as stressful or threatening. In Magnusson's longitudinal research it was found that boys with low adrenaline excretions at age 13 were far more likely to show a later pattern of persistent criminal activity than were individuals who had high adrenaline excretions. For the latter group, presumably, the perception of a situation as stressful and threatening acted as a deterrent to engagement in criminal activity, a deterrent that was not present for those with low adrenaline excretion.

Another wrinkle can be added to these findings. Three groups were formed in terms of patterns of later criminal activity: no later crime, teen offenders (recorded crime only before age 18), and persistent offenders (recorded crime during teenage years and in adulthood). Would the three groups show differences in hyperactivity and adrenaline excretion during early adolescence? What was found were clear differences between the three groups. On hyperactivity (i.e., motor restlessness and concentration difficulties), the no crime group showed the lowest scores, the persistent offenders the highest scores, with scores for the teen offenders falling between the two. In terms of adrenaline secretion, only the persistent offender group had a low level of secretion. In other words, the relation between lower physiological reactivity and antisocial behavior held only for the persistent offenders. In sum, males with a persistent criminal career were found to be characterized by adolescent patterns of high hyperactivity and low physiological reactivity (low adrenaline excretion), males with records as juvenile offenders only were found to be characterized by adolescent patterns of somewhat high hyperactivity only, and males without adolescent or adult records of criminal activity were found to be characterized by low hyperactivity and high physiological reactivity (high adrenaline excretion) (Figures 6.1, 6.2).

What do these findings illustrate? Recall the three noteworthy characteristics of Magnusson's longitudinal research. First, we have seen a detailed description of what it takes to do longitudinal research. Second, we have seen an emphasis on both biological and psychological variables. Third, we have seen an emphasis on patterns of relationships rather than on relationships between single variables and later outcomes. The second and third points relate to Magnusson's emphasis on an interactionist, holistic perspective on individual development. According to this perspective, biological and psychological variables are involved in a constant interplay, as is the individual with the environment. And, development must be understood in terms of the interplay among patterns of variables within the individual rather than in terms of single variables alone. The individual functions as an organismic whole rather than as a bunch of separate parts.

Before moving on to findings from other longitudinal research, let us consider Magnusson's commitment to longitudinal research and his contrast of such research to cross-sectional research. Magnusson suggests that it is only longitudinal research

Figure 6.1   Persistent hyperactivity for three categories of males: no crime, teenage crime, and teenage and adult crime.

The data indicate an association between criminal activity, particularly persistent criminal activity (teen & adult) and hyperactivity.

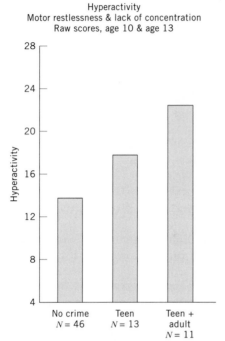

(From "Individual Development: A Longitudinal Perspective," by D. Magnusson, 1992, *European Journal of Personality, 6,* p. 131. Reprinted by permission of John Wiley & Sons, Inc.)

that could have led to an understanding of the kinds of relationships among variables seen in the previously mentioned findings for male and female development. Not that these are the entire story of what determines such patterns of development, since evidence also was found of the importance of home environment factors. However, he suggests that the changes in relationships among variables at different points in time, and the delineation of subgroups, could only have been observed through longitudinal research:

> Any historian who claimed to understand historical developments in Europe at a given time merely by conducting a cross-sectional study with the aid of information from daily newspapers from different countries on a given day would not be taken seriously but would become a justified object of derision. A meterologist who attempted to understand meterological processes by cross-sectional measures of temperature, wind velocity, relative humidity, and other aspects of weather at various locations in Sweden on a given day would probably trigger the same reaction. Cross-sectional studies are obviously important for the study of some narrow aspects of the individual development process. However, both an analysis of the phenomena involved and empirical research

Figure 6.2 Adrenaline excretion for three groups of males—no crime, teenage crime, and teenage and adult crime—in two independent situations.
The data indicate an association between lower physiological reactivity (adrenaline excretion) and persistent antisocial behavior (teen & adult).

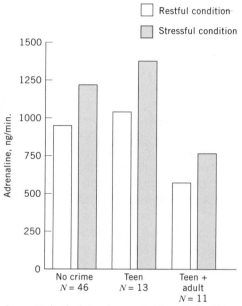

Adrenaline excretion versus criminality
During teenage years or teenage years
and adulthood

(From "Individual Development: A Longitudinal Perspective," by D. Magnusson, 1992, *European Journal of Personality, 6,* p. 132. Reprinted by permission of John Wiley & Sons, Inc.)

demonstrate the necessity of supplementing cross-sectional studies with systematic, long-term, prospective studies to a far greater extent than hitherto.

Magnusson, 1992, p. 135

The Longitudinal Research of Jack and Jeanne Block.

In this section we focus on a longitudinal study initiated by Jack and Jeanne Block. Let us start, however, by considering the earlier longitudinal research by Jack Block. In an important 1971 book, *Lives Through Time,* Jack Block reported the results of research on subjects studied in junior high school, in senior high school, and in their 30s. In this book Block (1971) expressed his commitment to longitudinal research as follows:

Psychologists are now increasingly drawn toward longitudinal studies for the ineluctable reason that there simply is no other way by which certain questions regarding development, cause and effect may be approached. Correlational, cross-sectional, or experimental methods have great and suggestive contributions to make toward an understanding of these bases of behavior. But these approaches do not encompass time and the trajectory of individual lives.

p. 3

Block was picking up on research begun earlier by members of the University of California (Berkeley) Institute of Human Development. Although there were considerable data on the subjects, there also were many problems: (1) Much of the data were not in a form that could be quantified. (2) There were missing data for many subjects. (3) Over time procedures and methods of testing changed, presenting problems in continuity of evaluation. (4) There was a lack of agreement on the focus of concern and in conceptual language. How could such data, albeit on the same individuals, be organized for comparative purposes in terms of longitudinal investigation? What Block did was to have judges evaluate each of the subjects, at each point in time, in terms of a *Q-sort* description. For example, as adults the subjects were interviewed extensively. On the basis of these interviews, judges described each subject by sorting 100 statements from the **California Q Set** into the following distribution, ranging from statements most characteristic of the individual at one end to statements least characteristic of the individual at the other end: 5,8,12,16,18,16,12,8,5. This distribution represents a normal distribution of the statements. Illustrative statements include the following: "Is critical, skeptical, not easily impressed." "Is a talkative individual." "Seeks reassurance from others."

The use of these Q-descriptions meant that although the data on the subjects varied for the time period involved (junior high school, senior high school, adulthood), a common set of descriptors could be employed. And, since the items were distributed by the raters in terms of a normal distribution, correlations could be computed to determine the agreement among ratings for different time periods. Finally, different judges were used to make the ratings at the different time periods. Thus, the ratings at one period could not have biased those of another period. Through such procedures Block attempted to overcome the problems noted earlier and to capture the development of personality over time.

What did Block find? Only a few of the major findings will be presented here. First, Block found evidence of considerable personality continuity in terms of statistically significant correlations between personality ratings made at the three different time periods. Continuity was greater between junior high school and senior high school than between senior high school and adulthood. Although statistically significant, the correlations generally were low, particularly over more extended periods of time. For example, the across-time average correlations on a measure of psychological adjustment were as follows: .56 for junior high school to senior high school, .28 for senior high school to adulthood, and .22 for junior high school to adulthood.

Second, there were important male-female differences in overall change and in the variables indicative of continuity. For example, between the period of senior high school and adulthood, males, relative to females, changed significantly toward a narrowing of interests and less responsiveness to humor. On the other hand, during this period females, relative to males, broadened their interests and became more ambitious and more sympathetic. In terms of overall level of psychological adjustment, females appeared to have a particularly difficult time in high school but were of the same overall level of adjustment in adulthood.

Third, there was enormous diversity among subjects in the amount of consistency shown over time. For example, whereas the overall (i.e., all personality measures) across-time correlation for males between junior high school and senior high school was .77, the range of correlations for individuals was from -.01 to 1.00. Similarly, whereas the overall across-time correlation for females between junior high school and senior high school was .75, the range of correlations for individuals was -.02 to 1.00. Thus, what was characteristic of the sample as a whole said relatively little about any particular subject.

In sum, using Q-sort judgments from independent judges at three points in time, Block found evidence of considerable consistency, greater for shorter than for longer periods of time, with evidence of differences in consistency for different personality characteristics, between males and females, and among individuals.

We can turn now to the longitudinal study begun in 1968 by Jack Block and Jeanne Block (J. Block, 1993; J. H. Block & Block, 1980). This study is of particular significance because of the variety of data obtained, recognition of the importance of gender differences in patterns of development, and the investigation of important personality constructs. In regard to the latter, although investigating a wide variety of personality variables, the Blocks were particularly interested in studying developmentally two personality constructs they believed to be of central theoretical importance—*ego-control* and *ego-resiliency.*

Ego-control refers to the individual's characteristic expression or containment of impulses, feelings, and desires. It relates to the individual's ability to delay, to inhibit action, and to be insulated from environmental distraction. Individuals fall along a continuum, ranging from overcontrol at one end to undercontrol at the other end. Overcontrolled individuals are overly constrained and inhibited, unduly delay gratification, and tend to show minimal expression of emotion. In contrast, undercontrolled individuals are expressive, spontaneous, and unable to delay gratification and have many but relatively short-lived enthusiasms and interests. Both extremes are viewed as less adaptive than midpoints on the continuum.

Ego-resiliency refers to the extent to which the individual can modify his or her level of ego-control to meet the demands of the situation. In other words, the ego-resilient person demonstrates flexibility and adaptiveness in meeting changing life circumstances and is able to plan and to be organized at times as well as to be spontaneous and impulsive at other times. Individuals range on a continuum from unresilient to resilient, expressing increasing degrees of adaptive functioning.

The Blocks began their investigation of these as well as other personality characteristics with the study of 128 children from two nursery schools in the Berkeley, California area. The sample of children was selected to be diverse in terms of parental income, parental education, and ethnicity (65% white, 27% black, 6% Asian, 2% Chicano). Extensive individual assessments of the children were conducted at ages 3, 4, 5, 7, 11, 14, 18, and 23. At age 23, 104 of the original sample of 128 subjects were assessed—a remarkably low rate of attrition given the time period involved. During the eight assessment periods a wide variety of data were obtained on each subject: life history data (L-data); ratings by teachers, parents, or other knowledgeable observers (O-data); data from experimental procedures or standardized tests (T-data); and self-report data (S-data). An effort was made to assess personality characteristics through multiple measures to achieve dependability and generalizability. When over-

SPOTLIGHT ON THE RESEARCHER

JACK BLOCK:
Studying Personality the Long Way

My interest in personality development was an inevitable consequence of prior interest in ego-control and ego-resiliency, two constructs my late wife, Jeanne, and I had formulated as integrative ways of conceptualizing personality systems. If these two constructs were indeed theoretically crucial, it became important to study their origins and developmental paths. For this kind of inquiry, only longitudinal research—studying the same individuals over time, from their early years onward—could suffice. The longitudinal method is uniquely suited for the study of personality development.

My book, *Lives Through Time* (1971), based on longitudinal information gathered by others, was a first effort to identify personality continuities and some of their antecedent factors. But our later study, begun in 1969 and continuing, of 128 three-year-olds now approaching age 30, was our personal, more focused, and more intensive effort to understand why people turn out as they do. Our research has demonstrated, in many ways, the essential coherence of personality development and the implications of early character structure for later character structure. For a long time, such coherence has been denied by many psychologists. As examples of the coherence of personality development, we have found reliable and important personality differences between the sexes in regard to developmental self-concept and other aspects of personality, that drug use in late adolescence can be foretold by personality characteristics observed at age 3, and that depressive tendencies in young adulthood can be foretold by dispositions identifiable in nursery school.

Many other findings are coming in as we harvest a study planted and nourished for many years. Lying ahead for this longitudinal research is deeper and longer inquiry into the behavioral outcomes of early personality characteristics, particularly with regard to psychopathology.

all evaluations were needed, Q-sorts were obtained from trained observers. For example, at age 3 each child was described using the *California Child Q-Set* by three nursery school teachers trained to use the Q-sort in this context. At age 14, four psychologists described each subject on the *California Adult Q-Set*. At each age the Q-set descriptions of each subject were combined to form a composite, in an attempt to rule out individual idiosyncrasies in observation and judgment. As in the earlier Block study, the assessors at each age were entirely different so as to maintain the independence of each data set. In sum, LOTS of data (L,O,T,S-data) were obtained, including multiple measures of many concepts and data of different kinds. This is a major feature of this study.

Although data collection and analysis continue, what has been reported to date? Let us begin with the concepts of ego-control and ego-resiliency. What is the path of development over time? It is clear that there is change over time—there is a developmental increase in ego-control and ego-resiliency. These changes in absolute scores would be expected. What of changes in relative scores? Do people over time maintain their relative positions on ego-control and ego-resiliency? Regarding ego-control, the evidence suggested that "from an early age individual differences in the level of ego-control are identifiable and continue to distinguish people for at least the next 20 years and, from the evidence of other studies, even beyond" (J. Block, 1993, p. 34). This was true for both males and females. The average correlation between two time periods was .48, with correlations between pairs of time periods ranging from a low of .22 (age 3 and age 18 for females) and a high of .82 (age 3 and age 4 for males).

Aside from consistency over time, ego-control measured at age 3 was found to be associated with peer behavior at age 7. Children low in ego-control at the earlier age were found to be more aggressive, more assertive, less compliant, and less inhibited at age 7 than children high in ego-control at age 3. While children very high in ego-control at age 3 tended to be shy at age 7, those low in ego-control at age 3 tended to be aggressive, teasing, and manipulative in their peer relations at age 7 (J. H. Block & Block, 1980; D. M. Buss, Block, & Block, 1980). In a study of adolescents, 14-year-olds rated as high on ego-control were found to demonstrate a high ability to delay gratification in an experimental setting and were described as responsible, productive, and ethically consistent (Funder & Block, 1989).

Concerning ego-resiliency, the findings were different for males and females. For males, there was evidence of continuity in individual differences in ego-resiliency over a period of 20 years. The mean between-age correlation on ego-resiliency for males was .43, ranging from a low of .22 (ages 3 and 23) to a high of .65 (ages 3 and 4, 11 and 14). However, for girls there was virtually no relation between resiliency scores during the childhood years and ego-resiliency in adolescence or adulthood. For females the mean between-age correlation was .21, with a range from a negative correlation of .28 between ages 4 and 14 to a high of .68 between ages 3 and 4. For girls, ego-resiliency scores during the early years and between the ages of 14 and 23 tended to correlate fairly well. However, between the ages of 11 and 14, during the period of puberty, there appeared to be a break in the relationship.

What of the other variables studied? Block (1993) reports the following observations:

1. Males and females were found to differ in the course of their self-esteem scores. For males, self-esteem increased during the course of adolescence whereas for females there was a decrease during this time, paralleling the findings reported by Magnusson in his Swedish study.

2. Boys who were to experience parental divorce, relative to boys whose parents were to remain married, were characterized by undercontrol of impulse and as being troublesome. Rather than being a consequence of divorce, the behavioral problems of these children appeared to exist prior to the divorce: "Children's behavioral problems may be present years before the formal divorce actually occurs. Indeed, the family discord often characterizing the period before parental separation may well have serious consequences for the children involved" (Block, 1993, p. 29).

3. At age 14, the use of marijuana was associated with ego-undercontrol in both sexes. The use of harder drugs reflected low ego-resiliency in addition to low ego-control.

4. The early antecedents of depression appeared to differ between males and females. Boys who were depressed at age 18 tended to be unsocialized, aggressive, and undercontrolled as children. On the other hand, girls who were depressed at age 18 tended to be intropunitive, oversocialized, and overcontrolled as children (Block, Gjerde, & Block, 1991).

As noted, the data collection and analysis in this study continue. However, in terms of what has been described we can see the diversity of findings based on a wide variety of data, the importance of considering sex differences in the developmental trajectory of various relationships, and the potential value of the concepts of ego-control and ego-resiliency. In addition, the Q-sort method appears to offer considerable potential for relating observations based on different kinds of data from different stages of development (Ozer, 1993).

The Minnesota Parent-Child Project

In this third, and final description of a longitudinal project, we consider the question of continuity in development from infancy through adolescence (Sroufe, Carlson, & Shulman, 1993). This project is presented because it starts at such an early point in time—infancy; it focuses on a concept of growing importance and interest—**attachment;** and it focuses on the development of an important part of personality—interpersonal relationships.

Let us once again take a brief detour so that we can become familiar with the conceptual and methodological background for the study. Work in the area of *attachment theory* is largely based on the early theoretical work of the British psychoanalyst John Bowlby and the empirical work of the psychologist Mary Ainsworth (Ainsworth & Bowlby, 1991; Bretherton, 1992; Slade & Aber, 1992). Bowlby was trained as a psychoanalyst and was interested in the effects of early separation from parents on personality development. Such separation was a major problem in England during World War II when many children were sent to the countryside, far from their parents, to be safe from enemy bombing in the cities. Following the war Bowlby began two research projects on the effects of separation, one *retrospective*, involving the recollections of individuals separated from their parents between the ages of 1 and 4 for health reasons, and the other *prospective*, involving the study of children as they underwent separation from their parents to enter institutions for health reasons. In his conceptual work, Bowlby was largely influenced by developments in two fields of biology: *ethology*, which focuses on the study of animals in their natural environment, and *general systems theory*, which focuses on general principles of operation of all biological systems. In terms of ethology, Bowlby was particularly struck with Lorenz's description of the imprinting phenomenon, noted earlier in the discussion of critical periods. Lorenz's description of the separation distress and proximity seeking of birds who had become imprinted on the mother, and of the strong bond that was not based on oral gratification, appeared to match Bowlby's observations of infants and young children.

Bowlby's clinical observations and reading of the ethological literature led him to formulate a theory of the development of the *attachment behavioral system* (ABS). According to the theory, the developing infant goes through a series of phases in the development of an attachment to a major caregiver, generally the mother, and the use of this attachment as a "secure base" for exploration and separation. The ABS is viewed as something programmed within infants, a part of our evolutionary heritage that has adaptive value. Thus, attachment behaviors such as crying, cooing, babbling, smiling, and sucking all serve the function of maintaining closeness of contact with the mother. At the same time, as the infant begins to wander and explore the environment, particularly around the end of the first year, the attachment relationship provides a secure base for exploration. Here the infant feels secure to explore but also feels secure that it can return to proximity to the mother if in need of comfort. As a further part of the development of the ABS, the infant develops **internal working models** or mental representations (images), associated with affect, of itself and its primary caregivers. It is these internal working models, based on interactional experience, that provide the basis for the development of expectations of future relationships. In this aspect, that is, in the emphasis on the importance of early emotional relationships for future relationships, attachment theory is similar to psychoanalytic object relations theory, a development out of psychoanalytic theory that emphasizes how early experiences influence the ways in which individuals perceive themselves and relate to others.

A major turning point in the empirical work on this issue occurred with the development by Ainsworth of the **Strange Situation procedure.** In this procedure an infant, generally about one year of age, is placed in an unfamiliar setting with a stranger, in both the presence and the absence of the infant's caregiver. The infant is allowed to play with toys that are present and then, at prescribed intervals, the mother leaves the room and then returns to reunite with the infant. At various intervals a stranger is introduced, with the infant sometimes left alone with the stranger before the mother returns to the room. The point here is to observe the behavior of the infant in relation to the mother under conditions of an unfamiliar setting, in the presence and absence of a stranger, and under conditions of separation and reuniting with the mother.

Based on a scoring scheme for observations of infant behavior during the Strange Situation, infants are placed in one of three attachment categories: (1) anxious-avoidant infants, (2) securely attached infants, (3) anxious-resistant infants. Briefly, anxious-avoidant infants (about 20% of infants) readily explore the environment, register little protest over separation from the mother, and are relatively accepting of the stranger, even in the absence of the mother. When the mother returns, these children show avoidance behavior in terms of turning, looking, or moving away. In contrast, infants who show secure attachment (about 70% of the sample) show ready exploration and acceptance of the stranger in the presence of the mother but are more sensitive to the departure of the mother (e.g., they cry or search for her) and when the mother returns show greeting behavior (e.g., they smile and initiate interaction). These infants also are readily comforted by the mother and readily return to exploration and play once reunited with her. Finally, the anxious-resistant infants (about 10%) have difficulty separating to explore, are wary of the stranger, and have difficulty reuniting with the mother upon her return. Upon reunion these infants may mix pleas to be picked up with squirming and insistence that they be let down.

Armed with the theory and familiarity with the classification of infant attachment patterns, we can return to consideration of the Minnesota Parent-Child Project. Based primarily on the work of Bowlby and Ainsworth, this project focuses on the infant caregiving system as the core out of which personality is formed (Sroufe et al., 1993). Thus, individual differences found during an early developmental period are hypothesized to relate to observed later differences in personality development, in particular in terms of the formation of social relationships. The project began in 1974–1975 with the recruitment of 267 women in the third trimester of pregnancy. Infants and caregivers were seen in a variety of contexts seven times during the first year, twice in each of the next three years, and yearly through age 13. A variety of information was obtained (e.g., temperament, intelligence, parent-child interaction, peer relationships) and observations were conducted in the home, laboratory, and school. After 13 years, about two-thirds of the original sample remained in the study.

Do individual differences in attachment in infancy, measured via the Strange Situation, relate to later differences in social and emotional behavior? The results of this project as well as others suggest that this indeed is the case. Thus, securely attached infants were rated by preschool teachers and independent observers as less dependent than either anxious or resistant infants. In addition, the securely attached infants were found to show greater ego-resiliency than children in the other groups. This association between infant attachment pattern and ego-resilient behavior continued to be found through middle childhood.

As hypothesized, relationships also were found between infant attachment patterns and peer relationships. In terms of preschool behavior, securely attached infants were found to participate more actively in the peer group, and were more positive in their peer interactions, than were members of the two other groups. This relation held whether quality of peer relationships was rated by independent observers, by teachers, or by children's ratings of one another. These children also were found to demonstrate greater empathy and to deal more easily with rebuff than was true for children from the other two groups. Finally, differences were found in the kind of behavior members of each group elicited from teachers. Securely attached children elicited warm behavior from teachers whereas those showing an earlier pattern of resistant attachment elicited unduly nurturant and caretaking behavior. Children with the earlier pattern of avoidant attachment elicited controlling and occasional angry behavior. Thus, it is suggested that "children actively create their environments based on their history of experiences" (Sroufe et al., 1993, p. 325).

Do such patterns continue through early and middle childhood (ages 10-11)? It would be expected that relationships between infant attachment pattern and later behavior would increasingly be difficult to find because of changes in the way needs and fears are expressed and because of the variety of intervening influences as time goes on. According to the theory, early attachment influences and internal working models are seen as exerting powerful influences on later development but are not seen as immutable. Nevertheless, evidence of such relationships has been found. For example, relative to members of the other two groups, those earlier grouped as securely attached were found to show greater self-confidence and self-esteem, to set higher goals and show greater persistence in these goals, to be less dependent, to spend more time in group activities, and to form close friendships (Table 6.3).

Preliminary data also are available concerning adaptation during the adolescent

TABLE 6.3 **Correlations Between Attachment Security at Age 2 Years and Summer Camp Ratings in Middle Childhood**

The data indicate that attachment patterns established early in life (age two years) are associated with later personality characteristics.

Variable	r	p
Emotional health	.35	.011
Self-confidence	.34	.012
Social competence	.36	.007
Social skills	.33	.013
Ego-resiliency	.32	.019

Note: Number of subjects ranged from 44 to 47.

Source: "Individuals in Relationships: Development From Infancy," by L. A. Sroufe, E. Carlson, and S. Shulman, 1993, in *Studying Lives Through Time* (p. 330), edited by D. C. Funder, R. D. Parke, C. Tomlin-son-Keasay, and K. Widaman, Washington, DC: American Psychological Association.

years (ages 14–15). Here too ratings on emotional health, self-esteem, ego-resiliency, and peer competence favor those with histories of secure attachment. In sum, independent ratings at points extending over a period of 14 years demonstrate a relation between early attachment patterns and later social and emotional development. What is suggested is a coherence to the development of personality wherein change occurs but continuity can be seen between infant patterns and later patterns of behavior. Thus, it is suggested that "prior adaptation and history are not 'erased' by change. Earlier patterns may be reactivated, and early history adds to current circumstances in predicting current adaptation" (Sroufe et al., 1993, p. 317). Such continuity is assumed to occur because of the development of self-maintaining patterns of interaction rather than because of any permanent establishment of a personality structure. Thus, continuity is assumed to exist because of the development of patterns of individual-environment interaction rather than because of the development of fixed structures or the operation of fixed environments. And, room is left for change to occur as a result of powerful relationship experiences that are different from those experienced earlier. In other words, there is a tendency to confirm internal working models but powerful new relationships can lead to the development of new internal working models.

Before concluding our discussion of the importance of early attachment, it may be useful to note that a number of studies have suggested a relation between early attachment patterns and patterns of adult romantic relationships (Bartholomew &

Horowitz, 1991; Collins & Read, 1990; Feeney & Noller, 1990; Hazan & Shaver, 1987, 1994; Simpson, 1990). For example, secure attachment styles have been found to be associated with relationship experiences of happiness, friendship, and trust; avoidant styles with fears of closeness, emotional highs and lows, and jealousy; and anxious/ambivalent styles with obsessive preoccupation with the loved person, a desire for union, extreme sexual attraction, emotional extremes, and jealousy. A relation also has been reported between attachment style and coping strategies. In a study of responses of Israelis to the Iraqi missile attacks during the 1991 Gulf War, securely attached people were found to experience less distress and to seek more social support than members of either of the other two groups. Avoidant individuals experienced more somatic difficulties, hostility, and avoidance whereas anxious/ambivalent individuals experienced more generalized signs of stress and used emotion-focused coping strategies such as attempting to change the way they felt (Mikulciner, Florian, & Weller, 1993). Although these findings fit with attachment theory and the findings reported in the Minnesota project, it is important to keep in mind that attachment style here is defined in terms of adult responses to questionnaires rather than in terms of objective measures taken in infancy. In addition, because these results are not based on longitudinal research, continuity of development is inferred rather than observed.

Having expressed these words of caution, and keeping them in mind, we can consider a recent report suggesting that adult romantic love styles are related to early experiences in the family (Waller & Shaver, 1994). In this research adult MZ (identical) and DZ (fraternal) twins and their spouses completed a questionnaire designed to measure their attitudes toward love. Such attitudes were viewed as related to attachment style. Comparisons were made of similarity of responses of MZ twins, DZ twins, and spouses to determine whether genetic similarity was associated with similarity of attitudes toward love. In other words, the study followed the standard form used by behavior geneticists as described in Chapter 5; that is, degree of trait similarity was examined in relation to degree of genetic similarity. As can be recalled, such studies typically have indicated an important genetic contribution to almost every personality characteristic and little evidence of shared environmental influences. In contrast to such findings, this research found that genes were not important determinants of attitudes toward romantic love. And, beyond this, the shared family environment seemed to play the major role in shaping the attitudes. As the authors note, these findings can be considered remarkable:

> In contrast to other attitude dimensions and personality traits, romantic love styles are not strongly influenced by heritable factors. . . . Moreover, in stark contrast to findings from previous twin studies of attitudes and personality traits, shared environmental effects play a substantial role in determining both trait variation and family resemblance on attitudes toward romantic love. These results suggest that shared experiences, not shared genes, account for similarities in love attitudes.

> Waller & Shaver, 1994, p. 272

Why should the findings in relation to love attitudes be so different from findings in relation to other personality characteristics? We do not have an answer to this question right now, but the authors speculate that love attitudes, and attachment styles, are inherently relational. Rather than involving the individual alone, they involve relationships between people. It is suggested that such interpersonal, relational attitudes are learned in childhood as a result of experiences with parents and observations of parental relationships. Although these results await further confirmation, and it remains to be demonstrated that actual behavior is in accord with expressed attitudes, for the first time we have impressive evidence of negligible genetic influence and strong shared environmental influence on an important aspect of personality functioning.

ADDITIONAL LONGITUDINAL EVIDENCE OF RELATIVE STABILITY AND RELATIVE CHANGE

It is not easy to summarize the findings of large and complex studies. However, perhaps we can summarize the findings from the studies discussed in the previous section by suggesting that they demonstrate qualitative change and consistent, coherent personality development over time. At the same time, there is evidence of gender differences and of considerable individual variability in the degree of coherence and consistency.

There is evidence from other studies indicative of greater or lesser degrees of stability and change over time. Although we have cautioned that "biologically-genetically influenced" does not mean fixed or unchanging, it is the case that relative stability has been suggested for intelligence and basic temperament traits that also are viewed as having strong genetic components. Over time the views concerning the stability and malleability of intelligence have varied markedly. Some time ago Bloom (1964), in reviewing the literature, concluded that there was increased stability of IQ scores with age and for shorter periods of time over longer periods of time. A more recent review reaches similar conclusions (Humphreys, 1992). However, it should be noted that over the 10-year interval of ages 8 and 18, the correlation between measures of intelligence at the two points in time is only .28 (Humphreys & Davey, 1988). In addition, there is evidence that changes on the order of 15 points in IQ scores can be obtained if active environmental efforts are pursued during the early years of development (Bloom, 1964; Schiff, Duyme, Dumaret, & Tonkiewicz, 1982; Turkheimer, 1991).

Turning to temperament, the developmental psychologist Jerome Kagan has been studying groups of children designated as "inhibited to the unfamiliar" and "uninhibited to the unfamiliar" (Kagan & Snidman, 1991a, 1991b). The proposed trait is similar to shyness or inhibition and is seen as having a biological substrate. According to Kagan, a majority of the children assigned to each group at age 4 months retain membership in that group at least through the 8th year of life. At the same time, there is evidence that many of the children change category membership. Thus, about one-third of the inhibited children at age 2 were not particularly shy at 3 1/2 years of age. Change in these children seemed particularly tied to having mothers who were not overly protective and placed reasonable demands on them (Kagan, Arcus, & Snidman, 1993).

Finally, a number of studies suggest relative stability on the five factors emphasized by trait theorists (i.e., OCEAN), *once adulthood has been reached* (Costa & McCrae, 1994; McCrae & Costa, 1990). Over intervals ranging from 3 to 30 years, the median correlation between scores on the five traits is about .65, leading McCrae and Costa, two leading five-factor theorists, to conclude that despite possible changes in life circumstances, personality is pretty much fixed by age 30. These theorists go on to suggest that about three-fifths of the variance in scores on personality traits is stable over the *full adult life span* and conclude that somewhere between age 21 and age 30 personality takes its final, fully developed form—for most of us, by the age of 30, our personality is set like plaster (Costa & McCrae, 1994). It is not just those traits that show substantial genetic contributions, however, but also attitudes; that is, there is evidence of the persistence of adult attitudes over lengthy periods of time (Alwin, Cohen, & Newcomb, 1991).

Note that these researchers emphasize greater stability and consistency than the previously mentioned suggestions of qualitative change that still reflect consistency and coherence. However, we must be cautious about taking too dogmatic and definitive a view in this regard. Many psychologists conduct research in this area with a bias in favor of finding stability, with the concern that if they did not find stability, the utility of the concept of personality would be questioned (Helson, 1993; Helson & Stewart, 1994). As a result, they are led to ignore evidence of change in other studies and even within their own findings. Thus, there is evidence that as identical twins grow up they grow apart in personality (McCartney, Harris, & Bernieri, 1990), that the majority of children categorized as insecurely attached (anxious-avoidant and resistant) in infancy do not grow up to have serious emotional difficulties (Lewis, 1991; Lewis, Feiring, McGuffog, & Jaskir, 1984), and mean and median correlations mask enormous individual variability in patterns of stability and change. For an individual, even three-fifths stability in trait scores, as emphasized by Costa and McCrae, leaves enormous room for change in the organization of personality functioning.

SOME THOUGHTS ON STABILITY AND CHANGE IN PERSONALITY AND THE QUESTION OF PROCESS

One can find evidence for both stability and change in personality. This is particularly the case when individual rather than group data are considered. How much one or the other is emphasized depends upon the area of personality considered, the measures used, and the biases of the investigators (Pervin, 1994b). Generally we know that change is most possible during periods of rapid development (Bloom, 1964). For most human characteristics, such development occurs during the early years of life. In addition, we know that agreement between measures tends to be greater between shorter periods of time than over longer periods of time, and between periods when there is little phenotypic change in the characteristic of interest as opposed to periods during which there is considerable phenotypic change. However, we by no means have knowledge or understanding of the boundary conditions of change in any important personality characteristic or of the processes fostering stability and change.

The issue of process needs to be of particular concern to us. In other words, we need to be concerned with the question of variables in the person and in the environment that foster stability or change in personality functioning. It is one thing to provide evidence of stability or change, it is another to demonstrate understanding of the processes involved. At this point we have a glimpse of the processes within the individual and the environment that foster stability and consistency in personality. For example, we have evidence that individuals seek self-verification, that they elicit reactions from others that maintain their self-perceptions and ways of behaving, that they select environments consistent with their own personalities, and that others treat them in ways consistent with the images formed of them. As people reach adulthood they tend to narrow and stabilize the range of friendships. All of these forces within the individual, in the environment, and in individual-environment transactions operate to produce relative stability and consistency.

At the same time, we know that change, often substantial change, occurs. Here, however, we have a less clear picture of the processes involved. We know that change occurs in psychotherapy, and that the therapeutic relationship appears to be important, but we are very unclear about the change process or processes involved in the various forms of therapy. We also know that powerful environments can produce change, even in adults. Finally, we know that life contains a large element of unpredictability, and that chance encounters and dramatic social or economic events can lead to significant change (Bandura, 1982; Lewis, 1991, 1995). However, we have hardly begun to scratch the surface in our understanding of the boundaries of change in various areas and of the individual and environmental forces conducive to substantial change.

SOME CONCLUDING POINTS RELEVANT TO LONGITUDINAL RESEARCH

In this chapter we have had an opportunity to consider the contributions of longitudinal research, in terms of both the strengths of the methodology and actual findings. It is clear that longitudinal research has much to offer to the study of personality. It also is clear that such research requires courage, patience, and adequate funds. As we have seen, it is not just a question of adequate conceptualization and methodology, but also the ability to maintain subject involvement over extended periods of time.

At the same time, it is important to be aware of a number of issues relevant to such research. Perhaps the most basic issue relates to our understanding of process. No matter how frequently assessments are made in the studies reviewed, there are important gaps in time. And, for all of the data gathered, generally relatively little is known about the individual. For the most part, what is painted are general brush strokes of personality development, colored by the societal forces operating during the time period involved and the culture of which the subjects are a part. The differences found for males and females in many of the studies give testimony to the importance of such factors in personality development.

Despite the statistically significant correlations reported, we should be aware of the individual differences involved and the remaining variance to be accounted for. Perhaps the point is best made by consideration of the difference between prospective and retrospective studies (Lewis, 1990b). As Freud once noted, as we look back on the development of the individual, the path seems all too clear. On the other hand, we would hardly have been able to predict from the child what was to unfold in the adult. Similarly, as we trace relationships back, that is retrospectively, the connections generally are clearer than if we try to predict forward, that is prospectively.

Consider, for example, the finding that 80% of 6-year-old boys identified as being at risk for emotional problems or actually clinically disturbed were found to have been assigned to the avoidant- or resistant-attachment categories in infancy. But if one took all boys classified as insecurely attached (avoidant and resistant) at age 1 and predicted that they would be at risk or clinically disturbed at age 6, one would be right in only 40% of the cases (Lewis et al., 1984). The reason that retrospective power is greater than predictive power is that far more boys were classified as insecurely attached than were later diagnosed at risk or disturbed. Thus, the clinician or researcher viewing later pathology would have a clear basis for suggesting a strong relationship between pathology and early attachment difficulties. On the other hand, focusing on the data in terms of prediction would still suggest a relationship, but a much more tenuous one, and also the importance of other variables.

The conclusion that there is an important difference between predictive power and retrospective power is all the more impressive if we consider the further follow-up results of this research (Lewis & Feiring, 1994). Here the same children were followed through age 13. In addition to the infancy ratings of attachment, ratings of current (age 13) psychological adjustment were obtained from the subjects as well as from teachers. Finally, measures of the subjects' memories of their early childhood relationships were obtained. Would the early measures of attachment relate to current adjustment and would the subjects' memories correspond to their actual childhood relationships? What was found was sobering. First, early childhood attachment status did not predict outcomes of early adolescent disturbance, either in terms of the subjects' or teachers' ratings. Second, early attachment status was not related to the teenagers' recollections of their early childhood relationships. Subjects with insecure attachments at 1 year were no more likely to describe their childhoods as negative than were subjects classified as securely attached. Third, a relation was found between current adjustment and recollection of the past. Teenagers with positive current adjustments had positive recollections of their past, while children with negative current adjustments had negative recollections.

This study demonstrates the problems of using subject recollections of the past, exactly one of the problems corrected for by longitudinal research. However, the results further brought into question the predictive utility of scores obtained in infancy for adolescent adjustment. The results of the Minnesota longitudinal study are more encouraging in this regard, but the data are still being analyzed and correlations rather than predictive relationships were emphasized. It is possible that statistically significant correlations will be found that, at the same time, provide for only weak predictive relationships. In other words, we do not as yet know whether there is a difference in findings between the two studies or whether the findings are similar but in one case statistically significant correlations are emphasized while in the other case the weakness of predictive power is emphasized.

In sum, then, we can conclude that there is evidence of consistency and coherence in personality, but there also is evidence of difficulty in predicting individual life trajectories. To return to the two points of view introduced at the beginning of this chapter, "You could always tell that . . . " and "Who could have predicted that . . . , " one can find evidence supportive of each. There is sufficient evidence of continuity that one can see relationships but sufficient uncertainty that prediction generally is problematic. The processes governing these relationships are still to be determined. Thus, studying personality longitudinally remains not only studying personality the hard way, but also involves coming to grips with the inherent uncertainty in the unfolding of individual lives.

MAJOR CONCEPTS

Phenotype.   The outer appearance as opposed to the genotype or underlying structure.

Genotype.   The underlying structure as opposed to the phenotype or outer appearance.

Stage theories.   Theories that emphasize fixed sequences or stages of development associated with specific ages (e.g., Freud's psychosexual stages of development).

Erogenous zone.   According to Freud, a part of the body that is a source of tension or excitation.

Narcissistic personality.   In psychoanalytic theory, a type of personality associated with the oral stage in which the world is viewed mainly in terms of the self and there is an excessive sense of entitlement.

Identity versus role diffusion.   Erikson's stage of development in which the person struggles to establish a sense of identity, or continuity as to who he or she is, as opposed to being without a sense of continuity or direction (role diffusion).

Critical period.   The concept that a particular time period is critical for the development of a characteristic, with the characteristic perhaps not developing if certain things do not occur during that time period.

Sensitive period.   The concept that a characteristic is particularly sensitive to influence during a particular time period.

Longitudinal research.   An approach to research emphasizing the study of the same subjects over an extended period of time.

Cross-sectional research.   An approach to research emphasizing the study of the same characteristics in subjects of different age groups.

California Q-Set.   A Q-sort set of personality characteristics used by the Blocks to study personality longitudinally.

Ego-control.   The Blocks' concept for the person's characteristic expression or containment of impulses, feelings, and desires.

Ego-resiliency.   The Blocks' concept for the extent to which people can modify their level of ego-control to meet the demands of the situation.

Attachment.   The concept developed by Bowlby emphasizing the early formation of a bond between child and caregiver, generally the mother, that is seen as having important implications for later social and emotional development.

Internal working models.   Bowlby's concept for the mental representations, associ-ated with affect, of the self and others that are developed during the early years of development and that form the basis for expectations concerning future relationships.

Strange Situation procedure.   The test situation developed by Ainsworth as a measure of attachment style in infants.

SUMMARY

1. The chapter considers the question of longitudinal stability or the stability of personality over time. The challenge here is to be able to recognize underlying (genotypic) continuity despite apparent (phenotypic) change. More generally, it is to account for both stability and change in personality over the life course.

2. Stage theories of development emphasize a fixed sequence or fixed progression of stages, each with its own defining characteristics and age of occurrence. Freud's psychosexual stages of development and Erikson's psychosocial stages of development are illustrative stage theories of development.

3. Questions such as the following have been raised in regard to stage theories: Does development proceed according to a fixed sequence? Is there uniformity of development across domains of personality functioning during a particular stage of development? Should the concept of critical periods, associated with stage theories, be replaced by that of sensitive periods?

4. In comparison to cross-sectional research, longitudinal research allows for the study of the development process as it unfolds. Such studies are useful for considering both stability and change in personality development. In considering change we must be careful to distinguish between different kinds of change: absolute-relative, quantitative-qualitative, phenotypic-genotypic, continuous-discontinuous. Magnusson's Swedish study of development and adjustment, the Blocks' research on ego-control and ego-resiliency, and the Minnesota parent-child project on the implications of early attachment for later social and emotional development illustrate longitudinal research on personality development.

5. Longitudinal studies provide evidence of qualitative change and consistent, coherent personality development over time. At the same time, there is evidence of considerable individual variability in degree of stability and kind of change.

6. It is suggested that how much stability and change are emphasized relative to one another depends on the area of personality considered, the measures used, and the biases of the investigator. We need to know more about the boundary conditions of change, the person and environmental variables that influence stability and change, and, most of all, the processes involved.

PART

III

TOPICS IN PERSONALITY RESEARCH

We now have had the chance to consider differing research strategies, the units of personality, and issues concerning personality determinants and development. In this section we turn to personality research in regard to specific topics rather than broad, general issues. The selected topics represent those areas of personality research currently receiving the greatest attention. However, an attempt has been made to focus on areas of longlasting significance rather than on those that are more of a fad. This, of course, is a difficult decision to make. We know that fads exist in personality research, as in most other areas of researech. For example, the 1950s were known as the decade of AAA, with a tremendous proportion of personality research focused on the concepts of achievement, authoritarianism, and anxiety. None of these represents as significant a focus of current investigation as was true for that period, and thus there is no chapter dedicated specifically to any one of them. Which of the current research topics will be listed in a text 40 years from now remains to be seen. In the meantime, the topics that follow represent an effort to capture both what is characteristic of research being conducted today and what may be of longlasting significance. In covering these topics I also have tried to return periodically to the research approaches and units of personality previously considered.

In the chapters that follow we begin with consideration of what I view as a major issue throughout virtually all personality research—how important are unconscious aspects of our personality functioning and how are we to measure them? For a long time this was a neglected topic in the field, although the concept of the unconscious always has been emphasized by psychoanalysts. Today there is considerable research being done in this area, from a psychoanalytic perspective as well as from other perspectives. From consideration of the unconscious, we move on to consideration of the concept of the self. What could be more central to personality than the ways in which we perceive ourselves? Yet, as will be seen in Chapter 8, over the course of the years personality psychologists have had greater and lesser interest in the concept of the self. In addition, we now are beginning to consider the significant cultural differences that exist in how the self is understood and the importance given to it in society. In Chapter 9 we return to the motive concept and consider the question of how people move from *thinking* about something to *doing* something, that is, from thoughts and plans to action. As noted earlier in the text, a focus on cognitive processes was part of the cognitive revolution. With time, however, interest shifted from "pure cognition" to how cognition is related to processes such as motivation and affect. Attention to the person's movement from thinking to doing is expressive of this shift. The topics covered in Chapter 10—emotion, adaptation, and health, also are expressive of this shift. In this chapter we have a chance to consider the role of emotion in personality functioning. In addition, we consider research on how people cope with stress and the implications of such efforts for their physical and psychological well-being. In the remaining two chapters in this section, we consider the nature of maladaptive psychological functioning and processes of therapeutic change, and then the issue of personality assessment.

This, then, is a broad sweep of what lies ahead. Today there is a great deal of activity in the area of personality psychology. The following chapters give a sense of the vitality and breadth of research present in the field.

THE UNCONSCIOUS

CHAPTER OVERVIEW

In this chapter we consider a wide variety of phenomena suggesting that at times people are unaware of internal and external stimuli that influence how they think, feel, and behave. Although the topic remains controversial, most personality psychologists accept the existence of such unconscious or nonconscious influences. We consider here the evidence in support of the existence of such influences and their potential importance for personality research generally.

Questions to Be Addressed in This Chapter

1 What is meant by the concept of the unconscious?

2 What evidence is there for the influence of unconscious processes on our thoughts, feelings, and behavior?

3 How does the concept of the unconscious suggested by information-processing theories differ from that suggested by psychoanalytic theory?

4 If we accept the importance of unconscious processes, what are the implications for the use of self-report data in personality research?

We come now to the first of the chapters on special topics in personality research and begin with one that is exceedingly important and complex—the unconscious. The view taken here is that this topic is central to our research on, and understanding of, personality. In fact, significant progress in the field will be difficult to achieve until we have some way of assessing the importance of unconscious processes in the psychological functioning of individuals. A somewhat similar view is suggested by Lazarus (1993b) in relation to work on emotion and adaptation: "A psychology that does not entail unconscious processes would be inadequate. It is necessary to face up to the scientific difficulties inherent in the concept" (p. 344).

The concept of the unconscious is of the utmost importance both theoretically and methodologically. From a theoretical standpoint, in personality psychology we have widely differing views of the importance of unconscious phenomena. Consider Freud's suggestion that we are "lived" by unknown, unconscious, and at times uncontrollable forces, as well as his suggestion that "psychoanalysis aims at and achieves nothing more than the discovery of the unconscious in mental life" (1924, p. 397). Compare such a view with that of the social cognitive theorist Albert Bandura: "While people are not fully conscious of every aspect of their thinking, neither is their thinking largely unconscious. People generally know what they are thinking" (1986, p. 125). What we have here are two very different views concerning the importance of unconscious phenomena in personality functioning. The differences are so fundamental that they reflect basic differences in the views of human nature and lead to interest in different kinds of phenomena that are studied in different ways: Freud emphasizes the clinical study of dreams and Bandura experimental investigation.

This takes us to the second matter of importance, the implications of views of unconscious processes for research. We consider this matter in greater detail later in the chapter. For now, however, we can note that a theory such as Freud's, one that places a great deal of emphasis on the unconscious, will not place a great deal of faith in reports people make about their thoughts and feelings, and perhaps even their behaviors as well. If we are "lived" by unknown forces, then how much stock can be placed in what people say they are thinking, feeling, or doing? On the other hand, we can note that Bandura's view will allow for, perhaps even encourage, the use of self-report data. If people generally know what they are thinking, then we can have faith in what they say concerning their thoughts. If such is the case, then it makes sense to make use of such data to study relationships among thoughts, feelings, and action.

In addition to the importance of the unconscious for theory and research, one's view of the unconscious has important moral and legal implications. From a moral standpoint, to what extent can people be held responsible for their behavior if they can be governed by unknown, uncontrollable forces? Can one be held accountable for something one did not "intend" to do, if by intent we mean a conscious decision to act? Does someone saying "I didn't mean to do that; I did it unconsciously" alter our response to the act? And, if so, how do we distinguish between the person who "truly" did something for unintentional, unconscious reasons and the person who "uses" such an explanation as an excuse? If a friend "forgets" to do something he or she promised to do, how do we separate out whether such forgetting is due to having too much on his or her mind, to an unconscious wish not to do it, or to a conscious decision not to do it and use "I forgot" as an excuse?

Very much the same matters apply in legal situations. A jury often has to decide whether a crime was committed with intent, where intent is equated with consciousness. In addition, juries have to make judgments concerning the accuracy as opposed to the distortion in people's memories. Such judgments can be particularly problematic when a long period has intervened between the original event and the recovery of the memory, and when events of major emotional significance are involved. Were such memories "buried" in the unconscious? Is it possible for someone to forget an event of major significance for a number of years and then to remember what was previously forgotten? Issues such as this are arising more frequently as cases of recall of childhood sexual abuse are reported. In one highly publicized case, a man stood trial for the murder of a young girl 20 years earlier, with the major evidence being the recovered memory of the event by his daughter. Using this case as a backdrop for discussion of the reality of repressed memories, a psychologist who is an expert on memory and eyewitness testimony raises the following questions: "How common is it for memories of child abuse to be repressed? How are jurors and judges likely to react to these repressed memory claims? When the memories surface, what are they like? and How authentic are the memories" (Loftus, 1993, p. 518)?

To examine briefly one final legal situation, is it possible for people's behavior to be influenced by messages delivered to them through their unconscious, or, as it is called in the field, subliminally? Such an issue was raised when a group of parents claimed in a lawsuit that the suicides of their sons were influenced by the subliminal message "Do it!" in the music of the rock group Judas Priest. The parents lost their case against the rock group, but the potential effects of subliminal messages remain a matter of considerable legal, as well as psychological, importance.

In sum, for many reasons it is important that we consider carefully what we mean by the unconscious and the evidence concerning its importance for psychological functioning. Before considering an illustrative range of phenomena, it should be recognized that there is no such thing as "an unconscious." So far as we know, there is no structure that can be located as constituting "the unconscious." Rather, what we call the **unconscious** consists of a set of contents and processes that is not available to awareness (consciousness) yet is potentially capable of influencing psychological functioning. What we call *the unconscious* consists of thoughts and feelings that, while not available at the time to consciousness, may influence other conscious and unconscious thoughts, feelings, and behaviors. What we call *the unconscious* consists of the processes through which such effects occur. In sum, although at times we may speak of *an unconscious*, in reality we are speaking of contents and processes that have an effect on the person's psychological functioning without the person's being aware of them or their effects.

ILLUSTRATIVE PHENOMENA

In this section we consider phenomena illustrative of unconscious processes and the effects of these processes. We take a broad sweep here, including phenomena that some, but not other, psychologists would consider illustrative. At this time, there are differing views as to which phenomena should be considered illustrative of unconscious processes and how such phenomena should be measured. Therefore, it seems wise to begin with a broad sweep and then see whether categories of unconscious phenomena can be formed.

1. *Subliminal Perception.* There is considerable evidence that stimuli too weak to be consciously perceived may nevertheless have an effect on perception and other psychological processes (Kihlstrom, 1987, 1990). The term used for such phenomena is **subliminal perception;** *subliminal* refers to the fact that the stimulus is presented below the threshold for conscious perception. For example, subjects shown a picture of a duck at a speed too fast for conscious perception draw more duck-related images when asked to draw a nature scene than do subjects shown a picture without a duck image in it (Eagle, Wolitzky, & Klein, 1966). Thus, the duck image is perceived and has an effect on later thought processes although subjects cannot report what was initially flashed to them on the screen. Similar effects can be demonstrated with auditory perception. For example, in a **dichotic listening task** the subject is instructed to attend to stimuli presented in one ear while different stimuli are presented in the other ear. Although the person reports no awareness of the stimuli presented in the unattended channel (ear), the stimuli nevertheless have an effect on subsequent behavior.

   At one time there was the suggestion that subliminal advertising might be used to get people to buy particular products (e.g., images of coke and popcorn might be flashed subliminally on the screen in a movie theatre to increase consumption of these products) (Morse & Stoller, 1982). In an antishoplifting effort, several department stores played subliminal messages such as "If you steal, you'll get caught" (Wortman & Loftus, 1992). Overall, research suggests that such advertising and antitheft efforts are not successful; that is, they do not get people to do things they would not ordinarily do or stop them from doing things they ordinarily do (Loftus & Klinger, 1992). There recently has been an increase in popularity of self-help audiotapes that present calming or motivating messages subliminally. However, systematic research raises questions concerning the effectiveness of such tapes other than through the suggestion involved in purchasing the tapes in the first place (Greenwald, Spangenberg, Pratkanis, & Eskenazi, 1991). In sum, there is clear evidence of subliminal perception effects on psychological processes but the extent and conditions of such effects remain to be determined.

2. *Implicit Memory.* **Implicit memory** involves the effects of events that occur or material learned for which the person reports no memory (Schachter, 1987). This is in contrast to *explicit memory,* when the person consciously recalls the events or material. Such implicit memory effects can be seen in patients who have experienced some brain damage. However, they also have been demonstrated experimentally. For example, subjects who learn a list of paired words and numbers will later learn the same pairs more easily than pairs not originally learned, even though they report no recall or recognition of the previously learned pairs (Nelson, 1978). Kihlstrom (1987, 1990) suggests that such implicit

memory effects are similar to the subliminal perception effects in that both involve the effects on psychological processes of events that are not accessible to conscious awareness. Kihlstrom suggests the term **implicit perception** for the subliminal perception effects. However, he also notes that in the case of implicit memory the events initially were available to conscious awareness, whereas in the case of implicit perception (subliminal perception) this was not the case.

3. *Dissociative Phenomena.* **Dissociative phenomena** involve occasions when major aspects of a person's functioning are kept out of awareness or are not integrated into the rest of the person's psychological functioning. Such experiences range from the mild and fairly common, such as forgetting a long stretch of driving, to the serious and relatively uncommon, such as forgetting major segments of recent time, as in someone forgetting where he or she has been for the past few days. At the extreme are cases of *multiple personalities,* in which the person has multiple, separate personalities that at times act independently of one another; some may be aware of the others and some may not. Once considered rare, multiple personalities are being reported in increasing frequency, to the extent that it is considered by some to be the psychological disorder of the 1990s (Kluft & Fine, 1993).

Dissociative phenomena are viewed by clinicians as efforts to block out of awareness events of extreme stress and trauma. Such processes are seen in military personnel during war when the combatant may forget a complete battle episode. The availability of the episode to awareness is demonstrated, however, with the administration of a drug called sodium pentothal or "truth serum" (Grinker & Spiegel, 1945). A scale to measure individual differences in the tendency toward dissociation has been developed (Bernstein & Putnam, 1986). Subjects are asked to indicate the frequency with which they have experiences such as the following: (1) find youself in a place with no idea of how you got there; (2) listen to someone talk and then realize you didn't hear part or all of what was said; (3) find yourself dressed in clothes you don't remember putting on; (4) experience your body as not belonging to you; (5) find yourself having things you don't remember buying.

4. *Blindsight.* Individuals with brain injuries may demonstrate unusual deficits in sensory functioning, retaining one aspect of sensory functioning while losing another. Thus, there have been instances in which patients with brain injuries report being unable to see yet they are able to respond correctly to stimuli when required to do so. For example, the patient might report being unable to see a pencil on the table but be able to pick it up. Such phenomena have been termed *blindsight* (Weisskrantz, 1986). Of related interest, although different in cause, are cases of hysterical blindness, in which the person is unable to see but there is no physical deficit. In one such case reported in the literature, a man who had been blind for two years and was unresponsive to psychiatric and drug treatment was helped to regain his vision through reinforcement for correct responses to a light stimulus (Brady & Lind, 1961). The successful regaining of his sight through the application of Skinnerian principles of be-

havior modification demonstrated the psychological rather than physical basis for the problem.

5. *Hypnosis.* Hypnosis alters the person's state of consciousness in response to the actions of another person (i.e., the hypnotist). Under such conditions, the person being hypnotized may fail to experience pain under normally painful conditions, may upon instruction from the hypnotist fail to remember experiences that occurred under hypnosis (i.e., posthypnotic amnesia), and may upon termination of the hypnosis perform actions suggested by the hypnotist during the hypnotic period (i.e., posthypnotic suggestion) (Kihlstrom, 1987). In the case of posthypnotic suggestion, the person may be unaware of performing the act and/or the origin of the behavior in the hypnotist's suggestion. Although interpretations of hypnotic phenomena vary, there is no question concerning the alteration of states of consciousness involved (Bowers, 1992).

6. *Subliminal Listening.* In his bestselling book *Peace, Love and Healing* (1989), the physician Bernie Siegel reports cases of what he calls *subliminal listening,* that is, cases in which patients in a coma or under anesthesia can hear even though they are not conscious. He also suggests that although many such patients do not recall what they heard, they can be affected by what they heard. He reports his own experiences, and those of others reported in reputable medical journals, of information heard at the unconscious level affecting subsequent behavior, attitudes, and health. Although there have been some reports of learning information during sleep, some recent research casts doubt upon such phenomena (Wood, Bootzin, Kihlstrom, & Schachter, 1992).

7. *Telling More Than We Know.* When asked to give reasons for their behavior, people give explanations. However, their explanations often have little to do with the real reason, even if they are attempting to be totally honest and forthcoming. For example, if customers are asked why they purchased a particular item, they may give a reason that makes sense to them even if it can be demonstrated that something else caused their selection (Nisbett & Wilson, 1977). Customers might say that they selected the item on the basis of brand when it can be demonstrated that place on the shelf made a difference. Retailers are well aware of the importance of shelf space placement for purchases, even if customers generally do not include this variable in their conscious decision making. In other words, there are hidden or unconscious influences on the decisions and judgments people make because they are not able to monitor certain processes and the actual causal agents are not part of their conscious decision-making repertoire.

8. *Conditioning Without Awareness.* In the 1930s a somewhat forgotten study was conducted in which subjects were classically conditioned to stimuli without conscious awareness, what was called *unconscious perception.* In this study (Diven, 1937), subjects received a shock to the word *barn.* In addition to showing signs of anxiety (i.e., galvanic skin response, a physiological indicator of sweat gland activity) in response to the word *barn,* they showed such signs in relation to three other classes of words: (1) the word *red,* which always preceded presentation of the word *barn;* (2) whichever word followed the

word *barn*; and (3) all words having a rural association (e.g., hay, plow, pasture, sheep) in contrast to the lack of an anxiety reaction in response to words with an urban association (e.g., pavement, subway, streetcar). In other words, the anxiety reaction generalized to other stimuli associated by contiguity in time or in *meaning* with the stimulus that was followed by shock. What was particularly striking about this result was that it occurred even when the subject failed to recognize that the word *barn* was the signal for the shock. In other words, there was generalized anxiety to meaning-related stimuli even though the person was unaware of the original stimulus signal for the shock. Through unconscious perception, one can develop fears for which there is no conscious explanation.

Subsequent research has demonstrated similar effects. In one experiment city names embedded in material presented to the nonattended channel in a dichotic listening task were followed by shock. Evidence was found of anxiety responses to these words as well as to associated stimuli even though the subjects were not aware of the words being followed by shock. Once more there was evidence of conditioning without awareness as well as generalization of such conditioning, again without awareness, to meaning-related stimuli (Corteen & Wood, 1972).

Beyond such research, there is evidence of what is called **vicarious learning** or **vicarious conditioning**, in which, for example, a child perceives a parent express an emotion in regard to a stimulus and learns to experience the same emotion in response to the stimulus (Bandura, 1986; Mineka et al., 1984). Thus, a child may unconsciously acquire fear and disgust responses by observing a parent express such emotional responses to particular stimuli; that is, direct experience itself is not required for the conditioning process to occur.

9. *Automatic (Routinized) Processes.* Many things we think and do occur automatically, without our expending conscious effort in the process. Many such operations originally were learned consciously while others were learned unconsciously. In either case, however, they become so routinized or automatic as to be unconscious. Illustrations of such **automatic processes** are following the rules of grammar, tying one's shoes, and typing. Although we have learned most of the rules for correct grammar in speech, most of us cannot spell out these rules; that is, they have been acquired unconsciously and remain unconscious. In tying our shoes and typing, the rules once were learned but often we have to struggle to relate them in the present. Could you tell someone how to tie a shoe or locate on the typewriter (or computer keyboard) the letters *x*, *m*, or *p*?

10. *Repression.* The concept of **repression** lies at the heart of psychoanalytic theory. In repression a thought or memory associated with anxiety, that once was conscious, is "made to become" unconscious and kept unconscious by a protective barrier. As in implicit memory, the event originally was registered in consciousness. In contrast to ordinary forgetting, however, in repression an active barrier against remembering is suggested, raising the question: How can the mind know what it isn't supposed to know? Psychoanalysts present considerable clinical evidence in support of the concept of repression, involving many

cases of previously forgotten material that is recalled in the process of analysis. As noted earlier in the chapter, many cases of recall of earlier experiences of child abuse are currently being reported. Such cases involve the recall of experiences forgotten for many years. However, it has been difficult to demonstrate the processes of repression and lifting of repression in the laboratory. There is evidence that individuals assessed as "repressors" recall fewer negative childhood experiences and have fewer early memories than do individuals assessed as "nonrepressors" (P. J. Davis & Schwartz, 1987). At this time there are differing views among psychologists as to the viability of the concept of repression, with some remaining committed to the concept as formulated by psychoanalysts and others suggesting a process similar to that of implicit memory (Erdelyi, 1985; Greenwald, 1992).

Ten phenomena have been presented as illustrative of unconscious processes. They cover a wide range of phenomena, with possible overlap among categories. Some psychologists would accept some of these phenomena as illustrative of unconscious processes, while other psychologists would accept different ones. In this regard it is important to be aware that there is not an agreed upon definition of what constitute unconscious phenomena. Nor is there agreement concerning how such phenomena should be measured. Although to this day some psychologists are prepared to reject the concept of the unconscious, most psychologists not only accept the existence of such phenomena but emphasize their importance in many aspects of our functioning:

> Our conclusion, perhaps discomforting for the layperson, is that unconscious influences are ubiquitous. It is clear that people sometimes plan and then act. More often than not, however, behavior is influenced by unconscious processes; that is, we act and then, if questioned, make our excuses.
>
> Jacoby, Toth, Lindsay, & Debner, 1992, p. 82

BRIEF HISTORICAL OVERVIEW

Having considered the phenomena of concern to us, we can proceed with a brief historical review to provide a context for discussion of current theory and research. Although many people associate the concept of the unconscious with Freud, its history dates further back (Ellenberger, 1970; Pekala, 1991). However, Freud's emphasis on an unconscious that was the storehouse for a host of sexual and aggressive drives and memories was new. According to Freud, his discovery of the extent to which we are influenced by unknown, uncontrollable forces was a third blow to the self-image of humans, following those of Copernicus's discovery that the earth is not the center of the universe and Darwin's discovery that we do not exist independently of other members of the animal kingdom.

Early in the history of experimental psychology, introspection was used as the major method of investigation. As part of the study of consciousness, subjects in the laboratories of Wundt and Titchener were trained to observe their perceptions, images, and feelings (Kihlstrom, 1987). With the rise of Watsonian behaviorism, study of consciousness (and thereby unconsciousness) was rejected as a legitimate area of inquiry. The interest was in behavior, that is, in overt behavior that did not require verbal self-report and that could be reliably observed and measured. Turning in good part to the study of animal behavior, there was an interest in what organisms *do* rather than in what they *think*, and an interest in external reinforcers that regulate behavior rather than in internal thought processes.

Psychoanalysts, of course, had maintained their interest in the internal workings of the mind, in particular of the unconscious mind. And there were some academic psychologists, such as Henry Murray, who retained a theoretical and research interest in such processes (Chapter 1). It was not until the 1950s, however, that systematic research started to be conducted on unconscious processes. On the one hand, interest developed in sleep research and the importance of unconscious processes in dream formation (Fisher, 1960; Shevrin & Luborsky, 1958). And, on the other hand, the "New Look" in perception was developing. Dating back to the late 1940s and early 1950s, the New Look movement emphasized the perceiver as an active participant in the perception process, not just a passive recorder of external stimuli (Bruner, 1992). In some striking experiments, it was demonstrated that the size of more valuable coins was overestimated relative to the size of less valuable coins, particularly on the part of poor children relative to rich children (Bruner & Goodman, 1947). It also was demonstrated that words of greater value to subjects could be recognized more readily than words of lesser value (Postman, Bruner, & McGinnies, 1948). Finally, psychoanalytically inclined researchers were demonstrating individual differences in the ways in which needs or motives influenced perception (Klein, 1951, 1954).

In sum, what was evolving during the 1950s was an interest in how personality processes are involved in perception. In addition, some psychodynamically oriented psychologists developed an interest in how needs influence what is perceived and how the person can unconsciously guard against the perception of threatening stimuli (perceptual defense). However, more traditional psychologists were critical of such efforts, suggesting flaws in the research designs as the basis for the findings reported. In the words of one of the participants in this period,

> Psychoanalytically committed investigators were, of course, inclined to take the view that everything was "seen" through the judas eye of the unconscious mind prior to getting into consciousness, but the more conservative critics (i.e., the main body of American experimental psychologists) would have none of it.
>
> Bruner, 1992, p. 781

Then, along came the cognitive revolution (Chapter 3). What is interesting here is that the cognitive revolution paved the way for a return to an interest in thinking and consciousness. However, in its use of the computer as a metaphor, there was an interest in rational thinking associated with consciousness rather than the irrational thinking associated by many with the unconscious. This was the case, at least, in the early beginnings of the cognitive revolution. In time, cognitive psychologists as well as personality and social psychologists returned to an interest in unconscious processes, both from a psychoanalytic perspective as well as an information-processing perspective. Such interest has grown to the extent that, in the words of one leader in the field, "After 100 years of neglect, suspicion, and frustration, unconscious processes have now taken a firm hold on the collective mind of psychologists" (Kihlstrom, 1992, p. 788).

As we shall see, many issues remain in regard to our understanding of unconscious processes. As previously noted, however, what is largely not in dispute is the importance of such processes. In the next section we consider two approaches to these phenomena, the psychoanalytic and the information processing. Followers of these two approaches are in agreement concerning the existence of unconscious processes but disagree concerning how these processes operate.

THE DYNAMIC UNCONSCIOUS OF PSYCHOANALYSIS

We return here to consider in greater detail the concept of the unconscious as elaborated by Freud. To this day it remains a bedrock concept of psychoanalytic theory, perhaps *the* bedrock concept! According to psychoanalytic theory, psychic life can be described in terms of the degree to which we are aware of phenomena: the *conscious* relates to phenomena we are aware of at any given moment, the *preconscious* to phenomena we can be aware of if we attend to them, and the *unconscious* to phenomena that we are unaware of and *cannot* be aware of except under special circumstances.

It is important to recognize the difference between the preconscious and the unconscious. Whereas preconscious phenomena are available to consciousness if we attend to them, unconscious phenomena require special circumstances to reach the level of consciousness. At this moment I am conscious of writing this paragraph and not of what I did yesterday. However, the latter is in my preconscious and available to consciousness if I turn my attention in that direction. Other memories are stored in my unconscious and are not available to consciousness, even if my attention is directed to the past, unless special circumstances are created to reduce the barrier against recall of these experiences. For Freud, particularly during the early years of psychoanalysis, much of therapy was directed toward making conscious what was previously unconscious. Thus, the recall of early memories was an important element of the therapeutic process.

In addition, it is important to recognize that although Freud emphasized the repressed part of the unconscious, he also suggested that other phenomena were part of the unconscious and were there for other than protective reasons (Shevrin, 1992). However, the former were of particular interest to Freud.

The unconscious emphasized by Freud and current analysts is known as the **dynamic unconscious**. Three qualities are associated with it. First, the operations of unconscious processes are *qualitatively different* from those of conscious processes. Whereas our conscious cognitive processes generally are rational and operate according to the rules of logic, our unconscious processes often are illogical. According to psychoanalytic theory, anything is possible in terms of the operations of the unconscious. For example, within the unconscious opposites can stand for the same thing, events of different periods may coexist, distant places may be brought together, and large things may fit into small spaces. According to the theory, the functioning of the unconscious is seen in dreams, slips of the tongue, psychotic thought, symbolic works of art, rituals, and in some aspects of the thinking of young children.

A second important aspect of the dynamic unconscious is that it contains wishes, drives, or motives. In other words, there is a motivational component to the contents of the unconscious. According to psychoanalytic theory, the contents of the dynamic unconscious are always pushing for expression and can be kept from awareness only through the operation of a protective barrier. The defenses represent the protective barrier that keeps the contents of the unconscious from reaching awareness. These defenses, such as repression, are themselves unconscious. In other words, both the contents of the unconscious and the operations of the defenses to keep these contents unconscious are not available to awareness. This raises the question of how we can be aware of the need to defend against something without being aware of what it is we are defending against. How can the mind be aware of something so as to act against it without such awareness reaching the level of consciousness? We shall return to this question later on.

Finally, related to this second aspect, the unconscious is filled with conflicts (Shevrin, 1992). According to the theory, conflicts such as those between two wishes or between a wish and a fear are important elements in the life of the unconscious.

The Freudian Unconscious. The Freudian unconscious emphasizes motivational explanations for phenomena such as slips of the tongue.

In sum, according to Freud, major portions of psychic life are unconscious and operate according to principles different from those of conscious life. Unconscious processes can be seen as dynamic in the sense of expressing the interplay among forces, either between conflicts within the unconscious (e.g., wishes and fears) or between the push from within the unconscious against the protective barrier of the defenses.

As noted in Chapter 1, Freud used clinical investigation to study unconscious processes. In particular, he was interested in unconscious processes as they operated in dreams and psychological symptoms. The analysis of dreams was seen by Freud to be the "royal road" to an understanding of the unconscious. He was more interested in describing unconscious phenomena and in understanding psychological symptoms as expressions of the unconscious than he was in defining a scientific concept. Thus, his descriptions of the workings of the unconscious often have a metaphorical quality to them, as when he speaks of "the unconscious" or says that we are "lived by unknown forces." In addition, he was so impressed with his clinical observations that he did not feel the need for experimental corroboration. Thus, when an American psychologist wrote to Freud of his experimental evidence in support of motivated forgetting, Freud was politely encouraging but indicated that the concept did not require such experimental evidence (Rosenzweig, 1941).

Having said this, is there experimental evidence in support of the concept of the dynamic unconscious? We can trace the beginnings of such efforts to the work of Otto Poetzl (1917), a Viennese neuropsychologist who produced the classic experimental study of the effects of unconscious stimuli on psychic functioning (Ionescu & Erdelyi, 1992; Shevrin, 1992). Poetzl, influenced by Freud, presented subjects with pictorial stimuli at a level below conscious perception. In other words, subjects could not report the contents of the pictorial stimuli. On the following day, he had subjects report their dreams of the previous night and draw elements of them. What he found was that elements of the pictorial stimuli that could not be reported at the time of presentation found their way into the subjects' dreams; that is, what could not be reported as perceived was not only perceived but also influenced the contents of that evening's dreams.

Although Poetzl's work was largely neglected for many years, experimentally oriented analysts later came to see it as an important contribution. These later efforts were part of the New Look in perception of the 1940s and 1950s, noted in the earlier historical review. Poetzl's findings were replicated and extended into the areas of free association and perception; that is, stimuli not consciously perceived were found to influence free associations and perceptions. As part of this research it was discovered that subjects appeared to have a need to dream: If awakened during dream sleep, they appeared to try to make up for the lost time for dreaming (Fisher, 1956, 1965). Although this finding could be interpreted on other grounds, at the time it was taken as support for Freud's idea that the function of the dream was to preserve sleep by transforming thoughts that might awaken the person into symbolic images.

Poetzl's findings also influenced work in the area of subliminal perception and perceptual defense. Early research on subliminal perception within the psychoanalytic framework has already been described. This involved demonstrations that stimuli not perceived at the level of conscious awareness could influence subsequent perceptions, images, and dreams. Such demonstrations do not, however, suggest that psychodynamic or motivational forces are involved. Yet, the operation of such forces is key to the definition of the dynamic unconscious. Work in the area of perceptual defense seemed to provide such a demonstration. In an early and influential piece of research, subjects were found to require more time to see emotionally toned words, such as *penis* and *whore*, than was required to perceive neutral words such as *apple* and *dance* (McGinnies, 1949). This research was criticized on a number of methodological grounds (e.g., Did subjects identify the emotionally toned words earlier but were reluctant to verbalize them to the experimenter? Were emotionally toned, "taboo" words less commonly seen and therefore more difficult to perceive than neutral words?) and gradually fell into disfavor.

More recent experimental research on the dynamic unconscious has been done on what is called **subliminal psychodynamic activation** (Silverman, 1976, 1982; J. Weinberger, 1992; J. Weinberger & Silverman, 1987). In this research, there is an effort to stimulate unconscious motives without making them conscious. In general, the experimental procedure involves using a tachistoscope to show subjects material related to wishes or fears that are expected to be either threatening or anxiety-alleviating. Observations then are made as to whether the expected effects occur. In the case of threatening wishes, the material being presented subliminally (below the threshold for conscious recognition) is expected to stir up unconscious conflicts and thus increase psychological disturbance. In the case of an anxiety-alleviating wish, the material being presented subliminally is expected to diminish unconscious conflict and thus decrease psychological disturbance. In either case what is key is that the content that is upsetting or relieving to various groups of subjects is predicted beforehand on the basis of psychoanalytic theory and the effects occur only when the stimuli are perceived subliminally or unconsciously.

We can consider here three relevant pieces of research. The first concentrates on arousing positive, anxiety-alleviating wishes (Silverman & Weinberger, 1985). These studies are based on the psychoanalytic view that many people, and particularly some patient populations, have wishes to merge or unite with the good mother of early childhood (i.e., the comforting, protective, nurturing mother). In illustrative research, the stimulus MOMMY AND I ARE ONE is presented subliminally to schizophrenic patients. The assumption is that these individuals have strong wishes to merge with the good mother representation and therefore will find such messages pleasurable or anxiety-alleviating. The effects of such messages are contrasted to those of a neutral message such as PEOPLE ARE WALKING. In some cases a threatening message such as MOMMY IS GONE also is presented subliminally. The research to date suggests that presenting the message MOMMY AND I ARE ONE subliminally to these patients indeed lessens their pathology and enhances their progress in therapeutic and educational settings (Weinberger, 1992).

The second illustration involves a test of the concept of the Oedipus complex, involving the young boy's fear of castration by his father as a result of his competitive wishes for his mother. In this research stimuli were presented subliminally to subjects. The stimuli were designed to activate unconscious conflicts and either intensify or alleviate these conflicts. The stimulus chosen to intensify the oedipal conflict was BEATING DADDY IS WRONG, whereas that selected to alleviate such conflict was

BEATING DADDY IS OK. In addition, a number of other stimuli were presented, such as the neutral stimulus PEOPLE ARE WALKING.

Before the subliminal presentation of one of these stimuli, subjects were tested for performance in a dart-throwing competition. Performance in such competition was measured again following the subliminal presentation of one of the three messages. The prediction, based on psychoanalytic theory, was that the BEATING DAD IS WRONG message would intensify oedipal conflicts and lead to poorer performance whereas the message BEATING DAD IS OK would alleviate such conflicts and lead to improved performance. The neutral message was expected to have no specific effects on performance. As indicated in Table 7.1, this is exactly what was found to be the case (Silverman, Ross, Adler, & Lustig, 1978).

A few additional points about this research are noteworthy. First, the results were not obtained when the stimuli were presented above threshold. The psychodynamic activation effects appear to operate at the unconscious rather than at the conscious level. Second, the experimental stimuli had to relate to the motivational state of the subjects and the response measured had to be sensitive to changes in this motivational state. In this case, subjects were first "primed" with picture and story material containing oedipal content and then the task was presented as one involving competition. In sum, the subjects were primed to an increased competitive motivation level; the stimuli presented subliminally related to such motivation; and the performance measure reflected changes in such motivational levels.

The third piece of research again involves the activation of conflicts and the observation of effects on dynamically related behaviors. In contrast to the previously presented research, here groups differing in theoretically significant ways were compared. Normal college women and women with eating disorders were compared in terms of how many crackers they would eat following subliminal presentation (i.e., at a speed of 4 milliseconds) of three messages: MAMA IS LEAVING ME, MAMA IS LOANING IT, MONA IS LOANING IT. Although subjects were told they were participating in tests of visual and taste discrimination, in fact the study was designed to

TABLE 7.1 Oedipal Conflict and Competitive Performance

The data indicate that the unconscious arousal of the oedipal conflict (BEATING DAD IS WRONG) can interfere with competitive performance whereas the unconscious alleviation of these conflicts (BEATING DAD IS OK) can enhance competitive performance.

DART SCORE	BEATING DAD IS WRONG	BEATING DAD IS OK	PEOPLE ARE WALKING
TACHISTOSCOPIC PRESENTATION OF THREE STIMULI			
Mean, Prestimulus	443.7	443.3	439.0
Mean, Poststimulus	349.0	533.3	442.3
Difference	−94.7	+90.0	+3.3

Source: Partial results adapted from "Simple Research Paradigm for Demonstrating Subliminal Psychodynamic Activation: Effects of Oedipal Stimuli of Dart-Throwing Accuracy in College Men," by L. H. Silverman, D. L. Ross, J. M. Adler, and D. A. Lustig, 1978, *Journal of Abnormal Psychology, 87,* p. 346. Copyright 1978 by the American Psychological Association. Adapted by permission.

test the hypothesis that subjects with eating disorders would increase their eating in response to the MAMA IS LEAVING ME message relative to the other subjects and the other messages. As indicated in Table 7.2, the crucial message affected the cracker eating of only the eating disorder group. In addition, this effect was not found when the stimuli were presented above threshold (200 ms) (Patton, 1992).

These three studies are illustrative of the subliminal psychodynamic activation effects derived from psychoanalytic theory. By now about 100 such studies have been reported that on the whole support the theory and the existence of the effect. At the same time, the results remain controversial both within and outside psychoanalytic circles (Balay & Shevrin, 1988). Part of the problem here lies in the fact that the results have not always been replicable, although one recent review suggests that the overwhelming body of evidence supports the existence of these effects. According to this reviewer, "the reason the work has been and may remain controversial is that it does not seem to fit into what is accepted in present-day academic psychology and even has the flavor of magic" (J. Weinberger, 1992, p. 176).

Before concluding our discussion of the psychoanalytic, dynamic unconscious, we should return to consideration of the concept of repression. As noted, this concept is a fundamental one in psychoanalytic theory and has assumed increasing importance in society today as there are increased reports of the recovery of forgotten experiences of early sexual abuse (Loftus, 1993). At this point, one can say that there is evidence suggestive of the existence of repression. One can cite here not only clinical evidence but also two kinds of experimental evidence as well. First, in the phenomenon known as **state-dependent memory**, people can recapture memories of events previously forgotten when they are in the same mood as at the time of the original experience (Bower, 1981). In other words, memories acquired in one mood state are accessible only when people are later in the same mood state. Otherwise, they may not be able to recall the memories. Such a phenomenon is of interest

TABLE 7.2   Number of Crackers Eaten After Exposure to Message

The data indicate that unconscious arousal of anxiety (MAMA IS LEAVING ME, 4 ms) in subjects with an eating disorder can lead to increased eating activity. These effects are not apparent in subjects without an eating disorder or when stimuli are presented above the threshold for conscious perception (200 ms).

	MAMA IS LEAVING ME	MAMA IS LOANING IT	MONA IS LOANING IT
Eating disorder			
4 ms ($N = 10$)	19.40 ($SD = 5.48$)	8.20 ($SD = 2.56$)	7.80 ($SD = 3.34$)
200 ms ($N = 10$)	9.60 ($SD = 3.47$)	9.56 ($SD = 3.30$)	9.00 ($SD = 3.41$)
No eating disorder			
4 ms ($N = 10$)	8.50 ($SD = 1.57$)	8.20 ($SD = 2.91$)	
200 ms ($N = 10$)	8.60 ($SD = 3.10$)	8.60 ($SD = 2.84$)	

Source: "What Does It All Mean?," by J. S. Masling, 1992, in R. F. Bornstein and T. S. Pittman (Eds.), *Perception Without Awareness*, 266, New York: Guilford. Adapted from "Fear of Abandonment and Binge Eating," by C. J. Patton, 1992, *Journal of Nervous and Mental Disease, 180*, pp. 484–490. Reprinted by permission of Guilford Publications, Inc.

because certain affects or moods are created during psychoanalytic treatment that might foster the recovery of such state-dependent memories.

The second line of experimental evidence supportive of the concept of repression involves individual differences in subjects high and low on measures of repression. As noted earlier, there is evidence that repressors recall fewer negative emotions from childhood and their earliest such memories are from a later age than is true for nonrepressors (P. J. Davis & Schwartz, 1987). One could also note evidence of **hypermnesia**, or the increased recall of stimuli with time (Ionescu & Erdelyi, 1992). At the same time, it should be clear that at this point there is no solid body of experimental evidence testing two key elements of the psychoanalytic concept of repression—that the forgetting is motivated by the reduction of anxiety and that the barrier against recall is lifted under specific, demonstrable conditions. Unfortunately, the conditions necessary to replicate the clinical observations of repression are very difficult to duplicate in the laboratory. Thus, the concept remains controversial outside psychoanalytic circles. Finally, there is no known method for evaluating the validity of recovered memories, whether of sexual abuse or of other events.

Before turning to the cognitive, information-processing view of unconscious processes, let us return to the fundamental question concerning the psychoanalytic, dynamic unconscious: *How can the mind unconsciously know what it is not supposed to know?* Fundamental to the dynamic view of the unconscious is the action of opposing forces, most particularly the conflict between processes pressing for expression and awareness (e.g., wishes) and processes pressing to keep threatening thoughts, feelings, and wishes out of awareness (e.g., defenses). How can such unconscious processes operate against other unconscious processes? How can we unconsciously be "aware" of a thought or wish so as to prevent it from reaching consciousness?

An understanding of such operations is problematic only if we assume two levels of awareness—unconscious and conscious. However, the problem is taken care of if we are prepared to consider the possibility of multiple levels of unconsciousness (Bowers, 1992). In other words, some unconscious processes may operate at deeper levels of the unconscious than other processes. Those at less deep levels, although still unconscious, may exert some control over those at the deeper levels. Thus, defensive processes, such as repression, may be at less deep levels of unconsciousness and exert control over memories, thoughts, and wishes that are even more unconscious. Just as there may be varying levels of consciousness (i.e., preconscious and conscious), there may be varying levels of unconsciousness.

I am reminded here of two patients. The first came to therapy because he felt that he was not sufficiently in touch with his feelings. In the course of therapy he became aware that when he started to experience certain feelings, such as anger, he would immediately feel tense. He recalled that as a child feelings of anger immediately led to the threat of abandonment. He then "decided" it was best not to feel angry. It was as if whenever he would start to feel angry he would say: "Don't feel that way and don't recognize that feeling." It all began to happen so quickly and become so automatic that, over time, he no longer was aware that he was doing it. He now was unconsciously defending against what he was unaware of. In fact, there were times in therapy when he fleetingly had a feeling but was "unaware" of it. Yet, his face and body would express the feeling. When asked to attend to what was going on, he became aware of the fleeting feeling that he had "decided" to bypass and ignore! Once more, this all happened so rapidly that he was not even aware of what he was doing (i.e., defending himself against a feeling) or what he was doing it against (i.e., the feeling of anger associated with anxiety).

In the second case, a depressed patient reported that she did not think about her career and therefore it was not relevant to her depression. When we started to talk about her uncertainty about whether she could succeed at what she wanted to be, she said: "I don't want to talk about that; it makes me too nervous." Further discussion led to her talking about how frightened she was of failure and also how guilty she felt about possibly not continuing in the field that everyone always had planned for her. It now was less painful not to think about the whole thing. In this case, she was somewhat aware of the process of "not thinking" and of the guilt and anxiety associated with not advancing in the field that had been selected for her. Yet, she often would report that her only problem was not having the energy to commit herself to the work that needed to be done. With this reasoning, she both avoided the threat of failure and the guilt associated with choosing another career. In addition she punished herself by saying that she was lazy and just not hard working enough.

In these clinical illustrations we see how individuals can be unaware, fleetingly aware, or only vaguely aware of thoughts and feelings that are painful to them and then rapidly turn their attention elsewhere, so rapidly that the process has gone unnoticed. Under conditions of support and encouragement, they can become aware of what they are doing and what they are struggling to defend against. However, even in therapy generally there is initial resistance to this process, without awareness of the resistance. It is a little like avoiding using an injured hand without being aware of doing so, except that in the case of the dynamic unconscious the lack of awareness is all the greater—it is all unconscious rather than partly preconscious. Once more, it is these processes that are so striking to the psychoanalyst that are so difficult to duplicate in the laboratory.

THE COGNITIVE UNCONSCIOUS

We turn now to consider what has been called the *cognitive unconscious* (Kihlstrom, 1987). This view of the unconscious is associated with current cognitive, information-processing theory. The modern high-speed computer is the model for understanding cognitive processes and, in this case, unconscious processes. According to this view, a number of processes may be run simultaneously on the computer without one process being "aware" of the other processes. In addition, a distinction often is made between *controlled* and *automatic processing of information*. **Controlled information processing** is rational and under the flexible control of the individual; **automatic information processing** is unintentional, involuntary, or uncontrollable and occurs outside of awareness. In addition, controlled cognitive processes are seen as being effortful, as when we focus our attention on solving a problem; automatic cognitive processes are seen as being effortless, as when we tie our shoe or drive a car. Controlled cognitive processes take up a lot of storage and attentional capacity, that is, for example, one has to think about all of the rules of the road when first learning to drive; automatic cognitive processes take up little storage and attentional capacity. Although automatic processes may not always have every one of these characteristics, such processes are characterized by being unintentional, involuntary, effortless, and occurring outside of awareness (Bargh, 1992). Finally, then, controlled processes are associated with conscious processing of information and automatic processes with unconscious or nonconscious processing of information. The cognitive unconscious involves all cognitive processes that are unavailable to awareness, regardless of the reason they are unavailable. Within this context, it is suggested that "the cognitive unconscious encompasses a very large portion of mental life" (Kihlstrom, 1987, p. 1446).

In what follows, we consider evidence of unconscious influences on memory and perception, and then unconscious influences on feelings and attitudes toward others. We then go on to consider the importance of automatic, unconscious cognitive processes for personality.

UNCONSCIOUS INFLUENCES ON MEMORY AND PERCEPTION

Jacoby (Jacoby & Kelley, 1992; Jacoby, Lindsay, & Toth, 1992; Jacoby, Toth et al., 1992) uses a model of placing unintended or unconscious influences in opposition to conscious (controlled) or intentional processes to demonstrate the importance of the former. For example, consider the following experiment demonstrating the "false fame" effect. In the first phase of the experiment, subjects are asked to read a list of names of nonfamous people (e.g., Sebastian Weisdorf). Half the subjects read the list with full attention, the other half with divided attention (attention was divided by subjects simultaneously monitoring a string of digits presented auditorially). In the second phase, subjects read a list of names that includes the names of famous people, the names of additional nonfamous people, and the names of the nonfamous people presented in the first phase. The subjects are asked to make fame judgments of the names and are informed that all of the names from the first phase list are indeed nonfamous. In other words, if subjects could remember the names from the first phase, they could be sure these were not famous people. On the other hand, if subjects read the name but could not remember it, the effect of "unconscious" familiarity might lead them to rate the name as famous in the second phase of the experiment. In sum, the latter unconscious, "false fame" effect was acting in opposition to the conscious recall effect.

Remember that in the first phase of the experiment, subjects were divided into full attention and divided attention groups. Would one expect a difference in performance in the two groups? As hypothesized, subjects who studied the names with full attention could recognize the nonfamous names from the first list when they appeared on the second list. In comparison, subjects who studied the names with divided attention were much more likely to mistakenly judge the earlier nonfamous names as famous when they appeared on the second list. In other words, reading the names under conditions of divided attention provided the basis for an unconscious influence on memory that was not true for the group that read the list with full attention. The unconscious influence of misinterpreting familiarity as fame occurred in the divided attention group but not in the full attention group.

In an experiment on unconscious influences on perception, Jacoby (Jacoby, Allan, Collins, & Larwill, 1988) presented previously heard and new sentences to subjects. These sentences were presented against a background of white noise of varying degrees of loudness and the subjects were asked to judge the loudness of the noise. Subjects mistakenly judged the background noise of the previously heard sentences as less loud than the background noise of the new sentences. In other words, in actuality subjects could hear the previously heard sentences more easily because of familiarity but instead judged the background noise to be less. That is, the subjects were unable to recognize the effect of memory on perception and thus had the subjective experience of a lower level of noise. This effect was found to be automatic in that it held even when subjects were told about the effect of prior perception and were told to avoid it. The subjects continued to judge the background noise accompanying previously heard sentences as less loud than that accompanying the new sentences. The effect was unconscious and automatic in that subjects could not be aware of and control it.

UNCONSCIOUS INFLUENCES ON FEELINGS AND ATTITUDES TOWARD OTHERS

For some time psychologists had been aware of evidence that repeated exposure to stimuli could increase their attractiveness (Zajonc, 1968). Most psychologists assumed that such an increase in positive affective response was due to conscious recognition. However, subsequent research demonstrated that these same positive exposure effects could be produced even when the exposures were too brief to be consciously perceived (Kunst-Wilson & Zajonc, 1980; W. R. Wilson, 1979). In other words, consciously knowing that the object was familiar was not necessary for the positive feelings effect to occur—subjects could feel more than they could know from conscious awareness.

This line of research was extended by social psychologists to demonstrate how attitudes toward others might be influenced unconsciously. In one study different groups of subjects were presented with lists of words with differing proportions of hostility words, ranging from 0% to 80%, all at a level below recognition. They then were given a description of a person that was ambiguous with regard to hostility and asked to rate the person on several trait dimensions. Despite not perceiving the words, subjects rated the person increasingly more negatively as the proportion of hostile words to which they were exposed increased (Bargh & Pietromonaco, 1982).

In another study demonstrating the unconscious effects of stimuli on the perception of others, subjects in one group (experimental group) were exposed to an experimenter who acted in an impatient, impolite fashion while subjects in a second group (control group) were exposed to the same experimenter who in this case acted in a polite fashion. Subjects in both groups then went to another room for a second study and were asked to choose "whoever was available" among the experimenters. Of the two experimenters made available, one looked very much like the experimenter in the first part of the study while the second did not. Despite their being unaware of the basis for their selection, subjects in the experimental group who had been exposed to the "impatient experimenter" showed a significantly greater tendency to avoid the similar-looking experimenter than did subjects in the control group who were exposed to the "polite experimenter" (Figure 7.1). Further evidence that this effect was unconscious came from the fact that subjects in the experimental group did not later rate their interaction with the first experimenter more negatively than did subjects in the control group (Lewicki, 1985). In sum, the effects of the earlier experience on social behavior were automatic and unconscious.

A final illustration of unconscious influences on attitudes and social behavior comes from a study of subliminal conditioning of attitudes (Krosnick, Betz, Jussim, & Lynn, 1992). In this study, two groups of subjects were shown a series of pictures of the same person. For one group of subjects, the pictures were preceded by subliminal exposure to positive affect-arousing pictures while subjects in the other group were subliminally exposed to negative affect-arousing pictures. Illustrative positive affect-arousing pictures were of a bridal couple, a group of people playing cards and laughing, and a couple in a romantic setting. Illustrative negative affect-

Figure 7.1   The three experimenters who conducted the experiment on the biasing effects of single instances.

Despite their being unaware of the basis for their selection, subjects exposed to experimenter (A) acting in an impolite way subsequently showed a significantly greater tendency to avoid a similar looking experimenter (B) in favor of a different looking experimenter (C) than did subjects exposed to experimenter (A) acting in a polite way.

A   B   C

(From "Nonconscious Biasing Effects of Single Instances on Subsequent Judgments," by P. Lewicki, 1985, *Journal of Personality and Social Psychology, 48.* Photos provided by author.)

arousing pictures were of a skull, a werewolf, a face on fire, and a bucket of snakes. After being shown the common group of slides of the target person, at a level above threshold, subjects in both groups filled out a questionnaire in which they reported their attitudes toward the target person, their beliefs about her personality, and their beliefs about her physical attractiveness.

Would the prior subliminal exposure to positive or negative affect-arousing stimuli influence the ratings and would it do so to different degrees for the three types of ratings—attitudes, beliefs about her personality, and beliefs about her physical attractiveness? What was found was that subjects in the positive affect-arousing group had more positive attitudes toward the target person and gave her more positive personality ratings but did not give her more positive physical attractiveness ratings (Table 7.3). Presumably the latter occurred because more objective data concerning the target's physical attributes were available from the photographs than was true for her personality characteristics. In sum, attitudes toward the target were conditioned by prior subliminal exposure to stimuli, again demonstrating the unconscious elements of such attitude formation.

The research in this section demonstrates unconscious influences on attitudes and social behavior. Such influences are important because they are widespread and often highly resistant to change. In fact, they may form the basis for many stereotypes and forms of prejudice. In our development we may experience subliminal exposure to attitudes toward other groups. Such exposure may lead to our forming emotional biases toward members of these groups, without our being aware of the biases or the basis for them. Because they may be based on affective conditioning, and because they are unconscious and automatic, they may also be highly resistant to corrective information. Such unconscious influences may be even more important than conscious influences in attitude formation.

TABLE 7.3 Attitude, Personality Beliefs, and Attractiveness Beliefs for Positive and Negative Conditions

The data indicate that subliminal exposure to positive and negative affect-arousing stimuli can affect our responses to others. These effects are greater when information is ambiguous (e.g., attitudes, personality judgments) than when more objective information is available (e.g., physical attractiveness).

	CONDITION			
Dependent Measure	Positive	Negative	Difference	P
Attitudes	5.34	5.06	0.28	.049
Personality beliefs	5.26	5.06	0.20	.062
Attractiveness beliefs	4.14	4.15	−0.01	.490
n	64	64		

Note: Ratings could range from 1 to 7; higher numbers indicate more favorable attitudes and beliefs.
Source: "Subliminal Conditioning of Attitudes," by J. A. Krosnick, A. L. Betz, L. J. Jussim, and A. R. Lynn, 1992, *Journal of Personality and Social Psychology, 18,* p. 157. © Sage Publications, Inc. Reprinted by permission.

CHRONICALLY ACCESSIBLE CONSTRUCTS

Until now we have considered, within the framework of the cognitive unconscious, the role of unconscious processes in memory, perception, attitudes, and interpersonal behavior. We come now to the way in which such processes may operate within the individual. The concept used to define such processes is **chronically accessible constructs** or automatic processes for perceiving and interpreting the world. In Chapter 3 we considered Kelly's constructs or ways of interpreting the world. The concept of chronically accessible constructs suggests that there are ways in which the individual views the world that are automatic; that is, they are readily activated with little information (Bargh, 1989; Higgins, 1989). Chronically accessible constructs have some or all of the qualities of automatic cognitive processes—they are unintentional, efficient, lacking in control, and lacking in awareness. Chronically accessible constructs also refer to ways of viewing the self because less attention is required to process self-relevant information than non–self-relevant information (Bargh, 1992). Such constructs also are utilized with greater frequency and with less effort or directed attention than other kinds of constructs (i.e., those that are used infrequently and require support, attention, and conscious control). Chronically accessible constructs also bias our perception and memory in the direction of confirmation of these constructs. In other words, once certain constructs become chronically accessible or automatic, they bias us toward perceiving and remembering events that confirm the constructs as opposed to events that would disconfirm and change the constructs. If we believe that we are good, we are likely to perceive and remember events in ways that confirm our goodness. On the other hand, if we believe that we are bad, we are likely to perceive and remember events in ways that confirm our badness. The same is true for other chronically accessible constructs we may have about ourselves or the world around us.

It should be clear that considerable individual differences exist in the kinds of chronically accessible constructs that exist within the person. What is common to all people is the effect of these constructs, an effect that is common to all automatic, unconscious processes. What is unique to the individual is the nature of the chronically accessible constructs involved. What is of particular importance in terms of personality functioning are the chronically accessible constructs individuals have about who they are, who they might be, who they should be, and who they should not be. As we shall see in the following chapter on the self, the sense of what we might become can be a powerful motivator, and discrepancies between who we believe we are and who we believe we should be can be sources of emotional distress. These influences can be particularly powerful to the extent that, as expressed through chronically accessible constructs, they are largely unconscious and uncontrollable (Higgins, 1989).

SUMMARY

In this section we have considered unconscious phenomena from the standpoint of cognitive, information-processing theory. The emphasis here is on the importance of cognitive processes that are not available to awareness. Such processes are described as being automatic, rather than controlled, and as lacking awareness and being unintentional and involuntary. Automatic processes are fast and efficient. They do not require much effort or room for storage in consciousness. On the other hand, such processes affect perception, memory, attitudes toward others, and attitudes toward ourselves that are outside of our conscious awareness and control. The ultimate effects of such processes will vary depending on the individual and circumstances involved. These effects will also vary depending on how available they are to be brought into awareness and under conscious control.

COMPARISON OF THE DYNAMIC AND COGNITIVE VIEWS OF THE UNCONSCIOUS

We can now turn to a comparison of the two views of the unconscious, the dynamic view of psychoanalytic theory and the cognitive view of information-processing theory. Both views emphasize the importance of unconscious processes and the influence of such processes on thought, feeling, and action. However, there are fundamental differences between the views and, to a striking extent, they have had limited influence on one another.

That individuals can be influenced, in important ways, by information below the level of conscious awareness is a view held in common by proponents of the psychoanalytic and information-processing views. What, then, are the differences between them and how fundamental are they? Let us consider four fundamental differences between the two points of view. First, the *contents* of the two views of the unconscious tend to be quite different. According to the psychoanalytic view, the major contents of the unconscious are sexual and aggressive wishes, fantasies, thoughts, and feelings. According to the information-processing view, the contents of the unconscious are primarily thoughts that may have no special motivational significance for the individual. According to Eagle (1987), "the psychoanalytic 'dynamic unconscious' is, above all, an unconscious of aims, motives, and drives, in contrast to a cognitive unconscious of thought processes and ideas" (p. 161).

Second, the *functions* of the unconscious are different according to the two views. In the psychoanalytic view, unconscious processes serve a defensive function; that is, they protect the individual from painful thoughts, feelings, and memories. The information-processing view suggests no such defensive function. According to this view, cognitions are unconscious because they cannot be processed at the conscious level, because they never reached consciousness, or because they have become overly routinized and automatic. Thus, information-processing theorists have particular difficulty with the psychoanalytic emphasis on the defenses of self-deception and repression (Greenwald, 1992; Higgins, 1989). For them it is unnecessary to assume such complex processes. Instead, one can emphasize the simpler concept of implicit memory to suggest that events once consciously perceived no longer are readily available to awareness. Implicit memories can then become explicit, that is, conscious, for a variety of reasons. Thus, "this implicit-becomes-explicit memory account is far simpler in its theoretical interpretation than the psychoanalytic account, which requires a sophisticatedly cognizant (and near omniscient) unconscious agency" (Greenwald, 1992, p. 773).

The third difference between the two views relates to the *qualitative nature* of unconscious processes. According to the psychoanalytic view, the "language" of the unconscious is fundamentally different from the "language" of conscious processes. Cognitive processes of the unconscious are characterized as being illogical and irrational. Symbols, metaphors, dreams are all expressions of unconscious cognitive processes. In contrast, conscious cognitive processes generally follow the rules of logic and rationality. According to the cognitive view, no fundamental differences in quality need exist between unconscious and conscious cognitive processes. Unconscious processes can be as intelligent and logical as those of conscious processes. Kihlstrom, a proponent of this view, makes the following contrast:

> The psychological unconscious documented by latter-day scientific psychology is quite different from what Sigmund Freud and his psychoanalytic colleagues had in mind in Vienna. Their unconscious was hot and wet; it seethed with lust and anger; it was hallucinatory, primitive, and irrational. The unconscious of contemporary psychology is kinder and gentler than that and more reality bound and rational, even if it is not entirely cold and dry.

Kihlstrom, Barnhardt, & Tataryn, 1992, p. 789

The fourth, and final, contrast involves *availability to consciousness*. For psychoanalysts, elements of the dynamic unconscious are not readily available to consciousness. Because of the defensive barriers against their reaching consciousness, special circumstances must be provided for the contents of the unconscious to reach consciousness. This can occur in the dream because the true nature of the unconscious wishes is disguised. In analysis they can come forth because the free-association process, in which the patient is encouraged to say whatever comes to mind, provides for a loosening of the controls of defensive processes. In analysis, the emphasis on symbols, slips, hidden meanings, and possible motives behind "unintentional" acts all combine to put the patient more in touch with his or her unconscious. And, when unconscious memories that have been repressed are recalled, the assumption is that they are recalled in the same form that they existed in the unconscious and, for the most part, in the same form that events were initially experienced. Thus, the analyst tends to assume that the recalled memory existed in the same form in the unconscious until then and that the memory has remained the same since the event first took place.

On the other hand, the cognitively oriented person is likely to emphasize that the recall of events from the unconscious follows the regular laws of memory and what is recalled likely has undergone a process of transformation since the original event took place. This is partly why analysts are much more likely than cognitive psychologists to believe patient reports of early events, the latter questioning the relationship between current recall and what actually occurred at an earlier point in time (Loftus, 1993).

SPOTLIGHT ON THE RESEARCHER
JOHN F. KIHLSTROM:
The Psychological Unconscious

My interest in unconscious mental processes developed gradually and in some ways accidentally—through one of those "random encounters" that are so important in shaping who we are. As a high-school student I read some of Freud's work, but his ideas never attracted me. As a college student at Colgate University, I was very interested in existentialist approaches to personality and originally wanted to try to study them quantitatively. But, as a psychology major, I was apprenticed to a professor—William E. Edmonston, now retired—who ran a hypnosis laboratory, and I fell into that. It wasn't until I got to graduate school, doing hypnosis research with Martin Orne and Fred Evans, that I realized the historical connection between hypnosis and hysteria (now called the dissociative and conversion disorders) and began to view hypnosis as a laboratory technique for studying unconscious mental life.

For the first few years I was narrowly focused on hypnosis, and especially posthypnotic amnesia (which remains a major interest of mine). A major influence was Jack Hilgard's neodissociation theory of divided consciousness, which suggested that cognitive structures or ideas could be "split off" or dissociated from one another and not be accessible to consciousness. However, there were other empirical and theoretical developments that interested me. First, Schneider and Shiffrin (among others) articulated the notion of automatic (as opposed to controlled) processing. Then, Anthony Marcel published the first convincing demonstration of the processing of complex information in the absence of conscious awareness. Later on, Dan Schacter published his now classic review of the explicit-implicit distinction in memory, suggesting that memories of past performance could influence performance *in the absence of conscious recall* (i.e., implicit memory as opposed to explicit memory). By the late 1980s, the field of psychology was beginning to experience a wholesale revival of interest in the psychological unconscious—with the idea that mental representations and processes could influence experience, thought, and action outside of conscious awareness and independent of conscious control. People doing hypnosis research began to connect with a wider group of colleagues, and these colleagues had more reason to take hypnosis research seriously.

At this point, in the mid-1990s, I think we have good evidence for dissociations in the areas of perception, learning, memory, and thinking—what might be called the cognitive unconscious. Some of this evidence comes from hypnosis research, but most of it comes from other paradigms involving both brain-damaged patients and normal subjects. Now we can go beyond mere existence proofs, to look at the differences between conscious and unconscious mental life. What is the difference between a percept, memory, or thought that is conscious and one that is not? What limitations are there on unconscious processing? How can we render something unconscious that once was conscious? And how can we bring into consciousness something that is unconscious? Now that we have good evidence for unconscious cognitive processes, does it make sense to think of unconscious emotional and motivational processes as well?

These are the same sorts of questions that Freud asked, but our modern view of unconscious mental life is quite different from Freud's. Freud's unconscious was irrational, hallucinatory, full of primitive affects and impulses. By contrast, the psychological unconscious of modern psychology is cognitive, rational, and propositional. Most important, we have agreed-upon rules by which we can infer the existence of unconscious percepts and memories from the results of formal experiments, whereas Freud was limited to speculations, which could never be tested, about the cases that he studied. But the point of this work is not to test Freudian theory—I was never interested in that. Rather, it is to integrate the notion of unconscious mental life—a notion that has intrigued both experimental and clinical psychologists—with general psychological theory.

In sum, we have four major differences between the psychoanalytic view of the dynamic unconscious and the information-processing view of the cognitive unconscious (Table 7.4). The clinical evidence so compelling to the psychoanalyst leaves the experimental psychologist more than somewhat puzzled and unconvinced. For the latter, the experimental testing of Freudian hypotheses is "hard to come by and positive findings rarer still" (Kihlstrom, 1990, p. 447). Thus, it is small wonder that the two views have so little impact upon each other.

When the magnitude of these differences is considered, one can question whether the dynamic unconscious and the cognitive unconscious are the same thing. Although there is some overlap, very different phenomena are included in the two categories. Many of the phenomena emphasized by analysts as part of the dynamic unconscious are rejected entirely by most cognitive psychologists (e.g., interpretations of the unconscious meanings of dreams and slips of the tongue, accidents, or errors). On the other hand, most of the phenomena emphasized by cognitive psychologists as representative of unconscious processes would be seen by analysts as of little interest and part of what psychoanalysts consider the preconscious—that which is not currently in consciousness but can be brought to awareness if attention is directed there.

TABLE 7.4   Comparison of Two Views of the Unconscious: The Dynamic Unconscious and the Cognitive Unconscious

Dynamic (Psychoanalytic) View	Cognitive (Information-Processing) View
1. Content emphasis on motives and wishes.	1. Content emphasis on thoughts.
2. Emphasis on defensive functions.	2. Focus on nondefensive functions.
3. Emphasis on illogical, irrational unconscious processes.	3. Absence of fundamental differences between conscious and unconscious processes.
4. Special conditions necessary for what was unconscious to become conscious.	4. Normal laws of perception and memory apply.

Perhaps part of the problem at this point is that more than just two or three categories (i.e., conscious, preconscious, unconscious) are necessary to do justice to the variety of phenomena described in this chapter. Perhaps, as suggested earlier, thoughts and experiences can occur at a variety of levels of awareness (Bowers, 1992). And, some thoughts and experiences can have some of the qualities of one category and some of the qualities of another category. For example, some automatic thoughts are outside of awareness but others are not, and some are uncontrollable but others are not (Bargh, 1989). In sum, we can accept the importance of unconscious phenomena without being bound by a particular theoretical focus or rigid definition of categories. As Kihlstrom et al. note, "After 100 years of neglect, suspicion, and frustration, unconscious processes have now taken a firm hold on the collective mind of psychologists" (1992, p. 788). Given the complexity of the phenomena and past history of neglect, we need to be patient and open to a wide range of possibilities as research goes forward.

IMPLICATIONS FOR THE USE OF SELF-REPORT MEASURES

It can readily be seen how acceptance of the importance of unconscious processes raises serious questions concerning personality assessment, in particular in regard to the use of self-report. If people are not aware of many aspects of their functioning and the causes of their behavior, how can we count on them to be good reporters?

Interestingly enough, questions concerning the use of self-report data in psychological investigations are raised by proponents of both the dynamic unconscious and cognitive unconscious points of view. However, not surprisingly the reasons are somewhat different. For proponents of the dynamic unconscious, motivational and defensive processes are expected to bias self-report data, limiting their validity. In an earlier chapter we quoted Henry Murray's comment that captures the essence of this view: "Children perceive inaccurately, are very little conscious of their inner states and retain fallacious recollections of occurrences. Many adults are hardly better" (Murray, 1938, p. 15).

Murray believed that subjective reports often were unreliable and inaccurate because of cognitive and motivational reasons—that is, because of people's limited ability to perceive and recall accurately and because of unconscious repression. To correct for such problems, Murray suggested the use of projective tests, as well as other kinds of data. This tradition has, as earlier noted, been followed by McClelland and others who suggest that self-report data and projective test data are two different kinds of data. It need not be the case that one kind of data is better than the other but that they are different, each with its own value and each relating to other variables in different ways. Thus, fantasy measures of the need for achievement relate to behavior in different ways than do self-report measures of need for achievement (Koestner & McClelland, 1990). Whereas fantasy measures are taken to be more indicative of motives, self-report measures are taken to be more indicative of values.

Motives and values are different aspects of one's personality and therefore it is not surprising that the two kinds of measures would relate to different kinds of behavior.

Somewhat more surprising may be the questioning of self-report data on the part of more cognitively oriented psychologists, although there is not unanimity of opinion in this regard. In 1977 attention was drawn to this matter by an article partially titled "Telling More Than We Can Know" (Nisbett & Wilson, 1977). The authors began by noting that in our daily lives we answer many questions concerning the basis for our choices, judgments, and behavior. For example, we answer questions such as: Why do you like that person? and Why did you do that? Similarly, personality psychologists ask such questions on a wide variety of self-report questionnaires. The assumption is that people have some insight into why they behave as they do, that they have some privileged information that is not available to the outside observer. Is there reason to believe that such is the case?

The authors of the article, Nisbett and Wilson, argue, to the contrary, that people often are unaware of their behavior and the reasons for their behavior. As a result, there is a lack of correlation between verbal reports and actual behavior. For example, the authors point to research suggesting that people are increasingly less likely to help others in distress as the number of bystanders increases—the well-known "bystander effect" (Latane & Darley, 1970). Yet, people do not spontaneously report that the presence of others influences their helping behavior and specifically reject such influence when it is mentioned as a possibility. To take another example, Nisbett and Wilson report two studies in which customers were asked to judge the relative merits of four different nightgowns and four different pairs of nylon stockings. The customers indicated their choice and the basis for it. The data clearly indicated that estimates of the relative quality of articles of clothing was influenced by the position of the articles—articles to the right being judged of higher quality than those to the left. For example, the right-most stockings were preferred almost four times as often as the left-most stockings. Yet, subjects never gave position as a reason for their selection. Further, when asked about a possible effect of position of the article, the customers rejected any such suggestion that this was a possible influence on their selection.

In reviewing a wide variety of such studies, Nisbett and Wilson (1977) came to the conclusion that asking subjects about the influences on their behavior was of little value in terms of understanding the actual bases for behavior. It is not that people are unwilling to give answers to the questions posed to them, it is that they are unable to give accurate answers—they tell more than they can know! Where, then, do their answers come from? The suggestion is that we carry around within us implicit causal theories for our own behavior and that of others. Just as we have implicit theories of personality (Chapter 1), we have implicit causal theories as to why we and others behave as we and they do. When asked to give causal explanations, we do not rely on accurate observations alone but employ these implicit causal theories. In doing so, we do not even think of, or even reject, explanations that do not fit within the theory.

Similarly, in filling out rating scales or questionnaires, we respond in terms of some implicit theory of the kinds of traits or personality characteristics that go with one another rather than in terms of actual observations of behavior (Shweder & D'Andrade, 1980). Although interpretations such as these do not rule out motivational or defensive reasons for the inaccuracy of self-report data, it is important to recognize that the emphasis is on unconscious, nonmotivational, cognitive explanations. The suggestion is that people are unable to observe their own cognitive processes at work and often make errors in judgment and inference (Nisbett & Ross, 1980). Because of limitations in our cognitive-processing mechanisms, we tell more than we know and know less than we assume we know.

Other cognitively oriented psychologists come to a somewhat different conclusion, one that leaves more room for the potential utility of self-report data. These psychologists suggest that self-report data are much more useful when we can be assured that the subjects have attended to what they are being asked about. In other words, rather than being broad and speculative, the questions asked of subjects must be specific to that which is focal to their attention. In addition, it is suggested that in our daily lives we face repeated events (there is a redundancy to the information available to us), and therefore we have an opportunity to observe what may have been missed the first time around. In addition, our causal explanations reflect these repeated observations and are likely to be generally accurate, even if they are in error in a specific, unusual instance (Ericcson & Simon, 1980, 1993).

Thus, social cognitive psychologists such as Bandura (1986) argue that self-report data can be of enormous value to personality psychologists. According to Bandura, the questions we ask subjects must be focused and specific, occurring just before or concurrent with action on their part. Thus, subjects can be asked to make self-efficacy judgments, or judgments concerning their ability to perform specific tasks in specific situations. At the same time, while upholding the utility of certain kinds of self-report data, Bandura is critical of the use of broad, sweeping, general questions such as those asked on most personality questionnaires. In addition, he is critical of the use of projective tests based on the dynamic unconscious. The view of human behavior as determined by unconscious dynamic forces is seen as a form of "demonology" and "mystical thinking" that dates back to the dark ages (Bandura & Walters, 1963). From an adaptive standpoint, how could we be so influenced by such unconscious forces and still be able to function in the world?

In sum, proponents of the dynamic unconscious and some proponents of the cognitive unconscious question the utility of self-report data. Other proponents of the latter point of view suggest that at least some forms of self-report data can be quite valuable in our research. This would appear to be a reasonable argument, but the question then becomes *which* kinds of self-report data and how significant are such data? Or, to put the question another way, are there some aspects of personality functioning that are so governed by unconscious or nonconscious processes that self-report data become worthless in the study of them? And, if so, how important are these aspects of personality functioning and how else can they be studied?

The view taken here is that there are sufficient data concerning the importance of unconscious processes for personality functioning that we must be cautious and limited in our reliance on self-report data. Whether interpreted from the standpoint of the dynamic unconscious or the cognitive unconscious, significant aspects of our functioning are not available to awareness and self-report (Wilson, 1994). As noted in the introduction to this chapter, this presents some extremely serious methodological problems for personality researchers. It likely is the case that in the future we will need to rely on multiple sources of data in any investigation—self-report, fantasy measures, physiological data, and overt behavior. And, we will have to sort out the relationships among these different kinds of data, understanding why under some circumstances the data show greater agreement than they do under other circumstances. This is an enormously difficult task but in principle no different from the case of medical diagnosis, where many diagnostic tests can be useful but on occasion suggestive of different conclusions. And, some of these tests may be more useful in some situations and other tests more useful in different situations.

CONCLUSION

In this chapter we have considered a wide variety of unconscious phenomena and the effects of such phenomena on perception, memory, attitudes, and interpersonal behavior. We have seen how after almost a century of emphasis by psychoanalysts, and the relative neglect of such phenomena by academic psychologists, the operation and influence of unconscious processes have become an area of great research interest. Recognition of the importance of unconscious processes has achieved its rightful place as a fundamental issue for personality psychology.

At the same time that both clinical investigators and experimental psychologists have come together in this interest, they tend to differ in the phenomena of interest to them and their interpretations of these phenomena. The dynamic unconscious emphasized by psychoanalysts is characterized by motives, wishes, defenses, irrationality, and unavailability to consciousness. The cognitive unconscious emphasized by information-processing psychologists is characterized by problems in attention and storage capacity as well as nonconsciousness and automaticity. Although there is overlap between these two points of view, and between representatives of the two points of view, the dynamic unconscious and the cognitive unconscious remain quite different concepts. When considering the phenomena themselves, they appear to be so diverse that representatives of each point of view can accept some as illustrative but reject others. In addition, unconscious phenomena appear to be so diverse that we may need to think in terms of more than two, or even three, levels of consciousness, with some phenomena having characteristics of more than one level (Bargh, 1989; Bowers, 1992).

Given the diversity, richness, and importance of unconscious processes, we can see why appreciation of them leads to profound theoretical and methodological questions. How to incorporate an appreciation of unconscious processes into our understanding of personality functioning becomes a major theoretical question. How to evaluate their importance in relation to various measures of personality becomes a major methodological question. Of particular significance, as noted, is the extent to which we can rely on self-report data to assess important aspects of personality.

When we are only interested in how individuals perceive events, themselves, and others, at the conscious level, there is no problem in the use of self-report data. However, when we are interested in causal explanations, as opposed to reasons people give for action, and when we are interested in unconscious feelings about the self and others, the use of self-report data becomes more problematic. At one end, it would seem that when people are attending to events, are not overly emotionally or motivationally involved, and are not asked to rely excessively on long-term memory, they can be reasonably good observers and reporters. But, at the other end, when people are not attending carefully, when they are very emotionally involved or feeling threatened, or when they are asked to respond to events of the distant past, their observations and reports become more suspect. Where most of the phenomena of importance to personality psychologists lie, and where specific phenomena fall between the two, is a matter of disagreement among psychologists. Clearly much work remains to be done.

MAJOR CONCEPTS

Unconscious. Those thoughts, experiences, and feelings of which we are unaware.

Subliminal perception. Perception of stimuli below the threshold of awareness.

Dichotic listening task. A task in which the subject is instructed to attend to stimuli presented in one ear while different stimuli are presented in the other ear.

Implicit memory. Memory effects in the absence of conscious memory for the stimuli.

Implicit perception. Perception without conscious awareness, as in subliminal perception.

Dissociative phenomena. Occasions when major aspects of a person's functioning are kept out of awareness or are not integrated into the rest of the person's psychological functioning.

Vicarious learning, vicarious conditioning. The process through which emotional responses are learned by observing emotional responses in others.

Automatic processes. Routinized cognitive processes, some of which may be so routine as to be unconscious.

Repression. The psychoanalytic concept for the defense mechanism through which an idea, thought, or wish is dismissed from, and kept out of, consciousness.

Dynamic unconscious. The concept of the unconscious associated with psychoanalytic theory and the concept of repression.

Subliminal psychodynamic activation. The research procedure associated with psychoanalytic theory in which stimuli are presented below the perceptual threshold (subliminally) to stimulate unconscious wishes and fears.

State-dependent memory. The ability to recall events experienced while in a specific mood only when one is again experiencing that mood.

Hypermnesia. The increased recall of stimuli with time.

Controlled information processing. Information processing that is effortful and under the flexible control of the individual, in contrast to automatic information processing.

Automatic information processing. Information processing that is effortless and automatic and occurs outside of awareness,

in contrast to controlled information processing.

Chronically accessible constructs. Schemata, in particular self-schemata, that are readily activated with little information.

SUMMARY

1. Although differing views exist concerning the importance of unconscious phenomena for personality functioning, this chapter suggests that they are of great importance for theory and research (e.g., the use of self-report measures).

2. Although at times we speak of an unconscious, in reality we are speaking of contents and processes that may have an effect on personality functioning without the person being aware of them or their effects. Depending on one's point of view, diverse phenomena can be taken as illustrative of unconscious processes (e.g., subliminal perception, implicit memory, dissociative phenomena, blindsight, conditioning without awareness, automatic processes, repression).

3. Historically the concept of the unconscious has been controversial. Today, as illustrated by the psychoanalytic view of the dynamic unconscious and the information-processing view of the cognitive unconscious, there is considerable agreement concerning the existence of unconscious processes but disagreement concerning how they operate. Disagreement between proponents of the two points of view focuses on contents, functions, qualities of unconscious processes, and availability to consciousness.

4. The dynamic unconscious emphasized by psychoanalysts is associated with distinctive qualities, with motives, and with conflict. Although mainly based on clinical evidence, some experimental research (e.g., subliminal psychodynamic activation) lends support to the concept. However, at this point there is no solid body of experimental evidence demonstrating either motivated (i.e., defensive) forgetting or the lifting of repression under defined conditions.

5. The cognitive unconscious involves all cognitive processes (e.g., automatic processes, chronically accessible constructs) that are unavailable to awareness regardless of the reason for their unavailability. Within this context, there is considerable evidence of unconscious influences on memory, perception, feelings, and attitudes toward others.

6. Given the range of phenomena included in the concept of the unconscious and the differing psychoanalytic and information-processing views, it is suggested that more than two descriptive categories are needed (e.g., conscious, preconscious, nonconscious, unconscious). It also is suggested that thoughts and ex-

periences can occur at a variety of levels of awareness and have qualities associated with more than one category.

7. Proponents of the dynamic unconscious point of view as well as many proponents of the cognitive unconscious point of view question the use of self-report measures in personality research. On the other hand, some cognitively oriented psychologists suggest that such measures can be useful when subjects are asked specific questions about phenomena to which they have attended.

THE CONCEPT OF THE SELF

8

CHAPTER OVERVIEW

In this chapter we consider research on the concept of the *self*, currently one of the most investigated topics in the field. We consider how a sense of self develops, alternative ways in which personality theorists have conceptualized the self, and motives that may be associated with the sense of self. Finally, we consider individual differences in personality variables associated with the self, for example, individual differences in self-efficacy and self-consciousness.

Questions to Be Addressed in This Chapter

1   What do we mean by the concept of the self? Is the concept of the self necessary for personality psychology?

2   How does a sense of self develop?

3   Are we motivated more by a need for self-verification or by a need for self-enhancement? By the desire to be known for who we are or by the desire to be known for who we would like to be?

4   What are the implications of individual differences in such matters as belief in one's own competence? In focusing attention on one's self as opposed to focusing attention on external stimuli? In the extent to which standards set by oneself or by others are met?

The concept of the self, the way we perceive and experience ourselves, would appear to be of such obvious significance that one can hardly imagine it not being a topic of interest to personality psychologists. Yet, periodically some psychologists have been led to ask: Is the concept of the self useful and necessary? The phenomena associated with the concept of the self seem so obvious; yet, when we try to study them empirically, it is often as if we are grasping at straws in the wind. As a result, as we shall see, periods of great interest in the self have alternated with periods of virtually complete rejection of it as a topic of useful inquiry.

WHY STUDY THE CONCEPT OF THE SELF?

Why is there a need to study the concept of the self? First, the concept of the self makes sense in terms of our daily lives and phenomenological experience. Terms such as *self-conscious, self-esteem, selfish,* and *self-love* give testimony to the importance of the self from an existential point of view. These terms and feelings associated with them form a major part of what patients talk about in virtually all forms of therapy. However the therapist construes what the patient is saying, in most cases the patient is experiencing dissatisfaction with some aspect of the self or with the total self.

Second, the self would appear to represent an important part of the way a person construes the world. The self emerges fairly early in infancy and begins to form an important part of the child's construction of the world. With our ability to differentiate ourselves from others and to reflect back upon ourselves, we use our self-concept as a way of evaluating and organizing information. As in any ongoing cognitive operation, new information concerning the self has to be evaluated against old concepts and then either be integrated into them or effect change in them. In other words, not only is the self experiential, but it is a concept with potentially important implications for the functioning of our cognitive system.

Finally, the concept of the self may be necessary to understand what otherwise appear to be discrepant or unrelated findings. For example, people perform differently when they are motivated, ego-involved, or self-involved as opposed to when they are not so involved. The concept of self appears to be necessary to understand such differences. Indeed, one might be tempted to say that the concept of the self is what gives organization and unity to the varied ways in which the person functions under differing conditions. Other than the concept of the self, is there any way in which we, as personality psychologists, can give expression to the organized, integrated aspects of human psychological functioning?

In sum, the self appears to be a major part of our experience and our construction of the world; it appears to play a major role in how we behave and to give unity to our functioning. Yet, as noted, historically there has been a waxing and waning of interest in the concept of the self. In 1975, when I began working on the book *Current Controversies and Issues in Personality,* I debated whether or not to include a chapter on the self. Today, one could hardly imagine not including such a chapter in a book on current research in personality. Hundreds of studies on the self are published yearly and there is major interest in the concept among psychoanalytic and social cognitive theorists. In this chapter we consider how these theorists have interpreted the self as well as what we have come to understand about the structure of the self and self-related psychological processes. Before doing so, however, let us briefly review the history of the concept so as to put current developments into historical perspective. In the course of considering this historical perspective, we also have a chance to discuss the thinking of some of the major self theorists of recent times.

THE WAXING AND WANING OF INTEREST IN THE SELF: A HISTORICAL PERSPECTIVE

The concept of the self was introduced into American psychology by William James in 1890. In a centennial anniversary article about the contributions of James, Markus (1990) noted that "although many aspects of James' theorizing about the self have been enormously influential, his notion of the self as the central object in mental life has been largely ignored" (p. 181). As Markus notes, James was "passionate" about the self and gave it central attention and emphasis. According to James, the self is central to all of our experience and we divide up the world into "me" and "not me." This distinction, and how we define "me" is based on our interactions with others, a view shared by later self theorists. Thus, according to this view our sense of self is a "looking-glass self" or reflective self that is based on our perception of how we look to significant others (Cooley, 1902; Mead, 1934). And, an important part of the "me" is the emotional tone of our self-feeling—our self-esteem.

Because James believed that social interactions were key to our self-concept and that our interactions vary according to setting and the individuals with whom we are interacting, he emphasized the importance of our having many selves. In a frequently quoted passage, James suggested that

> Properly speaking, a man has as many social selves as there are individuals who recognize him and carry an image of him in their head. But as the individuals who carry the images fall naturally into classes, we may practically say that he has as many different social selves as there are distinct groups of persons about whose opinion he cares.

1890, p. 294

According to this view of multiple selves, then, one might have a work self, a recreation self, a school self, a family self, and so on. Some people might have many such selves, others few such selves. However, these selves need not be isolated or fragmented from one another. Rather, they can be integrated in some way to form a more unified sense of self.

Because of the centrality of the self, James also believed that all psychological processes could be understood only in the context of an understanding of the self. For example, motivation is affected by whether the self is involved, and one "wills" action when an end state is seen as self-relevant. In other words, what permits us to act in voluntary ways, to do what we intend to do and avoid what we do not intend to do, is our perception of the relevance of action for the self (Cross & Markus, 1990).

With the rise of behaviorism, there was a decline in interest in the self. J. B. Watson (1919, 1930), the father of behaviorism, was opposed to the study of internal processes and the use of phenomenological self-report. It was the objective measurement of overt behavior that was the task of psychologists, and thus study of the self was excluded as a proper domain for investigation by scientific psychologists. During the 1940s there was a surge in interest in the concept, particularly in the work of Gordon Allport and Carl Rogers. We have already noted Allport's (1937) groundbreaking personality book, which contained a chapter on the self. As did James, Allport considered many topics that occupy the attention of today's personality psychologists—consciousness of the self, self-esteem, and the capacity of people to deceive themselves. Although always interested in the unity of personality, it was not until somewhat later that Allport (1961) emphasized the central role of the self in the organization of personality. Rogers's emphasis on the self as fundamental to experience will only be noted here since we will shortly consider it in depth.

Despite the emphasis on the self by Allport, Rogers, and others, in 1955 Allport found it necessary to address the question: Is the concept of the self necessary? A review at the end of the decade suggested that there were many problems with the research that had been done to that time (Wylie, 1961). More specifically, the problems involved many different definitions of the concept of self, many different measures of the self, and poor agreement among the various measures. Is the self mainly feelings, concepts, or perceptions of our behavior? Do we have one self or many selves? Is there a "public self" and a "private self," a "conscious self" and an "unconscious self"? And, if so, how do all of these selves relate to one another and to behavior? Is self-report an adequate basis for measurement of the self or are other techniques, such as projective tests, necessary? If multiple measures are used, how should the results be related to one another?

Questions such as these seemed so complex, though so necessary, and the efforts to answer them so faulty, that as of 1960 prospects for further progress did not seem bright. Thus, in 1973 the question of whether the concept of the self was necessary was again asked (Epstein, 1973). The cognitive revolution was replacing behaviorism as the predominant model in psychology, but for the most part personality psychologists remained wary of embracing the concept of the self. However, since that time the topic has returned with a vengeance. Just why this is the case is not clear. One reason may be that social and personality psychologists began to apply concepts from cognitive psychology to the field of personality. Thus, Markus (1977) suggested that the self be treated as a cognitive structure or schema. As such, **self-schemas** represent cognitive generalizations about the self that are derived from past experience. Like all schemas, self-schemas organize and guide the processing of information, in this case information concerning the self. But the application of cognitive principles to personality cannot be the total explanation for the return of interest in the self, since other theorists, such as psychoanalysts, also demonstrated renewed interest; yet they were largely untouched by the cognitive revolution. Perhaps there were more general forces building in society that led personality psychologists to focus on the self, forces that led to what has been called the "me generation" of the 1980s.

In sum, we can see from this brief review what an uneven career the concept of the self has had, emphasized at one point yet neglected at another, recognized as of fundamental importance in the drama of life yet so elusive as to frustrate continuously those who struggle to grab hold of it in scientific ways. Throughout, dating back to James over 100 years ago, psychologists have never been able to quite let go of their concern with the self. And, as we shall see during the course of this chapter, fundamental questions and issues have remained: When and how does the self develop? Is there one self or are there many selves? If many selves, how are they organized so that we do not all feel as if we are multiple personalities? If we vary from situation to situation, and from time period to time period, what is it that provides us with a sense of unity and identity? If part of the self is what we think and what we feel, then what is the relation between cognitive and affective aspects of the self? What is the relation of the self to behavior: If we viewed ourselves differently would we necessarily behave differently? If we behaved differently would we necessarily view ourselves differently? Finally, can we have unconscious self-perceptions? If so, how important are they and how can we assess them? We have enough questions to concern us. Let us turn to the efforts to provide answers.

DEVELOPMENT OF THE SELF

When and how does the self develop? Is the infant born with a self and, if not, how can we tell that a self is emerging? It is easy enough to ask adolescents and adults to tell us about themselves, but what do we do with an infant or young child? And, are humans alone in the capacity to have a sense of self?

Developmental psychologists have been concerned with the self and have conceptualized various stages in the development of self-understanding from infancy through adolescence (Damon & Hart, 1988; Harter, 1983). First, let us begin with a distinction between *self-perception* and *self-consciousness*. Various terms are used by developmental psychologists, but the basic point here is the distinction between the infant's *perception* that it exists separate from other persons or physical objects and the child's ability to reflect back upon itself, that is, the development of **self-consciousness.** Some refer to self-perception and self-consciousness as the *existential self* and the *categorical self* (Lewis & Brooks-Gunn, 1979) and others to a distinction drawn by William James between the "I" and the "Me," the "I" referring to the self that acts and observes, and the "Me" to the self that is observed or is the object of self-knowledge (Damon & Hart, 1988; Harter, 1983).

Two points are noteworthy about this distinction made by developmental psychologists. First, in referring to the development of the self, it must be clear which aspect of self-functioning is being considered. Second, cognitive developments are important components of self-development, with the development of self-consciousness representing a qualitative development beyond self-perception. Thus, while it is recognized as possible that other species are capable of self-perception, it is suggested that self-consciousness is limited to humans and the great apes (e.g., chimpanzees) (Lewis, 1992a).

THE SELF AS SEPARATE FROM OTHER PEOPLE AND OBJECTS: SELF-PERCEPTION

How is the infant able to develop a sense of itself as distinct from other people and objects, to be aware of itself as a separate entity? Developmental psychologists suggest that by around 3 months the infant has begun to make self-other differentiations (Lewis, 1990a, 1990b). In good part this is based on sensory differences associated with the bodily self as opposed to the nonbodily self (Butterworth, 1992; Harter, 1983; Lewis & Brooks-Gunn, 1979). For example, the sensations from touching its own body are different from those from touching other objects, from biting its own hand or foot or from biting the hands and feet of others or biting other physical objects. To take another illustration, the experience of visual flow is different when moving one's own head than when remaining stationary while observing other objects move. In addition, there is evidence that infants respond differentially to their own sounds than they do to the sounds of other infants. As early as one day after birth infants will cry less to the sound of their own cry than to the sound of another baby crying (Martin & Clark, 1982). Somehow the newborn infant is able to recognize its own vocalizations and discriminate them from those of other babies.

In addition to these sensory discriminations, early after birth infants are able to demonstrate the learning of contingencies between movement of their hand or foot and changes in surrounding objects (Lewis, Sullivan, & Brooks-Gunn, 1985). For example, the infant observes that moving its arms has an effect on the mobile that hangs in its crib. The relation between such movements and effects is different from that observed for the arm movements made by others; that is, there is a difference in action-outcome contingency between its own actions and the actions of others (Rovee-Collier, 1993). Awareness of such differences in action-outcome contingencies contributes to development of the perceived self.

Finally, there is the growing development of object permanence and thereby the sense of self, as well as others, as constant across a variety of situations. Because something is out of sight does not mean that it no longer exists, and because something changes in appearance does not mean that it no longer is the same object. Now the infant recognizes itself to be the same "John" or "Karen" whether it is in one room or another or whether it is playing with siblings, playmates, or the dog.

In sum, between the period of time when the infant is 3 months and when it is about $1\frac{1}{2}$ years, there is the development of a sense of perceived self. The perceived self involves the understanding that one's body is continuous across situations, that one's body has experiences different from those of other objects, and that outcomes can be contingent on one's own actions. Through these cognitive and motor skill developments, there is the development of the self as an active, independent, causal agent.

THE DEVELOPMENT OF SELF-CONSCIOUSNESS

At around the age of 15 months, there is the development of self-awareness or self-consciousness—the ability to reflect back upon the self and treat the self as an object.

How are we to track the beginnings of self-consciousness? One test that has been used here is the ability to recognize oneself in a mirror. At what point does the infant show self-recognition in terms of understanding that its own image is reflected in the mirror? First, let us consider some research by Gallup (1970) on self-recognition in chimpanzees. What Gallup did was to study the reactions of chimpanzees to observing themselves in a mirror. Most animals upon seeing themselves reflected in a mirror will show little interest or treat the image as another member of the species. The male fighting Siamese fish, for example, upon viewing a mirror held up to the wall of a fish tank with a female member of the species present, will expand its fins and grow vibrant in color—exactly what it does when it observes a male competitor in the tank. In other words, the male fish perceives the image and responds to it as another male and potential competitor. What will chimpanzees do? Gallup found that initially they responded to their own reflection in a manner similar to the Siamese fish, treating the image as if it were another chimp and making threatening gestures and vocalizations. However, after a few days of experience with the mirrors, they were able to engage in self-directed behaviors such as using the mirror to groom parts of their bodies. What Gallup then did was to anesthetize the chimps and place a red, odorless dye on parts of their face. When the anesthesia wore off and they were placed in front of the mirror, would they recognize themselves and the red dye? Indeed, what Gallup found was that they immediately began to explore the marked portion of their face, indicating self-awareness.

At what point would infants show the same behavior? This was the question investigated by Lewis and Brooks-Gunn (1979). What they did was compare the mirror self-recognition behavior of three groups of infants: ages 9–12 months, 15–18 months, and 21–24 months. Before placing each child in front of the mirror, they had the child's mother wipe its nose with a handkerchief, at the same time placing a spot of red rouge on the nose. Since the wiping was a typical maternal activity, the child had no awareness of anything out of the ordinary. Would the child placed in front of the mirror then recognize and respond to the red dot? Would it respond in a way that demonstrated self-recognition?

What Lewis and Brooks-Gunn found was that the children age 9–12 months responded to their mirror image by smiling and touching it but did not specifically direct their behavior toward the red dot. In other words, they responded "socially" to their reflection as if it were another child, but they did not respond to the spot of red rouge in a way that indicated they were aware that they were looking at themselves. Such self-directed activity began to appear in the 15–18-month-old group and was very apparent in the 21–24-month-old group. While the children in the youngest age group showed some recognition of themselves in terms of recognizing their own movements in the mirror, again expressing contingency self-recognition, actual self-recognition was not generally evident.

Similar observations were made in some very clever comparisons by Lewis and Brooks-Gunn of responses to three kinds of television images: "live" images reflecting on a television screen what the infant was doing at the time, week-old images of the infant played on the television screen but recorded a week earlier, and television images of the activity of another baby. Would the infants respond differentially to the three images? Here too an important difference was found in the behavior of the 9–12-month- and 15–18-month-old children. While the children in the younger group

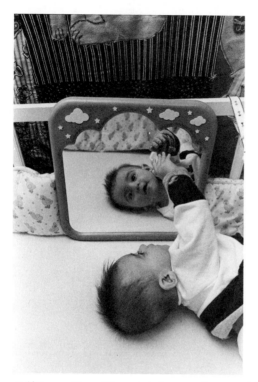

Self-Recognition. Although infants are interested in mirror reflections at an early age, recognition of self as expressed in self-directed mirror behavior does not develop until approximately 18 months of age.

showed a differential response to the live and week-old images, they did not distinguish between their self-images and those of another baby on the week-old tapes. In other words, once more they were using the contingent action between movement of their body and movement of the image on the screen as the cue for self-perception. On the other hand, children in the 15–18-month-old group did express differential responses to the self and other week-old images, again indicative of self-recognition. Thus, both the mirror self-recognition test and the video images test indicated that self-recognition in terms of specific features begins at about 15 months and is well established by 2 years of age (Table 8.1).

Does self-recognition, in particular mirror self-recognition, mean self-consciousness, the ability to reflect back upon the self? Can we rely on the data from mirror self-recognition research as a criterion for self-recognition and the development of self-consciousness? Some psychologists suggest not. Lewis (1990a, 1992b), however, points out that the view that self-consciousness develops at around 15 months fits with other developments that are occurring at the same time. First, at about that time the child is beginning to use language in a way that differentiates between the self and others. Second, at about that age the child begins to show what Lewis calls **self-conscious emotions,** that is, the emotions of embarrassment, pride, and shame.

TABLE 8.1   Summary of Main Stages in Mirror and Video Self-Recognition Tasks During Infancy

Stage	Age	Description
Unlearned attraction to images of others	First 3 months	[Little systematic research in first 3 months]
Contingency detection	Between 3 and 8 months	Interest in mirror reflection; approaches, touches, smiles, behaves "socially" to reflection
Self as permanent object	Between 8 and 12 months	Awareness of stable categorical features of self; locates objects attached to body using mirror image; differentiates contingent from noncontingent video tape-recordings of self
Self-other differentiation	Between 12 and 15 months	Uses mirror to locate others in space; differentiates own video image from others' video images
Facial feature detection	Beginning about 15 months, well established by 2 years	Recognition based on self-specific features; success in "rouge removal" tasks

Source: "Origins of Self-Perception in Infancy," by G. Butterworth, 1992, *Psychological Inquiry, 3,* p. 104. Reprinted by permission of Lawrence Erlbaum Associates, Inc.

According to Lewis, in contrast to other emotions, such as fear, emotions such as shame depend on the development of self-consciousness. Thus, one does not see evidence of shame prior to the development of self-consciousness. The price of the development of self-consciousness is the potential for feeling that one's self is bad and must be hidden from others—the emotion of shame.

SUMMARY OF THE DEVELOPMENTAL PERSPECTIVE

To summarize the perspective of developmental psychologists, distinct qualitative developments can be recognized in the development of the self. The important developments are those of self-perception and self-consciousness. Although infants cannot be asked about their sense of self, their behavior in various situations can be analyzed to indicate if they are differentiating between self-action and the action of others and if they are responding in terms of self-recognition and self-awareness. These observations of differential behavior of infants of different ages are linked to other observations reflecting developments in other areas. In particular, there is an overall effort to relate developments in the sense of self to other kinds of cognitive development.

THREE VIEWS OF THE STRUCTURE OF THE SELF

In this section we consider three theoretical views of the self—phenomenological, psychoanalytic, and cognitive. These three views represent the major efforts to conceptualize the self and most, although not all, self theorists fit into one or another of the categories.

THE PHENOMENOLOGICAL THEORY OF CARL ROGERS

We have already noted that Carl Rogers emphasized the concept of the self at a time when it was being neglected by most other personality psychologists. Rogers did not begin with an interest in the self. In fact, at first he thought that it was a vague, scientifically meaningless term. However, as he listened to clients expressing their problems and attitudes, he found that they tended to talk in terms of a self. Beginning in 1947, Rogers emphasized the concept of the self as a part of personality. Over the next 40 years he increasingly emphasized its importance and attempted to explore it both clinically and empirically.

Rogers emphasized the phenomenological approach—the attempt to understand people in terms of how they view themselves and the world around them. According to this position (Rogers, 1951), each person perceives the world in a unique way. These perceptions make up the individual's **phenomenal field,** which includes both conscious and unconscious perceptions. But the most important determinants of behavior, particularly in healthy people, are the perceptions that are conscious or capable of becoming conscious. Although the phenomenal field is essentially a private world of the individual, we can attempt to perceive the world as it appears to individuals, to see the world through their eyes and with the psychological meaning it has for them.

A key part of the phenomenal field concerns the self, constituting those perceptions and meanings that are represented in terms of "I," "me," or "self." The self-concept represents an organized and consistent pattern of perceptions. Although the self changes, it always retains this patterned, integrated, organized quality. As an organized set of perceptions, the self clearly is not a *homunculus*—a little person inside us. The self does not "do" anything. The person does not have a self that controls behavior. However, as an organized set of perceptions the self does influence how we behave. The self both reflects experience and influences experience. In addition to the self, each person has an *ideal self,* representing the self concept that the individual would most like to possess. It includes the perceptions and meanings that potentially are relevant to the self and that are valued highly by the individual.

According to Rogers, the early self grows largely out of perceptions of the parents' appraisals. The child's self-esteem, or personal judgment of its worthiness, grows out of these perceptions. With parental approval and support, the child can incorporate new experiences into its sense of self. In this case, there is a state of *congruence* between self and experience. On the other hand, if the parents impose conditions on the basic self-worth of the child (i.e., valuing the child under some but not other conditions), then experiences that threaten the sense of self-worth will be perceived as threatening and may be rejected. In other words, experiences that are *incongruent* with the self-structure may be denied or distorted, resulting in a condition of **self-experience discrepancy.** It is the imposition of conditions of self-worth, leading to the need to reject experiences incongruent with the self-structure, that lies at the heart of the formation of psychopathology. Originally Rogers emphasized the need for self-consistency in relation to the functioning of the self-system. Developed by Lecky (1945), the concept of **self-consistency** emphasizes the need on the part of the individual to function in accordance with and preserve the self-system. It is consistency and the maintenance of the self-structure that is seen as important. Although Rogers originally embraced this view, and never rejected it, he gradually placed greater emphasis on the need to maintain a sense of self associated with conditions of worth. Here there is greater emphasis on the need to maintain a *positive* image of the self than the need to maintain a *consistent* image. As we shall later see, considerable attention has recently been directed to investigation of the need for consistency (self-consistency or self-verification) and the need for a positive image (self-enhancement). At the same time, it should be observed here that what was important to Rogers was being honest with oneself in terms of recognizing experience and allowing it to become part of the self-system. For example, recognizing the feeling of anger and allowing the sense of oneself as sometimes an angry person would be important even if one preferred to see oneself as never angry.

Although impressed with the self-statements of clients, Rogers felt the need for an objective definition of the concept of the self, a way to measure it, and a research tool. He began with categories of self-statements made in recorded therapy sessions and then turned to the **Q-sort method.** As noted in relation to Block's longitudinal research in Chapter 6, the Q-sort was used to develop personality measures based on observer judgments; here the Q-sort was used to measure the self-concept. As in the previously described research, the person is given a set of statements consisting of personality characteristics. The subject sorts the statements into those most and least self-descriptive, according to a normal distribution (e.g., 100 cards into 11 categories with 2,4,8,11,16,18,16,11,8,4,2 statements in the categories). In addition, this procedure was used to measure the ideal self, with statements categorized according to the extent to which they fit with "least like my ideal self" at one end to "most like my ideal self" at the other end.

Because the self-statements and ideal self-statements to be sorted by subjects were the same and arranged according to the same normal distribution, it was possible to develop a quantitative measure of the difference between the self and the ideal self. This self–ideal self discrepancy score could then be related to other measures. In early research, the size of the self–ideal self discrepancy was related to measures of psychological well-being, with small self–ideal self discrepancies being associated with better well-being. In addition, changes in the size of the discrepancy score were found to be associated with progress in psychotherapy, with the size of the discrepancy becoming smaller as progress occurred. However, over time interest in the Q-sort as a measure of the self and ideal self declined, in part because subjects could distort or be defensive about their ratings. Was a small discrepancy between self and ideal self ratings a reflection of well-being or of defensiveness, that is, an inability to recognize one's deficiencies? In addition, Rogers became more interested in the experience of the individual and the ways in which feelings were incorporated into the self-system than in discrepancies between perceptions of the self and ideal self.

To summarize the work of Rogers, we can note his emphasis on the self during periods when the concept was in disfavor, and his efforts to develop objective measures of phenomena that were clinically significant. To his credit, Rogers always attempted to integrate his sensitivity as a clinician with his respect for the methods of and standards for obtaining scientific data. In addition, Rogers recognized the importance of both affective and cognitive aspects of the self, as well as conscious and unconscious aspects. Because he was not sure how to measure unconscious self-perceptions objectively, and he believed conscious self-perceptions were in any case of greater importance, his focus was on parts of the self that were available to awareness and self-report. Finally, Rogers emphasized both the need for consistency and the need for positive regard in relation to the self, gradually placing increased emphasis on the latter. More than anything, his efforts were directed toward helping individuals to be more aware and accepting of their experiences.

THE PSYCHOANALYTIC CONCEPT OF THE SELF

As developed by Freud, psychoanalytic theory did not include major emphasis on the concept of the self. Some analysts have suggested that the German word that was translated as *ego* could as well have been translated as *self.* However, whatever the merits of this view, the concept of the self was not a major part of classical psychoanalytic theory. The emphasis, rather, was on the drive-instincts and the conflicts between them and reality or the superego.

Sullivan's Interpersonal School of Psychiatry

Which is not to say, however, that neglect of the concept of the self has been true for all analysts or is true for contemporary psychoanalytic theory. The American psychiatrist Harry Stack Sullivan (1892–1949) developed an alternative approach to psychoanalysis, the **interpersonal school of psychiatry.** Influenced by earlier self theorists such as Cooley and Mead, Sullivan (1953) placed great emphasis on the social, interpersonal basis of the development of the self, most particularly on the early relationship between the infant and mother. According to Sullivan, the self develops out of feelings experienced while in contact with others and from *reflected appraisals* or perceptions by the child as to how it is valued or appraised by others. Important parts of the self, particularly in relation to the experience of anxiety as opposed to security, are the "good me" associated with pleasurable experiences, the "bad me" associated with pain and threats to security, and the "not me" or parts of the self that are rejected because they are associated with intolerable anxiety.

Object Relations Theory

Over the past 30 years psychoanalysts have had both clinical and theoretical interests in problems of self-definition and vulnerability to blows to self-esteem (Kernberg, 1976, Kohut, 1977). There has been interest in how, during the earliest years, a person develops a sense of self and then attempts to protect its integrity. Analysts concerned with such questions are known as object relations theorists (Greenberg & Mitchell, 1983). The focus in **object relations theory** is on relationship seeking rather than on instinctual gratification, as is true in classical psychoanalysis. The emphasis among object relations theorists is on how experiences with important people in the past are represented as aspects of the self, aspects of others, or aspects of self-other relationships and then how these self-representations affect relationships in the present (Baldwin, 1992).

Despite subtle differences among object relations theorists, they are united by this common emphasis on the early development of mental representations of the self, others, and self in relation to others (Cooper, 1993; Westen, 1992). What are the common elements to the object relations theorists' views concerning the self and self-representations? Westen (1992) has noted five common elements. First, self-representations in object relations theory are seen as multidimensional. Each individual has many representations of the self that are based on a variety of elements, including sounds and smells. In addition, as noted, these self-representations can be isolated from one another or in conflict with one another as well as integrated into a cohesive sense of self. These self-representations can also be partial or total, relating to a part of the self (e.g., "This part of me is bad, shameful") or to the total self (e.g., "I am bad, worthless").

Second, according to object relations theorists the representations of self are heavily affect laden. In fact, one could say that the individual's self-representations are organized according to their association with various affects, a view not terribly different from some current cognitive views of the nature of the organization of memory for experiences associated with strong emotion. Thus, self-representations might be organized according to whether they are associated with joy, sexual arousal, sadness, or shame.

Third, representations of the self are associated with motives in terms of wishes and fears. This motivational emphasis on self-representations follows from their association with affect. Because at the most basic level the self-representations are associated with pleasure or pain (pleasurable or painful affect), they take on the motivational qualities of wishes and fears. For the most part one seeks to replay positive self-representations and representations of relationships with others and avoid those associated with negative affect (fears).

Fourth, representation of the self can be conscious or unconscious. The emphasis on unconscious self-representations is not surprising given the importance of the unconscious in psychoanalytic theory (Chapter 7). It should be recognized here that what is being suggested is that not only are some self-representations *not conscious* because they are habitual, routine, or automatic, but that some self-representations are *unconscious* or unavailable to consciousness. This is either because they were formed at a time prior to the development of language and more advanced cognitive skills or because they have been repressed. As with other aspects of psychoanalysis, part of therapy is to enable the patient to become aware of self-representations that have been repressed for defensive purposes. When they are made conscious, they can be examined in the light of more adult, rational cognitive processes.

Fifth, as suggested in many of the previous comments and illustrations, the individual develops not just representations of the self but representations of others and of the self in relation to others. The affect that is at the core of representations holds for relationships as well as for the self. Thus, the internal working models emphasized by Bowlby (Chapter 6) are not just working models of the self but of relationships between the self and others. In fact, it is these relationship working models that are at the heart of attachment theory and its relevance to the formation of adult romantic relationships (Baldwin, Fehr, Keedian, Seidel, & Thomson, 1993; Hazan & Shaver, 1994).

To these five elements we can add a sixth. This is the suggestion that representations of the self, of others, and of the self in relation to others are organized into a system. The system of self-representations is what is known as the self-system and the individual tries to maintain a sense of cohesion, coherence, or integration among the elements of the system. This systems view was suggested in the first point concerning the multidimensionality of the self-representations. However, it is worth noting as a separate point because it is central to clinical work and is not characteristic of all theoretical views of the self. In terms of clinical work, many object relations theorists suggest that various forms of psychopathology can be understood in terms of the individual's efforts to maintain a cohesive self (Kohut, 1977). In other words, even painful repesentations of the self may be maintained because they are experienced as necessary for the sense of a cohesive as opposed to a fragmented self. In this sense one might prefer to be "bad" rather than to be confused or have no sense of self at all.

According to object relations theorists, what one sees in psychotherapy is the interplay among these self, other, and self in relation to other representations that date back to infancy and childhood. For example, a person may have self-representations of being both very fragile and totally invulnerable, of being very weak and virtually omnipotent, of being entitled to everything that is needed or desired and totally undeserving. Such self-representations are seen as dating back to early and emotionally intense relationships with significant others, including peers. As such, they are seen as not necessarily functioning according to cognitive processes associated with adulthood—how else could one simultaneously maintain such contradictory views of the self? For example, a key self-representation for one patient was that of having "Dumbo ears" because in childhood he was teased about parallels between his large ears and the Disney elephant character Dumbo. Another patient had a self-representation as one of the ugliest men on earth because of his large nose, which in childhood had been compared to that of Pinocchio. In both these cases the self-representations were conscious but the depth of feeling associated with them and the role they played in the patients' experiences of self and relationships with others were not consciously appreciated.

In sum, we have here a view of the self based largely on clinical work with patients, emphasizing many traditional psychoanalytic points such as the importance of early experiences and the unconscious, and, as we shall see, differing in important ways from more cognitive views of the self. Although efforts are being made to develop systematic means for assessing the nature of individual self-representations, largely through the analysis of therapy transcripts, the basic elements of the psychoanalytic–object relations view of the self are derived from clinical work with patients. In particular, of late they are derived from work with patients who struggle with unrealistic views of the self, who struggle with others to affirm these unrealistic views, and who struggle to maintain a cohesive sense of self. The basis for such theoretical work is quite different from that of social cognitive views of the self, to which we now turn.

SOCIAL COGNITIVE VIEW OF THE SELF

The social cognitive view of the self is based on concepts and research methods drawn from cognitive psychology. However, one can go back to the work of George Kelly (1955) to see key aspects of the cognitive emphasis. As described in Chapter 3, Kelly developed a theory of personal constructs: People, like scientists, observe events and formulate concepts or constructs to organize phenomena and predict the future. A construct, like a schema, is a way of perceiving, construing, or interpreting events. Constructs are organized in a system, with superordinate constructs higher in the construct system and subordinate constructs lower in the construct system. Within the construct system there are core constructs, those that are basic to the construct system and are not readily changed; and there are peripheral constructs, those less basic that can be altered without serious consequences for the rest of the system.

Where does the concept of the self fit within such a theoretical system? In personal construct theory the self is a person or role to which constructs are applied. In addition, however, the self may also be a construct, generally a core and superordinate one. Remember that all constructs have two poles. The opposite pole for the construct of self may be not self, forming the *self–not self* construct. However, it is possible for the other pole to be something else. Or, for example, the person may have a *good me–bad me* construct rather than a superordinate construct of the self that involves good and bad parts. In any case, Kelly's theory would suggest that one forms a construct such as self–not self on the basis of observing similarities and differences between oneself and others. And, on the basis of such observations, other constructs are applied to the self, subordinate to the self construct. For example, in the case of a person tested on Kelly's Role Construct Repertory Test to determine his or her construct system, constructs such as the following were formed: self-satisfied–self-doubting, unsure of self–self-confident, and self-sufficient–needs other people (Pervin, 1993a). These as well as other constructs were applied to the self and used to define it.

One final point may be worthy of note in relation to Kelly's theory. This is his emphasis on the importance of the construct system for predicting events as well as the problem if the system cannot provide for such prediction. Kelly emphasized the importance of consistency within the construct system—consistency permits predictions to be made. An inconsistent construct system in which predictions cancelled one another out would be problematic indeed. He also suggested that anxiety occurs when one experiences events that lie outside the construct system and threat is experienced when there is the danger of comprehensive change in the construct system. In terms of the self, then, one would seek to be able to predict one's own behavior and would experience anxiety when behaving in ways that did not fit one's self-concept. And, one might resist comprehensive change in the construct system as it applies to the self because of the threat associated with such change. Thus, people in therapy may seek changes in the ways they view themselves but also resist these changes because of the threat associated with them. In particular, people would be expected to resist change in core ways of construing the self even if such change is otherwise deemed desirable.

Despite the cognitive emphasis and brilliance of Kelly's theory, it had relatively little influence on the development of a social cognitive approach to the self. This would appear to be because personal construct theory was developed at a time when interest in the self was somewhat dormant and because Kelly's theory was not associated with some broader model or approach to research. Later, Epstein (1973, 1990, 1992) developed a view of the self that had many elements in common with Kelly's view. According to Epstein, the self is an organized conceptual system or theory. People have theories about themselves just as they have theories about other parts of the world. As such, the self contains many components (i.e., many selves), organizes information (experience), and guides action. In agreement with Kelly, Epstein suggested that parts of the self-theory are conscious and other parts are not conscious and that people are motivated to preserve the consistency and integrity of their self-theory. In addition, Epstein suggested that people are motivated to maximize pleasure and reduce pain, to maintain relatedness to others, and to enhance self-esteem. These motivations were part of an experiential as well as a cognitive emphasis in Epstein's theory. Such motivational emphases, which perhaps would fit with some of Rogers's views, were not part of Kelly's system. Indeed, as noted in Chapter 3, Kelly rejected the need for a motivational concept and instead suggested that people seek prediction, and the consistency in the construct system that provides for prediction, because that is the way they are. For Kelly, no further explanations were needed.

Although Epstein's views also were well received, once more they had little impact on the field. No new paradigm or way of viewing people was being presented, nor was there the suggestion of a new approach to research. The situation was quite different in regard to a cognitive, information-processing approach to the concept of the self. Here the person could be viewed as very much like a computer that processes information, some of which is organized around a category called the self. The cognitive revolution had brought with it such a model of the person, and cognitive psychologists were hard at work using the information-processing model conceptually and empirically. Could such a model be applied to the self?

Consider here a groundbreaking study by Markus (1977). Markus suggested that people form cognitive structures about the self just as they do about other phenomena. Such cognitive structures are called *self-schemata*. Note that Markus used the term *schemata* to refer to the plural of schema. Today the term *schema* is used for both the singular and the plural. However, consistent with her earlier usage, we will use the term *schemata* in discussing Markus's research. Self-schemata are cognitive generalizations about the self, derived from past experience, that organize and guide the processing of self-related information. Based on this conceptualization, Markus compared subjects who rated themselves as independent or dependent, that is, subjects for whom these self-schemata were relevant, to subjects who did not show any clear tendency to rate themselves as independent or dependent, that is, subjects for whom these self-schemata were not relevant. Subjects in the former groups were *schematic* for the independent-dependent self-schema; those in the latter groups were *aschematic*. Would subjects in these two groups differ in their cognitive functioning? That is, would the availability of relevant self-schema influence cognitive performance? Indeed, Markus found that individuals with a self-schema for independence functioned differently from those with a self-schema for dependence, and both functioned differently from individuals without a self-schema related to either independence or dependence. Subjects with self-schemata were able to process relevant information more rapidly, to give more schema-relevant illustrations, and to resist information that was incongruent with their self-schemata than were individuals without the relevant self-schemata. In other words, Markus demonstrated that people with particular self-schemata, such as independence and dependence, *process* relevant information with ease, *retrieve* relevant behavioral evidence with ease, and *resist* evidence contrary to their self-schemata.

Following that research, Markus and others gathered additional evidence suggesting that once self-schemata are established, they influence a wide variety of cognitive processes. For example, there is evidence that we attend to and learn self-relevant information more quickly than information that is not relevant to the self, that we can recall self-relevant information better than nonrelevant information, and that we not only resist information discrepant with our self-schemata but we actively elicit from others self-relevant or self-confirming information (Fong & Markus, 1982; Markus & Sentis, 1982; Swann & Read, 1981). In sum, Markus suggested the following: (1) Self-schemata can be viewed as cognitive structures that function similarly to other cognitive structures. (2) All incoming stimuli are evaluated according to the relevance to the self. (3) There is a self-confirming bias.

Note that none of these suggestions is in conflict with what was proposed by Kelly or Epstein. What is different, however, is the framework within which the concept and research procedures are situated. A further illustration of the application of the cognitive, information-processing model to the concept of the self may be useful in this regard. Cantor and Kihlstrom (1987, 1989) suggest that the self-concept be treated like any other concept or category. If one considers a concept such as *vehicle,* one can think of many types of vehicles that can be arranged in a hierarchy (Rosch, Mervis, Gray, Johnson, & Boyes-Braem, 1976). For example, cars, buses, and trucks all represent types of vehicles. Within the car category, there are subtypes such as four-door sedan and sports car. Within the truck category, there are subtypes such as pick-up truck and trailer truck. What is suggested is that there is a multiplicity of selves, called a **family of selves,** that can similarly be arranged in a hierarchy. For example, as noted earlier, one might have a work self, family self, social self, and alone self. Within each of these selves there might be further subselves. For example, within the family, there might be a child self, sibling self, and a partner self.

Where do the multiplicity of selves in the family of selves come from? There exist a variety of possibilities and individuals will have unique selves and organizations of selves. Thus, in contrast to the previous illustration, other individuals might organize their selves hierarchically in terms of affects, with a happy self and an unhappy self at the top of the hierarchy and various subtypes of happy and unhappy selves lower in the hierarchy. Cantor and Kihlstrom suggest, however, that most self-hierarchies are organized in terms of situational contexts, as in the first illustration. In other words, people recognize that their self-constructions vary from situational context to situational context. At the same time, there are overlapping resemblances among the contextual selves. Thus, just as the various types of cars have some resemblances and some differentiating features, the self in various contexts has some resemblances and differentiating features. What I am like at school may be clearly distinct from what I am like at home, but there is some overlap or common features between the two, at least enough for me to recognize them both as me.

How, then, do we arrive at a sense of unity, a sense of who we are despite all the contextual variation? Cantor and Kihlstrom suggest three bases for the sense of integration within the family of selves. First, the overlapping resemblances give us a sense of unity. Perhaps our prototypic self contains key elements that unite the various subselves. Second, unity to the self is given by our autobiographical record, our sense of continuity over time. Third, we may always be able to focus on a basic, core self. Whereas in our daily functioning we switch selves according to the situational context, using in each context what is called a **working self-concept** (Markus & Kunda, 1986), we always are able to return to focus on some basic level of self-conception. Thus, an answer is provided to the question of why we are not all multiple personalities—because of overlapping resemblances, an autobiographical record, and a basic or core self-conception.

In sum, the social cognitive view of the self includes an emphasis on both the structural aspects of the self and the ways in which the self-concept influences further information processing. At this point it might seem as if the social cognitive self is a somewhat cold, removed self relative to the phenomenological self or the psychoanalytic self. In fact, the original social cognitive conceptualization of the self did have a "cold" quality to it. However, over time greater emphasis has been given to affective and motivational variables. For example, it is recognized that each member of the family of selves can be associated with affect and, as noted, affect itself may be the basis for the categorization of some selves. In addition, Markus has developed the concept of **possible selves,** representing what people think they might become, what they would like to become, and what they are afraid of becoming (Markus & Nurius, 1986; Markus & Ruvolo, 1989). In this sense, possible selves not only serve to organize information but also have a powerful motivational influence, directing us toward becoming certain things and away from becoming other things.

Before concluding our discussion of the social cognitive self, it is important to note the extent to which attention recently has been given to cultural differences in the conception of the self (Kitayama, 1992; Markus & Kitayama, 1991; Triandis, 1989; Triandis, McCusker, & Hui, 1990). In societies emphasizing the individual self, such as our own, one's identity is based on unique qualities associated with the individual. When asked "Who are you?" most Americans respond with their name and what they do. In societies emphasizing the group, one's identity is based on ties to other members of the group. When asked "Who are you?" persons from such a society might answer in terms of the town they come from and the family they are part of. In individualistic societies, one's identity is based on what one owns and what one accomplishes. Value is placed on being independent and self-sufficient. In collectivist societies, one's identity is based on membership in a group, the collective self, and value is placed on conformity. In the former, the private self is emphasized, in the latter, the public self.

The Self. The nature and importance of the self has been found to vary in different cultures.

Suggested here is that the very nature of the self, the information that is emphasized and the implications of that information for social behavior, can vary enormously from culture to culture. Indeed, one can even ask about the boundaries of the self. Most Americans, if asked about their "true self," would locate it somewhere within the body; but in India, the true self is the spiritual self that lies outside the body. The very nature of the self is different in the two societies. Thus, it is not surprising that cultural differences exist in the basis for one's self-esteem. Whereas American students play up their uniqueness to enhance their self-esteem, Japanese students do not show this bias. In addition, for American students positive feelings and pride are associated with achievement; for Japanese students such feelings are associated with feelings of connectedness to others. For the Japanese students accomplishment, in the sense of individual achievement, is associated with negative feelings. Whereas American students seek to stand out, Japanese students follow the Japanese saying "nails that stick up are pounded down" (Markus, 1992).

Motivational Processes Relevant to the Self: Self-Verification and Self-Enhancement

In the previous discussion we were primarily concerned with structural aspects of the self. In this section we give more focused attention to motivational processes. Two classes of motivational processes have been emphasized in relation to the self—consistency and enhancement. Consistency, also called **self-verification,** refers to

SPOTLIGHT ON THE RESEARCHER

HAZEL ROSE MARKUS:
In Search of the Meaning of a Self

In the early 1960s my family moved from England to San Diego, California to join my father's brothers and their families. The three families often spent their weekends and vacations together. In the course of making plans for an upcoming vacation, we would collectively review the trips of the year before. My uncle would say something like "Let's go to the lake again. The swimming was fantastic; there's that great rock to dive from. Remember how much fun we had on the day we all went water-skiing?" My *other* uncle, a prophet before his time with respect to low-fat, preservative-free diets would interrupt, "I can't believe you would think of going back there—the food was poisonous, filled with chemicals; and there is nothing but junk to eat at that lodge." At this point, my aunt, who was always mindful of the bottom line would claim that the lodge had been very expensive and that since we didn't spend much time there, perhaps we should camp this year. "No," my mother would protest, camping would mean even more bugs than we had to endure last year, and she would recount in detail all events involving mosquitos, black flies, and spiders. On one occasion when I was 11 or 12 years old and this type of discussion was in full swing, I remember asking myself, "Which trips were those they are talking about? Did I go?"

It was as if we had all gone not on one big happy (in its own semidysfunctional way) family vacation, but instead on separate trips to different worlds. Thinking about my vacations, I couldn't remember any bugs; I thought the food was delicious (especially the cinnamon rolls that made the walk to the village more than worth the trip); I don't suppose it occurred to me that the accommodations had to be paid for; and while I certainly *did* remember the water-ski trip my uncle was referring to, I hardly remembered it as fun. It had been my first trip and no one had bothered to tell me to let go of the rope when I fell. I nearly drowned, or so I recalled. That my uncle recalled this trip as an all-time vacation highlight amazed me. On this occasion, I remember looking around my aunt's big dining room table and I knew we had all been at the same place at the same time. It could be documented. Yet each of us appeared to have summered separately. Each had lived out our vacations and packaged them for thought and memory quite individually in terms of our own concerns and fears.

It seems to me now that my amazement at the vast differences to be found in the lived worlds of the people in my relatively homogeneous family was the source of my interest in the self and personality. Many years later, I found that William James had written about his surprise in learning that the "internal landscapes" of people in similar conditions could be so different. More recently I have come across a quote by E. Sapir that captures this sentiment. He wrote, "The worlds in which different societies live are distinct worlds, not merely the same world with different labels attached." It seemed to me that the worlds in which the members of my extended family lived were distinct worlds, not merely the same world with different labels attached.

By the time of my dissertation research, I had become interested in the self and the sources and consequences of the specific concerns that gave form and definition to the self, and that simultaneously lend order, coherence, and structure to one's lived experience. I called these structures for knowing—schemas—self-schemas. Self-schemas function to give our lives their individually tailored and custom-crafted form. My colleagues and I, who worked on the functions of self-schemas, hoped to understand how they provide continuity to our lived experience, how they let us tune into some features of the world rather than others, how they shape our memory, and how they provide the contours of the anticipated future. This work was completed during a time when interest in cognition and cognitive processes was at its height. The dominant metaphor for the mind was the computer, so in studies of self-schemas, we concentrated on what we called the "information-processing" consequences of self-schemas.

Now I think many researchers are more broadly interested in the affective, motivational, and interpretive consequences of these interpretive structures, and in their role in self-making and world-making. My current studies are closely related to these early interests in many ways, but they focus on differences among cultural groups rather than on differences among people. Like members of the same extended family, cultural groups construct and highlight very different features of the shared world. European-American culture emphasizes individuality, independence, and the right and the need to be one's own person. In contrast, many Asian cultural groups emphasize not a given person's individuality, but instead the fundamental interdependence among people and the importance of being a member or a participant of the group. These different emphases reflect, in part, different understandings of what it means to be a person or a "self," and different notions of what is good and what is moral.

The goal of my current research, a goal shared with many pursuing cultural psychology, is to examine the consequences of this divergence in core cultural schemas for our ways of thinking, feeling, and acting. A concern of this research, a concern that I believe is becoming increasingly significant in personality and social psychology is to understand how our intensely private, personal internal lives (including our prevailing self-schemas) are shaped and conditioned by a variety of cultural, historical, economic, and sociopolitical factors. This requires careful attention to the recurrent interpersonal episodes that give form to everyday life. The general direction of this research is to blur or dissolve the hard and fast boundaries that our previous research has forged between the individual and the sociocultural, the self and the collective, or the person and the situation and to view these phenomena not as separate forces that must contend with each other, but instead as interdependent realities that must be coordinated because they require one another.

an individual's attempts to find agreement among self-perceptions and between self-perceptions and incoming information: We seek to be known for who we are or believe ourselves to be. **Self-enhancement** refers to the attempt to find information that will maintain or raise self-esteem: We seek to be known for who or what we would like to be.

An emphasis on self-consistency has already been seen in the theories of Kelly and Epstein. It is a motive that has been emphasized by many other theorists as well (Aronson, 1992; Schlenker & Weigold, 1989). Why should people seek self-consistency? First, consistency provides a sense of cohesion and integration whereas a lack of internal consistency is associated with conflict and stress. Second, consistency allows for predictability whereas a lack of consistency means that we are unable to predict how we are going to behave. In this sense there are both cognitive and emotional motivations for self-consistency, cognitive in terms of the need to be able to predict events and emotional in the sense of tension and conflict associated with the lack of consistency. It should not be surprising that a need for internal consistency would lead to a need for self-verification, that is, a need to have others verify who we think we are. There is a need to bring our inner, private selves and our outer, public selves into line with one another (Fleming & Rudman, 1993). We will select situations that will confirm our self-concept, even if the information received is not beneficial to our self-esteem. In other words, the need for self-verification may be so great that we are prepared to accept negative information to preserve our self-concept. And, the need to avoid disruption of our sense of self may be so great that positive events may be injurious to our health if we have negative self-images (Brown & McGill, 1989). In sum, the suggestion here is that people are motivated to promote self-consistency and to have their self-concepts verified by others.

But what of the need for positive regard and self-esteem? Don't we have a need to preserve a positive image of ourselves? Once more many theorists support an emphasis on the need for self-enhancement, the need for self-esteem maintenance, or the motive to believe in one's moral and adaptive adequacy (Greenberg, Pyszczynski, Solomon, & Rosenblatt, 1990; Greenwald & Pratkanis, 1984; Schlenker & Weigold, 1989; Steele, 1988; Steele & Spencer, 1992; Steele, Spencer, & Lynch, 1993; Tesser, 1988). According to this view, people seek information in a self-serving fashion, recall successes better than failures, are more likely to attribute success rather than failure to themselves, and are more likely to see good in themselves than in others. But what of the acceptance of negative information concerning the self? According to this view, self-inconsistency can be tolerated unless it suggests self-inadequacy. When we seem to prefer negative information about ourselves, it is not because of the need for self-verification, but rather because we fear that an unrealistically positive evaluation will lead to disillusionment and eventually greater blows to our self-esteem (Steele & Spencer, 1992). Seeking to maintain and enhance our self-esteem, we use *reflection processes* and *comparison processes,* bolstering our self-esteem through association with others held in high regard (reflection) and by avoiding comparison to such individuals (Tesser, Pilkington, & McIntosh, 1989). Most of us would like to be known as friends of important figures (reflection) but not to be compared to them.

Operation of the need for self-esteem would appear to produce less paradoxical effects than that of the need for consistency. The tendency to interpret events in a self-enhancing way makes more intuitive sense than our being at times uncomfortable with compliments, positive events, or success. However, the need to preserve our self-esteem can produce some untoward effects. For example, through self-handicapping maneuvers, we may put barriers in the way of our success so that failure can be attributed to the barrier (Tice, 1991). Thus, an individual using a self-handicapping strategy may "purposely" come late for an important interview. If he or she does not get the job, the person can blame it on coming late rather than on something personal that might represent a greater blow to self-esteem. Or, we may be self-effacing so as to not disappoint ourselves or others with our performance. Beyond this, the pain of blows to our self-esteem may be so great that we seek escape from self-awareness through alcohol, drugs, binge eating, or even suicide (Baumeister, 1990, 1991; Heatherton & Baumeister, 1991).

Is one or the other view correct? Do we seek the "true" or the "good," the honesty of self-verification or the warm glow of self-enhancement? What happens when the two motives conflict? If push comes to shove, do we prefer accurate feedback or positive feedback, the disagreeable truth or what fits our fancy, to be known for who we are or to be adored for who we would like to be (Pelham, 1991; Strube, 1990; Swann, 1991, 1992)? What happens when our cognitive need for consistency or self-verification conflicts with our affective need for self-enhancement, what Swann has called the *cognitive-affective crossfire* (Swann, Griffin, Predmore, & Gaines, 1987; Swann, Pelham, & Krull, 1989)?

Swann (1992) has been one of the most active investigators of this question. For the most part he is impressed with the motive for self-verification, even at the price of negative information. Thus, he illustrates the unhappy consequences of a negative self-concept with the description of an attractive, pleasant, intelligent woman who leaves men who like her and is attracted to men who are unkind to her, verifying thereby her own negative self-concept. But beyond such fascinating clinical anecdotes, and quips such as Groucho Marx's "I'd never join a club that would have me as a member," Swann provides empirical evidence to support his point of view. In a test of the hypothesis that people seek self-verifying partners, Swann gave subjects with favorable self-evaluations and unfavorable self-evaluations their choice of interacting with one of two evaluators. The descriptions of the evaluators, who actually were fictitious, consisted of comments written about the subjects, one set being favorable and the other unfavorable. Would all the subjects prefer to interact with the evaluator giving positive feedback, in line with the self-enhancement motive, or would different choices be made by those with positive self-evaluations and those with negative self-evaluations, as suggested by the self-verification hypothesis?

What Swann found was a clear difference in preference for interaction partners between the two groups (Swann, Stein-Seroussi, & Giesler, 1992). In line with the self-verification hypothesis, people with positive self-concepts preferred to interact with "evaluators" who gave favorable evaluations and people with negative self-concepts preferred to interact with "evaluators" who gave unfavorable evaluations (Figure 8.1). In addition, other experimental evidence suggests that people with negative self-concepts will respond to praise by seeking out feedback about their limitations and will remain committed to self-verifying partners even if their partners are critical of them (Swann, Hixon, & De La Ronde, 1992; Swann, Wenzlaff, Krull, & Pelham, 1992).

Does the need for self-verification of negative self-concepts suggest that such people are masochistic? Swann does not think so, since rather than preferring totally negative information they seek only negative information that confirms their negative self-evaluations. In their areas of strength, people with overall negative self-evaluations do seek favorable feedback. What Swann suggests is that people with negative self-evaluations are themselves caught in a cognitive-affective crossfire between the preference for negative feedback that is congruent with their self-concept and positive feedback that will enhance their self-esteem. He suggests that whereas initially people under such conditions might prefer positive feedback, upon further comparison of such feedback to their self-concept they opt for self-verification: "When the self-concept is negative, the desire for self-verification will override the desire for positive evaluations" (Swann, 1992, p. 16).

Figure 8.1 Preferences for interaction partners.

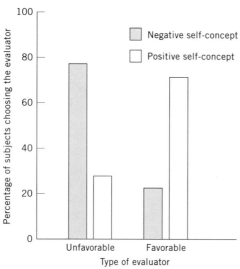

(From "Seeking 'Truth,' Finding Despair: Some Unhappy Consequences of a Negative Self-Concept," by W. B. Swann, Jr., 1992, *Current Directions in Psychological Science, 1,* p. 16. Reprinted with the permission of Cambridge University Press.)

Swann's evidence is impressive and provides a basis for understanding why negative self-concepts are often so difficult to change. In the course of efforts to improve their self-concept, such as in psychotherapy, people with negative self-concepts are interacting with others and are biased toward accepting information from others that validates their negative self-view. In a statement that appears to be sympathetic toward psychoanalytic models, Swann suggests that "a growing body of research suggests that the relationships children form with their primary caretakers will later help them—or haunt them—as they mature. Our data suggest that people's self-concepts may be an important vehicle through which childhood relationships are carried forward through life" (1992, p. 18).

At the same time, we need not be so unimpressed with the power of the need to protect one's self-esteem and the affective element of the cognitive-affective crossfire. There may be a balance between the cognitive need for consistency and the affective need for self-esteem or self-enhancement. When circumstances suggest a need for reality, self-consistency motives may predominate; when reality constraints are weak or self-esteem needs are great, self-enhancement motives may predominate (Schlenker & Weigold, 1989). In Swann's research the subjects often are forced to choose between the two, and to do so under conditions that may foster an emphasis on honesty and self-consistency. Under other conditions, however, people may be satisfied to stop with the good feeling associated with positive feedback rather than moving on to check whether the information fits with their self-concept (Sedikides, 1993). And, under other conditions people are able to use self-deception and self-handicapping devices to protect their self-esteem. Research indeed exists suggesting both individual differences in the need for self-enhancement and the conditions under which the need for self-enhancement or self-verification may be greater. In terms of individual differences, research suggests that highly narcissistic individuals— that is, those preoccupied with themselves and their importance—show a particular bias toward evaluating their performance in a self-enhancing, positive way relative to the performance of others (John & Robins, 1994; Robins & John, 1994). In terms of conditions, there is evidence that, during dating, individuals are concerned with self-enhancement—that is, with being evaluated favorably by their date—whereas in marriage or committed relationships individuals are concerned with self-verification, that is, with being seen by their partners as they see themselves to be: "Marriage apparently precipitates a shift from a desire for positive evaluations to a desire for self-verifying evaluations" (Swann, De La Ronde, & Hixon, 1994, p. 857).

In sum, we have evidence for the importance of two motivational processes associated with the self—the need for self-consistency and the need for self-enhancement. There is considerable evidence in support of each, justifying attention to the importance of the self in regard to personality and motivation. Clearly there is evidence of the power of the need for self-verification, even when the result is further verification of a negative self-concept. Although in contradiction to a pure pleasure-pain principle of operation, the need for consistency gives testimony to the utility of accuracy and predictability in our daily functioning. At the same time, it remains to be determined under which circumstances the cognitive need for consistency or the affective need for self-enhancement will predominate. The winner in the cognitive-affective crossfire remains to be determined.

COMPARISON OF THE SOCIAL COGNITIVE AND PSYCHOANALYTIC VIEWS OF THE SELF

In a 1992 article Westen, a scholar of both the psychoanalytic and social cognitive literatures, examined the two views and asked: Can we get our selves together? Westen noted the many similarities between the two points of view, suggesting that the growing convergence might come as a surprise to readers of only one or the other literature. He then asked: "Are we, then, one happy family, with cognitive and psychoanalytic psychologists marching proudly together under the banner of the self?" (Westen, 1992, p. 4).

Clearly an integration of the social cognitive and psychoanalytic views would have much merit. Each has distinct contributions but each also has distinct limitations. For example, Westen suggests that the psychoanalytic conceptualization of the self lacks an empirical base and ignores cultural differences. Although social cognitive theory is strong in just these areas, according to Westen it lacks the depth of psychoanalysis, for example, the attention given in object relations theory to the complex interactions among affective and motivational processes. Since the weaknesses of one appear to be the strengths of the other, why not an integration?

Westen's question was addressed by representatives of each point of view. What was their conclusion as to whether the two selves could be put together to form a unified self? The answer was not very encouraging. Although members of each group recognized the contributions of the other, they were at least equally impressed with the other's limitations and their own unique contributions. Thus, the drama and power of the self observed in the clinical context was sufficiently impressive to the psychoanalysts to make them reluctant to move toward the approach emphasized by the social cognitivists. And, members of the latter group were sufficiently impressed with the conceptual and methodological advances being made that they were reluctant to give up their methodological rigor for the drama of the self observed by clinicians.

What are other stumbling blocks to integration, an idea that would appear to have so much merit? At one time a major stumbling block was the lack of contact between members of the two groups. But, as suggested, there now exist individuals in each "camp" who are familiar with and respectful of the work of members of the other camp. Rather, the problem would appear to be one of fundamental conceptualization and approach to research. Three central issues relate to conceptualization: (1) the importance of unconscious self-representations; (2) the importance of early experiences in the formation of self-representations; and (3) the affective and motivational power of these self-representations, particularly in terms of their dynamic interplay. Psychoanalysts emphasize the importance of unconscious self-representations, the importance of early experiences in their formation and ongoing functioning, and the dynamic interplay among self-representations. Conflict among self-representations, for example, is a matter of major importance and interest. Social cognitivists are more interested in conscious self-schema, or nonconscious self-schema controlled by automatic cognitive processes, in current self-representations or current selves associated with memories of the past, and with the ability of individuals to differentiate among members of the family of selves. Interfacing with these differences are the differences in approaches to research, the one emphasizing clinical work and the other experimental work. Thus, although the idea of putting the various selves together would appear to have merit, and although we may be coming closer to the point at which a true integration is possible, at this time the two approaches remain separate and distinct, at best second cousins in the family of selves.

INDIVIDUAL DIFFERENCES IN THE SELF AND SELF-PROCESSES

In the previous discussion we considered general principles concerning the structure of the self and processes related to the self. Differences between groups of subjects have often been noted, but the general emphasis has been on common principles. In this section we consider the implications of individual differences in various aspects of the self.

BANDURA'S SELF-EFFICACY CONCEPT

In the early years of social cognitive theory, or, as it was called then, social learning theory, the concept of the self was virtually neglected (Bandura & Walters, 1963), in keeping with the early behavioral emphasis. Then, influenced by the cognitive revolution, in 1977 the concept of *self-efficacy* took center stage as a part of the theory (Bandura, 1977b). Self-efficacy relates to the perceived ability to cope with specific situations. It relates to the judgments people make concerning their ability to meet specific demands in specific situations. It should be clear that the social cognitive concept of self refers to processes that are part of the person's psychological functioning. The person does not have a structure called "the self," but rather self-conceptions and self-control processes that may vary from time to time and situation to situation. Thus, earlier concepts of the self were criticized for being too global and for their neglect of situational variability in how we view ourselves. As noted earlier, in the social cognitive view there are many selves, a family of selves, and, in terms of self-efficacy beliefs, many different such beliefs. Although individuals differ in their self-efficacy beliefs, because of their situational specificity one would not consider self-efficacy to be a personality trait. In terms of understanding the person and daily behavior, it is the self-efficacy beliefs associated with specific tasks and situations that are considered to be much more fundamental than any overall sense of self-efficacy or self-esteem.

According to Bandura, there are four determinants of our self-efficacy beliefs: actual performance accomplishments, vicarious experiences, verbal persuasion, and emotional arousal (Bandura, 1986). *Actual performance accomplishments* are the most important source of self-efficacy information. Through experience individuals gain knowledge of what they are good at and what their weaknesses are, of their competencies and their limitations. *Vicarious experiences* enable us to observe the successes and failures of others, evaluate ourselves in relation to them, and develop self-efficacy beliefs accordingly. Thus, through a process called observational learning (see Chapter 3), we learn about the world and ourselves through observing others. Not everything needs to be experienced directly to be learned. Through *verbal persuasion* we are influenced by the attitudes and beliefs communicated by others concerning what we are able to do. Confidence in us communicated by parents, partners, or friends can make a big difference in our self-efficacy beliefs as compared to expressions of doubt and lack of confidence. On the other hand, such expressions of confidence must be followed by actual accomplishment for them to contribute meaningfully to our sense of self-efficacy. Finally, through awareness of our own *emotional arousal* we receive information concerning our self-efficacy in a situation—the sense of threat and pounding of the heart associated with potential failure as opposed to the exhilaration associated with anticipated success.

As noted, self-efficacy beliefs are relevant to situations and tasks. They affect one's judgments concerning the likelihood of success in a situation, although it may also be recognized that success is influenced by factors outside one's control. Self-efficacy beliefs may be strong or weak, strongly resistant to change or swinging like a yo-yo from one extreme to another. Thus, whereas some individuals retain a sense of self-efficacy in situations despite continuous frustration and disappointment, others find their sense of self-efficacy continuously buffeted by each instance of success and failure. In addition, self-efficacy beliefs may be relatively realistic or unrealistic. In terms of the latter, we may know extremely self-effacing individuals who are reluctant to believe in their accomplishments or extremely grandiose individuals whose beliefs concerning what they are able to accomplish far exceed what they are actually able to do.

Self-efficacy beliefs are important because they influence which activities we engage in, how much effort we expend in a situation, and how long we persist at a task, as well as our emotional reactions while anticipating a situation or being involved in it. Clearly, we think, feel, and behave differently in situations in which we feel confident of our ability than in situations in which we are insecure or feel incompetent. Thus, individuals will differ in their thoughts, motivation, emotions, and performance in situations according to differences in their self-efficacy beliefs. In a relevant piece of research Bandura and Cervone (1983) studied the effects of goals and self-efficacy beliefs on motivation and persistence at a task. In this research, subjects performed a strenuous activity with or without goals and with or without feedback information that would influence their self-efficacy beliefs. Following some initial activity, subjects rated how satisfied or dissatisfied they would be with the same level of performance in a following session as well as the level of perceived self-efficacy for various possible performance levels. Their performance effort was then measured in the following session. Subsequent effort was found to be most intense when subjects were both dissatisfied with substandard performance and high on self-efficacy judgments for good performance (Figure 8.2). In other words, high self-efficacy beliefs clearly play a role in maintaining task persistence (Bandura, 1989b). Increasing and strengthening self-efficacy beliefs also is an important part of therapeutic efforts to have patients confront fearful situations and avoid relapse after engaging in efforts to break compulsive eating, drinking, and smoking patterns of behavior (Bandura, 1986).

One of the more fascinating research efforts of late has been that of relating self-efficacy beliefs to health (A. O'Leary, 1985, 1992). Central to this work is the relation of perceived self-efficacy to the functioning of the body's immune (disease-fighting) system. There is evidence that excessive stress can lead to impairment of the immune system, whereas improvement of the ability to ameliorate stress can enhance its functioning (O'Leary, 1990). In an experiment designed to examine the impact of perceived self-efficacy of control over stressors on the immune system, Bandura and his associates found that perceived self-efficacy indeed enhanced immune system functioning (Wiedenfeld et al., 1990).

In this research, subjects with a phobia (excessive fear) of snakes were tested under three conditions: a baseline control phase involving no exposure to the phobic stressor (snake), a perceived self-efficacy acquisition phase during which subjects were assisted in gaining a sense of coping efficacy, and a perceived maximal self-efficacy phase once they had developed a complete sense of coping efficacy. During these phases, a small amount of blood was drawn from the subjects and analyzed for the presence of cells that are known to help regulate the immune system. For example, the level of helper T cells, known to play a role in destroying cancerous cells and viruses, was measured. These analyses indicated that increases in self-efficacy beliefs were associated with enhanced immune system functioning, as evidenced by the increased level of helper T cells (Figure 8.3). Thus, although the effects of stress can be negative, the growth of perceived efficacy over stressors can have valuable adaptive properties at the level of immune system functioning.

To summarize the work on self-efficacy beliefs, it is clear that such beliefs play an important role in our motivational and emotional lives, with important implications for our performance and health. What also is important to recognize is the social cognitive emphasis on specific self-efficacy beliefs as opposed to generalized beliefs that would have a traitlike quality. Thus, Bandura has never been drawn to develop a questionnaire measure of self-efficacy. Although he accepts the value of self-report as a measure of self-efficacy, the research effort is on experimental situations in

Figure 8.2 Mean percentage changes in motivational level under conditions combining goals and performance feedback as a function of different combinations of levels of self-dissatisfaction (S-Dis) and perceived self-efficacy for goal attainment (S-Eff).
This graph illustrates the importance of both self-dissatisfaction with substandard performance and high perceived self-efficacy for motivation. Subjects who were both self-dissatisfied and highly self-efficacious displayed the largest performance gains, whereas those who were low on both displayed the least performance gains.

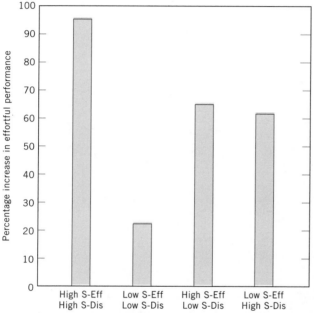

(From "Self-Evaluation and Self-Efficacy Mechanisms Governing the Motivational Effect of Goal System," by A. Bandura and D. Cervone, 1983, *Journal of Personality and Social Psychology, 45,* p. 1024. Copyright 1983 by the American Psychological Association. Reprinted by permission.)

which individual differences in relevant self-efficacy beliefs already exist or are manipulated by the experimenter.

SNYDER'S SELF-MONITORING CONCEPT

Although social cognitive theorists generally emphasize the importance of situational variables, they recognize individual differences in the importance attached to such cues. In other words, individuals differ in the extent to which they monitor or regulate their behavior according to situational cues. Snyder (1974, 1987) has developed a scale to measure such individual differences (Table 8.2). The high **self-monitoring** individual is highly sensitive to cues of situational appropriateness and regulates his or her behavior accordingly. In an extreme form, such a person can be a chameleon, always changing to meet the situation and never being sure of who he or she is. On the other hand, the low self-monitoring individual is less attentive to social information and generally behaves more in accord with internal feelings and attitudes. In an extreme form, such an individual can show insensitivity to the feelings and wishes

Figure 8.3   Changes in helper T cells during exposure to phobic stressor while acquiring perceived coping self-efficacy and after perceived coping self-efficacy develops to maximal level.
The data indicate that the growth of perceived self-efficacy during periods of stress was associated with enhanced immune system functioning (i.e., increased helper T cells).

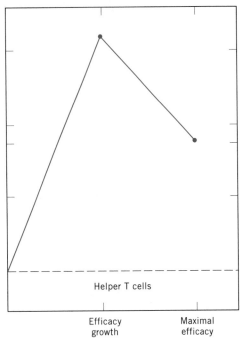

Helper T cells

| Efficacy | Maximal |
| growth | efficacy |

(From "Impact of Perceived Self-Efficacy in Coping With Stressors in Components of the Immune System," by S. A. Wiedenfeld et al., 1990, *Journal of Personality and Social Psychology, 59*, p. 1089. Copyright 1990 by the American Psychological Association. Adapted by permission.)

of others. A moderate amount of self-monitoring would balance sensitivity to changing situations and the views of others with independence and fortitude.

A variety of differences have been found between high self-monitoring (HSM) and low self-monitoring (LSM) scores. Some of these are described by Snyder as follows:

1. HSMs are better able to express and communicate emotions and expressive behavior intentionally than are LSMs.
2. HSMs are better able to deceive others in face-to-face interviews than are LSMs.
3. HSMs are better able to infer the emotional state of others correctly than are LSMs.
4. HSMs are more discriminating about situations and more variable in their behavior across situations than are LSMs.
5. HSMs generally appear to other people to be more friendly, outgoing, and extraverted and less worried, anxious, or nervous than are LSMs.
6. HSMs are less influenced in their self-presentations by changes in mood states than are LSMs.

TABLE 8.2 Illustrative Items and Scoring for the Self-Monitoring Scale

My behavior is usually an expression of my true inner feelings. (F)

At parties and social gatherings, I do not attempt to do or say things that others will like. (F)

When I am uncertain how to act in a social situation, I look to the behavior of others for cues. (T)

I sometimes appear to others to be experiencing deeper emotions than I actually am. (T)

I laugh more when I watch a comedy with others than when alone. (T)

In different situations and with different people, I often act like very different persons. (T)

T = True, F = False

Source: "Self-Monitoring of Expressive Behavior," by M. Snyder, 1974, *Journal of Personality and Social Psychology, 30,* p. 537.

7. HSMs remember more information about other people and make more inferences concerning the traits of others than do LSMs.

In sum, while situations are important, personality also is important in influencing the extent to which external as opposed to internal cues will be influential. Another perspective on this issue is presented in the next section.

CARVER AND SCHEIER'S CONTROL THEORY AND PRIVATE VERSUS PUBLIC SELF-CONSCIOUSNESS

Carver and Scheier (1981, 1990) have developed a model of human functioning (control model) that uses principles of control systems functioning and emphasizes individual differences in the extent to which people attend to private as opposed to public aspects of the self. The basics of their control systems model of self-regulation can be understood by thinking of a room thermostat, a mechanical control device for regulating room temperature. A thermostat is set at a desired room temperature that can be considered a set point or standard. The temperature in the room is then assessed and if it is below the desired level, the heat is turned on. If the temperature is above the standard, the air conditioning is turned on. The thermostat operates in an ongoing way to regulate the temperature, maintaining it at the level or standard set by a person.

In a similar way, Carver and Scheier suggest that we can consider the ways in which people set standards and then test the extent to which they are meeting the set standard. If too high a standard is perceived, the personality system will be set in motion to reduce the discrepancy between the standard and perceived level. For example, if we are not performing up to the standard we have set for ourselves, motivation and effort will be set in motion to reduce the size of the discrepancy. This is an ongoing process, just as is the working of the room thermostat. In addition, each individual may have many such standards and levels of control. These are arranged in a hierarchy with some standards and levels of control being superordinate, or more important and influential than others.

Individual differences can enter into the system in a number of ways. Individuals can differ in the levels and kinds of controls included in their self-regulatory system. A particular individual difference variable emphasized by Carver and Scheier is the private or public focus of attention of the self. Early in this research, prior to development of the control model, a scale was developed to measure individual differences in private and public self-consciousness—the Self-Consciousness Scale (Fenigstein, Scheier, & Buss, 1975). This scale consists of 10 items measuring *private self-consciousness,* 7 items measuring *public self-consciousness,* and 6 items measuring *social anxiety*. Illustrative items are shown in Table 8.3. As the items suggest, individuals high on **private self-consciousness** look inside themselves and attend to their own feelings, desires, and standards. Individuals high on **public self-consciousness** attend much more to what others may be thinking about them, to the self they are presenting to others, and to external standards. Individuals high on social anxiety tend to be easily embarrassed and anxious in social situations.

What are the implications of focusing more on the private self as opposed to the public self? People high on private self-consciousness tend to have more intense feelings and to be clearer about their feelings than people low on private self-consciousness. They tend to be higher in the agreement between their self-reports of behavior and actual behavior and to have more developed self-concepts than individuals low on private self-consciousness (A. H. Buss, 1980; Nasby, 1985). People high on public self-consciousness tend to be sensitive and reactive to the cues of others. If rejected by others they are likely to feel hurt and also are likely to change their stated views to conform to the perceived public norm. Individuals low on this trait are less likely to be emotionally influenced by the reactions of others and less likely to change their stated views to conform to the external norm.

Of course, circumstances can make any of us turn our attention toward our private

TABLE 8.3   Illustrative Items on the Self-Consciousness Scale

Private Self-Consciousness

1. I'm always trying to figure myself out.
2. I reflect about myself a lot.
3. I'm generally attentive to my inner feelings.
4. I'm constantly examining my motives.

Public Self-Consciousness

1. I usually worry about making a good impression.
2. I'm concerned about what other people think of me.
3. I'm self-conscious about the way I look.

Social Anxiety

1. It takes me time to overcome my shyness in new situations.
2. I get embarrassed very easily.
3. Large groups make me nervous.

Source: "Public and Private Self-Consciousness: Assessment and Theory," by A. Fenigstein, M. F. Scheier, and A. H. Buss, 1975, *Journal of Consulting & Clinical Psychology, 43,* p. 524.

self or our public self. Being alone, for example, can turn us toward introspection and our private self. Having to speak before an audience or being photographed can focus our attention on our public selves. However, Carver and Scheier suggest that individuals differ in how sensitive they are to these stimuli, those high on private self-consciousness being more sensitive to the private self and those high on public self-consciousness being more sensitive to the public self. Thus, individual differences exist in the ordinary focus of attention and in the sensitivity to stimuli leading in the direction of one or the other focus of attention. In both cases individuals are led to monitor their behavior in relation to a standard. However, the focus of attention, on private aspects of the self as opposed to public aspects of the self, is different in the two cases.

HIGGINS'S THEORY OF SELF-GUIDES

E. Tory Higgins has developed a theory of self-guides that comes as close as any model to integrating aspects of the social cognitive and object relations views of the self (Higgins, 1987, 1989; Strauman & Higgins, 1993). According to Higgins, **self-guides** represent standards for individuals to meet. Like other self-schema, they are cognitive structures that influence the way information is processed. Because they are frequently used, self-guides have the quality of *chronically accessible constructs*—schemata that are readily activated with little information (Chapter 7). As such, they may also be automatic and nonconscious; that is, the individual may use them automatically and be unaware of the schema being used.

In light of this discussion, Higgins's concept of self-guides would seem to be part of a fairly traditional social cognitive view. There is a particular emphasis on self-standards, but the emphasis clearly is social cognitive. However, Higgins also emphasizes a strong developmental and affective-motivational component to his theory. From a developmental standpoint, he suggests that self-guides result from early social learning experiences that are associated with emotional consequences for meeting or failing to meet standards. Of particular importance in this regard are two kinds of self-guides—the *ideal self* and the *ought self*. The **ideal self** represents the attributes that ideally we would like to possess, that is, the attributes important others hold for us and we hold for ourselves. The **ought self** represents the attributes we feel we should possess, that is, the duties, responsibilities, and obligations others hold for us and we hold for ourselves. The ideal self is associated with positive outcomes and is derived from the positive affect associated with attaining standards set by important figures from one's early environment. The ought self is associated with negative outcomes and is derived from the negative affect associated with not fulfilling duties and responsibilities set forth by important figures from one's early environment.

According to Higgins's self-discrepancy theory, we are motivated to reduce discrepancies between how we actually see ourselves and how ideally we would like to be (actual self–ideal self discrepancies) and between how we actually see ourselves and how we ought to be (actual self–ought self discrepancies). The reason for this is that in our early interactions, we associate positive affect with the meeting of these ideal and ought standards, and negative affect with not meeting them.

In his research on self-guides, Higgins uses a "Selves Questionnaire." Subjects are asked to list traits or attributes describing each of a number of self-states such as actual self, ideal self, and ought self. Subjects also rate the extremity with which each attribute applies to the particular self-state. It is important to note that subjects spontaneously generate these attributes rather than checking them off on some list. This is done to ensure selection of those attributes that are important and accessible for the particular subject. Discrepancies between self-states are then calculated in terms of differences between characteristics associated with the self and those associated with the self-guides—actual/ideal (AI) discrepancy and actual/ought (AO) discrepancy. For example, a subject might list *smart* in the ideal self and *dumb* in the actual self, leading to a mismatch or discrepancy on this attribute.

Research has indicated that these discrepancies have important and different emotional implications. AI discrepancies are associated with sadness, disappointment, and dissatisfaction, while AO discrepancies are associated with anxiety, worry, and agitation. In the former case (AI), the person is vulnerable to sadness because of the loss of positive outcomes. Hopes, wishes, or ideals have not been fulfilled. In the latter case (AO), the person is vulnerable to anxiety because of the threat of punishment for failing to meet obligations. Although both are negative outcomes, the particular nature of the outcome, in terms of self-guide discrepancies, is what determines the specific nature of the emotional consequence. In a result reminiscent of the finding of a relation between low self-efficacy and poor functioning of the immune system, a relation has been found between activation of the AI and AO discrepancies and poorer functioning of the immune system. In contrast to this, it is suggested that positive or self-congruent appraisals may have stress-buffering, immune-enhancing effects (Strauman, Lemieux, & Coe, 1993).

Another aspect of this research is the use of what are called *priming procedures* to activate particular self-guides or actual/self-guide discrepancies. In one illustrative study, subjects completed the "Selves Questionnaire." On the basis of these data, two groups of subjects were formed—one with high AI and AO discrepancy scores and one with low AI and AO discrepancy scores. Subjects in both groups were asked to fill out a mood questionnaire that included dejection emotions (e.g., sad, disappointed) and agitation emotions (e.g., tense, nervous). Subjects indicated the extent to which they were feeling each emotion on the questionnaire. Then, half the members of each group were assigned to an *ideal* priming condition and the other half to an *ought* priming condition. In the ideal priming condition, subjects were asked to describe the attributes they and their parents hoped they would have and the changes over the years in these hopes and aims. In the ought priming condition, subjects were asked to describe the attributes they and their parents believed it was their duty or obligation to have and the changes over time in these beliefs. These priming conditions were used to highlight or bring into focal attention the ideal and ought self-guides, and thereby the discrepancies between actual self-views and the self-guides. Following this the subjects again filled out the mood questionnaire.

Would priming result in a change in mood? Would the changes be different for subjects in the two groups? The prediction was that subjects who were high in both types of self-discrepancies would experience an increase in negative mood as a result of priming, whereas this would not be the case for subjects low in these discrepancies. If anything, such subjects might feel better as a result of focusing on the goals they had met. Further, a more specific prediction was that the effect would be specific to the discrepancy whose accessibility was temporarily increased by the priming manipulation—increased dejection with the ideal priming condition and increased agitation in the ought priming condition. Indeed, in accord with the predictions, ideal priming increased dejection in the high but not the low discrepancy subjects and ought priming increased the agitation in the high but not the low discrepancy subjects (Higgins, Bond, Klein, & Strauman, 1986). These results are indicated in Table 8.4 and illustrate how the moods of dejection and anxiety can be influenced by momentary contexts if the person has the relevant self-discrepancy guide. Presumably people with these discrepancies between self and self-guide are made to feel negative moods both by their own internal reflections and by specific situational events that makes these discrepancies more accessible.

Although all children learn ideal and ought self-guides, the specifics and emotional power of the guides and the magnitude of the AI and AO discrepancies vary from person to person. Because of their particular orientation toward parental standards, first-born children have been found to be more strongly oriented toward the standards of others and their AI and AO discrepancies are associated more with emotional distress than is the case for later-borns (Newman, Higgins, & Vookles, 1992).

Recent research has attempted to relate self-guides to childhood memories and vulnerability to emotional distress (Strauman, 1992a, 1992b). For example, are self-guide discrepancies associated with particular kinds of autobiographical memories? In line with what the theory predicts, AI discrepancy subjects retrieve childhood memories containing dysphoric content while AO discrepancy subjects retrieve childhood memories associated with anxious content. Once more, while both types of discrepancies are associated with childhood memories containing negative affect, the specific nature of the affect varied between members of the two groups. In another aspect of this research, subjects were followed over the course of a 3-year period. Evidence was found for stability in the attributes individuals associated with their selves as well as for the size of the self/self-guide discrepancies.

The evidence to date clearly suggests a picture of self-guides as important cognitive

TABLE 8.4   Mean Change in Dejection Emotions and Agitation Emotions as a Function of Level of Self-Discrepancies and Type of Priming

The data indicate that ideal priming increased dejection in subjects with high discrepancies but not the low discrepancy subjects. Ought priming increased agitation in the high but not the low discrepancy subjects.

Level of self-discrepancies	IDEAL PRIMING		OUGHT PRIMING	
	Dejection emotions	Agitation emotions	Dejection emotions	Agitation emotions
High actual:ideal and actual:ought discrepancies	3.2	−0.8	0.9	5.1
Low actual:ideal and actual:ought discrepancies	−1.2	0.9	0.3	−2.6

Note: Each of eight dejection emotions and eight agitation emotions was measured on a 6-point scale from *not at all* to *a great deal.* The more positive the number, the greater the increase in discomfort.
Source: "Self-Discrepancy: A Theory Relating Self and Affect," by E. T. Higgins, 1987, *Psychological Review, 94,* p. 329. Copyright 1987 by the American Psychological Association. Reprinted by permission.

structures that influence our processing of information and our emotional and motivational functioning. The social cognitive component of the theory is clear in the
emphasis on the self and self-guides as cognitive structures. However, we can also
see an object relations theory component in terms of the emphasis on early affective
experiences and the strong affect associated with the self and self-guide representations developed during the early years. The emphasis on the disturbing psychological
consequences of many of these discrepancies also fits with object relations theory,
as well as with Rogers's emphasis on the importance of discrepancies between the
self and ideal self. Relative to object relations theory, however, there is virtually no
emphasis on unconscious representations of the self or unconscious self-guides.
Relative to Rogers, what is different is the social cognitive framework within which
the theory is presented and the associated experimental procedures that are used.

FINAL REFLECTIONS ON THE SELF

In this chapter, we have considered the historical waxing and waning of interest in
the concept of the self, the various models of the structure of the self and self-related
processes, and illustrative approaches to individual differences. Clearly the self is an
area of major current interest. It is too important a personality concept to go away
or disappear altogether. The position taken here is that it will not again disappear
from the literature although its place of centrality may be lessened, particularly as
other cultural conceptions of the self are further explored. In relation to the different
approaches, it is clear from the presentation that the social cognitive approach is
gaining increased influence and is becoming more diverse in the aspects of the self
that are investigated. The central elements of this approach are the view of the self
as a cognitive structure made up of many selves or categories and following the
principles of operation of other cognitive structures. But this emphasis is not anti-
thetical to the psychoanalytic emphasis or the Rogerian, phenomenological emphasis.
This is particularly the case as social cognitive self theorists emphasize the importance
of affect as a part of the cognitive structures, often as a central organizing element
of these structures.

Nor would there appear to be disagreement concerning the importance of early
experiences in the formation of the self and self-standards, if Higgins's work can be
taken as illustrative of the social cognitive view. Most social cognitive theorists probably would place greater emphasis on the potential for change in the self-structure
than would psychoanalysts, but this may be more an issue of ideology than one of
practicality. Members of both groups likely would agree that some self-structures are
highly resistant to change and others are much more amenable to change. The key
point of difference would appear to be the relative emphasis on unconscious self-
representations, with psychoanalysts emphasizing unconscious elements and social
cognitive theorists emphasizing the conscious elements. Rogerians, with their recognition of defensive processes that prevent experiences from reaching awareness
but with their emphasis on phenomenology and the use of self-report, would appear
to fall between the two. This, then, would appear to be the greatest barrier to getting
our selves together. It is unclear whether future developments will provide for putting

the selves together, at least in some form better than a Humpty-Dumpty figure. This author believes that this will occur and that it will include an important emphasis on nonconscious and unconscious self-representations.

MAJOR CONCEPTS

Self-schema. An organized knowledge structure about the self, derived from past experience, that guides the processing of self-related information.

Self-consciousness. The ability to reflect back upon the self.

Self-conscious emotions. Emotions that require the ability for self-consciousness to be experienced (e.g., shame, pride).

Phenomenal field. Rogers's term for the stimuli perceived by the individual.

Self-experience discrepancy. Rogers's emphasis on experiences that are incongruent with the self-structure.

Self-consistency. The concept, developed by Lecky and used by Rogers and others, emphasizing the need to preserve a consistent self structure (i.e., cognitions relating to the self that are not inconsistent with one another).

Q-sort method. An assessment procedure in which the subject sorts statements into categories following a normal distribution. Used by Rogers as a measure of self, ideal self, and self-ideal discrepancy.

Interpersonal school of psychiatry. The term used to describe Harry Stack Sullivan's approach to personality and therapy.

Object relations theory. A psychoanalytic approach emphasizing humans as relationship seeking rather than instinct gratification seeking and the importance of mental representations of experiences with early significant figures.

Family of selves. Cantor and Kihlstrom's concept for the organized multiplicity of selves.

Working self-concept. Markus's concept for the self-schema being used in a particular situational context.

Possible selves. Markus's concept for the self-schema representing what people feel they may become.

Self-verification. The process, emphasized by Swann, of seeking information that verifies one's self-concept.

Self-enhancement. The process of seeking information that will maintain or enhance one's self-esteem.

Self-monitoring. Snyder's concept for the extent to which individuals monitor or regulate their behavior according to external or internal cues.

Private self-consciousness. Carver and Scheier's concept relating to the extent to which individuals focus on their own feelings and standards.

Public self-consciousness. Carver and Scheier's concept for the extent to which individuals focus on what others may be thinking of them and on external standards.

Self-guides. Higgins's concept for standards concerning the self that the individual feels should be met.

Ideal self, ought self. Two categories of self-guides, the former relating to attributes the individual would like to possess and the latter relating to attributes the individual feels should be possessed (i.e., duties, responsibilities, obligations).

SUMMARY

1.   Although interest in the self has waxed and waned, today it is one of the most researched topics in the field of personality. The concept of the self merits study because of its importance in phenomenological experience, in how we process information, and in organizing personality functioning.

2.   Developmental psychologists distinguish between self-perception, the infant's perception that it exists separate from other persons or physical objects, and self-consciousness, the ability to reflect back upon oneself. The development of self-perception is based in good part on the awareness of sensory differences associated with the body and with the learning of action-outcome contingencies. The development of self-consciousness is traced to approximately age 15 months, based on self-recognition research and an understanding of other cognitive developments occurring at that time.

3.   Three views of the self were considered: phenomenological, psychoanalytic, and social cognitive. Interest in the phenomenological self is illustrated in the work of Carl Rogers. Rogers was particularly interested in the organization of the self, in self-consistency, and in the individual's efforts to avoid the state of incongruence or discrepancy between self-concept and experience.

4.   Although Freud did not emphasize the concept of the self, it has achieved prominence among object relations theorists interested in the development of mental representations of the self, others, and self in relation to others, as well as in individual efforts to avoid blows to self-esteem and to maintain a cohesive sense of self. The self-representations emphasized by object relations theorists are multidimensional, affect laden, associated with motives and possible conflicts, and often unconscious.

5.   The social cognitive view of the self is based on concepts and research methods drawn from cognitive psychology. The self is treated as an important schema that influences the processing of a great deal of information and has implications for motivation and behavior. There is an emphasis on a multiplicity of selves (e.g., family of selves, possible selves) and cultural variation in the fundamental nature of the self. Social cognitive theorists also emphasize the importance of self-relevant motivational processes such as the motives for self-verification and self-enhancement.

6.   Although there is evidence of an interest in integrating the psychoanalytic and social cognitive views of the self, fundamental differences in content emphasized and research methods utilized have limited progress in these integrative efforts.

7.   There is considerable evidence of interest in individual difference variables associated with the concept of the self (e.g., Bandura's self-efficacy, Snyder's self-monitoring, Carver and Scheier's self-consciousness, Higgins's self-guides). Research associated with these variables demonstrates the importance of self-representations for cognition, affect, motivation, and interpersonal relationships.

THE PATH FROM THINKING TO ACTION

CHAPTER OVERVIEW

How is it that we move from thought to action, from intending to do something to actually doing it? In this chapter we consider the nature of purposive, goal-directed behavior. Relevant research on concepts such as personal projects, personal strivings, and life tasks is considered. Finally, we are led to ask whether we always operate rationally in our goal-directed behavior and why we sometimes experience breakdowns in volition; that is, we find that we are not able to do what we intend to do or feel compelled to do what we do not intend to do.

Questions to Be Addressed in This Chapter

1 How can we understand the process of going from thought to action? From the idea of some goal to the pursuit of it?

2 Is it useful for personality psychologists to make use of concepts such as will, intention, and volition, or are they best left to philosophers?

3 What would a theory of goal-directed behavior look like? How are goals acquired and do people operate rationally in their pursuit of goals?

4 How can we understand situations in which people cannot get themselves to do what they "want" to do or cannot stop themselves from doing what they "do not want" to do?

We know what it is to get out of bed on a freezing morning in a room without a fire, and how the very vital principle within us protests against the ordeal. Probably most persons have lain on a certain morning for an hour at a time unable to brace themselves to the resolve. We think how late we shall be, how the duties of the day will suffer; we say, "I *must* get up, this is ignominious," etc.; but still the warm couch feels too delicious, the cold outside too cruel, and resolution faints away and postpones itself again and again just as it seemed on the verge of bursting the resistance and passing over into decisive act. Now how do we *ever* get up under such circumstances?

James, 1892, p. 424

James's description of the struggle to get out of bed in the morning probably is familiar to everyone. For the rare individual who has not experienced this particular situation, there are many other illustrations of the struggle to get oneself to do something one wants or intends to do or to avoid doing what one does not want or intend to do. Philosophers have struggled with understanding such phenomena, using terms such as *will* and *volition*. What is the nature of will and volition—that is, the ability to regulate behavior and act upon our intentions? What is it that permits us to have a sense of will and volition? Do animals act with will and volition? Does my dog show intentional behavior when she takes my hand with her paw and "tells me" that she wants to be petted? Does the squirrel in my backyard show intentional behavior when he "sizes up" the problem of getting to the food in the bird feeder and alternatively selects different paths as I try to block each one?

For the most part, psychologists have been reluctant to use terms such as *intention, will,* and *volition*. They seem to be such vague, nebulous terms, better left to philosophers. Certainly behaviorists were not interested in such terms since they took us to the study of overt behavior and away from the mind. But even nonbehaviorists have been wary of the study of such phenomena. How are we to know when something is done intentionally, whether it be by a dog, a child, or the defendant in a criminal matter (Lewis, 1990c)? And how are we as psychologists to understand what is meant by the use of willpower? Do some people have greater willpower than others, over some things but not other things? Are some acts more voluntary than others, and, if so, are we to rely completely on subjective report or can we develop more objective measures?

Given the complexity of these questions, it is easy to see why psychologists have been wary of confronting them. Yet, can a science of personality ignore such questions that seem so fundamental to our experience? To return to James's illustration, we all know what it is to struggle with such feelings. Probably some of our most difficult moments consist of such struggles. And, when one considers what is going on at such times, some of the most basic processes of psychological functioning appear to be involved—thoughts or *cognitions* of what one should be doing, *motives* for doing it or not doing it, and *conflict* between motives and feelings *(affect)* associated with the struggle. Perhaps one could add as well the *trait* of Conscientiousness, since isn't it the conscientious person who is so self-disciplined and persevering that he or she makes the decisive act of getting out of bed before resistance takes over?

Although neglected in the past, there are signs that psychologists, in particular personality psychologists, are making an effort to come to grips with such questions. Part of the cognitive revolution, as noted earlier, was the introduction of the model of the person as an information-processing machine. And, as noted in the discussion of goal theory in Chapter 4 and of Carver and Scheier's control theory of self-regulation in Chapter 8, part of this model is an interest in **purposive behavior,** the orientation of the person or machine toward some target or end point. An interest in purposive behavior in humans brings to our attention the question of how we translate intention into action, in how we move from the thought or mental representation of a goal to the actual pursuit of it (Cantor, 1990a; Frese & Sabini, 1985; Kuhl & Beckmann, 1985; Scheier & Carver, 1988). It brings into play cognitions, motives, and dispositions (traits) to behave in particular ways. An interest in purposive behavior addresses questions such as how we define for ourselves a career objective and then make plans to pursue it. On a more immediate basis, an interest in purposive behavior addresses questions such as how we make plans for our day and how we go about making decisions when given a choice among activities—whether to work or socialize, eat or exercise, become involved with this or that person. And, as we shall see at the end of the chapter, an interest in purposive behavior brings to our attention problems of volition, those puzzling but terribly important times when we cannot do what we want to do or feel compelled to do what we do not want to do.

Such problems in volition are of particular importance because they seem to violate the sense of ourselves as reasonably rational beings—that we are capable of making reasonable decisions about what we want and then of choosing accordingly. The foremost model of such a rational being is what has been called *expectancy-value theory,* previously discussed in Chapter 3. According to expectancy-value theory, when faced with a decision concerning action, we choose that action that has the highest estimated payoff value. Payoff value is determined by how valuable an outcome is to us and the probability of that outcome. Thus, in our decision-making behavior we make some quick calculations concerning the probability of the behavior leading to what we want and the value of what we want. A multiplicative relationship is assumed between probability or expectancy and value, thus the formulation of *expectancy × value theory.* Whether we decide to work or play is determined by the probability of each leading to a particular end point or goal and the value we associate with that goal. Whether we decide to become involved with this or that person is determined by our estimate of the probability of success with each and the value we associate with success with each. A very rational decision-making model of people! Let us explore some of these models for choice behavior, then go on to consider them within the context of a more general theory of goals, and then, finally, consider research efforts to look at the process of translating goals into action as well as individual differences in goals and goal-directed processes.

RATIONAL CHOICE BEHAVIOR: EXPECTANCY X VALUE THEORY

We consider here some of the major figures in expectancy-value theory. To make sure we understand the theory, let us take the illustration given by Weiner (1992) of decision making by a bettor at a horse race. What the bettor does is compute the odds or probability that each horse will win the race and multiply that by the utility or payoff for a win by each horse to arrive at a **subjective expected utility (SEU)** for each choice. The horse with the highest SEU is the one on which the bet is placed. In this case, bettors have their own subjective probability for each horse's winning the race, but the value or payoff is determined by the track. Of course, another part of the "payoff" or utility may be being right or picking the winner. Thus, for some people it is not just the amount of money that is involved in gambling but the idea of being right or the thrill of being a "big winner." The point here is that expectancies and values are subjective matters, varying with the individual involved.

TOLMAN'S MODEL OF PURPOSIVE BEHAVIOR

One of the early proponents of an expectancy-value model was the cognitive learning theorist Edward Chase Tolman (1925, 1932). Tolman was a psychologist of theoretical and experimental brilliance whose contributions unfortunately are neglected today. Far ahead of his time, he emphasized cognitive processes over stimulus-response connections. He was a learning theorist who accepted much of the behaviorist framework, yet he was impressed with the patterned, goal-directed quality of behavior rather than its more mechanical, reflexlike characteristics. And, not only were purpose and cognition true of humans, they were true of rats as well!

Tolman emphasized the importance of cognitive factors in learning. He believed that animals learn cognitive maps or expectancies about which behaviors lead to what results, rather than learning mechanical stimulus-response connections. Because of his emphasis on cognitive variables such as expectancies over drive variables, Tolman was criticized for leaving rats (or humans) "buried in thought" (Guthrie, 1952, p. 143). A similar charge was made against early supporters of the cognitive revolution for their emphasis on "cold" cognition and their neglect of motivation and affect (Pervin, 1980). However, Tolman did recognize the importance of motivation and *value* in performance or action. Thus, he was impressed with the *persistence until* character of behavior—the persistence of activity independent of that which initiated it and until a particular end point (goal) has been reached. The emphasis on goals having values, together with the emphasis on expectancies, provides the basis for Tolman's expectancy-value theory. These qualities defined for Tolman the purposive character of behavior in animals and humans.

LEWIN'S LEVEL OF ASPIRATION RESEARCH

At around the same time that Tolman was developing his views, the noted social and personality psychologist Kurt Lewin also was developing a theory of goal-directed behavior. Lewin was not afraid to use concepts such as intention, need, and will in relation to his purposive, goal-directed view of behavior. His emphasis on expectancies and value, or *valence* as he defined the positive or negative value associated with a goal, is seen most clearly in his work on **level of aspiration** (Lewin, Dembo, Festinger, & Sears, 1944). Level of aspiration research studies how subjects go about setting standards or goals for future performance, including estimates of the difficulty of the task and their own levels of ability. For example, subjects might be asked to set distances from which they could sink a basket in basketball. After success at a short distance, subjects would attempt their shot from a greater distance. Feelings of success and failure are associated with an evaluation of the relationship between the set level of aspiration (goal) and actual performance, with greater experience of success associated with reaching higher levels of aspiration (more difficult goals) and greater experiences of failure associated with not reaching lower levels of aspiration (easier goals)—"Look at how good I am" versus "I couldn't even do that." Individuals in level of aspiration studies make choices based on the probability of success and the value of success, the latter depending in part on the perceived difficulty of the task (Figure 9.1).

ROTTER'S EXPECTANCY-VALUE MODEL

In the 1940s learning theorists debated the relative merits of Tolman's emphasis on cognitive variables and Hull's emphasis on drive and reinforcement variables. As noted in Chapter 3, the personality and clinical psychologist Julian Rotter (1954) made use of both points of view to develop an expectancy-value model and social learning approach to personality. His work, together with that of George Kelly, has been described as seminal in setting the stage for current cognitive approaches to personality (Cantor, 1990a). According to Rotter, the behavior potential or likelihood of a specific behavior in a given situation is a function of the expectancy of reward and the reward value of the goal—that is, behavior potential in a situation is a function of expectancy $\times$ value. Once more, it is important to note that expectancy and value are subjective and will vary from individual to individual in any given situation. Further, according to Rotter a situation can be described in terms of the consequences the individual associates with various behaviors in the situation. For each possible behavior in a situation the individual associates the probability of an outcome and the value of that outcome. Two situations are similar to the extent that their outcome contingencies are seen as similar in terms of probability and value. Thus, the person can be predicted to behave similarly in similar situations, similarity again being defined in terms of subjective outcome contingencies. Although not perfect, there is

Figure 9.1 Four points in a typical sequence of events in a level of aspiration situation. Level of aspiration researchers were particularly interested in two questions: (1) What determines the goal or level of aspiration (#2)? (2) What determines the reaction to achievement or nonachievement of the goal or set level of aspiration (#4)?

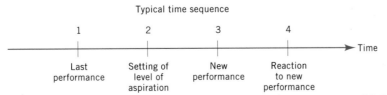

(Adapted from "Level of Aspiration," by K. A. Lewin, T. Dembo, L. Festinger, and P. S. Sears, 1944, in *Personality and the Behavior Disorders,* p. 334, by J. McV. Hunt, Ed., New York: Ronald Press.)

evidence that, at least in terms of subjective report, individuals do behave similarly in situations seen as similar in terms of their outcome contingencies (i.e., expectancy x value of each behavioral outcome in the situation) (Champagne & Pervin, 1987).

This emphasis on situational determinants of behavior is an important part of social learning and social cognitive theory, and an important distinguishing feature between it and trait theory (Mischel, 1968). However, one must keep in mind that it is the person who is defining the expectancies and outcome values associated with the behaviors in a situation. Thus, part of personality is just such expectancies and outcome values that the person defines as part of each situation (Mischel, 1973). In addition, as noted in Chapter 3, Rotter emphasized *generalized expectancies,* which refer to expectancies that tend to hold across situations. In other words, in addition to expectancies concerning behavior-outcome relationships in specific situations, individuals, as a result of their life history, hold generalized beliefs about themselves and the world.

Other theories emphasizing an expectancy-value model have been developed (Weiner, 1992) and have been influential in both general motivational research and organizational-industrial settings (Locke & Latham, 1990). As noted, the common elements are the emphasis on subjective expectancies and values leading to rational choices based on the maximization of subjective expected utility. Although expectancies and values are assumed to depend on past experience, greater or lesser attention may be given to the specific processes associated with such developments. Often research has focused on what the individual will do when faced with specific choices as opposed to how the person initiates activity. Most of all, these expectancy-value models have not been set within the context of a full model of purposive, goal-directed behavior. In the next section we consider an outline of such a model and then turn to research efforts based on goal-related concepts.

THE STASIS AND FLOW OF BEHAVIOR: TOWARD A THEORY OF GOALS

Today there are many goal concepts and theories of goal system functioning (Carver & Scheier, 1982, 1990; Ford, 1992; Klinger, 1977; Pervin, 1983, 1989). The following discussion is illustrative of many of the essential elements of such views, although it also contains elements with which proponents of alternative views might disagree or would emphasize to a different extent. It was developed to come to grips with the social learning, social cognitive theory emphasis on the variability of behavior from situation to situation and the trait theory emphasis on the stability of behavior across situations.

One year I had subjects log their behavior over the course of many days. For each situation lasting 20 or more minutes, the subject described the situation and their behavior in it. A fairly obvious observation became apparent—people are both stable and variable in their functioning, having both characteristic ways of behaving (stability) and varying their behavior to meet changing needs and circumstances. This is what I have called the *stasis and flow of behavior.* People are both stable and changing in the course of their daily lives and any theory of personality must account for this interplay between stability and change, between stasis and flow. To be rigidly the same in all situations would hardly be adaptive, and this is equally true for the condition of being buffeted like a ping-pong ball from situation to situation.

In addition to the observation of both stability and change, observation of the daily flow of behavior points out another fact: For most people there is a patterned, organized quality to their behavior and this organization seems directed toward end points or goals. Rather than being bounced around like ping-pong balls, people actively pursue end points or goals and develop plans or strategies to achieve these goals. Thus, there is a pattern to behavior that can only be appreciated by the study of behavior across diverse situations and over extended periods of time. Indeed, one could go so far as to say that *personality is the interplay between stability and variability as the individual maintains coherence and goal-directedness while responding to the demands of particular situations.* From this standpoint human behavior is complex, determined by multiple forces, purposive or goal-directed, and adaptive to both the person's need for a sense of continuity and coherence as well as the need to be able to adjust flexibly to situational demands. What follows is an effort to capture these elements.

1. *The patterned, organized quality of human behavior suggests that it is directed toward end points or* **goals;** that is, behavior is motivated and the concept of goals is suggested as a useful motivational concept. Goals can be complex or simple, very important or of lesser importance, of short-term importance (e.g., do well in this game) or of long-term significance (e.g., become a competent professional or have a good family life). It is important to distinguish between goals, which are desired end points, and *plans*, which represent the routes or paths toward attaining a goal: I have a goal of becoming an engineer and my plan is to take engineering courses. Although there is enormous variability in the goals of individuals, and how these goals are organized, most individuals share certain categories of goals (Table 9.1).

2. *Goals have cognitive, affective, and overt behavioral properties associated with them.* The cognitive component of a goal consists of the mental representation or image of the goal. One cannot have a goal without some representation of what one is striving toward, just as the home thermostat cannot control room temperature without some representation of the "desired" temperature. However, having a representation of the goal does not mean that all goals are conscious, just as we would not characterize the thermostat as having a conscious goal. We often are aware of our goals, but sometimes we are not. Sometimes self-report is an accurate measure of the individual's motivational system but at other times it is not; that is, although at times people can tell us why they are doing what they are doing, at other times they may not be able to account for their behavior or may give reasons that are more socially acceptable than the real causes of the behavior. This reflects the difference between *reasons* and *causes*, the former referring to the explanations people give and the latter to the actual determinants of behavior. For example, a person might say that they neglected to do something because they forgot or had too

TABLE 9.1   Goals Categories Derived From Subject Ratings of Goals in Situations

Goal Category	Illustrative Goals
1. Self-esteem, approval	Maintain self-esteem, avoid failure, gain acceptance, avoid rejection, advance career, compete successfully, assert self, avoid shame
2. Relaxation, fun, friendship	Have fun, increase intimacy, relax, establish friendship, give affection, avoid loneliness
3. Aggression, power	Hurt someone, avoid dominance or control, avoid feeling weak, influence or control others
4. Reduce tension, conflict, threat	Reduce anxiety, avoid rejection, avoid conflict or disagreement, do the "right" thing, avoid feeling guilty, avoid blame or criticism
5. Affection, support	Give affection, provide support or help, increase intimacy

Source: "The Stasis and Flow of Behavior: Toward a Theory of Goals," by L. A. Pervin, 1983, in *Personality: Current Theory and Research* (p. 36), by M. M. Page (Ed.), Lincoln: University of Nebraska Press. Reprinted from the 1982 Nebraska Symposium on Motivation by permission of the University of Nebraska Press. Copyright 1983 by the University of Nebraska Press.

much to do, rather than that they consciously or unconsciously did not want to do it.

In addition to cognitive or mental representations, goals have affects or emotions associated with them. Goals are associated with pleasure or pain. One seeks to attain things associated with pleasure and to avoid things associated with pain. However, the range of affects associated with goals is far more complex than just pleasure or pain. One can experience pride in one's success or shame in one's failure, love for one's partner or contempt for one's enemy. It is important to recognize that what is being suggested here is that it is the affective component of goals that gives them their motivational power.

Finally, in addition to these cognitive and affective properties, goals are associated with behavioral plans. Such plans include cognitive representations of activities that are necessary to achieve each goal and some assessment of one's ability to perform the necessary activities.

3. *A person's goals are organized in a hierarchical structure that at the same time provides for fluid, dynamic functioning.* What is suggested here is that goals are organized in a hierarchy with some goals being superordinate and some subordinate. One may have a superordinate goal of being happy in life or of being a good person, with subordinate goals of having a family, career, or both in the former case and subordinate goals of helping others and being moral in the latter case. However, the structure of the system can change so that what is generally of greater importance can be subordinated to a goal that generally is of lesser importance. For a rat, the goal of eating is sometimes more important than drinking, and sometimes the reverse is true. For humans, being a good person may generally be superordinate to having fun but sometimes having

fun may assume superordinate status. Thus, while having an overall goal structure, the person is able to adapt that structure to meet varying internal and external demands.

Another important aspect of goal systems is that the goals within the system can be integrated or in conflict. Two goals are in conflict when the pursuit of one interferes with the pursuit of the other.

4. *The dynamics of goal system functioning involve the activation, maintenance, and termination of goal-directed activity.* What is it that activates the pursuit of a goal? How are we able to maintain pursuit of a long-term goal over extended periods of time and often through great adversity? When do we finally stop pursuing a goal? These are questions that involve the dynamics of goal system functioning. What is suggested is that goals are always present in the system, just as programs are stored in a computer. A goal can be activated by an external stimulus or by an internal stimulus such as a physiological stimulus (e.g., hunger or thirst), a thought, or an image. Once a goal is activated, cognitive effort is directed toward assessment of how the goal might best be achieved. Assessment involves something similar to what the expectancy-value model suggests—an estimate is made of the value or importance of the goal and the likelihood of success in achieving it. Activity is maintained in the pursuit of the goal through continued focus on the mental representation, through periodic accomplishment of subgoals, and through self-reinforcement in terms of emotions such as pride and shame (Bandura, 1986). In other words, to sustain effort over the long term we must establish a serial organization to our goals, with subdivisions of immediate and long-term goals, and be able to say to ourselves that we are doing a good job or that we are not doing a good job and more effort must be expended. The affects associated with meeting what Higgins calls *ideal* and *ought* self-standards (Chapter 8) are relevant here. Finally, we terminate goal-directed activity when the goal is achieved, when a satisfactory level of goal attainment has been achieved, or when an assessment is made that further activity would be fruitless. In each case another goal takes precedence over the one formerly directing activity.

Certain principles of the dynamics of goal system functioning should be kept in mind. Three are particularly noteworthy. First, most complex behavior involves the interplay of many goals at one and the same time. For example, we may seek a career to satisfy many goals. This is the principle of **multidetermination.** Second, the same goal can be reached through various means or plans. There is more than one way to be popular or successful. This is the principle of **equipotentiality** or the potential for a goal to lead to many different behaviors; in other words, "There's more than one way to skin a cat." Third, the same behavior can be expressive of the operation of many different goals. A smile can express genuine warmth or hide hostile feelings, and a laugh can express pleasure in hearing a joke or the effort to mask social anxiety. This is the principle of **equifinality** or the potential for many different goals to lead to the same behavior; in other words, "You can't judge a book by its cover." It is suggested that these three principles, multidetermination, equipotentiality, and equifinality, are basic to understanding the dynamic aspects of goal system functioning.

Goal Theory. One of the challenges for theories of motivation is to explain how people are able to maintain effort over extended periods of time toward the achievement of distant goals.

5. *Development involves the increased elaboration of the cognitive, emotional, and behavioral aspects of the goal system.* A theory of goals must describe how goals are acquired as well as the development of goal systems. It has been suggested that the motivational power of goals is derived from their association with affect. According to the view presented here, in the course of development the person comes to associate affects with people, objects, places, things, and so on. The association of affect with some person or thing can be based on direct experience, such as classical conditioning, or the observation of others, as in vicarious conditioning (Bandura, 1986). Almost anything can become a goal in terms of its association with affect.

   The association of affect with persons and things is likely to be particularly intense during the early years of life. Thus, many of our strongest and longest-lasting preferences and aversions are derived from the early years. For example, most people have strong food and odor preferences and aversions that date back to childhood and are very difficult to change. At the same time, affective associations do change in the course of development and thereby new goals are attained and some goals drop out. Allport's (1961) concept of *functional autonomy* also has relevance here. Allport suggested that activity that once served a drive or need may become pleasurable and an independent motive in its own right. In terms of the theory being presented, an activity that originally was performed in the service of a goal may take on goal properties itself because of its association with positive affect. For example, the person originally may study to get good grades but eventually may enjoy studying for its own sake, the activity having become functionally autonomous from its initial roots.

It should also be noted that in the course of development the person acquires increased cognitive capacities. These capacities provide for greater complexity of organization of goals and more complex organization of plans for achieving goals. With development the person is able to think of more things he or she might want to achieve or avoid, as well as more ways in which these things can be achieved or avoided. With development the person also is better able to think far into the future and to delay present pleasure for the sake of anticipated pleasure (Mischel, 1990). Finally, in terms of behavior, development involves increased behavioral skills and capacities that can facilitate goal attainment.

It should be clear that what is being described is the development of a goal system, that is, of a complex network of interrelated goals and plans. Thus, developments in relation to one part of the goal system can have implications for other parts of the system. A change in the affective associations of one goal can have implications for the affective value of related goals, and the skills developed for the attainment of one goal can be used for the attainment of another goal.

6. *Psychopathology can be understood in terms of the absence of goals, goal conflict (e.g., between wishes and fears), or problems in the implementation of goals. Therapy involves reorganization of elements of the goal system or of ways in which goals can be attained.* Goals are based on affect, broadly speaking, positive and negative affect. Therefore one can speak of goals in terms of wishes and fears, end points one seeks (wishes) and end points one seeks to avoid (fears). Sometimes people are in distress because of a lack of goals. This may be particularly true during late adolescence or early adulthood, when career objectives have yet to be defined, or during the period of retirement, when a replacement has to be found for the work activity that otherwise occupied a significant part of one's life. More often people are in distress because of conflict between goals. For example, people often experience approach-avoidance conflicts between the goal of intimacy (approach) and the goal of avoiding blows to one's self-esteem (avoidance). The task of therapy then is to help the person to find means of integrating formerly conflicting goals—in the previous example, to be able to obtain intimacy without fear of significant loss of self-esteem. It should be noted here that therapy can involve specific goal conflicts but can also involve a reorganization of the goal system. This need not involve the making of a new goal system but rather establishing new linkages among goals and greater general integration within the goal system. This view of therapeutic change is similar to Kelly's (1955) emphasis on change in the structure of one's personal construct system, except that goals rather than constructs are being emphasized. Through such developments the person remains basically the same yet experiences fundamental change.

What has been attempted here is a broad conceptualization of goal system functioning. The emphasis is on the dynamic, system aspects of functioning and the interplay among cognition, affect, and behavior. As noted, such functioning has similarities to other views that emphasize the purposive, goal-directed nature of personality functioning. Clearly it is influenced by models associated with the cognitive revolution that emphasize feedback and control systems. At the same time, it also is influenced by much earlier views of organisms as motivated, purposive, and goal-directed (Pervin, 1983). Perhaps what distinguishes it most from other current models is the emphasis on affect, in particular on the role of classical conditioning of affect in the acquisition of goals. Most other models give less attention to affect and the question of how goals are acquired in the first place, a point to which we shall return later in the chapter. Perhaps another point of differentiation is the recognition of the potential importance of unconscious goals, although no means of assessing such goals is offered. For now, however, let us begin with this broad conceptualization and consider various programs of research that have emphasized goals and the movement of the person from thought to action.

GOALS, SELF-REGULATION, AND ACTION: PROGRAMS OF RESEARCH

In this section we consider specific research programs that have focused on goal concepts. In some cases there also is a focus on *self-regulation* or internal processes that monitor progress toward goal attainment. In most cases there is an effort to link cognitive, affective, and motivational variables in a comprehensive picture of the movement of the person toward action. As we shall see, there are differences among the approaches to be considered. What unites them for discussion here, however, is the common emphasis on the goal concept as a way of conceptualizing the person's thought and action.

BANDURA'S MODEL OF GOALS-STANDARDS AND SELF-REGULATION

Reference has been made in a number of places to the social cognitive theory of Albert Bandura—in Chapter 3 in relation to cognitive units of personality and in Chapter 8 in relation to his emphasis on self-efficacy beliefs. Here we focus on his approach to motivation. Bandura (1989b, 1990) increasingly has attended to affective and motivational processes. However, he clearly continues to embed his motivational work in a cognitive framework: "The capability for self-motivation and purposive action is rooted in cognitive activity. Future events cannot be causes of current motivation or action. However, by cognitive representation in the present, conceived future events are converted into current motivators and regulators of behavior" (1989b, p. 19). As suggested in the previous presentation of a theory of goals, it is the representation of goals, a cognitive activity, that influences behavior in the present. Bandura emphasizes the cognitive activity involved in representing goals, in anticipating likely outcomes from various actions, in making attributions for past successes and failures, and in making self-efficacy estimates.

Let us consider Bandura's view of the action process as it unfolds, paying particular attention to his emphasis on these cognitive variables and the role they play in self-regulation. We can start the action process with the presence of a goal or standard. According to Bandura, **internal standards** represent goals for us to achieve and bases for expecting reinforcement from others or from ourselves. What activates the person is the establishment of a goal or standard, an estimate of the effort needed to meet the standard, and the anticipated consequences of meeting or not meeting the standard. Two things are particularly important to keep in mind in this regard. First, Bandura is emphasizing internal reinforcers as well as external reinforcers in relation to meeting or not meeting standards. Thus, pride in accomplishment and guilt or shame in failure are seen as powerful internal forces of self-regulation. It is through such processes of **self-reinforcement** that we are able to maintain behavior over extended periods of time in the absence of external reinforcers. Second, Bandura is suggesting that the motivatonal power is not derived from the goals themselves but rather from the fact that people respond evaluatively to their own behavior. In other words, goals set the standards for positive or negative self-evaluation in terms of progress toward or movement away from achieving goals (1989b, p. 27).

Is there evidence of the motivational significance of goals? In research on effortful performance, Bandura (1989b) has demonstrated that people who set no goals for themselves show less effort and are surpassed in performance by those who set low goals, who in turn are surpassed in effort and performance by those who set more challenging goals for themselves (Figure 9.2). Having set a standard or goal, the person makes some estimate of the best plan or strategy for achieving the goal and the amount of effort required. In pursuing the goal, the person relies on feedback information concerning progress toward the goal. In a relevant research project (Bandura & Cervone, 1983), subjects performed a strenuous activity under one of four conditions: goals with feedback on performance, goals alone, feedback alone, and absence of goals and feedback. Following this activity, described as part of a project to plan and evaluate exercise programs for postcoronary rehabilitation, subjects rated how self-satisfied or self-dissatisfied they would be with their performance in further strenuous activities and their effortful performance was again measured. In accord with the hypothesis, the condition combining goals and performance feedback had a strong motivational impact, whereas neither goals alone nor feedback alone had comparable motivational significance (Figure 9.3). In sum, both goals and feedback information are required for effortful performance.

From earlier discussions of Bandura's work, it should be apparent that self-efficacy beliefs play a major role in the self-regulatory process. Indeed, in the previously discussed research measures also were obtained for perceived self-efficacy for various possible performance levels. In accord with the hypothesis, and as represented in Figure 8.2, subsequent effort was most intense when subjects were both dissatisfied with substandard performance and high on self-efficacy judgments for good attainment. Neither dissatisfaction alone nor positive self-efficacy judgments alone had a comparable effect, thereby providing support for the theory that goals have motivating power through self-evaluative and self-efficacy judgments.

Figure 9.2   Mean increases in motivational level under conditions of performance feedback alone depending on whether people continue to perform the activity without goals or spontaneously set low or high goals for themselves.
This graph illustrates the importance of self-set goals for motivation.

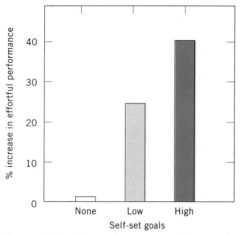

(From "Self-Regulation of Motivation and Action Through Internal Standards and Goal Systems," by A. Bandura, 1989, in *Goal Concepts in Personality and Social Psychology,* p. 28, by L. A. Pervin, Ed., Hillsdale, NJ: Erlbaum. Reprinted by permission of Lawrence Erlbaum Associates, Inc.)

Figure 9.3   Mean percentage increase in effortful performance under conditions varying in goals and performance feedback.
This graph illustrates the importance of goals and performance feedback information for motivation.

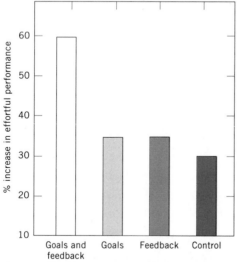

(From "Self-Evaluative and Self-Efficacy Mechanisms Governing the Motivational Effect of Goal Systems," by A. Bandura and D. Cervone, 1983, *Journal of Personality and Social Psychology, 55,* p. 1021. Copyright 1983 by the American Psychological Association. Reprinted by permission.)

The motivational effects of self-efficacy judgments are many. First, self-efficacy judgments have an effect on the level of commitment to the goal. As noted, self-efficacy beliefs affect how much effort is expended. They also affect which kinds of challenges the person will undertake and how long he or she will persevere in the face of obstacles. In other words, ordinarily we will undertake more difficult challenges only if we have some sense that we are capable of meeting them. And, we are unlikely to persevere if we believe that further effort is probably futile. Second, self-efficacy judgments have an effect on our emotional reactions to the task and the productivity of our efforts. Thus, it has been demonstrated that people with high self-efficacy beliefs for a particular task experience less stress during the task, as measured by increases in heart rate, than do individuals who perceive themselves to be inefficacious (Figure 9.4). Perceived inefficacy and the movement toward abandonment of goal striving also are associated with depressive affect as opposed to the more positive mood associated with perceived efficacy and continued goal striving (Figure 9.5). Further complicating matters for the person with low perceived self-efficacy is

Figure 9.4   Percentage changes in heart rate displayed by perceived self-efficacious and perceived self-inefficacious subjects while they received instructions for the problem-solving task, coped with the task demands, and later appraised their perceived self-efficacy. This chart illustrates that people with high self-efficacy beliefs experience less stress (increase in heart rate) associated with problem-solving than do people with low self-efficacy beliefs.

(From "Perceived Self-Efficacy in Coping With Cognitive Stressors and Opioid Activation," by A. Bandura, D. Cioffi, C. B. Taylor, and M. E. Brouillard, 1988, *Journal of Personality and Social Psychology, 55,* p. 484. Copyright 1988 by the American Psychological Association. Reprinted by permission.)

Figure 9.5   Percentage change in depressive mood for people combining strong perceived self-efficacy with goal adherence (SE + G +); weak perceived self-efficacy with goal adherence (SE-G +); and weak perceived self-efficacy with goal abandonment (SE-G-)
This graph illustrates the association of depressive mood with low self-efficacy beliefs and continued goal striving.

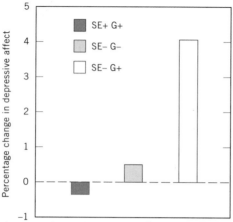

(From Bandura and Abrams, 1986. Published in "Self-Regulation of Motivation and Action through Internal Standards and Goal Systems," by A. Bandura, 1989, in *Goal Concepts in Personality and Social Psychology*, p. 61, by L. A. Pervin, Ed., Hillsdale, NJ: Erlbaum. Reprinted by permission of Lawrence Erlbaum Associates, Inc.)

that when faced with complex decisions, his or her thinking becomes erratic and indecisive. In other words, low self-efficacy beliefs may operate to impair the cognitive activities so vital for goal pursuit.

A third way in which self-efficacy beliefs play an important role in goal performance is their effect on the setting of further standards. As is clear from the previous discussion, self-efficacy beliefs affect emotional and cognitive reactions to discrepancies between standards and performance. Whether one becomes motivated or discouraged by not meeting a standard is influenced by one's self-efficacy beliefs concerning the potential value of further effort. In addition, self-efficacy beliefs affect reactions to the attainment of goals as well. Greater joy is derived from attributing success to one's own competence and ability than to luck. And, the individual is more likely to set new and higher standards for performance if he or she feels more confident of his or her ability to meet these higher standards.

The setting of new and higher standards upon goal attainment is an important matter for Bandura since it completes and recycles the self-regulatory process. According to Bandura, "After people attain the standard they have been pursuing, those who have a strong sense of self-efficacy generally set a higher standard for themselves. Adopting further challenges creates new motivating discrepancies to be mastered" (1990, p. 92). In other words, attaining the goal does not result in a ceasing of activity. Rather, the person sets a higher standard of performance. Since it is the anticipated self-evaluative consequences rather than the goals themselves that are of motivational importance, attaining the goal results in further initiation of goal-directed effort. The setting of another standard recycles the process of motivated behavior described earlier.

Before concluding our discussion of Bandura's theory, a word should be said about the distinctions he makes among types of goals. These distinctions can be of particular value to individuals who struggle with motivational problems. Are some goals likely to be more motivating than others? Bandura suggests that *specific, challenging, realistic,* and *short-range* goals are more conducive to self-motivation than are *ambiguous, unrealistic, nonchallenging,* and *long-range* goals. Explicit standards are seen as promoting better goal-directed performance than are general intentions to do one's best. In terms of challenge, Bandura suggests that people work harder and perform better for higher goals. Although people may eventually reject unrealistically demanding goals, they generally will remain steadfast to challenging goals and prefer them to goals that seem to be too easy or unchallenging.

Finally, we can consider the comparative effects of proximal (short-range) goals relative to distal (long-range) goals. Consider here Bandura's (1989b, p. 44) words of wisdom:

> Self-motivation is best sustained through a series of proximal subgoals that are hierarchically organized to ensure successive advances to superordinate goals.
> . . . Pursuit of a formidable goal can sustain a high level of motivation provided it is broken down into subgoals that are challenging but clearly attainable through extra effort. To strive for unreachable goals is to drive oneself to unrelenting failure.

What is being suggested is that one can have long-term goals but personal advancement is best accomplished through the translation of these distal goals into more immediate subgoals. Then, as one comes closer to realizing distal goals, their attainment will seem more possible than was the case earlier. Not surprisingly, in this regard, in a study of children deficient and uninterested in mathematics, proximal goals compared favorably relative to distal goals or no goals at all in relation to improving performance, increasing self-efficacy, and increasing intrinsic interest in mathematics (Bandura & Schunk, 1981; Figure 9.6). In sum, a person having motivational difficulties might want to consider if his or her goals are too vague, unrealistic, or set too far into the future without translation into the present. Put more positively, to increase the motivational power of goals, they should be specific, realistically challenging, and tied to the future through more immediate pursuits.

We have here Bandura's theory of goals and self-regulation, heavy in its emphasis on cognitive processes. In terms of the theory, cognitive processes enter into the setting of standards or goals, the operation of self-efficacy beliefs, and the operation of self-evaluative processes. The theory has similarities to other models presented. For example, one can think here of Higgins's emphasis on self-standards (ideal and ought) and the control theory emphasis on reducing discrepancies between the standard and actual level of functioning. However, important differences also are noteworthy. In relation to the control theory of Carver and Scheier (1981, 1990), discussed in the previous chapter, Bandura suggests that his theory places much greater emphasis on the person as an active agent in setting goals and standards. He

Figure 9.6   Level of intrinsic interest in arithmetic activities shown by children in different goal conditions when given free choice of activities.
This graph illustrates the association of intrinsic interest with proximal goals as opposed to distal goals or no goals.

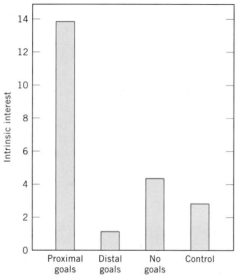

(From "Cultivating Competence, Self-Efficacy, and Intrinsic Interest," by A. Bandura and D. H. Schunk, 1981, *Journal of Personality and Social Psychology, 41*, p. 593. Copyright 1981 by the American Psychological Association. Reprinted by permission.)

suggests that in their model the person does nothing after achieving the standard whereas in his model the person sets a new standard through anticipation of self-evaluative consequences of meeting the new standard. Thus, in his model the person is seen as more proactive and self-regulatory than in control theory.

One can also compare Bandura's theory to expectancy-value theory. Although once more there are similarities, Bandura notes that his model places greater emphasis on problematic judgmental processes and on the importance of self-efficacy beliefs than is the case for expectancy-value theories. In terms of judgmental processes, Bandura suggests that sometimes people operate in terms of cognitive biases or incomplete information. It is not that they necessarily are irrational, but that they make erroneous probability or expectancy estimates due to cognitive biases and limits in their information-processing skills. And, he suggests that one must distinguish between outcome expectancies and self-efficacy beliefs if one wants to improve prediction of behavior. According to Bandura, people behave differently depending on whether or not they believe their ability will influence the outcome. This is not just a question of locus of control but of self-estimates concerning requisite skills to meet the demands of the situation. In addition, Bandura suggests that the implications of an outcome will differ depending on whether or not it is seen as contingent upon one's efficacy.

Finally, Bandura emphasizes the motivating power of expected self-evaluative consequences rather than the motivating power of goals themselves, as suggested in the initial presentation of a theory of goals. According to Bandura, the pleasure is not in the goal itself but in the pursuit of it. One is never satisfied to rest on one's laurels but must ever be engaged in the process of setting new standards for attainment. There are two possible problems with this model. First, although Bandura presents experimental evidence in support of the view that it is self-dissatisfaction and feedback information that are important for motivation, he does not rule out the potential for pleasure in the goal itself. His results may be particularly biased by a research emphasis on performance situations rather than on other kinds of situations in which goals are involved. For example, is it not possible to take continuing pleasure in a certain level of intimacy without necessarily seeking ever-higher levels of intimacy? Is friendship, sex, or a book ever "good enough" without having to always meet a higher standard?

Second, an exclusive emphasis on self-evaluative consequences begs the question of where goals come from in the first place. In fact, Bandura suggests that goals are acquired on the basis of direct reinforcement by others or through observing others set and meet standards, the latter involving the processes of observational learning and vicarious conditioning. However, in either case there is emotion involved— directly through the reinforcement by others or indirectly through vicariously experiencing the emotions of others meeting or not meeting standards. In other words, it would appear from the model that goals (standards) do have affect associated with them rather than just with the process of moving toward or away from them. According to this view, we may feel good and reward ourselves for getting closer to the goal (standard), but this does not preclude full enjoyment of the goal itself. It feels good to win the prize not just because one has "done a good job" but because the prize itself is satisfying.

PERSONAL PROJECTS, PERSONAL STRIVINGS, AND LIFE TASKS

A number of personality psychologists have recently emphasized the intentional structure of personality in relation to specific, individualistic, and context-relevant goals. Different names are given for these goals, such as *current concerns* (Klinger, 1977), *personal projects* (Little, 1989; Palys & Little, 1983), *personal strivings* (Emmons, 1989a, 1989b), and *life tasks* (Cantor, 1990a). However, as noted, they share an emphasis on goal-directed behavior and thus can be considered together in this section. Here we consider research relevant to personal projects and personal strivings and, because of its more elaborate theoretical development, consider the concept of life tasks in the next section.

Little's Research on Personal Projects

Little (1989; Palys & Little, 1983) defines a **personal project** as an extended set of personally relevant actions intended to achieve a personal goal. Personal projects may range from seemingly trivial pursuits of daily life, such as "doing the laundry," to lifetime obsessions, such as "liberate my people." At any one time a person may be involved with few or many personal projects. According to Little, "personal projects are natural units of analysis for a personality psychology that chooses to deal with the serious business of how people muddle through complex lives" (1989, p. 15).

How are personal projects to be assessed? Little suggests the use of the Personal Projects Analysis (PPA) method. The first step in this method is the elicitation of the person's personal projects. Thus the method is primarily self-report. Subjects are free to list any personal projects they believe are relevant to them, as many or as few as they like. Illustrative personal projects are given in Table 9.2. Subjects typically give approximately 15 illustrative projects. Subjects then are asked to rate each personal project on a number of dimensions, including importance, enjoyment, difficulty, progress, positive impact, and negative impact. The effort here is to obtain information relevant to the meaning, structure, stress, and efficacy associated with each personal project as well as the person's personal project system as a whole: Are the projects experienced as worthwhile or worthless? Are the projects experienced as organized or in disarray? Are the demands of the projects experienced as exceeding the person's capacity to cope with them? Does the subject experience progress in relation to the personal projects and anticipate continuing with them?

The PPA method leaves considerable room for individuals to respond in terms of their own perceptions and experiences. It also is flexible in that the researcher can add dimensions of special interest along which the subject rates the personal projects (e.g., importance, difficulty, likelihood of achievement). In addition, subjects can be

TABLE 9.2 Examples of Personal Projects Generated by University Students in Phase 1 of PPA

Finish my history essay
Set time aside for spiritual life
Watch Toronto beat up on Detroit
Meet new friends
Develop a philosophy of life
Gain more cerebral friends
Get laid
Be more attentive to my brother
Lose 15 pounds
Care for my dying aunt
Let fingernails grow
Get wasted over Christmas
Write the GRE
Figure out mom and dad

Source: "Personal Projects Analysis: Trivial Pursuits, Magnificient Obsessions, and the Search for Coherence," by D. Little, 1989, in *Personality Psychology: Recent Trends and Emerging Directions* (p. 18), by D. M. Buss and N. Cantor (Eds.), New York: Springer-Verlag. Reprinted by permission of Springer-Verlag.

asked questions such as whether each project facilitates, conflicts with, or is unrelated to the other projects. Analysis of the individual's personal projects matrix (ratings of the projects along the dimensions) can be done in terms of content, overall scores on the dimensions, and structure. For example, Little reports that although personal projects can be put into a hierarchy, they are best understood in terms of a lattice structure. In other words, rather than being organized in a hierarchical ladder fashion, personal projects have multiple interconnections. Each personal project may have multiple connections to other projects as well as multiple reasons for existing as a project and multiple means of being carried out. Analysis of ratings of the cross-impacts of personal projects, whether they facilitate, conflict with, or are unrelated to one another, gives a sense of the overall level of conflict as opposed to coherence in the system. In sum, personal projects are treated as systems rather than as isolated units.

What are the implications of such analyses? Little notes a relationship between reports of life satisfaction and ratings of projects as low in stress and high on positive outcome and control. According to him, satisfactions and disaffections with life are centered in the domains of stress and efficacy associated with one's personal projects. Project outcome, the extent to which people believe their projects are likely to be successfully completed, is the single best predictor of life satisfaction and depressive affect. In accord with Bandura, Little suggests that "our sense of efficacy in bringing our personal projects to successful completion . . . seems to be a pivotal factor in whether we thrive emotionally or lead lives of perhaps not so quiet desperation" (1989, p. 25). Also in accord with Bandura is the finding that short-term projects that are enjoyable and moderately difficult are more satisfying than projects of longer range from which little immediate enjoyment is derived (Palys & Little, 1983).

Another interesting aspect of this line of research has been the effort to relate personal projects to other personality concepts such as traits. Are personality traits and personal projects related to one another? Little used the NEO-PI (Chapter 2) as a measure of personality traits and found a strong pattern of relationships between personal project variables and trait variables. Most noteworthy was a relationship between Neuroticism scores on the NEO-PI and high personal project scores for stress, difficulty, negative impact, lack of control, lack of progress, and poor anticipated outcome. In addition, scores for Conscientiousness on the NEO-PI were found to be correlated with enjoyment, control, outcome, and progress ratings on personal projects.

In sum, Little's work on personal projects emphasizes the intentional and system aspects of personality functioning. Efforts are underway to investigate the functioning of personal projects in relation to specific situational and interpersonal contexts, as well as to establish linkages with other personality variables.

Emmons's Research on Personal Strivings

Emmons (1989a, 1989b) defines a *personal striving* as a coherent pattern of goal strivings that represents what an individual is typically trying to do. Personal strivings refer to the typical types of goals that a person hopes to accomplish in different situations. Illustrative personal strivings are "Make attractive people notice me," "Have as much fun as possible," "Do as many helpful things for people as I can," and "Avoid arguments whenever possible." It is important to note here that personal strivings include both things one is trying to obtain or experience as well as things one is trying to avoid. Personal strivings can be either positive or negative and individuals differ in the extent to which life is made up of positive as opposed to negative strivings.

A number of further distinguishing features of personal striving are noted by Emmons. First, they are idiographic or unique to the individual, particularly in terms of the goals that cluster together to form the personal striving as well as the ways in which the person goes about expressing the personal striving. Although personal strivings are idiographic, common or nomothetic categories of personal strivings can be formed. Illustrative categories and associated personal strivings are given in Table 9.3.

A second characteristic of personal strivings involves cognitive, affective, and/or behavioral components, either in conjunction with or independent of one another. For example, the striving of "being a good person" might involve all of these components whereas the striving of "achieving a spiritual oneness with God" might lack a behavioral component. Third, although personal strivings are reasonably stable, they are not fixed. What a person is trying to do varies from situation to situation and can change as life changes. Personal strivings reflect our continuing development throughout the life span. Fourth, achieving a particular instance of a personal striving does not mean that one no longer strives for that goal. One can feel good about being a good person in a particular instance but still seek other opportunities to be a good person, and one can avoid blows to one's self-esteem in particular instances while still seeking to avoid such blows in other instances. Finally, for the most part personal strivings are assumed to be conscious and available to self-report: "The position taken here is that people are able to report when solicited what they are trying to accomplish. . . . There is much to admire in Weiner's declaration that 'the

TABLE 9.3   **Striving Content Categories**

Category	Example
Positive	"Think of the needs of others"
Negative	"Not let too many people get close to me"
Intrapersonal	"Avoid worrying about financial setbacks"
Interpersonal	"Persuade others that I am right"
Achievement	"Work toward higher athletic capabilities"
Affiliation	"Be friendly with others so they will like me"
Intimacy	"Help my friends and let them know I care"
Power	"Force men to be intimate in relationships"
Personal growth/health	"Develop a positive self-worth"
Self-presentation	"Be concerned about my physical appearance always"
Autonomy	"Make decisions on my own"

Source: "The Personal Striving Approach to Personality," by R. A. Emmons, 1989, in *Goal Concepts in Personality and Social Psychology* (p. 100), by L. A. Pervin (Ed.), N.J.: Lawrence Erlbaum Associates. Reprinted by permission of Lawrence Erlbaum Associates, Inc.

royal road to the unconscious is less valuable than the dirt road to consciousness' " (Emmons, 1989b, p. 101). Emmons does leave room for the possibility that individuals are not conscious of their strivings, and even the possibility that the strivings can be unconscious. However, the basic assumption remains that people are able to report accurately on their goals in a realistic, nondefensive manner (Emmons, King, & Sheldon, 1993).

Emmons also takes a systems view of personal strivings. He sees personal strivings as organized in a hierarchy, with some superordinate to others. In addition, personal strivings can be linked to or independent of one another, and integrated or in conflict with one another. As we shall see, Emmons has done some quite interesting research on conflict among personal strivings. And, in accord with the principles of equipotentiality and equifinality noted earlier, Emmons suggests that a personal striving can be achieved through many different plans of action (equipotentiality) and any one action can express a variety of strivings (equifinality). In addition, in accord with the principle of multidetermination, action can involve the interplay of many different personal strivings. Thus, there is a complex relation between personal strivings and specific behaviors.

How are personal strivings to be assessed? Four steps are involved in such an assessment (Emmons, 1989b). In the first step, subjects are asked to list all of their personal strivings, defined as "the things that you typically or characteristically are trying to do in your everyday behavior"; and illustrative positive and negative strivings are provided. Individuals vary in the number of strivings reported, ranging from 10 to over 40, with an average of around 16. In the second step, subjects are asked to write down the actual ways they go about trying to succeed in each of their strivings. In terms of the framework presented earlier, these are plans for achieving goals. For example, the personal striving of "try to spend more time relaxing" might be associated with activities such as exercising, calling up friends to get together, and drinking. On the average, subjects give four to five ways of accomplishing each personal striving.

In the third step, subjects select 15 of their strivings and rate them on dimensions such as valence (positive or negative value), ambivalence (how much unhappiness is felt upon successful action), importance, probability of success, clarity, and difficulty. Factor analysis of the provided dimensions indicates three factors: *degree of striving* (value, importance, commitment), *success* (past attainment and probability of success), and *ease* (opportunity and low level of difficulty). It is interesting to note here that these fit quite well with the expectancy-value model.

In the fourth step, the subject compares each striving with every other striving in relation to the question: "Does being successful in this striving have a helpful or harmful (or no effect at all) on the other striving?" This involves a 15 by 15 matrix leading to the identification of strivings that facilitate or are in conflict with one another. An interesting aspect of this matrix is that the relations between strivings are not reciprocal; that is, one striving can facilitate another but the reverse may not be true. For example, "getting good grades" would facilitate "getting into graduate school" but the reverse would not be true. Generally such a difference is due to one personal striving being higher in the hierarchy than the other, but it also can be due to different linkages with other personal strivings. For each individual the amount of overall instrumentality or conflict in the personal construct system can then be calculated.

With this conceptualization and method of assessment, what kinds of studies have been done and what have been the findings? We can consider four areas of research: subjective well-being, conflict and ambivalence, self-complexity and affective reactivity, and personal strivings and traits.

Subjective Well-Being.   The focus of subjective well-being research has been on positive affect, negative affect, and life satisfaction. To obtain measures of their subjective well-being, subjects recorded their moods and thoughts four times a day for 21 consecutive days. This method is called an *experience-sampling method (ESM)* and involves individuals wearing a beeper that signals them at random moments throughout their waking hours to record aspects of their immediate experience. It is a method used to study private experience under as natural conditions as possible.

Emmons (1986) found that positive affect is associated with striving for important goals and the sense of past fulfillment of strivings; negative affect with ambivalence, conflict, and low subjective probability of success in achieving strivings; and life satisfaction with the sense of importance of one's personal strivings, the sense that they facilitate or are instrumental in relation to one another, and a high probability of success. In addition, in accord with expectancy-value theory, commitment to personal strivings was associated with high expectancy for success in the achievement of valued personal strivings. In sum, there were somewhat varied relationships between the criteria for subjective well-being and specific aspects of the personal strivings structure but all made theoretical sense.

Conflict and Ambivalence.   Emmons makes the valuable distinction between conflict and ambivalence, the former expressing a struggle between two or more strivings and the latter expressing mixed feelings about success in achievement of any one striving. In other words, conflict is related to two or more goals and ambivalence to the same goal. Emmons (Emmons & King, 1988) found that individuals with a lot of conflict and ambivalence in regard to their personal strivings also experience negative affect and low life satisfaction as determined by the experience sampling method. In another study, conflict and ambivalence within the personal strivings structure were related to scores on a well-being scale; records of visits to the student health center; number of different illnesses; and daily reports of anxiety, depression, and physical complaints as well as of positive and negative affect (Emmons & King, 1988). As predicted, conflict and ambivalence were found to be associated with high levels of anxiety, depression, negative affect, and psychosomatic complaints (Table 9.4). Even more striking was the fact that these measures of ambivalence and conflict were related to measures of physical symptoms a year later even when differences in initial level of illness were removed as a factor.

The suggestion made is that conflict and ambivalence may be particularly bad for one's health when they involve the expression of emotion. For example, conflict between wishes to confide in others and fears of doing so may lead to rumination

TABLE 9.4 **Correlations of Striving Conflict and Ambivalence With Psychological and Physical Well-Being**

The correlations indicate that conflict and ambivalence scores are associated with negative affect and health complaints.

Psychological Well-Being	Conflict	Ambivalence
Psychological		
Positive affect	−.11	−.34[b]
Negative affect	.21	.18
DPQ Well-Being Scale	−.07	−.11
Anxiety	.17	.27[a]
Depression	.19	.34[b]
Physical		
Somatization	.24[a]	.19
Daily symptoms	.14	.13
Health center visits	.27[a]	.12
Number of illnesses	.31[b]	.21

Note: $N = 48$. [a]$p < .05$. [b]$p < .01$.

Source: "The Personal Striving Approach to Personality," by R. A. Emmons, 1989, in *Goal Concepts in Personality and Social Psychology* (p. 105), by L. A. Pervin (Ed.), Hillsdale, NJ: Erlbaum. Reprinted by permission of Lawrence Erlbaum Associates, Inc.

and chronic physiological arousal that is associated with eventual physical illness. This possible relationship is being explored further through the development of an Ambivalence Over Expressing Emotion Questionnaire (AEQ). Illustrative items include "Often I'd like to show others how I feel, but something seems to be holding me back" and "I try to show people that I love them, although I am afraid that it may make me appear weak or vulnerable." Results to date suggest that conflict over expressing emotion is detrimental to well-being although neither expressiveness nor lack of expressiveness (without conflict) per se is associated with psychological or physical well-being (Emmons, et al., 1993).

Personal Strivings and Traits.   Finally, in terms of the relation between personal strivings and traits, Emmons has investigated the personality trait of narcissism and found that individuals scoring high on a measure of narcissism have different personal strivings than those scoring low on such a measure. For example, subjects high on narcissism have personal strivings such as efforts to dominate and manipulate people and to dress fashionably whereas subjects low on narcissism have personal strivings such as efforts to make their parents proud, to be aware of others' feelings, and to please others. What was striking about these findings was that these differences in personal strivings were confirmed by reports of peers (Emmons, 1989b).

In sum, Emmons focuses on the individualistic, idiographic nature of personal strivings to establish general, nomothetic relationships such as that between high conflict and low subjective well-being. There is an interest in not only the content of personal strivings, but also in their structure—how many strivings there are, the relationships among them, and the number of alternative plans for achieving them. Emmons views his approach as compatible with Carver and Scheier's (1981) control theory. He views personal strivings and traits as distinct concepts but also as related to one another—a personal striving can be fulfilled through many different behaviors (equipotentiality) and the same behavior can express the action of many different strivings (equifinality).

Cantor's Research on Life Tasks

The final illustration of work on goal-related concepts and the transformation of intentions into actions is the theoretical and research approach of Cantor (1990a, 1994; Cantor & Langston, 1989; Cantor & Zirkel, 1990). Her work is particularly germane to this chapter because, in an important 1990 paper, she specifically addressed the issue of movement from thought to behavior (Cantor, 1990a). Cantor's work must be seen in the context of a cognitive or social cognitive approach to personality, and we have already been in touch with aspects of her thinking in Chapters 3 and 8. As detailed in her writings with Kihlstrom (Cantor & Kihlstrom, 1987, 1989), Cantor emphasizes the adaptive aspects of personality functioning, in particular the adaptive aspects of cognitive functioning. The emphasis is on **social intelligence** or the cognitive competencies and knowledge individuals can use as they attempt to solve the problems of daily life. Cantor's work has ties to the earlier work of theorists such as Kelly, Rotter, Bandura, and Mischel. It emphasizes such cognitive functions as discriminations among situations, the representation of goals and development of plans for achieving goals, the representation of a self with a past history as well as possible selves for the future, and the development of coping strategies and self-regulatory mechanisms. Of particular importance is the emphasis on the idiographic meanings situations and events have for people as well as the situational specificity of personality functioning. Thus, broad-band traits are rejected in favor of an emphasis on processes that lead to adaptive efforts to cope with the demands of specific situations and events.

In relation to the translation of cognition into action, the movement as described by Cantor from "having" to "doing," three concepts are emphasized: *schema, life tasks,* and *cognitive strategies.* Schema refer to organizations of information. As we have seen, people have self-schema, including possible selves, other-schema, goal schema, plan schema, and **event schema.** The latter refer to scripts that represent expected sequences of action in specific situations (e.g., cocktail party script or seminar participant script) as well as to specific *if-then hypotheses* people formulate concerning relations between actions and outcomes (e.g., "If I express anger then people will reject me," "If I enjoy myself too much then something bad will happen," "If I open myself up to others then they will be supportive").

The concept of *life tasks* is similar to that of the earlier noted concepts of current concerns, personal strivings, and personal projects. **Life tasks** refer to the individual's translation of goals into specific tasks on which to work during particular life periods and within specified contexts. It is important to recognize once more that these goals are seen as specific to contexts and to periods of life; that is, individuals devote their time and energy to different goals in different situations, and the nature of their goals changes during the course of life. Life tasks are idiographic and vary not only in content but also in how broad they are and whether they are primarily experienced as self-imposed or as imposed by others. It is assumed that the majority of life tasks are conscious and available to self-report, although a person does not necessarily always reflect upon them. Finally, cognitive strategies are the means by which individuals work on their current life tasks. They involve the appraisal of situations, planning for outcomes, memory of past experiences, and self-regulatory efforts such as delay of gratification (Mischel, 1990). They involve efforts not only to solve external problems but to do so in accord with internal emotions, needs, and values.

Cantor suggests that the best time to study the operation of life tasks and cognitive strategies is during major life transitions. During periods of significant change in one's interpersonal or work life, more attention is given to goals and how they can be pursued. Such transitions are seen as providing real-life analogies to laboratory tasks. The transitions from high school to college and then on to a career are illustrative of such periods, and Cantor has developed a research project involving the study of University of Michigan undergraduates from their first year of college through their senior year. Begun in 1984, a wide variety of data was collected at various points during the subjects' college careers: questionnaire data concerning family background, self-concept discrepancy measures following Higgins's approach (Chapter 8), symptom checklists and satisfaction self-reports, activity reports, objective information concerning academic performance, and life-task and strategy information. At the initiation of the project subjects were asked to list their current life tasks (i.e., those things they believed they were working on in their lives) and to rank them in order of importance. An average of 8.3 tasks was reported, ranging from the very abstract ("maturing beyond my high school mentality") to the concrete and immediate ("finding a girlfriend" or "finding a boyfriend"). The students were asked to code their freely generated tasks into three categories of achievement tasks (getting good grades, planning for the future, managing time) and three categories of interpersonal tasks (being on one's own away from family, developing an identity, and making friends). The six consensual tasks were then rated on dimensions such as importance, enjoyment, difficulty, challenge, and control. Basic to these dimensions, as determined by factor analyses of the ratings, were three areas: negative aspects of tasks (e.g., stressful, difficult, time consuming), rewarding aspects (e.g., enjoyment, progress), and matters of personal control (e.g., control, initiative). Subjects also were asked to list the concrete situations to which these tasks applied and their plans for handling them. Finally, as in the Emmons research, subjects were asked about the degree to which effort on each task facilitated or interfered with the pursuit of other tasks. Here a general conflict was found between the pursuit of academic tasks and the pursuit of social life tasks (Cantor & Langston, 1989).

Strategies were assessed through questionnaires and through semistructured interviews. Two strategies were determined to be of special significance, one in the academic realm and the other in the social realm. In the academic realm, a distinction was made between optimists and *defensive pessimists* (Norem, 1989; Norem & Cantor, 1986). In anticipation of achievement tasks, optimists feel relatively little anxiety and have high expectations. On the other hand, defensive pessimists "play out worst case scenarios," set low expectations, and take concrete steps to prepare for task demands. In terms of actual performance, optimists and defensive pessimists did not differ in past academic performance or in first semester performance. Thus, the defensive pessimists tend to be the students who others see as always being worried when they have nothing to be worried about.

Both optimism and defensive pessimism are seen as adaptive coping strategies for achievement tasks, with each strategy working better for different individuals. The optimists' outlook helps them focus on positive performance expectancies and avoid thinking about what might go wrong. Defensive pessimists' strategy seems to allow them to harness the anxiety associated with academic performance. Thus, their playing out of worst case scenarios and preparing for not doing well seem to calm them without interfering with their commitment to the pursuit of the task at hand. At the same time, it is clear that this strategy perpetuates anxiety. These differences in strategies did not carry over into the social realm; that is, whether or not an individual was an optimist or defensive pessimist in relation to achievement tasks was not predictive of their method of handling of social tasks.

In the social realm, differences were found among students in terms of what is called *social constraint*. The strategy of social constraint mainly has to do with social anxiety. It resembles defensive pessimism but focuses on the social realm. Individuals high on social constraint tend to be other-directed and anxious about their social performance. Whereas most students reported enjoying their social tasks more than their academic tasks, these students reported more stress and negative feelings in the social realm. The adaptive value of the strategy seems to lie in the use of others to guide one's social actions and the protection of self-esteem through being a follower and observer rather than a leader. Thus, this strategy provides for at least some participation in social activity. In terms of context-specificity, once more it is important to note that the negative cognitions of those high on social constraint did not generalize to other domains. Overall, those high on social constraint were no more depressed or negative about life and themselves than were those low on social constraint.

In sum, in considering the path to action, Cantor focuses on the life tasks people choose for themselves and the strategies they use to solve the problems associated with these tasks. As noted, there is an emphasis on cognitive activity, but life tasks and strategies are also seen as associated with emotion and possible behaviors. Beyond the cognitive emphasis, three aspects of the approach are noteworthy. First, it clearly is idiographic in its emphasis on the unique meanings individuals give to situations, events, themselves, and life generally. Second, the focus is on the adaptive process and generally there is an optimism concerning the efforts of people to solve life's problems. The emphasis tends to be on successful adaptation rather than problematic adaptation. Third, as part of the emphasis on successful adaptation, there is an emphasis on discriminative abilities, flexibility, and context specificity:

> Generalized deficits seem to be the exception not the rule in social intelligence. More typically, self-efficacy varies considerably for an individual across different task domains and individuals construct different task goals and use differentially

SPOTLIGHT ON THE RESEARCHER

NANCY CANTOR:

The Dynamics of Personality in Context

As an adolescent in the 1960s, I took Erikson to heart, bringing the struggle for identity to new heights, or to new depths as my parents might add. Accordingly, from my viewpoint, personality develops and grows through the individual's participation in and struggles with the tasks deemed important in their social-cultural life context. As psychologists, as parents, as peers, we too often act as if individuals "have" personalities, forgetting that what people "do" or try to do, and with whom they do it, can define and redefine who they are and who they will become. Thus, in thinking about personality, I begin with the premise that human beings are motivated to become fuller participants in their cultures and that few of us find it easy to take on culturally valued and personally relevant tasks.

In graduate school, I listened to Walter Mischel, and what I heard was not the pessimism of then traditional personality theory, illustrated by trait theory and psychoanalytic theory, but the optimism of flexibility—people really didn't have to be pigeonholed by who they "were" but could be described in terms of what they were "doing." Even better, the "doing" side of personality could include the cognitive work we do as well as overt performances. With John Kihlstrom, I worked on developing a problem-solving framework for personality in which the thoughts, feelings, and efforts of individuals are given form and function by the life tasks on which they work and their daily use of cognitive-behavioral strategies. Our social intelligence perspective examines the ways in which individuals think creatively about their own potential and about possible worlds in which they might live. We assume that "intelligent" thought and nonrigid action serve a fundamental human function enabling people to participate energetically in the culturally valued tasks of daily life.

Our work extends beyond the laboratory to encompass the task pursuits of individuals in their everyday worlds—how people respond to setbacks, how they anticipate problems or distract themselves in the face of anxiety, who they turn to when self-doubts get out of hand, and when they decide it is best to go on to the next task. Through experience-sampling and daily diary methods, we try to chart the dynamic ups and downs of individuals' efforts to participate in the life of their culture—in order to see both what people do and to what ends they do it. In this regard, I see the challenge for future work in our field as residing in methodological innovations that will provide a fuller picture of the dynamics of personality in context. To face that challenge, we need to go beyond debates about consistency to describe and explain the personality processes that are involved in individual attempts to take part in the tasks of their ever-changing life contexts. From this vantage point, personality flexibility and learning are more important for well-being than stability or consistency, because tasks change as do the opportunities for and constraints on our preferred "solutions." Therefore, I suppose that I have not strayed far from Erikson or Mischel in my message.

effective strategies to meet those goals in the various domains of their goal-directed pursuits.

Cantor & Langston, 1989, p. 159

COMMON ELEMENTS, DIFFERENCES, AND UNANSWERED QUESTIONS

In this section we have considered four approaches to goals and the effort to achieve goals through action: Bandura's work on goals and self-efficacy, Little's work on personal projects, Emmons's work on personal strivings, and Cantor's work on life tasks. They share features in common, with the goals model presented earlier in the chapter and with the efforts of Dweck (Chapter 4) as well as others working in this area (e.g., Carver & Scheier, 1988; Ford, 1992; Klinger, 1977; Kuhl & Beckman, 1985). What unites them is a common emphasis on the purposive, goal-directed nature of activity. Cognitive processes are emphasized, but affect and overt behavior are considered as well. In fact, it is the interrelationships among thinking, feeling, and doing that probably are of particular concern. In addition, for the most part there is an emphasis on assessing goal-directed activity in real-life situations and over time, on the value of idiographic analyses as well as the formulation of general laws, and on the system properties of goal structures and processes.

At the same time, there are differences among them and questions that remain to be addressed. We will focus on two points (Pervin, 1989): First, there is the question of consciousness of goals. The four personality psychologists whose work has been considered in this section all emphasize the person's ability to be conscious of and to report goals. They suggest that individuals often are not focusing their conscious attention on these goals or on the pursuit of them; that is, they may be involved with them on an automatic (nonconscious) basis but are able to bring them into awareness or consciousness when necessary. The research methods used all involve the study of goals that can be articulated by individuals. At the same time, the goals model presented earlier in the chapter suggests the existence of unconscious goals that individuals are not able to articulate or report. For example, consider the work on attachment discussed in Chapter 7. It is likely that many individuals are not aware of their attachment behavior, the goals involved in this behavior, or the working models of others and the interpersonal relations that are involved in these pursuits. The view taken here is that some goals, including goals of considerable importance, are unconscious and that currently we are without adequate methods for the assessment of such goals or the role they play in daily life.

Second, there is the question of where goals come from. The basis upon which goals are acquired has all too frequently been neglected by psychologists. In essence the question here is what gives goals their motivating power. The most common response to this question is the association of goals with affect (Pervin, 1983, 1989). The goal theory presented earlier gave particular attention to the process of classical conditioning in this regard. In other cases the role of affect is not specifically stated but is implicit in the discussion of the relation of goals to motivation. Thus, for example, both Mischel (1973) and Bandura (1986) do not specifically emphasize the role of affect in motivation but do talk about self-evaluative responses (e.g., pride and disappointment) to meeting performance standards. Other goal theorists, however, do not address the question at all. What is suggested is that much more attention needs to be given to how goals are acquired, become functionally autonomous, and are relinquished.

Not unrelated to these two points is the question of breakdowns in goal-directed, self-regulatory functioning. It is this area that we now consider.

BREAKDOWNS IN SELF-REGULATION AND THE PROBLEM OF VOLITION

This chapter began with a quote from William James concerning will—what is it that makes us able to get out of a warm bed on a cold morning? This led us to consider theories of goal-directed action or purposive behavior. For the most part, these theories have a rational quality to them. Expectancy-value theory has a rational choice quality, with people choosing that behavior or outcome deemed to have the highest expected utility based on value and probability. And, for the most part, the research considered presents a very optimistic picture of the person functioning to adapt to internal and external demands. Yet, in my work as a therapist I am struck with the problems people have in relation to goal-directed functioning, will, or, what I refer to as problems in volition (Pervin, 1991). Here too we can return to James:

> If we compare the outward symptoms of perversity together, they fall into two groups, in one of which normal actions are impossible, and in the other abnormal ones are irrepressible. Briefly, we may call them respectively the obstructed and the explosive will.
>
> James, 1892, p. 436

William James was interested in will and voluntary action. He emphasized what he called *ideo-motor action* or the view that the bare idea of a movement's effects is sufficient to produce the movement itself. In other words, we get up out of bed because of the thought of doing so—"we think the act, and it is done" (p. 423). But why, then, is it often so difficult to get up out of bed? James suggested that in such cases there were competing ideas that interfered with our resolve. But what of those cases in which we cannot overcome such interferences, in which we cannot by resolve or strength of will get ourselves to do what we want to do? James referred to such instances as cases of unhealthiness of will. Thus, the previous quote refers to the two types of unhealthy will: obstructed will and explosive will. According to James, action may involve the interplay between impulsive and inhibitory forces. These two forces are always operating together, and the consequence represents the outcome of the balance between the opposing forces. Obstructed will, then, occurs when the impulsion is insufficient or inhibition is in excess, while the explosive will occurs when impulsion is exaggerated or inhibition is defective. In sum, in any particular case of the breakdown of volition, there may be too much or too little impulsion and too much or too little inhibition.

To his great credit, James addressed a problem too long neglected by psychologists—will and the problem of breakdowns in will, volition, or self-regulation. One semester I asked students in a large introductory personality course to indicate any problem in volition that concerned them and the reasons for it. Almost every student listed one or more such difficulties, the most frequent being the problems of procrastination and overeating. Almost all could list some reason for the difficulty but generally these were merely statements of the problem rather than causal analyses. Thus, a student might report "I feel that I should write the paper but I just can't get myself to sit down and do it" or "I know how many calories that food has and how I want to lose weight but I just feel as if I have to have it."

The problem of procrastination illustrates what James called obstructed will, the problem of overeating explosive will. The former involves problems of *inhibition* in that people are inhibited from doing what they say they want to do. The latter involves problems of *addiction*, not necessarily in the sense of an addiction to drugs or smoking, but in the sense of a compulsive desiring, wanting, or "craving." I have seen many patients with problems of inhibition or addiction. One patient could not get himself to hand in papers on time even though it meant the potential ruin of his career. Until close to the end of his treatment, he came late to almost every appointment, from a few minutes late to the point when just a few minutes remained in the session. Another patient was inhibited in relation to women. He was a quite successful and attractive man who very much wanted to marry. However, as soon as he started to get close to a woman he was overcome with barriers and ended the relationship, only to begin the cycle anew with another woman. When he was not with women he was lonely; with them he was uncomfortable.

In contrast to such problems in inhibition, some of my patients have found themselves "compelled" to do things they did not want to do. They were addicted to certain things—to work, to visiting prostitutes, to eating fattening foods, or to calling 800 or 900 telephone numbers for explicit sexual conversations. Some of these may seem exaggerated but, as noted, almost everyone suffers from an inhibition or addiction of one kind or another. Not only that, but many people suffer from both inhibitions and addictions, as in the patient who could not get herself to clean house or file insurance forms and also was addicted to foods that were threatening to her health. In all of these cases people are unable to self-regulate; they are unable to do the very thing that would seem to make most rational sense, the very thing that would seem to make most sense from their own expectancy-value point of view, their subjective expected utility.

Personality psychologists do not have much to offer in the way of understanding such phenomena, perhaps little more insight into the problem than James had with his emphasis on conflicting forces. Most cognitive theories focus on problems in attention. Problems in volition reflect a breakdown in attentional focus; the inhibited person cannot focus on the intended goal and the addicted person cannot focus on an alternative goal. The answer to such problems is to refocus attention to the desired goal. This analysis makes apparent sense since clearly these problems in volition involve problems in attentional focus. However, what are we to tell the person who cannot redirect his or her attention, the person who says, "I try to focus on writing the paper but my mind just drifts and becomes blank," or the person who says, "I try to think about what I really want to do but I become obsessed with a wish or thought"? In other words, the problem of attentional focus is indeed part of the problem, but it is descriptive rather than explanatory. Taking oneself out of the problematic situation often helps to refocus attention, but whatever the otherwise adaptive capacity of human thought, people often take their "blank minds" or "obsessed minds" with them wherever they are.

Are such problems in volition basically problems in self-efficacy? Certainly they are problems in efficacy since the person cannot perform the necessary actions to cope with the demands of particular situations. But are they problems in self-efficacy in terms of the person's perception of his or her ability to meet the demands of the situation? The answer here is not clear-cut. Most people in these situations would acknowledge their inability to exercise will; to break through their inhibitions; or to stop their compulsive, addictive behavior. However, many people have complete faith in their self-efficacy. There are drinkers and smokers who claim that they can stop any time they want. As we know, self-efficacy beliefs often are quite discrepant with reality: People believe that they cannot do what in fact they are able to do or that they can do what in fact they are unable to do. And, in many cases, shifts in self-efficacy beliefs can occur with enormous speed: The person feels enormously self-confident at one moment and enormously anxious and doubtful at another moment.

What must be emphasized here is that we are not talking about bizarre behavior characteristic of a minority of strange individuals. Rather, to one extent or another we are talking about daily human behavior. So how can we include such phenomena in our models of goal-directed action? It would seem that problems of inhibition are somewhat easier to explain than are those of addiction. Problems of inhibition for the most part appear to involve anxiety; that is, the person cannot do what he or she wants to do because anxiety is associated with it. The man who seeks intimacy also is afraid of intimacy and the person who seeks to turn in his work on time is afraid of the evaluation of the work or of submitting to deadlines. On the other hand, how are we to explain the power of addictions? Physiological explanations alone will not suffice since such explanations are questionable for smoking and drinking let alone for gambling, eating, and sexual addictions. The view taken here is that in these cases there has been a powerful process of classical conditioning, of the association of positive affect with an act or behavior that otherwise violates people's wishes and overrides their executive control system. What perhaps is involved here is not terribly different from the powerful food and odor preferences and dislikes most of us have, preferences and dislikes that were acquired early in life and often remain remarkably difficult to change (Rozin & Zellner, 1985).

Undoubtedly this is not a satisfactory solution to the problem. Much research will need to be done. The point in discussing it in this section is twofold. First, it brings to the forefront a problem with all current models of purposive behavior—in addressing the question of translating thought into action, they either do not address problems in such movement or do not provide satisfactory answers to the problem. Problems in volition seem to violate the assumptions of these models and therefore would seem to have something valuable to contribute to an extension of them. Second, problems in volition bring us back to the two questions raised earlier, the question of unconscious goals and the question of where goals come from. When volition breaks down, people often have difficulty stating what their goals are, and certainly *why* they are having such difficulty in pursuing the goal that they do have in mind. People struggling with inhibition often are not aware that another goal is in conflict with the one that is staring them in the eye; and people struggling with an addiction generally are puzzled by the power of the goal that dominates their attention and effort. And, particularly in this case, how do such goals achieve their power? We can be impressed with the ability of people to do what they intend to do, to construct a goal hierarchy and match specific goals to specific situations, and to shift goals as situations require or as life changes require. We can be impressed with the ability of people to develop strategies, to delay, to reward themselves for accomplishments and punish themselves for failures, in sum, to self-regulate. At the same time, we must be impressed with the breakdowns in self-regulation, with the instances when people are unable to translate thought into action or, of perhaps even greater significance, the instances when people are moved to action when they would otherwise choose to think and behave differently.

MAJOR CONCEPTS

Purposive behavior.   Behavior directed toward an end point or goal.

Expectancy × value theory.   A theory of motivation emphasizing the probability of action as a function of the expectancy of achieving an outcome multiplied by the value of the outcome.

Subjective expected utility (SEU).   The subjective probability of an event multiplied by the value of the event.

Level of aspiration.   In Lewin's research, the goal or standard set by an individual for future performance.

Goal.   The mental representation of an end point toward which the organism strives.

Multidetermination.   The concept indicat-

ing that a complex act has multiple determinants or goals.

Equipotentiality.   The concept indicating that a goal can lead to different plans or behaviors to achieve the goal.

Equifinality.   The concept indicating that the same outcome can be a result of the expression of many different goals.

Self-regulation.   The ability of the organism to regulate itself toward the attainment of a goal.

Internal standards.   Bandura's concept for the individual's standards or goals that play a crucial role in the self-regulation of behavior over extended periods of time.

Self-reinforcement.   The organism's ability to reinforce itself for progress toward a goal, which plays an important role in the self-regulation of behavior over extended periods of time.

Personal project. Little's concept of an extended set of personally relevant actions intended to achieve a personal goal.

Personal striving. Emmons's concept of a coherent pattern of goal strivings representing what an individual is typically trying to do.

Social intelligence. Cantor and Kihlstrom's term for the cognitive competencies and knowledge individuals can use as they attempt to solve the problems of daily life.

Event schema. A type of schema representing a script of sequences of action in specific situations (e.g., cocktail party).

Life task. Cantor's concept for the individual's translation of goals into specific tasks that can be worked on during specific periods of time and in specific contexts.

SUMMARY

1. In the past, psychologists have been reluctant to use terms such as *intention, will,* and *volition.* However, there is evidence of increased interest in purposive, goal-directed behavior, that is, in how people translate the idea of a goal into action.

2. Expectancy-value theory represents a rational model of human decision-making behavior and is expressed in Tolman's work on purposive behavior in animals, in Lewin's work on level of aspiration, and in Rotter's social learning theory.

3. A model of goal system functioning was presented that emphasizes stability and variability in the individual's efforts to maintain coherence and achieve goals in the face of changing situational circumstances. Goals have cognitive, affective, and behavioral properties associated with them. Goal system functioning is characterized by the principles of multidetermination, equipotentiality, and equifinality.

4. Bandura emphasizes the process of self-regulation in the pursuit of meeting standards. Internal reinforcers (i.e., self-reinforcement), external reinforcers, and feedback information are important in relation to goal-directed activity. Explicit, realistic, and challenging goals are particularly conducive to self-motivation.

5. Little's work on personal projects, Emmons's work on personal strivings, and Cantor's work on life tasks illustrate current research on goal-directed activity. Life satisfaction and subjective well-being are associated with having goals that are low in stress, high in perceived likelihood of positive outcome, and high in perceived control (Little), as well as being associated with low conflict and low ambivalence (Emmons). Cantor emphasizes the concept of social intelligence, particularly in terms of life tasks and cognitive strategies (e.g., defensive pessimism, social constraint).

6.   The problem of volition, that is, why people cannot do what they intend or want to do, is seen as an issue of major importance to purposive theory. At this point there is not a satisfactory explanation for problems in volition or the breakdown of self-regulation.

EMOTION, ADAPTATION, AND HEALTH

10

CHAPTER OVERVIEW

In this chapter we consider the importance of emotion for personality functioning. Various views concerning the innate, universal aspects of emotion are considered as well as those emphasizing more individualistic aspects. From there we move on to consider how people cope with emotional, stressful events and the implications of their coping methods for physical and psychological well-being. The overall view is that the emotions people experience and how they cope with emotionally taxing events form an important part of their personality and have important implications for their health.

Questions to Be Addressed in This Chapter

1 To what extent are emotions innate and universal?

2 What means do people use to cope with stress and to what extent are there individual differences in these coping methods?

3 Is there evidence of a relation between personality and psychological and physical health?

4 To what extent is personality reflected in the different emotions experienced by the individual as well as in the organization of these emotions?

If we were to use our own experience as a starting point for personality research, certainly one of the areas of greatest emphasis would be emotions, or, as they are often referred to in the literature, *affects*. Feelings are an important part of our daily existence and, as we shall see, likely play an important role in our psychological adjustment and physical well-being. Yet, for considerable periods of time they have been neglected by psychologists generally and personality psychologists in particular. Much like work on the self, work on affects has waxed and waned with shifts in what was deemed to be important by psychologists and in the research methods that were in favor at the time.

Interest in the emotions, and their relation to adaptation and health, goes far back in human history. The Greeks emphasized temperamental types characterized by different degrees of emotionality and different kinds of emotion. The great biologist Darwin was interested in emotions, particularly in the continuity of expression of emotions in animals and people, that is, that many of the same basic emotions and accompanying facial expressions exist in both (Figure 10.1). In line with his more general theory, Darwin viewed emotions and their communication to others as having functional or adaptive value. The great American psychologist William James, in his *Principles of Psychology* (1890), emphasized the importance of emotion. Thus, the basis for the continued study of emotion had been set. This indeed was the case during the early years of the field of psychology. However, with the development of Watsonian behaviorism in the 1920s there was a decline in interest in emotions. As expressed by the later proponent of behaviorism, B.F. Skinner: "The exploration of the emotional and motivational life of the mind has been described as one of the great achievements in the history of human thought, but it is possible that it has been one of the great disasters" (1974, p. 165). The cognitive revolution of the 1960s changed the face of psychology, but it did little at first to foster the study of emotion. As noted by Silvan Tomkins, at the time a lone voice emphasizing the importance of affects whose work eventually became extremely influential, "the cognitive revolution was required to emancipate the study of cognition. . . . An affect revolution is now required to emancipate this radical new development from an overly imperialistic cognitive theory" (1981, p. 306).

Well, the affect revolution that Tomkins believed was required appears to have occurred. Today, psychologists are actively engaged in the study of the structure and determinants of emotions, and personality psychologists are actively engaged in the study of individual differences in emotions and the relation of these individual differences to other aspects of personality functioning (Pervin, 1993b). Thus, after a lengthy period of neglect, emotion is taking its rightful place as a central area of concern to personality psychologists. And, if this area has been neglected in this text until now, it is time to attend to research in this important area of investigation. We begin with a brief overview of the place of emotion in traditional personality theory, move on to a discussion of current theory in the area, and then proceed to relate the emotions to efforts on the part of the organism to adapt to stress and the implications of these adaptations for psychological and physical well-being—thus, the title of the chapter: Emotion, Adaptation, and Health.

Figure 10.1 Illustrative facial expressions in chimpanzees.
These are drawings from photographs and descriptions. Many of the facial expressions are similar to facial expressions of emotion in humans.

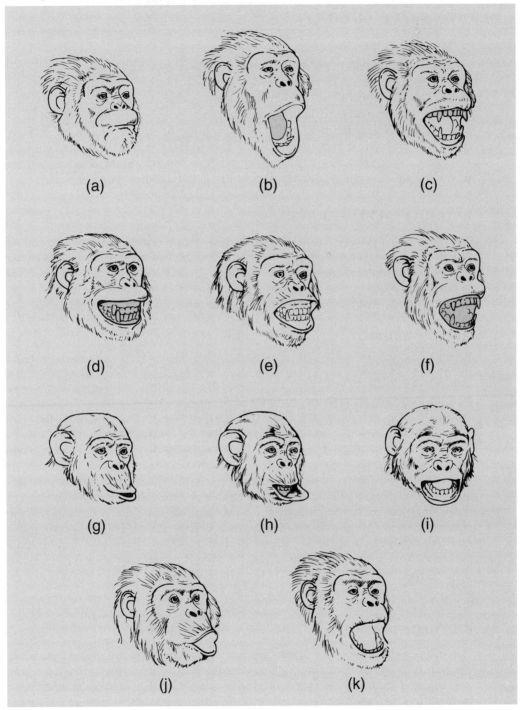

(a)

(b)

(c)

(d)

(e)

(f)

(g)

(h)

(i)

(j)

(k)

(From "Facial Expressions of Emotion in Nonhuman Primates," by S. Chevalier-Skolnikoff, 1973, in *Darwin and Facial Expression*, p. 72, by P. Ekman, Ed., New York: Academic Press. Reprinted by permission of Academic Press.)

AFFECT WITHIN THE CONTEXT OF TRADITIONAL PERSONALITY THEORY

In this section we consider briefly the place of affect in the major theoretical approaches to personality: psychodynamic; phenomenological/humanistic; trait; and social cognitive, information processing. The main point to be made here is that affect, particularly the affects of anxiety and depression, has been considered within the context of each of these theoretical approaches. However, for the most part affect has not been considered to be a central element in the organization of personality (Izard, 1993b; Lewis & Michalson, 1983; Malatesta, 1990; Pervin, 1993b). As we shall see, what is suggested in this chapter is that how the person organizes his or her emotional life *is* a central defining characteristic of that individual's personality.

PSYCHOANALYTIC THEORY

Affect clearly plays a central role in psychoanalytic theory, perhaps a more central role than in any of the other major theoretical approaches to personality. This is true in terms of both the range of affects considered and the role of affect in the total organization of personality. Within the psychoanalytic literature one can find reference to virtually every affect, not only to common affects such as anxiety, guilt, and depression, but also to others such as shame, jealousy, envy, and optimism that are only now becoming affects of interest to psychologists. And, it is suggested that certain character types are disposed toward experiencing some affects rather than others. For example, as seen in Chapter 6, in Erikson's psychosocial stages of development, the first three stages are associated with the affects of mistrust, shame, and guilt, respectively. In addition, in terms of the role of affect in the organization of personality, the role of anxiety is emphasized in relation to almost all aspects of personality functioning, particularly in relation to the mechanisms of defense.

Even though they are considered to be important within the context of psychoanalytic theory, affects typically have been viewed as secondary to the drives or instincts. Thus, whereas major attention was given to drive or instinct theory, less attention was given to the development of a theory of affects. Although interested in the phenomena of a wide range of affects, analysts have traditionally given the greatest attention to the affects of anxiety and depression. Finally, it is important to note that although emphasis is given to affect as conscious experience, analysts have also emphasized the importance of painful affects that are repressed or otherwise defended against. Thus, not only anxiety but other painful affects such as guilt and shame may be part of the unconscious functioning of the person.

PHENOMENOLOGICAL THEORY: CARL ROGERS

Because of the attention Carl Rogers gave to phenomenology and experience in his research and clinical work, one might have expected him to have developed a highly differentiated theory of affects. Yet, it is interesting to find that there are no references to affect terms in the indexes to some of Rogers's most significant works (Rogers, 1951, 1961). There is an emphasis on feelings and experience generally, and positive and negative feelings more specifically, but rarely to any one affect. Rogers emphasized the importance of therapeutic change in the manner of experiencing the self and the world, a change from unrecognized, unowned, and fixed feelings to known, accepted, and fluid feelings, but he did not suggest a shift in the nature of the specific affects experienced, from depression to joy, shame to pride, or hate to love, for example.

As was true for Freud, Rogers gave major attention to anxiety and defense in his personality theory. Anxiety was viewed as the result of a discrepancy between experience and the self-concept, in particular when such discrepancies were associated in the past with the loss of positive regard from others. In other words, Rogers suggested that individuals strive to maintain a concept of the self, in particular a concept of the self associated with positive regard from others, and experiences incongruent with this self-concept arouse anxiety and lead to defensive maneuvers. In the terms discussed in Chapter 8, Rogers emphasized both the motive for self-consistency or self-verification and the motive for self-enhancement. However, beyond this, he did little to elaborate upon why individuals experience affects other than anxiety, or to define how the various affects are organized differentially in various personalities.

TRAIT THEORY

Temperament has always been a fundamental part of trait theory. Indeed, one can suggest that the basic traits, whether viewed within the context of a three-factor or a five-factor model (Chapter 2), consist of temperaments. To some extent moods and affects are associated with the various trait factors. For example, the affects of anxiety, hostility, and depression are associated with Neuroticism, whereas warmth and positive emotions are associated with Extraversion. As we shall see later in the chapter, some trait theorists emphasize the broad dimensions of positive and negative affect/mood and suggest important implications of these dimensions for health and well-being (Tellegen, 1985, 1991; D. Watson & Clark, 1991, 1993; Watson & Tellegen, 1985). In addition, traitlike individual differences in affect intensity, or the level of reactivity and variability of emotional reactivity, are emphasized (Larsen, 1991).

People often use trait terms to describe emotional states (e.g., aggressive, friendly, warm). Thus, it is not surprising that trait theorists would include some recognition of this area of functioning within their descriptive taxonomy (Plutchik, 1980). At the same time, it should be clear that trait theorists give attention to broad dimensions of mood or temperament rather than to specific affects. To an even greater extent than was true for psychoanalytic and phenomenological theory, there is no articulated theory of affects or any elaboration of the role of the organization of affects within the individual for general personality functioning. Rather, trait theorists for the most part emphasize principles of genetics and biology/physiology to account for broad and largely stable individual differences in temperament.

SOCIAL COGNITIVE, INFORMATION-PROCESSING THEORY

For a long time cognitive theories left the person in thought, devoid of emotion or action. Kelly's (1955) personal construct theory recognized the importance of affects such as anxiety, fear, and threat, but the emphasis was on constructs; and, on the whole, human emotions remained outside the range of the theory. Bandura (1986) emphasizes the importance of affective responses acquired through direct experiences or observational learning (i.e., vicarious conditioning, Chapter 3), in particular the affects of anxiety and depression. According to Bandura, anxiety is the emotional response to feelings of low self-efficacy in relation to negative outcomes, whereas depression is the emotional response to feelings of low self-efficacy in relation to positive outcomes. Thus, one experiences anxiety when feeling unable to manage situations in which psychological or physical harm is possible, and one experiences depression when feeling unable to manage situations in which rewards may be lost. Mischel does not list emotions among the major personality variables in his cognitive social theory of personality.

Starting from a "cold" cognitive position, social cognitive and information-processing approaches to personality have increasingly turned toward an interest in affect, in terms of both how cognitive processes influence affect and how affect influences cognitive processes (Isen, 1993; Singer & Salovey, 1993). At the same time, the range of affects considered by these personality theorists has been relatively limited. When efforts have been made to consider a broader range of affects, the emphasis has been on cognitive attributions that lead to the experiencing of these affects and not on individual differences or the relation of various affects to the rest of personality functioning.

A CENTRAL ROLE FOR AFFECT IN PERSONALITY

In this section we have briefly considered the place of affect in traditional approaches to personality. Two points stand out. First, with the possible exception of psychoanalytic theory, the major approaches to personality give minimal attention to affects other than anxiety and depression. Second, in no case is affect emphasized as a major organizing element in personality functioning.

What might such an approach look like? First, attention would be given to a wider range of affects than is considered in most personality theories. Attention would be given not only to anxiety and depression, but to affects such as shame, envy, jealousy, disgust, pride, and love. Individual differences would be considered not just in terms of scores on particular affects, but on individual patterns of relations among the affects (Izard, 1993b; Malatesta, 1990; Pervin, 1993b). For example, it would not only be important to know whether the individual had a high or low score on an affect such as anxiety, but also to know how that score compared with the person's scores on other affects. In other words, it would be important to consider personality in terms of individual patterns of affects.

Second, in such a theory affect would be given central status, rather than being an accompaniment or consequence of drives, cognitions, or the like. In such a theory affect would be given a central place in the organization of personality, with an emphasis on the implications of emotion for thought, action, and motivation. In other words, such a theory of personality would emphasize a broadened range of affects, patterns of affects, and the central place of affect in the organization of personality functioning. In the next section we turn to efforts that have been made to develop at least some components of such a theory (Table 10.1).

TABLE 10.1 **Elements of a Central Role for Affect in Personality**

1. Emphasis on a broad range of affects.
2. Emphasis on the patterning or organization of affects within the individual.
3. Affect as central to the organization of personality (e.g., influences on thought, motivation, and action).

BASIC EMOTIONS THEORY

In this section we consider the view that there are basic, universal emotions that play a central role in personality functioning. There are three key figures in this view, although others hold similar or related views. The central figure is Silvan Tomkins (1962, 1963, 1991), who, as earlier noted, for some time was the main one who emphasized the importance of affect as an area of inquiry. In addition, there is the research of two individuals who were influenced by Tomkins, Paul Ekman (1992a, 1992b, 1993, 1994) and Carroll Izard (1991, 1992, 1993a, 1993b, 1994).

There are a few basic principles to **basic emotions theory,** or **differential emotions theory** as it is called by Izard. First, it is suggested that there are basic, fundamental, or primary emotions that are universal. The exact number of basic emotions varies somewhat from theorist to theorist, generally ranging from 8 to 14. The 8 basic affects suggested by Tomkins are: *interest-excitement, enjoyment-joy, surprise-startle, distress-anguish, disgust-revulsion-contempt, anger-rage, shame-humiliation, fear-terror.* The basic emotions emphasized by Izard in the Differential Emotions Scale and representative items for each scale are given in Table 10.2.

According to this view, the affects are innate and part of our evolutionary heritage. In agreement with Darwin, it is suggested that these affects have evolved because of

TABLE 10.2 **Representative Items on the Differential Emotions Scale**

Basic Emotion	Representative Scale: In your daily life, how often do you
1. Interest	Feel like what you're doing or watching is interesting
2. Enjoyment	Feel happy
3. Surprise	Feel like you feel when something unexpected happens
4. Sadness	Feel unhappy, blue, downhearted
5. Anger	Feel angry, irritated, annoyed
6. Disgust	Feel like things are so rotten they could make you sick
7. Contempt	Feel like somebody is "good for nothing"
8. Fear	Feel afraid, shaky, and jittery
9. Guilt	Feel like you ought to be blamed for something
10. Shame	Feel like people laugh at you
11. Shyness	Feel shy, like you want to hide
12. Hostility inward	Feel you can't stand yourself

Source: "Stability of Emotion Experiences and Their Relations to Traits of Personality," by C. E Izard, 1993, *Journal of Personality and Social Psychology, 64,* p. 851.

their adaptive value. They are signals to us and to others that action is necessary. We do not learn to be afraid, startled, disgusted, or angry, although we do learn when, where, and in response to which stimuli to respond with these affects. For example, although there appear to be universal stimuli for disgust, namely those having contamination properties, what is considered to be disgusting by some individuals or cultures can be considered a source of joy by others (e.g., eating ants can be considered disgusting or a delicacy) (Rozin & Fallon, 1987).

Second, the basic, universal emotions have unique features. Most significantly, each affect is associated with a pattern of facial movement involving specific facial muscles. This pattern of facial movement or facial expression, unique to each affect, is innate and universal. It can be seen in young infants as well as adults, and in members of differing cultural groups (Figures 10.2a–10.2d). According to Ekman, "the strongest evidence for distinguishing one emotion from another comes from research on facial expressions" (1992a, p. 175). In cross-cultural research conducted independently by Ekman and by Izard, it has been demonstrated that members of vastly different cultures select comparable emotion terms to fit facial expressions. In other words, members of different cultures share the same basic facial expressions associated with the basic emotions and can recognize these facial expression–emotion relationships in one another (See Figure 10.2a–10.2d). At the same time, it is recognized that individuals differ in the intensity of their facial expressions, and cultures have what are called *display rules* concerning the appearance of each emo-

Figure 10.2a   Illustrative facial expressions of affect in children.

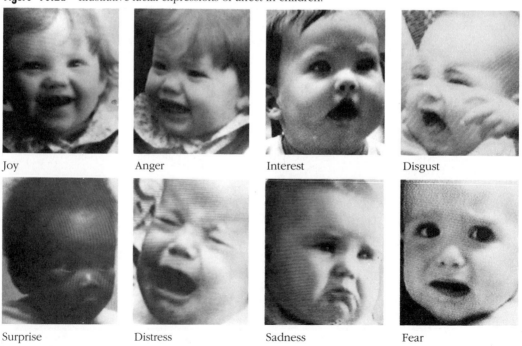

Joy   Anger   Interest   Disgust

Surprise   Distress   Sadness   Fear

(Photo provided by C. Izard)

Figure 10.2b   Illustrative facial expressions of affect in adults.

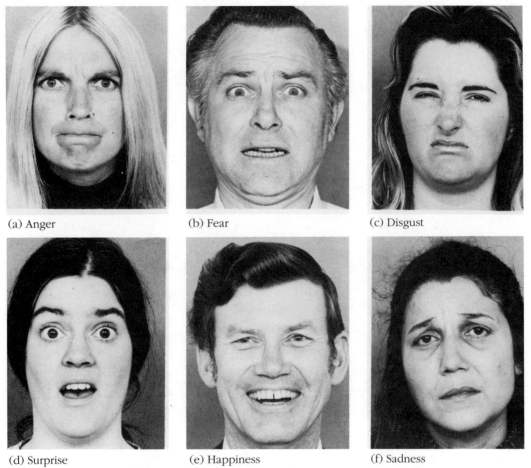

(a) Anger   (b) Fear   (c) Disgust

(d) Surprise   (e) Happiness   (f) Sadness

(Photos reproduced by permission of P. Ekman)

tion. In addition to the universality of these facial expressions, it is suggested that the basic emotions have distinctive physiological patterns of response associated with them.

Third, the affect system is the primary motivational system. It is suggested that emotions, rather than drives, have an energizing or motivational effect. Emotions have the capacity to organize and maintain sets of thoughts and actions. Thus, many thoughts and memories are organized in terms of their association with the same affect, as is true for many behavioral responses (Bower, 1981; Singer & Salovey, 1993). The importance of affect for motivation was seen in the presentation of goal theory in Chapter 9, a view greatly influenced by the work of Tomkins.

Fourth, as a result of constitutional factors as well as experience, individuals differ in the frequency and intensity with which particular emotions are experienced. According to Izard, "a major general function of the emotions and emotion system is

Figure 10.2c   Illustrative facial expressions of affect in subjects from the Fore of New Guinea (clockwise from top left: happiness, sadness, disgust, anger).

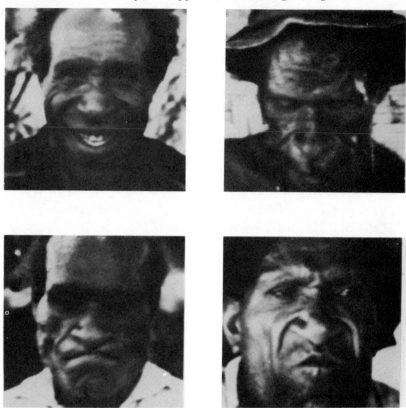

(Photos reproduced by permission of P. Ekman)

the organization of traits and dimensions of personality" (1993b, p. 637). Since affects are motivational and organize cognition and action, it is not surprising that they would be central to an individual's personality. And, as each emotion influences thought and action in relatively distinctive ways, specific emotions help to shape specific traits in each individual. Thus, the discrete emotions of interest, enjoyment, and shyness have been found to be related to the trait of Extraversion (shyness is negatively correlated with Extraversion), while the discrete emotions of sadness, contempt, fear, shame, and guilt have been found to be related to the trait of Neuroticism. In addition, as would be expected from such relationships with traits, there was evidence of stability of individual differences in discrete emotion scores over a 3-year period (Izard, Libero, Putnam, & Haynes, 1993).

In sum, basic emotion theorists suggest that there are innate, universal emotions that are part of our evolutionary heritage, have adaptive value, and have universal expressions and distinctive physiological properties. These emotions have importance for motivation, cognition, and action and play a central role in the organization of personality functioning. Although the basic nature of each affective response is

Figure 10.2d Percentage agreement in judgment of photographs of facial expressions across cultures.
The data indicate that members of different cultures can recognize facial expression-emotion relationships in one another.

	United States (N = 99)	Brazil (N = 40)	Chile (N = 119)	Argentina (N = 168)	Japan (N = 29)
	97% Happiness	95% Happiness	95% Happiness	98% Happiness	100% Happiness
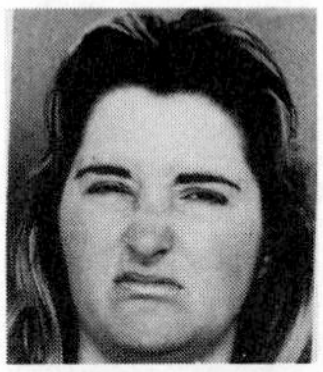	92% Disgust	97% Disgust	92% Disgust	92% Disgust	90% Disgust
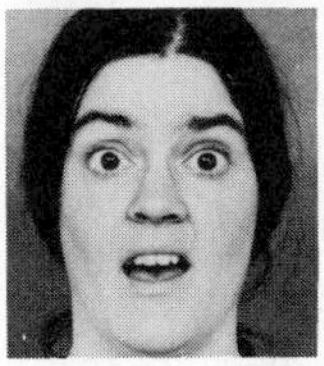	95% Surprise	87% Surprise	93% Surprise	95% Surprise	100% Surprise
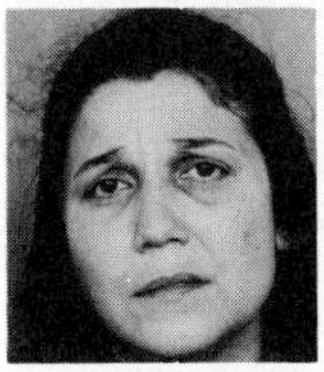	84% Sadness	59% Sadness	88% Sadness	78% Sadness	62% Sadness
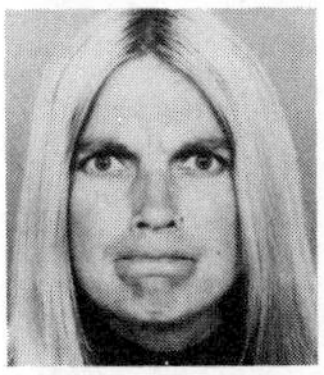	67% Anger	90% Anger	94% Anger	90% Anger	90% Anger
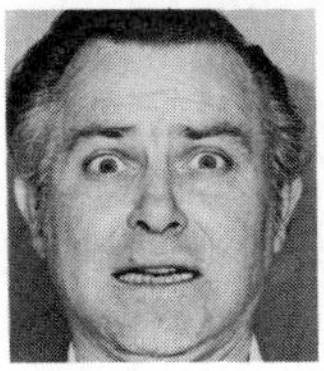	85% Fear	67% Fear	68% Fear	54% Fear	66% Fear

(Photos reproduced by permission of P. Ekman. From "Cross-Cultural Studies of Facial Expression," by P. Ekman, 1973, in *Darwin and Facial Expression,* p. 207, by P. Ekman, Ed., New York: Academic Press. Reprinted by permission of Academic Press.)

innate and universal, it is recognized that there are learned associations between each emotion and specific stimuli as well as cultural rules concerning when and how each affect is to be expressed. What is important to recognize here is that a number of basic, discrete emotions are being suggested rather than a simple positive-negative feeling state dichotomy or a general state of arousal that is then influenced by specific cognitions to form a specific emotion. What also is important to recognize is that affect is seen as fundamental or central to personality functioning, both in terms of its organizing function relative to thought and action and in terms of individual differences in the frequency and intensity with which the affects are aroused and expressed.

Before concluding this section on basic affects, it should be noted that many, perhaps all, of these points remain controversial. Thus, some theorists and researchers question the view of basic, universal emotions and the evidence of universal facial expressions and distinctive physiological responses (Davidson, 1992; Ortony & Turner, 1990). Many of these critics emphasize the role of cognitive factors to a much greater extent than do basic emotion theorists. They point out that there is a lack of agreement among basic emotion theorists concerning the number of basic emotions and that the specific meaning of each emotion differs in many cultures even if members of the various cultures are prepared to identify facial expressions in the same way (Shweder, 1993; G. M. White, 1993; Wierzbicka, 1992). Whatever the eventual outcome of such debate, what cannot be ignored is the immense contribution made by basic emotion theorists in bringing this area to the forefront of psychological investigation. In addition, what should not be ignored is the potential contribution to be made to our conceptualization of personality functioning.

EMOTION AND ADAPTATION

In this section we tie the study of emotion to the problem of adaptation—how people attempt to cope with emotion to meet situational demands and accomplish personal goals. We will rely heavily on the work of Richard Lazarus, whose 1991 book *Emotion and Adaptation* attempted to establish exactly this relationship. We will trace the historical development of Lazarus's work from an emphasis on stress and coping to a broader concern with emotion and adaptation (Lazarus, 1991, 1993b).

Lazarus's research on stress began in the 1950s and led to the 1966 publication of *Psychological Stress and the Coping Process,* which has shaped work in the stress field until the present. In his early research Lazarus showed stress-inducing films to subjects. In one film a series of operations were being performed as part of a male rite of passage in a tribe in Australia; in another film bloody work accidents (e.g., a worker fatally impaled on a board thrust from a circular saw; a worker's finger cut off) were shown. Influenced by psychoanalytic theory, Lazarus was interested in how the motives and efforts of individuals to cope with threat influenced the degree of stress experienced. Messages were presented with the films to influence the defense used by the subject. For example, the messages "The people in the film are not hurt or distressed by what is happening" and "These accidents didn't really happen but were staged for their effect" were used to encourage the defense mechanism of denial. Degree of stress in relation to the films and accompanying messages was measured by self-reports of stress and physiological recordings of the heart rate and skin conductance levels (i.e., sweat gland activity) of the subjects. In this research Lazarus found that the messages associated with the films had a powerful influence on the degree of stress experienced. In sum, experienced stress reflected both the degree of perceived threat and the defensive process employed by the individual to cope with that threat.

Lazarus then moved from an emphasis on ego defenses to a broader cognitive conceptualization and defined *appraisal* as a basic mediator of stress reactions. According to the theory outlined in his landmark book, stress occurs when the person views circumstances as taxing, exceeding his or her resources, and endangering well-being (Lazarus, 1966). Involved in this process are two stages of cognitive appraisal. In **primary appraisal,** the person evaluates whether there is anything at stake in the encounter, whether there is a threat or danger. For example, is there potential harm or benefit to self-esteem? Is one's personal health or that of a loved one at risk? In **secondary appraisal,** the person evaluates what, if anything, can be done to overcome the harm, prevent harm, or improve the prospects for benefit. In other words, secondary appraisal involves an evaluation of the person's resources to cope with the potential harm or benefit evaluated in the stage of primary appraisal. In sum, the degree of stress experienced is a result of these two appraisal processes— one evaluating the degree of potential harm or threat and the other the potential for successful coping with the threat.

Lazarus suggests that primary and secondary appraisal are universal aspects of the coping process. However, in a stressful situation various means of coping are available to master or tolerate the circumstances appraised as taxing the individual's resources. Research on the diverse means used by subjects to cope with stress led to the development of the Ways of Coping Scale, a questionnaire measure of eight coping strategies (Folkman, Lazarus, Dunkel-Schetter, DeLongis, & Gruen, 1986; Table 10.3). In particular a distinction is made between problem-focused forms of coping (e.g., efforts to alter the situation) and emotion-focused forms of coping (e.g., emotional distancing, escape-avoidance, seeking social support). Research based on the use of this questionnaire suggests the following conclusions (Lazarus, 1991):

1. People differentiate among situations in their appraisals. In other words, individual appraisals are sensitive to environmental conditions.

2. There is evidence of both stability and variability in the methods individuals use to cope with stressful situations. Although individuals do show tendencies to favor particular coping methods, most individuals use a variety of coping methods depending on the specific context. In other words, coping reflects both personality and situational influences.

3. In general, the greater the reported level of stress and efforts to cope, the poorer is the physical health of the individual and the greater is the likelihood of psychological symptoms. In contrast, the greater the sense of mastery, the better is the physical and psychological health.

4. Although the value of a particular form of coping depends on the context in

TABLE 10.3 Illustrative Items From the Ways of Coping Scale

Scale	Illustrative Item
Confrontative coping	I expressed anger to the person who caused the problem.
Distancing	I made light of the situation and refused to get too serious about it.
Self-controlling	I tried to keep my feelings to myself.
Seeking social support	I talked to someone to find out more about the situation.
Accepting responsibility	I realized I brought the problem on myself.
Escape-avoidance	I wished that the situation would go away or somehow be over with.
Planful problem-solving	I knew what had to be done; so I doubled my efforts to make things work.
Positive reappraisal	I changed or grew as a person in a good way.

Source: "The Dynamics of a Stressful Encounter: Cognitive Appraisal, Coping, and Encounter Outcomes," by S. Folkman, R. S. Lazarus, C. Dunkel-Schetter, A. DeLongis, and R. Gruen, 1986, *Journal of Personality and Social Psychology, 50,* p. 996.

which it is used, in general planful problem-solving ("I made a plan of action and followed it" or "Just concentrated on the next step") is a more adaptive form of coping than escape-avoidance ("Hoped a miracle would happen" or "Tried to reduce tension by eating, drinking, or using drugs") or confrontative coping ("I let my feelings out somehow" or "I expressed anger to those who caused the problem").

A number of aspects of this approach are noteworthy. First, there is an emphasis on what Lazarus calls a *cognitive mediational approach.* What is emphasized is the meaning or cognitive appraisal of the situation. Second, stress is conceived in terms of an individual-environment relationship. What is stressful for one person is not necessarily stressful for another. Thus, ordinarily one cannot speak of a stressful stimulus per se but rather must speak of a relation between the degree of potential harm perceived and the perceived resources to cope. Stress is not in the stimulus or object, but in the relation between the person and the event. Third, stress and coping are viewed in process rather than trait terms. Rather than viewing approaches to coping as fixed parts of the person, Lazarus suggested that individuals make use of a variety of coping methods depending on their preferred mode and the adaptive requirements of the situation: "Although stable coping styles do exist and are important, coping is highly contextual, since to be effective it must change over time and across different stressful conditions" (Lazarus, 1993a, p. 8). Finally, it can be noted that Lazarus viewed the coping process as occurring at both conscious and unconscious levels. The person may sometimes be aware but at other times unaware or unconscious of the method being used to cope with stress. In sum, Lazarus's stress and coping model emphasizes cognitive, mediational processes, individual-environment relationships, personality and contextual influences, and conscious and unconscious processes.

Over time Lazarus came to consider stress as part of a broader view of emotions—

thus the title of his book *Emotion and Adaptation* and the title of this section. Lazarus developed a cognitive-motivational-relational theory of emotions. It is cognitive in terms of its emphasis on appraisal processes and beliefs about the self and world, motivational because it involves the motives or goals with which the person encounters the environment, and relational in its emphasis on the relationship between the individual and the environment. Lazarus suggests that each emotion has a *core relational theme* that defines the harm or benefit in an adaptational encounter that is associated with each emotion. The core relational themes associated with specific emotions are presented in Table 10.4.

As can be seen, the core relational theme emphasizes the perceived or appraised motivational relevance and consequences for the individual. In other words, the emotion experienced by a person is influenced by the extent to which the encounter touches upon personal goals and the extent to which it thwarts or facilitates these goals (Smith & Lazarus, 1990). Negative emotions are associated with appraisals that important goals are being thwarted in the encounter, whereas positive emotions are experienced when appraisals are made that important goals are being facilitated. In addition, it is suggested that the individual makes other appraisals in each encounter that influence the specific nature of the emotion experienced. For example, when anger is experienced the person has made the appraisal that the thwarting of goals is due to the action of someone else; that is, there is blaming of the other. In contrast, with guilt there is self-blame for the thwarting of goals. Appraisals also are made of the potential for change in the situation. The emotion of hope is associated with the

TABLE 10.4 Core Relational Themes for Each Emotion

Anger	A demeaning offense against me and mine.
Anxiety	Facing uncertain, existential threat.
Fright	Facing an immediate, concrete, and overwhelming physical danger.
Guilt	Having transgressed a moral imperative.
Shame	Having failed to live up to an ego-ideal.
Sadness	Having experienced an irrevocable loss.
Envy	Wanting what someone else has.
Jealousy	Resenting a third party for loss or threat to another's affection.
Disgust	Taking in or being too close to an indigestible object or idea (metaphorically speaking).
Happiness	Making reasonable progress toward the realization of a goal.
Pride	Enhancement of one's ego-identity by taking credit for a valued object or achievement, either our own or that of someone or group with whom we identify.
Relief	A distressing goal-incongruent condition that has changed for the better or gone away.
Hope	Fearing the worst but yearning for better.
Love	Desiring or participating in affection, usually but not necessarily reciprocated.
Compassion	Being moved by another's suffering and wanting to help.

Source: Emotion and Adaptation (p. 122), by R. S. Lazarus, 1991, New York: Oxford University Press. © Reprinted by permission of Oxford University Press.

appraisal that a negative situation can be ameliorated or a positive situation produced, whereas the emotion of sadness is associated with the appraisal that loss is irrevocable. These appraisals are similar to those emphasized by attribution theorists (e.g., Weiner, Chapter 4). What is done here, however, is to put them in the context of motivational, relational encounters and the appraisal processes emphasized in the stress and coping research.

To appreciate the details of Lazarus's model, it may be useful to think of the processes along a time dimension. From this standpoint we can think of a person entering into a situation with specific motives or goals and beliefs about the self and world. Events then occur with implications for the relevant goals and beliefs. This is the relational, person-environment aspect of the model. As part of primary appraisal, the person evaluates the potential harms and benefits relevant to the goals; that is, motivational relevance and consequence are appraised. As part of secondary appraisal, the person evaluates the causes of the event, resources for coping with it, and the implications for the future. The result of these appraisals, expressed in the core relational theme, is the experiencing of a specific emotion and the making of decisions concerning coping efforts. In sum, the person enters into a situation with motives or goals and beliefs about the self and world; and events occur that are appraised (primary and secondary appraisal) in relation to these goals and beliefs, leading to the experience of emotion and coping efforts. This process may be represented as follows:

$$\text{motives} \longrightarrow \text{events} \longrightarrow \text{primary appraisal and secondary appraisal}$$
$$\longrightarrow \text{emotions} \longrightarrow \text{coping}$$

Although useful for representational purposes, a few words of caution should be noted in relation to this process or flow chart. First, the representation might seem to suggest that this is a one-time process, whereas Lazarus suggests that the person is continuously engaged in encountering the environment, making appraisals, experiencing emotions, making coping efforts, and changing goals. This recycling of the process can occur very rapidly. Second, the representation might seem to suggest that a person experiences but one emotion in a situation, whereas in fact many emotions may be experienced, depending on the core relational themes associated with the situation. Thus, clearly it is possible for the person to experience both anger and anxiety, anger and guilt, sadness and compassion, or other combinations of two or more emotions in the same emotional situation. Third, the representation might seem to suggest that this is a rational and conscious process, that is, that the person deliberately and consciously makes these appraisals and decisions. However, Lazarus suggests that this process need not be intentional or conscious. To the contrary, the process can be rapid, automatic, and at times unconscious. Although emotions involve processes of cognitive appraisal, these processes can be automatic and unconscious; that is, the person may experience an emotion without being aware of just why it is being experienced. Keeping in mind the point that this is a much more complex process than can be represented by a flow chart, the representation may still be of use in understanding the processes involved in the experiencing of emotion and efforts at adaptation.

Where does personality enter into this conceptualization? Lazarus's approach is both nomothetic and idiographic, emphasizing common elements to all emotion and adaptation processes as well as the unique meanings and appraisals made by the individual. Personality enters in at every aspect of the process. Individuals differ in the kinds of motives or goals with which they enter into situations, in the kinds of appraisals they are likely to make, and in their preferred coping methods. All of these enter into the emotions that will be experienced. Therefore, it is clear that individuals will differ in the kinds of emotions they experience in specific situations, in the connections they make among the emotions, and in the overall level of experiencing each emotion.

It may be useful at this point to pause and compare Lazarus's views with those presented earlier as part of basic emotions theory. Lazarus's views are similar in that he believes that emotions are part of our evolutionary heritage and serve an adaptive function. For example, the adaptive function of anger is to remove or undo the source of harm, whereas the adaptive function of sadness is to get help and support or disengage from a lost commitment. In addition, Lazarus believes that there are biological, psychological, and sociocultural components to emotion. The biological component involves the physiological response pattern associated with each specific emotion. In addition, each emotion is associated with a feeling state and a tendency toward particular actions. However, the specific emotion experienced depends upon the relational and appraisal components of the process. These components are very much subject to influence by cultural processes and individual experience. The theory of core relational themes suggests that if a person appraises his or her relationship to the environment in a particular way, then a specific emotion results: "The *if* in the formula provides for the flexibility and complexity made possible by intelligence and culture; the *then* provides the biological universal linking cognition to the emotional response" (Smith & Lazarus, 1990, p. 624). Finally, Lazarus would be in agreement with basic emotions theorists in according affect a central place in the organization of personality.

Despite this corresponding emphasis on evolutionary and biological processes, and the importance given to affect in the organization of personality, Lazarus's view is quite different from that of the basic emotion theorists. Most significant is his far greater emphasis on cognitive processes and personal meanings that are regarded as the basis of all emotion. According to basic emotions theorists, cognitive processes can be involved in the activation of specific emotions, but they are not necessarily involved. Emotions can be activated by stimulation of parts of the brain, by biochemical or neurochemical processes, by facial expressions and bodily postures, and by tastes and odors (Izard, 1993a). From this standpoint, cognition is perhaps a sufficient but not a necessary condition for the experiencing of an emotion, at least one of the basic emotions:

> The emotions system preceded the cognitive system in evolution and outpaces it in ontogeny. It is highly adaptive for animals to be able to feel before they think, as in the case where pain elicits withdrawal or pain-induced anger motivates defensive actions. It is equally adaptive for the preverbal infant (as young as 3 weeks) to smile at caregivers and begin establishing attachment bonds that greatly increase the chances of survival.

Izard, 1993a, p. 73

SPOTLIGHT ON THE RESEARCHER

RICHARD S. LAZARUS:

Appraisal and Personal Meaning in Stress, Coping, and Emotion

When I came on the scene in the late 1940s, very few psychologists were interested in stress. I came to see stress, and the emotions associated with it, as a major problem of human adaptation in everyday life. Most of the important struggles and transitions of life, such as going to school; performing in public; taking tests; managing problems at work; getting along with others; dealing with parents, siblings, and teachers; aging; and undergoing life-threatening illness, involve stress. In some ways, however, stress is less important than the way people cope with it; dysfunctional coping makes stress worse and contributes to mental and physical illness.

In addition to purely intellectual issues, an important reason for my interest was personal. I viewed my childhood and adolescence as very stressful, and I felt that my emotions got out of hand too easily. I wanted to understand what was going on in my own life struggles and to be able to apply what I learned to myself and others who needed help.

It soon became evident that the stressful demands of living did not have the same effect on all people. Some showed impairment in their functioning; others showed no evident effects; and the functioning of still others was improved. In contrast to the traditional normative emphasis in psychology, we had to take *individual differences* into account. And as a psychologist with strong clinical interests, I was attracted to general principles that could have application to individuals in trouble. As La Rochefoucauld put it, "It is easier to know man in general than to understand one man in particular."

I became convinced that we needed to understand what it was about individuals as well as the environmental conditions they faced that accounted for whether people suffered from stress and in what ways. My central thesis was that the ways people *appraise* and *cope with* the personal significance of what is happening shape their emotional lives. This thesis is effectively captured in the words Shakespeare put into Hamlet's mouth (Act I, Scene 2), that "There is nothing either good or bad but thinking makes it so." In turn, appraisal and coping, and the emotions they arouse, are influenced by individual differences in *goal hierarchies* and *beliefs about self and world.*

The research I did with motion picture films in the early 1960s demonstrated that if you change the way people construe what is happening in a movie that is disturbing to watch, you can greatly influence the levels of stress they display. *Psychological Stress and the Coping Process,* which I published in 1966, examined theoretical approaches to stress and empirical research on them from this standpoint. I would like to think that this work contributed to the rapid expansion of interest in a cognitive-mediational approach to stress and coping, both in professional and lay circles. It was followed up later in *Stress, Appraisal, and Coping* (1984) by myself and Susan Folkman.

More recently, I presented a cognitive-motivational-relational theory of the emotions in which I examined each emotion from the standpoint of its essential meaning for the individual and the appraisal process that resulted in that meaning (Lazarus, 1991). Since stress involves many different emotions, perhaps as many as 15 or more, studying the emotions people experience in adaptational encounters offers a far more powerful analysis of what is happening psychologically than the study of stress, per se, which is typically treated as a unidimensional variable (Lazarus, 1993b).

Thus, knowing that the reaction is anxiety, anger, guilt, hope, or pride tells us much more about individuals and what they are dealing with in their lives than the knowledge that they are experiencing a particular amount of stress. Each emotion carries a distinctive meaning that the individual constructs about his or her relationships with others. Appraisal and coping have become widely accepted—indeed, dominant—concepts in our present-day efforts to understand the emotional life and its role in adaptation.

Given the changing fads and fashions of psychology, it would be foolhardy to predict the future. Instead, statements about what we might hope for would be more sensible. I hope that in the future there will be a greater willingness on the part of psychologists to study what psychology has repeatedly shied away from—namely, the personal, relational meanings that lie behind our emotions and, indeed, much of what we do to cope. Complex, evaluative judgments, called *appraisals*, produce these meanings. How this works then becomes a central theoretical and research task.

I also hope that the coping process, which refers to the diverse ways we adapt to the world and regulate our emotions, will continue to stimulate research interest. The measurement of coping and its effectiveness in facilitating adaptation are among the most important riddles on which a thorough understanding of our emotional lives depends (Lazarus, 1993a).

But it is not enough to study coping and emotion interindividually (between persons) or via questionnaires. In-depth study, which is costly and time consuming, is needed, in which the construction of meaning and the coping process are studied intraindividually (within the same person, over time and across situations). The great challenge now is to examine the processes involved naturalistically, longitudinally, and in depth, while paying close attention to evidence of unconscious processes, such as ego defenses that may lie beneath the surface of our actions and reactions.

In the next section we turn to the implications of emotion and adaptation for psychological and physical health. First, however, it may be worthwhile highlighting again some of the major components of Lazarus's approach since they relate to themes developed in earlier chapters. First, there is an emphasis on both biological and psychological processes. Second, there is an emphasis on both cognitive and motivational (goal) processes. Third, there is an emphasis on individual-environment relationships and processes, including recognition of the importance of personality and situation or context variables. As a result, people are understood to be both stable and varying in their emotional responses and coping efforts. Fourth, his approach is both nomothetic and idiographic, emphasizing principles common to the adaptive efforts of all individuals as well as the unique meanings people are capable of attaching to events (Table 10.5).

EMOTION, ADAPTATION, AND HEALTH

Lazarus suggests that the kinds of emotions we experience and the ways in which we cope with life's stresses have implications for psychological and physical health.

TABLE 10.5   Major Elements of Lazarus's Approach to Emotion and Adaptation

1. Both biological and psychological processes emphasized.
2. Both cognitive and motivational processes emphasized.
3. Emphasis on individual-environment relationships.
4. Emphasis on both stability and change, personality and context, in emotional responses and coping efforts.
5. Approach is both nomothetic and idiographic.

The view that mind and body are interconnected is not new. In more recent times, psychoanalysts suggested that psychological conflicts could result in disturbances in bodily functioning, what are called *psychosomatic disorders* (Alexander, 1950). In these cases, the psyche, or mind, is influencing the soma, or body. What is important to recognize is that the disturbance in bodily functioning is real, as, for example, in disorders such as hypertension and ulcers. In the psychoanalytic view of the time, specific psychological conflicts were associated with specific physical disorders. For example, conflicts over dependency needs and the wish to be fed might result in stomach ulcers. This view ran into difficulties when it was hard to demonstrate empirically what was suggested by some clinical observation—a link between specific conflicts and specific physical disorders. More recently there has been a return to interest in the link between mind and body, although current approaches are more empirical and no longer based on the psychoanalytic model. In addition, there is an effort to determine the exact link between psychological processes and bodily processes, that is, to understand and measure the biological processes intervening between thoughts or feelings and the formation of illness (Contrada, Leventhal, & O'Leary, 1990).

We have already seen in earlier chapters evidence of efforts to link psychological processes to psychological and physical well-being. For example, suggestions were made of links between the Type A behavior pattern and risk for coronary heart disease; between internal, stable, and global attributions for negative events and depression; between low self-efficacy beliefs and poorer functioning of the immunological system; between self-ideal and self-ought discrepancies and poorer functioning of the immunological system; and between goal conflicts and more frequent psychological and physical complaints. Research in each of these areas continues. Current evidence suggests that hostility is the toxic element of Type A behavior (Contrada, Leventhal, & O'Leary, 1990). In addition, the Type A style of vigorous, explosive speech and the potential for hostility has been contrasted to a Type C or cancer-prone personality (Temoshok, 1987). Whereas the Type A individual is angry, hostile, and explosive, the Type C person has an emotionally avoidant style, particularly in relation to negative affects. Whereas the Type A individual presents the picture of someone tense and ready to explode, the Type C person presents a pleasant, cheerful, or impassive face to the world. And, although not very robust, there is evidence that the Type A person is at somewhat greater risk for the development of coronary heart disease, and the Type C person is at somewhat greater risk for the development of cancer (Contrada et al., 1990). In each case the suggestion is made that there is a constitutional, predisposing factor that interacts with particular emotional struggles and coping efforts to produce physiological responses detrimental to the well-being of the person. More generally, there is growing evidence that stress and negative affect are related to poorer immunological system functioning and greater susceptibility to infectious disease (Cohen, Tyrrell, & Smith, 1993; Cohen & Williamson, 1991; A. O'Leary, 1990).

In the sections that follow, we consider three areas of investigation concerning the relation between personality and health: optimism, negative affectivity, and suppression of emotion. These three areas currently are active areas of research and can be related to content covered earlier in the text.

OPTIMISM AND HEALTH: THE POWER OF POSITIVE THINKING

In recent years books on the best-seller list have suggested that optimism and positive mood are good for your health (Cousins, 1979; Siegel, 1986). Is there evidence to substantiate such claims? Is there evidence of the power of positive thinking? Over much of the past decade, Scheier and Carver (1993) have been investigating the relation between optimism and health. **Optimism** is defined as the belief that good, as opposed to bad, things will generally occur in one's life. We have already come across the work of Scheier and Carver in relation to their research on public and private self-consciousness (Chapter 8) and their control theory of goal-directed functioning (Chapter 9). As part of their theory, they suggest that positive affect is associated with the rate of movement toward goals and negative affect with the rate of movement away from goals (Carver & Scheier, 1990). In other words, emotions are related to goals and reflect "how things are going" in relation to goals. Emotion is tied not only to experienced rate of movement toward or away from goals but to expectancies concerning progress. Thus, positive emotion is associated not only with actual goal progress but with expected progress, and negative emotion is experienced in relation to negative expectancies concerning progress.

In addition to situation-specific expectancies, Scheier and Carver suggest that people develop generalized expectancies, a view similar to that suggested by Rotter (Chapter 3). Optimism, then, is seen as an important personality characteristic involving generalized expectancies concerning the future. People are viewed as falling along a continuum from pessimists (people who generally expect bad things to occur) at one end to optimists (people who generally expect good things to happen) at the other end. A test has been developed to measure individual differences on this continuum, the Life Orientation Test, or LOT (Scheier & Carver, 1985; Table 10.6). Research suggests that individual differences along the pessimism-optimism dimension are relatively stable over periods as long as 3 years, even in the face of individual catastrophe (Scheier & Carver, 1987, 1993). Although there is some evidence that the LOT scale could be used to identify people along two separate dimensions, an optimism dimension and a pessimism dimension, Scheier and Carver have decided to view optimism and pessimism as opposite poles of a single dimension.

Do individuals differing in dispositional optimism, defined by scores on the LOT, differ in their psychological and physical well-being? According to Scheier and Carver, a growing number of studies suggest that "optimists routinely maintain higher levels

TABLE 10.6   Illustrative Items from the Life Orientation Test (LOT)

1. In uncertain times, I usually expect the best.
2. I always look on the bright side of things.
3. I'm a believer in the idea that "every cloud has a silver lining."
4. I rarely count on good things happening to me. (Reverse scoring)

Source: Scheier, M. F., & Carver, C. S. (1985). Optimism, coping, and health: Assessment and implications of generalized outcome expectancies. *Health Psychology, 4,* 219–247.

of subjective well-being during times of stress than do people who are less optimistic" (1993, p. 27). For example, optimists have been found to adjust better than pessimists to the transition to college, and optimism has been found to be associated with lower levels of distress in women with breast cancer (Aspinwall & Taylor, 1992; Carver et al., 1993.) But the effects of optimism seem to extend beyond making people feel better. In research on the implications of this personality characteristic for physical well-being, dispositional optimism was studied in relation to recovery from coronary artery bypass surgery (CABS). Dispositional optimism was assessed prior to surgery and related to patient physical recovery and general well-being 6–8 days and 6 months postoperatively. Dispositional optimism was found to be associated with a faster rate of physical recovery during the period of hospitalization, with a faster rate of return to normal life activities subsequent to discharge, and with postsurgical quality of life 6 months later (Scheier et al., 1989). In sum, dispositional optimism had a broad effect on patient recovery from CABS. Note that in this case not just self-report data were used, but behavioral data concerning recovery as well. In sum, there is evidence for the importance of dispositional optimism for both psychological and physical well-being.

How is one to account for this relationship? Scheier and Carver suggest that coping mechanisms play an important role in mediating the effects of optimism on well-being (Carver et al., 1993; Scheier & Carver, 1993). Their research in this area began with investigation of the relation between individual differences in optimism-pessimism and methods of coping. Building on the distinction made by Lazarus and his co-workers between problem-focused coping (i.e., action that has the goal of removing or circumventing the source of stress) and emotion-focused coping (i.e., attempts to reduce or eliminate the emotional distress associated with a situation), they suggested that both situational factors and personality factors would influence choices of coping devices. In terms of situations, problem-focused coping is more likely in situations in which people believe that something can be done about the source of stress, emotion-focused coping is more likely when people believe that little can be done about the situation. Optimists and pessimists would be expected to differ in the strategies they use to cope with stress, optimists being more likely to use problem-focused coping methods and pessimists emotion-focused coping methods.

In a test of these relationships, subjects completed the LOT and the Ways of Coping Scale. Subjects were asked to describe the most stressful situation they have encountered in the last 2 months and the extent to which they thought the situation was controllable. Optimism scores then were correlated with scores for various coping

I happen to believe a nasty disposition is good for your health.

Optimism and Health. Research suggests a relation between methods of coping with stress and health. Generally, a positive, optimistic disposition appears to be better for one's health than a negative, pessimistic disposition.

mechanisms for situations described as controllable, situations described as uncontrollable, and across all situations. Optimism was found to be positively associated with problem-focused coping, especially when the situation was perceived to be controllable.

In a follow-up of this result, Scheier and Carver had subjects complete the LOT and, several weeks later, indicate how they would respond to five hypothetical situations described as being stressful but potentially controllable. One situation read as follows:

> It is a week before finals begin. You look in the exam schedule, and suddenly realize that three of your five final exams are on the same day. All three courses are the ones that you have been finding difficult. As it happens, all three courses are in your major.

Scheier, Weintraub, & Carver, 1986, p. 1261

LOT scores were correlated with scores for the use of various coping methods, derived from the subjects' descriptions of how they would respond to each of the five situations. As can be seen in Table 10.7, optimism was significantly associated

TABLE 10.7   **Correlations Between Optimism and Dimensions of Coping**

The correlations indicate a positive association between optimism and active coping, and a negative association with disengagement and focusing on/expressing feelings forms of coping.

Coping dimension	Correlations
Problem-focused coping	.14[a]
Suppression of competing activities	.21[b]
Seeking social support	.20[b]
Focusing on/expressing feelings	− .21[b]
Disengagement	− .30[b]
Positive reinterpretation	.07
Self-blame	− .09

[a] $p < .05.$ [b] $p < .01.$

Source: "Coping With Stress: Divergent Strategies of Optimists and Pessimists," by M. F. Scheier, J. K. Weintraub, and C. S. Carver, 1986, *Journal of Personality and Social Psychology, 51,* p. 1261. Copyright 1986 by the American Psychological Association. Reprinted by permission.

with problem-focused coping and the suppression of competing activities and was negatively associated with emotion-focused coping (i.e., tendency to focus on and express feelings; tendency to disengage) (Scheier, Weintraub, & Carver, 1986).

In later research designed to study the relation between dispositional optimism and coping, Scheier and Carver developed their own measure of coping styles (COPE) and administered this to subjects along with the LOT, Rotter's Internal-External Locus of Control Scale (Chapter 3), and a number of other personality measures. Once more, optimism was positively associated with active coping and planning, and negatively associated with the focus on emotions, denial, and disengagement. Internal locus of control followed a similar but by no means identical pattern of relationships (Carver, Scheier, & Weintraub, 1989; Table 10.8).

Returning to the breast cancer study noted earlier in which optimism was related to lower levels of distress, subjects completed the COPE scales in terms of how they responded to the stressors associated with diagnosis and surgery. Optimism was positively associated with accepting the reality of the situation, humor, and making the best of things. It was negatively associated with denial, avoidance, and disengagement from coping efforts. The evidence suggested that the differences in coping efforts served as the vehicle by which optimistic women were less vulnerable than pessimistic women to distress (Carver et al., 1993).

What is to be concluded from this research? Scheier and Carver suggest the following:

Research from a variety of sources is beginning to suggest that optimists cope in more adaptive ways than do pessimists. Optimists are more likely than pessimists to take direct action to solve their problems, are more planful in

TABLE 10.8   Correlations Between Coping Scales and Measures of Optimism and Locus of Control

The correlations indicate an association between optimism and active coping, and a negative association between optimism and focus on emotions, denial, and disengagement. Similar but not identical relationships hold for internal locus of control.

COPE scales	Optimism ($n = 476$)	Control ($n = 476$)
Active coping	.32[b]	.21[b]
Planning	.25[b]	.14[b]
Suppression of competing activities	.08	.04
Restraint coping	.20[b]	.09
Seeking social support—instrumental	.10[a]	.02
Seeking social support—emotional	.07	−.07
Positive reinterpretation and growth	.41[b]	.16[b]
Acceptance	.19[b]	.02
Turning to religion	.15[b]	−.02
Focus on and ventilation of emotions	−.11[a]	−.16[b]
Denial	−.27[b]	−.19[b]
Behavioral disengagement	−.34[b]	−.20[b]
Mental disengagement	−.14[b]	−.12[b]
Alcohol-drug disengagement	−.11[a]	−.02

[a] $p < .05$, two-tailed. [b] $p < .01$, two-tailed.

Source: "Assessing Coping Strategies: A Theoretically Based Approach," by C. S. Carver, M. F. Scheier, and J. K. Weintraub, 1989, *Journal of Personality and Social Psychology, 56,* p. 276. Copyright 1989 by the American Psychological Association. Reprinted by permission.

dealing with the adversity they confront, and are more focused *in their coping efforts.* Optimists are more likely to accept the reality of the stressful situations they encounter, and they also seem intent on growing personally from negative experiences and trying to make the best of bad situations. In contrast to these positive coping reactions, pessimists are more likely than optimists to react to stressful events by trying to deny that they exist or by trying to avoid dealing with problems. Pessimists are also more likely to quit trying when difficulties arise.

1993, pp. 27–28

Implicit in this statement is the suggestion that optimism is good for people, and the authors go on to ask whether this is always true. They suggest that generally optimism is good although it can lead to poorer outcomes if one is overly optimistic in unproductive ways (e.g., sitting and waiting for good things to happen) or if it is used inflexibly in uncontrollable situations for which emotion-focused coping may be more adaptive. However, they also note that research suggests that optimists seem to be directed toward active coping rather than passive waiting and denial, and they seem to be able to be flexible in their use of coping methods when situations preclude more active, problem-focused efforts. Thus, they conclude that optimism is beneficial for mental and physical functioning.

NEUROTICISM AND NEGATIVE AFFECTIVITY

In this section we consider the personality construct of **negative affectivity (NA)** or the disposition to experience aversive emotional states such as anxiety and depression (as well as other negative affects such as anger, disgust, and contempt), to have a negative view of the self, and to be introspective and dwell on the negative side of the self and the world (L. A. Clark & Watson, 1991; D. Watson & Clark, 1984, 1992, 1993). NA is viewed as a personality trait expressing a general negative condition across situations and over time. It is seen as being related to the traits of neuroticism and anxiety and has been found to be associated with clinical anxiety and depression (D. Watson, Clark, & Carey, 1988), but it is broader in its manifestations. Individuals high on NA are not seen as *unable* to experience joy, excitement, or enthusiasm. Rather, the high NA individual is defined in terms of the *tendency* to experience negative emotions, distress, and upset. This point is important because it suggests two dimensions of affect, positive affect (PA) and negative affect (NA); and individuals can be high on one, the other, or both. For example, a person may have many experiences of both joy and distress, primarily joy or distress, or rarely experience either.

What is the relation of NA to health? Clearly, NA is associated with distress and poor psychological well-being. It is related to marital and job dissatisfaction and to high levels of perceived stress and conflict. But what about physical health? Here we find a relation between NA and reports of health complaints. But, and here we come to an interesting and important twist, a number of studies report that NA (and neuroticism) is related more to health complaints than to actual physical disease (Costa & McCrae, 1987; D. Watson, 1988; D. Watson & Pennebaker, 1989). In other words, although NA may be related to health complaints, one cannot automatically assume a corresponding relation between NA and actual health difficulties such as hypertension or lowered immunological system functioning. In fact, evidence is reported to suggest that NA is largely unrelated to coronary disease, cancer, or probability of death (Watson & Pennebaker, 1989).

The following portrait is presented of individuals high on NA:

> They complain of angina but show no evidence of greater coronary risk or pathology. They complain of headaches but do not report any increased use of aspirin. They report all kinds of physical problems but are not especially likely to visit their doctor or to miss work or school. In general, they complain about their health but show no hard evidence of poor health or increased mortality.

D. Watson & Pennebaker, 1989, p. 244

In sum, to establish a relation between a personality variable such as NA and health, there must be measures of health that are independent of subjective self-report.

Now, we come to a rather interesting question. It might have struck the reader that NA seems to have characteristics similar to other personality concepts previously discussed. Neuroticism has already been mentioned, but one could also note a similarity to the depressive attributional style. Indeed, it is suggested that NA is related to the tendency to make internal, stable, and global attributions for negative events (L. A. Clark & Watson, 1991). Therefore, attributional style is seen as a component of NA rather than as some independent variable. But what of optimism-pessimism? Doesn't the individual high on NA seem rather pessimistic? Indeed, here too it is suggested that "of all the constructs that we are considering, optimism-pessimism is perhaps the one most clearly synonymous with NA. Certainly the two constructs overlap conceptually" (L. A. Clark & Watson, 1991, p. 228). But, if NA and pessimism-optimism are so closely related, why don't measures of NA duplicate some of the findings associated with use of the LOT?

At the present time we do not have a satisfactory answer to this interesting and troubling question. It may be that NA emphasizes negative affect, and positive affect is the important component of optimism. In other words, it may be that one is not the reverse of the other and that more attention has to be paid to the relation between positive and negative affects rather than just to one or the other type of affect alone. Some support for such a point of view comes from research on the adjustment of students to college where it was found that negative mood and positive mood were distinct variables with different relationships to coping methods. For example, positive mood was related to active coping and the seeking of social support whereas negative mood was related to avoidance (Aspinwall & Taylor, 1992). Such research suggests that the positive mood part of optimism may be more critical than the absence of negative mood to successful coping and health.

Scheier and Carver reject the view that optimism is related to attributional style or to neuroticism and negative affectivity. They suggest that optimism has a demonstrated relation to physical health, beyond self-reports of health complaints, and comes out as a different variable than neuroticism or anxiety in analyses of scores on multiple personality measures (Scheier et al., 1989). At this point we are left with a question to be answered by further research!

In sum, the concept of NA is important because of its presentation as a broad trait variable related to psychological distress and reports of somatic complaints. Research on NA is important because it suggests the need for objective measures of health in addition to self-report measures to establish personality–physical health relationships. In addition, it raises the important, if at times troubling question of the relation among personality concepts; that is, to what extent are concepts with different names independent, overlapping, or identical concepts?

SUPPRESSION OF THOUGHTS AND EMOTIONS: WHAT HAPPENS WHEN PEOPLE TRY NOT TO THINK OR FEEL CERTAIN THINGS?

The image of psychoanalytic therapy, with some degree of accuracy, is that it promotes the free expression of feeling. Is such free expression of feeling desirable and is the suppression or denial of feeling necessarily bad for your health? This has become a quite fascinating area of investigation and will be the focus of concern in this section. But first, let us begin with the questions of how able we are to control and suppress our thoughts and feelings and what happens when we try to do so.

Wegner's Research on the Effects of Thought Suppression

Let us begin this part of the story with a discussion of Daniel Wegner's research program on the effects of thought suppression. In his beginning research in this area, Wegner had subjects verbalize their stream of consciousness for a 5-minute period during which they were asked not to think of a white bear. Reporting their stream of consciousness by speaking into a tape recorder, they were to ring a bell every time they said "white bear" or a "white bear" came to mind. This was designated as the suppression session. Following this, subjects were asked to report their stream of consciousness into a tape recorder and ring the bell whenever they mentioned or had the thought of "white bear." In other words, the second session was identical to the first except that in this session, called the expression session, they were asked to "try to think of a white bear." Another group of subjects was given the identical directions except that they experienced the expression session first and the suppression section second.

What might one guess about the frequency of "white bear" thoughts and mentions? Would the frequency differ in expression as opposed to suppression sessions? Would it make a difference which session was experienced first? Subjects did have more frequent "white bear" thoughts and mentions in the expression sessions than in the suppression sessions. This probably comes as no surprise. However, what was striking was the difficulty subjects had in suppressing "white bear" thoughts. Subjects reported thinking about a white bear more than once per minute when instructed to try not to think of a white bear! What was even more striking, however, was the effect of initial thought suppression. Subjects in the expression session following suppression reported far more "white bear" thoughts than did subjects in the expression session when this session occurred first. As indicated in Figure 10.3, what was particularly striking was that the frequency of bell rings, indicating "white bear" thoughts, increased over the course of the 5-minute period in the expression period following suppression, whereas the frequency of bell rings decreased over time in every other measurement period (in the initial expression group for both periods and the initial suppression group for the suppression period). In other words, initial suppression produced a rebound effect or surge in "white bear" thoughts during the following expression period, an effect that increased during the 5-minute period. Thus, the researchers noted the paradoxical effect of thought suppression producing a preoccupation with the suppressed thought, something that probably comes as no surprise to any student who has tried to suppress thoughts about food while trying to diet (Wegner, Schneider, Carter, & White, 1987).

So much for "white bear" thoughts. But what of more interesting thoughts, thoughts that have feelings associated with them? Exciting thoughts? In a follow-up experiment, Wegner (Wegner, Shortt, Blake, & Page, 1990) had subjects think aloud as they followed instructions to think about or not think about the following topics: sex, dancing, the subject's mother (Mom), and the university's dean of students (Dean). Once more subjects were asked to report whatever came to mind while speaking into a tape recorder. In the thought suppression period, subjects were asked to report when a thought came to mind. For example, in relation to the suppression of sexual thoughts, subjects were told "Please continue, but now do not think about sex; if the thought comes to mind, please mention it." This was in contrast to the

Figure 10.3   Bell rings per minute over the 5-minute periods.

This chart depicts the number of bell rings per minute, indicating "white bear" thoughts, during 5-minute expression and suppression periods for two groups of subjects (expression following suppression and suppression following expression). Reports of "white bear" thoughts only increased during the expression period that followed suppression, suggesting a surge or rebound effect due to the earlier efforts at suppression.

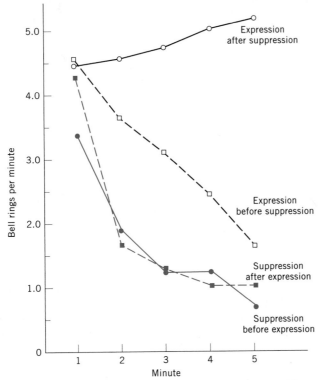

(From "Paradoxical Effects of Thought Suppression," by D. M. Wegner, D. J. Schneider, S. R. Carter, and T. L. White, 1987, *Journal of Personality and Social Psychology, 53*, p. 8. Copyright 1987 by the American Psychological Association. Reprinted by permission.)

expression period when subjects were instructed "Please continue, but now do think about sex; if the thought comes to mind, please mention it." In addition to the monitoring of the relevant thoughts, ongoing skin conductance levels were assessed as a measure of arousal. In sum, this study compared the effects of efforts to suppress an exciting thought (i.e., sex) to efforts to suppress more neutral thoughts (e.g., dancing, Mom, Dean) and had a physiological measure of arousal as well as recordings of thought frequency.

What might the results look like? Would frequency of thought during the suppression period differ among the four topics? And, what of the measure of arousal? Would arousal levels differ among the four topics? In other words, would suppression instructions have a differential effect on exciting thoughts as opposed to neutral thoughts? First, in relation to the thought frequency measure, once more it was found that thoughts about the topic were more frequent during expression than during suppression, but that even during suppression the thoughts did not go away. But, perhaps much to one's surprise, the pattern or results for thoughts of sex were no different from those for the neutral topics; that is, the thought frequency measure gave no indication that sexual thoughts were any more difficult to express or suppress than the less exciting thoughts. However, a strikingly different pattern was noted in relation to the skin conductance level measure of arousal. As seen in Figure 10.4, here there was a greater increase in arousal (deviation of skin conductance level from baseline) when the thought was sex than was true for any of the other thoughts. Arousal was even greater during the suppression period of thoughts about sex than during the expression period, although this difference was not statistically significant (Wegner, Shortt, Blake, & Page, 1990).

Wegner (1992, 1994) concludes from this and additional research that the suppression of an exciting thought—the thought of sex—can promote excitement and later intrusions of the exciting thought. Indeed, an exciting thought may be even more stimulating after suppression than during free expression. Not only are people not always able to control their thoughts, but often they are unable to control their emotions. The implications of these results are described as follows:

> The suppression of exciting thoughts, from this perspective, may be responsible for the perpetuation of unwanted emotional reactions. . . . The person tries to

Figure 10.4   Deviation of skin conductance level from baseline (in μmhos) during the suppression or expression of four target thoughts.

This graph illustrates increases in arousal (deviation of skin conduction level from baseline) during periods of suppression or expression of sexual thoughts, in contrast with suppression or expression of other thoughts.

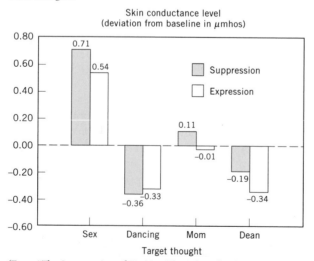

(From "The Suppression of Exciting Thoughts," by D. M. Wegner, G. W. Shortt, A. W. Blake, and M. S. Page, 1990, *Journal of Personality and Social Psychology, 58,* p. 412. Copyright 1990 by the American Psychological Association. Reprinted by permission.)

suppress the exciting thought and so introduces a new measure of excitement. With the emotion newly charged, the motive to suppress further is itself energized, and the process recycles to produce yet a more powerful emotional response. . . . In other words, thought suppression may be a necessary part of the development of phobia, panic, and inappropriate anxiety. Unfortunately, what people believe to be the medicine turns out to produce the disease. A similar conclusion might be reached regarding the perpetuation of positive emotional responses such as infatuations, addictions, or obsessions.

Wegner et al., 1990, p. 417

It is important to note that Wegner distinguishes between the concept of suppression and the Freudian concept of repression. Whereas **suppression** involves the intentional, conscious removal of a thought from attention, repression involves the unintentional, unconscious removal of a thought from attention and memory: "Suppression is a street battle raging in the forefront of the mind, not a few random muggings hidden deep in its alleyways" (Wegner, 1992, p. 195). In addition, whereas Freudian theory emphasizes the defensive aspects of the process of repression, Wegner suggests that the effects of efforts at thought suppression are consequences of normal cognitive processes. According to what he calls *ironic process theory,* Wegner (1994) suggests that under conditions of time pressure or stress, efforts at mental control produce unintended, ironic effects, that is, effects that are the very opposite of those that are desired.

Pennebaker's Research on the Effects of the Inhibition of Emotion

But can the suppression of thoughts and emotions affect the body? Conversely, can the confiding of thoughts and expression of feeling have therapeutic effects for health? Here we turn to the research of James Pennebaker. In an initial piece of research, Pennebaker found that subjects who tried to be deceptive showed evidence of tension in their overt behaviors (changes in eye movement and facial expression) and in their level of physiological arousal. The suggestion was made that long-term inhibition might be a factor in psychosomatic disease (Pennebaker & Chew, 1985). This suggestion fit with the general model of psychosomatic disorders previously noted; that is, the inhibiting or holding back of thoughts and feelings is associated with stress and the potential for disease. Following this, Pennebaker set out to examine whether the reverse could occur, that is, whether the expression of thoughts and feelings associated with stress could reduce the negative effects of inhibition. His hypothesis was that actively confronting upsetting experiences, through writing or talking, would reduce the negative effects of inhibition. In the research he had healthy undergraduates write about either traumatic experiences or superficial topics for four days (Pennebaker, Kiecolt-Glaser, & Glaser, 1988). Would writing about traumatic experiences have therapeutic effects? To determine whether writing about one or the other topic had a differential effect on health, Pennebaker recorded the number of health center visits during a 15-week period prior to the study and a 6-week period following the four days of writing. In addition, he took measures of immune system functioning, blood pressure levels, and subjective distress.

It is hard to believe that just writing about traumatic experiences during a 4-day period could have profound effects on health. Yet, this is exactly what was found. As indicated in Figure 10.5, students writing about their traumatic experiences showed a decline in health center visits during the study, whereas the control group, those who were writing about superficial experiences, showed an increase in health center visits. In addition, similar differential effects favoring the group writing about traumatic experiences were shown for measures of immune system functioning, blood pressure level, and subjective distress. Beyond this, the subjects writing about traumas were divided into two groups: one that had written about topics they had previously not discussed (high disclosers), and the other that did not write about such topics (low disclosers). The greatest health improvements were shown by the high disclosers, that is, by those who wrote about topics they had previously held back from telling others (Pennebaker, Kiecolt-Glaser, & Glaser, 1988).

Pennebaker concluded from this research that "opening up" or confiding in others has healing power (Pennebaker, 1990). He went on to study the effects of opening up in real-life crisis situations such as the San Francisco earthquake (1989) and the Gulf War (1991). What he did was to follow the course of people's thoughts, discussions, and dreams during the weeks following each crisis. After the San Francisco earthquake, he interviewed by phone residents of California and Texas. Individuals were called at random and interviewed for a 10-minute period 1, 2, 3, 6, 8, 16, 28, or 50 weeks after the earthquake. Respondents were asked how many times they had talked about and had thought about the earthquake during the previous 24 hours

Figure 10.5   Mean health center illness visits for the periods before and during the experiment. (Note that the standard deviation for visits per month ranged from .12 to .40, averaging .26 over the four observations.)

The data illustrate how students writing about their traumatic experiences (trauma group) showed a decline in health center visits, whereas the students writing about superficial experiences (control group) showed an increase in health center visits. (The latter increase probably reflected normal seasonal illness rates during the period of investigation.)

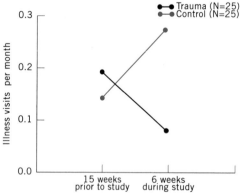

(From "Disclosure of Traumas and Immune Function: Health Implications for Psychotherapy," by J. W. Pennebaker, J. K. Kiecolt-Glaser, and R. Glaser, 1988, *Journal of Consulting and Clinical Psychology, 56,* p. 243. Copyright 1988 by the American Psychological Association. Reprinted by permission.)

as well as about their moods and interpersonal relationships. The data indicated that Bay Area residents talked and thought about the earthquake to a considerable extent during the first 2 weeks following the event. However, during the next 5 weeks respondents greatly reduced their discussions yet many continued thinking about the quake. In other words, for many there was a shift from talking and thinking about the event to only thinking about it. During this period, roughly weeks 3 through 8 following the quake, subjects reported an increase in negative moods as well as arguments with family members and co-workers. In addition, they reported an increase in dreams about the quake. These increases did not occur for the respondents in the other cities, those not directly affected by the quake. In addition, aggravated assault rates greatly increased in the Bay Area during this period. These increased signs of distress disappeared, however, approximately 8 weeks after the catastrophe.

Parallel findings occurred in relation to the Gulf War. In this case there was a random calling of Dallas residents each week of the war and in the 6 weeks following its conclusion. In addition, college students and respondents to a newspaper questionnaire were sampled during this period. As indicated in Figure 10.6, once more subjects reported talking and thinking about the war during the initial 2 weeks of the war, but then there was a great drop in their talk relative to their thoughts. This was true for all three samples. In addition, again following the earlier results, during the

Figure 10.6   Self-reported number of thoughts and conversations in the previous 24 hours concerning the Persian Gulf War among 361 Dallas-area residents (approximately 30 respondents at each time point). To control for extreme responses, subjects who reported thinking or talking about the war more than 25 times in the previous 24 hours were assigned a value of 25 times.
This chart illustrates that during the first few weeks following a crisis situation (Gulf War), there is both thinking and talk about the event, and then a greater drop in talk relative to thoughts in the following weeks.

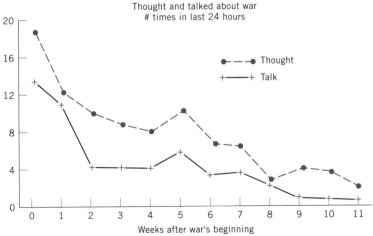

(From "Social Mechanisms of Constraint," by J. W. Pennebaker, 1993, in *Handbook of Mental Control,* p. 214, by D. W. Wegner and J. W. Pennebaker, Eds., Englewood Cliffs, NJ: Prentice Hall. Copyright 1993. Reprinted by permission of Prentice-Hall, Inc., Englewood Cliffs, NJ.)

3rd to 8th week there was an increase in reports of physical symptoms, anxiety, arguments, and war-related dreams (Figure 10.7) (Pennebaker, 1993).

What is one to conclude from such findings? Pennebaker (1993) proposes a three-stage model of coping with trauma. During the first stage, an emergency phase, people's thoughts and talk revolve around the trauma. This provides a level of social support. During the second stage, an inhibition phase, thoughts continue to revolve around the trauma but relevant talk declines. Often this is because others are reluctant to continue the talking. Pennebaker suggests that during this phase there may be a conspiracy of silence. Thus, about 4 weeks after the Bay Area earthquake, T-shirts began appearing with the saying "Thank you for not sharing your earthquake experience." Because of these social constraints, people may be forced to inhibit their feelings, with untoward consequences for health and well-being. Finally, in the third stage, called the adaptation phase, there is a reduction in thoughts as well as talk and a reduction in stress. Presumably the time required for each phase varies according to the event and the trauma involved.

Pennebaker's research calls to mind Emmons's work mentioned earlier in relation to goals and action. This research emphasized conflict over emotional expression, with the implications of such conflict for well-being (Emmons et al., 1993). It perhaps also may be related to work assessing the implications of the defense mechanism of repression for health. Research suggests that repressors show greater physiological reactivity to threat than do individuals who allow for more conscious recognition of feelings (Weinberger, 1990). While such comparisons can be made, Pennebaker himself does not view the processes he is investigating as comparable to those associated with the psychoanalytic concept of repression.

Figure 10.7   Percentage of San Francisco residents (n = 175) who reported at least one dream about the earthquake in the previous week and the percentage of Dallas residents (n = 281) reporting at least one dream about the war. The x-axis refers to the number of weeks following the earthquake (for the San Francisco sample) and the outbreak of the Persian Gulf War (for the Dallas sample).
This chart illustrates the increase in dreams about a crisis situation during the period when talk declines relative to thoughts (see Figure 10.6).

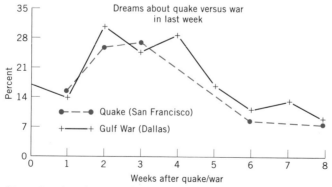

(From "Social Mechanisms of Constraint," by J. W. Pennebaker, 1993, in *Handbook of Mental Control,* p. 215, by D. W. Wegner and J. W. Pennebaker, Eds., Englewood Cliffs, NJ: Prentice Hall. Copyright 1993. Reprinted by permission of Prentice-Hall, Inc., Englewood Cliffs, NJ.)

SPOTLIGHT ON THE RESEARCHER

JAMES W. PENNEBAKER:
The Healing Powers of Confiding in Others

How did I ever begin studying disclosure and health? I suppose I was guided by a number of seemingly unrelated observations that intuitively were related. From childhood, I remember being mesmerized by religious faith healers I saw on television. The ritual, the prayers, and the fervent beliefs of the healer and "healee" all worked together to bring about seemingly magical health improvements. After I went to college, I noticed that whenever there were major conflicts with my parents (I was a hippie; they weren't), I tended to get sick when I would return home for a visit. Later, I discovered how writing about my feelings seemed to improve my mood and even how I felt. As a young faculty member, some interviews I had with polygraphers from the FBI revealed that after people confessed to their crimes, they became physiologically relaxed.

As I thought about all of these phenomena, a common theme emerged: Not talking about your problems is bad; confronting them is good. Many famous writers, philosophers, and psychologists knew this long before I did. In fact, I suspect that my grandmother told me this as a child. So what is the big deal?

In almost all primitive cultures, people know that there is a close link between mental and physical health. In our culture for the last century, we have mindlessly adopted a simple medical model of health: All physical illnesses must have physical causes and, therefore, benefit from physical treatments. Now, we profess surprise at learning that emotions and stressors directly or indirectly influence every system within our bodies. The fact that disclosure influences physical health is surprising only if we think that the mind and body are independent entities. Putting traumatic or emotional experiences into words—as we see in writing, praying, undergoing psychotherapy, talking with friends, or confessing to the police—helps to organize our thoughts and feelings, thereby reducing the biological upheavals of stress.

I am particularly excited by some future directions within the disclosure and health world. What kind of people naturally disclose their feelings and who are those people who naturally clam up? Recent work in behavior genetics and childhood shyness points to some powerful early determinants. Other research is hinting that people may be most at risk for health problems if they are naturally open and talkative but are punished for voicing their true feelings.

At least two other potential gold mines exist for future personality researchers. First, we need to better understand language in natural human interactions. What is it about putting emotional experiences into words that influences both the experiences and the emotions themselves? Second, we must explore the role of culture in defining and interpreting personality and behaviors to a far greater degree. Are some personalities physically and mentally healthier in some societies and not others?

And while future personality researchers are at it, perhaps they could also figure out when, why, and for whom faith healing works.

Summary

In sum, a variety of lines of research, from differing theoretical perspectives, combine to suggest that emotional inhibition, whether conscious (i.e., suppression) or unconscious (i.e., repression), can have negative health consequences. It would appear that active coping efforts, the use of social support, and reasonable levels of emotional regulation are generally useful and positive for one's health. On the other hand, efforts to suppress, inhibit, or deny emotions that leave the person in conflict and inner turmoil appear to have negative consequences for health.

CONCLUSION

We now have come full circle in our discussion of emotion, adaptation, and health. The topic of emotion has been brought back to center stage as an area of interest, both in its own right as well as in terms of its implications for thoughts, motivation, and health. In addition, recognition has been given to the importance of people's efforts to cope with external and internal sources of stress. Finally, the implications of affect and coping for psychological and physical well-being have been illustrated.

In each of these areas we see the study of processes that hold for all individuals as well as emphasis on the importance of individual differences. In each of these areas we see evidence of the influence of situations or context as well as the importance of individual styles or dispositions. Thus, although certain emotions are more likely in some situations than in others, individuals vary in the likelihood of their experiencing particular emotions. And, although some coping mechanisms are more likely in some situations than others, individuals vary in their characteristic use of different coping devices. Finally, although there is evidence of stages in the process of adapting to trauma, individuals differ in the intensity and duration of the stages, as well as the consequences for psychological and physical health. The areas of emotion, adaptation, and health turn out to be profitable areas of investigation from a personality standpoint. Perhaps of even greater significance for personality psychologists is the opportunity offered by such research to observe the functioning of the person as a whole. In other words, along with the importance of individual differences in each of these areas, great importance can be attached to the ways in which the pieces relate to one another as part of the overall functioning of the personality system.

MAJOR CONCEPTS

Basic emotions theory. The view that there are basic, universal emotions that are part of our evolutionary heritage.

Differential emotions theory. Izard's theory suggesting that there are basic, fundamental, or primary emotions that are universal.

Primary appraisal. Lazarus's concept for the first stage of appraisal in which the person evaluates whether or not there is a threat or danger.

Secondary appraisal. Lazarus's concept for the second stage of appraisal in which the person evaluates what can be done to overcome harm, prevent harm, or improve the prospects for benefit.

Optimism. Positive expectancies about the future. Scheier and Carver use the con-

cept of dispositional optimism to refer to the person's characteristic generalized expectancy for positive outcomes.

Negative affectivity (NA). The disposition to experience aversive emotional states such as anxiety and depression, to have a negative view of the self, and to dwell on the negative side of the self and the world.

Suppression. The conscious, intentional effort to remove thoughts or feelings from awareness.

SUMMARY

1. Affects are emphasized in psychoanalytic theory but viewed as secondary to drives or instincts. Rogers emphasized the phenomenology of experience but did not develop a differentiated affect theory. Trait theorists give greater attention to broad dimensions of mood or temperament than to specific affects. Social cognitive theorists increasingly are interested in affect, but the range of affects considered is limited. Beyond depression and anxiety, then, within traditional personality theory there has been limited attention to the affects and in no case has affect been emphasized as a major organizing element of personality functioning.

2. Basic emotions theory (Tomkins, Ekman) and differential emotions theory (Izard) suggest that there are basic, fundamental, or primary emotions that are universal. These emotions are viewed as important for motivation, cognition, and action and play a central role in the organization of personality functioning.

3. Lazarus has attempted to relate work in the area of emotion to that of adaptation and motivation. Beginning with work on appraisal processes in stress, he developed a cognitive-motivational-relational theory of emotions and suggested that each emotion is associated with a core relational theme.

4. Research suggests a relation among emotion, coping mechanisms, and health (i.e., immunological system functioning). For example, there is evidence of a relation between optimism and health as well as between negative affectivity and health.

5. Wegner's research suggests that efforts at thought suppression produce unintended, ironic effects that are the very opposite of those that are desired (e.g.,

efforts at thought suppression lead to the increased awareness and excitability of unwanted thoughts).

6.   Pennebaker's research on the inhibition or expression of thoughts and feelings following traumatic experiences suggests problematic aspects to the former (inhibition) and healing aspects to the latter (expression, release).

MALADAPTIVE PERSONALITY FUNCTIONING AND PROCESSES OF CHANGE

11

CHAPTER OVERVIEW

Can personality theory and research help us understand people's psychological difficulties and how to help them with these difficulties? This would seem to be a reasonable task for personality psychology. In this chapter we consider three approaches to maladaptive personality functioning and therapeutic change—trait, psychoanalytic, and cognitive. The focus is on how each approach describes, explains, and offers prescriptions for the treatment of psychological difficulties. Finally, consideration is given to the question of whether therapeutic procedures associated with these approaches are distinctive in their effects or share common therapeutic elements.

Questions to Be Addressed in This Chapter

1 What is the nature of maladaptive personality functioning? How do the various theories of personality describe and explain maladaptive personality functioning?

2 How can changes in maladaptive personality functioning be produced? To what extent does each of the major theoretical models of personality suggest a procedure for producing change?

3 Is there evidence of the differential effectiveness of various forms of therapy? Is there evidence that specific forms of therapy are associated with different kinds of change? Or, does the evidence suggest that the various forms of therapy lead to similar processes of change?

In the last chapter we considered the relation of personality to physical health and emotional well-being. In this chapter we extend that discussion further to the relation of personality theory to maladaptive psychological functioning (i.e., psychopathology) and therapeutic change. We focus our attention on the three major theoretical orientations current in the field today—trait, psychoanalytic, and social cognitive/information processing, and their relevance to an understanding of processes of maladaptive functioning and therapeutic change.

In restricting our attention to these three orientations, we will not be able to consider every approach current in the field today. For example, attention will not be given to the client-centered therapy of Carl Rogers or to behavioral approaches associated with S-R and Skinnerian learning theory. However, consideration of the trait, psychoanalytic, and cognitive approaches is adequate to examine the diversity of ways in which current personality theory is associated with models of maladaptive personality functioning and therapeutic change.

DESCRIPTION, EXPLANATION, AND PRESCRIPTION

Gerald walked into my office clearly in great distress. He began this first session with the statement that life was now pretty much over for him—at the age of 23! His hands shook and he started to sob as he described the series of events that had brought him to this point. A couple of months ago he broke up with his girlfriend, the only truly serious relationship he ever had with a woman. Then, after over a year of self-doubt, he decided that law was not the field for him and dropped out of law school. Finally, his religious faith had been badly shaken. What was to become of him? Was there any hope? His past accomplishments seemed trivial in comparison to his current failures. His parents were professionally successful, happily married, religiously committed. He could never be the person they represented. Was there any point in going on?

This vignette is of an actual person who came to me for treatment. A few of the details have been changed to protect confidentiality, but the essence of the story is real and probably familiar to many readers. Along with our compassion for Gerald's plight, we can be concerned with three questions: (1) What is the best way of describing his difficulties and those of others in psychological distress? (2) How can we account for or explain the problems? Why is Gerald having these problems and experiencing this enormous amount of anxiety and depression? (3) How can he be helped? What do we know about how people change that can lead to a prescription for therapeutic procedures that will help him to get on with his life and not face such turmoil in the future? In sum, along with our compassion we are concerned with the problems of *description, explanation,* and *prescription* in relation to problematic psychological functioning.

The concepts of maladaptive or pathological personality functioning and therapeutic change are central elements in a course in abnormal psychology. Why, then, should they be covered in a personality text? These topics are, and should be, central to personality theory; that is, an explanation of "normal" and "pathological" functioning, of adaptive and maladaptive functioning, as well as an understanding of why people do and do not change, is a fundamental part of a comprehensive theory of personality. It is hard to imagine a scientific understanding of diseases of the body that is not based on an understanding of normal body functioning. Put another way, knowledge of normal functioning facilitates an understanding of disturbances in such functioning. An understanding of normal and abnormal aspects of bodily functioning go hand in hand. Why should this be any different for psychological processes?

The situation is more complex in regard to treatment. Here the tie between understanding and treatment is less clear. One can have an understanding of the causes of a disease but not a remedy for it. For some forms of cancer and for AIDS, our understanding of the disease process outpaces treatment procedures. On the other hand, it is possible to have effective treatment procedures without a knowledge of how they work. This often is the case when a drug is known to be effective in the treatment of an illness although the process through which it works is unclear. For example, aspirin for the treatment of pain and tranquilizers for the treatment of psychosis were known to be effective before the basis for their effectiveness was discovered. To the extent that psychological processes follow a similar path, we may understand aspects of maladaptive personality functioning without being able to effect changes in them, and we may discover effective change processes that work for unknown reasons or for reasons different from those suggested by practitioners. As we shall see at the end of the chapter, teasing apart the effective components of various forms of psychotherapy remains a challenging task, even when the procedures themselves are of demonstrated efficacy.

The ideal theory of personality would cover all aspects of personality functioning. Current theories are a long way from this ideal and tend to concentrate on particular aspects of personality functioning. Each theory has a *range of convenience,* a range of phenomena covered by the theory, and a *focus of convenience,* particular phenomena that are given focal attention. In discussing the trait, psychoanalytic, and social cognitive/information-processing approaches to maladaptive functioning and adaptive change, it should be clear that they differ in the extent to which these phenomena are part of their range and focus of convenience. For example, psychopathology and psychotherapy are a particular focus of psychoanalysis. In contrast, proponents of the five-factor model of trait theory have just begun to direct their attention to the area of psychopathology and have not yet begun to tackle the area of psychotherapy. Thus, these areas of personality lie outside the focus of convenience of this theoretical approach. In considering the contributions of the alternative theoretical approaches to our understanding of maladaptive functioning and change, we must keep in mind the extent to which these are aspects of the focus of convenience of each approach.

TRAIT THEORY

In Chapter 2 we considered trait units of personality and noted earlier models, such as that of Eysenck, and later models, such as the five-factor model (FFM) or Big Five model. These models will be presented here to illustrate the relevance of trait theory to maladaptive functioning and therapeutic change.

EYSENCK'S TRAIT THEORY

Not only has Eysenck been a major contributor to the development of a trait approach to personality theory, but he has established clear linkages of the theory to the problems of psychopathology and change. According to Eysenck (1979, 1990), a person develops neurotic symptoms because of the joint action of a biological system and experiences that contribute to the learning of strong emotional reactions to fear-producing stimuli. Thus, the vast majority of neurotic patients tend to have high Neuroticism and low Extraversion scores (Eysenck, 1982, p. 25). In contrast, criminals and antisocial persons tend to have high Extraversion and high Psychoticism scores. Such individuals show weak learning of societal norms.

As noted earlier, Eysenck views the operation of the biological system, which has a strong genetic (inherited) component to it, as key to the development of pathological functioning. The trait of Neuroticism is associated with the experiencing of negative affect states, including anxiety, depression, and hostility (Zuckerman, 1991). According to Eysenck, people high on Neuroticism tend to be emotionally labile and frequently complain of worry and anxiety as well as of bodily aches (e.g., headaches, stomach difficulties, dizzy spells). The relation between high Neuroticism scores and complaints of physical and psychological distress was also noted in Chapter 10. Such individuals, because of an inherited constitution, respond quickly to stress and show a slower decrease in the stress response once the danger has disappeared than is true for more stable (low Neuroticism) individuals. In terms of the introversion-extraversion dimension, it is suggested that because of differences in inherited biological functioning, introverts are more easily aroused by events than extraverts and more easily learn social prohibitions. In addition, learning for introverts appears to be more influenced by punishments, whereas extraverts are more influenced by rewards. Other trait theorists who emphasize the importance of inherited differences in biological functioning similarly stress the importance of individual differences in the potential to experience positive and negative emotional states as key to the development of psychological disorders (Cloninger, 1986, 1987; Gray, 1987).

As can be seen, Eysenck attempts to tie together biologically based individual differences in conditioning or learning and the development of psychopathology. Despite the strong genetic contribution to the development of psychological disorders, Eysenck claims that one need not be pessimistic concerning the potential for treatment. A frequent, outspoken critic of psychoanalytic theory and therapy, Eysenck played a major role in the development of the treatment approach known as **behavior therapy,** or the application of learning principles to the treatment of disorders of psychological functioning. Since neurotic behavior involves the learning of maladaptive responses, therapeutic treatment of such behaviors involves the unlearning or extinction of such learned responses (Eysenck, 1979; Eysenck & Martin, 1987). Although he has not himself actively pursued the development of therapeutic approaches, Eysenck has consistently been a spokesperson for the application of learning-based procedures in the treatment of psychological disorders.

THE FIVE-FACTOR MODEL (FFM) AND PERSONALITY DISORDERS

> An emergent and still-growing consensus on the FFM suggests that this is a comprehensive classification of personality dimensions that may be a conceptually useful framework for understanding personality disorders. . . . Trait psychologists know that individual differences in most characteristics are continuously distributed, and it seems reasonable to hypothesize that different forms of psychopathology might be related to normal variations in basic personality dispositions.
>
> Costa & Widiger, 1994, pp. 1–2

The application of the FFM to personality disorders is a relatively recent development (Costa & Widiger, 1994; Trull, 1992; Widiger, 1993). Basically it is a descriptive approach to personality disorders; that is, personality disorders are described in terms of extreme scores on the Big Five factors. The question asked is whether personality pathology can be seen as the extreme of normal traits and, if so, "why not measure it this way?" (Soldz, Budman, Demby, & Merry, 1993, p. 51). According to supporters of the model, it (the FFM) "is largely sufficient for characterizing normal and abnormal personality functioning" (Widiger, 1993, p. 82).

Two Illustrative Applications

Since this is not an abnormal psychology text, we will not consider the various forms of personality disorders and their accompanying trait characteristics in detail. However, two examples will be given to illustrate the use of the FFM. The first example involves the *compulsive personality disorder*. The essential feature of this personality disorder is a restricted ability to express warm and tender emotions. Other defining characteristics are perfectionism; excessive devotion to work and productivity to the exclusion of pleasure; indecisiveness; preoccupation with rules, details, and procedures; and concern with dominance-submission issues in relationships. In psychoanalytic terms, compulsive people have the qualities of the anal personality (Chapter 6). In terms of the FFM, such individuals score high on Conscientiousness and low on Extraversion. There also is a tendency for them to score high on Neuroticism and low on Agreeableness (Soldz et al., 1993; Trull, 1992).

The second illustration is that of the **narcissistic personality disorder.** The essential feature of individuals with this personality disorder is a grandiose sense of self-importance or uniqueness. Other defining characteristics are exaggeration of achievements and talents; preoccupation with fantasies of unlimited success, power, brilliance, or beauty; constant need for attention and admiration; sense of entitlement; problems in empathy; and experience of rage, shame, humiliation, or emptiness in response to perceived criticism or defeat. In terms of the FFM, such individuals score extremely low on Agreeableness, high on Extraversion, and high on Openness to Experience. Their low scores on Agreeableness are due primarily to their low scores on the facets of Modesty (indicating arrogance and conceit), Altruism (indicating self-centeredness, selfishness, and exploitation), and Tendermindedness (indicating lack of empathy) (Corbitt, 1994). (See Table 2.2 for a description of the complete range of facets.) They do not necessarily score high on Neuroticism except for the facet or component of Vulnerability (Soldz et al., 1993; Trull, 1992; Widiger, 1993).

In sum, it is proposed that the FFM is a useful way of conceptualizing and differentiating among personality disorders. Each of the five factors is important in one or more of the personality disorders, and each diagnosis has been found to be correlated with extreme scores on one or more of the five dimensions. The difference between normal and disordered personality functioning is that a personality-disordered person's traits are extreme and rigid; that is, personality dysfunction is characterized by extreme and inflexible expressions of otherwise normal ways of thinking, feeling, and behaving (L. A. Clark, Vorhies, & McEwen, 1994).

Applications to Problematic Interpersonal Behavior

Some personality psychologists emphasize interpersonal variables as basic units (Carson, 1969, 1991; Kiesler, 1991). Wiggins (1991; Wiggins & Pincus, 1992) has developed a circumplex model based on the dimensions of Dominance-Submission and Love-Hate (Figure 11.1). He and proponents of the FFM agree that the two models are complementary in that the same personality traits can be located in relation to either model. The suggestion is that most of the various personality disorders can be located on the interpersonal circumplex presented in Figure 11.1

Figure 11.1   Circumplex model of interpersonal behavior.
Wiggins's circumplex model of interpersonal behavior is based on the two dimensions of Dominance-Submission and Love-Hate. The eight points in the figure represent interpersonal traits along the circumplex. The model is viewed as complementary to the five-factor model of personality traits.

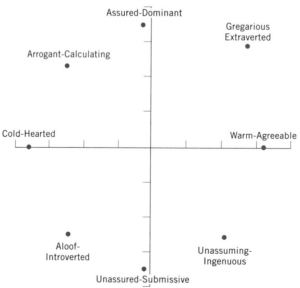

(Adapted from "Circular Reasoning About Interpersonal Behavior: Evidence Concerning Some Untested Assumptions Underlying Diagnostic Classification," by J. S. Wiggins, N. Phillips, and P. Trapnell, 1989, *Journal of Personality and Social Psychology, 56,* p. 297. Copyright 1989 by the American Psychological Association. Reprinted by permission.)

(Wiggins, Phillips, & Trapnell, 1989). For example, the narcissistic personality disorder can be located in the Arrogant-Calculating section of the circumplex, defined by the interpersonal traits of arrogance, egotism, and to some extent dominance.

In sum, the effort here is to develop a model of interpersonal behavior that encompasses both normal and abnormal interpersonal traits and that can be related to the FFM. Although many of the personality disorders seem to fit well within Wiggins's interpersonal circumplex, some do not (e.g., compulsive personality disorder), probably because personality disorders include problems in thinking and feeling as well as in interpersonal behavior. To include such additional characteristics, it is suggested that traits associated with the FFM must be used as well (Pincus & Wiggins, 1990; Widiger, 1994).

DESCRIPTION, EXPLANATION, AND PRESCRIPTION AND THE FIVE-FACTOR MODEL

Where does the five-factor model leave us in relation to Gerald and other individuals in psychological distress? Following from the previous discussion, Gerald would be described as high on the Neuroticism factor, most specifically high on the Anxiety and Depression facets (see Table 2.2). The former would describe his being tense and jittery, the latter his overwhelming feelings of sadness, hopelessness, loneliness, and guilt. In addition, he likely would be described as high on the Conscientiousness factor, most specifically in terms of his high aspiration level (Achievement Striving) and adherence to ethical principles and moral obligations (Dutifulness). But, does this provide us with an adequate description of Gerald and his struggles? And, even if the description is adequate, does it provide us with an explanation for his difficulties? Finally, how are we to proceed in terms of helping Gerald? How are his anxiety and depression to be alleviated, and how is he to be helped to avoid such crises in the future?

Here we come to the exact nature of the criticism of the FFM of personality disorders (Benjamin, 1993; L. A. Clark, 1993; Davis & Millon, 1993; Schacht, 1993; Tellegen, 1993). Criticism involves the three major points of description, explanation, and prescription. First, there is the suggestion that the model does not include some important aspects of personality functioning and gives insufficient detail about the individual. In the words of one critic, the FFM leaves the person a stranger (McAdams, 1992). We are without an appreciation of the unique attributes of Gerald and of how these and other characteristics relate to one another. We know that Gerald is a conscientious person struggling with anxiety and depression, but do we know him? Do we know that he sometimes has functioned as a capable leader and at other times fled from challenging tasks? Can we appreciate the fact that he has been independent in many ways but now seeks either to have his situation taken care of for him or to be left alone to suffer the misery he feels he deserves?

Perhaps description beyond what is offered is not necessary. But what, then, of explanation? Here critics suggest that we are without an explanation for Gerald's difficulties. Why did he have the problems with his girlfriend that he did and why did the breakup result in such a profound sense of loss? Why did he choose to be a lawyer and then become so disillusioned with pursuit of this career? And, why was it at this point that his religious beliefs were so shattered and with such tumultuous consequences? In many ways we can understand anxiety and depression as a result of loss and blows to one's self-esteem, but this is not what is described. And, why the depth of response in terms of complete collapse and thoughts of suicide?

Finally, there is the issue of prescription. How can we be of help to Gerald? Here critics suggest that the FFM may be useless as a guide for individual treatment; that is, it lacks a model for psychotherapy or change. Stability rather than change is emphasized, and processes of change currently lie outside the range of convenience of the model. Other than relying upon procedures suggested by behavior therapists or therapists from other orientations, the model has nothing to offer in terms of helping Gerald with his current situation and plans for the future.

Despite these criticisms, proponents of the model suggest that "in time it will be the five-factor model that will prove to be sufficient for characterizing not only the normal but also the maladaptive, abnormal personality" (Widiger, 1993, p. 140). In addition, it is suggested that the model can be useful for matching individuals with specific traits to therapists with specific traits or therapeutic procedures that fit their personality. For example, a procedure involving considerable exploration would not be appropriate for an individual low on the Openness to Experience factor. Thus, proponents of this trait model suggest that it is a good beginning effort at classification, and that explanation and prescription will have to follow from such descriptive-classificatory efforts.

THE TRAIT MODEL AND PERSONALITY DISORDERS: SUMMARY

The trait model of personality emphasizes broad dispositions in behavior. Eysenck's three-factor model suggests that disorders in personality functioning are due to maladaptive learning associated with genetically based individual differences in physiological functioning. In his emphasis on the role of learning in the development of pathological behavior, Eysenck simultaneously emphasized the application of learning principles, in the form of behavior therapy, to the treatment of these disorders.

The FFM, and interpersonal models that are associated with it (e.g., Wiggins's), views personality disorders as consisting of extreme, maladaptive forms of normal personality traits. The emphasis here is on the descriptive character of the personality disorders. In contrast to Eysenck's work, there has been no effort to tie these descriptive characteristics to a theory of the formation of the disorders or a theory of therapeutic change. On the other hand, much greater effort has been made to establish systematic links between traits and the various personality disorders than is true in Eysenck's work. For the most part, the nature of maladaptive functioning and therapeutic change is not part of the focus of convenience of either trait approach.

PSYCHOANALYTIC THEORY

As indicated earlier, psychopathology and psychotherapy are very much a part of the focus of convenience of psychoanalytic theory. The theory evolved out of clinical practice, and developments to this day are based on clinical experience. Beyond this, we shall see that the psychoanalytic view of maladaptive functioning and of thera-peutic change differs in fundamental ways from that of trait theory.

PSYCHOPATHOLOGY

The psychoanalytic view of maladaptive functioning emphasizes the affect of anxiety and the mechanisms of defense, or ways of coping with anxiety (Masling & Bornstein, 1993). In addition, there is an emphasis on conflict, most specifically conflict between wishes (needs, motives, instincts) and fears. According to classical psychoanalytic theory, during the course of development the child experiences various instincts or wishes. Different instincts-wishes are associated with the different stages of devel-opment (Chapter 6). During the oral stage the infant may wish to incorporate or bite, during the anal stage to soil or defy, and during the phallic stage to enjoy sexual feelings in relation to the parent of the opposite sex. The important point here is that the developing child is experiencing a variety of feelings and wishes. If the child is punished for these feelings and wishes, or experiences the threat of loss or aban-donment in relation to them, he or she will come to associate them with anxiety. In other words, the developing child comes to believe that if these feelings and wishes are recognized and expressed, pain or punishment will ensue.

What is the vulnerable child to do? According to psychoanalytic theory, because anxiety is a painful affect the child learns to defend against the anxiety and the wish or desire. For example, the child may deny that he or she has the wish-feeling associated with anxiety, may remove all feeling associated with the experience so there is less threat involved, and may forget (repress) all memories of events or otherwise remove the threat associated with the feeling or desire. Although initially there may be some awareness that this is being done, over time it takes on an automatic quality. Not only is the person not aware of using a defensive maneuver, but he or she is unaware of what is being defended against. As a patient of mine said in a therapy session when he was struggling with some painful feelings: "I have the feeling that I am approaching something but as soon as I do I feel a wall coming down, a barrier against feeling these things. It just seems so automatic that I can't do anything about it and I just don't know what it's about."

When this state has been reached, there has been a successful defensive maneuver, successful in the sense that the person does not have to experience anxiety or the threat associated with the feeling or wish. On the other hand, there is a cost associated with the successful defense. The cost is losing touch with a part of one's internal life. In addition, the person may avoid future situations that threaten to similarly arouse the painful emotion of anxiety and thereby never learn that other situations may be different from the original one associated with anxiety. For example, contact with women or men may be avoided because of a domineering, punitive mother or father, precluding the potential for learning that other women and men are different. And, finally, the person may be left with underlying feelings of guilt or shame, that is, the vague sense that he or she is bad, inferior, or contemptible.

Feelings of guilt and shame bring us to the topic of depression. According to psychoanalytic theory, depression involves the loss of self-esteem that is dependent on ideals or standards being fulfilled. In depression there is the feeling "I have lost everything; now the world is empty" or "I have lost everything because I do not deserve anything. I hate myself" (Fenichel, 1945, p. 391). Because the person believes he or she has not met ideals or the strict standards of the superego, he or she is filled with self-reproach. The self-reproach is manifest in lowered self-esteem, feelings of inferiority, and feelings of worthlessness. The anger that might otherwise be directed outward at another person or the situation associated with failure and loss is now turned against the self in the form of self-reproach and self-flagellation. Rather than being angry at others, the depressed person is angry at the self: "I deserve to be punished, disliked, abandoned." In sum, the emphasis is on the feelings of guilt, self-reproach, and loss of self-esteem associated with the failure to meet the strict ideals and standards of the superego.

The psychoanalytic theory of psychopathology is somewhat more complicated than this in its details, but the essence of the model is conflict between a wish and the threat of punishment or pain associated with expression of the wish. In technical terms, it is the conflict between the instinctual wishes of the id and the threat of punishment from the outside world or from the superego in the form of guilt. However, one need not use these technical terms to appreciate the emphasis on conflict between wishes and fears, as well as between perceived accomplishments and standards (i.e., superego), that is central to the theory. Within this context maladaptive functioning is expressed in a number of ways. As indicated, the person loses touch with some aspect of his or her internal life and retains some negative picture of the self. In addition, he or she remains fearful of approaching certain situations that may no longer be of harm. Finally, because of the anxiety that underlies this process, there is a rigid aspect to the person's functioning. In fact, rigidity perhaps is the defining characteristic of defensive, maladaptive personality functioning. Extreme anxiety interferes with flexible, adaptive functioning.

It is important to note that the processes described occur unconsciously. According to psychoanalytic theory the person is unaware of the wish-feeling and the defense against it. The process is not just automatic in the sense that it is habitual and therefore nonconscious, but it is unconscious because it is repressed! It is not only that the person is unaware, but there is a barrier (i.e., defense) against becoming aware—thus, my patient's spontaneous expression of the feeling that as he started to become vaguely aware of something a wall or barrier seemed to come down and it was lost to him—the operation of the defensive process. What was once conscious, the wish-feeling and the threat associated with it, now is gone from consciousness. Whereas once there was awareness of the sexual or angry feeling, and of the threat associated with it, now there is a lack of consciousness and perhaps only an occasional sense of anxiety as something associated with the repressed wish-feeling occurs to the person.

OBJECT RELATIONS THEORY

What has been presented is a fairly traditional view of the psychoanalytic model of psychopathology. However, new developments have occurred in psychoanalytic theory. Of particular importance, as noted in Chapter 8, are developments associated with object relations theory. As described earlier, the focus for object relations analysts is on how important people of the past are represented as aspects of the self, others, and self-other relationships. These representations are both cognitive, in terms of mental images, and affective, in terms of the association of strong emotions with them. The emphasis is on the person as relationship seeking rather than on drive gratification. In addition, object relations theorists place great emphasis on the self, the ways in which various parts of the self are experienced, and the extent to which the person experiences the self as integrated and cohesive as opposed to fragmented and fragile. Generally the emphasis in relation to psychopathology is on problematic representations of the self and others and on vulnerability to blows to the sense of self and self-esteem. Illustrations of such problematic representations and vulnerability follow.

Narcissistic Personality Disorder: Comparison With Trait Theory

As noted, object relations theorists have been interested in disorders of self-representation. Of particular interest to them, and to us in relation to the earlier discussion of trait theory, is the narcissistic personality disorder. According to object relations theorists, the development of a healthy sense of self and a healthy narcissism involves the development of a clear sense of one's separateness and individuality, a reasonably stable sense of self-esteem, a pride in one's accomplishments, and the ability to be aware of and responsive to the needs of others while responding to one's own needs. The narcissistic personality involves a disturbance in the sense of self and a vulnerability to blows to self-esteem. The narcissistic person has a continuous need for the admiration of others and lacks empathy with the feelings and needs of others. This lack of empathy is due to the intense preoccupation with the self and to the difficulty in recognizing others as separate individuals with their own needs.

How do such characteristics develop? As noted, basically the object relations theory explanatory model emphasizes the nature of the early object (person) relations and the psychological state of the child developing a sense of self and self-esteem. In the case of the narcissistic personality disorder, there are parents or parental figures who are unempathic, insensitive to the needs and feelings of the child, focused on their own needs, and capable of being extremely attentive and admiring at one moment and disinterested or deprecating at another moment. In other words, the parents send mixed messages to the child, that he or she is both "special" or "exceptional" and "deficient" or "inadequate." Thus, the child does not have adequate empathic role models, feels that he or she cannot trust others for self-esteem, and vacillates in self-evaluations between grandiosity and worthlessness. Because of the preoccupation with the self, and the lack of empathic models, there is a difficulty in being empathic to the needs of others. In sum, there is an explanation in terms of earlier experiences with significant others and the representations of self and others that were developing at a time critical for the development of a sense of self.

This portrayal of the narcissistic personality disorder comes from clinical practice. The characteristics described match many of those noted in the context of trait theory. And, efforts have been made to develop questionnaire measures of narcissism (Murray, 1938; Raskin & Hall, 1979; Table 11.1). However, despite similarities to the trait description of the narcissistic personality disorder, the object relations view remains fundamentally different. Of particular importance is the fact that the disorder is seen

TABLE 11.1   **Illustrative Items from Questionnaire Measures of Narcissism**

Murray's Narcissism Scale (1938, p. 181)
I often think about how I look and what impression I am making upon others.
My feelings are easily hurt by ridicule or by the slighting remarks of others.
I talk a good deal about myself, my experiences, my feelings, and my ideas.

Narcissism Personality Inventory (Raskin & Hall, 1979)
I really like to be the center of attention.
I think I am a special person.
I expect a great deal from other people.
I am envious of other people's good fortune.
I will never be satisfied until I get all that I deserve.

within the context of a theoretical framework and a theoretical explanation is given for the pattern of associated characteristics (Kernberg, 1976; Kohut, 1971; Millon, 1981).

Object Relations, Attachment, and Depression

As a further illustration of this approach, we can consider the problem of depression. In Chapter 6 we considered Bowlby's emphasis on development of the *attachment behavioral system* and his concept of *internal working models* or mental representations associated with affect. In that chapter it also was suggested that early attachment patterns are related to later social and emotional behavior, as well as to romantic relationships. Current theory suggests that an important contributor to depression is the early development of impaired mental representations or internal working models of a caregiving relationship; that is, impaired mental representations based on disturbed early relationships create a vulnerability to later depession (Blatt & Bers, 1993a, 1993b; Blatt & Homann, 1992).

Perhaps the best way to appreciate the essence of this view is to follow some specific research linking internal working models to depression (Carnelley, Pietromonaco, & Jaffe, 1994). In this research the authors proposed that attachment theory provides a framework for understanding the thoughts and behaviors of depressives in their relationship functioning. Specifically it was proposed that children who experience rejection and coldness develop a working model of the self as unlovable and incompetent and a working model of others as unreliable, cold, and distant. The development of such models leads to expectations of rejection and failure, expectations that may distort perceptions of events and even unintentionally elicit behaviors from others that confirm their view that they are unworthy of another's love. In sum, in addition to negative representations of the self, the model suggests that as a result of negative experiences with a primary caregiver, there is the development of an insecure working model of adult attachment and a vulnerability to depression (Figure 11.2).

Following from this model, the researchers hypothesized that less positive childhood experiences would be associated with an insecure attachment style and greater vulnerability to depression than would more positive childhood experiences. In a study to test these hypotheses, a measure of depression was administered to under-

Figure 11.2   Hypothesized associations among predictors of relationship functioning. Both adult attachment style and depression may result from less positive childhood experiences with a primary caregiver, and they also may exert a reciprocal influence (curved line). Also, adult attachment style or depression may influence relationship functioning (solid line indicates a suggested strong link, dotted line a suggested weaker link).

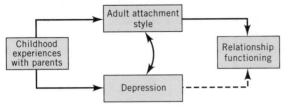

(From "Depression, Working Models of Others, and Relationships Functioning," by K. B. Carnelley, P. R. Pietromonaco, and K. Jaffee, 1994, *Journal of Personality and Social Psychology, 66*, p. 129. Copyright 1994 by the American Psychological Association. Reprinted by permission.)

graduate women. On the basis of the scores on the measure, depressed and non-depressed groups were formed. The subjects then completed questionnaires assessing a variety of parent-child relationship characteristics suggested by attachment theory. For example, subjects separately rated their mother and father in terms of whether they were accepting or rejecting (e.g., "My Mother [Father] gave me the feeling that she [he] liked me as I was") and whether they encouraged independence as opposed to being overprotective (e.g., "When I was a child, my Mother [Father] encouraged me to make my own decisions"). In addition, the subjects completed questionnaire measures of adult working models of attachment. On the basis of their responses to these questionnaires, they were assigned to one of three attachment-style groups: *secure* ("It is relatively easy for me to become emotionally close to others"), *fearful* ("I want emotionally close relationships, but I find it difficult to trust others completely, or to depend on them"), and *preoccupied* ("I am uncomfortable being without close relationships, but I sometimes worry that others don't value me as much as I value them") (Bartholomew & Horowitz, 1991).

Would a link be found between reports of childhood experiences and attachment style? Would depressed and nondepressed subjects differ in their reports of childhood experiences with parents and in their adult attachment styles? Consistent with the model, reports of childhood experiences were indeed found to be linked to later adult attachment style. Women who reported less positive childhood experiences with both parents were characterized by the less secure attachment styles (i.e., fearful, preoccupied) relative to women who reported more positive childhood experiences. A similar, although not as strong, link was suggested between early experiences with controlling mothers and fathers and the development of these insecure attachment styles. In addition, again consistent with the model, a link was established between reports of negative childhood experiences with parents and depression; that is, depressed women were more likely than nondepressed women to report less positive childhood experiences. Finally, depression status was significantly correlated with each of the two insecure attachment styles, fearful and preoccupied; that is, depressed women were more likely than nondepressed women to have insecure attachment styles. In sum, the data supported the view that early childhood experiences are associated with the development of internal working models and attachment styles that make the person vulnerable to the development of depression.

In a second study by Carnelley, Pietromonaco, and Jaffe (1994), married women recovering from depression were compared to nondepressed married women in terms of early childhood experiences and attachment style. In addition, a measure of marital relationship adjustment was obtained. The results here were less conclusively supportive of the model than in the first study. However, evidence was found for links between negative childhood experiences with mother and a fearful attachment style, between less positive experiences with mother and father and depression, and between depression and a fearful attachment style. In addition, attachment style was found to be related to marital adjustment and relationship functioning; that is, women who were more fearful or preoccupied showed poorer marital adjustment and less supportive exchanges with their spouses than did more securely attached women.

In sum, consistent with attachment theory the researchers found that depression was associated with an insecure working model of attachment. In addition, depression was found to be associated with less positive early relationships with parents. A link was suggested between the development of an insecure attachment style and vulnerability to depression. It is important to recognize that this study made use of recollections of early experiences. Thus, it might be that current states of depression and current attachment difficulties bias the recollection of childhood experiences. This indeed is a potentially serious problem in such research. However, other research involving observation of depressed mother–child interactions lends support to the hypothesized link between the development of early internal working models of attachment and vulnerability to depression (Blatt & Homann, 1992).

THERAPEUTIC CHANGE

If this is what psychopathology or maladaptive personality functioning is about, then how is change to occur? Essentially the psychoanalytic model of pathology is a learning model; that is, maladaptive functioning represents fixation or the lack of new learning in relation to experiences occurring in childhood. As a result, the person does not learn that it is possible to have different feelings, that outcomes may be different, that relationships can be different, and that he or she can develop a different picture of the self, one associated with less guilt or shame and more self-esteem. Although not itself a formal theory of learning, it nevertheless is a learning model. Therefore, it is not surprising that analysts view the psychoanalytic process as a learning process in which the patient can reexperience old conflicts and solve them now in a different, more adaptive way.

The vehicle for this learning process to occur is the **transference.** In the course of psychoanalysis, the patient develops attitudes, wishes, and feelings toward the analyst that correspond to those experienced earlier in relation to significant figures (e.g., mother, father) from childhood. Although the term may suggest something strange and unique to the analytic situation, in fact there is nothing unusual about transference. As research indicates, we all respond to some people, in some situations, in ways that suggest that they remind us, consciously or unconsciously, of earlier figures associated with conflict and anxiety (Thorne, 1989). People who experience rage and anxiety in relation to a domineering boss or partner, people who feel jealous when someone gets something they hoped to get, people who feel envious of the success of others regardless of their own success, and people who feel they must satisfy the needs of others even at the expense of their own pleasure are all expressing transference in the course of their daily lives.

What makes transference different in psychoanalysis is that it can be expressed, studied, and understood in the context of a safe environment and a trusted therapist. Thus, in the course of analysis, the patient can experience rage at the analyst and fear the analyst's retaliation yet also know that the analyst is there to help and will not retaliate. In the course of analysis the patient can become jealous of other patients who are thought to get more time or who are fantasized to be of greater interest to the analyst. Or, the patient can become engaged with the analyst in a power struggle over bills or time or who will speak and how the session is to be conducted. All of these can and do occur as part of the transference that develops in the analytic process. However, as noted, they are not unique to the analytic process. Each is experienced in daily life as well; but in daily life, the person is unaware of what is going on and unable to study it in sufficient depth. In the therapeutic transference situation there is an opportunity to become aware of and examine these maladaptive ways of relating to others and the self.

Psychoanalytic theory has always emphasized a cognitive component and an affective component to therapeutic change. In the early development of the theory, it was the cognitive component that was emphasized. What was important was that the person recall what had been repressed—what was unconscious was now to become conscious. The goal of analysis was the uncovering of all that had been repressed, the recovery of buried memories. In addition, there was an emphasis on the process of insight; that is, the patient was to understand his or her unconscious conflicts and their roots in childhood. Although both the recovery of repressed memories and the gaining of insight involve cognitive processes, making conscious what otherwise is unconscious, both involve emotion as well.

As time has gone on, analysts have given even greater attention to the emotional component of the therapeutic process. In this sense, the power of the transference is in the fact that it is a real-life encounter, that it involves intense feelings and the reexperiencing of old conflicts. It is because of this that the transference provides for what has been called the *corrective emotional experience* (Alexander & French, 1946). The corrective emotional experience involves the recognition by patients, at a feeling level, that things can be different, that they need not be afraid of their wishes or punish themselves with excessively strict standards. In good part the corrective emotional experience occurs because the analyst acts differently than did the parents or other figures who were prominent in the patient's emotional development. It is in this sense that the therapeutic process is a learning process; that is, there is a resumption of growth where, because of conflict and anxiety, adaptive learning failed to occur or maladaptive learning did occur.

Are there reasons why change may not occur? Psychoanalytic theory suggests that change can be a difficult process. In addition to therapist limitations, patients are not always ready and eager to change. Substantive change generally is painful. In psychoanalytic therapy it involves reexperiencing old fears and at times coming to grips with less than flattering wishes and self-images. In addition, change means uncertainty: "I know what things are like now but could they be worse when they change? I know that I don't fully like myself or my life now, but how do I know I'll like myself or life better if things change? I know how to function now but what am I supposed to do while I'm examining all these old issues?"

Because change involves uncertainty, anxiety, and potential loss as well as gain, most patients resist as well as seek change. In psychoanalysis the term *resistance* technically refers to the patient's not following the cardinal rule of free associating and saying whatever comes to mind. However, more broadly resistance involves all the ways in which the person, consciously or unconsciously, resists change. This may take the form of forgetting an appointment, sleeping past an appointment time, coming late, failing to attempt things that make sense to try (e.g., a shy person calling someone for a date or speaking to someone who approaches him or her at a party), or continuing to do things that make sense to stop (e.g., provoking arguments with a partner or boss). In attempting to understand and explain why and how people change, we also must attempt to understand and explain why people find it so difficult to change. The concept of resistance is important in this regard.

As with the theory of pathology, the theory of treatment is more complicated than what has been presented. However, what we have here is the essence of the psychoanalytic model of therapeutic change. It involves learning, in good part through the transference, that certain thoughts and feelings need no longer be anxiety arousing or guilt producing and that they can be handled in more adaptive ways.

DESCRIPTION, EXPLANATION, AND PRESCRIPTION AND THE PSYCHOANALYTIC MODEL

As we did in our discussion of trait theory, we can once more consider where we are left in relation to Gerald and other individuals with psychological difficulties. First, in terms of description, psychoanalytic theory and object relations theory seem to provide the basis for an excellent description of Gerald's difficulties. His feelings about himself are well described by the theories, as are his problems in romantic relationships. Gerald suffers from the overly strict standards and self-blame described by psychoanalysts. His idealization of his most recent partner and devastation upon being disappointed in the relationship, together with his past history of difficulty in developing close relationships, fit with the insecure attachment styles described by object relations theorists and attachment theorists.

The model also offers an explanation for Gerald's difficulties. In fact, the suggestion that either a loss of self-esteem or a loss of a love relationship is the immediate cause of depression fits his situation exactly. In Gerald's case he experienced disappointment in regard to both career choice and romance. Beyond this, there is evidence of development of strict standards (i.e., superego) at an early age and of an ambivalent relationship with his mother, who at times was extremely nurturing and indulgent and at other times very critical and rejecting. In adult life he formed ambivalent relationships with women, seeking closeness with them but always remaining fearful of rejection and not being able to establish real intimacy.

Finally, we come to prescription. The models being considered suggest a method of alleviating Gerald's depression and helping him to establish more meaningful relationships in the future. Presumably in the course of therapy he would come to see how strict, unrealistic, and harsh his standards were. He would come to see the price he paid for his feelings of guilt and anger turned inward. This would be done both through an analysis of current patterns in relation to patterns established early in life as well as through an analysis of experiences in the transference or therapeutic situation itself. Thus, he might have the opportunity to find out whether the therapist evaluated him as harshly as he evaluated himself and whether the therapist would reject him if he were not the "model patient."

Having said all this, does research suggest that analysis "works" and that it works in this way? In other words, can we assess the changes that occur? Do they match the changes described earlier? Can we trace the process of change during the course of therapy to determine the therapeutic ingredients of change? This is a tall order for research and, as we shall discuss in greater detail at the end of the chapter, an enormously complex matter. Perhaps there is no more difficult task for personality research than to assess personality change and the therapeutic process as it relates to this change.

We will have more to say about outcome research later in the chapter but suffice it here to say that evaluation studies of psychoanalysis or psychoanalytically oriented therapy do not provide great cheer for proponents (Crits-Christoph, 1992; Elkin et al., 1989; Sloane, Staples, Cristol, Yorkston, & Whipple, 1975; Wallerstein, 1989). This is not to say that such therapy is not effective but rather that it has not been demonstrated to be generally more effective than other forms of therapy, no more effective at producing particular kinds of change. At the present time, analytically oriented researchers are focusing their attention on trying to understand what in the analytic process promotes change, as opposed to evaluating whether or not change occurs (Luborsky, Barber, & Beutler, 1993; Messer & Warren, 1990). The greatest emphasis is on the nature of the therapeutic relationship, in particular the ability of the therapist to offer interpretive comments to the patient at a time and in a way that will lead to insight and growth. In other words, rather than focusing on a wholesale evaluation of the process, there is an effort to assess the extent to which key therapeutic ingredients are present and the impact of their presence or absence on change.

SOCIAL COGNITIVE/INFORMATION-PROCESSING APPROACHES

In this section we consider approaches to maladaptive functioning and change associated with the third model—social cognitive/information-processing approaches. In many ways theorists and practitioners of this approach are a much more diverse group than are those following the trait or psychoanalytic approaches.

Basically cognitive approaches include all theories and practices that focus on how the person processes information, that is, the processes of attending, encoding, storing-remembering, and retrieving information. Included here are concepts such as attributional beliefs (e.g., Seligman, Weiner), schema generally and self-schema in particular, dysfunctional thoughts, and irrational beliefs. Fundamental is the view that it is cognitions and cognitive processes that determine problematic emotions and behaviors, and it is these cognitions and cognitive processes that must be changed for the person's psychological well-being to improve. In relation to this, the therapist generally is seen as an active participant in the change process, challenging the patient to examine his or her cognitions and to carry out experiments in alternative ways of thinking and behaving.

Three approaches are considered in this section of the chapter. These are selected because of historical interest, because they are representative of the diversity within the group as a whole, and because they have been influential on theory or practice.

KELLY'S PERSONAL CONSTRUCT THEORY

In Chapter 3 we considered Kelly's (1955) personal construct theory as illustrative of an early cognitive approach to personality. As noted, Kelly viewed the person as a scientist with a theory or construct system, constructs being ways of interpreting or viewing events. The purpose of the construct system is to predict events. Like a theory, the better the construct system the greater the range of events the person can predict with accuracy. Individuals differ in the constructs they use to interpret the world and in the ways in which their construct systems are organized.

How is such a system to relate to maladaptive psychological functioning and to therapeutic change? Not surprisingly, Kelly viewed psychopathology in terms of disordered functioning of the construct system and therapy in terms of procedures to help the person develop new and better constructs as well as a more integrated construct system. What is meant by disordered functioning of the construct system? A poor scientist is one who retains a theory and makes the same predictions despite research failures. Similarly, Kelly interpreted psychopathology in terms of the preservation of one's constructs despite repeated invalidation of them. A poor scientist is one who shapes the data to fit the theory or who makes different parts of the theory fit the data even if the parts no longer add up. Similarly, Kelly interpreted psychopathology in terms of the person's distorting events to fit the construct system or of using the construct system in such chaotic ways that its structure no longer made sense. For example, Kelly suggested that people could make their constructs excessively *permeable* (allowing almost any content into it) or *impermeable* (allowing almost no new information in). Or, people could *tighten* the functioning of the construct system so that the same predictions are made regardless of circumstances, or *loosen* the functioning so that predictions became so varied as to border on the chaotic.

Why might such disturbances in the functioning of the construct system occur? According to Kelly, disorders of the construct system are responses to anxiety, fear, and threat. These are familiar terms but were defined by Kelly in ways that applied to his personal construct theory. Thus, **anxiety** occurs when one's constructs do not apply to events, **fear** when a new construct is about to enter the construct system, and **threat** when the person is aware of imminent, comprehensive change in the construct system. In other words, disorders of the construct system are responses to the sense that one's construct system is not working well, that one is at a loss as to how to understand and predict events, and that significant change in the construct system may be necessary. But, since such change is associated with threat, the effort may be directed toward preservation of the construct system, albeit in a contorted and distorted form. Thus, rather than extending and fine-tuning the construct system, people may make their constructs excessively permeable or impermeable and may make excessively tight or loose predictions. Or, they may act in hostile ways so as to coerce others to behave in ways congruent with the predictions of their construct system.

Perhaps the reader already has discovered something very striking about Kelly's view of maladaptive construct system functioning—basically it is a model of anxiety and defense (Pervin, 1993a). Although fundamentally different from Freud's model of anxiety and defense, it nevertheless is a model of these concepts. The source of anxiety is not in the instincts or wishes but rather in problems of prediction. The response is not a defense against recognition and expression of the instinctual wish but rather against comprehensive change in the construct system. Despite these fundamental differences, however, there is a parallel view of disordered functioning of the construct system as a response to anxiety, fear, and threat.

What, then, of therapeutic repair and growth? Kelly has a vastly different model of therapy than did Freud. If the problem is that the person is functioning as a poor scientist, then the solution is to help him or her become a better scientist. How is this to be done? According to Kelly, one must encourage the person to adopt an *invitational mood* in which new ideas and hypotheses can be explored. The therapist must help to establish an *atmosphere of experimentation* in which new constructs (hypotheses) can be tried on for size, experiments can be performed to explore new data, and constructs (hypotheses) concerning the self and others can be revised on the basis of empirical evidence. Acting as much like a mentor as a therapist, certainly more like a mentor than a blank screen on which the patient may project his or her transference reactions, Kelly attempted to help the patient design experiments, test out new ways of behaving, and consider new ways of construing events. Therapy was nothing less than the reconstruction of the construct system, and the therapist played a major role in attempting to provide an atmosphere and specific experiences that would facilitate such reconstruction.

As noted earlier in the text (Chapter 3), Kelly's views have not had a major direct impact on personality theory. And, although there is an active group of personal construct therapists, his views about therapy have not had a broad impact on therapeutic practice. Why this is the case remains an interesting question since, in the light of developments in cognitive therapy, clearly he had much to say.

BANDURA'S SOCIAL COGNITIVE THEORY

Bandura was trained as a clinician. Although he has focused on developing a theory of basic personality functioning, he has retained an interest in understanding maladaptive functioning and in designing procedures for therapeutic change. Bandura views these areas as a necessary part of a comprehensive personality theory. And, he suggests that treatment procedures should be applied only after the basic mechanisms involved are understood and the methods adequately tested.

According to Bandura (1986), maladaptive behavior is the result of dysfunctional learning. Such learning occurs as the result of either direct experience or exposure to inadequate models. In the latter case, through observational learning and vicarious conditioning of emotional responses, the person learns maladaptive expectancies, emotional responses, and behavioral responses. Through direct experience and exposure to inadequate models the person may develop **dysfunctional self-evaluations,** most notably perceptions of low self-efficacy or perceived inefficacy. Perceived self-efficacy is the perception that one can perform tasks required by a situation or cope with a situation. Perceived inefficacy is the perception that one cannot perform the necessary tasks or cope with the demands of the situation. Thus, perceptions of low self-efficacy or inefficacy are fundamental to all maladaptive psychological functioning. Increases in the positive nature of self-efficacy beliefs are viewed as fundamental to all therapeutic change.

As we have seen, Bandura emphasizes the importance of feelings of self-efficacy for health. According to research already presented, perceived self-efficacy is associated with the functioning of the body's immune system. Perceived inefficacy also is viewed as fundamental to the experiences of anxiety and depression (Bandura, 1988, 1989a). According to Bandura, perceived inefficacy in relation to threatening events leads to anxiety and perceived inefficacy in relation to rewarding outcomes leads to depression. In the case of anxiety, people believe that they are without resources to cope with the threat. This is similar to Lazarus's emphasis on the process of secondary appraisal (Chapter 10). The perception of the inability to cope with the situation may be complicated further by the perceived inability to cope with the anxiety itself—a fear-of-fear response that can lead to panic (Barlow, 1991). In the case of depression, people believe that they are unable to gain desired rewarding outcomes. This may be because either their self-efficacy beliefs are low or their standards for gaining rewards are excessively high. Thus, when they fall short of their exacting standards, they blame themselves and their lack of ability or competence for what has happened.

What is to be done in relation to the problem of low self-efficacy? According to Bandura, change in self-efficacy beliefs is the core of all processes of psychotherapeutic change. The treatment approach emphasized by social cognitive theory is the acquisition of cognitive and behavioral competencies through modeling and guided participation. In **modeling,** desired activities are demonstrated by various models who experience the positive consequences or at least no adverse consequences. Generally, the complex patterns of behavior are broken down into subskills and increasingly difficult subtasks so as to ensure optimal progress. In **guided participation,** the individual is assisted in performing the modeled behaviors. Although Bandura accepts the importance of maladaptive and irrational beliefs, and the potential value of exploration of such beliefs, he also suggests that experience is a necessary part of real change in self-efficacy beliefs. It is the experience of mastery that leads to a therapeutic increase in perceived self-efficacy. Thus, he has an active, experiential view of what is necessary for therapeutic change.

The research literature suggests that modeling treatments can be effective in redressing deficits in social and cognitive skills and in increasing self-efficacy beliefs. However, the boundaries of such treatments are unknown. That is, it remains to be demonstrated that modeling and guided participation treatments can be used to change self-efficacy beliefs in cases of severe anxiety, severe depression, and other forms of psychological dysfunction. How these methods would be applied to other personality disorders, such as the narcissistic personality disorder, is unknown. The concept of self-efficacy has been a major contribution to the social cognitive literature and is used in many psychotherapy evaluation studies. However, the direct impact of social cognitive theory on therapeutic practice has been limited.

BECK'S COGNITIVE THEORY AND THERAPY

Probably no cognitive approach to understanding and treating maladaptive personality functioning has been more influential than that of Aaron Beck. Trained as a psychiatrist and psychoanalyst, and working with depressed patients, Beck began to be impressed with the irrational, maladaptive cognitive beliefs of his patients. Becoming disenchanted with psychoanalytic techniques, he developed a cognitive approach to therapy. According to Beck (1987), psychological difficulties result from negative schema concerning the self and others, automatic thoughts, and dysfunctional assumptions.

Beck's view of psychopathology is best seen in relation to the problem of depression, where his work originated and has had its greatest impact. His model of depression emphasizes three negative schema, known as the **cognitive triad of depression.** These involve views of the self, the world, and the future—the self as a loser, the world as frustrating, and the future as bleak. Negative views of the self include self-statements such as "I am inadequate, undesirable, worthless." Negative views of the world include statements such as "The world makes too many demands on me and life represents constant defeat." Negative views of the future include statements such as "Life will always involve the suffering and deprivation it has for me now." In addition, the depressed person is prone to faulty information processing, such as magnifying everyday difficulties into disasters and overgeneralizing from a single instance to the belief that "Nobody likes me."

In sum, Beck's cognitive model of psychopathology emphasizes the role of automatic, erroneous beliefs (schema) and maladaptive information processing (e.g., faulty appraisals) in the creation of negative, painful affects and maladaptive behavioral responses. It is maladaptive cognitions that lead to problematic emotions and psychological difficulties. Different disorders are distinguished by the patterns of beliefs-schema associated with them. For example, in depression these thoughts concern failure and self-worth, whereas in people with anxiety problems they concern danger (Clark, Beck, & Brown, 1989). The task of cognitive therapy is to help the person identify and correct these distorted conceptualizations, dysfunctional beliefs, and faulty information-processing methods. The therapy involves specific learning experiences designed to teach the person to monitor negative, automatic thoughts; to recognize how these thoughts lead to problematic feelings and behaviors; to examine the evidence for and against these thoughts; and to substitute more reality-oriented interpretations for the problematic cognitions. In addition to the examination of beliefs for their logic, validity, and adaptiveness, behavioral assignments are used to help the person test maladaptive cognitions and develop their

SPOTLIGHT ON THE RESEARCHER

AARON T. BECK:

Cognitive Underpinnings of Personality Disorders

When I was treating patients back in the late 1950s, I noticed that they showed a specific type of cognitive bias in the way that they construed their life experiences—past, present, and future. Depressed patients showed a systematic interpretive bias in terms of defeats or deprivations; anxiety patients in terms of threats and personal vulnerability; and angry patients in terms of being wronged in some way. The clinical observations were confirmed by a number of systematic studies of both clinical and nonclinical subjects.

With the recognition that underlying many of the symptom disorders such as anxiety and depression there was a personality disorder, I started to focus on the cognitive underpinnings of the personality disorders. I discovered that each of these disorders could be characterized by an idiosyncratic set of beliefs. The dependent personality, for example, had beliefs such as "If I do not have somebody to help or care for me, I will be unable to function." The beliefs of the avoidant personality would run like this: "Since it would be intolerable for me to have rejection, I must stay away from any situation in which I would be vulnerable." It became clear that these beliefs are not confined simply to psychopathological groups but are characteristic—to a lesser degree—of people in general.

Our therapeutic work consisted of modifying the patients' faulty thinking and their dysfunctional beliefs. Some of my former students extended the basic research to a wide variety of conditions, including post-traumatic stress disorder, panic disorder, bipolar disorders, and schizophrenia and also a variety of so-called medical disorders such as chronic back pain, colitis, and chronic fatigue syndrome. Each of these conditions has its own configuration of idiosyncratic beliefs and biased thinking.

My current and future work is proceeding in the direction of tying the cognitive approach more closely to cognitive psychology and developmental psychology. Current studies are examining the kind of processing that goes on in the various disorders (e.g., automatic versus controlled processing), subliminal perception, and memory in each of the disorders. We are looking at two dimensions of personality—autonomy (individuals whose sense of self depends on self-definition, self-control, and self-worth) and sociotropy (individuals whose sense of self depends on close interpersonal relationships)—to determine how these relate to vulnerability to depression, how they are expressed in the symptomatology, and how they affect patients' reactions to group as opposed to individual therapy and placebo versus pharmacotherapy. Our future studies also will include assessing various predictors of suicide (such as hopelessness and low self-esteem concept) in a general medical population.

hypothesis-testing skills. In general the treatment focuses on specific target cognitions that are seen as contributing to the problem.

Beck's approach to the treatment of depression can be seen in a recently published case study (Young, Beck, & Weinberger, 1993). The case involved a young woman suffering from depression, marital conflict, and difficulty coping with her children. The therapy began with the elicitation of her automatic thoughts and negative self-schema. For example, one automatic thought was that she was not going to get any better, that she would forever be trapped in her situation. One of her schema was that people did not really care about her. Another was that she was incompetent. These negative thoughts and negative schema were not unconscious, in the sense of being repressed, but were nonconscious in the sense that they were automatic and she was not aware of them until they were examined with the help of the therapist.

Following elicitation of the dysfunctional thoughts and schema, the therapist engaged the patient in what is called the process of *collaborative empiricism*. In this process the therapist and patient act as a collaborative team in examining, much as scientists might do, the problematic thoughts and schema. For example, each time the patient viewed herself as "stupid" or "incompetent," she and the therapist examined the basis for such self-descriptions. Was she "stupid" for not having previously been aware of these automatic thoughts or was the therapist able to be aware of them because of his training? Was making a mistake an indication of being incom-

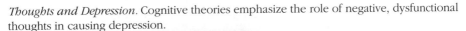

Thoughts and Depression. Cognitive theories emphasize the role of negative, dysfunctional thoughts in causing depression.

petent or was it part of being human? Could she be expected to demonstrate competence or gain competence if she stayed in bed much of the day? In addition to such examination and rational analysis, the therapist gave her specific tasks and homework assignments. For example, she was asked to keep a daily record of her dysfunctional thoughts and to consider alternative thoughts and explanations for events. In addition, she was to practice new ways of thinking and behaving. Problems were broken down into *graded tasks* or smaller steps so that progress could be made and the sense of self-efficacy increased. For example, writing a major paper might be broken down into smaller tasks of writing an outline and specific paragraphs. Whereas the task of writing a major paper might seem overwhelming, that of writing an outline and a few paragraphs would seem more manageable.

The focus on problematic cognitions and the active, structured, problem-focused approach to treatment are clear in this illustration. The patient described was helped to overcome her depression in the course of 20 sessions. In addition, she decided that she could manage on her own without having to depend on her unreliable, nonsupportive husband. When problems arose in treatment, they were viewed as attitudinal difficulties rather than as signs of resistance; that is, on such occasions the therapist looked for evidence of other faulty cognitions rather than viewing them as motivated, defensive maneuvers.

Clearly what is being described here is a very different model from that of psychoanalysis. Do cognitive therapists function differently than psychodynamic therapists? A comparative analysis of verbatim transcripts of psychodynamic and cognitive therapy sessions suggests that indeed this is the case (E. E. Jones & Pulos, 1993). In this research therapy sessions were rated in terms of the presence or absence of various characteristics seen as relevant to one or another form of therapy. Although the two forms of therapy were found to share some features (e.g., self-image is a focus of discussion), there also were major differences between them (Table 11.2). In the psychodynamic therapies, there was an emphasis on the evocation of affect, on bringing troublesome feelings into awareness, on integrating current difficulties with past life experiences, and on using the therapist-patient relationship as a change agent. On the other hand, in cognitive therapies there was an emphasis on the control of negative affect through the use of rationality and the use of support, encouragement, and reassurance on the part of the therapist. Of course, these fit with the differences emphasized by the two approaches to treatment.

Outcome Research

Does cognitive therapy work? A number of outcome studies suggest that cognitive therapy is an effective treatment procedure, in particular in the treatment of depressed patients (Chambless & Gillis, 1993; Elkin et al., 1989; Hollon, Shelton, & Davis, 1993; Imber et al., 1990; K. D. O'Leary & Wilson, 1987; Robins & Hayes, 1993). However, it has not been demonstrated to be more effective than other forms of treatment. In addition, how cognitive therapy works and whether the changes produced are specific to this form of therapy remain unclear (Robins & Hayes, 1993), an issue that we will return to at the end of the chapter. Perhaps most significant from a theoretical standpoint, it has not yet been demonstrated that the key ingredients of therapeutic change are the changes in beliefs and ways of processing information (Hollon,

TABLE 11.2 Illustrative Differences Between Psychodynamic and Cognitive-Behavioral Therapies

Characteristics of Psychodynamic Treatment

1. Therapist is sensitive to patient's feelings, attuned to patient, empathic.
2. Therapist focuses on patient's feelings of guilt.
3. Therapist identifies a recurrent theme in patient's experience or conduct.
4. Therapist emphasizes patient's feelings to help him or her experience them more deeply.
5. Patient's feelings or perceptions are linked to situations or behavior of the past.
6. Sexual feelings and experiences are discussed.

Characteristics of Cognitive-Behavioral Treatment

1. Discussion centers on cognitive themes (i.e., about ideas or belief systems).
2. Therapist behaves in a teacher-like (didactic) manner.
3. Specific activities or tasks for patient to attempt outside of session are discussed.
4. Therapist presents an experience or event in a different perspective.
5. Real versus fantasized meanings of experiences are actively differentiated.
6. Therapist gives explicit advice and guidance (versus defers even if pressed to do so).

Source: "Comparing the Process in Psychodynamic and Cognitive-Behavioral Therapies," by E. E. Jones and S. M. Pulos, 1993, *Journal of Consulting and Clinical Psychology, 61,* pp. 312–313.

DeRubeis, & Evans, 1987; Whisman, 1993). In other words, it may be that changes in cognitive beliefs and methods of processing information accompany, or even follow, emotional and behavioral changes.

Cognitive Therapy: Past, Present, and Future

In a review of the past, present, and future of cognitive therapy, Beck concludes that "cognitive therapy has fulfilled the criteria of a system of psychotherapy by providing a coherent, testable theory of personality, psychopathology, and therapeutic change . . . and a body of clinical and empirical data that support the theory and the efficacy of the theory" (1993, p. 194). It is clear that Beck's theory and approach to therapy have had a noteworthy impact on the field. However, one can take issue with such an unqualified positive evaluation. First, even supporters of cognitive therapy describe it as "a promising, but as yet not adequately tested" treatment procedure (Hollon et al., 1993, p. 270). Perhaps more important from a personality text standpoint, cognitive therapy hardly stands as a "coherent, testable theory of personality." Cognitive therapy has a focus of convenience, the nature of dysfunctional cognitive processes and procedures for change in such processes. There is, however, much more to personality than this and so far cognitive therapy has done little to extend its focus or range of convenience.

SOCIAL COGNITIVE MECHANISMS IN PSYCHOPATHOLOGY

Dodge (1993) recently reviewed the social cognitive mechanisms present in maladaptive functioning, emphasizing conduct disorders and depression. His review is useful in trying to pull together the diverse concepts emphasized by social cognitive/information-processing approaches.

Dodge notes that a person's behavioral response in a situation can be viewed as following a sequence of cognitive, information-processing steps. The first step in the process is the encoding of the stimulus situation. This involves selective attention to particular kinds of information. The second step involves forming a mental representation, which is an elaboration of pure perception—what is stored in memory has meaning associated with it. When the mental representation is accessed or retrieved, it is brought into awareness with its associated cognitive and emotional features. This accessing of such mental representations as well as possible responses constitutes the third step in the process. In the fourth step there is an evaluation of the alternative possible responses in terms of moral criteria and/or the anticipated consequences associated with each response. As Dodge notes, although possible responses are generally subjected to such evaluation, a response can be triggered without evaluation and without inhibitory control. Such regulatory failure can be due to developmental immaturity or excessive emotional arousal. The concepts of delay of gratification and impulse control are relevant here. Finally, following these four steps there is enactment of the selected response. The concept of skill is relevant to the adequacy with which the selected response will be enacted. In sum, the four information-processing steps prior to enactment are encoding, mental representation, accessing of possible responses, and evaluation of possible responses in terms of anticipated consequences.

Dodge goes on to suggest that problems can occur at each step of the process. For example, aggressive individuals may be biased toward attending to hostile cues in others whereas depressed individuals may be biased toward cues that have negative implications for their self-esteem. In the second step of the process, mental representation, attributions of causality, such as those emphasized by Seligman, Weiner, and Dweck, are particularly important. Whereas attributions of hostile intent set the stage for aggressive responses, helplessness attributions set the stage for depression. It is here that the functioning of the person's schema or constructs becomes particularly important as new information is incorporated into preexisting cognitive structures or results in changes in these structures. Dodge contrasts the cognitive functioning of aggressive and depressed children at this stage as follows:

> Both aggressive and depressed children display deviant patterns of mental representation, but these patterns differ. Aggressive children are deficient at interpreting peer intention cues, and their errors are biased in the direction of presumed hostility by others. The hostile attributions lead aggressive children to engage in retaliatory angry aggression. Depressed children also interpret the peers' behavior as hostile, but they attribute blame for peers' behavior to the self, that is, to internal, global, and stable causes. Depressed children also engage in distorted thinking and overgeneralization from negative events. Hypothetically, these attributional patterns and cognitive errors then trigger depressive symptoms.

Dodge, 1993, pp. 567–568

Moving to the third step, Dodge suggests that problems can arise in relation to the accessing of mental representations and response possibilities. Once more there may be a bias toward accessing particular representations and responses. There may be a rigidity with which representations and responses are accessed or, due to limited schema, a paucity of alternatives that can be accessed. Again contrasting aggressive and depressed children, the former may be able to think only of hostile responses whereas the latter may be able to think only of passive responses. For each, alternative knowledge structures are either not there or not readily accessed. In the fourth step, that of evaluating and selecting responses, Bandura's self-efficacy beliefs are particularly important. Given the choice, people will select for enactment responses for which they have high self-efficacy beliefs and which they believe are likely to produce positive consequences. The person's goals, standards, plans, and strategies play a crucial role in this stage of the process.

Finally, in the stage of enactment both cognitive and behavioral skills are involved. Maladaptive responses can follow from poor selection, but they can also follow from deficient skill in enacting the properly selected response. The response will then impact upon the stimulus situation that follows. For example, depressed individuals not only have a tendency to perceive facial expressions in others in inaccurate ways, but also respond to such perceptions in ways that are likely to make others have a negative response to them (Persad & Polivy, 1993). In such a case, people's behavior operates to confirm their distorted expectancy ("self-fulfilling prophecy") and the sequence is recycled.

Dodge's contrast between the development of aggressive conduct disorders and depressive disorders is presented in Figure 11.3. What he suggests is that early experiences lead to the development of particular knowledge structures and methods

Figure 11.3   Models of the development of conduct disorder and depression.
Dodge's social cognitive model of maladaptive psychological functioning suggests that early experiences lead to the development of knowledge structures and ways of processing information that then lead to the enactment of problematic behaviors.

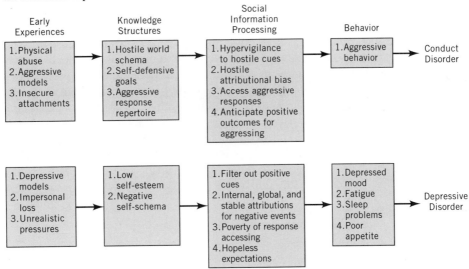

(From "Social-Cognitive Mechanisms in the Development of Conduct Disorder and Depression," by K. A. Dodge, 1993, *Annual Review of Psychology, 44,* p. 579. Reproduced with permission from the Annual Review of Psychology, Volume 44, copyright 1993 by Annual Reviews.)

of processing information. Particular forms of maladaptive functioning are linked to differences in early experiences and associated ways of processing information. Thus, different forms of maladaptive behavior can be understood in terms of differences in the information-processing steps described earlier. It should be noted that Dodge does not suggest that every act follows the entire sequence or that the person processes only one sequence at a time. However, the model is suggested as a useful way of conceptualizing the various steps of the process from event perception to response enactment, as well as a useful way of conceptualizing the maladaptive ways of processing information that can occur along the way. Although not discussed by Dodge, presumably one could similarly suggest therapeutic methods for affecting change at each step of the process.

DESCRIPTION, EXPLANATION, AND PRESCRIPTION AND THE COGNITIVE MODEL

In this section we have considered a number of different approaches that collectively represent social cognitive/information-processing approaches to maladaptive functioning and therapeutic change. How can we evaluate what they have to offer in terms of description, explanation, and prescription? And, how do they relate to Gerald's difficulties? These approaches appear to do a satisfactory job of describing psychological difficulties, particularly in terms of the description of problematic, dysfunctional cognitions. At the same time, it should be clear that the range of difficulties analyzed from this standpoint still is limited. The focus of convenience has mainly been on the problems of anxiety and depression, and to a lesser extent problems in social behavior (e.g., aggression, poor delay of gratification).

Within this context, it is not surprising that much of Gerald's difficulties are well described by these approaches, most particularly by Beck's cognitive model of depression. Gerald indeed came in with the cognitive triad of depression, possessing negative schema concerning himself, the world, and the future. He also was extremely self-critical, interpreting any evidence of his being less than perfect as evidence of his being a failure. It was hard for him to believe that anyone could respond to him or his behavior in a nonevaluative, nonjudgmental way. Until discussed in therapy, he was not aware that almost all his constructs were evaluative and that it was possible for people to respond to him in terms of other constructs.

In terms of explanation, we can understand Gerald's difficuties, and those of other patients, in terms of faulty cognitions, schema, and appraisals. An explanatory model is offered. However, at this point the causal link between the cognitions and the problematic emotions and behaviors remains to be determined. Are the faulty cognitions the *cause* of the difficulties or are they *correlated* with the difficulties, that is, part of the difficulties but not the cause of them? Do the cognitions precede the psychological difficulties? What happens to them when the difficulties recede? And, why do difficulties recur if the problematic cognitions and cognitive processes have been corrected? These are challenging questions for any theoretical model but are particularly crucial in relation to the model under consideration.

Prescription is part of the focus of convenience of this approach, as noted, particularly in relation to anxiety and depression. Thus, the illustration of Beck's approach gives us a clear sense of what the cognitive therapist would do to help Gerald. The focus would be on his problematic schema and dysfunctional thoughts. These would be held up for examination and critical analysis. His excessive standards would be assessed and his past accomplishments, of which there were many, would be considered. In addition, efforts would be made to get him out of the house and out of his seclusion built upon shame over his failures. In a supportive, encouraging manner the therapist would help him to design specific projects that were meaningful, manageable, and useful in restoring his sense of self-esteem.

ISSUES RELEVANT TO THE ANALYSIS OF MALADAPTIVE FUNCTIONING AND THERAPEUTIC CHANGE

In this section we consider issues relevant to the differing views of maladaptive personality functioning and therapeutic change.

SITUATION, DOMAIN SPECIFICITY

The trait, psychoanalytic, and social cognitive models differ in the extent to which they emphasize situations and contexts as opposed to broad dispositional tendencies. No theory of personality suggests that behavior is independent of context. However, the models differ in the extent to which behavior is seen as context-dependent. In this regard, social cognitive theory stands apart from trait theory and psychoanalytic theory. Social cognitive theorists suggest that functioning is highly context-specific, that the person differentiates among situations and responds accordingly. Although maladaptive functioning may be more rigid, and therefore demonstrates less differentiation among situations, it still is seen as relatively context-specific. In contrast, trait and psychoanalytic models emphasize much greater consistency across situations and contexts.

SYSTEM FUNCTIONING

The concept of a system suggests that different parts are operating in conjunction with one another, that the functioning of one part is influenced by the functioning of the other parts. From this standpoint, maladaptive functioning expresses not just problematic aspects of parts of the system, but problematic functioning of the system as a whole. For example, a systems model would emphasize conflict among thoughts and feelings as well as maladaptive aspects of particular thoughts or feelings. In this context, the psychoanalytic model is the most systems oriented of the three (Pervin, 1989). The psychoanalytic model clearly emphasizes the dynamic interplay among forces (motives, drives, instincts) that can be operating in conjunction with, or in opposition to, one another. In contrast, at least at the present time, the trait model emphasizes the independent operation of each trait or the additive influence of particular traits. Originally the social cognitive model did not emphasize a systems perspective. However, with the more recent emphasis on conflicts among goals and possible selves, a greater systems emphasis has begun to emerge.

The difference in this regard between the psychoanalytic model and the two other models can be seen in the associated views of therapeutic change. According to psychoanalytic theory, it is not just individual responses that change but basic relations among structural units. In contrast, in Eysenck's behavioral approach to treatment, as well as in the cognitive therapy approaches, there is an emphasis on changes in specific maladaptive behaviors and cognitions. The difference can also be seen in relation to the attention given to why people do not change. As noted earlier, in psychoanalysis considerable attention is given to the concept of resistance, that is, to the parts of the person that resist change and make change difficult. Resistance is understood to be an inevitable part of the dynamics of system functioning and system change. In contrast, behavioral and cognitive approaches give far less attention to the concept of resistance (Wachtel, 1982).

EMPHASIS ON UNCONSCIOUS INFLUENCES

The psychoanalytic model emphasizes unconscious influences to a greater extent than either of the other two models. In the early days of psychoanalysis, the bringing into consciousness of what formerly was unconscious was seen as the central task of therapy. Today, many analysts would still view this as the central task although others would view it as an accompaniment of other changes (e.g., the corrective emotional experience). At the other extreme, there is the trait model's neglect or rejection of the importance of unconscious influences. In the middle would be social cognitive theory and cognitive therapies. Social cognitive theory emphasizes nonconscious, automatic cognitive processes and the influences of such processes on feelings and behavior (Chapter 7). For the most part, cognitive therapies emphasize irrational and maladaptive thoughts that can be verbalized by patients or readily attended to with the assistance of the therapist. At the same time, many cognitive therapists increasingly are attending to thoughts that are outside the patient's awareness, corresponding to cognitive theory's greater interest in such cognitive processes. As described by two representatives of this point of view,

> This is an interesting turn of events for an approach that developed in the 1950s out of a rejection of conceptualizations that utilized the notion of unconscious motivation and thought. . . . To be sure, this does not make any of the cognitive therapies equivalent to psychoanalysis, but it does demonstrate the wisdom of some of Freud's clinical insights.
>
> Davison & Neale, 1994, p. 584

COGNITION, AFFECT, AND BEHAVIOR

What are the relations among thoughts, feelings, and behavior? Historically this has been a major issue for psychology with various models emphasizing the predominance of one over the other. In terms of the issues under consideration, different models can emphasize the greater importance of one or the other in relation to maladaptive functioning and therapeutic change (Pervin, 1984). In the early days of behavior therapy, attention was focused almost exclusively on behavior. This was particularly the case with approaches influenced by the learning theorist B.F. Skinner. With the development of cognitive therapies, greater attention was paid to thoughts and how irrational thoughts can lead to maladaptive feelings. Psychoanalysts attach importance to disturbances in reality testing (i.e., the ability of the individual to perceive events realistically and cope with them accordingly) and to cognitive processes more generally. In addition, many psychoanalytic researchers currently emphasize the importance of concepts such as schema and pathogenic beliefs (i.e., problematic beliefs about the self and other people that are developed during childhood) (Horowitz, 1991; Weiss & Sampson, 1986). Indeed, there is evidence of a convergence of psychoanalytic and cognitive views concerning the role of negative self-schema in depression (Ouimette & Klein, 1993; Segal & Muran, 1993). However, the major emphasis in psychoanalysis is on the affects. This can be seen in the emphasis on anxiety in relation to psychopathology and on the transference and corrective emotional experience in relation to therapy. As seen in Table 11.2, in psychodynamic treatment the focus is on feelings and experience whereas in cognitive therapy it is on cognitive themes (i.e., ideas or belief systems).

CHANGES PRODUCED AND PROCESSES OF CHANGE

In this final issue, we consider a set of complicated questions: Do different therapies produce different changes or are the changes comparable? Do the different therapies produce change in different ways or are there common change processes to all forms of therapy (Lambert & Bergin, 1992)? As illustrated in Table 11.3, changes can be similar or different in relation to the various therapies and produced through common or different processes. Proponents of each form of therapy would like to believe that their method of change is best, at least best for specific disorders or for producing particular kinds of change. Proponents of each model would like to believe that they have identified the key elements of maladaptive functioning and that their therapeutic procedures are specifically designed to affect change in these elements. In a somewhat simplified form, one could say that behavior therapists seek to alter problematic, maladaptive behaviors through the use of learning principles, that psychoanalysts seek to alter feelings through the use of the analytic situation as a growth experience (i.e., transference), and that cognitive therapists seek to alter problematic, maladaptive cognitions through rational analysis and the testing of hypotheses in daily life. But is there evidence that the changes produced are different and that different change processes are the causes of these different changes?

We have already noted the lack of evidence for the differential effectiveness of various forms of treatment (Elkin et al., 1989; Imber et al., 1990; Stiles, Shapiro, & Elliot, 1986). Similarly, there is a lack of evidence that the changes produced by each form of therapy are different from one another. Proponents of each form of therapy may suggest that the changes are different, and someday research may uncover such differential change, but until now it has been difficult to find. To take one illustration of the problem, consider the relation of cognitive change to the alleviation of depression. If we study cognitions at the beginning and end of therapy with depressives,

TABLE 11.3   Relations Between Processes of Therapeutic Change and Changes in Maladaptive Personality Functioning

Different forms of therapy can have common processes of change that lead to either similar or different changes in personality. On the other hand, these forms of therapy may involve different change processes that lead to either similar or different outcomes. Some psychologists argue that all forms of therapy lead to similar outcomes as a result of the same basic change processes, whereas others argue that each form of therapy leads to unique changes that are a result of distinctive change processes.

| | | CHANGES PRODUCED | |
		Common to All Forms of Therapy	Unique to Each Form of Therapy
PROCESSES OF CHANGE	Common	Same processes in all forms of therapy lead to same changes.	Same processes in all forms of therapy lead to different changes.
	Different	Different procedures lead to common changes or outcomes.	Different procedures lead to different changes in different forms of therapy.

we would expect to find specific cognitive changes along with the alleviation of depression. There is evidence that this is the case (Hollon et al., 1993; Robins & Hayes, 1993). However, does this mean that the cognitive changes are *causing* the alleviation of depression as opposed to *accompanying* or perhaps even *following* the change in depression? A critical question such as this remains to be answered (Brewin, 1989; Hollon et al., 1987; Whisman, 1993). Although this illustration focuses on cognitive therapy, similar examples could be given for other forms of therapy as well. Specific effects in association with specific forms of treatment remain to be demonstrated.

This discussion suggests the possibility of common outcomes in association with different therapies. Does this mean that different procedures are leading to the same outcomes or is it more likely that all therapeutic procedures contain common therapeutic ingredients? Are the change processes more similar than different, the therapeutic ingredients more common than separate? Much of the current thinking in the field suggests that this might be the case, that is, that there are common factors operating in all forms of therapy (Garfield, 1992; Goldfried, Greenberg, & Marmor, 1990; Lambert & Bergin, 1992; Roberts, Kewman, Mercier, & Hovell, 1993). Such a common factor appears to lie in the therapeutic working relationship, most particularly in the support and warmth that is a part of this relationship. One can think here of the work long ago by Carl Rogers (1966) on the necessary and sufficient conditions of therapeutic change. According to Rogers, three conditions are necessary and sufficient for therapeutic change to occur—therapist unconditional positive regard for the client (warmth, acceptance), empathic understanding on the part of the therapist, and congruence or honesty on the part of the therapist. Rogers viewed these as determining the therapeutic climate that he believed to be the essential ingredient of all therapeutic change.

Might it be the case that the various forms of therapy indeed lead to common changes produced through common pathways? And, if so, what would be the implications of this for our views of maladaptive functioning and change? For our theories of personality more generally? The view taken here is that further research, with more sophisticated measures and larger samples of patients and therapists, will find otherwise. That is, we will ultimately find that the changes produced by different forms of therapy are somewhat different and that, in addition to a common core of necessary conditions, there are distinctive therapeutic elements to the various forms of therapy. This is not to say that one form of therapy will win out over all others, but rather that different therapies will be found to produce different effects, at least for some kinds of people and for some therapists. However, this remains a belief and the current literature does not offer much support for it.

COMPARISON OF THE ALTERNATIVE MODELS

In this chapter we have considered what can go wrong in the personality functioning of individuals and how maladaptive patterns of thinking, feeling, and behaving can be changed. Questions of maladaptive functioning, or psychopathology, and of processes of therapeutic change, whether occurring inside or outside of therapy, have been seen as basic to our understanding of personality more generally. In this light, we have considered the trait, psychoanalytic, and social cognitive models of maladaptive functioning and change. The three models can be seen to differ in the extent to which maladaptive functioning and therapeutic change fall within their range and focus of convenience. In addition, the three models can be seen to differ in their emphasis on what needs to be changed and how it is to be changed (Table 11.4). Although there are differences among individuals within each model, common positions and points of emphasis on specific issues do stand out (e.g., context specificity; systems functioning; the importance of unconscious influences; and relations among thoughts, feelings, and behaviors).

Despite the suggestion by most proponents of each of the models that there are different changes being produced by different procedures, we have seen that research has yet to find such differences. The case for differential methods producing differential effects remains to be made. It may be that changes in behaviors and traits, or changes in feelings and conflicts, or changes in self-efficacy beliefs and irrational thoughts are key to therapy. However, we must also be prepared to consider the possibility that personality constitutes a system in which change of one kind tends to lead to changes of another kind, that is, that thoughts, feelings, and behaviors change in conjunction with one another. In addition, although it may be that there are different methods of change or different change processes, it also may be that the necessary and sufficient conditions of change are the same for all methods and

TABLE 11.4 Comparison of Trait, Psychoanalytic, and Cognitive Models of Maladaptive Personality Functioning and Therapeutic Change

	Trait Theory	Psychoanalytic Theory	Cognitive Theory
	DISORDERED PERSONALITY FUNCTIONING		
Relevant Concepts	Extreme scores on traits	Conflict between wishes and fears and anxiety and defense; harsh superego (guilt); internal working models	Maladaptive, irrational cognitions (schema, self-evaluations, thoughts) and cognitive processes
	THERAPEUTIC CHANGE		
	Behavior therapy; stability emphasized	Transference; make unconscious conscious; corrective emotional experience	Modeling and guided participation; identify and correct faulty cognitions; collaborative empiricism
Focus of Convenience	Low	High	Moderate-High
Emphasis on Domain Specificity	Low	Low	High
Emphasis on System Functioning	Low	High	Low-Moderate
Emphasis on Unconscious Influences	Low	High	Low-Moderate
Relative Emphasis on Cognition, Affect, Behavior	Behavior	Affect	Cognition

Note: Focus of convenience relates to the extent to which maladaptive personality functioning and therapeutic change are emphasized in the theory.

kinds of change. Answers to questions such as these are bound to have implications for any current or yet to be developed theory of personality.

MAJOR CONCEPTS

Behavior therapy. The application of learning principles to the treatment of disorders of psychological functioning.

Narcissistic personality disorder. A personality disorder characterized by a grandiose sense of self-importance or uniqueness, a constant need for attention and admiration, a sense of entitlement, problems in empathy, and vulnerability to blows to self-esteem with a resulting sense of shame, humiliation, and rage.

Transference. In psychoanalysis, the patient's development toward the analyst of attitudes and feelings rooted in past experiences with parental figures.

Anxiety, fear, threat (Kelly). In Kelly's personal construct theory, anxiety occurs when the person recognizes that his or her construct system does not apply to the events being perceived; fear occurs when a new construct is about to enter the person's construct system; and threat occurs when the person is aware of an imminent, comprehensive change in his or her construct system.

Dysfunctional self-evaluations. Bandura's emphasis on maladaptive self-evaluations, such as low self-efficacy beliefs or excessively high standards for self-reward, that may develop as a result of direct experience or vicarious conditioning associated with exposure to inadequate models.

Modeling. Bandura's concept for the process of reproducing behaviors learned through the observation of others.

Guided participation. A treatment approach emphasized by social cognitive theory in which a person is assisted in performing modeled behaviors.

Cognitive triad of depression. Beck's description of the cognitive factors or schema that lead to depression, involving negative views of the self, world, and future.

SUMMARY

1. Three approaches to personality (trait, psychoanalytic, cognitive) were considered in terms of the description, explanation, and treatment of maladaptive personality functioning.

2. Trait theory, as represented by the five-factor model, suggests that personality disorders can be understood as extremes of basic personality traits such as Neuroticism, Extraversion, Conscientiousness, Agreeableness, and Openness to Experience. Each disorder is described in terms of a pattern of high and low scores on the basic traits, and the traits are seen as relevant to one or more of the disorders identified by clinicians working in the field. However, explanation and suggestions for methods of therapeutic change for the most part lie outside the focus of convenience of the theory.

3. Psychopathology and change are areas within the focus of convenience of psychoanalytic theory, based as it is on clinical work with patients. Psychoanalytic theory focuses on conflicts between wishes and fears, and on defenses against anxiety in the description and explanation of maladaptive personality functioning. The emphasis is on early childhood experiences and unconscious processes. Psychoanalysis is seen as a learning process in which, in part through the analysis of transference reactions, the unconscious is made conscious and there is the opportunity for a corrective emotional experience.

4. Recent developments in object relations theory focus on the person as relationship seeking and on the internal working models or mental representations that are associated with affect, may be conscious or unconscious, and date back to early experiences in childhood. Research was presented suggesting that problematic internal working models, in the form of insecure (avoidant, preoccupied) attachment styles, may form a link between negative childhood experiences and later depression.

5. Cognitive theory includes a number of different approaches, illustrated in the works of Kelly, Bandura, and Beck. Generally these approaches focus on maladaptive and irrational cognitions that are viewed as causing problematic emotions and behaviors. Kelly's personal construct theory focuses on threats to the construct system and the need for therapy to help the person develop new constructs and new ways of predicting events, that is, to become a better scientist. Bandura's social cognitive theory focuses on the role of negative, maladaptive self-efficacy beliefs in anxiety and depression. Modeling and guided participation are suggested as useful procedures for change and all therapeutic change is viewed as being the result of changes in self-efficacy beliefs. Beck's views are illustrated in his approach to depression, which emphasizes the cognitive triad of depression (i.e., negative schema concerning the self, world, and future). Therapy involves the identification and correction of dysfunctional beliefs and negative schema through what is described as collaborative empiricism, that is, through an active, structured, collaborative effort between therapist and patient to logically examine beliefs and develop new ways of behaving.

6. The three approaches can be compared in terms of their relative emphasis on issues such as domain specificity; system functioning; unconscious influences; and relations among cognition, affect, and behavior. The issue of whether different therapeutic procedures produce different kinds of change is highly complex. At this point there is evidence of the effectiveness of therapy, but there is not evidence for specific procedures producing specific kinds of change.

PERSONALITY ASSESSMENT

12

CHAPTER OVERVIEW

Can our personality measures be used to make accurate predictions concerning how people will perform on specific tasks or in specific jobs? In this chapter we consider the strengths and limitations of the various kinds of data—self-report data, life-history data, ratings by observers, and experimental data—personality psychologists use in their research and applied efforts. We also consider the extent to which observations from these data sources lead to similar conclusions and predictions, that is, whether the different data sources lead to equivalent or different pictures of the person. The general theme in the chapter is that different theories of personality are associated with different kinds of data and that we need multiple methods of personality assessment in our research and applied efforts.

Questions to Be Addressed in This Chapter

1 Suppose you were asked to select individuals to serve as spies and saboteurs during war. How would you go about the task? Which personality characteristics would be crucial and how would you assess candidates in relation to them?

2 What are the strengths and limitations of different personality measures? For example, although self-ratings provide considerable information, can they be validated by the ratings of observers? To what extent are subjects able to give deceptive pictures of themselves? If we use fantasy measures, what is the relation of fantasy to overt behavior?

3 What evidence is there of the utility of personality data in making real-life predictions and decisions?

4 How can personality assessment methods adjust for diversity in subject populations?

5 What is the relation between personality theory and personality assessment?

In this chapter we consider questions concerning the assessment of personality. Throughout the previous chapters we have considered a great variety of personality data—questionnaires, scales, ratings, measures of responses to experimental situations, physiological data, and so on. Thus, throughout the text we have been concerned with questions of **personality assessment**. Why, then, a separate chapter on assessment? The term *assessment,* as opposed to *measure* or *test,* suggests two things. First, it suggests an effort to gather many kinds of information about an individual in order to understand the various parts of personality or personality as a whole. This is in contrast to a measure or test that considers only a specific aspect of the individual's personality. Second, the term *assessment* suggests that the information obtained will be used to make a prediction or decision of some consequence. For example, the person may be assessed relative to job employment or assignment to a particular form of psychotherapy. Thus, the term suggests an interest in broader aspects of personality functioning and an interest in utilizing the information obtained in making a prediction or decision.

A chapter on personality assessment allows us to pull together much that has been previously considered and to address new issues as well. It allows us to consider questions such as the following: What is the relation of different types of data to one another? What is the utility of personality data in making real-life predictions and decisions? What is the relation between personality theory and personality assessment? Before turning to these and related questions, however, let us begin with a story. The story involves what has been called a "milestone study" in the history of personality assessment—the effort to assess the suitability of individuals to serve as U.S. undercover agents during World War II (OSS Assessment Staff, 1948; Taft, 1959; Wiggins, 1973). What follows is the story of the efforts of a group of psychologists, led by Henry Murray, to assess individuals on a broad variety of personality measures to determine those who were fit to serve behind enemy lines as resistance leaders, spies, and saboteurs.

THE ASSESSMENT OF MEN BY THE STAFF OF THE OFFICE OF STRATEGIC SERVICES

The Office of Strategic Services (OSS), forerunner to the Central Intelligence Agency, was created in 1942 to select and train agents to gather strategic information and conduct destructive operations behind enemy lines. As part of the effort, a selection board was established based on the model used by the British, itself based on the selection approach developed by the Germans. The task of the selection staff, mainly although not exclusively consisting of psychologists, was to decide whether a candidate was suitable for such an effort and to make recommendations concerning the specific tasks appropriate for that individual (e.g., spying, sabotage, resistance leader). The staff had to operate under tremendous time constraints, conditions of considerable uncertainty, and great stress in terms of the consequences of incorrect decisions, in particular the recommendation of someone as fit for service who ultimately would turn out to be unsatisfactory. Since this was war time, there was not the luxury of scholarly consideration of measures, procedures, and so forth. Of particular help would have been the opportunity to do a task or criterion analysis, that is, a study of the actual skills required by agents in the field and the personality characteristics of successful agents. Not only that, but the selection staff did not usually know which task or assignment was being considered for the individual. Thus, they had to assess the candidates on a broad range of characteristics thought to be relevant to the potential set of undercover assignments.

What skills and personality characteristics are necessary or desirable for an individual serving in such a capacity? Perhaps the image of James Bond comes to mind. Does this mean that we look for James Bond–type individuals and reject those who do not fit the model? What the staff did was to formulate a list of abilities and personality characteristics thought to be desirable for work as an undercover agent. The resulting list is presented in Table 12.1. Then the staff set out to develop a procedure to assess candidates on the relevant characteristics. The decision was made to use, wherever possible, multiple techniques to assess any one characteristic. Thus, the assessment staff obtained data from interviews, informal observations, performance in specific individual and group tasks, and projective tests such as the Rorschach and TAT. As one illustration of a test situation used by the assessment staff, candidates were told to assume a new identity with a cover story and to answer questions honestly only when they were told they were in "X condition." Later they were interviewed concerning a stressful task they had performed. Could the candidate now be tricked into breaking cover under the presumed conditions of interest and support but when "X condition" had not been announced? Although in some cases the procedure used resulted in an objective quantitative score, in most cases the staff made ratings of the candidate on each task performed and the relevant characteristics.

We have already covered a number of important assessment issues—definition and analysis of the criterion toward which one is trying to predict, development of a list of relevant abilities and personality characteristics, and specification of tests or procedures to be used for the assessment of these abilities and characteristics. Now we come to the issue of how the data will be organized to make a prediction. One possibility, generally favored by assessment psychologists, is to study the relation of

TABLE 12.1   General and Special Qualifications for OSS Overseas Service

General Qualifications

1. *Motivation for assignment:* war morale, interest in proposed job.
2. *Energy.and initiative:* activity level, zest, effort, initiative.
3. *Effective intelligence:* ability to select strategic goals and the most efficient means of attaining them; quick practical thought—resourcefulness, originality, good judgment—in dealing with things, people, or ideas.
4. *Emotional stability:* ability to govern disturbing emotions, steadiness and endurance under pressure, snafu tolerance, freedom from neurotic tendencies.
5. *Social relations:* ability to get along well with other people, good will, team player tact, freedom from disturbing prejudices, freedom from annoying traits.
6. *Leadership:* social initiative, ability to evoke cooperation, organizing and administering ability, acceptance of responsibility.
7. *Security:* ability to keep secrets; caution, discretion, ability to bluff and to mislead.

Special Qualifications

8. *Physical ability:* agility, daring, ruggedness, stamina.
9. *Observing and reporting:* ability to observe and to remember accurately significant facts and their relations, to evaluate information, to report succinctly.
10. *Propaganda skills:* ability to apperceive the psychological vulnerabilities of the enemy; to devise subversive techniques of one sort or another; to speak, write, or draw persuasively.

Source: Assessment of Men (pp. 30–31) by the OSS Assessment Staff, 1948, New York: Rinehart.

each variable to the criterion and then to study how combinations of variables might best be used to predict the criterion. For example, if interested in who will make the best salesperson, one might determine how each of a number of skill and personality variables relates to sales success and then determine the best combination of scores for predicting the criterion of sales success. Alternatively, one could develop a picture of the ideal type of person for the job and then come up with an overall assessment of how close the individual comes to this ideal. In this holistic approach, generally emphasized by clinicians, it is the total person who is assessed rather than individual variables or combinations of variables.

Because the OSS assessment staff could not first study the relation of individual measures to performance, and because of the great amount and variety of information collected, a more clinical approach to the organization of information was taken. In addition, as leader of the effort, Henry Murray was clearly disposed toward such a clinical, holistic approach. Thus, the staff operated as a diagnostic council in which data were presented, reports were read, and observations shared, leading to the development of consensus ratings of the candidate on the relevant characteristics (see Table 12.1). Finally, the staff made an overall judgment of the suitability of the candidate for assignment as well as judgments of the relative suitability for different assignments such as saboteur or resistance leader.

So, we now have considered another assessment question, that of how to organize the data so as to make a prediction. And, finally we come to the end of the story and the last assessment issue—how well did they do? What was the predictive utility or predictive validity of the effort? Here, unfortunately, we have a less than satisfactory answer. The details of this part of the story are complex but basically involve a very important issue—how do we evaluate the results of an assessment effort? What is the criterion to be used as a measure of the success of the assessment effort? In this case, do we use an objective measure such as whether the agent lived or died? This would hardly seem satisfactory since performance need not have been related to this outcome measure—many successful agents died in the course of making a monumental contribution to the war effort. So, perhaps we have to turn to a more subjective measure such as ratings of performance. But, who is to rate the agent's performance? In this case, each assessed candidate who went overseas received four assessments: by the assessment staff based overseas, by the agent's immediate supervisors, by the staff considering the agent for further assignment once a tour of duty had been completed, and by the staff appraising the candidate upon return from duty. Each of these probably seems a reasonable possibility as the basis for rating the agent's performance, and one would expect all four to be in reasonable agreement. Assessment psychologists rarely have things so easy. The average correlation among appraisal ratings from the four methods was .52, not a very impressive record of agreement!

So, we might ask, how did the original assessment staff do relative to each of the four methods of evaluating final performance? Here, once more, the record is somewhat disappointing. The correlations between the assessment staff's ratings and the four types of final appraisal ranged between .08 and .53, averaging less than .30. The authors of the final report were led to conclude that "none of our statistical computations demonstrates that our system of assessment was of great value" (OSS Staff, 1948, p. 423). However, at least one outstanding personality psychologist suggests that the staff may have been too critical of itself in this regard. Further analysis of the data suggested that even these low correlations could have been of value in improving the predictive effort. In such a case, eliminating but a few of the individuals who otherwise would have incorrectly been assigned to overseas duty represents a substantial contribution. Thus, this psychologist concludes his review of the effort as follows:

> This remarkable volume must be considered as ranking among the most significant treatises on personality assessment ever written. The authors were painfully aware of the difficulties of conducting an assessment program in the absence of a satisfactory criterion analysis, with assessment procedures of unknown validity, in a situation in which adequate appraisals of the outcomes were not possible.
>
> Wiggins, 1973, p. 539

However one might be led to evaluate the OSS assessment results, the point here has been to illustrate certain points and note certain issues. These may be listed as follows:

1. How does one go about defining the personality characteristics relevant to the problem or criterion of interest?
2. How does one decide which is the best measure of each personality charac-

teristic? If multiple measures are used for each characteristic, as might seem reasonable and as was done in the OSS project, what does one do if the measures do not agree? That is, what does one do if there is low agreement or low reliability among measures of the particular characteristic?

3. How does one organize the information so as to make a prediction? Does one do it on a more holistic basis or on a less global basis? Is more information always useful or can too much information be overwhelming?

4. How does one decide on the proper criterion or measure to which one is trying to predict? In some cases such a criterion may be obvious, such as sales as a measure of success for a salesperson. However, in other cases the criterion may be less obvious and more ambiguous, such as that of success as a therapist or as a leader. In other words, our evaluation of the success of the assessment effort may depend partly on the criterion measure used. That is, in some cases the validity of a personality test, scale, or rating will depend on the criterion it is being measured against.

Personality assessment is a sufficiently complex field that we will not be able to give definitive answers to all of these questions. However, with the OSS story in mind, we are in a better position to address these as well as other questions that will arise.

TYPES OF PERSONALITY DATA

As noted at the beginning of this chapter, in the course of this text we have had an opportunity to consider a variety of personality data. The personality measures discussed have included questionnaires, ratings, responses to experimental tests, preferences, and physiological measures (Table 12.2). It may be useful to group this diverse array of measures into categories. Block (1993), as noted in Chapter 6, distinguishes among four categories of personality measures: *L-data, O-data, T-data,* and *S-data (LOTS)*. L-data consist of life-record or life-history data. Past history of accomplishment or criminality would be illustrative of such data. When accurate records are kept, such data can be quite objective and informative about the person. O-data consist of observer ratings by parents, teachers, spouses, or peers. We have seen O-data used by Magnusson in teacher ratings of hyperactivity, by Sroufe in ratings of attachment, and by Block in terms of Q-sort descriptions of individuals at different points in time. Ratings were the fundamental measure used by the OSS staff in its assessment project, both in terms of the initial assessment of candidates and the final evaluation of performance. Ratings have the advantage of being able to assign an overall score to diverse data. For example, the OSS staff made use of a variety of data to arrive at a rating for each candidate on each of the relevant variables. As used by Block and Block (1980) in their longitudinal work, they also provide for comparison across ages when different testing procedures have been used. However, ratings are inherently subjective and, as seen in the OSS project, often unreliable in terms of agreement among raters. Ratings may be averaged to arrive at a reasonable score.

TABLE 12.2   Illustrative Personality Measures Noted in Previous Chapters

Measure	Type of Data	Concept	Psychologist	Chapter
TAT	T	Achievement motive	Murray; McClelland	1
Structured interview	S	Type A	Friedman & Rosenman	1
EPI	S	Traits	Eysenck	2
NEO-PI	S	Traits	Costa & McCrae	2
EFT	T	Cognitive style	Witkin	3
Rep Test	S	Personal construct	Kelly	3
I-E Scale	S	Generalized expectancies	Rotter	3
ASQ	S	Attributional style	Seligman & Peterson	3
Approach-avoidance	T	Conflict	Miller	4
SIDE	S	Home environment	Dunn & Plomin	5
Ratings	O	Hyperactivity	Magnusson	6
Criminal records	L	Criminality	Magnusson	6
California Q-set	O	Ego-control, ego-resilience	Block	6
Dart throwing	T	Unconscious	Silverman	7
Partner preference	S	Self-verification	Swann	8
Helper T cells	T	Self-efficacy beliefs	Bandura	8
Free responses	S	Personal projects, personal strivings, life tasks	Little; Emmons; Cantor	9
Ways of Coping	S	Coping	Lazarus	10
LOT	S	Optimism	Scheier & Carver	10
GSR	T	Arousal	Wegner	10
Dreams	S	"Opening up"	Pennebaker	10

L = Life-record data
O = Observer data
S = Self-report data
T = Objective test data

However, as noted, ratings always involve an element of subjectivity; and when there is disagreement among raters, an average rating may be a highly questionable measure of the personality characteristic of interest to the researcher.

T-data are derived from experimental procedures or standardized tests. In many ways they represent the objective and experimental ideal. The use of T-data was seen most clearly in Bandura's work on performance in relation to goals and in research using physiological measures of stress (e.g., heart rate, galvanic skin conductance, immunological system functioning). What should be noted here, however, is that often T-data are used in conjunction with other kinds of data. Thus, Bandura uses performance data in conjunction with subject ratings of self-efficacy beliefs, and physiological measures of stress often are used in conjunction with responses to questionnaires assessing coping style. T-data in personality research most typically are used to test a hypothesis concerning personality functioning rather than as a basis for emphasizing individual differences. Such data typically represent a very limited sampling of the person's behavior with uncertain generalizability to functioning in more naturalistic settings.

To the extent that individual differences are emphasized in personality research, S-data or self-report data constitute a major portion of such research. This should be clear from the many illustrative questionnaires and self-report scales that have been presented throughout the text. Self-report data have the advantage of quickly sampling a broad range of phenomena of interest to the researcher. Questionnaires are easily administered to large groups of subjects, in particular college students who must satisfy a course requirement of serving as a subject, and are easily scored. Some psychologists argue that self-report data can be useful as long as subjects are asked to report on things they have attended to and that do not rely excessively on memory or broad judgments (Ericsson & Simon, 1980). Critics of self-report data argue that people often consciously or unconsciously give inaccurate pictures of themselves, that people often make erroneous causal attributions for their actions, and that people may respond more to the way items are phrased than to their content (D. N. Jackson & Messick, 1958; Nisbett & Wilson, 1977; Wilson & Stone, 1985). Illustrative of this problem of ***response style*** is the tendency to agree or disagree with items regardless of their content, what has been called the "tendency to acquiesce." Thus, subjects may have a preference for responses such as "Like" and "Agree" (yea-sayers) or "Dislike" and "Disagree" (nay-sayers) (Jackson & Messick, 1967; Wiggins, 1973).

We have considered here four categories of personality data and made some brief comments about some of the strengths and limitations associated with each type of data. What is important to recognize is that there are different types of data that the personality researcher can obtain and that each type of data may be more or less suitable for different purposes (Moskowitz, 1986). Although personality researchers typically become committed to one or another type of data, and there are periods of time during which one or another type of data falls into disfavor, it is possible to use more than one type of data in a single piece of research or in an extended program of research. For example, as noted, Bandura makes use of self-reports of self-efficacy beliefs, performance measures in goal-setting situations, and measures of immunological system functioning. Similarly, both Lazarus and Carver and Scheier make use of questionnaires and physiological measures in their research on stress, coping, and health. At least one expert in the field has called for more "integrative methodological pluralism" in the conduct of personality research, a view that goes back to the work of Henry Murray and may be gaining increased support today (Craik, 1986).

A RETURN TO CONSIDERATION OF RELIABILITY AND VALIDITY

Chapter 1, on research methods, discussed the common goals of reliability and validity in all personality research. It was noted that reliability relates to the replicability of observations and validity to the accuracy of the measure used or data obtained. Now that we have discussed many different research efforts, it may be useful to consider these important concepts in greater detail.

Reliability expresses the need for ensuring that a measure of personality reflects true and systematic variation in the subject rather than error, bias, or random variation. Many different kinds of reliability relate to personality tests. Perhaps the simplest kind relates to whether administering the test on more than one occasion will result in comparable scores for the same person—this is known as **test-retest reliability.** Assuming that the personality concept being measured is a stable one and not unduly influenced by minor situational events, one would expect that taking the test on more than one occasion would lead to comparable scores, fulfilling the requirement of replicability of observation.

However, suppose that the very act of taking the test alters the nature of the response. Suppose that there is a practice effect or that the person's responses to the second administration of the test will be influenced by recall of responses to the first administration. In these cases the second test is not an independent assessment and therefore not suitable as a reliability check. To handle such problems, in some cases alternate forms of a test have been developed. Since the alternate forms are presumed to be parallel or equivalent, the extent of agreement of scores on the two tests constitutes another form of reliability—**alternate form reliability.** Although the development of alternate or parallel forms of tests is common for intelligence and aptitude tests, it is far less common for personality tests. An illustrative exception would be the two forms of the Sixteen Personality Factor Questionnaire (16 P.F.) developed by Cattell as a measure of personality traits.

When the test is of sufficient length, reliability may be checked by comparing subject responses to one-half of the test with responses to the other half—**split-half reliability.** Subject responses to the first half may be compared to those to the second half, or, more typically, responses to odd-numbered items compared to those to even-numbered items. This form of reliability tells something about the internal consistency of the test, that is, whether different parts of the scale are measuring the same thing.

These forms of reliability all relate to the consistency of subject response, certainly a requirement of a test of a personality characteristic assumed to be stable. Two other kinds of reliability relate to the person obtaining the data. The first is **scorer reliability.** Two persons scoring a test should come up with the same score for the same subject. Today there are machine scoring programs for many of the major personality tests. In this case, scoring reliability is assured. However, for other tests machine scoring is not available or a trained scorer is required. Many personality researchers make use of fantasy material, such as responses to TAT cards, that require the researcher to score the responses according to a prescribed procedure (C. P. Smith, 1992). Such data cannot be scored by machine and generally considerable training is required to ensure scorer reliability.

A second type of reliability relating to the person making use of the data is **interpreter reliability.** Interpreter reliability is a factor when the assessor goes beyond the scores obtained to make a rating or formulate a personality description. We already observed the problems that can arise in relation to the OSS study of appraisals of performance. There the four methods of appraisal showed poor agreement or low criterion reliability, creating problems for the staff seeking to determine the utility of its assessment efforts. Interpreter reliability is often a problem when clinical data are involved. Given the same set of observations concerning an individual, clinicians may be led to very different formulations of the subject's personality. Another place where such problems often arise is in the use of projective tests such as the Rorschach Inkblot Test. This test can be scored with considerable reliability. And, there are resulting personality descriptions that can be made with considerable interpreter reliability (Exner, 1993). However, when psychologists interpreting the Rorschach go beyond prescribed rules of interpretation, they do so at the risk of loss of interpreter reliability. At that point one no longer is working with a reliable measure but rather, at best, with a creative and insightful artist.

In sum, these forms of reliability constitute the basis for establishing the replicability of personality observations, in terms of both the responses of the subject and the scoring and interpretation of the observer. Scorer and interpreter reliability always are a necessary part of a scientific endeavor. As noted in the first chapter, the essence of science is that the observations of one investigator can be repeated, checked, or replicated by another investigator. There is no need to "take the word" of an investigator or assume honesty or infallibility. Indeed, unfortunately it is not uncommon for honest errors to be made in scoring or statistical analysis, and for published results to fail to be replicated by other investigators.

The degree of reliability required for consistency of subject response will depend on the characteristic being measured and the circumstances under which it is being measured. For example, one would expect two measures of height taken within a short time span to show high agreement but would not expect measures taken at ages 2 and 20 to show much agreement. Similarly, one would expect two measures of weight taken under comparable circumstances to show high agreement but would not expect a measure of an athlete's weight prior to an athletic event to correspond to the measure obtained following that event.

For personality measures, one would expect high agreement between measures taken at different points in time and under different circumstances only to the extent that the personality characteristic being measured is assumed to be stable with regard to time and situation. For the most part, personality psychologists tend to assume a fair amount of stability over time in the characteristics of interest to them as well as a fair amount of stability over roughly comparable situations. However, the degree of assumed stability, particularly in regard to situations, differs among psychologists of different orientations. For example, trait psychologists emphasize generality of response across situations while social cognitive psychologists emphasize the situation or context-dependent nature of personality functioning. Trait psychologists would expect much greater consistency of behavior in terms of characteristics such as honesty, sociability, and dominance than would social cognitive psychologists. Thus, these two views hold different implications for the kinds of response consistency or reliability that are expected and required, although both would insist on observer reliability.

We now have had a chance to explore the concept of reliability in greater depth than in the first chapter and will seek to do the same for the concept of validity. In the earlier chapter it was suggested that validity had to do with the truth or accuracy of the measure. The validity of a test involves the accuracy with which it measures what it purports to measure. As with reliability, a number of kinds of validity can be differentiated. In **concurrent validity,** scores derived from a test are found to correspond to those derived from another test. For example, scores derived from a short test of a personality concept might correspond to those derived from the lengthier version, giving the short test evidence of concurrent validity. Or, scores derived from a questionnaire might be found to correspond to scores derived from a lengthier interview procedure. In fact, the Minnesota Multiphasic Personality Inventory (MMPI), the most frequently used personality questionnaire, was in good part derived as a replacement for extensive psychiatric diagnostic interviews.

In **predictive validity,** scores derived from a test are found to correspond to measures of performance obtained at some later date. For example, a measure of mechanical aptitude would be expected to predict who would succeed in a related training program, and a measure of artistic aptitude would be expected to differentiate between those who later demonstrated artistic ability and those who did not. To take two further examples, closer to personality research, a measure of need for achievement would be expected to predict business success and a measure of the trait of Conscientiousness, as measured by the NEO-PI questionnaire, would be expected to predict job performance.

The concepts of concurrent validity and predictive validity are reasonably straightforward. Now we come to a third kind of validity, one both more complex and more central to personality theory and research—*construct validity* (Campbell & Fiske, 1959; Cronbach & Meehl, 1955). **Construct validity** relates to the gathering of research evidence in support of a personality concept or construct as well as a measure of that construct. In many ways it is similar to the gathering of evidence in support of a theory; that is, it involves an ongoing process of formulating and testing hypotheses. To the extent that research findings support the hypotheses, there is increasing evidence to support the personality construct and the measure of the construct. If research findings do not support the hypotheses, then there is a problem with the construct, the measure of the construct, or both.

Perhaps it is best to view the concept of construct validity within the context of an actual research program. Consider, for example, the concept of a Type A behavior pattern noted in Chapter 1. The history of this research begins with the clinical observation by two cardiologists of a possible link between a pattern of personality characteristics and risk of heart disease (Friedman & Rosenman, 1974). The cardiologists observed that many younger patients suffering from cardiac disorders had a particular constellation of behavioral characteristics, including competitive achievement striving, a sense of time urgency, and aggressiveness. A *structured interview (SI)* procedure was developed to measure individual differences in this regard. In the SI, both content of responses and expressive style were measured, the latter in terms of characteristics such as vocal speed, volume, and explosiveness. Later, a questionnaire was developed to measure individual differences in Type A characteristics—the Jenkins Activity Survey (JAS) (Jenkins, 1979). So far, so good. We have a concept, Type A personality characteristics, and measures, the SI and the JAS. But the story now starts to become complicated and brings us to the heart of construct validity. In ensuing research, two problems started to emerge. First, results associated with the SI did not always correspond to those associated with the JAS. Which was the more valid measure? The results using the SI seemed more consistent with the theory than did those using the JAS, suggesting greater validity for the SI as a measure of the Type A pattern. However, even the results using the SI were somewhat inconsistent. Further research suggested that while the cardiologists had defined the Type A pattern in terms of multiple characteristics, the key ingredient was hostility (Contrada, Leventhal, & O'Leary, 1990). In other words, the hostility component seemed key to the relation to risk of heart disease. Part of the reason for the limited success of the JAS appears to be that it did not sufficiently tap the hostility component. So, through research we have the gradual redefinition of a concept and the development of greater trust in a particular measure. At this point, much research remains to be done; and the Type A concept as a contributing ingredient to risk for coronary disease, as well as the SI measure, remains somewhat controversial. In other words, there is evidence in support of the construct and the measure of the construct, but much research needs to be done to establish their construct validity.

It should now be clear why the concept of construct validity is so fundamental to personality research. Often in personality research we have two or more investigators who use different tests to measure what appear to be the same or very similar concepts. Yet, results with the two instruments differ. For example, there is evidence that a questionnaire measure of the need for achievement and a fantasy measure of the need for achievement show different relationships to achievement behavior (Koestner & McClelland, 1990). Here we must decide, in the light of research evidence, whether one or the other is a better measure of the need for achievement, or whether, perhaps, the two are measuring different concepts.

At the time that this chapter was being written, a research report appeared that further illustrates the problem being considered. The investigators were interested in exploring whether a measure of explanatory style could be derived from TAT protocols that would correlate with or match the measure derived from the Attributional Style Questionnaire (ASQ) discussed in Chapter 1. Further, the question was asked whether scores derived from a fantasy (TAT) protocol would relate to depressive symptoms in the same way as other measures of explanatory style. What the researchers found was that scores for explanatory style could be derived from TAT protocols and that such scores did correlate with a measure of depression. Indeed, the scores correlated with depression on the same order as did scores derived from the ASQ (.21 to .31 correlations between the measures of explanatory style and depression). However, and here's the rub, the two measures of explanatory style, the one derived from the TAT pictures and the other from the ASQ, showed very modest correlations with one another! In fact, the two measures correlated lower with one another than either did with the measure of depression. Apparently each measure was picking up a different aspect of explanatory style that related to depression (Peterson & Ulrey, 1994). In sum, each measure could be argued to be a measure of explanatory style and associated with depression, but they certainly were not equivalent measures or substitutes for one another.

To take another example, recall that in Chapter 10 there was discussion of the relation between the concept of negative affectivity and the concept of optimism, as well as the measures of the two concepts. Is optimism the reverse of negative affectivity and, if so, shouldn't the measures associated with the two concepts be negatively correlated? And, if the concepts and measures are comparable, shouldn't research using the two concepts lead to similar conclusions? On the other hand, suppose the results are not comparable, as suggested by Scheier and Carver. Then, we must review the nature of the research findings and decide whether they are competing concepts and measures or different concepts and measures. And, if they are competing concepts and measures, which has the greater degree of research support, that is, the greater degree of construct validity? In sum, construct validity involves research findings that support both the concept being proposed and the measure of the concept. It is for this reason that it is so fundamental to personality research.

SOME QUESTIONS RELEVANT TO PERSONALITY ASSESSMENT

Personality assessment plays an important role in business settings where employment decisions need to be made and in clinical settings where diagnoses and treatment decisions are important. However, our concern here is primarily with personality research. Therefore, although the questions considered will at times relate to matters of practical concern, the primary focus is on issues relating personality assessment to personality research.

RELATIONS BETWEEN SELF AND OBSERVER RATINGS

What is the relation of self-ratings to ratings by observers? A review of the research covered in the text indicates the extent to which personality research involves self-report data (S-data). Such data may include responses to questionnaires but may also involve mood ratings, memories, health complaints, dreams, and thoughts. We have already noted the concerns some personality psychologists have expressed in regard to S-data. Murray, as noted, suggested that "children perceive inaccurately, are very little conscious of their inner states and retain fallacious recollections of occurrences. Many adults are hardly better" (1938, p. 15). From a quite different standpoint, Nisbett

(Nisbett & Ross, 1980; Nisbett & Wilson, 1977) raises questions about how well subjects are able to report on their mental processes—do they have access to information unavailable to the observer and, if so, how able are they to make this information available to others? Thus, for reasons concerning defensive processes as well as limitations in what people can know about themselves, many psychologists raise serious questions concerning the validity and utility of S-data.

What is the response of those who make use of S-data? On the one hand, some argue that statements made on questionnaires can be treated as data without treating the statement as accurate. The argument here runs that whether someone reports health complaints on a questionnaire is important regardless of whether the self-report matches actual disease. The suggestion is that it is an empirical question as to how useful that self-report statement is. Without necessarily believing that it is true, we can establish empirical relations between the statement and other phenomena. For example, self-reports of being concerned about the feelings of others may relate to other observations regardless of whether individuals making such statements are independently judged to be concerned about the feelings of others. In this sense, self-report data are to be treated as any other data (e.g., pressing a lever in a reaction time experiment or a physiological response). Their importance lies in the connections that can be made between them and other data rather than in their truth or accuracy per se.

A somewhat different view suggests that people can make accurate self-reports depending on what it is that they are asked to report on. Here the suggestion is that people generally are able to give accurate reports concerning themselves if the questions are specific and relevant to recent events, as opposed to global judgments that require the analysis of an enormous amount of information. For example, Bandura (1986) argues that self-efficacy judgments relative to specific tasks and at the time that the task is about to be performed can be useful even if more general trait judgments are not. In response to critics of the use of S-data who argue that people are defensive (Murray) or that people cannot report on their thought processes (Nisbett), Bandura asks:

> By what means, and for what purposes, would nonconscious cognitive operations that regulate behavior be barred from consciousness, leaving people with largely irrelevant or misleading conscious thoughts? . . . While people are not fully conscious of every aspect of their thinking, neither is their thinking largely unconscious. People generally know what they are thinking.

1986, pp. 124, 125

An even stronger argument in support of S-data is made by Funder (1989, 1993), who suggests that there is considerable evidence that people often are reasonably accurate judges of their own personality characteristics. How would one evaluate such a matter? One approach is to ask whether self-judgments are matched by those of others who know the person. We have already seen in Chapter 2 that there is evidence of a statistically significant level of agreement between self-ratings and ratings by peers and spouses on the Big Five factors (McCrae & Costa, 1990). Funder has attempted to define the variables that make for accuracy of judgments. What he has done is gather self-judgments and peer judgments of personalities of subjects as well as obtain responses to personality questionnaires and records of actual behavior in laboratory situations and daily life. Thus, he is able to consider both the general relation between self-judgments and the judgments of others as well as the specific determinants of more and less accurate judgments.

Funder is relatively impressed with the level of agreement between self-judgments and peer judgments. Beyond this, he suggests that it is easier to make personality judgments about some people than others and that it is easier to make judgments about some personality characteristics than about others. Most critical here appears to be the observability of the behavior relevant to the characteristic to be judged (Funder & Dobroth, 1987). Traits that are easily observable lead to good self-other agreement, whereas those that are less readily observable lead to poorer self-other agreement. For example, the trait of sociability shows relatively good self-other agreement because the behaviors defining Extraversion are revealed directly in social behavior. In contrast, the trait of Neuroticism shows poorer self-other agreement because its behaviors are less visible. Many opportunities to observe the behaviors relevant to the trait also facilitates self-other agreement. In addition, there appear to be relevant sex differences. Evidence exists of greater self-other agreement concerning the trait of dominance for men than for women, but the reverse is true for the trait of friendliness (Moskowitz, 1990). Here the suggestion is that men and women are able to give accurate self-reports, as determined by agreement with the judgments of others, on different characteristics.

Let us now consider the question of self-report accuracy as evaluated relative to the criterion of reports by peers and other observers. First, there is the question of overall agreement. Here we find evidence of statistically significant levels of agreement, which is impressive evidence of validity to many researchers who make use of self-report measures. These correlations are described as "substantial" and as "evidence that both ratings and self-reports are useful ways to measure personality, with at least as much truth as error" (McCrae & Costa, 1990, p. 38). However, those who question the validity and utility of self-report measures are likely to see the cup as half empty rather than half full, with room for as much error as truth. Psychologists who see the cup as at least half full argue that those who know the person better generally show greater agreement with self-reports than do observers who have had minimal contact with the person. Such improved agreement might reflect greater accuracy with more opportunity for observation, but it also might reflect greater agreement resulting from discussion and verbal agreement between the person and a close acquaintance.

When comparing self and spouse ratings, the nature of the agreements and disagreements is at least as interesting as the overall levels. Let us consider here the scores by a husband and wife on the NEO-PI, a measure of the Big Five factors as well as facets for three of the five factors (Table 12.3). The material is taken from a case used to illustrate the relevance of different personality theories and assessment devices to the same individual (Pervin, 1993a). As can be seen, the subject (the husband) and his wife show good agreement on the general pattern of scores and relatively good agreement on four of the five factors—Extraversion, Agreeableness, Openness to Experience, and Conscientiousness. They agree that his outstanding trait is his Extraversion and that he is very low on Agreeableness, although he sees

TABLE 12.3 NEO-PI Self Ratings and Ratings by Wife

Domain Scales		Raw Score	SELF T-Score*	Range	Raw Score	WIFE T-Score	Range
(N)	Neuroticism	110	71	Very high	47	39	Low
(E)	Extraversion	141	77	Very high	144	71	Very high
(O)	Openness to Experience	118	50	Average	105	45	Average
(A)	Agreeableness	37	15	Very low	38	25	Very low
(C)	Conscientiousness	69	61	High	65	54	Average

Facet Scales		Raw Score	Facet T-Score	Range	Raw Score	Facet T-Score	Range
Neuroticism Facets							
(N1)	Anxiety	21	66	Very high	2	29	Very low
(N2)	Hostility	27	87	Very high	15	57	High
(N3)	Depression	14	55	Average	3	32	Very low
(N4)	Self-consciousness	11	44	Low	2	27	Very low
(N5)	Impulsiveness	23	69	Very high	18	61	High
(N6)	Vulnerability	14	63	High	7	47	Average
Extraversion Facets							
(E1)	Warmth	22	49	Average	26	55	Average
(E2)	Gregariousness	23	69	Very high	26	69	Very high
(E3)	Assertiveness	28	75	Very high	29	70	Very high
(E4)	Activity	30	81	Very high	30	77	Very high
(E5)	Excitement-seeking	23	67	Very high	22	67	Very high
(E6)	Positive emotions	15	44	Low	11	35	Low
Openness to Experience Facets							
(O1)	Fantasy	13	43	Low	6	30	Very low
(O2)	Aesthetics	7	31	Very low	13	42	Low
(O3)	Feelings	32	82	Very high	24	61	High
(O4)	Actions	17	54	Average	17	57	High
(O5)	Ideas	24	59	High	24	54	Average
(O6)	Values	25	60	High	21	55	Average

* T-Score = standardized score with x̄ (mean) = 50, σ (standard deviation)
Source: NEO-PI (Costa & McCrae) Psychological Assessment Resources, Inc.

himself as even lower on this trait than does his wife. They both see him as average in Openness to Experience and average to slightly high on Conscientiousness. However, there is a noteworthy difference in the scores on Neuroticism—the husband views himself as very high and his wife views him as low on this trait. The NEO-PI report for him states: "Individuals scoring in this range [for Neuroticism] are prone to experience a high level of negative emotion and frequent episodes of psychological distress. They are moody, overly sensitive, and dissatisfied with many aspects of their lives." The NEO-PI report based on his wife's ratings of him states: "Individuals scoring in this range are emotionally well-adjusted and infrequently experience episodes of psychological distress. They are not sensitive or moody, and have few complaints about life." As can be seen from the facet scores, the wife sees him as lower on every component of Neuroticism than he sees himself. Is this because he knows some things about his feelings that she doesn't? Does this correspond to the earlier reported finding of greater agreement on observable traits such as Extraversion and lesser agreement on less easily observed traits such as Neuroticism? Or, does he use a different scale for measuring Neuroticism and such feelings as anxiety, depression, and hostility? From the data it is hard to decide between these as well as other possible explanations for the discrepancy. In any case, one is left with the task of evaluating the level of agreement between the two. Is the cup half or more than half full based on the overall level of agreement, or is the cup half or more than half empty because of the noteworthy disagreement in a major component of one's internal psychological life and personality? What would the subject and his wife say if presented with this pattern of scores? Is it the basis for harmony or for problems in misrepresentation of one another?

Discussion of the specific areas of disagreement between this person and his wife takes us to the second question that can be asked: What can we say about the kinds of self-reports that are likely to be more accurate and trustworthy? The evidence suggested by Funder and his co-workers suggests that in addition to some people being easier to judge than others, some traits are easier to judge than others. In addition, some people are better judges of themselves or of others. These observations make sense and add to our understanding of the issue of self-other agreement on personality ratings. But what do they suggest about the validity of self-reports? To what extent do people know themselves and to what extent do they, as Murray suggested, have faulty recollections and faulty knowledge of their inner states? And, if some people are better self-reporters than others, can we distinguish among people in this regard? If some traits can be judged more accurately, are we in a position to know on which traits a person is more likely to give accurate self-reports? And, if we are interested in the overall assessment of personality, how much of importance to the individual's personality is likely to be subject to accurate self-report and how much is likely subject to distortion? How much of the essentials of personality is easily observable and how much is difficult to observe?

As can be seen, these are complex and difficult questions. We also appear to be without clear-cut answers to them. In part the answer depends on how one reads the data and in part on the aspects of personality that are of interest to the researcher. Most personality researchers would likely agree about the boundary conditions of S-data, that is, the areas in which such data are likely to be trustworthy and the areas in which they are likely to be questionable. On the other hand, that leaves a potentially large gray area of disagreement, an area in which some researchers are likely to feel much more comfortable than others in the use of S-data.

THE POTENTIAL FOR DECEPTION

How able is the subject to intentionally deceive the assessor or give a false personality picture? This issue is not unrelated to the previous one. With the first question there was an implicit assumption that the subject was attempting to give an accurate self-report; here the question concerns the ability to intentionally distort or give a false personality picture. This issue is of considerable importance in applied personality assessment in which, for example, the candidate for a position may be tempted to present a particularly favorable self-representation. Or, a person might be eager to present a particularly unfavorable self-picture in order to be deferred from military duty or to be entitled to benefits because of a psychological illness. I am reminded here of the time my son was required to take a personality inventory during an employment interview. When he came home he asked if I thought he should have answered some of the questions in a way that would have given an even more favorable picture of himself. I advised answering such tests honestly, for a variety of reasons, one of which will become evident shortly.

Although the assessment issue being addressed here is particularly relevant to applied settings, it has relevance to personality research as well. Ordinarily we assume that subjects in our research are being honest and cooperative. If anything, there is evidence that some subjects wittingly or unwittingly speculate about the researcher's hypothesis and then attempt to give supporting data in the interest of being a good subject and advancing science (Orne, 1962). However, we know that sometimes subjects are intentionally uncooperative or dishonest, and at other times are sufficiently bored by the research that they answer questions in a careless manner.

What have personality assessment psychologists done about this problem? Some have built in checks on the honesty and care with which the subject is responding. We can consider here the MMPI, mentioned earlier as the most frequently used objective personality measure. The original version of the MMPI was developed in the 1940s to differentiate among individuals with various kinds of psychiatric illness. Over time it increasingly was used as the basis for development of a wide variety of personality scales and practical applications. The MMPI consists of 10 clinical scales, relating to various psychiatric diagnoses, and three validity scales. The latter three scales are relevant to the issue being addressed here. The validity scales serve as a check on whether the subject is "faking good," "faking bad," responding in a defensive manner, or responding in a careless manner. It was partly because of my knowledge of the existence of such scales that I advised my son to answer his employment questionnaire honestly. Often validity scales are part of such assessment devices and people seeking to present themselves in a particularly favorable or unfavorable light may be discovered.

What do such scales look like? Consider whether you would answer true or false to questions such as the following: "I get angry sometimes." "I see things, animals, or people around me that others do not see." "At times I feel like swearing." Individuals who attempt to "fake good" on personality tests answer many questions in a statistically infrequent way, in particular to suggest that they always tell the truth, never have negative feelings, and behave as well privately as they do in the company of others. Individuals who attempt to "fake bad" on personality tests also answer questions in a statistically infrequent way that is not diagnostic of any specific pathology. These people appear intent upon presenting themselves in a deviant or unusual manner. Individuals who are defensive are guarded in their responses and deny common personal inadequacies. Such individuals are viewed as trying to protect a self-image, even to themselves, rather than as "faking good" or being consciously deceptive. Finally, carelessness can be determined by repeating some items and seeing whether the person answers in an inconsistent, unreliable manner.

The use of such validity scales in the development of the MMPI was a remarkable achievement. Other personality inventories have adopted similar methods to determine whether subjects are responding in an honest and careful manner. For example, the California Psychological Inventory (CPI) (Gough, 1987), a popular measure of normal personality characteristics, includes scales to measure whether the person is trying to make a good impression ("fake good"), exaggerate problems ("fake bad"), or responding carelessly. Some personality inventories, however, do not include such scales. The NEO-PI includes a final item that asks respondents if they have answered the questions honestly and accurately. A negative response is seen as invalidating the questionnaire, but a positive response is not questioned or otherwise examined (NEO-PI Manual, 1985). A check for careless responding in terms of extended repeats of single responses is used, but otherwise subjects are assumed to be responding honestly (NEO-PI Manual Supplement, 1989). Two recent reviews of this test question this assumption, particularly in regard to its use in applied settings (Hess, 1992; Widiger, 1992).

We do not know the extent of the problem of deceptive responding to personality questionnaires. Clearly it seems reasonable to assume that this is less of a problem in a research setting than in applied settings, but the true extent of the problem in the research setting has not been determined. What is clear from the inclusion of measures of "faking good" and "faking bad" is that respondents often do intentionally try to distort the picture of themselves to be derived from S-data.

THE RELATION OF FANTASY TO BEHAVIOR

What is the relation of fantasy measures to behavior? We come here to personality measures that have been developed in part to address problems suggested in the previous discussion. Murray, for example, specifically suggested the Thematic Apperception Test (TAT) as part of "an attempt to discover the covert (inhibited) and unconscious (partially repressed) tendencies of normal persons" (1938, p. 529). Although some clinicians use a systematic scoring method to derive measures of individual needs or motives from the TAT, most interpret the stories produced in a holistic and subjective manner. When fantasy measures have been developed for research purposes, much more care has been taken to develop systematic scoring methods and to validate the derived measures (C. P. Smith, 1992).

The forerunner of the use of fantasy measures such as responses to TAT cards in research was the work on achievement motivation discussed in Chapter 4. This research actually began with an effort to alter the content of fantasy experimentally (Atkinson & McClelland, 1948). Men from a naval submarine base who had been without food for varying amounts of time (1 hour, 4 hours, 16 hours) were presented with pictures and requested to write stories about them. The stories were then scored in terms of a variety of categories that might be expressive of these deprivation conditions—food-related imagery, themes of food deprivation, statements of a desire for food, and so on. A "need for food" score was computed for each story and a total score was obtained for all the stories written by each subject. The results showed a clear relationship between the period of food deprivation and the amount of "need for food" expressed in the stories. Thus, there was a relation between motive strength, as determined by hours without food, and amount of "need for food" imagery, suggesting that the content of fantasy productions could be used as a measure of motive strength.

Using this research as a base, McClelland and his co-workers set out to develop a measure of one motive, the achievement motive (McClelland, 1961; McClelland et al., 1953). The basis of this motive is positive affect associated with successful performance as judged against standards of excellence. The design used to develop a measure of the need for achievement, or n Ach as it is called, was to manipulate experimentally the level of achievement motivation in two groups and then to observe the differences in their fantasy productions. In one group the achievement motive was aroused by telling the subjects that they were taking tests to measure their intelligence and leadership abilities. As part of a further effort to increase the level of the achievement motive, after taking one of the tests some subjects were told that they had done poorly. This group represented the *failure group* in whom achievement motivation would be expected to be high. The other group, the *relaxed group,* was told that they were taking some tests being used for developmental purposes. After taking further tests, subjects were asked to write brief, 5-minute stories to a series of pictures, some of which had been taken from the TAT and others that were designed with this specific motive in mind (Chapter 4). As in the "need for food" research, it was found that stories written under the conditions of arousal of the achievement motive differed in significant ways from those written under the relaxed condition. Stories written under the aroused conditions contained much more achievement imagery (i.e., stories with a goal of success in competition with a standard of excellence; stories with actors behaving in ways that produce success; stories of positive feelings associated with success). This permitted the development of a scoring scheme to measure the n Ach in individual subjects. In other words, there was a personality construct, n Ach, and a fantasy measure of the construct.

What followed was a research program over a number of years that represented one of the most ambitious efforts by a personality psychologist. Individuals high in achievement motivation were found to outperform those low in achievement motivation on a wide variety of tasks and societies high on achievement motivation were found to have higher levels of productivity and economic growth than societies low in achievement motivation (Koestner & McClelland, 1990). Other motives explored were the power motive and the affiliation motive (Winter, 1992). Evidence was presented that the level of such motives can play an important role in life events. For example, levels of power and affiliation motives can affect whether war or peace occurs (Winter, 1993). Most recently McAdams (1992) has developed a fantasy measure of the *intimacy motive,* defined as a recurrent preference or readiness for experiences of warm, close, and communicative interaction with other persons (Chapter 4). Subjects high in intimacy motivation, as measured by scores on imaginative stories, have been found to be rated by peers as significantly more "sincere" and "loving" and less "dominant" than subjects low in intimacy motivation. Subjects high in intimacy motivation also show greater eye contact, smiling, and laughter in one-on-one conversations than do subjects low in intimacy motivation.

For some time there has been a debate concerning the relation of fantasy to behavior. It is clear from the research that fantasy often expresses a motive that is expressed, under the right circumstances, in behavior. On the other hand, it also is true that people often have fantasies, such as hostile fantasies or sexual fantasies, that are never expressed in behavior. Thus, fantasy has a complex relation to observable behavior. But what of the relation between fantasy measures and self-report measures? Do they correspond or do they measure different things? McClelland (1980; McClelland et al., 1989) has strongly argued that self-report measures and fantasy measures are two different types of measures that show different relationships with behavior. And, as was seen earlier in the chapter in the discussion of measures of explanatory style, self-report and fantasy measures do not always correlate well. In other words, we have here an issue in construct validity!

McClelland suggests that self-report questionnaires may measure something closer to a value than a motive. Thus, although scores on both self-report measures and fantasy measures can be demonstrated to show a relation to behavior, he suggests that motive scores derived from fantasy measures show better relations to behavior in unconstrained situations, are better predictors of behavior over time, and show better relations to behavior in the absence of social reinforcers. As one illustration of the difference in functioning associated with scores on the two types of measures, individuals high on a fantasy measure of n Ach will outperform low scorers on challenging tasks, but not on easy or overly difficult tasks. In other words, they are sensitive to the challenge aspect of the situation. In contrast, self-report measures of the achievement motive do not show such a sensitivity to the nature of the challenge associated with the task (Koestner & McClelland, 1990).

In sum, to answer the question introduced in this section, there is clear evidence that objective measures of motives can be derived from fantasy material and that these measures can be demonstrated to relate to important aspects of personality functioning. At the same time, it is clear that fantasy has a complex relation to behavior, with motives being expressed only under certain conditions and some fantasies never being expressed in behavior at all. In addition, it seems clear that a distinction needs to be made between self-report and fantasy measures. Even when the same term is used, the evidence suggests that they are measures of at least somewhat different constructs.

UTILITY FOR PREDICTION

How predictive are personality measures? Are personality measures useful in predicting behavior? It is clear that relationships can be demonstrated between individual differences on personality measures and differences in functioning in various situations. Virtually every chapter in this text has demonstrated that individuals differing on some personality characteristic differ in other aspects of their behavior as measured by independent means. But suggesting that individual differences in personality matter is different from suggesting that we have personality measures with strong predictive validity. The results of the OSS assessment staff should give us reason for pause in this regard. At the same time, it may be difficult to address this question in a global fashion. Some personality measures may be better predictors than others, and some may be more useful for some purposes than others.

A particularly important concept in relation to prediction using personality measures is that of *bandwidth* versus *fidelity*. As discussed in Chapter 2, **bandwidth** refers to the breadth of phenomena to which a personality concept or measure relates. A measure with broad bandwidth relates to a wide range of phenomena whereas a measure with narrow bandwidth relates to a limited range of phenomena. **Fidelity** refers to the sensitivity of the measure to the phenomena of interest. A measure showing high fidelity suggests great sensitivity to phenomena whereas one with low fidelity is associated with little sensitivity. As noted in Chapter 2, one can think of the analogy of two radios, one with great bandwidth and little fidelity, the other with little bandwidth and great fidelity. The former may be able to pick up many stations from great distances, but the sensitivity to distinctions between stations close to one another or the signal from particular stations may be low. In contrast, the second radio may be able to pick up only stations within a certain range, but within this range it is exquisitely sensitive to each and every station. An analogy can also be made to Kelly's (1955) suggestion that each construct system and each theory has a range of convenience and a focus of convenience. The range of convenience relates to the range of phenomena included within the theory, while the focus of convenience relates to the specific phenomena covered particularly well by the theory. As Kelly noted, personal construct systems and personality theories differ in their range of convenience and focus of convenience. Similarly, personality measures differ in bandwidth and fidelity.

What is the significance of this distinction between bandwidth and fidelity? First, it suggests that comparison of the predictive utility of two personality measures must include consideration of their comparative bandwidth and fidelity. One personality questionnaire may offer limited utility for a broad range of predictions while another questionnaire may offer considerable utility for a limited range of predictions. Such differences would have to be taken into account in comparing the predictive utility of the two measures. One would need to ask useful or predictive for which phenomena and what range of phenomena? It often is the case that bandwidth and fidelity are negatively correlated—bandwidth is gained at the cost of fidelity and fidelity is gained at the cost of bandwidth.

Second, consideration can be given to personality constructs associated with various theories. Take, for example, the debate between trait theorists and social cognitive theorists concerning the consistency of behavior across situations. To a certain extent, the issue can be framed in terms of whether there is evidence of consistency in behavior and the importance of personality relative to situational influences—the person-situation controversy. From this standpoint trait theorists emphasize stability and consistency to a much greater extent than do social cognitive theorists. However, it also is possible to consider the issue in relation to bandwidth and fidelity. Such consideration suggests that the trait concept expresses considerable bandwidth relative to fidelity, and that social cognitive concepts emphasize fidelity relative to bandwidth. In other words, trait concepts reflect general characteristics of an individual's functioning over a broad range of situations but are relatively weak at differentiating among situational contexts, while social cognitive concepts reflect the sensitivity of individuals to situational or contextual variables but provide little in the way of broad descriptions of the individual's functioning. Ideally, we would have concepts and measures that are both broad in bandwidth and high in fidelity. However, as noted, all too often the two work in opposition to one another.

Returning to the question of the predictive utility of personality measures, perhaps this issue has been addressed most specifically in the area of employment and the assessment of job performance. For many years there was considerable skepticism concerning the predictive utility of personality measures for personnel selection. However, a review of the literature suggests "a revival of interest in recent years in the potential validity of personality measures, stimulated in part by advances in basic research in personality" (Schmidt & Ones, 1992, p. 638). Supporters of the use of personality measures point to the predictive validity of such measures in relation to criteria such as earnings and managerial effectiveness (Hogan, 1991). Not surprisingly, some of the recent research in this area has focused on the Big Five traits, and the suggestion is made that "personality measures, when classified within the Big Five domains, are systematically related to a variety of criteria of job performance" (Goldberg, 1993, p. 31).

Despite such enthusiastic endorsements, two words of caution are in order. First, personality measures relate in complex ways to job performance in different areas and to different measures of job performance (Hough, 1992). Consider, for example, the relation between personality constructs and job proficiency in managers and executives as opposed to health care workers (Table 12.4). Whereas scores on the achievement trait are positively related to job proficiency in managers and executives (.18), they are negatively related to job proficiency in health care workers (−.24). Other correlations show similar differences between the two groups.

Table 12.5 presents the relation of nine personality constructs to eight different measures of job performance. As noted by Hough, "the correlations indicate that all

TABLE 12.4 Validities of Personality Constructs Within Job Proficiency Criterion

These correlations of personality constructs—traits with measures of job performance suggest that prediction of performance is a difficult task. In addition to the generally low correlations, the same personality measure relates differently to performance in different jobs.

| Personality Constructs | JOB PROFICIENCY | | | | | |
| | MANAGERS AND EXECUTIVES | | | HEALTH CARE WORKERS | | |
	No. of Correlations	Sum of Samples	Mean Correlation	No. of Correlations	Sum of Samples	Mean Correlation
Affiliation	—	—	—	1	65	.00
Potency	67	10,080	.18	12	500	.05
Achievement	6	445	.18	1	65	− .24
Dependability	22	3,213	− .03	15	758	.24
Adjustment	39	6,203	.11	14	752	.08
Agreeableness	19	2,718	.07	4	168	.19
Intellectance	11	1,616	.09	4	168	− .06
Rugged individualism	6	860	.03	1	72	− .04
Locus of control	—	—	—	—	—	—
All personality scales	170	25,135	.11	52	2,548	.11

Source: "The 'Big Five' Personality Variables—Construct Confusion: Description Versus Prediction," by L. M. Hough, 1992, *Human Performance, 5,* p. 150. Reprinted by permission of Lawrence Erlbaum Associates, Inc.

TABLE 12.5 Relationship Between Personality Constructs and Job-Performance Constructs
In addition to personality measures being differentially related to different jobs (Table 12.4), they can be differentially related to various measures or criteria of job performance.

| | JOB-PERFORMANCE CONSTRUCT | | | | | | | | |
| Personality Construct | OVERALL PERFORMANCE | | | TECHNICAL PROFICIENCY | | | IRRESPONSIBLE BEHAVIOR | | |
	No. of Corre- lations	Sum of Samples	Mean r	No. of Corre- lations	Sum of Samples	Mean r	No. of Corre- lations	Sum of Samples	Mean r
Affiliation	31	3,782	.02	2	736	.06	1	667	.01
Potency	248	30,642	.09	23	17,001	.02	14	38,578	− .06
Achievement	31	3,182	.19	6	15,554	.02	4	19,476	− .19
Dependability	114	21,029	.07	13	25,327	.05	69	98,676	− .24
Adjustment	186	28,587	.11	23	9,364	.05	9	21,431	− .15
Agreeableness	69	12,722	.04	4	7,837	.02	4	24,259	− .08
Intellectance	36	10,888	.01	2	700	.16	2	1,414	− .15
Rugged individualism	32	3,410	.05	3	153	.01	1	7,923	.00
Locus of control	11	2,517	.19	2	8,333	.06	2	8,333	− .12

Source: "The 'Big Five' Personality Variables—Construct Confusion: Description Versus Prediction," by L. M. Hough, 1992, *Human Performance, 5,* pp. 152–153. Reprinted by permission of Lawrence Erlbaum Associates, Inc.

nine personality constructs have a different pattern of correlations with criteria. In addition, each of the personality constructs appears useful for predicting at least one job-performance construct" (1992, pp. 151–152). In sum, different personality measures are important in relation to different jobs and different criteria of job performance.

The second note of caution concerns the magnitude of the relationships observed. Review of the correlations in Tables 12.4 and 12.5 indicates that in no case does a correlation reach above .30. As indicated in Table 12.4, the average correlation of the nine personality scales was .11 with the measure of job proficiency in each of the two job categories. Although small correlations can lead to important increases in predictive success, my own evaluation of such results is that they do not constitute impressive evidence of the utility of personality measures in the prediction of job success. In particular, intelligence often is an important component of job success and it is not clear to what extent these measures would add to the predictive value of intelligence. Finally, Hough (1992) suggests that the Big Five are too limited a picture of personality for the prediction of important life outcomes.

Where do we stand, then, in relation to the utility of personality measures in the prediction of behavior? During the discussion in this section, we have noted a number of considerations. A distinction was made between bandwidth and fidelity, with the note that a personality measure might be strong in relation to one and weak in relation to the other. In addition, it was noted that personality measures show complex and not terribly strong relations to various measures of job performance in different occupations. At this point the evidence seems clearest that intelligence,

TABLE 12.5 continued

SALES EFFECTIVENESS			CREATIVITY			TEAMWORK			EFFORT			COMBAT EFFECTIVENESS		
No. of Corre-lations	Sum of Samples	Mean r	No. of Corre-lations	Sum of Samples	Mean r	No. of Corre-lations	Sum of Samples	Mean r	No. of Corre-lations	Sum of Samples	Mean r	No. of Corre-lations	Sum of Samples	Mean r
1	667	.19	2	116	−.25	—	—	—	1	667	.00	2	600	−.02
7	1,111	.25	11	550	.21	39	2,307	.08	16	17,156	.17	9	2,695	.08
2	162	.27	2	116	.14	3	233	.14	4	15,530	.21	1	300	.13
5	2,236	.06	5	268	−.07	25	1,340	.17	11	25,408	.14	5	1,490	.08
3	778	.18	8	442	−.05	31	2,067	.13	15	9,562	.16	13	3,880	.19
—	—	—	3	174	−.29	7	329	.17	1	7,666	.15	1	300	−.04
1	667	.15	1	58	.07	1	667	.11	1	667	.11	1	300	−.07
—	—	—	1	58	.01	4	306	.06	2	198	−.03	2	595	.25
1	667	.19	—	—	—	—	—	—	6	9,039	.13	—	—	—

achievement motivation, and conscientiousness play a role in most kinds of success in most occupations. However, beyond this the relations tend to be weaker and less consistent. Although we can point to evidence of the importance of personality for performance in important life outcomes, much work remains to be done in this area.

Before leaving the topic of prediction, at least brief note should be made of a historical controversy, that between clinical and statistical prediction. The issue involves how assessment data are to be combined to make predictions. As seen in the work of the OSS staff, a general personality picture of the subject was drawn up and used as the basis for prediction. The approach was clinical and holistic. But what if, instead, the staff had used a formula combining individual test scores to make the predictions. Would the results have been better? In 1954, Paul Meehl wrote a classic book, *Clinical Versus Statistical Prediction,* that addressed this question. Are personality data better combined "mechanically," according to some statistical formula, or are they best combined clinically and intuitively? Is it better to use a statistical formula or clinical judgment? Or, as Meehl (1957) subsequently put it: "When shall we use our heads instead of the formula?" (p. 268)

The clinical versus statistical issue became extremely heated and to this day can trigger strong debate between those favoring each approach. Those favoring the clinical approach describe the statistical approach as "pedantic, trivial, forced, rigid, and sterile," while those favoring the statistical approach describe the clinical approach as "mystical, vague, hazy, crude, sloppy, and muddleheaded." Unfortunately, as is often the case in such debates, many different issues got fused and confused. Argument began to center not only on *how* data were to be combined but *which* data were to be used. For example, should projective test data (e.g., Rorschach, TAT) be used or should questionnaire data such as scale scores on the MMPI be used? And, jobs were threatened. Could the clinician be replaced by a computer that would automatically make predictions based on test scores?

Once more the matter is complex and we will not get into all of the issues. In part, there is the general question of whether there is a known basis for prediction or the availability of a formula. For example, suppose an assessment staff was asked to pick astronauts to go to the moon before any astronauts had ever been selected and their performance evaluated. There would be no directly comparable data available to the assessment staff to be used as the basis for prediction. Or, suppose a treatment decision is being made about a patient with some idiosyncratic features that cannot be included in a known statistical formula.

Although such cases are important and involve times when judgments in the absence of predictive formulas need to be made, they are in the minority. In the majority of cases, evidence exists concerning the relation of the personality data to the criterion. In such cases, evidence suggests that the statistical method outperforms the clinical approach. Clinical skills are important in many areas, but computers appear to be far better at taking large amounts of data and combining them in a systematic manner. Of course, prior research is necessary for this to be done. But, once the prior research has been done, the computer is a more systematic processor of information than a clinician. In these cases, as Meehl suggested, clinicians are better off leaving the work to the computer and directing their skills to other areas.

DIVERSITY AND PERSONALITY ASSESSMENT

To what extent are personality measures equally applicable to members of different racial, ethnic, and cultural groups? We now come to an issue of great import to personality theory, research, and assessment—the equal applicability of personality assessment measures to members of diverse cultural groups. As asked in a review of the literature: "Can a researcher legitimately compare two different cultures using chosen tests, records, or interviewers? Do the results mean the same? Can a practitioner apply assessment equally in more than one culture?" (Sundberg & Gonzales, 1981, p. 478)

Perhaps the best way of beginning discussion of the importance of appreciating cultural differences is to take some illustrations from the business world. A report in the *New York Times* (October 3, 1993) titled "Don't Sell Thick Diapers in Tokyo" describes the problem of "cultural arrogance" in relation to cross-cultural selling. A large American company tried to sell the same disposable diapers in Japan that it sells in the United States. However, Japanese mothers change their babies' diapers more than twice as often as American mothers, and they preferred a thinner diaper that was easier to store and use. A second illustration is a commercial comparing the effectiveness of the company's detergent relative to another company's detergent, a standard practice in U.S. commercials. In Japan this was not effective because the Japanese emphasize harmony and publicly polite business dealings. Another commercial by an American company showed a Japanese man walking into the bathroom while his wife bathed using a soap that was said to make women more attractive. Japanese women took great offense to the commercial because it is bad manners for a husband to disturb his wife's privacy in this way. Thus we see the problems of trying to do business in a foreign culture without understanding the rules, norms, rituals, and meanings of behavior that are part of that culture!

In psychology, the issue has been raised most clearly in relation to intelligence tests. Can the same test be used with members of different groups and be considered equally fair and valid for all groups? In one of the most important books written by a psychologist, one that all concerned students should be aware of, *The Science and Politics of IQ,* Kamin (1974) demonstrated how IQ tests were used to keep immigrants from Eastern Europe out of the United States in the 1920s. Psychologists suggested that IQ tests were accurate measures of native or inborn intelligence rather than measures of exposure to American language and culture. What Kamin calls the associated "race hypothesis" suggested that as the proportion of Nordic blood decreased, the intelligence level decreased in a comparable fashion. He went on to draw analogies to current uses of IQ test data. The version of the Wechsler Adult Intelligence Test used until a number of years ago included the following two items: What does the saying "One swallow doesn't make a summer" mean? What does the saying "Shallow brooks are noisy" mean? Most current students have never heard these sayings but they were commonly used 40 years ago.

For tests of personality assessment, the issue has been raised most clearly in relation to the MMPI. As noted, the MMPI was developed in the early 1940s and is the most frequently used objective personality inventory. It has been translated into many foreign languages and used in countries throughout the world. The first edition, the only edition until it was revised recently, was based on the responses of individuals living in Minnesota at the time. In a critique of the use of the test with minority groups, Gynther (1972) raised the question of whether the use of norms based on the scores of white Americans discriminated against black Americans. He pointed out that blacks score higher on a number of MMPI scales, which some psychologists interpret as evidence of greater pathology. However, inspection of differences in response to particular items suggests an alternative explanation. For example, blacks were far more likely than whites to endorse items such as the following: "I believe I am a condemned person." "People say insulting and vulgar things about me." "I am very religious (more than most people)." Differences in response on items such as these can reflect differences in cultural values, beliefs, and experiences rather than psychopathology. Others have criticized Gynther's view of racial bias in the MMPI, suggesting that the test can be used with equal predictive validity for blacks and whites (Pritchard & Rosenblatt, 1980). In response, Gynther (Gynther & Green, 1980) presents data indicating that compared with whites, more black normals are likely to be falsely identified as pathological, and fewer black patients are likely to be incorrectly classified as normal. In other words, both false positives (normals diagnosed as pathological) and false negatives (pathological individuals diagnosed as normal) work against blacks.

In an effort to be sensitive to these issues, the second edition of the MMPI included a number of changes. First, the standardization group for the development of the scales represented a broader sampling of U.S. residents and included a proportionate representation of blacks. Second, sexist language and outmoded idiomatic expressions were deleted. However, the standardization sample for the second version included an underrepresentation of Hispanics and Asian Americans. Although one reviewer suggests that such unrepresentativeness "appears unlikely to compromise the test in most settings" (Nichols, 1992, p. 565), such a conclusion would seem premature, particularly given the influence of these test scores on important life decisions.

The problem is no less serious in personality research, even if the practical implications are less troublesome. The vast majority of the published personality literature is based on studies with American subjects, mostly college students at that. To what extent do the findings hold for members of different cultures? To what extent are the principles cross-cultural and universal? Sometimes cross-cultural work is done in which the same questions are asked of members of a different culture or a questionnaire is translated into a foreign language. However, this ignores the possibility that the members of a different culture would not pose the question in that way in the first place. This point was noted in Chapter 8 during discussion of cultural differences in the concept of the self. In addition, it is possible that a questionnaire developed in a different culture would have a different structure altogether. Although there is evidence of some universality of the Big Five personality factors, for example, there also is evidence that there is not perfect overlap in the factors in different cultures (Yik & Bond, 1993). In addition, other factors may be necessary to include personality characteristics emphasized in different cultures.

In sum, anyone involved with personality theory, research, and assessment must be aware of cultural diversity. The world is carved up in different ways by members of different cultures and the same words, even when accurately translated from one language to another, take on different meanings in the context of different cultures. This does not mean that it will be impossible to formulate general principles of personality functioning that hold for members of all cultural groups. However, it does mean that such generality cannot be assumed automatically.

THE RELATIONSHIP BETWEEN PERSONALITY THEORY AND PERSONALITY ASSESSMENT

In Chapter 1 a relation was suggested between different personality theories and different research methods. For example, a link was suggested between clinical methods and psychoanalytic theory, the correlational approach and emphasis on individual differences and trait theory, and the experimental approach and social cognitive theory. As can be seen in the research reported throughout the text, each theoretical approach can be conducted within the context of each of the research methods. The theory-method relationship is not absolute. However, the roots of the alternative theoretical models lie in different research traditions. Thus, it has been suggested that there is tie between the kind of data obtained in each research approach and the phenomena emphasized by each theoretical approach.

Does such a link exist in relation to assessment? That is, does a link exist between theoretical traditions and approaches to personality assessment? Here too it may be suggested that although virtually any assessment method can be used in association with any personality theory, a link between assessment method and personality theory does exist. What is this link? Some time ago Campbell (1957) suggested that assessment methods could be differentiated along three dimensions: structured-unstructured, disguised-undisguised, and voluntary-objective. The *structured-unstructured* dimension relates to how much room is left for the subject to respond in an individualistic way. An unstructured interview leaves the subject much more freedom of response than does a structured interview. Similarly, a projective test such as the Rorschach or TAT leaves the subject much more freedom to respond than does a questionnaire with true-false or yes-no alternative responses. The *disguised-undisguised* dimension relates to whether the subject is aware of how responses will be interpreted. For example, according to the phenomenological approach of the Rogerian interview, the interest is in how the subject views the world. There is no disguise involved. On the other hand, on the Rorschach the examiner will interpret the subject's responses in terms of symbols and possible unconscious meanings that often would come as a surprise to the subject. One can also think here of McClelland's contrast between fantasy measures of motives that need not be conscious as opposed to questionnaire measures of values. Finally, the *voluntary-objective* dimension relates to whether the subject expresses a choice or preference (i.e., voluntary response) as opposed to being required to give the correct answer as on an objective performance test.

Is there a link between the personality theories and the assessment devices differentiated in terms of these dimensions? The suggestion here is that such a link indeed exists. Psychoanalytic theories tend to be associated with unstructured and disguised tests such as the Rorschach and TAT. When experimental procedures are used, procedures such as subliminal psychodynamic activation (Chapter 7) are emphasized. In terms of data interpetation and prediction, there tends to be an emphasis on holistic analyses of the personality. Recall that this was the procedure used by the OSS staff and its diagnostic council, led by Henry Murray who was sympathetic to the psychoanalytic point of view. In contrast, trait theories tend to be associated with structured, nondisguised tests such as the NEO-PI questionnaire. As noted, although some questionnaires make use of validity scales to check on the honesty with which subjects are responding, the authors of the NEO-PI suggest that no such scales are necessary—it is assumed that most subjects are capable of accurate self-report and generally are motivated to be honest in their responses. In addition, when predictions are made on the basis of such assessment information, they generally involve the use of specific scales rather than holistic descriptions.

Finally, social cognitive theories tend to be associated with performance tests or objective test data. Although self-report measures are in some cases accepted, such as Bandura's use of self-efficacy measures, there are limitations emphasized in the use of such measures and the general preference is for more objective measures. As noted in Chapter 9, Cantor makes use of self-report data as measures of life tasks. However, once more these are associated with specific contexts and generally related to other objective measures of behavior. In other words, when self-report measures are used by social cognitive theorists, they tend to be situation- or context-specific rather than global measures of functioning, as would be true for trait measures. In addition, it is rare for social cognitive theories to be associated with fantasy measures (e.g., Stewart, 1992), and virtually never is there an emphasis on even more disguised assessment measures such as the Rorschach.

As with the link between research methods and personality theories, the link between assessment methods and theories is not necessarily perfect or always existent. However, it is suggested that a link does exist. In other words, here too different theories of personality are associated with different kinds of data and an emphasis on different kinds of personality measures. The point can be made quite graphic by comparing the data from different assessment measures on one subject. For some time I taught a class on personality assessment. I would divide the class into four groups of students, each of which would study the same subject with the use of a different set of personality tests. One group would read the subject's autobiography and conduct an interview. Another group administered the Rorschach and TAT tests, thereby emphasizing projective test data. The third group never met the subject but had access to responses to questionnaire measures of personality traits. Students in the fourth group had a sampling of the three kinds of data. At the end of the semester all students were asked to formulate their impressions of the subject and predict to some data that were not available to them. Inevitably the students were surprised to observe how different were their impressions of the subject. In addition, they were struck with how different their predictions were, with each group best predicting to data that were most similar to the data they had in hand.

A similar point has been made in a case presented elsewhere (Pervin, 1993a). The case involves an individual tested at the time he was an undergraduate and then followed over the course of 25 years. He took the Rorschach and TAT as an undergraduate. On the former, on one card he gave the following response: "Some sort of Count, Count Dracula. Ready to grab, suck blood. Ready to go out and strangle some woman." His TAT stories often had themes of sadness and hostility. The psychoanalyst who interpreted these stories described him as "vacillating between expressing sadistic urges and experiencing a sense of victimization. . . . He is confused about what meaningful relationships two people can have. At the same time, he craves attention, needs to be recognized, and is often preoccupied with sexual urges." The description was at least somewhat different in terms of the subject's self-picture. Although concerned about his inability to become involved with women and uncertainty about a future career, he described himself as intelligent, friendly, sincere, kind, humane, and basically good. Generally there was a good match of self to ideal self, although he wished to be warmer and more industrious. On the questionnaire (16 P.F.), his responses led to the picture of a person who is bright and outgoing but also insecure, easily upset, and somewhat dependent. Twenty years later he took some additional tests. On the NEO-PI his responses led to the picture of a person low on Agreeableness and high on Extraversion and Neuroticism. At the same time, in relation to social cognitive concepts, he described his major goals as being a good parent, becoming less critical and more accepting of his wife and others, and feeling better about his professional work. In terms of competence and self-efficacy beliefs, he considered himself to be very bright and functioning at a very high intellectual level, although not as creative as he would like to be. He believed that he was very socially skilled: "I can pull off anything and have a lot of confidence in myself socially." Overall he had positive self-efficacy beliefs, believing that he could do most things well (e.g., socially, professionally, athletically). His main doubts about himself revolved around his ability to be genuinely giving and accepting, as well as his ability to be creative.

These are only sketches of vast amounts of data obtained at different points in time from a variety of assessment methods. However, they are sufficient to illustrate the point that at least a somewhat different picture emerges from the different sources of data. At times there is overlap and correspondence; at times there are strikingly different pictures; and at times there are just different points that are emphasized. What is being suggested here is that these differences correspond to the different theoretical concepts and approaches emphasized by different theories of personality. In other words, theory, research, and assessment are part and parcel of one another. It is not necessarily the case that one or another approach is right or wrong, but rather that each may be giving a different glimpse of the true complexity of the individual personality. On the other hand, where different types of data lead to specific and contradictory conceptions of an individual's personality or predictions of behavior, then one or more of the measures must be invalid.

CONCLUSION

What are the implications for us if the previous statement is true, that is, that the various personality theories and associated assessment devices give glimpses of the complexity of individual personality functioning? First, it means that we will want to be wary of fruitless debate about which theory is right or which assessment device is better. Rather, we may want to consider whether some theories are more relevant than others to some phenomena and whether some personality measures are better than others for some purposes. Second, it suggests that we will want to be wary of personality theories and assessment measures that result in simple pictures of people. The psychological world of most people is fairly complex, consisting of a variety of thoughts, feelings, and action tendencies, with the potential for functioning in more and less adaptive ways, depending on the context, the stress created in them, and the suitability of their methods of coping. Some people know, and research has demonstrated, that people can be given a fictitious, generally applicable personality sketch and believe that it is individually diagnostic of them (Forer, 1949). As students of the field, we should be far more discerning and sophisticated in our evaluation of personality measures. Finally, in line with a suggestion noted earlier in this chapter, there appears to be a need for methodological pluralism (Craik, 1986). If people are as complex as is being suggested, then what is needed are multiple methods of assessment used in an integrated manner. In other words, from an assessment standpoint the task before us may be to understand how each of the available approaches has something to offer and, what is most challenging of all, to understand how the pieces of the personality puzzle can be fit together. This was the task that the OSS staff set for itself. Fifty years later, without the demands of a wartime effort, we should be in a better position to accomplish the task today.

MAJOR CONCEPTS

Personality assessment.   The use of personality measures toward the goal of understanding an individual's personality and making a prediction concerning performance.

Response style.   The tendency of people to respond to a self-report instrument in terms of the way items are phrased rather than in terms of their content (e.g., tendency to acquiesce).

Test-retest reliability.   The form of reliability indicating the extent to which scores obtained on one occasion are comparable to scores obtained on another occasion.

Alternate form reliability.   The form of reliability indicating the extent to which scores on two tests agree and therefore can be used as alternate measures of the concept.

Split-half reliability.   The form of reliability indicating whether scores on one half of the test are comparable to scores on the other half.

Scorer reliability.   The form of reliability indicating the extent of agreement between two or more scorers of responses to a test.

Interpreter reliability.   The form of reliability indicating the extent of agreement between two or more interpreters of responses to a test.

Concurrent validity.   The form of validity indicating the extent to which scores derived from one test are comparable to scores derived from another test (e.g., MMPI scores and psychiatric interview).

Predictive validity.   The form of validity indicating the extent to which scores obtained from a test predict later performance.

Construct validity.   The form of validity indicating the extent to which research evidence supports a personality concept and the measure of that concept.

Bandwidth.   The range of behaviors covered by a personality concept or personality measure.

Fidelity.   The specificity with which a personality concept or personality measure can be used to describe or predict behavior.

SUMMARY

1. Personality assessment involves the effort to gather personality-relevant information about an individual toward the goal of making a relevant prediction or decision. The OSS selection study illustrates questions concerning the kinds of data to be obtained, how the data will be organized to make predictions, and how the success of the effort will be evaluated.

2. Throughout the text various personality measures have been used (i.e., Block's L-data, O-data, T-data, and S-data). Each type of data has its distinctive set of strengths and limitations.

3. Consideration was given to the various kinds of reliability that are necessary to establish replicability of personality observations, as well as to the various kinds of validity that are possible. Particular attention was given to construct validity, which involves the progressive accumulation of evidence in support of a concept and a measure of that concept. Without generally accepted measures for most personality concepts, for example, on the order of a thermometer to measure temperature, we are required to demonstrate the construct validity of our measures.

4. The chapter considered the evidence concerning the accuracy of self-report data. Evidence suggests that people can be reasonably accurate judges of their own personality characteristics and that self-observer ratings can show reasonable agreement. At the same time, the potential for self-deception and self-observer disagreement leaves many personality psychologists cautious concerning extensive reliance on self-report measures.

5. Many personality assessment methods build in checks on whether the subject is answering honestly or attempting to deceive the examiner.

6. There is considerable evidence that scores derived from fantasy measures of motives (e.g., n Ach, n Power, n Intimacy) can be related to important behavior. However, the relation of fantasy to behavior appears to be complex and fantasy measures of a personality construct generally show only weak agreement with self-report measures of the concept.

7. The concepts of bandwidth and fidelity are useful in evaluating the predictive utility of different personality measures. A personality measure may be strong in relation to bandwidth or fidelity and weak in relation to the other. In addition, personality measures tend to show complex and often not very strong relations to diverse measures of performance (e.g., in different occupations). The clinical versus statistical prediction issue highlights the question of how data should be organized to maximize predictive validity.

8. How to recognize cultural diversity in personality assessment and research is an important issue in the field. This involves the phrasing of items in questionnaires

(e.g., avoiding sexist language) and the use of appropriate norms for scoring and predictive purposes. It also involves awareness that the framing of a research question may be culturally biased.

9. A link was suggested between personality theory and personality assessment; that is, different theories are associated with different kinds of data. It further was suggested that, given the complexity of personality, there is a need for methodological pluralism or multiple methods of personality assessment.

CONCLUSION: CURRENT ISSUES AND THE PROSPECTS FOR THE SCIENCE OF PERSONALITY

13

CHAPTER OVERVIEW

In this chapter we review some issues covered in previous chapters and consider some new ones. Rather than trying to answer specific questions, we focus here on broad issues in the personality field that cover many specific topics. Such issues include how general or situation-specific behavior is, how fixed or malleable personality is, and whether one or another research strategy is best for the field. In general there is an emphasis on going beyond ideological positions to appreciate the complexity of the field and its subject of investigation—the person.

In the preceding chapters we have considered research covering much of the field of personality. Questions have been raised and answers provided to the extent permitted by current knowledge in the field. Here we return to broader questions, some considered earlier and others not. Until now I have tried to be objective in presenting the field to the student; here I will be much more explicit about my own point of view.

A DEFINITION OF PERSONALITY

Until now we have avoided a definition of personality. It may seem strange to weave our way through much of the field without defining the topic itself. We generally are taught to begin with a definition. How can we talk about what has not been defined? But, in fact, scientists in more advanced fields than psychology often investigate phenomena for which they do not have an adequate definition.

Over the years personality has been defined in a variety of ways, allowing each researcher to investigate the phenomena viewed as particularly important, without the field itself accepting a common definition. Having said this, it is time to take the plunge and offer a definition of what it is that we have been considering in this text:

> Personality is the complex organization of cognitions, affects, and behaviors that gives direction and pattern (coherence) to the person's life. Like the body, personality consists of both structures and processes and reflects both nature (genes) and nurture (experience). In addition, personality includes the effects of the past, including memories of the past, as well as constructions of the present and future.

A number of points in this definition are worthy of emphasis and clarification. First, often the field of personality has been defined in terms of the study of individual differences. As I see it, individual differences are a part of the field of personality. The research included in this text gives clear testimony to the importance attached to individual differences. However, I view the organization of the parts of the person into a total functioning system as the defining characteristic of the personality field.

The analogy can be made to the study of the functioning of the body. We may be interested in how the body functions as a total system, as well as in individual differences. However, it is the organization of bodily functioning that is central to our concern rather than individual differences in particular parts. The point was made many years ago as follows:

> Ordinary definitions of personality put emphasis on individual differences in a way that has been, I think, detrimental to progress in theory and research. . . . If anatomists had proceeded in the same way as personality psychologists, we would know a great deal about minor variations in the location of the heart without ever realizing that for just about everyone everywhere it is located in the chest just slightly to the left of center. The above is not to deny the importance of individual differences; but until we know more about basic processes of personality, it is difficult to know how to fit the differences in.
>
> Sechrest, 1976, p. 4

I agree with what is being said here except that I would add emphasis to the organized aspects of personality functioning. It is not just the basic processes, but how these processes function in relation to one another that is key.

A second element to the definition is the emphasis on cognition, affect, and behavior—what we think, feel, and do. Often these aspects are considered in isolation. For example, the emphasis may be on cognitions or on emotions. Sometimes one is viewed as determining the others. For example, cognitions may be seen as determining emotions. In my own view, what we think, feel, and do are always influencing one another. What we focus our attention on influences our mood, but our mood also influences the direction of our attention. Our mood influences our behavior, but our behavior and its consequences have implications for our mood. Thus, personality includes the interrelations among thoughts, feelings, and behavior. It is the organization of these elements, in terms of the ongoing interactions among them, that is central to personality.

Third, there is a time dimension that must be included. Personality can operate only in the present. However, the past exerts an influence on the present through current structures and memories. In addition, the future exerts an influence on the present through expectations and goals. Our dreams of the future are as much a part of personality as are our memories of the past and our perceptions of the present. As noted in the text, the future cannot determine the present but our views of the future can do so. Clearly the person with a negative schema for the future will feel and behave very differently from the person with a positive future schema.

Having emphasized these points, it is clear that in my view personality is complex. Not only does personality include many things (e.g., cognitions, affects, behaviors), but it includes the organization of these units. It is this complexity of organization that is key to the definition of personality and that has been emphasized at various times throughout the text. Given this complexity, and given the uniqueness of each individual studied, it is no wonder that progress in the field has been so difficult to achieve.

RESEARCH STRATEGIES

In the first chapter we considered three research strategies—clinical, correlational, experimental. The strengths and limitations of each approach, as well as the common goals of reliability and validity, were noted. In the course of the text we have had the opportunity to consider efforts to utilize these approaches toward the goal of understanding personality functioning. Although occasional efforts to use multiple approaches have been noted, for the most part the tendency in the field is to use one or another approach and one or another kind of data—life history, observer ratings, objective tests, and/or self-reports (LOTS). Not only that, but the tendency is to emphasize the strengths of the approach being taken and the limitations of alternative approaches. Those who favor the clinical approach emphasize the richness of the data and the limited applicability of many experimental findings to "real-life" situations. Those who favor the correlational approach emphasize the utility of self-report measures and the importance of individual differences. They are critical of the nonquantitative nature of much clinical research and the limited range of phenomena that can be investigated in the laboratory. Finally, those who favor the experimental approach emphasize the importance of control over the variables of interest and are critical of research that relies on self-report measures or clinical reports of what occurs in the therapeutic setting.

Such divergence of emphasis on research procedures is not unique to personality psychologists. As noted in Chapter 1, psychologists studying memory debate the relation between findings gained from use of the laboratory approach and those gained from naturalistic observation. The issue of where and how memories are studied was highlighted recently in relation to the evaluation of memories of child abuse. Are memories of abuse as a child to be trusted? Concerned with the problem, the American Psychological Association set up an investigating panel known as the Working Group on the Investigations of Memories of Childhood Abuse. It consists of both researchers and clinical practitioners and its task was described as follows:

> Clinicians are more apt than researchers to accept their clients' reports of abuse when they are based on old memories, while researchers are, as a rule, more skeptical about the validity of memories that span many years with many intervening experiences. . . . Clinicians know one set of data and researchers know another. Our mission is to get those two data sets to overlap.
>
> American Psychological Association Monitor, November 1993, p. 44

Many questions are raised concerning research strategy. Is aggression best studied in the laboratory or in more natural settings? Are qualitative data, such as those often obtained in the clinical setting or in naturalistic observation, of scientific value or must all scientific data be quantitative? Can laboratory findings with relatively healthy subjects be used as the basis for therapeutic procedures with clinical populations (Weisz, Weiss, & Donenberg, 1992)? Can self-report measures of mental health be trusted or must clinical judgment be used to distinguish between the truly healthy and those who present the illusion of mental health based on the defensive denial of distress (Shedler, Mayman, & Manis, 1993)? These are among the issues debated in the field, not only in personality but in the field of psychology more broadly.

My own view is that most of these debates are useless and not constructive for the field. The value of qualitative data is accepted in other sciences such as biology and geology, why should it not be in psychology? Darwin's great discoveries were based on observation; why should such research be excluded from psychology? The point here is that we should not be ideological about how or where the data are obtained but focus only on the quality of the data. If the observations reported can be replicated by others and are relevant to important questions, then they should be valued regardless of whether they come from the clinic or the laboratory, and they should be valued regardless of whether they are obtained from self-report or objective measures. Beyond this, there is the need for research that utilizes multiple research procedures and multiple sources of data, as in the OSS study described in Chapter 12. Thus, I am very much in agreement with the following view expressed in relation to memory research:

> There is no question but that field research is important as a source for identifying variables for empirical investigation. However, to become fully informed, convergent methods of investigation are helpful, and the use of multiple meth-

ods—including interviews, laboratory simulations, staged events, field studies, autobiographical memory studies, and clinical studies—all contribute to further our knowledge of emotion and memory. . . . The approaches may differ, but there need not be—and there usually is not—any conflict between approaches: Normally they are complementary.

Christianson, 1992, p. 303

Unfortunately, psychologists do not find it easy to pursue such multiple approaches, either individually or collectively. Some years ago a number of members of my department and I decided to follow Murray's course and study a few subjects intensively. Each of us was interested in a different aspect of personality and each preferred one or another method of research. Why not select a few subjects for intensive study and relate the data obtained by each of us toward the goal of forming a comprehensive picture of the person? There was great initial enthusiasm for the idea but it never got off the ground. A few individuals left to teach elsewhere and the rest were so busy with their individual projects that they were unable to commit themselves to the collective endeavor. Thus, although collaborative research involving the intensive study of individuals with multiple research procedures is a worthy ideal, it is very difficult to implement in practice.

SPECIFICITY VERSUS GENERALITY

One of the most difficult and controversial issues for personality psychologists concerns how general or specific behavior is across situations and domains. The issue comes up most pointedly in the person-situation controversy (Chapter 2) and in the contrasting positions of trait psychologists and social cognitive psychologists. However, it seems to me that the issue is much broader in its ramifications and implications. The question is the following: Is personality functioning sufficiently consistent and stable across situations to permit broad generalizations or is it so specific to circumstances that such broad generalizations are not possible? Answers to this question are important not only for how personality is construed but for how it is investigated. And, the answers touch upon every area of research considered in this text: Can we talk about a global sense of self and self-esteem or must we talk about specific selves and specific self-efficacy beliefs? Is there a *self* or is there a *family of selves?* Do people have general goals or are their goals situation-specific? Can we speak of an individual's general coping style or are coping devices domain-specific? Do people have general attributional styles or do their attributions depend on the content and circumstances involved?

One possible solution to the problem is to suggest that we can treat something as general for some purposes and as specific for other purposes. For example, for some purposes we may want to speak of coping strategy (Chapter 10) as a general personality characteristic and for other purposes as domain-specific. For some purposes we may wish to consider someone as having a Type A personality or as being an extravert, though we recognize that he or she does not always exhibit Type A or extraverted personality characteristics. For some purposes, "most of the time" or "under most circumstances" may be good enough. Another possible solution is to suggest that we can treat something as general for some people but not for others. For example, we might distinguish between introverts and extraverts while recognizing that some people cannot be classified as either an introvert or an extravert in all situations.

It seems to me, however, that neither of these solutions is truly acceptable. In terms of the first suggestion, that for some purposes we focus on generalities and for other purposes on situational specificity, how do we know for which purposes, and for which people, we can operate in terms of broad generalities and for which we need to attend to situational variations? There are no principles to guide us, nor do I envision any being discovered. In terms of the second suggestion, that we think in terms of different groups of individuals, this leads us to a theory of personality for some people and not for others. For example, we may have a theory of introversion-extraversion that applies to only some proportion of the population. This hardly seems like a satisfactory state of affairs.

So where does this lead us? My belief is that we need to develop a theory of personality that recognizes both stability (consistency) and variability (situational specificity) in personality functioning. In other words, my belief is that we must recognize what I have called the stasis and flow of human behavior—that people have general patterns of functioning but also are capable of adapting to specific situational demands. In relation to goals or motives, for example, this means that people have a general goal system, but they are capable of revising goal priorities according to internal demands and external contingencies. We know that it makes sense to pursue social goals in some cases and work goals in other cases, to pursue having a good time in some situations and to pursue self-esteem goals in other situations. We recognize that we can meet multiple goals (e.g., both social and work goals) in some situations but not in others. We recognize that generally some things matter to us more than others but that what sometimes does not matter much can become very important. As we review our lives during the course of a week, month, or year, we are struck both with broadly consistent patterns as well as with the importance of occasional detours. It is this interplay between stability and change, between stasis and flow, that I believe to be the essence of personality. Thus, our task is not to ignore one and focus on the other, but to appreciate and understand the interplay between the two.

NATURE AND NURTURE, GENES AND CULTURE

Both genes and experience are important in personality development. As noted in Chapter 5, there is no gene without environment and no environment without genes. The two are constantly operating in relation to one another. Beyond this, the two always are operating to make humans similar to one another in some ways and different from one another in other ways. All humans share certain genetic characteristics that define them as human beings, male or female. Except for rare abnormalities, we all have two eyes, two ears, a brain, and so on. At the same time, except for identical twins each one of us is genetically unique. This contributes to enormous diversity, something that biologically is seen as desirable for the species. Similarly, culture operates to create both uniformity and diversity. Individuals within a culture tend to share certain beliefs and values. On the other hand, individuals from different cultures vary enormously in what they believe and value.

Over time there have been shifts in the importance attributed to genetic and environmental-cultural influences. And, there has always been some controversy about the relative importance of the two. As noted in Chapter 5, today we are witnessing a surge of interest in genetic contributions to personality, with behavioral geneticists suggesting that 40% to 50% of personality is genetically determined. Beyond this, it is suggested that many environmental effects are mediated by genetic influences; for example, people with different genes elicit different responses from the environment or select different environments. In the course of recognizing the importance of genetic influences, however, we cannot fail to be impressed as well with the importance of cultural influences. A biologist friend of mine is fond of saying that the only thing not influenced by genes is which language you speak. But, I think she would agree as well that probably there is no characteristic of interest to personality psychologists that is not influenced by the environment generally, and culture in particular—including which language you speak.

The importance of culture has been noted in a number of places in this text, most specifically in relation to the self (Chapter 8), in relation to displays of emotion (Chapter 10), and in relation to assessment (Chapter 12). In the course of writing this chapter I came across a rather amusing sports story that well illustrates the importance of culture. It involved a young pitcher from South Korea who had recently been signed by the Los Angeles Dodgers. During his first professional time at bat, he turned to the umpire and bowed, something not previously seen in American baseball. The young pitcher later explained: "We are taught in Korea to respect the elders. I was thanking him for all his effort and for being there for us."

If we know only one culture, it is hard for us to appreciate its importance and the potential for diversity in personality functioning. Many of the things we believe and do seem so natural that we can hardly imagine them otherwise. Thus, many American students are amazed to learn that members of other cultures have a completely different sense of the self. Many members of one culture find it difficult to navigate socially when in a very different culture. For example, although there appears to be a high degree of universality in the emotions that can be experienced, there is enormous cultural diversity in what elicits each emotion, how the emotions are experienced subjectively, and how they are shared socially (Scherer & Wallbott, 1994). Even within American society there are great cultural-ethnic differences in how emotions are experienced, labeled, displayed, and shared (Matsumoto, 1993). The South Korean pitcher who bowed to the umpire indicated that he could not see the umpire's expression since the umpire had his mask on. However, given the diversity of cultural rules for the display of emotions, it is not clear that the pitcher would have been able to interpret accurately what the umpire was feeling and expressing.

Culture influences virtually every aspect of our personality functioning. The goals we choose to follow and how we strive to achieve them are influenced by culture. For example, whether we view achievement in terms of individual effort or group cooperation, and whether we view success in terms of career goals or family goals are very much influenced by culture (Salili, 1994). Culture influences the way we interact with others through standards for what we consider acceptable and appropriate social behavior. And, apparently culture even influences the very nature of our biological functioning. For example, there is evidence that cultural beliefs about aging influence the degree of memory loss people experience in old age. A comparison of American and mainland Chinese stereotypes about aging and differences in memory performance in older adults (ages 59–91 years) finds that the Chinese have more positive views toward aging and their older people have better memory functioning: "The results suggest that a social psychological mechanism contributes to the often-reported memory decline that accompanies aging. That is, it is possible that in the United States, the negative stereotypes about how old people cognitively age, to which individuals starting at a young age are exposed, become self-fulfilling prophecies" (Levy & Langer, 1994, p. 996).

Given the evidence for the importance of both genetic and environmental-cultural influences, it is clear that arguments concerning the relative importance of one or the other hardly make sense. Rather, the task is to understand the constraints and opportunities set by both genes and culture, and most of all the process through which as biological beings we come to acquire cultural beliefs and practices. There are two analogies that I find useful in relation to these gene-environment interactions. The first, described in Chapter 5, is that of the movement of a ball down a landscape. The landscape represents what is genetically determined. The ball rolling down the landscape represents development and the influence of environmental forces. The path of the ball, that is, the unfolding of personality, always reflects the genetic landscape in interaction with environmental events. The second analogy is based on the computer, with hardware representing the genes and software the environmental-cultural influences. Obviously both hardware and software are necessary for a computer to run. The hardware sets certain constraints and potential for the software. Given the hardware, there is enormous diversity in the programs (software) that can be written. Beyond this, individual users of the standard hardware and software can create completely unique products, just as the individual personality is unique. At the same time that we are impressed with the uniqueness of the final product, however, we can be impressed with the hardware that represents the basic structure of the system as well as the software that represents the specific language and functions that can be used. Without this combination of elements, no final product would occur. To take this analogy one step further, as computers have become more sophisticated, as the "brains" of the system have evolved, software has become increasingly important and able to take on an increasing diversity of functions. In an analogous way, the development of the human brain has provided for increased capacity for thinking, feeling, and behaving in diverse ways. Although the influence of genes remains powerful, we are capable of being shaped in enormously diverse ways by culture and unique experiences.

MALLEABILITY-FIXITY, STABILITY-CHANGE

As noted in Chapters 6 and 11, personality psychologists are concerned with the extent to which personality is malleable and how change occurs. Genes clearly set limits to outcomes but they do not fix outcomes. The constraints set by genes may be broad or narrow, depending on the characteristic involved. Similarly, early experience appears to be important but not all-defining of personality characteristics. The impact of early experience depends on the intensity of the experience, how long it lasts, and the kinds of later experiences that occur. The person consistently maltreated in childhood over an extended number of years, and who does not receive better care in adolescence, is headed for trouble. However, constitutional (genetic) factors will clearly play a role in the outcome of such experiences, and the availability of at least some positive experiences and models can turn development in a more positive direction, particularly if later experiences are more positive and build upon any earlier positive experiences (Garmezy, 1993; Robins & Rutter, 1990).

Most personality psychologists appear to have a disposition to view personality as relatively malleable or relatively fixed, as open to change or as primarily stable due to genes and/or early experience. However, we really know relatively little about the boundary conditions for what is possible in personality development and about the factors that determine one or another course of development. We know that some people remain relatively stable over time while others change dramatically. We know that some experiences exert a lasting impact, at least on most people, while others appear to be of more transient significance. But why some experiences are so powerful and others so transient is not yet understood. And, as some psychologists have suggested, it may be that chance events play a far greater role in development than most of us currently believe.

The issues are similarly complex in relation to the processes of therapeutic change discussed in Chapter 11. Some personality psychologists are broadly optimistic concerning the potential for therapeutic change, while others are more skeptical. Each can point to evidence in support of his or her view, but in fact we have not yet been able to define *what* in personality can be changed *how*, that is, what can be changed by which methods. Global answers clearly will not do, just as it does not make sense to speak in terms of whether personality is malleable *or* fixed. There is evidence that at least some aspects of personality can change in positive ways, particularly in the context of a supportive, positive relationship. My own sense is that affects (emotions) are more difficult to change than cognitions (beliefs) and behaviors. But, the fact of the matter is that we still know relatively little about the processes of change, at least in terms of being able to say with confidence that a specific therapeutic procedure will result in specific therapeutic consequences, at least for specified individuals. Despite growing efforts to prescribe treatments for specific psychological difficulties, to a considerable extent our efforts are more on the order of belief and trial and error; that is, different therapists believe that their efforts are therapeutic and, on the whole, have a degree of success with some patients. However, *why* they are successful, with *which* patients, or why the procedures in the hands of some therapists are very effective while in the hands of other therapists are far less effective, is poorly understood.

In sum, as with the person-situation controversy and the nature-nurture controversy, we should avoid taking ideological positions in relation to a malleability-fixity controversy. In relation to the person-situation controversy, we have seen that the question needs to be framed in terms of *how* persons and situations interact to lead to behavior. Similarly, in relation to the nature-nurture controversy we have seen that the question needs to be framed in terms of *how* nature and nurture, genes and environment, interact to produce observed personalities. Thus, in relation to the malleability-fixity controversy, we should be prepared to focus our attention on *how* specific experiences or therapeutic procedures operate to produce change, at least in some individuals rather than in others. What is being suggested is that we remain skeptical of newspaper headlines or television programs that suggest easy answers to difficult questions, answers such as that "temperament is fixed" or that "psychotherapy is shown not to be effective." What is being suggested is that we appreciate the complexity of the questions being addressed and, as a result, recognize that only an understanding of the processes involved will lead to answers to the questions of concern to us.

RANGE OF CONVENIENCE AND FOCUS OF CONVENIENCE; BANDWIDTH AND FIDELITY

Here we return to concepts that have appeared in a number of places in the text. They can be helpful to us in obtaining a more differentiated picture of the field. The two pairs of concepts, range of convenience–focus of convenience and bandwidth-fidelity, are related. Each suggests that in evaluating theories and assessment devices we have to consider the range of phenomena covered and the areas of greatest applicability. In relation to the former, some theories of personality and some assessment devices are much more comprehensive than others; that is, they have a greater range of convenience or greater bandwidth. Comprehensiveness is certainly a desirable feature of a theory or assessment device, but it is not the only criterion for evaluation. Another is an appreciation for detail or accuracy of prediction, that is, quality of focus of convenience or fidelity.

Unfortunately, in the field of personality these two desirable features often play off one another. Comprehensive theories of personality often are weak in detail and research relevance, whereas theories elegant in their detail often provide for only limited coverage of personality phenomena. Similarly, broad personality assessment devices often are much weaker in their predictive power in relation to a specific task or job than assessment measures developed with the particular task or job in mind.

It seems to me that many of the differences among personality psychologists involve a preference for range of convenience or focus of convenience, for bandwidth or fidelity. Some are interested in the total picture, others in the specific parts. There are individuals who look at a card on the Rorschach inkblot test and focus on the inkblot as a whole, while others focus on small details. Similarly, my sense is that there are personality psychologists who prefer the grand sweep of things and others who prefer to focus on particular aspects of personality functioning.

The importance of the concepts of range of convenience–focus of convenience and bandwidth-fidelity is that they allow us to recognize differences in theories and assessment devices. Thereby they allow us to recognize the strengths and limitations of alternative theories and assessment devices. Rather than just saying one is better than the other, and perhaps being in the position of comparing apples and oranges, we are in the position of considering theories and personality measures in terms of both generality and specificity, and in terms of both strengths and limitations. For example, in Chapter 11 we noted that the field of therapy was outside the focus of convenience of trait theory but a part of the focus of convenience of psychoanalytic theory. As a comprehensive measure of personality, the Rorschach Inkblot Test is suggested to have considerable bandwidth, but limited fidelity compared to the Attributional Style Questionnaire, and even less fidelity compared to measures of self-efficacy beliefs in particular situations. In sum, in comparing and evaluating theories of personality and measures of personality we always want to keep in mind the issues of generality and specificity, range of convenience–focus of convenience and bandwidth-fidelity.

SOCIAL AND POLITICAL ASPECTS OF PERSONALITY THEORY AND RESEARCH

We come here to a topic not previously developed in the text. It involves the extent to which personality theories and personality measures are influenced by forces current in society at the time. The topic also involves consideration of the social and political implications of various theories and research findings. In the popular view, science is seen as involving the objective pursuit of truth and scientists are seen as purely rational individuals, at least in their scientific endeavors. Yet, the fact of the matter is that scientists are influenced by social forces operating at the time they are conducting their work. And, the findings of scientists often have political implications (Pervin, 1984). The physicists working on the atomic bomb were not neutral about their work or the idea of continuing to find more powerful means of destruction. The public was not neutral to Darwin's views. Freud's views of women, developed at a particular time and within a particular social context, have been criticized by modern feminists. So much for the fallacy of science as completely objective, rational, and politically insignificant.

I would like to consider briefly three illustrations of the point being made. The first relates to the issue of differences in intelligence. In a book that I recommend to students as one of the most socially significant ever written in the field, Kamin (1974) reviewed the history of the IQ concept and the history of IQ testing in America. Early efforts in the area of intelligence testing were directed toward development of a practical diagnostic instrument that could be used in the prescription of therapeutic efforts with individuals with low scores. In other words, the focus was on change and assistance. This work was done by Binet in France in the early 1900s. However, the pioneers of the mental testing movement in America associated Binet's test with the concept of "innate intelligence." According to Kamin, this association between IQ and innate intelligence fits with the sociopolitical views of these pioneers, specifically the views that members of some ethnic and racial groups were innately more intelligent than members of other ethnic and racial groups.

Kamin suggests that during the 1920s these views became associated with significant decisions concerning social policy and social action. IQ tests were used to demonstrate that vast numbers of immigrant Jews, Hungarians, Italians, and Russians were feebleminded. Leaders of the mental testing movement proclaimed that they were measuring native or inborn intelligence rather than exposure to American customs or privileged environments. The "race hypothesis" suggested that as the proportion of Nordic blood decreased, the intelligence level decreased in comparable fashion. And, according to Kamin, the data from intelligence testing played a role in passage of the Immigration Act of 1924, which imposed quotas designed to restrict immigration of the "biologically inferior" people of southeastern Europe. In other words, scientific "facts" were used to support social and political views. In 1994, "facts" concerning the malleability of intelligence are being used to explain differences between economic classes and to justify termination of special educational programs (Herrnstein & Murray, 1994).

The second illustration involves the science and politics of sex differences. Here we turn to a paper by Shields (1975) that analyzed interest in the psychology of differences between men and women during the period between 1850 and the 1930s. Of particular importance is the fact that during this period research was primarily conducted by men; women were viewed according to their relationship to the male norm rather than as subjects for study in their own right. According to Shields, the prevailing social view was that women were intellectually inferior to men and therefore "it was left to the men of science to discover the particular physiological determinants of female inadequacy" (1975, p. 740). First there was the belief that men were intellectually superior to women because their brains were larger, as evidenced by their larger heads. Going beyond this, brain size was measured and indeed men were found to have larger brains.

However, a few problem arose. First, clearly there was no relationship between brain size and intelligence across species since many animals with large heads, and large brains, showed little evidence of high intelligence. But what of brain size relative to body size as opposed to absolute brain size? Here, according to Shields, the data suggested that women possess a proportionately larger brain than men. But what of parts of the brain as opposed to the total brain? Investigations of differences between men and women in specific parts of the brain proved to be of no greater comfort to the investigators. Yet, for many the hunt continued with an eye toward finding anatomical differences favoring male superiority. What Shields suggests is that there was a bias in terms of who conducted the research, how the research questions were framed, and which results were accepted. Results that favored the accepted social view were likely to be accepted unchecked whereas those that challenged the accepted social view were critically dismissed or subjected to every possible methodological criticism.

The third illustration involves controversy concerning current views expressed by behavior geneticists and evolutionary psychologists. A major figure in the area of behavior genetics recently took an extreme "nature" view and suggested that most children grow up to be individually different based on their individual genotypes:

> Being reared in one family, rather than another, within the range of families sampled makes few differences in children's personality and intellectual development. The data suggest that environments most parents provide for their children have few differential effects on the offspring. Most families provide sufficiently supportive environments that children's individual genetic differences develop.

Scarr, 1992, p. 3

This view was attacked by two developmental psychologists who suggested that considerable evidence indicates that what parents do or fail to do crucially affects development (Baumrind, 1993; J. F. Jackson, 1993). Beyond this, the view was attacked because of its implications for public policy, including the funding of intervention programs. In other words, concern was expressed that if the public believes that developmental outcomes are entirely due to genetic factors, there will be little support for environmental intervention programs.

All three of these illustrations relate to the nature-nurture issue but this is not the only issue on which personality psychologists differ or the only issue that has social and political implications. Although striking in regard to this issue, the importance of social and political forces in shaping research, as well as the importance of personality research for public policy, extends beyond the nature-nurture issue. Rather the point is the need for increased sensitivity to the social and political forces that act upon and are influenced by personality theory and research.

PROSPECTS FOR THE FUTURE

After this review of much of the current research in the field of personality and consideration of a number of broader issues, what can be said about the future of the field? My own view is cautiously, patiently optimistic. It is *optimistic* in the belief that important questions are being addressed by personality psychologists, in sophisticated ways, and that bright and talented young people increasingly are being drawn to the field. It is *cautiously* optimistic because we still have not had major breakthroughs and the history of the field is filled with fads for one or another topic of investigation. Thus, optimism must be tempered by a sense of the history of the field. In addition, optimism must be tempered by appreciation for the complexity of our task—an understanding of and explanation for human personality functioning.

This is why I say that I am *patiently* optimistic. The difficulty of the task is such that gains will come slowly. It is not that we are poorer scientists than physicists, chemists, and biologists. Rather, we have not been at our work for as long a period of time. And, as many would argue, given the uniqueness of the individual and the multitude of forces operating to shape individuals, understanding human personality is a far more difficult task than understanding particles, elements, or genes. For these reasons I am cautiously, patiently optimistic about the future of the field.

SUMMARY

1. A definition of personality was offered that emphasizes the organized, interrelated aspects of cognitive, affective, and behavioral functioning.

2. Clinical, correlational, and experimental strategies are all viewed as potential contributors to knowledge, with no one strategy intrinsically better than the other. Similarly, different kinds of data (LOTS) are viewed as useful in the study of personality. Collaborative research, involving multiple methods and kinds of data, is desirable but difficult to implement.

3. It is suggested that we need to develop a theory of personality that recognizes both stability (consistency) and variability (situational specificity), both stasis and flow, in personality functioning.

4. Both genes and environment operate to produce similarities and differences in people. The importance of culture and awareness of the diverse ways in which culture influences the view of the self and the expression of emotion was emphasized. Two analogies, that of a ball rolling down a landscape and that of computer hardware and software, are useful in appreciating the importance of both genetic and environmental influences.

5. There is evidence both of stability of personality over time and also of change. At this point we are not able to be specific about the boundary conditions of stability and change or about the processes that contribute to stability and change.

6. The concepts of range of convenience–focus of convenience and bandwidth-fidelity are useful in recognizing differences among personality theories and assessment devices, as well as in evaluating their strengths and limitations.

7. Like all other scientists, personality psychologists are influenced by social and political forces operating in society. In addition, the research of personality psychologists can influence public attitudes and social policy.

8. Understanding people is an enormously complex endeavor. Despite the difficulty and lack of a consensus concerning a particular theory, one can be cautiously optimistic about the future of the field.

REFERENCES

Abramson, L. Y., Garber, J., & Seligman, M. E. P. (1980). Learned helplessness in humans: An attributional analysis. In J. Garber & M. E. P. Seligman (Eds.), *Human helplessness* (pp. 3–37). New York: Academic.

Abramson, L. Y., Seligman, M. E. P., & Teasdale, J. D. (1978). Learned helplessness in humans: Critique and reformulation. *Journal of Abnormal Psychology, 87,* 49–74.

Ainsworth, M. D. S., & Bowlby, J. (1991). An ethological approach to personality development. *American Psychologist, 46,* 333–341.

Alexander, F. (1950). *Psychosomatic medicine.* New York: Norton.

Alexander, F., & French, T. M. (1946). *Psychoanalytic therapy.* New York: Ronald.

Allport, G. W. (1937). *Personality: A psychological interpretation.* New York: Holt, Rinehart and Winston.

Allport, G. W. (1955). *Becoming.* New Haven, CT.: Yale University Press.

Allport, G. W. (1958). What units shall we employ? In G. Lindzey (Ed.), *Assessment of human motives* (pp. 239–260). New York: Holt, Rinehart and Winston.

Allport, G. W. (1961). *Pattern and growth in personality.* New York: Holt, Rinehart and Winston.

Allport, G. W., & Odbert, H. S. (1936). Traitnames: A psycho-lexical study. *Psychological Monographs, 47* (1, Whole No. 211).

Alwin, D. F., Cohen, R. L., & Newcomb, T. M. (1991). *Political attitudes over the life span.* Madison: University of Wisconsin Press.

Anastasi, A. (1958). Heredity, environment, and the question "How?" *Psychological Reviews, 65,* 197–208.

Anderson, C. A., Jennings, D. L., & Arnoult, L. H. (1988). Validity and utility of the attributional style construct at a moderate level of specificity. *Journal of Personality and Social Psychology, 55,* 979–990.

Aronson, E. (1992). The return of the repressed: Dissonance theory makes a comeback. *Psychological Inquiry, 3,* 303–311.

Aronson, E., & Mettee, D. R. (1968). Dishonest behavior as a function of differential levels of induced self-esteem. *Journal of Personality and Social Psychology, 9,* 121–127.

Aspinwall, L. G., & Taylor, S. E. (1992). Modeling cognitive adaptation: A longitudinal investigation of the impact of individual differences and coping on college adjustment and performance. *Journal of Personality and Social Psychology, 63,* 989–1003.

Atkinson, J. W., & McClelland, D. C. (1948). The projective expression of needs: II. The effect of different intensities of the hunger drive on Thematic Apperceptions. *Journal of Experimental Psychology, 38,* 643–658.

Balay, J., & Shevrin, H. (1988). SPA is subliminal, but is it psychodynamically activating? *American Psychologist, 44,* 1423–1426.

Baldwin, M. W. (1992). Relational schemes and the processing of social information. *Psychological Bulletin, 112,* 461–484.

Baldwin, M. W., Fehr, B., Keedian, E., Seidel, M., & Thomson, D. W. (1993). An exploration of the relational schemata underlying attachment styles: Self-report and lexical decision approaches. *Personality and Social Psychology Bulletin, 19,* 746–754.

Banaji, M. R., & Crowder, R. G. (1989). The bankruptcy of everyday memory. *American Psychologist, 44,* 1185–1193.

Bandura, A. (1977a). *Social learning theory.* Englewood Cliffs, NJ: Prentice Hall.

Bandura, A. (1977b). Self-efficacy: Toward a unified theory of behavioral change. *Psychological Review, 84,* 191–215.

Bandura, A. (1982). Self-efficacy mechanism in human agency. *American Psychologist, 37,* 122–147.

Bandura, A. (1986). *Social foundations of thought and action: A social cognitive theory.* Englewood Cliffs, NJ: Prentice Hall.

Bandura, A. (1988). Self-efficacy conception of anxiety. *Anxiety Research, 1,* 77–98.

Bandura, A. (1989a). Human agency in social cognitive theory. *American Psychologist, 44,* 1175–1184.

Bandura, A. (1989b). Self-regulation of motivation and action through internal standards and goal systems. In L. A. Pervin (Ed.), *Goal concepts in personality and social psychology* (pp. 19–85). Hillsdale, NJ: Erlbaum.

Bandura, A. (1989c). Social cognitive theory. *Annals of Child Development, 6,* 1–60.

Bandura, A. (1990). Self-regulation of motivation through anticipatory and self-reactive mechanisms. *Nebraska Symposium on Motivation, 38,* 69–164.

Bandura, A. (1992). Self-efficacy mechanism in psychobiologic functioning. In R. Schwarzer (Ed.), *Self-efficacy: Thought control of action* (pp. 335–394). Washington, DC: Hemisphere.

Bandura, A., & Abrams, K. (1986). *Self-regulatory mechanisms in motivating apathetic and despondent reactions to unfulfilled standards.* Unpublished manuscript.

Bandura, A., & Cervone, D. (1983). Self-evaluative and self-efficacy mechanisms governing the motivational effect of goal systems. *Journal of Personality and Social Psychology, 45,* 1017–1028.

Bandura, A., & Cervone, D. (1986). Differential engagement of self-reactive influences in cognitive motivation. *Organizational Behavior and Human Decision Processes, 38,* 92–113.

Bandura, A., Cioffi, D., Taylor, C. B., & Brouillard, M. E. (1988). Perceived self-efficacy in coping with cognitive stressors and opioid activation. *Journal of Personality and Social Psychology, 55,* 479–488.

Bandura, A., & Rosenthal, T. L. (1966). Vicarious classical conditioning as a function of arousal level. *Journal of Personality and Social Psychology, 3,* 54–62.

Bandura, A., Ross, D., & Ross, S. (1963). Vicarious reinforcement and imitative learning. *Journal of Abnormal and Social Psychology, 67,* 601–607.

Bandura, A., & Schunk, D. H. (1981). Cultivating competence, self-efficacy, and intrinsic interest. *Journal of Personality and Social Psychology, 41,* 586–598.

Bandura, A., & Walters, R. H. (1963). *Adolescent aggression.* New York: Ronald Press.

Bargh, J. A. (1989). Conditional automaticity: Varieties of automatic influence in social perception and cognition. In J. S. Uleman & J. A. Bargh (Eds.), *Unintended thought* (pp. 3–51). New York: Guilford.

Bargh, J. A. (1992). Does subliminality matter to social psychology? In R. F. Bornstein & T. S. Pittman (Eds.), *Perception without awareness* (pp. 236–255). New York: Guilford.

Bargh, J. A., & Pietromonaco, P. (1982). Automatic information processing and social perception: The influence of trait information presented outside of conscious awareness on impression formation. *Journal of Personality and Social Psychology, 43,* 437–449.

Bargh, J. A., & Tota, M. E. (1988). Context-dependent automatic processing in depression: Accessibility of negative constructs with regard to self but not others. *Journal of Personality and Social Psychology, 54,* 925–939.

Barlow, D. H. (1991). Disorders of emotion. *Psychological Inquiry, 2,* 58–71.

Baron, R. A. (1987). Outlines of a grand theory. *Contemporary Psychology, 32,* 413–415.

Bartholomew, K., & Horowitz, L. M. (1991). Attachment styles among young adults: A test of a four-category model. *Journal of Personality and Social Psychology, 61,* 226–244.

Bateson, P., & Hinde, R. A. (1987). Developmental changes in sensitivity to experience. In M. H. Bornstein (Ed.), *Sensitive periods in development* (pp. 19–34). Hillsdale, NJ: Erlbaum.

Baumeister, R. F. (1990). Suicide as escape from self. *Psychological Review, 97,* 90–113.

Baumeister, R. F. (1991). Shirking the self-burden: The psychological unity of some extreme habits. In R. F. Baumeister (Ed.), *Escaping the self: Alcoholism, spirituality, masochism, and other flights from the burdens of selfhood* (pp. 636–654). New York: Basic Books.

Baumrind, D. (1993). The average expectable environment is not good enough: A response to Scarr. *Child Development, 64,* 1299–1317.

Beck, A. T. (1987). Cognitive models of depression. *Journal of Cognitive Psychotherapy, 1,* 27.

Beck, A. T. (1993). Cognitive therapy: Past, present, and future. *Journal of Consulting and Clinical Psychology, 61,* 194–198.

Benjamin, L. S. (1993). Dimensional, categorical, or hybrid analyses of personality. *Psychological Inquiry, 4,* 91–95.

Berger, S. M. (1962). Conditioning through vicarious investigation. *Psychological Review, 69,* 450–466.

Bernstein, E. M., & Putnam, F. W. (1986). Development, reliability and validity of a dissociation scale. *Journal of Nervous and Mental Disease, 174,* 727–735.

Bindra, D., & Scheier, I. H. (1954). The relation between psychometric and experimental research in psychology. *American Psychologist, 9,* 69–71.

Blatt, S. J., & Bers, S. A. (1993a). Commen-
tary. In Z. V. Segal & S. J. Blatt (Eds.), *The self in emotional distress* (pp. 164–170). New York: Guilford.

Blatt, S. J., & Bers, S. A. (1993b). The sense of self in depression: A psychodynamic perspective. In Z. V. Segal & S. J. Blatt (Eds.), *The self in emotional distress* (pp. 171–210). New York: Guilford.

Blatt, S. J., & Homann, E. (1992). Parent-child interaction in the etiology of dependent and self-critical depression. *Clinical Psychology Review, 12,* 47–91.

Block, J. (1971). *Lives through time.* Berkeley, CA: Bancroft.

Block, J. (1981). Some enduring and consequential structures of personality. In A. I. Rabin (Ed.), *Further explorations in personality* (pp. 27–43). New York: Wiley.

Block, J. (1993). Studying personality the long way. In D. C. Funder, R. D. Parke, C. Tomlinson-Keasey, & K. Widaman (Eds.), *Studying lives through time* (pp.9–41). Washington, DC: American Psychological Association.

Block, J. (1995). A contrarian view of the five-factor approach to personality description. *Psychological Bulletin,* in press.

Block, J., Gjerde, P. F., & Block, J. H. (1991). Personality antecedents of depressive tendencies in 18–year-olds: A prospective study. *Journal of Personality and Social Psychology, 60,* 726–738.

Block, J. H., & Block, J. (1980). The role of ego control and ego resiliency in the organization of behavior. In W. A. Collins (Ed.), *Development of cognitive, affect, and social relations: The Minnesota symposium in child psychology* (pp. 39–101). Hillsdale, NJ: Erlbaum.

Bloom, B. S. (1964). *Stability and change in human characteristics.* New York: Wiley.

Boneau, C. A. (1992). Observations on psychology's past and future. *American Psychologist, 47,* 1586–1596.

Booth-Kewley, S., & Friedman, H. S. (1987). Psychological predictors of heart disease: A quantitative review. *Psychological Bulletin, 101,* 343–362.

Boring, E. G. (1950). *A history of experimen-*

tal psychology. New York: Appleton-Century-Crofts.

Borkenau, P., & Ostendorf, F. (1989). Descriptive consistency and social desirability in self- and peer reports. *European Journal of Personality, 3,* 31–45.

Bornstein, M. H. (Ed.). (1987). *Sensitive periods in development.* Hillsdale, NJ: Erlbaum.

Bornstein, M. H. (1989). Sensitive periods in development: Structural characteristics and causal interpretations. *Psychological Bulletin, 105,* 179–197.

Bouchard, T. J., Jr., Lykken, D. T., McGue, M., Segal, N. L., & Tellegen, A. (1990). Sources of human psychological differences: The Minnesota study of twins reared apart. *Science, 250,* 223–250.

Bouchard, T. J., Jr., & McGue, M. (1981). Familial studies of intelligence: A review. *Science, 212,* 1055–1059.

Bower, G. H. (1981). Mood and memory. *American Psychologist, 36,* 129–148.

Bowers, K. S. (1992). *The problem of consciousness.* Paper presented at the August meetings of the American Psychological Association, Washington, DC.

Brady, J. P., & Lind, D. I. (1961). Experimental analysis of hysterical blindness. *Behavior Research and Therapy, 4,* 331–339.

Braungart, J. M., Plomin, R., DeFries, J. C., & Fulker, D. W. (1992). Genetic influence on tester-rated infant temperament as assessed by Bayley's Infant Behavior Record: Nonadoptive and adoptive siblings and twins. *Developmental Psychology, 28,* 40–47.

Brehm, S. S. (1992). *Intimate relationships.* New York: McGraw-Hill.

Bretherton, I. (1992). The origins of attachment theory: John Bowlby and Mary Ainsworth. *Developmental Psychology, 28,* 759–775.

Brewin, C. R. (1989). Cognitive change processes in psychotherapy. *Psychological Review, 96,* 379–394.

Briggs, S. R. (1989). The optimal level of measurement for personality constructs. In D. M. Buss & N. Cantor (Eds.), *Personality psychology: Recent trends and*

emerging direction (pp. 246–260). New York: Springer-Verlag.

Brown, J. D., & McGill, K. L. (1989). The cost of good fortune: When positive life events produce negative health consequences. *Journal of Personality and Social Psychology, 57,* 1103–1110.

Bruner, J. S. (1956). You are your constructs. *Contemporary Psychology, 1,* 355–356.

Bruner, J. S. (1992). Another look at New Look 1. *American Psychologist, 47,* 780–783.

Bruner, J. S., & Goodman, C. C. (1947). Value and need as organizing factors in perception. *Journal of Abnormal and Social Psychology, 42,* 33–44.

Buss, A. H. (1980). *Self-consciousness and social anxiety.* San Francisco: Freeman.

Buss, A. H., & Plomin, R. (1975). *A temperament theory of personality development.* New York: Wiley Interscience.

Buss, A. H., & Plomin, R. (1984). *Temperament: Early developing personality traits.* Hillsdale, NJ: Erlbaum.

Buss, D. M. (1989). Sex differences in human mate preferences: Evolutionary hypotheses tested in 37 cultures. *Behavioral and Brain Sciences, 12,* 1–49.

Buss, D. M. (1991). Evolutionary personality psychology. *Annual Review of Psychology, 42,* 459–492.

Buss, D. M. (1995). Evolutionary psychology: A new paradigm for psychological science. *Psychological Inquiry, 6,* 1–30.

Buss, D. M., Block, J. H., & Block, J. (1980). Preschool activity level: Personality correlates and developmental implications. *Child Development, 51,* 401–408.

Buss, D. M., Larsen, R. J., Westen, D., & Semmelroth, J. (1992). Sex differences in jealousy: Evolution, physiology and psychology. *Psychological Science, 3,* 251–255.

Butterworth, G. (1992). Origins of self-perception in infancy. *Psychological Inquiry, 3,* 103–111.

Campbell, D. T. (1957). A typology of projective tests and otherwise. *Journal of Consulting Psychology, 21,* 207–210.

Campbell, D. T., & Fiske, D. W. (1959). Convergent and discriminant validation by the multitrait-multimethod matrix. *Psychological Bulletin, 56,* 81–105.

Cantor, N. (1990a). From thought to behavior: "Having" and "doing" in the study of personality and cognition. *American Psychologist, 45,* 735–750.

Cantor, N. (1990b). Social psychology and sociobiology: What can we leave to evolution? *Motivation and Emotion, 14,* 242–254.

Cantor, N. (1994). Life task problem solving: Situational affordances and personal needs. *Personality and Social Psychology Bulletin, 20,* 235–243.

Cantor, N., & Kihlstrom, J. F. (1987). *Personality and social intelligence.* Englewood Cliffs, NJ: Prentice-Hall.

Cantor, N., & Kihlstrom, J. F. (1989). Social intelligence and cognitive assessments of personality. *Advances in Social Cognition, 2,* 1–59.

Cantor, N., & Langston, C. A. (1989). "Ups and downs" of life tasks in a life transition. In L. A. Pervin (Ed.), *Goal concepts in personality and social psychology* (pp. 127–167). Hillsdale, NJ: Erlbaum.

Cantor, N., & Zirkel, S. (1990). Personality, cognition, and purposive behavior. In L. A. Pervin (Ed.), *Handbook of personality: Theory and research* (pp. 135–164). New York: Guilford.

Carnelley, K. B., Pietromonaco, P. R., & Jaffe, K. (1994). Depression, working models of others, and relationships functioning. *Journal of Personality and Social Psychology, 66,* 127–140.

Carson, R. C. (1969). *Interaction concepts of personality.* Chicago: Aldine.

Carson, R. C. (1991). The social-interactional viewpoint. In M. Hersen, A. E. Kazdin, & A. S. Bellack (Eds.), *The clinical psychology handbook* (pp. 185–199). Elmsford, NY: Pergamon.

Carver, C. S., et al. (1993). How coping mediates the effect of optimism on distress: A study of women with early stage breast cancer. *Journal of Personality and Social Psychology, 65,* 375–390.

Carver, C. S., & Scheier, M. F. (1981). *Atten-tion and self-regulation: A control theory approach to human behavior.* New York: Springer-Verlag.

Carver, C. S., & Scheier, M. F. (1982). Control theory: A useful conceptual framework for personality, social, and health psychology. *Psychological Bulletin, 92,* 111–135.

Carver, C. S., & Scheier, M. F. (1985). Aspects of self and the control of behavior. In B. R. Schlenker (Ed.), *The self and social life.* New York: McGraw-Hill.

Carver, C. S., & Scheier, M. F. (1988). A model of behavioral self-regulation: Translating intention into action. *Advances in Experimental Social Psychology, 21,* 303–346.

Carver, C. S., & Scheier, M. F. (1990). Origins and functions of positive and negative affect: A control-process view. *Psychological Review, 97,* 19–35.

Carver, C. S., Scheier, M. F., & Weintraub, J. K. (1989). Assessing coping strategies: A theoretically based approach. *Journal of Personality and Social Psychology, 56,* 267–283.

Caspi, A., & Bem, D. J. (1990). Personality continuity and change across the life course. In L. A. Pervin (Ed.), *Handbook of personality: Theory and research* (pp. 549–575). New York: Guilford.

Cattell, R. B. (1943). The description of personality: Basic traits resolved into clusters. *Journal of Abnormal and Social Psychology, 38,* 476–506.

Cattell, R. B. (1945). The principal trait clusters for describing personality. *Psychological Bulletin, 42,* 129–161.

Cattell, R. B. (1956). Validation and interpretation of the 16 P.F. questionnaire. *Journal of Clinical Psychology, 12,* 205–214.

Cattell, R. B. (1965). *The scientific analysis of personality.* Baltimore: Penguin.

Cattell, R. B., & Eber, H. W. (1962). *Handbook for the Sixteen P.F. Test.* Champaign, IL: IPAT.

Chambless, D. L., & Gillis, M. M. (1993). Cognitive therapy of anxiety disorders. *Journal of Consulting and Clinical Psychology, 61,* 248–260.

Champagne, B., & Pervin, L. A. (1987). The relation of perceived situation similarity to perceived behavior similarity: Implications for social learning theory. *European Journal of Personality, 1,* 79–92.

Chevalier-Skolnikoff, S. (1973). Facial expressions of emotion in nonhuman primates. In P. Ekman (Ed.), *Darwin and facial expression* (pp. 11–89). New York: Academic.

Christianson, S. A. (1992). Emotional stress and eyewitness memory: A critical review. *Psychological Bulletin, 112,* 284–309.

Clark, D. A., Beck, A. T., & Brown, G. (1989). Cognitive mediation in general psychiatric outpatients: A test of the content-specificity hypothesis. *Journal of Personality and Social Psychology, 56,* 958–964.

Clark, L. A. (1993). Personality disorder diagnosis: Limitations of the five-factor model. *Psychological Inquiry, 4,* 100–104.

Clark, L. A., Vorhies, L., & McEwen, J. L. (1994). Personality disorder symptomatology from the five-factor model perspective. In P. T. Costa, Jr. & T. A. Widiger (Eds.), *Personality disorders and the five-factor model of personality* (pp. 95–116). Washington, DC: American Psychological Association.

Clark, L. A., & Watson, D. (1991). General affective dispositions in physical and psychological health. In C. R. Snyder & D. R. Forsyth (Eds.), *Handbook of social and clinical psychology* (pp. 221–245). Elmsford, NY: Pergamon.

Cloninger, C. R. (1986). A unified biosocial theory of personality and its role in the development of anxiety states. *Psychiatric Developments, 3,* 167–226.

Cloninger, C. R. (1987). A systematic method for clinical description and classification of personality. *Archives of General Psychiatry, 44,* 573–588.

Coan, R. W. (1966). Child personality and developmental psychology. In R. B. Cattell (Ed.), *Handbook of multivariate experimental psychology* (pp. 732–752). Chicago: Rand McNally.

Cofer, C. N. (1981). The history of the concept of motivation. *Journal of the History of the Behavioral Sciences, 17,* 48–53.

Cohen, S., Tyrrell, D. A. J., & Smith, A. P. (1993). Negative life events, perceived stress, negative affect, and susceptibility to the common cold. *Journal of Personality and Social Psychology, 64,* 131–140.

Cohen, S., & Williamson, G. M. (1991). Stress and infectious disease in humans. *Psychological Bulletin, 109,* 5–24.

Collins, N. L., & Read, S. J. (1990). Adult attachment, working models, and relationship quality in dating couples. *Journal of Personality and Social Psychology, 58,* 644–663.

Conley, J. J. (1985). Longitudinal stability of personality traits: A multitrait-multimethod-multioccasion analysis. *Journal of Personality and Social Psychology, 49,* 1266–1282.

Contrada, R. J., Leventhal, H., & O'Leary, A. (1990). Personality and health. In L. A. Pervin (Ed.), *Handbook of personality: Theory and research* (pp. 638–669). New York: Guilford.

Cooley, C. H. (1902). *Human nature and the social order.* New York: Scribner.

Cooper, S. H. (1993). The self construct in psychoanalytic theory: A comparative view. In Z. Segal & S. J. Blatt (Eds.), *The self in emotional distress* (pp. 41–67). New York: Guilford.

Corbitt, E. M. (1994). Narcissism from the perspective of the five-factor model. In P. T. Costa, Jr. & T. A. Widiger (Eds.), *Personality disorders and the five-factor model of personality* (pp. 199–203). Washington, DC: American Psychological Association.

Corteen, R. S., & Wood, B. (1979). Autonomic responses to shock-associated words in an unattended channel. *Journal of Experimental Psychology, 94,* 308–313.

Costa, P. T., Jr., & McCrae, R. R. (1985). *The NEO Personality Inventory Manual.* Odessa, FL: Psychological Assessment Resources.

Costa, P. T., Jr., & McCrae, R. R. (1987). Neuroticism, somatic complaints, and disease:

Is the bark worse than the bite? *Journal of Personality, 55,* 299–316.

Costa, P. T., Jr., & McCrae, R. R. (1988). From catalog to classification: Murray's needs and the five-factor model. *Journal of Personality and Social Psychology, 55,* 258–265.

Costa, P. T., Jr., & McCrae, R. R. (1992). *NEO-PI-R, Professional Manual.* Odessa, FL: Psychological Assessment Resources.

Costa, P. T., Jr., & McCrae, R. R. (1994). "Set like plaster?" Evidence for the stability of adult personality. In T. Heatherton & J. Weinberger (Eds.), *Can personality change?* (pp. 21–40). Washington, DC: American Psychological Association.

Costa, P. T., Jr., & Widiger, T. A. (Eds.). (1994). *Personality disorders and the five-factor model of personality.* Washington, DC: American Psychological Association.

Cousins, N. (1979). *Anatomy of an illness.* New York: Norton.

Craik, K. H. (1986). Personality research methods: An historical perspective. *Journal of Personality, 54,* 18–50.

Crandall, C. S. (1991). Do heavy-weight students have more difficulty paying for college? *Personality and Social Psychology Bulletin, 17,* 606–611.

Crits-Christoph, P. (1992). The efficacy of brief dynamic psychotherapy: A meta-analysis. *American Journal of Psychiatry, 149,* 151–158.

Cronbach, L. J. (1957). The two disciplines of scientific psychology. *American Psychologist, 12,* 671–684.

Cronbach, L. J., & Meehl, P. E. (1955). Construct validity in psychological tests. *Psychological Bulletin, 52,* 281–302.

Cross, S. E., & Markus, H. R. (1990). The willful self. *Personality and Social Psychology Bulletin, 16,* 726–742.

Csikszentmihalyi, M. (1975). *Beyond boredom and anxiety.* San Francisco, CA: Jossey-Bass.

Damarin, F. L., & Cattell, R. B. (1968). Personality factors in early childhood and their relation to intelligence. *Monographs of the Society for Research in Child Development, 33,* 1–95.

Damon, W., & Hart, D. (1988). *Self-understanding in childhood and adolescence.* Cambridge, England: Cambridge University Press.

Daniels, D., & Plomin, R. (1985). Differential experiences of siblings in the same family. *Developmental Psychology, 21,* 747–760.

Dashiell, J. F. (1939). Some rapprochements in contemporary psychology. *Psychological Bulletin, 36,* 1–24.

Davidson, R. J. (1992). Emotion and affective style: Hemispheric substrates. *Psychological Science, 3,* 39–43.

Davis, G. D., & Millon, T. (1993). The five-factor model for personality disorders: Apt or misguided? *Psychological Inquiry, 4,* 104–109.

Davis, P. J., & Schwartz, G. E. (1987). Repression and the inaccessibility of affective memories. *Journal of Personality and Social Psychology, 52,* 155–162.

Davison, G. C., & Neale, J. M. (1994). *Abnormal psychology: An experimental clinical approach.* New York: Wiley.

DeAngelis, T. (1993). APA panel is examining memories of child abuse. *American Psychological Association Monitor,* November, p.44.

Deci, E. L., & Ryan, R. M. (1985). *Intrinsic motivation and self determination in human behavior.* New York: Plenum.

Deci, E. L., & Ryan, R. M. (1991). A motivational approach to self: Integration in personality. *Nebraska Symposium on Motivation, 38,* 237–288.

Degler, C. (1991). *In search of human nature.* New York: Oxford University Press.

Diener, C. I., & Dweck, C. S. (1978). An analysis of learned helplessness: Continuous changes in performance, strategy and achievement cognitions following failure. *Journal of Personality and Social Psychology, 36,* 451–462.

Diener, C. I., & Dweck, C. S. (1980). An analysis of learned helplessness: The processing of success. *Journal of Personality and Social Psychology, 39,* 940–952.

Dienstbier, R. (Ed.). (1990). *Nebraska sympo-*

sium on motivation. Lincoln: University of Nebraska Press.

Diven, K. (1937). Certain determinants in the conditioning of anxiety reactions. *Journal of Psychology, 3,* 291–308.

Dodge, K. A. (1993). Social-cognitive mechanisms in the development of conduct disorder and depression. *Annual Review of Psychology, 44,* 559–584.

Dollard, J., & Miller, N. E. (1950). *Personality and psychotherapy.* New York: McGraw-Hill.

Don't Sell Thick Diapers In Tokyo. *New York Times,* October 3, 1993, p. D9.

Dunn, J. (1992). Siblings and development. *Current Directions in Psychological Science, 1,* 6–9.

Dunn, J., & Plomin, R. (1990). *Separate lives: Why siblings are so different.* New York: Basic Books.

Dweck, C. S. (1986). Motivational processes affecting learning. *American Psychologist, 41,* 1040–1048.

Dweck, C. S. (1991). Self-theories and goals: Their role in motivation, personality, and development. In R. D. Dienstbier (Ed.), *Nebraska Symposium on Motivation* (pp. 199–235). Lincoln: University of Nebraska Press.

Dweck, C. S., Chiu, C., & Hong, Y. (1995). Implicit theories and their role in judgments and reactions: A world from two perspectives. *Psychological Inquiry, 6,* in press.

Dweck, C. S., & Leggett, E. L. (1988). A social-cognitive approach to motivation and personality. *Psychological Review, 95,* 256–273.

Eagle, M. N. (1987). The psychoanalytic and the cognitive unconscious. In R. Stern (Ed.), *Theories of the unconscious and theories of the self* (pp. 155–189). Hillsdale, NJ: Erlbaum.

Eagle, M. N., Wolitzky, D. L., & Klein, G. S. (1966). Imagery: Effect of a concealed figure in a stimulus. *Science, 18,* 837–839.

Eaves, L. J., Eysenck, H. J., & Martin, N. G. (1989). *Genes, culture and personality: An empirical approach.* San Diego, CA: Academic.

Ekman, P. (1972). Universals and cultural

differences in facial expression of emotion. In J. Cole (Ed.), *Nebraska symposium on motivation* (pp. 207–283). Lincoln: University of Nebraska Press.

Ekman, P. (1973). Cross-cultural studies of facial expression. In P. Ekman (Ed.), *Darwin and facial expression* (pp. 169–222). New York: Academic.

Ekman, P. (1992a). An argument for basic emotions. *Cognition and Emotion, 6,* 169–200.

Ekman, P. (1992b). Are there basic emotions? *Psychological Review, 99,* 550–553.

Ekman, P. (1993). Facial expression and emotion. *American Psychologist, 48,* 384–392.

Ekman, P. (1994). Strong evidence for universals in facial expressions: A reply to Russell's mistaken critique. *Psychological Bulletin, 115,* 268–287.

Ekman, P., & Friesen, W. V. (1986). A new pan-cultural facial expression of emotion. *Motivation and Emotion, 10,* 159–168.

Ekman, P., Friesen, W. V., O'Sullivan, M., Chan, A., Diacoyanni-Tarlatzis, I., Heider, K., Krause, R., Le Compte, W. A., Pitcairn, T., Ricci-Bitti, P. E., Scherer, K., Tomita, M., & Tzavaras, A. (1987). Universal and cultural differences in the judgment of facial expressions of emotion. *Journal of Personality and Social Psychology, 53,* 712–717.

Elder, G. H., Jr. (1974). *Children of the Great Depression.* Chicago: University of Chicago Press.

Elder, G. H., Jr. (1979). Historical change in life patterns and personality. In P. B. Baltes & O. G. Brim, Jr. (Eds.), *Life-span development and behavior* (pp. 117–159). New York: Academic.

Elder, G. H., Jr., & Caspi, A. (1988). Economic stress: Developmental perspectives. *Journal of Social Issues, 44,* 25–45.

Elkin, I., et al. (1989). NIMH treatment of depression collaborative research program: I. General effectiveness of treatments. *Archives of General Psychiatry, 46,* 971–983.

Ellenberger, H. F. (1970). *The discovery of the unconscious.* New York: Basic Books.

Elliot, A. J., & Devine, P. G. (1994). On the motivational nature of cognitive dissonance: Dissonance as psychological discomfort. *Journal of Personality and Social Psychology, 67,* 382–394.

Elliot, E. S., & Dweck, C. S. (1988). Goals: An approach to motivation and achievement. *Journal of Personality and Social Psychology, 54,* 5–12.

Ellis, A., & Harper, R. A. (1975). *A new guide to rational living.* North Hollywood, CA: Wilshire.

Emmons, R. A. (1986). Personal strivings: An approach to personality and subjective well-being. *Journal of Personality and Social Psychology, 51,* 1058–1068.

Emmons, R. A. (1987). Narcissism: Theory and measurement. *Journal of Personality and Social Psychology, 52,* 11–17.

Emmons, R. A. (1989a). Exploring the relationship between motives and traits: The case of narcissism. In D. M. Buss & N. Cantor (Eds.), *Personality psychology: Recent trends and emerging directions* (pp. 32–44). New York: Springer-Verlag.

Emmons, R. A. (1989b). The personal striving approach to personality. In L. A. Pervin (Ed.), *Goal concepts in personality and social psychology* (pp. 87–126). Hillsdale, NJ: Erlbaum.

Emmons, R. A. (in press). Motives and life goals. In S. Briggs, R. Hogan, & W. Jones (Eds.), *Handbook of personality psychology.* Orlando, FL: Academic.

Emmons, R. A., & Diener, E. (1986). A goal-affect analysis of everyday situational choices. *Journal of Research in Personality, 20,* 309–326.

Emmons, R. A., & King, L. A. (1988). Conflict among personal strivings: Immediate and long-term implications for psychological and physical well-being. *Journal of Personality and Social Psychology, 54,* 1040–1048.

Emmons, R. A., King, L. A., & Sheldon, K. (1993). Goal conflict and the self-regulation of action. In D. W. Wegner & J. W. Pennebaker (Eds.), *Handbook of mental control* (pp. 528–551). Englewood Cliffs, NJ: Prentice Hall.

Epstein, S. (1973). The self-concept revisited, or a theory of a theory. *American Psychologist, 28,* 404–416.

Epstein, S. (1983). A research paradigm for the study of personality and emotions. In M. M. Page (Ed.), *Personality: Current theory and research* (pp. 91–154). Lincoln: University of Nebraska Press.

Epstein, S. (1990). Cognitive-experimental self-theory. In L. A. Pervin (Ed.), *Handbook of personality: Theory and research* (pp. 165–192). New York: Guilford.

Epstein, S. (1992). The cognitive self, the psychoanalytic self, and the forgotten selves. *Psychological Inquiry, 3,* 34–37.

Erdelyi, M. H. (1985). *Psychoanalysis: Freud's cognitive psychology.* New York: Freeman.

Ericsson, K. A., & Simon, H. A. (1980). Verbal reports as data. *Psychological Review, 87,* 215–251.

Ericsson, K. A., & Simon, H. A. (1993). *Protocol analysis: Verbal reports as data.* Cambridge, MA: MIT Press.

Evans, G. W., Palsane, M. N., & Carrere, S. (1987). Type A behavior and occupational stress: A cross-cultural study of blue-collar workers. *Journal of Personality and Social Psychology, 52,* 1002–1007.

Exner, J. E., Jr. (1993). *The Rorschach: A comprehensive system.* New York: Wiley.

Eysenck, H. J. (1970). *The structure of human personality.* London: Methuen.

Eysenck, H. J. (1977). Personality and factor analysis: A reply to Guilford. *Psychological Bulletin, 84,* 405–411.

Eysenck, H. J. (1979). The conditioning model of neurosis. *Behavioral and Brain Sciences, 2,* 155–199.

Eysenck, H. J. (1982). *Personality genetics and behavior.* New York: Praeger.

Eysenck, H. J. (1990). Biological dimensions of personality. In L. A. Pervin (Ed.), *Handbook of personality: Theory and research* (pp. 244–276). New York: Guilford.

Eysenck, H. J. (1992). Four ways five factors are not basic. *Personality and Individual Differences, 13,* 667–673.

Eysenck, H. J. (1993). Creativity and personality: Suggestions for a theory. *Psychological Inquiry, 4,* 147–178.

Eysenck, H. J., & Eysenck, S. B. G. (1975). *Manual of the Eysenck Personality Questionnaire*. London: Hodder & Stoughton.

Eysenck, H. J., & Martin, I. (Eds.). (1987). *Theoretical foundations of behavior therapy*. New York: Plenum.

Eysenck, S. B. G., Eysenck, H. J., & Barrett, P. (1985). A revised version of the psychoticism scale. *Personality and Individual Differences, 6,* 21–29.

Feather, N. T. (Ed.). (1982). *Expectations and actions: Expectancy-value models in psychology*. Hillsdale, NJ: Erlbaum.

Feeney, J. A., & Noller, P. (1990). Attachment style as a predictor of adult romantic relationships. *Journal of Personality and Social Psychology, 58,* 281–291.

Fenichel, O. (1945). *The psychoanalytic theory of neurosis*. New York: Norton.

Fenigstein, A., Scheier, M. F., & Buss, A. H. (1975). Public and private self-consciousness: Assessment and theory. *Journal of Consulting & Clinical Psychology, 43,* 522–527.

Festinger, L. (1957). *A theory of cognitive dissonance*. Evanston, IL: Row, Peterson.

Fisher, C. (1956). Dreams, images, and perception: A study of unconscious-preconscious relationships. *Journal of the American Psychoanalytic Association, 4,* 5–48.

Fisher, C. (1960). Subliminal and supraliminal influences on dreams. *American Journal of Psychiatry, 116,* 1009–1017.

Fisher, C. (1965). Psychoanalytic implications of recent research on sleep and dreaming. *Journal of the American Psychoanalytic Association, 13,* 197–303.

Fleming, J. H., & Rudman, L. A. (1993). Between a rock and a hard place: Self-concept regulating and communicative properties of distancing behaviors. *Journal of Personality and Social Psychology, 64,* 44–59.

Flink, C., Boggiano, A. K., & Barrett, M. (1990). Controlling teaching strategies: Undermining children's self-determination and performance. *Journal of Personality and Social Psychology, 59,* 916–924.

Folkman, S., Lazarus, R. S., Dunkel-Schetter, C., DeLongis, A., & Gruen, R. (1986). The dynamics of a stressful encounter: Cognitive appraisal, coping, and encounter outcomes. *Journal of Personality and Social Psychology, 50,* 992–1003.

Folkman, S., Lazarus, R. S., Guren, R. J., & Delongis, A. (1986). Appraisal, coping, health status and psychological symptoms. *Journal of Personality and Social Psychology, 50,* 571–579.

Fong, G. T., & Markus, H. (1982). Self-schemas and judgments about others. *Social Cognition, 1,* 191–204.

Ford, M. E. (1992). *Motivating humans*. Newbury Park, CA: Sage.

Forer, B. R. (1949). The fallacy of personal validation: A classroom demonstration of gullibility. *Journal of Abnormal and Social Psychology, 44,* 118–123.

Frese, M., & Sabini, J. (Eds.). (1985). *Goal directed behavior: The concept of action in psychology*. Hillsdale, NJ: Erlbaum.

Freud, S. (1924). *A general introduction to psychoanalysis*. New York: Permabooks (Boni & Liveright Edition).

Freud, S. (1953). *A general introduction to psychoanalysis*. New York: Permabooks. (Boni & Liveright Edition, 1924).

Frey, J. (1994). 1 is the fastball, 2 is the curve, 3 is a nice bow. *New York Times,* March 8, p. B11.

Friedman, H. S., & Booth-Kewley, S. (1988). Validity of the Type A construct: A reprise. *Psychological Bulletin, 104,* 381–384.

Friedman, M., & Rosenman, R. H. (1974). *Type A behavior and your heart*. New York: Knopf.

Funder, D. C. (1989). Accuracy in personality judgment and the dancing bear. In D. M. Buss & N. Cantor (Eds.), *Personality psychology: Recent trends and emerging directions* (pp. 210–223). New York: Springer-Verlag.

Funder, D. C. (1993). Judgments of personality and personality itself. In K. H. Craik, R. Hogan, & R. N. Wolfe (Eds.), *Fifty years of personality psychology* (pp. 207–214). New York: Plenum.

Funder, D. C., & Block, J. (1989). The role of ego-control, ego-resiliency, and IQ in delay of gratification in adolescence. *Journal of Personality and Social Psychology, 57,* 1041–1050.

Funder, D. C., & Colvin, C. R. (1988). Friends and strangers: Acquaintanceship, agreement, and the accuracy of personality judgment. *Journal of Personality and Social Psychology, 55,* 149–158.

Funder, D. C., & Colvin, C. R. (1991). Explorations in behavioral consistency: Properties of persons, situations, and behaviors. *Journal of Personality and Social Psychology, 60,* 773–794.

Funder, D. C., & Dobroth, K. M. (1987). Differences between traits: Properties associated with interjudge agreement. *Journal of Personality, 54,* 528–550.

Funder, D. C., Parke, R. D., Tomlinson-Keasey, C. A., & Widaman, K. (Eds.). (1993). *Studying lives through time: Personality and development.* Washington, DC: American Psychological Association.

Gallup, G. G., Jr. (1970). Chimpanzees: Self-recognition. *Science, 167,* 86–87.

Garfield, S. L. (1992). Major issues in psychotherapy research. In D. K. Freedheim (Ed.), *History of psychotherapy* (pp. 335–359). Washington, DC: American Psychological Association.

Garmezy, N. (1993). Vulnerability and resilience. In D. Funder, R. D. Parke, C. Tomlinson-Keasey, & K. Widaman (Eds.), *Studying lives through time* (pp. 377–398). Washington, DC: American Psychological Association.

Glass, D. C., & Carver, C. S. (1980). Helplessness and the coronary-prone personality. In J. Garber & M. E. P. Seligman (Eds.), *Human helplessness* (pp. 223–243). New York: Academic.

Goetz, T. E., & Dweck, C. S. (1980). Learned helplessness in social situations. *Journal of Personality and Social Psychology, 39,* 246–255.

Goldberg, L. R. (1981). Language and individual differences: The search for universals in personality lexicons. In L. Wheeler (Ed.), *Review of personality and social psychology* (pp. 141–165). Beverly Hills, CA: Sage.

Goldberg, L. R. (1990). An alternative "description of personality": The big-five factor structure. *Journal of Personality and Social Psychology, 59,* 1216–1229.

Goldberg, L. R. (1993). The structure of phenotypic personality traits. *American Psychologist, 48,* 26–34.

Goldfried, M. R., Greenberg, L., & Marmor, C. (1990). Individual psychotherapy: Process and outcome. *Annual Review of Psychology, 41,* 659–688.

Goldsmith, T. H. (1991). *The biological roots of human nature.* New York: Oxford University Press.

Gough, H. G. (1987). *Administrator's guide to the California Psychological Inventory.* Palo Alto, CA: Consulting Psychologists Press.

Gray, J. A. (1987). *The psychology of fear and stress.* Cambridge, England: Cambridge University Press.

Greenberg, J., Pyszczynski, T., Solomon, S., & Rosenblatt, A. (1990). Evidence for terror management theory: II. The effects of mortality salience on reactions to those who threaten or bolster the cultural worldview. *Journal of Personality and Social Psychology, 58,* 308–318.

Greenberg, J. R., & Mitchell, S. A. (1983). *Object relations in psychoanalytic theory.* Cambridge, MA: Harvard University Press.

Greenwald, A. G. (1992). Unconscious cognition reclaimed. *American Psychologist, 47,* 766–779.

Greenwald, A. G., & Pratkanis, A. R. (1984). The self. In R. G. Wyer & T. K. Srull (Eds.), *Handbook of social cognition.* (Vol. 3, pp. 129–178). Hillsdale, NJ: Erlbaum.

Greenwald, A. G., Spangenberg, E. R., Pratkanis, A. R., & Eskenazi, J. (1991). Double blind tests of subliminal self-help audiotapes. *Psychological Science, 2,* 119–122.

Griffin, D. R. (1992). *Animal minds.* Chicago: University of Chicago Press.

Grinker, R. R., & Spiegel, J. P. (1945). *Men under stress.* Philadelphia: Bakiston.

Guilford, J. P. (1975). Factors and factors of personality. *Psychological Bulletin, 82,* 802–814.

Guthrie, E. R. (1935). *The psychology of learning* (2nd ed.). New York: Harper.

Guthrie, E. R. (1952). *The psychology of learning.* New York: Harper.

Gynther, M. D. (1972). White norms and black MMPIs: A prescription for discrimination? *Psychological Bulletin, 78,* 386–402.

Gynther, M. D., & Green, S. B. (1980). Accuracy may make a difference, and does difference make for accuracy? *Journal of Consulting and Clinical Psychology, 48,* 268–272.

Hall, C. S., & Lindzey, G. (1957). *Theories of personality.* New York: Wiley.

Harlow, H. F. (1953). Mice, monkeys, men and motive. *Psychological Review, 60,* 23–32.

Harter, S. (1983). Developmental perspectives on the self-system. In P. H. Mussen (Ed.), *Handbook of child psychology* (Vol. 4, pp. 275–385). New York: Wiley.

Hazan, C., & Shaver, P. R. (1987). Romantic love conceptualized as an attachment process. *Journal of Personality and Social Psychology, 52,* 511–524.

Hazan, C., & Shaver, P. R. (1994). Attachment as an organizational framework for research on close relationships. *Psychological Inquiry, 5,* 1–22.

Heatherton, T. F., & Baumeister, R. F. (1991). Binge eating as escape from self-awareness. *Psychological Bulletin, 110,* 86–108.

Helson, R. (1993). Comparing longitudinal studies of adult development: Toward a paradigm of tension between stability and change. In D. Funder, R. D. Parke, C. Tomlinson-Keasey, & K. Widaman (Eds.), *Studying lives through time* (pp. 93–120). Washington, DC: American Psychological Association.

Helson, R., & Stewart, A. (1994). Personality change in adulthood. In T. F. Heatherton & J. L. Weinberger (Eds.), *Can personality change?* (pp. 201–225). Washington, DC: American Psychological Association.

Herrnstein, R. J., & Murray, C. (1994). *The bell curve: Intelligence and class structure in American life.* New York: Free Press.

Hess, A. K. (1992). Review of the NEO Personality Inventory. *Mental Measurements Yearbook, 11,* 603–605.

Hetherington, E. M., Reiss, D., & Plomin, R. (Eds.). (1994). *Separate social worlds of siblings: Impact of nonshared environment on development.* Hillsdale, NJ: Erlbaum.

Higgins, E. T. (1987). Self-discrepancy: A theory relating self and affect. *Psychological Review, 94,* 319–340.

Higgins, E. T. (1989). Continuities and discontinuities in self-regulatory self-evaluative processes: A developmental theory relating self and affect. *Journal of Personality, 57,* 407–444.

Higgins, E. T. (1990). Personality, social psychology, and person-situation relations: Standards and knowledge activation as a common language. In L. A. Pervin (Ed.), *Handbook of personality: Theory and research* (pp. 303–338). New York: Guilford.

Higgins, E. T., Bond, R. N., Klein, R., & Strauman, T. (1986). Self-discrepancies and emotional vulnerability: How magnitude, accessibility, and type of discrepancy influence affect. *Journal of Personality and Social Psychology, 51,* 5–15.

Hiroto, D. S. (1974). Locus of control and learned helplessness. *Journal of Experimental Psychology, 102,* 187–193.

Hoffman, L. W. (1991). The influence of the family environment on personality: Accounting for sibling differences. *Psychological Bulletin, 110,* 187–203.

Hogan, R. (1982). On adding apples and oranges in personality psychology. *Contemporary Psychology, 27,* 851–852.

Hogan, R. (1991). Personality and personality measurement. In M. D. Dunnette & L. M. Hough (Eds.), *Handbook of industrial and organizational psychology* (2nd ed., Vol. 2, pp. 873–919). Palo Alto, CA: Consulting Psychologists Press.

Hollon, S. D., DeRubeis, R. J., & Evans, M. D. (1987). Causal mediation of change in treatment for depression: Discriminating between nonspecificity and noncausality. *Psychological Bulletin, 102,* 139–149.

Hollon, S. D., Shelton, R. C., & Davis, D. D. (1993). Cognitive therapy for depression: Conceptual issues and clinical efficacy. *Journal of Consulting and Clinical Psychology, 61,* 270–275.

Horowitz, M. J. (Ed.). (1991). *Person schemas and maladaptive interpersonal patterns.* Chicago: University of Chicago Press.

Hough, L. M. (1992). The "Big Five" personality variables—construct confusion: Description versus prediction. *Human Performance, 5,* 139–155.

Hull, C. L. (1943). *Principles of behavior.* New York: Appleton.

Humphreys, L. G. (1992). Commentary: What both critics and users of ability tests need to know. *Psychological Science, 3,* 231–274.

Humphreys, L. G., & Davey, T. C. (1988). Continuity in intellectual growth from 12 months to 9 years. *Intelligence, 12,* 183–197.

Hundleby, J. D., Pawlik, K., & Cattell, R. B. (1965). *Personality factors in objective test devices: A critical integration of a quarter of a century's research.* San Diego, CA: Knapp.

Imber, S. D., Elkin, I., Watkins, J. T., Collins, J. F., Shea, M. T., Leber, W. R., & Glass, D. R. (1990). Mode-specific effects among three treatments for depression. *Journal of Consulting and Clinical Psychology, 58,* 352–359.

Ionescu, M. D., & Erdelyi, M. H. (1992). The direct recovery of subliminal stimuli. In R. Bornstein & T. S. Pittman (Eds.), *Perception without awareness* (pp. 143–169). New York: Guilford.

Isen, A. M. (1993). Positive affect and decision making. In M. Lewis & J. M. Haviland (Eds.), *Handbook of emotions* (pp. 261–278). New York: Guilford.

Izard, C. E. (1991). *The psychology of emotion.* New York: Plenum.

Izard, C. E. (1992). Basic emotions, relations among emotions, and emotion-cognition relations. *Psychological Review, 99,* 561–565.

Izard, C. E. (1993a). Four systems for emotion activation: Cognitive and noncognitive processes. *Psychological Review, 100,* 68–90.

Izard, C. E. (1993b). Organizational and motivational functions of discrete emotions. In M. Lewis & J. M. Haviland (Eds.), *Handbook of emotion* (pp. 631–641). New York: Guilford.

Izard, C. E. (1994). Innate and universal facial expressions: Evidence from developmental and cross-cultural research. *Psychological Bulletin, 115,* 288–299.

Izard, C. E., Huebner, R. R., Risser, D., McGinnes, G., & Dougherty, L. (1980). The young infant's ability to produce discrete emotion expressions. *Development Psychology, 16,* 132–140.

Izard, C. E., Libero, D. Z., Putnam, P., & Haynes, O. M. (1993). Stability of emotion experiences and their relations to traits of personality. *Journal of Personality and Social Psychology, 64,* 847–860.

Jackson, D. N. (1967). *Personality research form manual.* Goshen, NY: Research Psychologists Press.

Jackson, D. N. (1984). *Personality research form manual* (3rd ed.). Port Huron, MI: Research Psychologists Press.

Jackson, D. N., & Messick, S. (1958). Content and style in personality assessment. *Psychological Bulletin, 55,* 243–252.

Jackson, D. N., & Messick, S. (Eds.). (1967). *Problems in assessment.* New York: McGraw-Hill.

Jackson, J. F. (1993). Human behavioral genetics, Scarr's theory, and her views on interventions: A critical review and commentary on their implications for African American children. *Child Development, 64,* 1318–1332.

Jacoby, L. L., Allan, L. G., Collins, J. C., & Larwill, L. K. (1988). Memory influences subjective experience: Noise judgments. *Journal of Experimental Psychology, 14,* 240–247.

Jacoby, L. L., & Kelley, C. M. (1992). A process-dissociation framework for investigating unconscious influences: Freudian slips, projective tests, subliminal perception, and signal detection theory. *Current*

Directions in Psychological Science, 1, 174–179.

Jacoby, L. L., Lindsay, D. S., & Toth, J. P. (1992). Unconscious influences revealed. *American Psychologist, 47,* 802–809.

Jacoby, L. L., Toth, J. P., Lindsay, D. S., & Debner, J. A. (1992). Lectures for a layperson: Methods for revealing unconscious processes. In R. F. Bornstein & T. S. Pittman (Eds.), *Perception without awareness* (pp. 81–120). New York: Guilford.

James, W. (1890). *Principles of psychology.* New York: Holt.

James, W. (1892). *Psychology: Brief course.* New York: Holt.

Jenkins, C. D. (1979). The coronary-prone personality. In W. D. Gentry & R. B. Williams (Eds.), *Psychological aspects of myocardial infarction and coronary disease.* St. Louis: Mosby.

John, O. P. (1990). The "Big Five" factor taxonomy: Dimensions of personality in the natural language and in questionnaires. In L. A. Pervin (Ed.), *Handbook of personality: Theory and research* (pp. 66–100). New York: Guilford.

John, O. P., & Robins, R. W. (1994). Accuracy and bias in self-perception: Individual differences in self-enhancement and the role of narcissism. *Journal of Personality and Social Psychology, 66,* 206–219.

Jones, E. *The life and work of Sigmund Freud* (Vol. 1). New York: Basic Books, 1953; Vol. 2, 1955; Vol. 3, 1957.

Jones, E. E., & Pulos, S. M. (1993). Comparing the process in psychodynamic and cognitive-behavioral therapies. *Journal of Consulting and Clinical Psychology, 61,* 306–316.

Kagan, J. (1994). *Galen's prophecy.* New York: Basic Books.

Kagan, J., Arcus, D., & Snidman, N. (1993). The idea of temperament: Where do we go from here? In R. Plomin & G. E. McClearn (Eds.), *Nature, nurture and psychology* (pp. 197–210). Washington, DC: American Psychological Association.

Kagan, J., Arcus, D., Snidman, N., Feng, W. Y., Hendler, J., & Greene, S. (1994). Reactivity in infants: A cross-national comparison. *Developmental Psychology, 30,* 342–345.

Kagan, J. & Snidman, N. (1991a). Infant predictors of inhibited and uninhibited profiles. *Psychological Science, 2,* 40–44.

Kagan, J. & Snidman, N. (1991b). Temperamental factors in human development. *American Psychologist, 46,* 856–862.

Kahn, S., Zimmerman, G., Csikszentmihalyi, M., & Getzels, J. W. (1985). Relations between identity in young adulthood and intimacy at midlife. *Journal of Personality and Social Psychology, 49,* 1316–1322.

Kamin, J. (1974). *The science and politics of I.Q.* Hillsdale, NJ: Erlbaum.

Kelly, G. A. (1955). *The psychology of personal constructs.* New York: Norton.

Kelly, G. A. (1958). Man's construction of his alternatives. In G. Lindzey (Ed.), *Assessment of human motives* (pp. 33–64). New York: Holt, Rinehart and Winston.

Kenrick, D. T., Sadalla, E. K., Groth, G., & Trost, M. R. (1990). Evolution, traits, and the stages of human courtship: Qualifying the parental investment model. *Journal of Personality, 58,* 97–116.

Kernberg, O. (1976). *Object relations theory and clinical psychoanalysis.* New York: Aronson.

Kiesler, D. J. (1991). Interpersonal methods of assessment and diagnosis. In C. R. Snyder & D. R. Forsyth (Eds.), *Handbook of social and clinical psychology* (pp. 438–468). Elmsford, NY: Pergamon.

Kihlstrom, J. F. (1987). The cognitive unconscious. *Science, 237,* 1445–1452.

Kihlstrom, J. F. (1990). The psychological unconscious. In L. A. Pervin (Ed.), *Handbook of personality: Theory and research* (pp. 445–464). New York: Guilford.

Kihlstrom, J. F. (1992). Dissociation and dissociations: A commentary on consciousness and cognition. *Consciousness and Cognition, 1,* 47–53.

Kihlstrom, J. F., Barnhardt, T. M., & Tataryn, D. J. (1992). The cognitive perspective. In R. F. Bornstein & T. S. Pittman (Eds.), *Perception without awareness* (pp. 17–54). New York: Guilford.

Kitayama, S. (1992). Some thoughts on the cognitive-psychodynamic self from a cultural perspective. *Psychological Inquiry, 3,* 41–43.

Klein, G. S. (1951). The personal world through perception. In R. R. Blake & G. V. Ramsey (Eds.), *Perception: An approach to personality* (pp. 328–355). New York: Ronald.

Klein, G. S. (1954). Need and regulation. In M. R. Jones (Ed.), *Nebraska symposium on motivation* (pp. 224–274). Lincoln: University of Nebraska Press.

Klein, G. S. (1976). *Psychoanalytic theory: An exploration of essentials.* New York: International Universities Press.

Klinger, E. (1977). *Meaning and void: Inner experience and the incentives in people's lives.* Minneapolis: University of Minnesota Press.

Kluft, R. P., & Fine, C. G. (Eds.). (1993). *Clinical perspectives on multiple personality disorder.* Washington, DC: American Psychiatric Press.

Koestner, R., & McClelland, D. C. (1990) Perspectives on competence motivation. In L. A. Pervin (Ed.), *Handbook of personality: Theory and research* (pp. 527–548). New York: Guilford.

Kohut, H. (1971). *The analysis of the self.* New York: International Universities Press.

Kohut, H. (1977). *The restoration of the self.* New York: International Universities Press.

Krosnick, J. A., Betz, A. L., Jussim, L. J., & Lynn, A. R. (1992). Subliminal conditioning of attitudes. *Journal of Personality and Social Psychology, 18,* 152–162.

Kuhl, J., & Beckman, J. (Eds.). (1985). *Action control from cognition to behavior.* New York: Springer-Verlag.

Kunda, Z. (1987). Motivated inference: Self-serving generation and evaluation of causal theories. *Journal of Personality and Social Psychology, 53,* 636–647.

Kunst-Wilson, W. R., & Zajonc, R. B. (1980). Affective discrimination of stimuli that cannot be recognized. *Science, 207,* 557–558.

Lambert, M. J., & Bergin, A. E. (1992). Achievements and limitations of psychotherapy research. In D. K. Freedheim (Ed.), *History of psychotherapy* (pp. 360–390). Washington, DC: American Psychological Association.

Larsen, R. J., (1991). Emotion. In V. J. Derlega, B. A. Winstead, & W. H. Jones (Eds.), *Personality* (pp. 407–432). Chicago: Nelson-Hall.

Latane, B., & Darley, J. M. (1970). *The unresponsive bystander: Why doesn't he help?* New York: Appleton-Century-Crofts.

Lau, R. R. (1982). Origins of health locus of control beliefs. *Journal of Personality and Social Psychology, 42,* 322–324.

Lazarus, R. S. (1966). *Psychological stress and the coping process.* New York: McGraw-Hill.

Lazarus, R. S. (1991). *Emotion and adaptation.* New York: Oxford University Press.

Lazarus, R. S. (1993a). Coping theory and research: Past, present, and future. *Psychosomatic Medicine, 55,* 234–247.

Lazarus, R. S. (1993b). From psychological stress to the emotions: A history of changing outlooks. *Annual Review of Psychology, 44,* 1–21.

Lazarus, R. S. (1993c). Lazarus rise. *Psychological Inquiry, 4,* 343–357.

Lazarus, R. S., & Folkman, S. (1984). *Stress, appraisal, and coping.* New York: Springer-Verlag.

Leary, T. (1957). *Interpersonal diagnosis of personality.* New York: Ronald.

Lecky, P. (1945). *Self-consistency: A theory of personality.* New York: Island.

Lefcourt, H. M. (Ed.). (1984). *Research with the locus of control construct.* Orlando, FL: Academic.

Lepper, M. R., & Greene, D. (Eds.). (1978). *The hidden costs of reward.* Hillsdale, NJ: Erlbaum.

Levy, B., & Langer, E. (1994). Aging free from negative stereotypes: Successful memory in China and among the American deaf. *Journal of Personality and Social Psychology, 66,* 989–997.

Lewicki, P. (1985). Nonconscious biasing effects of single instances of subsequent judgments. *Journal of Personality and Social Psychology, 48,* 563–574.

Lewin, K. A., Dembo, T., Festinger, L., & Sears, P. S. (1944). Level of aspiration. In J. McV. Hunt (Ed.), *Personality and the behavior disorders* (pp. 333–378). New York: Ronald.

Lewis, M. (1990a). Challenges to the study of developmental psychopathology. In M. Lewis & S. M. Miller (Eds.), *Handbook of developmental psychopathology* (pp. 29–40). New York: Plenum.

Lewis, M. (1990b). Development, time, and catastrophe: An alternate view of discontinuity. In P. Baltes, D. L. Featherman, & R. Lerner (Eds.), *Life span development and behavior* (Vol. 10, pp. 325–350). Hillsdale, NJ: Erlbaum.

Lewis, M. (1990c). The development of intentionality and the role of consciousness. *Psychological Inquiry, 1,* 231–247.

Lewis, M. (1991). *Development, history and other problems of time.* Paper presented at the Jean Piaget Society meeting, May, Philadelphia, PA.

Lewis, M. (1992a). *Shame, the exposed self.* New York: Free Press.

Lewis, M. (1992b). Will the real self or selves please stand up? *Psychological Inquiry, 3,* 123–124.

Lewis, M. (1993). The emergence of human emotions. In M. Lewis & J. M. Haviland (Eds.), *Handbook of emotions* (pp. 223–235). New York: Guilford.

Lewis, M. (1995). *Unavoidable accidents and chance encounters.* New York: Guilford.

Lewis, M., & Brooks-Gunn, J. (1979). *Social cognition and the acquisition of self.* New York: Plenum.

Lewis M., & Feiring, C. (1994). Developmental outcomes as history. Unpublished manuscript. Robert Wood Johnson Medical School, New Brunswick, NJ.

Lewis, M. Feiring, C., McGuffog, C., & Jaskir, J. (1984). Predicting psychopathology in six year olds from early social relations. *Child Development, 55,* 123–136.

Lewis, M., & Michalson, L. (1983). *Children's emotions and moods: Developmental theory and measurement.* New York: Plenum.

Lewis, M., Sullivan, M. W., & Brooks-Gunn, J. (1985). Emotional behavior during the learning contingency in early infancy. *British Journal of Developmental Psychology, 3,* 307–316.

Little, B. R. (1989). Personal projects analysis: Trivial pursuits, magnificent obsessions, and the search for coherence. In D. M. Buss & N. Cantor (Eds.), *Personality psychology: Recent trends and emerging directions* (pp. 15–31). New York: Springer-Verlag.

Little, B. R., Lecci, L., & Watkinson, B. (1992). Personality and personal projects: Linking Big Five and PAC units of analysis. *Journal of Personality, 60,* 501–526.

Locke, E. A., & Latham, G. P. (1990). *A theory of goal setting and task performance.* Englewood Cliffs, NJ: Prentice-Hall.

Loehlin, J. C. (1992). *Genes and environment in personality development.* Newbury Park, CA: Sage.

Loftus, E. F. (1991). The glitter of everyday memory . . . and the gold. *American Psychologist, 46,* 16–18.

Loftus, E. F. (1993). The reality of repressed memories. *American Psychologist, 48,* 518–537.

Loftus, E. F., & Klinger, M. R. (1992). Is the unconscious smart or dumb? *American Psychologist, 47,* 761–765.

Luborsky, L., Barber, J. P., & Beutler, L. (1993). Introduction to special section: A briefing on curative factors in dynamic psychotherapy. *Journal of Consulting and Clinical Psychology, 61,* 539–541.

Lykken, D. T. (1971). Multiple factor analysis and personality research. *Journal of Experimental Research in Personality, 5,* 161–170.

Lykken, D. T., Bouchard, T. J., Jr., McGue, M., & Tellegen, A. (1993). Heritability of interests: A twin study. *Journal of Applied Psychology, 78,* 649–661.

Lykken, D. T., McGue, M., Tellegen, A., & Bouchard, T. J., Jr. (1992). Emergenesis: Traits that do may run in families. *American Psychologist, 47,* 1565–1577.

Magnusson, D. (Ed.). (1988). *Paths through life.* Hillsdale, NJ: Erlbaum.

Magnusson, D. (1990). Personality development from an interactional perspective. In L. A. Pervin (Ed.), *Handbook of personalitys: Theory and research* (pp. 193–222). New York: Guilford.

Magnusson, D. (1992). Individual development: A longitudinal perspective. *European Journal of Personality, 6,* 119–138.

Magnusson, D., Andersson, T., & Torestad, B. (1993). Methodological implications of a peephole perspective. In D. C. Funder, R. D. Parke, C. Tomlinson-Keasey, & K. Widaman (Eds.), *Studying lives through time* (pp. 207–220). Washington, DC: American Psychological Association.

Magnusson, D., & Torestad, B. (1993). A holistic view of personality: A model revisited. *Annual Review of Psychology, 44,* 427–452.

Mahler, M. S. (1963). Thoughts about development and individuation. *Psychoanalytic Study of the Child, 18,* 307–324.

Mahler, M. S., Pine, F., & Bergman, A. (1975). *The psychological birth of the human infant: Symbiosis and individuation.* New York: Basic.

Malatesta, C. Z. (1990). The role of emotions in the development and organization of personality. *Nebraska Symposium on Motivation, 36,* 1–56.

Marcia, J. E. (1966). Development and validation of ego-identity status. *Journal of Personality and Social Psychology, 4,* 551–558.

Marcia, J. E. (1980). Identity in adolescence. In J. Adelson (Ed.), *Handbook of adolescent psychology* (pp.159–187). New York: Wiley.

Markus, H. (1977). Self-schemata and processing information about the self. *Journal of Personality and Social Psychology, 35,* 63–78.

Markus, H. (1990). The willful self. *Personality and Social Psychology Bulletin, 16,* 726–742.

Markus, H. (1992). Quoted in the *APA Monitor,* October, p. 23.

Markus, H., & Cross, S. (1990). The interpersonal self. In L. A. Pervin (Ed.), *Handbook of personality: Theory and research* (pp. 576–608). New York: Guilford.

Markus, H., & Kitayama, S. (1991). Culture and the self: Implications for cognition, emotion, and motivation. *Psychological Review, 98,* 224–253.

Markus, H., & Kunda, Z. (1986). Stability and malleability of self-concept. *Journal of Personality and Social Psychology, 51,* 858–886.

Markus, H., & Nurius, P. (1986). Possible selves. *American Psychologist, 41,* 954–969.

Markus, H., & Ruvolo, A. (1989). Possible selves: Personalized representations of goals. In L. A. Pervin (Ed.), *Goal concepts in personality and social psychology* (pp. 211–241). Hillsdale, NJ: Erlbaum.

Markus, H., & Sentis, K. (1982). The self in social information processing. In J. Suls (Ed.), *Psychological perspectives on the self* (pp. 41–70). Hillsdale, NJ: Erlbaum.

Martin, G. B., & Clark, R. D. (1982). Distress crying in neonates: Species and peer specificity. *Developmental Psychology, 18,* 3–9.

Masling, J. M. (1992). What does it all mean? In R. F. Bornstein & T. S. Pittman (Eds.), *Perception without awareness* (pp. 259–276). New York: Guilford.

Masling, J. M., & Bornstein, R. F. (Eds.). (1993). *Psychoanalytic perspectives on psychopathology.* Washington, DC: American Psychological Association.

Maslow, A. H. (1954). *Motivation and personality.* New York: Harper.

Maslow, A. H. (1968). *Toward a psychology of being.* Princeton, NJ: Van Nostrand.

Maslow, A. H. (1971). *The farther reaches of human nature.* New York: Viking.

Matsumoto, D. (1993). Ethnic differences in affect intensity, emotion judgments, display rule attitudes, and self-reported emotional expression in an American sample. *Motivation and Emotion, 17,* 107–123.

McAdams, D. P. (1988). *Intimacy, power, and the life history.* New York: Guilford.

McAdams, D. P. (1992). The five-factor model in personality: A critical appraisal. *Journal of Personality, 60,* 329–361.

McCartney, K., Harris, M. J., & Bernieri, F. (1990). Growing up and growing apart: A developmental meta-analysis of twin studies. *Psychological Bulletin, 107,* 226–237.

McClelland, D. C. (1951). *Personality*. New York: Sloane.

McClelland, D. C. (1961). *The achieving society*. Princeton, NJ: Van Nostrand.

McClelland, D. C. (1980). Motive dispositions: The merits of operant and respondent measures. *Review of Personality and Social Psychology, 1,* 10–41.

McClelland, D. C., Atkinson, J., Clark, R., & Lowell, E. (1953). *The achievement motive*. New York: Appleton-Century-Crofts.

McClelland, D. C., Koestner, R., & Weinberger, J. (1989). How do self-attributed and implicit motives differ? *Psychological Review, 96,* 690–702.

McCrae, R. R. (1994). New goals for trait psychology. *Psychological Inquiry, 5,* 148–153.

McCrae, R. R., & Costa, P. T., Jr. (1990). *Personality in adulthood*. New York: Guilford.

McCrae, R. R., & Costa, P. T., Jr. (1991). Adding *liebe und arbeit:* The full five-factor model and well-being. *Personality and Social Psychology Bulletin, 17,* 227–232.

McCrae, R. R., & John, O. P. (1992). An introduction to the five-factor model and its applications. *Journal of Personality, 60,* 175–215.

McDougall, W. (1930). Hormic psychology. In C. Murchison (Ed.), *Psychologies of 1930* (pp. 3–36). Worcester, MA: Clark University Press.

McGinnies, E. (1949). Emotionality and perceptual defense. *Psychological Review, 56,* 244–251.

McGue, M., Bouchard, T. J., Jr., Iacono, W. G., & Lykken, D. T. (1993). Behavioral genetics of cognitive ability: A life-span perspective. In R. Plomin & G. E. McClearn (Eds.), *Nature, nurture, and psychology* (pp.59–76). Washington, DC: American Psychological Association.

Mead, G. H. (1934). *Mind, self and society*. Chicago: University of Chicago Press.

Meehl, P. E. (1954). *Clinical versus statistical prediction*. Minneapolis: University of Minnesota Press.

Meehl, P. E. (1957). When shall we use our heads instead of a formula? *Journal of Counseling Psychology, 4,* 268–273.

Messer, S. B., & Warren, S. (1990). Personality change and psychotherapy. In L. A. Pervin (Ed.), *Handbook of personality: Theory and research* (pp. 371–398). New York: Guilford.

Mikulciner, M., Florian, V., & Weller, A. (1993). Attachment styles, coping strategies, and post traumatic psychological distress: The impact of the Gulf War in Israel. *Journal of Personality and Social Psychology, 64,* 817–826.

Miller, G. A., Galanter, E., & Pribram, K. H. (1960). *Plans and the structure of behavior*. New York: Holt, Rinehart and Winston.

Miller, N. E. (1944). Experimental studies of conflict. In J. McV. Hunt (Ed.), *Personality and the behavior disorders* (pp. 431–465). New York: Ronald.

Miller, N. E. (1951). Comments on theoretical models: Illustrated by the development of a theory of conflict behavior. *Journal of Personality, 20,* 82–100.

Millon, T. (1981). *Disorders of personality*. New York: Wiley-Interscience.

Mineka, S. (1985). Animal models anxiety-based disorders: Their usefulness and limitations. In A. H. Tuma & J. D. Maser (Eds.), *Anxiety and the anxiety disorders*. Hillsdale, NJ: Erlbaum.

Mineka, S. (1987). A primate model of phobic fears. In H. Eysenck & I. Martin (Eds.), *Theoretical foundations of behavior therapy* (pp. 81–111). New York: Plenum.

Mineka, S., Davidson, M., Cook, M., & Klein, R. (1984). Observational conditioning of snake fear in rhesus monkeys. *Journal of Abnormal Psychology, 93,* 355–372.

Mischel, W. (1968). *Personality and assessment*. New York: Wiley.

Mischel, W. (1973). Toward a cognitive social learning reconceptualization of personality. *Psychological Review, 80,* 252–283.

Mischel, W. (1990). Personality dispositions revisited and revised: A view after three decades. In L. A. Pervin (Ed.), *Handbook of personality: Theory and research* (pp. 111–134). New York: Guilford.

Mischel, W., & Shoda, Y. (1995). A cognitive-affective system theory of personality: Reconceptualizing the invariances in personality and the role of situations. *Psychological Review,* in press.

Monson, T. C., Hesley, J. W., & Chernick, L. (1982). Specifying when personality traits can and cannot predict behavior: An alternative to abandoning the attempt to predict single-act criteria. *Journal of Personality and Social Psychology, 43,* 385–399.

Mook, D. G. (1987). *Motivation.* New York: Norton.

Morse, R. C., & Stoller, D. (1982, September). The hidden message that breaks habits. *Science Digest,* p. 28.

Moskowitz, D. S. (1986). Comparison of self-reports, reports by knowledgeable informants, and behavioral observation data. *Journal of Personality, 54,* 294–317.

Moskowitz, D. S. (1988). Cross-situational generality in the laboratory: Dominance and friendliness. *Journal of Personality and Social Psychology, 54,* 829–839.

Moskowitz, D. S. (1990). Convergence of self-reports and independent observers: Dominance and friendliness. *Journal of Personality and Social Psychology, 58,* 1096–1106.

Murray, H. A. (1938). *Explorations in personality.* New York: Oxford University Press.

Murray, H. A. (1951). Toward a classification of interaction. In T. Parsons & E. A. Shils (Eds.), *Toward a general theory of action* (pp. 434–464). Cambridge, MA: Harvard University Press.

Nasby, W. (1985). Private self-consciousness articulation of the self-schema, and recognition memory of trait adjectives. *Journal of Personality and Social Psychology, 49,* 704–709.

Nelson, T. (1978). Detecting small amounts of information in memory: Savings for nonrecognized items. *Journal of Experimental Psychology, 4,* 453–468.

Newell, A., Shaw, J. C., & Simon, H. (1958). Elements of a theory of human problem-solving. *Psychological Review, 65,* 151–166.

Newman, L. S., Higgins, E. T., & Vookles, J. (1992). Self-guide strength and emotional vulnerability: Birth order as a moderator of self-affect relations. *Personality and Social Psychology Bulletin, 18,* 402–411.

Nichols, D. S. (1992). Review of the MMPI-2. *Mental Measurements Yearbook, 11,* 562–565.

Nisbett, R., & Ross, L. (1980). *Human inference: Strategies and shortcomings of social judgment.* Englewood Cliffs, NJ: Prentice Hall.

Nisbett, R. E., & Wilson, T. D. (1977). Telling more than we know: Verbal reports on mental processes. *Psychological Review, 84,* 231–279.

Norem, J. K. (1989). Cognitive strategies as personality: Effectiveness, specificity, flexibility, and change. In D. M. Buss & N. Cantor (Eds.), *Personality psychology: Recent trends and emerging directions* (pp. 45–60). New York: Springer-Verlag.

Norem, J. K., & Cantor, N. (1986). Defensive pessimism: "Harnessing" anxiety as motivation. *Journal of Personality and Social Psychology, 51,* 1208–1217.

Novacek, J., & Lazarus, R. S. (1989). The structure of personal commitments. *Journal of Personality, 58,* 693–715.

O'Leary, A. (1985). Self-efficacy and health. *Behavior Research and Therapy, 23,* 437–451.

O'Leary, A. (1990). Stress, emotion, and human immune function. *Psychological Bulletin, 108,* 363–382.

O'Leary, A. (1992). Self-efficacy and health: Behavioral and stress-physiological mediation. *Cognitive Therapy and Research, 16,* 229–245.

O'Leary, K. D., & Wilson, G. T. (1987). *Behavior therapy: Application and outcome.* Englewood Cliffs, NJ: Prentice Hall.

Orne, M. T. (1962). On the social psychology of the psychological experiment: With particular reference to demand characteristics and their implications. *American Psychologist, 17,* 776–783.

Ortony, A., & Turner, T. J. (1990). What's basic about basic emotions? *Psychological Review, 97,* 315–331.

OSS Assessment Staff. (1948). *Assessment of men.* New York: Rinehart.

Ostendorf, F., & Angleitner, A. (1990). *On*

the comprehensiveness of the five-factor model of personality: Some more evidence for the five robust rating factors in questionnaire data. Paper presented at the Fifth European Conference on Personality, Rome, Italy.

Ouimette, P. C., & Klein, D. N. (1993). Convergence of psychoanalytic and cognitive-behavioral theories of depression. In J. M. Masling & R. F. Bornstein (Eds.), *Psychoanalytic perspectives on psychopathology* (pp. 191–223). Washington, DC: American Psychological Association.

Ozer, D. J. (1993). The Q-sort method and the study of personality development. In D. C. Funder, R. D. Parke, C. Tomlinson-Keasey, & K. Widaman (Eds.), *Studying lives through time* (pp. 147–168). Washington, DC: American Psychological Association.

Palys, T. S., & Little, B. R. (1983). Perceived life satisfaction and the organization of personal project systems. *Journal of Personality and Social Psychology, 44,* 1221–1230.

Patton, C. J. (1992). Fear of abandonment and binge eating. *Journal of Nervous and Mental Disease, 180,* 484–490.

Pedersen, N. L., Plomin, R., McClearn, G. E., & Friberg, L. (1988). Neuroticism, Extraversion, and related traits in adult twins reared apart and reared together. *Journal of Personality and Social Psychology, 55,* 950–957.

Pedersen, N. L., Plomin, R., Nesselroade, J. R., & McClearn, G. E. (1992). A quantitative genetic analysis of cognitive abilities during the second half of the life span. *Psychological Science, 3,* 346–353.

Pekala, R. J. (1991). Quantifying consciousness: An empirical approach. New York: Plenum.

Pelham, B. W. (1991). On confidence and consequence: The certainty and importance of self-knowledge. *Journal of Personality and Social Psychology, 60,* 518–530.

Pennebaker, J. W. (1990). *Opening up: The healing powers of confiding in others.* New York: Morrow.

Pennebaker, J. W. (1993). Social mechanisms of constraint. In D. W. Wegner & J. W. Pennebaker (Eds.), *Handbook of mental control* (pp. 200–219). Englewood Cliffs, NJ: Prentice Hall.

Pennebaker, J. W., & Chew, C. H. (1985). Behavioral inhibition and electrodermal activity during deception. *Journal of Personality and Social Psychology, 49,* 1427–1433.

Pennebaker, J. W., Kiecolt-Glaser, J. K., & Glaser, R. (1988). Disclosure of traumas and immune function: Health implications for psychotherapy. *Journal of Consulting and Clinical Psychology, 56,* 239–245.

Persad, S. M., & Polivy, J. (1993). Differences between depressed and nondepressed individuals in the recognition of and response to facial emotional cues. *Journal of Abnormal Psychology, 3,* 358–368.

Pervin, L. A. (1963). The need to predict and control under conditions of threat. *Journal of Personality, 31,* 570–587.

Pervin, L. A. (1975). *Current controversies and issues in personality.* New York: Wiley.

Pervin, L. A. (1980). *The cognitive revolution and what it leaves out.* Unpublished manuscript. Rutgers University, New Brunswick, NJ.

Pervin, L. A. (1983). The stasis and flow of behavior: Toward a theory of goals. In M. M. Page (Ed.), *Personality: Current theory and research* (pp. 1–53). Lincoln: University of Nebraska Press.

Pervin, L. A. (1984). *Current controversies and issues in personality.* New York: Wiley.

Pervin, L. A. (1985). Personality: Current controversies, issues, and directions. *Annual Review of Psychology, 36,* 83–114.

Pervin, L. A. (Ed.). (1989). *Goal concepts in personality and social psychology.* Hillsdale, NJ: Erlbaum.

Pervin, L. A. (Ed.). (1990). *Handbook of personality: Theory and research.* New York: Guilford.

Pervin, L. A. (1991). Goals, plans, and problems in the self-regulation of behavior:

The question of volition. In P. R. Pintrich & M. L. Maehr (Eds.), *Advances in motivation and achievement* (pp. 1–20). Greenwich, CT: JAI Press.

Pervin, L. A. (1993a). *Personality: Theory and research* (6th ed.). New York: Wiley.

Pervin, L. A. (1993b). Personality and affect. In M. Lewis & J. Haviland (Eds.), *Handbook of emotion* (pp. 301–312). New York: Guilford.

Pervin, L. A. (1993c). Pattern and organization: Current trends and prospects for the future. In K. Craik, R. Hogan, & R. N. Wolfe (Eds.), *Perspectives in personality* (pp. 69–84). Greenwich, CT: JAI Press.

Pervin, L. A. (1994a). A critical analysis of current trait theory. *Psychology Inquiry, 5,* 103–113.

Pervin, L. A. (1994b). Personality stability, personality change, and the question of process. In T. Heatherton & J. Weinberger (Eds.), *Can personality change?* (pp. 315–330). Washington, DC: American Psychological Association.

Pervin, L. A., & Yatko, R. J. (1965). Cigarette smoking and alternative methods of reducing dissonance. *Journal of Personality and Social Psychology, 2,* 30–36.

Peterson, C. (1991). The meaning and measurement of explanatory style. *Psychological Inquiry, 2,* 1–10.

Peterson, C., & Seligman, M. E. P. (1984). Causal explanations as a risk factor for depression: Theory and evidence. *Psychological Review, 91,* 347–374.

Peterson, C., Semmel, A., von Baeyer, C., Abramson, L. Y., Metalsky, G. I., & Seligman, M. E. P. (1982). The Attributional Style Questionnaire. *Cognitive Therapy and Research, 6,* 287–300.

Peterson, C., & Ulrey, L. M. (1994). Can explanatory style be scored from TAT protocols? *Personality and Social Psychology Bulletin, 20,* 102–106.

Pincus, A. L., & Wiggins, J. S. (1990). Interpersonal problems and conceptions of personality disorders. *Journal of Personality Disorders, 4,* 342–352.

Plomin, R. (1986). *Development, genetics, and psychology.* Hillsdale, NJ: Erlbaum.

Plomin, R. (1990a). *Nature and nurture.* Pacific Grove, CA: Brooks/Cole.

Plomin, R. (1990b). The role of inheritance in behavior. *Science, 248,* 183–188.

Plomin, R. (1993). Nature and nurture: Perspective and prospective. In R. Plomin & G. E. McClearn (Eds.), *Nature, nurture, and psychology* (pp. 457–483). Washington, DC: American Psychological Association.

Plomin, R. (1994). *Genetics and experience: The interplay between nature and nurture.* Newbury Park, CA: Sage Publications.

Plomin, R., & Bergeman, C. S. (1991). The nature of nurture: Genetic influence on "environmental" measures. *Behavioral and Brain Sciences, 14,* 373–427.

Plomin, R., Chipuer, H. M., & Loehlin, J. C. (1990). Behavioral genetics and personality. In L. A. Pervin (Ed.), *Handbook of personality: Theory and Research* (pp. 225–243). New York: Guilford.

Plomin, R., Coon, H., Carey, G., DeFries, J. C., & Fulker, D. W. (1991). Parent-offspring and sibling adoption analyses of parental ratings of temperament in infancy and early childhood. *Journal of Personality, 59,* 705–732.

Plomin, R., & Daniels, D. (1987). Why are children in the same family so different from each other? *Behavioral and Brain Sciences, 10,* 1–16.

Plomin, R., Emde, R. N., Braungart, J. M., Campos, J., Corley, R., Fulker, D. W., Kagan, J. S., Robinson, J., Zahn-Waxler, C., & DeFries, J. C. (1993). Genetic change and continuity from fourteen to twenty months: The MacArthur Longitudinal Twin Study. *Child Development, 64,* 1354–1376.

Plomin, R., & Neiderhiser, J. M. (1992). Genetics and experience. *Current Directions in Psychological Science, 1,* 160–163.

Plomin, R., & Rende, R. (1991). Human behavioral genetics. *Annual Review of Psychology, 42,* 161–190.

Plomin, R., & Saudino, K. J. (1994). Quantitative genetics and molecular genetics. In J. E. Bates & T. D. Wachs (Eds.), *Temper-*

ament: Individual differences at the interface of biology and behavior (pp.143–171). Washington, DC: American Psychological Association.

Plutchik, R. (1980). *Emotion: A psychoevolutionary synthesis.* New York: Harper & Row.

Poetzl, O. (1917). The relationship between experimentally induced dream images and indirect vision. *Psychological Issues Monograph, 1960, 2,* 46–106.

Postman, L., Bruner, J. S., & McGinnies, E. (1948). Personal values as selective factors in perception. *Journal of Abnormal and Social Psychology, 43,* 142–154.

Prince, M. (1906). *The dissociation of personality.* New York: Longmans, Green.

Pritchard, D. A., & Rosenblatt, A. (1980). Racial bias in the MMPI: A methodological review. *Journal of Consulting and Clinical Psychology, 48,* 263–267.

Psychological Assessment Resources. (1985). NEO-PI Manual. Odessa, FL.

Psychological Assessment Resources. (1989). NEO-PI-R Manual. Odessa, FL.

Raskin, R., & Hall, C. S. (1979). A narcissistic personality inventory. *Psychological Reports, 45,* 55–60.

Raskin, R., & Hall, C. S. (1981). The Narcissistic Personality Inventory: Alternate form reliability and further evidence of construct validity. *Journal of Personality Assessment, 45,* 159–162.

Raskin, R., & Shaw, R. (1987). *Narcissism and the use of personal pronouns.* Unpublished manuscript.

Read, S. J., Jones, D. K., & Miller, L. C. (1990). Traits as goal-based categories: The importance of goals in the coherence of dispositional categories. *Journal of Personality and Social Psychology, 58,* 1048–1061.

Roberts, A. H., Kewman, D. G., Mercier, L., & Hovell, M. (1993). The power of nonspecific effects in healing: Implications for psychosocial and biological treatments. *Clinical Psychology Review, 13,* 375–391.

Robins, C. J., & Hayes, A. M. (1993). An ap-

praisal of cognitive therapy. *Journal of Consulting and Clinical Psychology, 61,* 205–214.

Robins, L. N., & Rutter, M. (Eds.). (1990). *Straight and devious pathways from childhood to adulthood.* Cambridge, England: Cambridge University Press.

Robins, R., & John, O. P. (1994). Narcissus and self-awareness: Effects of visual perspective and narcissism on self-perception. Submitted manuscript. University of California, Berkeley.

Rogers, C. R. (1951). *Client-centered therapy.* Boston: Houghton Mifflin.

Rogers, C. R. (1956). Some issues concerning the control of human behavior. *Science, 124,* 1057–1066.

Rogers, C. R. (1958). A process conception of psychotherapy. *American Psychologist, 13,* 142–149.

Rogers, C. R. (1959). A theory of therapy, personality, and interpersonal relationships as developed in the client-centered framework. In S. Koch (Ed.), *Psychology: A study of science* (pp. 184–256). New York: McGraw-Hill.

Rogers, C. R. (1961). *On becoming a person.* Boston: Houghton Mifflin.

Rogers, C. R. (1966). Client-centered therapy. In S. Arieti (Ed.), *American handbook of psychiatry* (pp. 183–200). New York: Basic Books.

Rosch, E., Mervis, C., Gray, W., Johnson, D., & Boyes-Braem, P. (1976). Basic objects in natural categories. *Cognitive Psychology, 8,* 382–439.

Rose, R. J. (1988). Genetic and environmental variance in content dimensions of the MMPI. *Journal of Personality and Social Psychology, 55,* 302–311.

Rosenzweig, S. (1941). Need-persistive and ego-defensive reactions to frustration as demonstrated by an experiment on repression. *Psychological Review, 48,* 347–349.

Rotter, J. B. (1954). *Social learning and clinical psychology.* Englewood Cliffs, NJ: Prentice Hall.

Rotter, J. B. (1966). Generalized expectancies

for internal versus external control of re-inforcement. *Psychological Monographs,* 80 (Whole No. 609).

Rotter, J. B. (1971). Generalized expectancies for interpersonal trust. *American Psychologist, 26,* 443–452.

Rotter, J. B. (1981). The psychological situation in social learning theory. In D. Magnusson (Ed.), *Toward a psychology of situations.* Hillsdale, NJ: Erlbaum.

Rotter, J. B. (1990). Internal versus external control of reinforcement. *American Psychologist, 45,* 489–493.

Rovee-Collier, C. (1993). The capacity for long-term memory in infancy. *Current Directions in Psychological Science, 2,* 130–135.

Rowe, D. C. (1993). Genetic perspectives on personality. In R. Plomin & G. E. McClearn (Eds.), *Nature, nurture and psychology* (pp. 179–196). Washington, DC: American Psychological Association.

Rozin, P., & Fallon, A. E. (1987). A perspective on disgust. *Psychological Review, 94,* 23–41.

Rozin, P., & Zellner, D. (1985). The role of Pavlovian conditioning in the acquisition of food likes and dislikes. *Annals of the New York Academy of Sciences, 443,* 189–202.

Salili, F. (1994). Age, sex, and cultural differences in the meaning and dimensions of achievement. *Personality and Social Psychology Bulletin, 20,* 635–648.

Sandvik, E., Diener, E., & Seidlitz, C. (1993). Subjective well-being: The convergence and stability of self-report and non-self-report measures. *Journal of Personality, 61,* 317–342.

Scarr, S. (1992). Developmental theories for the 1990s: Development and individual differences. *Child Development, 63,* 1–19.

Scarr, S. (1993). Biological and cultural diversity: The legacy of Darwin for development. *Child Development, 64,* 1333–1353.

Schacht, T. E. (1993). How do I diagnosis thee? Let me count the dimensions. *Psychological Inquiry, 4,* 115–119.

Schachter, D. (1987). Implicit memory: His-tory and current status. *Journal of Experimental Psychology, 13,* 501–518.

Schafer, R. (1976). *A new language for psychoanalysis.* New Haven, CT.: Yale University Press.

Scheier, M. F., & Carver, C. S. (1985). Optimism, coping, and health: Assessment and implications of generalized outcome expectancies. *Health Psychology, 4,* 219–247.

Scheier, M. F., & Carver, C. S. (1987). Dispositional optimism and physical well-being: The influence of generalized outcome expectancies on health. *Journal of Personality, 55,* 169–210.

Scheier, M. F., & Carver, C. S. (1988). A model of behavioral self-regulation: Translating intention into action. *Advances in Experimental Social Psychology, 21,* 303–346.

Scheier, M. F., & Carver, C. S. (1993). On the power of positive thinking: The benefits of being optimistic. *Psychological Science, 2,* 26–30.

Scheier, M. F., Magovern, G. J., Sr., Abbott, R. A., Matthews, K. A., Owens, J. F., Lefebvre, R. C., & Carver, C. S. (1989). Dispositional optimism and recovery from coronary artery bypass surgery: The beneficial effects on physical and psychological well-being. *Journal of Personality and Social Psychology, 57,* 1024–1040.

Scheier, M. F., Weintraub, J. K., & Carver, C. S. (1986). Coping with stress: Divergent strategies of optimists and pessimists. *Journal of Personality and Social Psychology, 51,* 1257–1264.

Scherer, K., & Wallbott, H. G. (1994). Evidence for universality and cultural variation of differential emotional response patterning. *Journal of Personality and Social Psychology, 66,* 310–328.

Schiff, M., Duyme, M., Dumaret, A., & Tonkiewicz, S. (1982). How much could we boost scholastic achievement IQ scores? A direct answer from a French adoption study. *Cognition, 12,* 165–196.

Schlenker, B. R., & Weigold, M. F. (1989). Goals and the self-identification process:

Constructing desired identities. In L. A. Pervin (Ed.), *Goal concepts in personality and social psychology* (pp. 243–290). Hillsdale, NJ: Erlbaum.

Schmidt, F. L., & Ones, D. S. (1992). Personnel selection. *Annual Review of Psychology, 43,* 627–670.

Schreiber, F. R. (1973). *Sybil*. Chicago, IL: Regnery.

Scott, J. P., & Fuller, J. L. (1965). *Genetics and the social behavior of the dog*. Chicago: University of Chicago Press.

Sears, R. R. (1944). Experimental analysis of psychoanalytic phenomena. In J. McV. Hunt (Ed.), *Personality and the behavior disorders* (pp. 306–332). New York: Ronald.

Sechrest, L. (1976). Personality. *Annual Review of Psychology, 27,* 1–27.

Sedikides, C. (1993). Assessment, enhancement, and verification determinants of the self-evaluation process. *Journal of Personality and Social Psychology, 65,* 317–338.

Segal, Z. V., & Dobson, K. S. (1992). Cognitive models of depression: Report from a consensus development conference. *Psychological Inquiry, 3,* 219–224.

Segal, Z. V., & Muran, J. C. (1993). A cognitive perspective on self-representation in depression. In Z. V. Segal & S. J. Blatt (Eds.), *The self in emotional distress* (pp. 131–170). New York: Guilford.

Seligman, M. E. P. (1975). *Helplessness*. San Francisco: Freeman.

Shaver, P. R., & Brennan, K. A. (1992). Attachment styles and the "Big Five" personality traits: Their connections with each other and with romantic relationships. *Personality and Social Psychology Bulletin, 18,* 536–545.

Shedler, J., Mayman, M., & Manis, M. (1993). The illusion of mental health. *American Psychologist, 48,* 1117–1131.

Shevrin, H. (1992). Subliminal perception, memory and consciousness: Cognitive and dynamic perspectives. In R. F. Bornsein & T. S. Pittman (Eds.), *Perception without awareness* (pp. 123–142). New York: Guilford.

Shevrin, H., & Luborsky, L. (1958). The measurement of preconscious perception in dreams and images: An investigation of the Poetzl phenomenon. *Journal of Abnormal and Social Psychology, 58,* 285–294.

Shields, S. (1975). Functionalism, Darwinism, and the psychology of women: A study in social myth. *American Psychologist, 30,* 739–754.

Shoda, Y., Mischel, W., & Wright, J. C. (1994). Intra-individual stability in the organization and patterning of behavior: Incorporating psychological situations into the idiographic analysis of personality. *Journal of Personality and Social Psychology, 67,* 674–687.

Shweder, R. A. (1993). The cultural psychology of emotions. In M. Lewis & J. M. Haviland (Eds.), *Handbook of emotions* (pp. 417–431). New York: Guilford.

Shweder, R. A., & D'Andrade, R. G. (1980). The systematic distortion hypothesis. In R. A. Shweder (Ed.), *Fallible judgement in behavioral research* (pp. 37–58). San Francisco: Jossey-Bass.

Siegel, B. S. (1986). *Love, medicine, & miracle*. New York: Harper & Row.

Siegel, B. S. (1989). *Peace, love, and healing*. New York: Harper & Row.

Silverman, L. H. (1976). Psychoanalytic theory: The reports of its death are greatly exaggerated. *American Psychologist, 31,* 621–637.

Silverman, L. H. (1982). A comment on two subliminal psychodynamic activation studies. *Journal of Abnormal Psychology, 91,* 126–130.

Silverman, L. H., Ross, D. L., Adler, J. M., & Lustig, D. A. (1978). Simple research paradigm for demonstrating subliminal psychodynamic activation: Effects of oedipal stimuli on dart-throwing accuracy in college men. *Journal of Abnormal Psychology, 87,* 341–357.

Silverman, L. H., & Weinberger, J. (1985). Mommy and I are one: Implications for psychotherapy. *American Psychologist, 40,* 1296–1308.

Simpson, J. A. (1990). Influence of attachment styles on romantic relationships. *Journal of Personality and Social Psychology, 59,* 971–980.

Singer, J. A., & Salovey, P. (1993). *The remembered self.* New York: Free Press.

Skinner, B. F. (1974). *About behaviorism.* New York: Knopf.

Skinner, N. S. F., & Howarth, E. (1973). Cross-media independence of questionnaire and objective test personality factors. *Multivariate Behavioral Research, 8,* 23–40.

Slade, A., & Aber, J. L. (1992). Attachments, drives, and development: Conflicts and convergences in theory. In J. W. Barron, M. N. Eagle, & D. L. Wolitzky (Eds.), *Interface of psychoanalysis and psychology* (pp. 154–185). Washington, DC: American Psychological Association.

Sloane, R. B., Staples, F. R., Cristol, A. H., Yorkston, N. J., & Whipple, K. (1975). *Psychoanalysis versus behavior therapy.* Cambridge, MA: Harvard University Press.

Smith, C. A., & Lazarus, R. S. (1990). Emotion and adaptation. In L. A. Pervin (Ed.), *Handbook of personality: Theory and research* (pp. 609–637). New York: Guilford.

Smith, C. P. (Ed.). (1992). *Motivation and personality: Handbook of thematic content analysis.* New York: Cambridge University Press.

Snyder, M. (1974). Self-monitoring of expressive behavior. *Journal of Personality and Social Psychology, 30,* 526–537.

Snyder, M. (1979). Self-monitoring processes. *Advances in Experimental Social Psychology, 12,* 85–128.

Snyder, M. (1981). On the influence of individuals on situations. In N. Cantor & J. F. Kihlstrom (Eds.), *Personality, cognition, and social interaction* (pp. 309–329). Hillsdale, NJ: Erlbaum.

Snyder, M. (1987). *Public appearances/private realities: The psychology of self-monitoring.* New York: Freeman.

Soldz, S., Budman, S., Demby, A., & Merry, J. (1993). Representation of personality disorders in circumplex and five-factor space: Explorations with a clinical sample. *Psychological Assessment, 5,* 41–52.

Spence, D. P. (1982). *Narrative truth and historical truth: Meaning and interpretation in psychoanalysis.* New York: Norton.

Spence, D. P. (1987). *The Freudian metaphor.* New York: Norton.

Sroufe, L. A., Carlson, E., & Shulman, S. (1993). Individuals in relationships: Development from infancy. In D. C. Funder, R. D. Parke, C. Tomlinson-Keasey, & K. Widaman (Eds.), *Studying lives through time* (pp. 315–342). Washington, DC: American Psychological Association.

Stagner, R. (1937). *Psychology of personality.* New York: McGraw-Hill.

Stagner, R. (1961). *Psychology of personality* (3rd ed.). New York: McGraw-Hill.

Steele, C. M. (1988). The psychology of self-affirmation: Sustaining the integrity of the self. *Advances in Experimental Social Psychology, 21,* 261–302.

Steele, C. M., & Spencer, S. J. (1992). The primacy of self-integrity. *Psychological Inquiry, 3,* 345–346.

Steele, C. M., Spencer, S. J., & Lynch, M. (1993). Self-image resilience and dissonance: The role of affirmational resources. *Journal of Personality and Social Psychology, 64,* 885–896.

Stewart, A. J. (1992). Scoring manual for psychological stances toward the environment. In C. P. Smith (Ed.), *Motivation and personality: Handbook of thematic content analysis* (pp. 451–488). New York: Cambridge University Press.

Stiles, W. B., Shapiro, D. A., & Elliot, R. (1986). Are all psychotherapies equivalent? *American Psychologist, 41,* 165–180.

Strauman, T. J. (1992a). Self-guides autobiographical memory, and anxiety and dysphoria. *Journal of Abnormal Psychology, 101,* 87–95.

Strauman, T. J. (1992b). Self, social cognition, and psychodynamics: Caveats and challenges for integration. *Psychological Inquiry, 3,* 67–71.

Strauman, T. J., & Higgins, E. T. (1993). The

self construct in social cognition: Past, present, and future. In Z. Siegel & S. Batt (Eds.), *The self in emotional distress* (pp. 3–40). New York: Guilford.

Strauman, T. J., Lemieux, A. M., & Coe, C. L. (1993). Self-discrepancy and natural killer cell activity: Immunological consequences of negative self-evaluation. *Journal of Personality and Social Psychology, 64,* 1042–1052.

Strickland, B. R. (1989). Internal-external control expectancies: From contingency to creativity. *American Psychologist, 44,* 1–12.

Strube, M. J. (1990). In search of self: Balancing the good and the true. *Personality and Social Psychology Bulletin, 16,* 699–704.

Sullivan, H. S. (1953). *The interpersonal theory of psychiatry.* New York: Norton.

Sundberg, N. D., & Gonzales, L. R. (1981). Cross-cultural and cross-ethnic assessment: A review and issues. In R. McReynolds (Ed.), *Advances in psychological assessment* (Vol. 5, pp. 460–510). San Francisco: Jossey-Bass.

Swann, W. B., Jr. (1991). To be adored or to be known? The interplay of self-enhancement and self-verification. In E. T. Higgins & R. M. Sorrentino (Eds.), *Handbook of motivation and cognition* (pp. 408–450). New York: Guilford.

Swann, W. B., Jr. (1992). Seeking "truth," finding despair: Some unhappy consequences of a negative self-concept. *Current Directions in Psychological Science, 1,* 15–18.

Swann, W. B., Jr., De La Ronde, C., & Hixon, J. G. (1994). Authenticity and positivity strivings in marriage and courtship. *Journal of Personality and Social Psychology, 66,* 857–869.

Swann, W. B., Jr., Griffin, J. J., Jr., Predmore, S. C., & Gaines, B. (1987). The cognitive-affective crossfire: When self-consistency confronts self-enhancement. *Journal of Personality and Social Psychology, 43,* 59–66.

Swann, W. B., Jr., Hixon, J. G., & De La Ronde, C. (1992). Embracing the bitter "truth." *Psychological Science, 3,* 118–121.

Swann, W. B., Jr., Pelham, B. W., & Krull, D. S. (1989). Agreeable fancy or disagreeable truth? Reconciling self-enhancement and self-verification. *Journal of Personality and Social Psychology, 57,* 782–791.

Swann, W. B., Jr., & Read, S. J. (1981). Acquiring self-knowledge: The search for feedback that fits. *Journal of Personality and Social Psychology, 41,* 1119–1128.

Swann, W. B., Jr., Stein-Seroussi, A., & Giesler, R. B. (1992). Why people self-verify. *Journal of Personality and Social Psychology, 62,* 392–401.

Swann, W. B., Jr., Wenzlaff, R. M., Krull, D. S., & Pelham, B. W. (1992). The allure of negative feedback: Self-verification strivings among depressed persons. *Journal of Abnormal Psychology, 101,* 293–306.

Taft, R. (1959). Multiple methods of personality assessment. *Psychological Bulletin, 52,* 1–23.

Tellegen, A. (1985). Structures of mood and personality and their relevance to assessing anxiety with an emphasis on self-report. In A. H. Tuma & J. D. Maser (Eds.), *Anxiety and the anxiety disorders* (pp. 681–706). Hillsdale, NJ: Erlbaum.

Tellegen, A. (1991). Personality traits: Issues of definition, evidence and assessment. In D. Cicchetti & W. Grove (Eds.), *Thinking clearly about psychology: Essays in honor of Paul Everett Meehl* (pp. 10–35). Minneapolis: University of Minnesota Press.

Tellegen, A. (1993). Folk concepts and psychological concepts of personality and personality disorder. *Psychological Inquiry, 4,* 122–130.

Tellegen, A., Lykken, D. T., Bouchard, T. J., Jr., Wilcox, K. J., Segal, N. L., & Rich, S. (1988). Personality similarity in twins reared apart and together. *Journal of Personality and Social Psychology, 54,* 1031–1039.

Temoshok, L. (1987). Personality, coping style, emotion and cancer: Towards an integrative model. *Cancer Surveys, 6,* 545–567.

Tesser, A. (1988). Toward a self-evaluation model of social behavior. *Advances in Experimental Social Psychology, 21,* 181–227.

Tesser, A. (1993). The importance of heritability in psychological research: The case of attitudes. *Psychological Review, 100,* 129–142.

Tesser, A., Pilkington, C. J., & McIntosh, W. D. (1989). Self-evaluation maintenance and the mediational role of emotion: The perception of friends and strangers. *Journal of Personality and Social Psychology, 57,* 442–456.

Thigpen, C. H., & Cleckley, H. (1954). *The three faces of Eve.* Kingsport, TN: Kingsport Press.

Thorne, A. (1989). Conditional patterns, transference, and the coherence of personality across time. In D. M. Buss & N. Cantor (Eds.), *Personality psychology: Recent trends and emerging directions* (pp. 149–159). New York: Springer-Verlag.

Tice, D. M. (1991). Esteem protection or enhancement? Self-handicapping motives and attributions differ by trait self-esteem. *Journal of Personality and Social Psychology, 60,* 711–725.

Tolman, E. C. (1925). Purpose and cognition: The determiners of animal learning. *Psychological Review, 32,* 285–297.

Tolman, E. C. (1932). *Purposive behavior in animals and men.* New York: Century.

Tomkins, S. S. (1962). Commentary. The ideology of research strategies. In S. Messick & J. Ross (Eds.), *Measurement in personality and cognition* (pp. 285–294). New York: Wiley.

Tomkins, S. S. (1963). *Affect, imagery, consciousness: The negative affects.* New York: Springer.

Tomkins, S. S. (1981). The quest for primary motives: Biography and autobiography of an idea. *Journal of Personality and Social Psychology, 41,* 306–329.

Tomkins, S. S. (1991). *Affect, imagery, consciousness: Anger and fear.* New York: Springer.

Trapnell, P. D., & Wiggins, J. (1990). Extension of the Interpersonal Affective Scales to include the Big Five dimensions of personality. *Journal of Personality and Social Psychology, 59,* 781–790.

Triandis, H. C. (1989). The self and social behavior in differing cultural contexts. *Psychological Review, 96,* 506–520.

Triandis, H. C., McCusker, C., & Hui, C. H. (1990). Multimethod probes of individualism and collectivism. *Journal of Personality and Social Psychology, 59,* 1006–1020.

Trivers, R. (1972). Parental investment and sexual selection. In B. Campbell (Ed.), *Sexual selection and the descent of man: 1871–1971* (pp. 136–179). Chicago: Aldine.

Trull, T. J. (1992). DSM-III-R personality disorders and the five-factor model of personality: An empirical comparison. *Journal of Abnormal Psychology, 101,* 553–560.

Tryon, R. C. (1940). Genetic differences in maze learning in rats. In *National Society for the Study of Education.* Bloomington, IL: Public School Publishing.

Turkheimer, E. (1991). Individual and group differences in adoption studies of IQ. *Psychological Review, 110,* 392–405.

Wachs, T. D. (1992). *The nature of nurture.* Newbury Park, CA: Sage.

Wachtel, P. (Ed.). (1982). *Resistance: Psychodynamic and behavioral approaches.* New York: Plenum.

Waddington, C. H. (1957). *The strategy of genes.* New York: Macmillan.

Waller, N. G., & Shaver, P. R. (1994). The importance of nongenetic influences on romantic love styles. *Psychological Science, 5,* 268–274.

Wallerstein, R. S. (1989). The psychotherapy research project of the Menninger Foundation: An overview. *Journal of Consulting and Clinical Psychology, 57,* 195–205.

Wallston, K. A., & Wallston, B. S. (1981). Health locus of control scales. In H. M. Lefcourt (Ed.), *Research with the locus of control construct* (pp. 189–243). New York: Academic.

Watson, D. (1988). Intraindividual and interindividual analyses of positive and negative affect: Their relation to health complaints, perceived stress, and daily activities. *Journal of Personality and Social Psychology, 54,* 1020–1030.

Watson, D. (1989). Strangers' ratings of the five robust personality factors: Evidence of a surprising convergence with self-reports. *Journal of Personality and Social Psychology, 52,* 120–128.

Watson, D., & Clark, L. A. (1984). Negative affectivity: The disposition to experience aversive emotional states. *Psychological Bulletin, 96,* 465–490.

Watson, D., & Clark, L. A. (1991). *Preliminary manual for the Positive and Negative Affect Schedule* (Expanded Form). Unpublished manuscript, Southern Methodist University, Dallas, TX.

Watson, D., & Clark, L. A. (1992). On traits and temperament: General and specific factors of emotional experience and their relation to the five-factor model. *Journal of Personality, 60,* 441–476.

Watson, D., & Clark, L. A. (1993). Behavioral disinhibition versus constraint: A dispositional perspective. In D. W. Wegner & J. W. Pennebaker (Eds.), *Handbook of mental control* (pp. 506–527). Englewood Cliffs, NJ: Prentice Hall.

Watson, D., Clark, L. A., & Carey, G. (1988). Positive and negative affectivity and their relation to anxiety and depressive disorders. *Journal of Abnormal Psychology, 97,* 346–353.

Watson, D., & Pennebaker, J. W. (1989). Health complaints, stress, and distress: Exploring the central role of Negative Affectivity. *Psychological Review, 96,* 234–254.

Watson, D., & Tellegen, A. (1985). Toward a consensual structure of mood. *Psychological Bulletin, 98,* 219–235.

Watson, J. B. (1919). *Psychology from the standpoint of a behaviorist.* Philadelphia: Lipincott.

Watson, J. B. (1928). *The ways of behaviorism.* New York: Harper.

Watson, J. B. (1930). *Behaviorism.* Chicago: University of Chicago Press.

Watson, J. B., & Rayner, R. (1920). Conditioned emotional reactions. *Journal of Experimental Psychology, 3,* 1–14.

Watson, R. C. (1940). Genetic differences in maze learning in rats. *National Society for the Study of Education: The thirty-ninth yearbook.* Bloomington, IL: Public School Publishing Co.

Wegner, D. M. (1992). You can't always think what you want: Problems in the suppression of unwanted thoughts. *Advances in Experimental Social Psychology, 25,* 193–225.

Wegner, D. M. (1994). Ironic processes of mental control. *Psychological Review, 101,* 34–52.

Wegner, D. M., Schneider, D. J., Carter, S. R., & White, T. L. (1987). Paradoxical effects of thought suppression. *Journal of Personality and Social Psychology, 53,* 5–13.

Wegner, D. M., Shortt, G. W., Blake, A. W., & Page, M. S. (1990). The suppression of exciting thoughts. *Journal of Personality and Social Psychology, 58,* 409–418.

Weinberger, D. A. (1990). The construct reality of the repressive coping style. In J. L. Singer (Ed.), *Repression and dissociation: Implications for personality, psychopathology, and health* (pp. 337–386). Chicago: University of Chicago Press.

Weinberger, J. (1992). Validating and demystifying subliminal psychodynamic activation. In R. F. Bornstein & T. S. Pittman (Eds.), *Perception without awareness* (pp. 170–188). New York: Guilford.

Weinberger, J., & Silverman, L. H. (1987). Subliminal psychodynamic activation: A method for studying psychoanalytic dynamic propositions. In R. Hogan & W. Jones (Eds.), *Perspectives in personality: Theory, measurement, and interpersonal dynamics* (pp. 251–287). Greenwich, CT.: JAI Press.

Weiner, B. (1979). A theory of motivation for some classroom experiences. *Journal of Educational Psychology, 71,* 3–25.

Weiner, B. (1985). An attributional theory of achievement motivation and emotion. *Psychological Review, 92,* 548–573.

Weiner, B. (1990). Attribution in personality psychology. In L. A. Pervin (Ed.), *Handbook of personality: Theory and research* (pp. 465–485). New York: Guilford.

Weiner, B. (1991). Metaphors in motivation

and attribution. *American Psychologist, 46,* 921–930.

Weiner, B. (1992). *Human motivation.* Newbury Park, CA: Sage.

Weiner, B. (1993). On sin versus sickness: A theory of perceived responsibility and social motivation. *American Psychologist, 48,* 957–965.

Weiss, J., & Sampson, H. (1986). *The psychoanalytic process.* New York: Guilford.

Weisskrantz, L. (1986). *Blindsight.* Oxford: Oxford University Press.

Weisz, J. R., Weiss, B., & Donenberg, G. R. (1992). The lab versus the clinic. *American Psychologist, 47,* 1578–1585.

Werker, J. (1989). Becoming a native listener. *American Scientist, 77,* 54–59.

Westen, D. (1992). The cognitive self and the psychoanalytic self: Can we put ourselves together? *Psychological Inquiry, 3,* 1–13.

Whisman, M. A. (1993). Mediators and moderators of change in cognitive therapy of depression. *Psychological Bulletin, 114,* 248–265.

White, G. M. (1993). Emotions inside out: The anthropology of affect. In M. Lewis & J. M. Haviland (Eds.), *Handbook of emotions* (pp. 29–40). New York: Guilford.

White, R. W. (1959). Motivation reconsidered: The concept of competence. *Psychological Review, 66,* 297–333.

Widiger, T. A. (1992). Categorical versus dimensional classification: Implications from and for research. *Journal of Personality Disorders, 6,* 287–300.

Widiger, T. A. (1993). The DSM-III-R categorical personality disorder diagnoses: A critique and an alternative. *Psychological Inquiry, 4,* 75–90.

Widiger, T. A. (1994). LSB on the SASB, FFM, and IPC. *Psychological Inquiry, 5,* 329–332.

Wiedenfeld, S. A., Bandura, A., Levine, S., O'Leary, A., Brown, S., & Raska, K. (1990). Impact of perceived self-efficacy in coping with stressors in components of the immune system. *Journal of Personality and Social Psychology, 59,* 1082–1094.

Wiener, N. (1948). *Cybernetics.* New York: Wiley.

Wierzbicka, A. (1992). *Semantics, culture, and cognition.* New York: Oxford University Press.

Wiggins, J. S. (1973). *In defense of traits.* Unpublished manuscript. University of British Columbia, Vancouver, B C.

Wiggins, J. S. (1991). Agency and communion as conceptual coordinates for the understanding and measurement of interpersonal behavior. In D. Cicchetti & W. Grove (Eds.), *Thinking clearly about psychology: Essays in honor of Paul Everett Meehl* (pp. 89–113). Minneapolis: University of Minnesota Press.

Wiggins, J. S. (1992). Have model, will travel. *Journal of Personality, 60,* 527–532.

Wiggins, J. S., Phillips, N., & Trapnell, P. (1989). Circular reasoning about interpersonal behavior: Evidence concerning some untested assumptions underlying diagnostic classification. *Journal of Personality and Social Psychology, 56,* 296–305.

Wiggins, J. S., & Pincus, A. L. (1989). Conceptions of personality disorders and dimensions of personality. *Psychological Assessment, 1,* 305–316.

Wiggins, J. S., & Pincus, A. L. (1992). Personality: Structure and assessment. *Annual Review of Psychology, 43,* 473–504.

Wiggins, J. S., & Pincus, A. L. (1994). Personality structure and the structure of personality disorders. In P. T. Costa, Jr. & T. A. Widiger (Eds.), *Personality disorders and the five-factor model of personality* (pp. 73–93). Washington, DC: American Psychological Association.

Wilson, G. (1978). Introversion/extroversion. In H. London & J. E. Exner (Eds.), *Dimensions of personality* (pp. 217–261). New York: Wiley.

Wilson, T. D. (1994). The proper protocol: Validity and completeness of verbal reports. *Psychological Science, 5,* 249–252.

Wilson, T. D., & Stone, J. I. (1985). Limitations of self-knowledge: More on telling more than we can know. *Review of Personality and Social Psychology, 6,* 167–184.

Wilson, W. R. (1979). Feeling more than we

can know: Exposure effects without learning. *Journal of Personality and Social Psychology, 37,* 811–821.

Winter, D. G. (1973). *The power motive.* New York: Free Press.

Winter, D. G. (1988). The power motive in women and men. *Journal of Personality and Social Psychology, 54,* 510–519.

Winter, D. G. (1992). Content analysis of archival productions, personal documents, and everyday verbal productions. In C. P. Smith (Ed.), *Motivation and personality: Handbook of thematic content analysis* (pp. 110–125). Cambridge, England: Cambridge University Press.

Winter, D. G. (1993). Power, affiliation, and war: Three tests of a motivational model. *Journal of Personality and Social Psychology, 65,* 532–545.

Witkin, H. A. (1973). The role of cognitive style in academic performance and in teacher-student relations. *Educational Testing Service Research Bulletin.* Princeton, NJ: Educational Testing Services.

Witkin, H. A., Dyk, R. B., Faterson, H. F., Goodenough, D. R., & Karp, S. A. (1962). *Psychological differentiation.* New York: Wiley.

Witkin, H. A., Lewis, H. B., Hertzman, M., Machover, K., Meissner, P. B., & Wapner, S. (1954). *Personality through perception.* New York: Harper & Row.

Wood, J. M., Bootzin, R. R., Kihlstrom, J. F., & Schachter, D. L. (1992). Implicit and explicit memory for verbal information presented during sleep. *Psychological Science, 3,* 236–239.

Wortman, C. B., & Loftus, E. F. (1992). *Psychology.* New York: McGraw-Hill.

Wylie, R. C. (1961). *The self-concept.* Lincoln: University of Nebraska Press.

Yang, K., & Bond, M. H. (1990). Exploring implicit personality theories with indigenous or important constructs: The Chinese case. *Journal of Personality and Social Psychology, 58,* 1087–1095.

Yik, M. S. M., & Bond, M. H. (1993). Exploring the dimensions of Chinese person perception in indigenous and imported constructs: Creating a culturally balanced scale. *International Journal of Psychology, 28,* 75–95.

Young, J. E., Beck, A. T., & Weinberger, A. (1993). Depression. In D. H. Barlow (Ed.), *Clinical handbook of psychological disorders* (2nd ed., pp. 240–277). New York: Guilford.

Young, P. T. (1961). *Motivation and emotion.* New York: Wiley.

Zajonc, R. B. (1968). The attitudinal effects of mere exposure. *Journal of Personality and Social Psychology Monograph, 9,* Part 2.

Zuckerman, M. (1991). *Psychobiology of personality.* New York: Cambridge University Press.

PHOTO CREDITS

Chapter 1

Page 5: Max Halberstadt. Page 11: Courtesy American Museum of Natural History. Page 15: Bettmann Archive.

Chapter 2

Page 41 (top): McLaughlin/The Image Works. Page 41 (bottom): J. Berndt/Stock, Boston. Page 47 (top): Courtesy Paul T. Costa, Jr. Page 47 (bottom): Courtesy Robert R. McCrae.

Chapter 3

Page 76: Photo by Charlyce Jones, Courtesy Columbia University Department of Psychology. Page 81: © Etta Hulme, 1986 Fort Worth Star-Telegram. Reprinted by permission of NEA, Inc. Pages 82 and 84: Courtesy Albert Bandura. Page 85: Drawing by Opie; © 1978 The New Yorker Magazine, Inc.

Chapter 4

Page 97: Drawing by Handelsman; © 1972 The New Yorker Magazine, Inc. Page 104: Courtesy David C. McClelland. Pages 105 and 106: Courtesy Dan McAdams. Page 121: Courtesy Carol Dweck. Page 124: Frank Siteman/Stock, Boston.

Chapter 5

Page 141: Photo by D.C. Goings, Courtesy David M. Buss. Figure 5.1: Patricia Hollander Gross/ Stock, Boston. Page 151: Courtesy Robert Plomin.

Chapter 6

Page 174: Judy Gelles/Stock, Boston. Page 182: Courtesy Jack Block.

Chapter 7

Page 208: Illustration by Patrick McConnell, *Psychology Today,* February 1987. Copyright © 1987 American Psychological Association. Reprinted by permission from *Psychology Today.* Figure 7.1: Courtesy Pawel Lewicky. Page 222: Photo by UA News Services, courtesy John Kihlstrom.

Chapter 8

Page 238: Gale Zucker/Stock, Boston. Page 249: Alan Carey/The Image Works. Page 250: Courtesy Hazel Markus.

Chapter 9

Page 278: Lionel Delevingne/Stock, Boston. Page 297: Courtesy Nancy Cantor.

Chapter 10

Figure 10.2a: Courtesy Carroll E. Izard. Figure 10.2b,d: Courtesy Paul Ekman. Page 322: Courtesy Richard S. Lazarus. Page 327: Art by P. Steiner. Copyright © 1985 American Psychological Association. Reprinted by permission from *Psychology Today*. Page 339: Courtesy James Pennebacker.

Chapter 11

Page 364: Courtesy Aaron T. Beck. Page 365: Dion Ogust/The Image Works.

INDEX